1975

This book may be kept

FOURTEEN

Correctional Institutions

Correctional Institutions

Edited by

Robert M. Carter
University of Southern California

Daniel Glaser
University of Southern California

Leslie T. Wilkins
State University of New York, Albany

J. B. LIPPINCOTT COMPANY

Philadelphia   New York   Toronto

Library of Congress Catalogue Card No.: 70-37398
Printed in the United States of America.
Paperbound ISBN-0-397-47208-0
Clothbound ISBN-0-397-47266-8

for Austin H. MacCormick

Foreword

This anthology on correctional and penal institutions was designed to fill what heretofore had been a significant gap in the literature of corrections. In this volume, the editors have provided materials of sufficient scope to meet the needs of the campus community for a general, all-purpose text on institutions, as well as those of the correctional practitioner and administrator in reviewing the literature of the field. For the nonprofessional interested citizen, the anthology provides a general portrait of institutions in theory and in practice.

The complexity of correctional institutions historically, traditionally, operationally and legally are illuminated by this broad range of readings. The contributors of these theoretical, empirical and descriptive materials are administrators, practitioners, scholars and researchers from both within and without the field of corrections. This wide cross-section assures an overview of sometimes divergent perspectives of institutions. It is to be noted that the contributors to this anthology have made here and elsewhere major contributions to corrections in theory and in practice.

The editors themselves represent different disciplines—criminology, sociology and methodology—and have had divergent experiences in corrections in administration, practice and research. Their incisive judgment and informed perception are clearly revealed in the selections made.

Although the anthology presents an historical review of correctional and penal institutions as well as the current state of achievement, it serves a particular need in pointing to the requirements of the future. The needs and directions for future efforts—that which needs to be done, in contrast to that which has and is being accomplished—is clearly apparent in this volume. The increasingly complex challenge of crime to corrections demands insight and knowledge about both past and present so that the future may be more intelligently utilized.

E. K. NELSON, *Director*
School of Public Administration
University of Southern California
Los Angeles

Preface

The ways in which organized society has dealt with criminal offenders constitute a long and painful chapter in the history of man. In primitive societies, each individual dealt with wrongs done him or his family in his own way. The victim was motivated chiefly by ideas of revenge, retaliation, or compensation for loss of property.

Even as modern societies developed, the basic concept behind the intervention of government continued to be that of retribution—a balancing of the scales of justice.

In the beginning, the scales tended to be balanced on the side of the superior power of the state. The death penalty was the most common response to ordinary crime. It is recorded that in London, in January 1801, a seventeen-year-old boy was hanged for stealing a silver spoon. With a relatively small population there were eight hundred executions in a year in England alone toward the end of the sixteenth century. Then, even more than now, the recipients of these harsh punishments were mainly the poor and the underprivileged.

The Quakers provided the keystone around which modern penal reform developed in America, while concurrent reforms were taking place in England and on the Continent. Becarria[1] published his great Essay on *Crime and Punishments* in 1764. John Howard, the famous English philanthropist and prison reformer, High Sheriff of Bedfordshire, was a central figure in the movement.

Following the uprising of the common people and the advent of modern democracy in France and in America, the Quakers developed strong allies in their drive for humane treatment of offenders and the substitution of imprisonment for corporal and capital punishment.

These penal reforms were logical corollaries to the concepts set forth in the Declaration of Independence, to the effect that all men are created equal and are endowed with certain inalienable rights and that these include life, liberty, and the pursuit of happiness. These concepts came into even sharper focus in the adoption of the Bill of Rights, contained in the first ten Amendments to the American Constitution.

The translation of the rights expressed in the Constitution into statutes and practices has been a slow and tortuous process. It is, perhaps, relevant to point out that from their adoption in 1791 until 1865, our country still tolerated slavery, and that it has taken a long succession of controversial Supreme Court decisions, continuing up to this very day, to implement forcefully the concepts set forth so clearly and so simply 180 years ago.

The slowness with which we have moved is related to many factors, some economic, some philosophical, some political and administrative.

Fundamental Dichotomies in Basic Principles

The idea of retributive punishment is deeply rooted in the minds and emotions of man. This attitude, and this simple atavistic impulse to punish and to overpunish offenders, remains the central trunk of the administration of criminal justice throughout the world. Welded onto this central trunk, sometimes very insecurely, are ideas of human compassion, of deterrence of others who might offend, of the rehabilitation of offenders who must be reabsorbed into society after imprisonment, and the broader concept of the need for protection of the public from personal, economic, or social injury.

That all of these concepts are not completely compatible should be clear to any thoughtful person. To overpunish makes rehabilitation more difficult and at times impossible. To underpunish, or not to punish at all, belies the purposes of deterrence and fails, at least partially, in the broad objective of public protection.

While the social sciences have made long strides in understanding social phenomena, there is still no central, widely accepted, and scientifically supported theory of crime-causation.

The practice of retributive punishment is rooted in the belief that each man possesses a free will and by his own decisions and actions determines his course. At the other end of the continuum, there is the idea that man's behavior is mainly the result of his environment and his inheritance, as well as of the social and economic opportunities which are available to him in a complex society. We therefore continue to administer criminal justice on a basis of fundamental concepts which are confusing and often incompatible, particularly when applied to the factual circumstances of individual cases.

Administrative Fragmentation

Another basic problem which our criminal justice systems have faced from the beginning and continue to face, especially in America, is the fragmentation of the administrative entities which comprise the justice systems. First, we have the constitutional separation of powers into the judicial, legislative, and executive. Legislators are particularly prone to try to solve the crime problem by passing punitive laws, but, conversely, they fail to appropriate adequate funds to implement the administration of the criminal law, whether it be excessively punitive or not.

The police, because of their particular role in the game of maintaining peace and order, have difficulty in understanding the roots of delinquent and criminal behavior, and tend to respond more vigorously than any other segment of the system with demands for strong, punitive methods.

The courts, being in the province of the legal profession, are generally not only skilled but dedicated to assuring fair and equitable procedures in the process of determining guilt or innocence. On the other hand, when guilt has been established, the decision as to what disposition should be made of each individual case, in terms of public protection, deterrence, retributive punishment, or rehabilitation, leaves most judges in a deep quandry. They face each case at the point of sentence with variable combinations of compassion, anger, puzzlement, personal bias, and political anxiety, but almost never with the armamentarium of scientific knowledge which would help them to decide what disposition might best serve the total society within the limits of the law and public tolerance.

It is small wonder that the disposition and management of public offenders remains the most controversial phase of the administration of justice.

Intergovernmental Difficulties and Economic Problems

The American faith in local government has also contributed to vast difficulties in the administration of justice. The development of state prisons and correctional institutions for both adults and juveniles came about gradually because local jails and workhouses found it difficult to handle small numbers of the more serious offenders, classified as felons and serving relatively long sentences.

An important economic factor is also present in the shifting of this part of the penal and criminal load to the states because the long-term confinement of offenders in secure institutions is relatively expensive even if very little rehabilitative and retraining effort is made. Shifts in our economy have affected the taxing capacity of local government in a negative way. This makes it necessary that some of the tax revenues collected by the federal government and by the states be redistributed to local government or that some of the services normally rendered by local government be transferred upward to the state or federal level.

In the handling of offenders, this has opened up the temptation for local governments to commit cases to state or federal institutions where the law permits, not because this is necessarily the best solution to either society's or the offender's problems, but rather because the cost of the care and management of the case is shifted from one unit of government to another.

Measures have been taken both at the federal and at the state levels of government to insure equitable treatment of public school pupils, welfare recipients, and the like, but no similar efforts of any consequence are in effect in this country with respect to the management, control, and corrective treatment of public offenders.

This phenomenon is most visible in the disparities in institutional facilities, but it also affects the administration of the so-called community-based programs. Local jails and probation services vary widely in effectiveness, leadership, and financial support from one community to another.

SHIFTS IN CORRECTIONAL STRATEGIES

The acceptance of the use of imprisonment as the keystone in the treatment of public offenders was, as we have noted, an important change made more than a century and a half ago. It soon became apparent, however, that imprisonment alone did little to insure long-range public protection because less than 5 percent, even of those sent to state and federal institutions for the most serious crimes, die in prison, and an even smaller percentage of those committed for shorter periods of time to jails and juvenile institutions are not eventually released. So we found ourselves paying substantial sums of money to maintain residential establishments, and too often the only result of this expenditure was short periods of incapacitation.

The logic of the situation leads inevitably to the conclusion that there should be alternatives to incarceration wherever the public welfare can be equally well served. To those accustomed to the need to *punish* and *deter*, rather than to *control, treat,* and *rehabilitate,* the alternatives to imprisonment seem not only mild and lenient but emotionally unsatisfying both to victims and average citizens. Furthermore, the limited number of empirical studies of the relative effectiveness of available alternatives, such as fines, weekend sentences, probation supervision, and halfway houses, have not been dramatically convincing one way or the other.

The factor differentiating imprisonment and contemporary alternatives which is most apparent and easily demonstrated is that of financial cost. In terms of dollars expended per case the ratio runs at about $10 for incarceration to $1.00 for probation or other "community-based programs". If the current trend toward reducing the proportion of the persons convicted who are imprisoned is to continue, we must begin to spend more of the 90 percent saving on improving the quality and effectiveness of the non-prison alternatives.

Probation

The essential weakness of probation, as with many other aspects of the correctional process, is the lack of adequate numbers of qualified probation officers to supervise the caseload of the jurisdiction. Caseloads of individual officers may vary from one jurisdiction to another from as few as twenty-five to as many as three hundred. It is generally agreed by students in this field that adequate service for those who require supervision demands average caseloads of not more than thirty-five or forty per probation officer.

Probation officers are essentially caseworkers and belong to the people-helping services. They also have peace officer functions and therefore often find themselves faced with philosophical conflicts. However, as the use of probation has grown, in the last quarter-century in particular, it is gradually being recognized that the role of the probation officer is a specialized one, requiring specific training and skills, different in many respects from those required of the social agency caseworker and the public welfare worker.

It should be noted also that each caseload is made up of a diversity of offenders with widely disparate needs calling for new and highly sophisticated treatment approaches. Most overburdened probation personnel in the system today are ill-equipped either by training or opportunity to deal differentially with the kind of clientele they must serve.

Prisons

The conditions most characteristic of American prisons between World Wars I and II were enforced idleness, inadequate and untrained personnel, gross overcrowding, and indeed, an almost complete negation of the high-sounding principles enunciated at the first convention of prison executives at Cincinnati in 1870.

The failure of the prisons to rehabilitate, and the maintenance of conditions of idleness, overcrowding, and lack of programs, generally made many of them crucibles of crime and degradation rather than instruments of reformation and resocialization. It should come as no surprise, then, that the courts are rebelling against sending offenders to these institutions unless they feel it to be absolutely necessary as a measure of public protection. This movement away from imprisonment unfortunately has not been matched by well supported and effective alternatives.

The Indeterminate Sentence and Parole

During the last fifty years the earlier ideas of the indeterminate sentence began to come into wider use. The concept of the indeterminate sentence was advanced for two widely different reasons: first, because individual judges had such dissimilar ideas about the appropriate length of a sentence, there was great need for a system of sentencing which could insure some degree of consistency. Disparity in sentencing is still a major problem in most jurisdictions. The second justification for the indeterminate sentence was that, if rehabilitation and retraining were, in fact, to be supported by the law, the people who administer the system, rather than the courts, should determine, within some broad limits, the appropriate time to release an offender from an institution, dependent upon his readiness to assume a law-abiding role in free society. The first idea, it can be seen, is based upon the concept of equal justice, and the second, upon the unequal needs of individual offenders for training and treatment.

In a few states, wide discretion has been delegated to parole boards or parole authorities to fix the time limits of sentences for adult felons within statutory limits set by law for each offense and to grant release on parole (conditional release under supervision) within the terms so fixed. However, the second concept behind the indeterminate sentence has been relegated to a minor consideration in most of the states because the parole boards have been kept organizationally independent of the administrative and treatment personnel of the correctional establishment.

The practical consequence of this arrangement almost invariably has been that these independent lay parole boards have proven to be so vulnerable to unreasoned attacks, and to the resultant concern for the protection of the political figure who appoints and reappoints them, that they tend to err on the side of extreme conservatism, at tremendous public cost, without demonstrable evidence that their actions really support the totality of the public interest.

The statutes of every state are different, but where they provide for discretionary release "on parole", there are usually minimum terms provided for in the law. It is rare that any substantial number of offenders are released at the expiration of the minimum term. On balance, the net result of the adoption of greater indeterminancy in the sentencing and parole statutes in a state has been longer rather than shorter time served before release.

The popular notion which equates parole with leniency is 180 degrees wrong. Here we encounter the common phenomenon of public opinion being formed on a basis of a few well publicized "bad" cases without regard for the total parole picture.

POSTWAR INNOVATIONS IN CORRECTIONAL THEORY AND PRACTICE

Correctional institutions and programs received little nourishment during the Depression years of the 1930s and little public attention during World War II. But the ten years following the war saw the effects of fifteen years of neglect. Prison riots, parole scandals, and evidences of correctional maladministration became so common throughout the land that the public and responsible political leaders, for the first time in many years, began giving the correctional problem new attention.

Demands for the abandonment of the conventional prison for all except the few dangerous and irredeemable offenders have become commonplace.

A reappraisal of the decision-making process, both in the courts and in the parole boards, has been urged.

Responses to dissatisfactions with old programs have resulted not only in demands for improvements in them, but also in active attention to new alternatives. Innovation is the magic word in applications for experimental and demonstration funds.

The Ford Foundation, through the American Justice Institute, funded a survey of modern correctional practice in the Western world in 1959.[2]

The Congress in 1964 recognized the deplorable state of the correctional field by appropriating over two million dollars to conduct a three-year study of correctional manpower and training.[3]

President Johnson established a Commission on Law Enforcement and Administration of Justice (National Crime Commission) on July 23, 1963. Twenty of the Commission's recommendations published in 1967 deal directly with correctional matters.[4]

The basic thrust behind these and numerous other studies in the last decade lies in a deep dissatisfaction with the organization, the methods, and the results of correctional effort in all of its dimensions.

Upon the recommendation of Chief Justice Warren Burger, the American Bar Association in 1970 formed a high level *Commission on Correctional Facilities and Services,* intended to focus the attention of the country upon the needs for reform in our correctional systems.

A new revolution in correctional theory and practice is in the making now, at the beginning of the second century after the first statement of correctional principles in 1870.[5]

THE FUTURE OF CORRECTIONS

Predictions of things to come are, of necessity, a combination of hardheaded logic and hopeful expectation. Those which follow are no exception.

(1) Fewer offenders, and especially the younger ones, will be confined for long periods in custodial institutions.

(2) The programs of these institutions will place greater emphasis on preparation for release and reintegration into normal society and less on the prevention of escapes and on economic production, unless it contributes to occupational competence.

(3) The new correctional institutions for both youths and adults will be much smaller, perhaps less than a hundred residents each, and will be located in cities, not on farms as has been our tradition.

(4) There will be less and less of the sharp dichotomy between incarceration and parole- or probation-supervision. Offenders will move in and out among varying degrees of restraint. Work and training furloughs, weekend sentences, halfway houses, and similar community-based programs will become more common and more varied.

(5) Probation services will expand, but they will be better supported and will include a much wider variety of programs: hostels, group homes, training programs, job placements, sheltered workshops, psychiatric services, and special counseling.

(6) Post-institutional supervision (parole) will also exhibit changes in variety and character similar to those in the community programs for probationers.

(7) The character, composition, and function of parole boards will change. These boards, made up largely of lay persons appointed by state governors, are seldom well qualified for their decision-making tasks, and, to compound the problem, they are peculiarly vulnerable to the most reactionary influences in the society, which do not support the majority concept of rehabilitation as opposed to retribution.

(8) New forms of disposition tribunals, as substitutes for the conventional "sentencing" by judges and the term-fixing and paroling functions of lay parole boards will be developed.

(9) Community-based programs must make more and more use of related community resources, both public and private. To do this, the organization and management of the correctional services must be consolidated and coordinated in each community. It is now the rule rather than the exception in major cities, in an area say, ten miles square, to find from five to ten separate governmental agencies (federal, state, county and city), supervising several thousand probationers and parolees of all ages and both sexes. There is no valid excuse for the cost, confusion, and inefficiency of this arrangement.

(10) More and more attention will be given to the development of information systems making use of modern computer technology so that decision-makers throughout the justice system can operate on a basis of facts instead of opinion and guesswork.

(11) Empirical research methods will be employed more and more as the means of defining and refining the problems of crime and delinquency and of evaluating and testing the effectiveness of programs.

(12) From the standpoint of the offender who would seek to escape the

consequences of his behavior, the "New Corrections" will be far more difficult to evade than is the case under our present system; conversely, for those who need help, professionally competent assistance will be provided. And the long-term needs for public protection will be better served.

RICHARD A. McGEE, *President*
American Justice Institute
Sacramento

Contents

FOREWORD: E. K. Nelson   vii

PREFACE: Richard A. McGee   ix

SECTION I: *History and Current Status*

INTRODUCTION   3

1. Correction in Historical Perspective
   Thorsten Sellin   8

2. Development of Modern Correctional Concepts and Standards
   American Correctional Association   17

3. State Correctional Institutions for Adults
   *The President's Commission on Law Enforcement and
   Administration of Justice*   35

4. Juvenile Institutions
   *The President's Commission on Law Enforcement and
   Administration of Justice*   52

5. Local Adult Correctional Institutions and Jails
   *The President's Commission on Law Enforcement and
   Administration of Justice*   71

6. Our Sick Jails
   Richard A. McGee   88

7. The Federal Prison System
   U.S. Bureau of Prisons   99

8. Correctional Philosophy and Architecture
   Howard B. Gill   110

9. Patterns of Correction
   Garrett Heyns   128

SECTION II: *The Correctional Institution as a Community*

INTRODUCTION   145

10. Some Foundations for a Theory of Correction
    Clarence Schrag   149

11. The Prison Experience: The Convict World
    John Irwin   173

12. Sociology of Confinement: Assimilation and the Prison 'Rat'
    Elmer H. Johnson   193

13. The Social Relations of Persistent Offenders
    Gordon Trasler   203

14. Women in Prison
    David A. Ward and Gene G. Kassebaum   213

15. The Social Meaning of Prison Homosexuality
    John H. Gagnon and William Simon   221

16. Organizational Goals and Inmate Organization
    Bernard B. Berk   233

17. Patterns of Management and Adaptations to Organizational
    Roles: A Study of Prison Inmates
    Thomas P. Wilson   248

18. Measuring Inmate Change in Prison
    Daniel Glaser and John R. Stratton   263

SECTION III: *Specific Programs in Correctional Institutions*

INTRODUCTION   277

19. Standard Minimum Rules for the Treament of Prisoners
    International Commission of Jurists   281

20. Classification
    American Correctional Association   301

21. The Effectiveness of Correctional Education
    Daniel Glaser   318

22. Disciplinary Action and Counseling
    Daniel Glaser   329

23. Inmate Self Government
    J. E. Baker   340

24. Prison Industry
    Elmer H. Johnson   356

25. Preparing Prisoners for Their Return to the Community
    J. E. Baker   365

SECTION IV: *Fusion of Institutional and Community Programs*

INTRODUCTION   383

26. New Roles For Jails
    Mark S. Richmond and George W. Aderhold   385

27. Special Community Programs: Alternatives to Institutionalization
    *The President's Commission on Law Enforcement and
    Administration of Justice*   401

28. Some Directions for Citizen Involvement in Corrections
    Vincent O'Leary   417

29. The Prison of the Future
    Daniel Glaser   428

SECTION V: *Scientific Guidance of Institutional Policies*

INTRODUCTION   435

30. Sources of Resistance to Innovation in Corrections
    Donald R. Cressey   438

31. Impediments to Penal Reform
    Norval Morris   461

32. Ethical and Legal Issues in Experimentation With Offender
    Populations
    Gilbert Geis   488

33. Five Practical Research Suggestions for Correctional Administrators
    Daniel Glaser   499

34. Evaluation of Penal Treatments
    Leslie T. Wilkins   509

NOTES   524

INDEX OF NAMES, ORGANIZATIONS, AND PROGRAMS   547

INDEX OF SUBJECTS   551

History and Current Status

Introduction

Correctional institutions have multiple goals, as do most organizations—
and even most persons. Some of these goals are formally proclaimed or
readily recognized and may be called manifest purposes or functions;
others are subtle and hidden, but may be recognized by perceptive
observers as latent functions. Often the latent functions have more
influence on the way an institution is run than do the manifest functions.

This book's opening chapter is an introduction to the history of
correctional institutions, an essential topic if one is to understand their
present status. Its author is an internationally renowned criminological
scholar, the University of Pennsylvania's Professor Emeritus Thorsten
Sellin. He points out that the change from capital and corporal penalties
to confinement was a late development in the punishment of law-
breakers, and that initially the major purpose of confinement was the
exploitation of prisoners as laborers. Reform movements followed, inspired at first only by humanitarian sentiments, later reinforced by
democratic political philosophies, and finally by social science theories.
Today a mixture of these diverse motives and many latent private or
public interests in particular activities determine penal practices. New
concerns are continually superimposed upon old ones at correctional
institutions, but rarely are the old concerns completely abandoned.

The manifest goals proclaimed by prison officials in the current era are
most frequently dual: protection of the community and rehabilitation of
the offender. This is a semantic muddle, since protection of the community implies a variety of more specific goals, including rehabilitation of
the offender. Analysis of statements by lawmakers contending that prison

3

sentences should be the penalties for certain crimes, and of the arguments that prison officials submit in support of their budget requests, reveals that three broad purposes are most often claimed for correctional institutions: (1) deterrence of actual or potential offenders by making them fear prison sentences; (2) incapacitation of known offenders by holding them securely in custody; (3) rehabilitation of these offenders, so that they will have more interest in and capacity for legitimate alternatives to crime when they are released.

Two types of conflict among these goals often prevail. The first results from the fact that each goal makes different and competing demands on necessarily limited state funds and staff time. Time and money spent on counting or walling-in prisoners cannot be spent on educating them. Secondly, pursuit of one goal may impede achievement of another goal. Thus custodial restriction of prisoners that keeps them from contact with non-criminal persons in the free community may make them when released especially ill at ease and unable to adjust successfully in non-criminal occupations.

In addition to these officially proclaimed concerns, latent goals often creep into the activities of particular functionaries in all correctional organizations, and these may displace the official goals. Thus a prison industry manager's interest in showing a good production record may guide the assignments he gives inmate workers more than an interest in teaching them new skills. More pervasively, an interest in making their jobs easier can motivate institution personnel in any position to exert only a minimum effort, or to be far more concerned with keeping prisoners contented than with changing them.

Instead of conflicting with one another, multiple goals may sometimes be served simultaneously by a given prison activity. Thus restrictions on the freedom of movement of prisoners serves both to incapacitate them from committing crimes in the outside community and to make prison life less pleasant, hence presumably deterrent. The latter objective may be divided into *general* deterrence, to keep those who may contemplate committing a crime from trying it, and *individual* deterrence, to keep a person already convicted from risking reconfinement by committing crime again.

General deterrence of potential offenders by the prospect of imprisonment doubtless occurs, but is widely exaggerated. Experience everywhere has shown that unusually long prison sentences do not affect the crime rate. It is clear that when a man commits a criminal act he either: (1) thinks mostly of the risk of being caught, rather than the length of imprisonment; or (2) he is so emotionally involved in his act that he does not think of its consequences. In the first type of crime, such as a deliberately planned burglary or fraud, certainty of apprehension by the police and of conviction in the courts is a stronger deterrent than severity of imprisonment (assuming the penalty when caught is sufficient to make the crime not worthwhile). The second type of act is illustrated by the majority of murders, which result from the escalation of an argument among friends or relatives and the availability of lethal weapons; in such cases the murderer usually has been too overwrought to care about the consequences of his act, and does little to evade arrest.

Offenses that are committed with some rational deliberation, even if also committed with emotion, will not be seen as worth the penalty, if the penalty is certain and appreciable. Certainty of confinement imposed to incapacitate known offenders to prevent their committing further crimes is usually more than sufficient to be a general deterrent. Indeed, just the disgrace of being caught is an adequate deterrent for most people. The general deterrent effect of imprisonment, therefore, is not strengthened by increasing the length or restricting the conditions of imprisonment, but by greater efficiency of the police and the courts, in making penalties more certain.

Individual deterrence by imprisonment varies with the character of the particular prisoner. It depends greatly on his "prisonization"—his adjustment to "doing time". It also changes with his rehabilitation—the extent to which he comes to anticipate more gratification from alternatives to criminality than from crime. Thus neither general nor individual deterrence is directly affected by most efforts to have prisons increase their deterrent effects.

Incapacitation and rehabilitation are the two official goals of imprisonment, and their achievement may vary greatly with the performance of correctional officials. Incapacitation is the one goal which institutions are most successful in attaining. Few prisoners escape; most who do are quickly apprehended, and while persons confined commit some crimes against each other and against prison employees, they are largely prevented from preying on the outside community. Incapacitation is needed, however, only when rehabilitation is not achieved: when an offender no longer is a marked risk to the community we do not have to be concerned about the security of his custody. It follows that rehabilitation is the most essential and most variable goal of correctional institutions. This variability and centrality of rehabilitation justifies its being the chief concern of modern correctional management. It also justifies taking some risks of not achieving maximum incapacitation or deterrence if these risks result from measures which increase the prospects of rehabilitation.

A detailed history of change in prison emphasis and practice is presented in the chapter from the American Correctional Association's *Manual of Correctional Standards.* It stresses especially the world leadership of the United States in penal innovation during the nineteenth century. The Association draws heavily upon the writings of an elder statesman of American corrections, Austin H. MacCormick, to argue the case for rehabilitation, as opposed to punishment or deterrence as prison goals. They call the 1870s a "Golden Age of Penology" because it was then that the rehabilitation ideal was vigorously propagated by the birth of the reformatory movement and by a classic Declaration of Principles from the National Prison Association which preceded the present Association. Nevertheless, they also report on a variety of "Dark Age" prison characteristics that survived for more than a half-century after the 1870s. New rehabilitation efforts in the mid-twentieth century are then described, as well as a variety of continuing prison deficiencies.

Following this historical commentary, government sponsored surveys are drawn upon for systematic current descriptions of juvenile, local adult and state correctional institutions in the United States, together with an official description of the federal prison system. Each of these accounts includes statistics on staff and inmates, brief histories, statements of working philosophy, details of current programs, and descriptions of physical plants, administrative organization, and research or information activities.

The most neglected—yet in many ways the most influential—correctional institutions in the United States are the local jails. They receive about ten times as many offenders as the state and federal prisons, and usually are also the places of prior confinement for those in the latter establishments. Most urban jails house dozens of people in large cages, the mixture of personalities in each cage is fairly haphazard, and only one staff member supervises several such cages. Inmate control of other inmates is thus architecturally and administratively guaranteed. Therefore, homosexual rape, extortion and other domination by the most physically or verbally aggressive is a standard feature of jail life. Occasional screaming news reports about such scandals in a jail simply describe what is routine as though it were unusual. These conditions, combined with almost complete idleness—especially for those who are unsentenced—make jails much more criminalizing than most other correctional facilities. Richard A. McGee, whose remarkably creative career probably includes administrative authority over more man-years of correctional confinement than any other American, provides a masterful account of jail ailments as well as the potential "wonder drugs" for a considerable cure.

A special focus on architecture in relation to correctional philosophy is presented with acerbic alliteration by Howard B. Gill, perhaps the most colorful and critical of long-prominent commentators on American correction. His concise and trenchantly labeled typologies of prison architecture, philosophy, and personnel reflect extensive experience and scholarship. Whether or not one agrees with all of his charges against prevailing practice, or accepts fully his prescriptions for more ideal programs, his commentary will be thought-provoking.

The long career of the late Dr. Garrett Heyns included at various times the executive direction of all correctional institutions in the states of Michigan and Washington, and the direction of a federally sponsored Joint Commission on Correctional Manpower and Training. His description of "Patterns of Correction" in the United States focuses on the variety of state administrative organizations for managing correctional programs. These differ greatly in the autonomy they grant to correctional leadership, and in the extent to which they administratively integrate the various components of state correctional activity. Dr. Heyns' survey fittingly concludes our series of overviews of correctional institutions. It then becomes appropriate to seek an inner view of these institutions as communities.

1　Correction in Historical Perspective

THORSTEN SELLIN*

INTRODUCTION

A study of the changes that have occurred in our ideas of how to deal with offenders against the criminal law brings us into contact with one of the most fascinating and challenging aspects of social history, the history of punishment. It is, by and large, a sordid history; a record of our slow progress in finding effective means of reducing criminality by punishment; a record of much violence, brutality, torture, and indifference to human suffering, but also of charity, compassion, and honest search for methods of correctional treatment that will salvage rather than destroy those who are its objects. It is the purpose of this paper to attempt to disengage a few of the general trends that are discernible in that record and lay bare some of the conspicuous elements that compose these trends, especially since the Middle Ages.

To the casual student of the history of punishment and of the reasons given for its existence, character, and myriad forms, it would appear that there are two noticeable *purposes* of punishment and that while they are different in kind, they are not always completely separable. One of these purposes is the protection and conservation of the social interests or values which have been injured by the offender. It is a mundane purpose, nowadays often designated, especially abroad, by the term of social

* From the Symposium on Crime and Correction in *Law and Contemporary Problems* 23, 4 (Autumn 1958): 585–593. Published by the Duke University School of Law, Durham, North Carolina. Copyright © 1958 by Duke University. Reprinted by permission of the author and publisher.

defense. This protection is thought to be achievable by various *means*, such as (a) the extermination of the offender; (b) making him so fear punishment that he will commit no more crimes (deterrence); or (c) reforming, re-educating, or curing him by more positive methods. The second purpose is other-worldly, so to speak. It views punishment as being inflicted in order to save the offender's soul, this end being achieved by his repentance and atonement.

Next, we must consider the human *motives,* wishes, and desires that have led us to establish and apply punishments that would effect the means and thereby achieve the purposes or ends thereof. Prominent among these motive forces have been (a) a primitive desire for vengeance or retaliation; (b) compassion with sinners or unfortunate fellowmen; (c) a wish to exploit the offender's productive capacities; and (d) the hope to turn him into a law-abiding citizen by some kind of rational treatment or therapy.

Even though a case could be made for the claim that these purposes, means, and motives have always existed in the civilized world, history suggests that their respective shares in the scheme of things have not at all times been of equal proportions. Although there have been times and places when the salvation of the soul of the criminal may have appeared to be the main aim of punishment, the "protection of society" has usually been the dominant purpose, the more so as man has proceeded to exchange his fear of the unknown for a confidence in his ability to penetrate it. As for means and motives, their interplay and the roles of their constituent parts have undergone great changes in the course of time. Indeed, the story of the changes in social attitudes toward the offender is essentially the story of how the roles of the various means and motives of punishments have progressively lost or gained in importance.

And that story is inextricably interwoven with the history of cultural change in general; for the nature of punishments and the motives behind them reflect the fundamental character of the structure, the institutions, and the intellectual life of society; as these change, so do attitudes toward offenders, as well as the resultant ways of dealing with them. In surveying these last-mentioned changes, we shall examine separately (a) the retaliatory, (b) the exploitative, (c) the humanitarian, and (d) the re-educational-therapeutic elements in punishment. It is hoped that this examination will reveal something of the interrelationships and relative strength of these elements at different periods. The history we are studying is not like a ladder, on which each rung marks a clear division between one stage and the one above. It is more like a river, arising from several tributaries, some of which, owing to the operation of changing climatic factors, tend to grow more powerful, while others show signs of drying up; yet, all are adding their respective flow to the main stream.

THE RETALIATORY ELEMENT

No punishments illustrate the retaliatory element better than do capital and corporal penalties. The supreme penalty of death may well be the oldest of all punishments. In historical times, the manner of inflicting it has taken all conceivable forms, some of them designed to snuff out life speedily, others planned so as to prolong the agony of the victim as much as possible. The executioner's sword and the hangman's rope have been reasonably rapid methods, but those who have been burned at the stake, boiled or buried alive, broken on the wheel, or immured have known the full meaning of public vengeance and retaliation.

However, this penalty has undergone great changes in the last few hundred years and especially during the last century and a half. Where it was once employed in the case of all serious crimes in all nations, it has gradually become limited to very few crimes or has been abolished altogether.

Statistical data on the relative use of the death penalty in early times are rare, especially long-time series which indicate trends. A most interesting series of this kind, and the longest reliable one' so far produced, unfortunately, applies to only one community, the town of Malines in Belgium. It covers five centuries before the French Revolution and, therefore, antedates the more recent abolitionist trend. During these centuries, Malines had a population that remained rather constant in size, and the criminal law which it administered underwent no radical changes. Nevertheless, the annual average number of executions dropped from four during 1370–1400, to two during the sixteenth century, to one every four years during the eighteenth century.[6] There are good reasons for believing that this phenomenon was no isolated one, but was occurring in the rest of Europe.

It has been estimated that during the 150 years beginning with the reign of Henry VIII in England and ending with the Commonwealth, the annual average of 300 executions at Tyburn (London and Middlesex) during the first half century dropped to ninety during the last thirty-five years. A century later, during the five decades 1749–98, the annual average number of criminals executed in London and Middlesex each decade ran to thirty-one, twenty-one, thirty-six, fifty-three, and twenty-one, respectively. Most of the executions were for crimes against property.[7]

A growing sentiment against the death penalty manifested itself during the latter half of the eighteenth century. The philosophers of the Enlightenment gave it voice. Becarria's essay *On Crimes and Punishments* (1764) was not the first to advocate the removal of this penalty, but it was written at a time when the soil was ready to receive the seed it planted. It took several decades for its influence to be fully felt. During the nineteenth century, however, the death penalty was abolished in many countries or otherwise reduced in scope. This general trend has continued to the present day, in spite of local and temporary reversals, until we must conclude that what was once a highly acceptable method of dealing with criminals has become archaic in our Western culture and a vestigial organ in our body politic. . . .

What has been said about the death penalty is even more true of corporal punishments. Since imprisonment was an uncommon form of punishment prior to the eighteenth century, corporal punishments ranked next to the capital ones in importance. Branding, mutilation, and flogging were frequently in use. Only flogging has survived here and there in our Western culture. The whip did not disappear from British law until 1948, and it is still a legal form of punishment in Canada and some other Commonwealth countries, such as the Union of South Africa and Ceylon. Mutilation is still practiced in some parts of the Moslem world. In the United States, the traditional forms survived in several northern states until the early decades of the last century and in the South until some time after the Civil War. Delaware still retains the whipping post, but uses it only rarely nowadays. Indeed, that is something of an anachronism considering the step recently taken by Delaware to abolish the death penalty.

The retaliatory element is, of course, present in greater or lesser degree in other than capital or corporal punishments. It is present whenever the punishment inflicts suffering without regard to the offender's future rehabilitation, and it is clearly reflected in the vicious sentences to long prison terms that tend to be demanded and imposed when public sentiments have been aroused by some brutal crimes.

THE EXPLOITATIVE ELEMENT

Those who today complain that our prisons are great financial burdens on the taxpayer might well be surprised to learn that the use of prisons in connection with punishments developed for the purpose of exploiting the manpower of criminals and making them financially profitable. The use of criminals to build roads, fortifications, and public works goes back to ancient times. In ancient Rome, criminals were sometimes sent to labor in the mines and quarries. Mining continued, in many countries, to be a favorite way of exploiting criminals, partly because of the hazards such labor involved, and it is a curious fact that the first state prison in the United States—in Connecticut—was in a mine. Whatever might have been the form of exploitation, it is obvious that when such criminals were not engaged in work, they had to remain confined somewhere if they were to be counted on to complete their tasks; hence, the need for prisons that were mere places for the safekeeping of these unwilling laborers.

Perhaps the best illustration of penal servitude is the system of galley slavery which was introduced toward the end of the Middle Ages in the countries bordering on the Mediterranean Sea. The practice seems to have begun in France shortly before the middle of the fifteenth century and spread from there to nearby maritime countries. Gradually, many criminals who would otherwise have been sentenced to death or corporal punishments were committed to the galleys, warships peculiarly suited to the Mediterranean and propelled by rowers.

Numerous other illustrations could be given. The first state prisons in the United States were set up as institutions for the confinement of criminals sentenced to perform hard labor, and until relatively recent times, and still in some states, one of the chief elements of punishment has remained the financial exploitation of the prisoner's manpower. We need only mention the lease system of prison labor, which was not completely abolished until thirty-five years ago, and the system of contract labor for the benefit of private employers, which remained in many states until twenty-five years ago. The chain gangs are still remembered, and there can be little doubt that in many places, the improvements in living conditions in prison road camps have in part been motivated more by a need for maintaining healthy work crews than by a desire to rehabilitate offenders.

THE HUMANITARIAN ELEMENT

Humanitarian sentiments and feelings have played a large role in the transformation of punishments, especially since the beginning of the Christian era, for these feelings are closely bound up with religious beliefs. Charitable agencies, societies, etc., developed quite early for the purpose of bringing solace in some form to poor prisoners, visiting them, ransoming them, and burying them. All the early prison reformers were motivated by Christian charity and compassion, and these sentiments played a large role in the movement to reduce the use of corporal and capital punishments, improve conditions in jails, and lighten the burdens of imprisonment. The first programs of education of prisoners aimed to teach them to read religious books, and the first prison libraries were chiefly stocked with devotional literature. Humanitarian sentiments were largely responsible for the introduction of medical services to prisoners. The first prison society in the United States was formed to "alleviate the miseries of public prisons." Indeed, until recent times, penal reform has been to a large extent dictated not by a carefully studied plan to develop effective penal treatment, but by humanitarian sentiments.

THE TREATMENT ELEMENT

The greatest changes in our attitudes toward the offender have occurred during the last two centuries. They are attributable to two great movements which can be roughly traced back to ideas that reached fruition or were being foreshadowed in the late eighteenth century—the rise of a philosophy of democracy and the birth of the behavioral sciences. The former led to great political upheavals, and the latter produced a revolution in our views regarding the nature of the offender and his treatment.

The rationalists of the eighteenth century were convinced that research would be able to uncover not only the scientific laws that governed the inanimate world, but the laws that ruled social life and the behavior of man. The fumbling efforts to understand human behavior by physiognomics that culminated in the work of Lavater became more systematic in the researches of Gall, the father of "phrenology," whose ideas are no longer acceptable, but who fully understood their implications for penology. The leading brain anatomist of his age, Gall became convinced that the explanation of all human behavior was to be found in the structure of the brain; his studies of criminals confirmed him in that belief. It is not very important that his theories could not be substantiated, but it is important that they caused him to stress the need for the individualization of punishment. He regarded it as axiomatic that punishment should be fitted not only to the crime, but to the criminal as well, just as physicians who have diagnosed a disease must consider the nature of the patient when prescribing treatment.

In the demand for individualization of punishment, he received ample support from the infant science of psychiatry. Not long after the American Revolution, Benjamin Rush had studied what he called the diseases of the moral faculty. What he called anomia developed later in the clinical studies of Pinel, Esquirol, and Pritchard into what came to be known as moral insanity, a conception of the cause of crime which definitely placed the criminal into the category of the mentally diseased and hence in need for preventive care rather than punishment.

There is no need to describe here in any great detail the variety of researches or theories about the causation of crime which flourished during the last century nor their successors during the present century. Suffice it to say that whether we consider the individualistic theories of the criminal anthropologists, the hereditarians, the psychoanalysts, or the psychologists or the environmental theories of the positivists, the Marxians, the sociologists, and others, they all pointed in the same direction so far as the penal system was concerned; they all demanded that punishment be fitted to the punished and not to the crime, broadly speaking. To the investigators of the matrix and phenomena of human behavior, criminals were not all alike and should not be treated as if they were. The fact that two persons had committed the same crime was not, to them, a sound reason for giving them the same punishment. And as scientists, they easily arrived at the conclusion that the criminal should not be sentenced to a fixed and unalterable punishment, but that his correctional treatment should have flexibility if it were to meet society's demand for protection against him and to serve best his need for effective therapy.

It is obvious, that whatever humanitarian sentiments may have lurked in the recesses of the minds of those who called for a scientific basis for the treatment of the offender, this basis was not that of the humanitarians, nor of the retaliators or the exploiters. And who would question the enormous influence that the scientific movement has had on our penal system? We need only to look at the innovations of the last century to see how different the correctional system of a modern state is as compared with that of earlier days. At the beginning of the nineteenth century, fines, one or two forms of imprisonment, the death penalty, and perhaps the lash were the usual punishments; today, a variety of specialized institutions, probation, indeterminate sentences, parole, juvenile courts, etc., testify to the impact which the behavioral sciences have had on our legislation. The concept of individualized treatment has received general acceptance—within limits which may be modifiable but certainly not removable during the foreseeable future.

The mention of these limits brings us back to the democratic movement. We are told by the legal historian that justice was marked by great arbitrariness prior to the nineteenth century, at least on the continent of

Europe, and that it favored the ruling classes. The egalitarian political philosophy which matured during the eighteenth century brought significant changes. Even before Beccaria published his famous essay, Voltaire had called for the abolition of arbitrary punishments. Judges, he claimed, should act on the basis of well-formulated laws, so that citizens would no longer have to complain of arbitrary justice and judges would not have to fear the hatred of the people, since punishments would be dictated by law and not by the sentiments of the judge.[8]

Beccaria clarified the issue still further. Criminal law should be based, he said, on the concept of the equality of men. Definite punishments should be fixed by laws adopted by representatives of a political society based on the social contract. Courts should determine the guilt of the accused, but should not be allowed to interpret the law, since nothing would be more dangerous than to judge in accord with the "spirit of the law," for in that case, this spirit would depend on the judge's good or bad logic, his good or bad digestion, the strength of his emotions, or the frailties of the accused. The same judge might even, at times, impose different punishments for the same crime! There might be some inconveniences in the literal application of the law, but the legislature could always change it. Otherwise, the accused would become the slave of the judge. Exact punishments would also be most intimidating; therefore, a criminal code should be precise and clear. Parallel scales of crimes and punishments should be devised, and the degree of the offender's injury to society should determine the severity of his punishment.[9]

The impact of these ideas to which Becarria gave such a felicitous expression soon became apparent in the various reforms of the penal law which were made in the late eighteenth and the early nineteenth century in most countries. From the point of view of political philosophy, this was a victory for the demands of democracy, for the equality of all persons before the law, and for the principle of legality. From the point of view of penology, it meant the shift from capital and corporal punishments and torture, which were looked upon as instrumentalities of a feudal age, to punishments consisting of the deprivation of liberty and, therefore, more fitting for persons who had by their crimes forfeited their right to enjoy the privilege of freedom. The simple hedonistic philosophy by which Beccaria explained human motivation—and which Jeremy Bentham later was to make the foundation for his penal system—no doubt could have provided him with a basis for constructing a system requiring the individualization of punishment, but the intellectual climate of his day was not favorable. Dominated by the emerging political philosophy, he arrived at the antithesis of individualization—namely, equal punishments for equal crimes, the nature of the crime being the measure of the injury done by a criminal to society.

There is little need for stressing the fact that the penal philosophy embraced by the egalitarians and the correctional or treatment philosophy derived from the behavioral scientists are mutually incompatible. We have already noted the effect of the behavioral sciences on the penal system. A corollary effect may be noted in the administration of justice. With the increase of the number and variety of possible dispositions available to the courts, the arbitrary power of courts, which the egalitarians were desirous of destroying because of their mistrust of these agencies, has increased, and more and more discretionary power has been transferred to agencies of correctional administration.

CONCLUSION

The history of penal legislation during the last century has been one of compromise. The treatment philosophy has constantly made more inroads, but has now reached the point of diminishing returns, one might say. The hard core of the older philosophy which demands a life for a life or at least life imprisonment for a life and a considerable degree of proportionality between the seriousness of the crime and the severity of the punishment still remains strong, however.

2 Development of Modern Correctional Concepts and Standards

AMERICAN CORRECTIONAL ASSOCIATION*

To understand the modern correctional systems and services of America one should examine the gradual development of the ideas and attitudes embodied in our present correctional philosophy, standards, and procedures.

EARLY IDEAS OF RETRIBUTIVE PUNISHMENT

In primitive times, each individual dealt with wrongs done him as he saw fit. In taking personal revenge the retaliation, being unrestrained, frequently went far beyond the original wrong. Later, attempts were made to limit the retaliation to the extent of the injury. This was the intent of the ancient Judaic doctrine of "an eye for an eye, and a tooth for a tooth," commonly misinterpreted today. It was an injunction against inflicting on another, as retributive punishment, more injury than one had received at his hands.

As time passed, the practice of individual retaliation for wrongs suffered was no longer sanctioned. Any action that might endanger the sovereign or good order in his realm became an offense against the King's peace and was punished by the State. The list of what constituted wrongs against the King grew until practically all offenses against property or persons were considered public rather than private matters. Punishment

* From the *Manual of Correctional Standards* (Washington, D.C.: American Correctional Association, 1966), pp. 3–19. Copyright © 1966 by the American Correctional Association.

17

was still meted out on the basis of retribution, but it was inflicted by the State, not by the individual wronged, and within a framework of law, not under the vague sanction of ancient traditions and customs.

The death penalty is the most ancient of all penalties and was inflicted in every conceivable form in the Middle Ages. Burning at the stake, boiling in oil, beheading, breaking on the wheel, and drawing and quartering are but a few of the methods used in Europe in the 16th and 17th centuries. Torture was used to force the accused to confess guilt and disclose accomplices, and was also used as punishment. Other punishments included mutilations (cutting out the tongue, burning out the eyes, and cutting off the ears), branding, flogging, and such forms of public humiliation as the stocks and the pillory. In many instances punishments inflicted were worse than death, and often death itself followed.

REACTION AGAINST EXTREME PUNISHMENTS

The severity and frequency of the punishments and the inequitable way in which they were administered began to cause serious unrest among the common people. The penalties for the rich and the poor, the educated and the ignorant differed widely. In England, the number of offenses for which the death penalty was prescribed finally rose to over 350, and included the most trivial offenses. Sir Samuel Romilly's bill to abolish the death penalty for shoplifting in the amount of five shillings or more was passed by the Commons and defeated by the Lords six times between 1810 and 1820, and was not enacted until 1832.

Between 1811 and 1819 thousands of petitions from shopkeepers, manufacturers and bankers flooded the House of Commons, all on the same general lines: "that the archaic severity of the law made its enforcement impossible, and thus destroyed its deterrent effect; and that in the interest of public safety, milder punishments should be imposed." The resistance to change began to break down, however, only when Sir Robert Peel created the forerunner of the modern police forces in 1829. Ten years later the number of capital offenses was reduced to fifteen, and in 1861 to four.[10]

SEVERE COLONIAL CRIMINAL CODES

It was because of social and legal injustices, as well as desire to worship as they chose, that the early colonists, particularly the Pilgrims and the

Quakers, came to America. They brought with them from England and the Continent the idea of jails and workhouses, but only as detention places for accused persons and for the confinement of vagrants, paupers, beggars, and so on. Offenses which today would lead to imprisonment in a state prison, as well as offenses that would now be considered misdemeanors, were usually punished by fines, whipping, branding and mutilation, the stocks and the pillory. Hanging was the punishment for from ten to eighteen offenses in the various colonies.

EARLY COLONIAL INSTITUTIONS

Massachusetts and Pennsylvania share major credit for the early efforts in the colonies to substitute imprisonment for the corporal and capital punishments prescribed by the harsh English and colonial criminal codes. The first steps in that direction were short but significant. In 1632 the Massachusetts Bay Colony erected in Boston a small wooden structure that served as a prison for the entire colony for eighteen years until prisons were erected in other towns. The Colony of New Plymouth, founded by the Pilgrims in 1620, built a prison in 1638. In 1655, the General Court of the Massachusetts Bay Colony decided that each county should have a house of correction for the idle, drunkards, and other petty offenders, and a few institutions of this type were subsequently put in operation.

After the adoption of the Constitution in 1780, the first prison for the entire Commonwealth was established on Castle Island in Boston harbor in 1784–85. The courts sentenced men to hard labor for a term of years or life in this fortress-prison. Although it had been used for difficult prisoners as early as 1636, it was not sufficiently secure and construction of a new state prison was begun around 1800. In December, 1805, the Commonwealth's maximum security "penitentiary prison" at Charlestown received its first prisoner.[11]

REFORMS INITIATED BY QUAKERS

In 1676 the extremely severe criminal codes derived from England were made applicable to Pennsylvania, but in 1682 William Penn's first assembly passed "The Great Law," embodying the comparatively humane Quaker criminal code. The Pennsylvanians lived under this code until 1718, when it was repealed and the Quakers went back again under what was to them the yoke of barbarism. William Penn died one day before the date on which the advanced code of justice he had established was uprooted.

The Quakers had a particular abhorrence of the cruel and barbarous punishments called for by the criminal code under which Pennsylvania suffered for the half-century preceding the American Revolution, as Massachusetts had for more than a century. They and their allies, who included such non-Quakers as Benjamin Franklin, played a leading role in the reforms of the criminal code and penal procedures that gained momentum as soon as the War for Independence was won, and were written into Pennsylvania law in the early 1790's. The final triumph for the Quaker reformers came in 1794, when an Act was passed which reduced the list of capital crimes to first degree murder and prescribed imprisonment for the other offenses.

Usually considered the first prison established in America, although the Massachusetts prisons cited above actually antedated it by a century and a half, a cell-block in the Walnut Street Jail in Philadelphia was opened in 1790 as the penitentiary for the Commonwealth. The Western State Penitentiary was opened in 1826 and the Eastern State Penitentiary in 1829. (While this discussion is primarily concerned with early colonial reforms of the criminal codes, it is of historical interest to note that New York's first state prison [Newgate] was opened in 1791, New Jersey's in 1798, Kentucky's and Virginia's in 1800, Massachusetts' Charlestown Prison in 1805, Vermont's in 1809, Maryland's and New Hampshire's in 1812, Ohio's in 1816, New York's Auburn Prison in 1819, and its Sing Sing Prison in 1828.)

BASIS OF SOCIAL AND LEGAL REFORMS

These and other social and legal reforms flowed logically from what was in the minds of the colonists when they drew up the Declaration of Independence, which pronounced it a self-evident truth that all men are created equal and are endowed with certain inalienable rights which cannot be taken or bargained away. Chief among these rights are life, liberty and the pursuit of happiness. It was a basic assumption that the very purpose of the law was to protect these rights. This legal concept finds expression also in our modern belief in individualized treatment of the offender.

Our substantive criminal laws were for the most part borrowed from the English common law as set forth by Sir Edward Coke in his Third Institute. Many jurisdictions rejected the doctrine of common law crimes because they also included religious and political offenses, but borrowed as much as they desired by way of statutory enactments. The intent of our criminal laws is to punish the individual offender by imposing a penalty corresponding to the gravity of his offense. Such laws are therefore punitive rather than reformatory in character. All our other safeguards of individual rights seem somewhat in conflict with the philosophy of our criminal laws, and many states have felt it necessary to make provisions in their constitutions in substantially the following language: "The enforcement of the criminal laws of the State shall be based upon reformation and not upon vindictive justice."

MODERN PHILOSOPHY OF REHABILITATION

The modern philosophy of rehabilitation is put to practical application by the development of the three related and continous phases of the correctional process: probation, institutional training and treatment, and parole. The basic principles of probation and parole are now quite generally accepted by intelligent and informed citizens, although malad-ministration of these services leads to sharp criticism. There is no such general acceptance of the idea that a primary function of penal and correctional institutions is rehabilitation. It is necessary to state and re-state the arguments in support of that idea with respect to prisons, which the public generally thinks of as punitive agencies.

The following extracts from an article on this subject discuss the question of whether prisons protect society most effectively by being operated primarily for custody and punishment or for custody and rehabilitation.[12] It is obvious that the prison provides society some protection from crime by merely keeping offenders in custodial segregation for varying periods up to life imprisonment. It is equally obvious that this may or may not help solve the problem of crime in general, just as the segregation of lepers may or may not promote the prevention and cure of leprosy. Even with specific offenders, imprisonment has limited value as a protective device unless they are confined for life.

If, on the other hand, modern society sought to protect itself against those who are a menace to the persons or the purses of their fellow citizens by life imprisonment or other inordinately long sentences for all sorts of crimes, it would find itself eventually with an ever-increasing burden of criminals. It would deserve to, moreover, as a penalty for its abandonment of a defensible philosophy with respect to crime. The history of Elizabethan England, of Colonial America, and, indeed, all history, sounds a clear warning that society does not reduce crime but increases it by imposing penalties that those who make up society cannot accept as necessary and just.

It is contrary to progressive correctional philosophy and is becoming increasingly repugnant to the social conscience of our people to imprison an offender for a long period, without regard for his personal characteristics, merely because his custodial segregation affords society protection for the time being. There is a growing awareness among thoughtful people that society can never be truly protected by any procedure that does not deal justly and wisely with its individual members.

The theory that the prison can more effectively reduce crime and thus promote the protection of society by serving as an instrument of punishment cannot be discussed without reference to the theory of rehabilitation, for in practice the two theories run counter to each other at so many points. The debate on the punitive versus the rehabilitative theory has filled the pages of penological literature for generations. It is a debate that has not been conclusively ended on the world stage. So far as the United States is concerned, however, it is ended. It would be virtually impossible in America today to find a penologist of recognized standing who is willing to write or speak on the relative validity of the two theories except as a literary or oratorical exercise or as a task of restating what he considers self-evident truths.

The position he and his colleagues would take is that whatever validity the punitive philosophy may have in this country and century is so far out-weighed by the merits of the philosophy of rehabilitation that the latter should take unquestioned precedence in current penal thought. They would insist, moreover, that if punishment is to be considered an aim of imprisonment, it must be what the Germans termed "Zweckstrafe," or punishment for a purpose, rather than "Vergeltungs-strafe," or punishment as retribution.

Punishment as retribution belongs to a penal philosophy that is archaic and discredited by history. Our leading correctional administrators, if prisons were to be operated as instruments of retributive punishment, would refuse to accept appointments to administer them. They recognize that even if the idea of retribution by legal penalties is entirely sound today from the ethical standpoint, which they question in view of the known inaccuracies and inequities of our legal processes, it is not sound from the practical standpoint. It is impossible to determine what penalties provide the varying but exact amounts of retribution called for by a list of crimes ranging, for example, from theft of a handkerchief to murder. When it abandoned the use of the death penalty for the former and a great variety of other minor and major offenses, society posed for itself the impossible task of setting up a graded scale of crime values with commensurate penalties.

The task of producing a legal slide rule on which one can compute the exact degree of retribution called for by a crime committed by a person at a given time under specific conditions is still more impossible. The wide divergence in sentences for the same crimes imposed not only by courts in the United States but also by those of a single state and by the courts of the federal judicial system bear indisputable witness to our failure to develop exact scales of punishment or to use those we have even-handedly.

Retribution, moreover, implies the payment of a debt to society and expiation of one's offense. The very crimes that we are most anxious to prevent—murder, rape, and other crimes involving cruelty and violence—are those for which society can never exact adequate compensation by retribution nor the perpetrators make adequate payments by expiation. For these and other crimes it is impossible to pay one's debt to society and it is not good for the offender to believe that it is possible. Payment of a debt carries the implication that one is free to start running up a new account. This is all too often the view of prisoners who have served out the full length of a heavy retributive sentence of imprisonment.

Finally, if it were possible to use the prison as an instrument of retributive punishment with exactitude and justice, its use for such a purpose would defeat the achievement of so many more worthy purposes that the net result to society would not be gain but loss, not benefit but injury. The prison operated on the basis of a purely punitive philosophy would produce more criminals than it would prevent.

If we are to dismiss the idea of punishment as retribution, what of punishment for a purpose? What purpose could give validity to the use of the prison as an instrument of punishment? It is difficult to think of anything that can be admitted to consideration except deterrence. It is conceivable that under a system of law enforcement in which the apprehension and conviction of offenders are swift and certain, punishment by imprisonment could be so imposed and carried out that it would deter the ex-prisoner and other potential offenders from the commission of crime. Only the most unrealistic optimist, however, would claim that under the present system of law enforcement in the United States, deterrence can be effectively accomplished by punitive imprisonment. In the United States so small a percentage of all offenders are caught and convicted that what happens to them can have little effect on the great body of potential and actual violators of the law.

Many offenders, moreover, are the type that could not be deterred even if the odds were heavily against them. Included in this group are many insane, mentally defective, neurotic, and psychopathic persons, some with uncontrollable compulsive urges, especially in the sexual field. There are others who act impulsively, without weighing the costs, perhaps under the stress of anger or passion; others who plan their crimes, such as insurance murders, but whose cupidity of predatory desires outweigh their caution; still others whose recklessness makes unfavorable odds more, rather than less, attractive, and many who do not know whether the odds are in their favor or not and do not care. In these groups fall the great majority of the types of offenders we would like most of all to deter from crime, because of the nature and frequency of the crimes they characteristically commit.

In spite of these facts, strengthening the processes of law enforcement so that more offenders are imprisoned would undoubtedly result in some degree of deterrence, but what degree is by no means certain. There can be little doubt, furthermore, that emphasis on the use of the prison as an instrument of deterrence would result in a net loss rather than a net gain. To achieve the maximum deterrent effect it would be necessary either to impose excessively long sentences or to inflict harsh treatment and impose rigid restrictions and deprivations on the prisoners. The experience of centuries in Europe and America indicates that these methods not only defeat rehabilitation and increase recidivism but encourage in free society a brutalized viewpoint that fosters crime.

Experienced penologists do not dismiss the idea of punishment. They recognize the fact that being sent to a prison, however humanely it is operated, is punishment in itself. They know that it is impossible to make a prison so pleasant that the prisoners will not consider their imprisonment punishment. They believe it is neither necessary nor justifiable to add to the punishment inherent in loss of liberty, separation from one's friends and family, and the stigma of a prison sentence. Experience has convinced them that efforts to do so tend to reduce the number of offenders who become law-abiding citizens on release and to increase the number who continue in crime. They are certain that emphasis on the punitive theory of imprisonment works against rather than for the protection of society.

Penologists in the United States today are generally agreed that the prison serves most effectively for the protection of society against crime when its major emphasis is on rehabilitation. They accept this as a fact that no longer needs to be debated. The best thought in what was once called the penal field and is now significantly called the correctional field is directed toward developing institutional plants, personnel and programs that will accomplish the rehabilitation of as many offenders as possible and will enable those who cannot be released to adjust as well as possible to the restricted life of the prison. Although prison administrators know that a substantial percentage of adult offenders are not likely to be salvaged by any methods we have thus far developed, they direct their programs of rehabilitation to the presumably incorrigible as well as the probably reclaimable group, and consider only a small minority of prisoners as completely hopeless cases. This may seem to be an impractical and visionary viewpoint, but it is wholly realistic and is based on a clear-cut idea of what rehabilitation is and what it can accomplish.

The position taken by the proponents of the theory of rehabilitation may be summed up as follows: They do not rule out the necessity of custodial segregation, but consider custody a means to an end in the vast majority of cases, and an end in very few cases. They do not deny the desirability of achieving a deterrent effect if it can be done without impairing the effectiveness of rehabilitative programs that offer more assurance of good results than deterrence does. In short, they believe, all things considered, that the prison which is not geared toward rehabilitation as one of its primary aims stands condemned on its own evidence.

DEVELOPMENT OF ADULT CORRECTIONAL INSTITUTIONS

The colonial "prisons" described earlier in this chapter bore little resemblance to the correctional institutions of today.

The intent in establishing institutions for the confinement of long-term prisoners during the 1790's and early 1800's was not only to substitute imprisonment for corporal and capital punishment but also to get away from the evil conditions existing in the jails: congregate confinement, with men, women and children sleeping indiscriminately on the floors of filthy compartments, liquor sold at the jail bar, and neglect and brutality accepted as standard practice. Idleness compounded the bad effects of these conditions.

The concern of early reformers in America and Europe with the twin evils of congregate confinement and idleness in jails was carried into the prison field in the classic controversy between the proponents of the so-called Auburn and Pennsylvania Systems of prison operation. These systems or methods took their names from the New York State Prison at Auburn, opened in 1819, and the Eastern Penitentiary in Philadelphia, opened in 1829.

The basic difference between them was that Pennsylvania prisoners lived and worked in separate cells, each with its own small exercise yard, and Auburn prisoners lived in separate cells but worked in congregate shops. The cells at the Eastern Penitentiary were of the "outside" type and unusually large: $11^3/_4$ feet long and $7^1/_2$ feet wide. The Auburn cells were of the "inside" type. In the first block erected there were two-men cells and compartments for ten or more prisoners, but in the second block the cells were single and only 7 feet long and $3^1/_2$ feet wide.

In both systems strict silence rules were enforced and prisoners were confined to separate cells not merely to make discipline easier but also to prevent contamination of one prisoner by another. In the spirited controversy over the merits of these two systems which went on for years in this country and abroad, the proponents of both talked as often in terms of reformation as of punishment, but their ideas of how reformation could best be accomplished are indicated by the inscription over the door of the first New Jersey Penitentiary, opened in 1799: "Labor, Silence, Penitence."

The development of European prisons was largely on the Pennsylvania System pattern. On the other hand, most of the American prisons opened during the 19th century were patterned basically on the Auburn system, principally because congregate labor was found more efficient and profitable than the labor of men working alone at work-benches in their cells. There was little penal progress worthy of the name until the 1870's. A punitive philosophy predominated in the prison field and found expression in mass treatment, rigid repression and regimentation, silence rules, severe punishments, poor and insufficient food, confinement in small, unsanitary, poorly lighted cells, and lack of anything but the most rudimentary efforts at rehabilitation. The dollar sign was over the main gate of most institutions, and prison labor was exploited to the limit in chain gangs, contract shops and lease systems where shameful abuses went unchecked.

The 1870's was a period which, it appeared at the time, might mark the beginning of a "Golden Age of Penology." In this decade the Elmira (New York) Reformatory, the first reformatory for men, was opened with a program having rehabilitation, or reformation, as its aim and utilizing parole systematically for the first time in this country. The first separate institutions for women were opened in Indiana and Massachusetts. The National (later American) Prison Association was organized and at its first Congress, held in Cincinnati in 1870, adopted a Declaration of Principles so advanced in thought that it was re-affirmed in 1930 with few basic changes. The first International Prison Congress, held in London in

1872, was attended by the leading American advocates of prison reform and the total atmosphere of that Congress also was one of progress.

The advances in theoretical penology, however, were not matched by advances in practical application. The Elmira Reformatory, as well as the other early institutions patterned after it, failed to realize the high hopes of the founders because of their unrealistic faith in the effectiveness of unselective education for all and other mass treatment programs which eventually made the reformatories educational treadmills little better than the industrial treadmills which prisons had become. Little was known about individual differences, or of the motivations of criminal and delinquent behavior. The marks on which parole was granted were credited or withheld by personnel who had no professional training for correctional work as we understand it today, and were based on performance in programs which neither tested nor trained the inmates adequately. By 1910 it was generally admitted that the adult reformatory idea, as put into practice, was an almost complete failure. It was not until the 1930's that the reorganization of Elmira's educational program on modern lines led to a general reorganization of the institution, and it began at last to bring some of the hopes of the 1870's to reality.

In our prisons also, in spite of the ferment of reform in the 1870's, there was little progress until well into the 20th century. The conditions and practices existing prior to 1870 went on for another half-century and, in fact, some of them have persisted until the present. The worst abuses of the contract system of prison labor were not curbed until a series of restrictive federal laws, beginning with the Hawes-Cooper Act of 1929, effective in 1934, practically put prison contract industries out of business.

The last state operating the iniquitous lease system, under which prisoners were virtually sold into servitude, did not abolish it until 1928, and then only under the impact of public opinion aroused by successive scandals. Exposures of brutality in chain-gangs at about the same time started a trend which led gradually to the almost complete elimination of the use of chains in road-camps and other outdoor work projects. Some states and counties continue to use, especially with prisoners presenting serious escape risks, the so-called "step-chain," a chain fastened to a shackle on each ankle and short enough to make running impossible. This practice, however, is the exception rather than the rule.

Silence rules were still rigidly enforced in some prisons in every section of the country as late as 1928. Such rules are in use today in many institutions to some extent, but are usually enforced only in messhalls, chapels, in marching formations, and so on.

The number of states using flogging as official prison punishment has decreased greatly during the last four decades. It is still on the statute books in less than a dozen states, and not over half that number use this form of punishment. In the others where it is still permitted by law, it has been banned by edicts of governors or policies of correctional officials. The preceding statements refer to state institutions; there is no way of determining how many counties use flogging as punishment, either officially or surreptitiously.

In short, the punitive philosophy cast a heavy shadow over policy and practice in American prison systems not merely in the 1800's but well into the 20th Century. Correctional care, custody, training and treatment of the sort described in this *Manual,* and widely practiced today, were found in few institutions to more than a very limited extent four decades ago. By the time the century's halfway mark was reached, however, significant changes and advances had taken place. The correctional philosophy is now clearly predominant in the American institutional field, although some officials in actual practice give it little more than lip service.

In the period just before World War I the attacks on prison conditions which had been made intermittently since the early 1800's were given new impetus by the reports of commissions set up by New York and New Jersey to investigate their state prison systems. These commissions were headed respectively by Thomas Mott Osborn and Dwight Morrow. The bad conditions and practices the commissions' reports revealed and the exposure during and soon after the same period of even worse situations in the prisons of other states aroused public-spirited citizens throughout the country.

The major emphasis in that period, however, was on abolishing brutality, improving living conditions, and making prison life less destructive and embittering. Speakers usually denounced our "19th century bastilles," the bucket system, stripes, the silent system, such punishments as the lash, stringing up by the wrists, and the water cure, the evils of the contract and lease systems, and so on. There was also considerable talk of the need of establishing, or improving, such programs of rehabilitation as education, vocational training and medical services. But the necessity of eliminating glaring evils was so pressing that it was easy to postpone action on constructive programs until the task of removing destructive factors was completed. Conditions during World War I were not conducive to civilian prison progress, nor were the roaring 1920's, with bootlegging and gang warfare bringing the establishment of crime commissions and laws prescribing heavy mandatory sentences for many offenses in their train.

The year 1930 may well be accepted as the beginning of the modern era of prison progress. The event that gave it greatest impetus was the complete reorganization and reform of the Federal prisons which were raised from the status of a backward, neglected, and at times corrupt system to a position of preeminence among the prisons of the country. The rapid and steady progress made by the federal system from 1929–30 on had a strong influence on state prisons, for it demonstrated that practical programs of rehabilitation could be set up and operated effectively with adequate physical plants and, above all, qualified personnel. This is not to imply that there had been no progress in state prisons prior to that time. A number of states had established or improved educational and other rehabilitative programs, and here and there the domination of prisons by politics had been somewhat weakened. But progress in general had been slow, spotty and sporadic.

Progress in several states in the 1930's gave added strength to the influence exerted by federal prison progress. New York not only reorganized and revivified Elmira but opened the unwalled Wallkill Prison, then and now an outstanding institution. A strong educational program under expert direction was established by the State Department of Correction. New Jersey opened two medium security reformatories for males and one for women, and strengthened its classification, educational and medical programs. These are only a few instances of the steps of progress which were taken by states during the 1930's. This was a difficult period, with the depression forcing reductions in appropriations in the face of rising prison populations. There was one factor favorable to prisons during the depression, however: they were able to recruit well educated and highly skilled personnel who in ordinary times would not enter the prison service, and personnel of all types were also available through the Works Progress Administration and other relief programs.

World War II, following on the heels of the depression, was another period of mixed blessings. Personnel on all levels, including those in key positions, left to enter the armed services and institutions were seriously undermanned throughout the war. Fortunately, civilian crime went down and with it state prison populations shrank from 154,446 at the end of 1940 to 114,217 at the end of 1944. Prison industries boomed and produced war goods valued at over $138,000,000. Prisoners worked with a will, as well as volunteering for painful and dangerous medical experiments. Under a wartime relaxation of legal restrictions, prisoners in agricultural states were used in large numbers to gather crops which would otherwise have been lost.

During the post-war period two occurrences of vividly contrasting types took place. One was the wave of riots and other mass disorders which swept over prisons of every size, age and type in every section of the country in the 1950's. The other was the particularly striking progress made in two states, Texas and California, which set examples not only for their regional areas but also for the entire country. The progress in Texas took on added importance because it laid down guide-lines for other Southern states, several of which made marked progress in their prison systems in the 1950's: notably Alabama, Louisiana and North Carolina.

Space limits a detailed discussion of the riot wave. Every phase of the riots was widely publicized by newspapers, magazines, radio, television, and movies. The riots have been described and discussed in thoughtful books, articles and reports. An analysis of causal and contributory factors was made by the American Prison Association's Committee on Riots, which published its report in May 1953. After stating that "the immediate causes given out for prison riots are only symptoms of more basic causes," the report lists the fundamental causes as follows: A. Inadequate financial support, and official and public indifference; B. Substandard personnel; C. Enforced idleness; D. Lack of professional leadership and professional programs; E. Excessive size and overcrowding of institutions; F. Political domination and motivation of management; G. Unwise sentencing and parole practice.

No complete and definitive survey has been made of the effects of the riots on the prisons in which they occurred and on prisons in general. It is known that some institutions have been given public support for improvement of bad conditions, others became worse than ever under the weight of public condemnation, and others stood still. It is difficult to say in what degree stagnation and retrogression since the riots are due to the stiffening of public opinion against prisoners and against modern correctional methods, which many unthinking people hold responsible for the riots, and in what degree are due to soaring construction costs and salary scales, which make the replacement of archaic and inadequate physical plants and the provision of vitally needed personnel difficult or impossible for many states.

The reform of the Texas prison system, referred to above, began in 1947. A survey and report made by the Osborne Association had exposed abominable conditions on the prison farms, which constituted practically the entire prison system. A new head of the system was appointed and under his leadership a sweeping program of reform and reorganization was initiated and carried out. Personnel standards were raised, farm operations modernized, new institutions built and old facilities improved, brutal disciplinary methods abolished, and such rehabilitative programs as education, vocational training, classification, religion, and medical services were developed under competent personnel. A veritable transformation of the prison system took place, and a feature of the change highly appreciated by the taxpayers was the tremendous increase in farm production under the new methods and personnel, and the new morale they engendered.

The progress in California, beginning in 1944 and continued without slackening since that date, has brought its correctional system to the point where it is rated as sharing leadership in the United States with the federal system, which began similarly spectacular progress in 1929–30. Coincident with the rise in the state's population, in the 20 years since the Department of Corrections was established in 1944, California's prison population has risen in round numbers from 5,700 to 27,000 on December 31, 1964. This unprecedented increase presented the tremendous problem of providing housing capacity for the rapidly increasing number of prisoners. Under the leadership of career administrators, new institutions, some of them composed of several semi-autonomous satellite institutions, and two reception-guidance centers have been constructed, and a 2,300-bed naval hospital has been taken over to serve as the Department's Rehabilitation Center for drug addicts. The older institutions have undergone extensive renovation and reconstruction. The Department's forestry camp program has been greatly expanded by the construction of three conservation centers and increase in the number of camps. . . .

In contrast to the progress that has been made in the prisons of the country, there are two matters which must be of grave concern to the correctional field and to the public: idleness in prisons, and the deplorable situation in most of our county jails. In the all-important matter of providing work for prisoners there has been, except for the war period, retrogression instead of progress in many institutions. Our state prisons, all too often, are little better than "idle houses." Thousands of prisoners now have no work at all, other thousands have nothing to do except dawdle through years of semi-idleness on overmanned maintenance details. In some of our most prosperous states only a small percentage of the prisoners are employed in industries, and move at a pace which does not equip them for future employment in an outside industry.

There is no validity in the belief that prisoners cannot work and will not work. That idea was clearly refuted during World War II. It does not take a war, moreover, to establish a high and profitable production record in prisons. The federal prison industries and those of the few states that have set up a modern system of diversified industries to produce goods for the use of state departments and agencies have demonstrated that prison labor under good management, with the incentive of even a small wage, can lessen the burden of the taxpayer without unfair competition with free industry, and can pay long-range dividends in the preparation of prisoners to earn an honest living on release. The use of prison labor on farms, in forestry camps, and on other public works, providing indefensible methods of custodial control are not used, is profitable to the taxpayers and beneficial to the prisoners.

The so-called Work Furlough Plan, initiated in Wisconsin 20 years ago for jail prisoners, is now being used successfully by several states, notably North Carolina, with prisoners convicted of felonies. Under this plan, carefully selected prisoners are allowed to work during the day at jobs in the community, frequently those they held before being committed. They return to the institution at night. The employer deposits regular wages with the authorities, and a charge is made against them for the prisoner's "room and board." If his family is on relief, part or all of the costs are charged against the prisoner's account. This type of arrangement has resulted in substantial savings to the state or county. It has also helped prisoners to maintain their self-respect, to keep their families together, and to go out when their sentences end with jobs and frequently with savings.

American county jails have been often described as the penal (they cannot properly be called correctional) institutions that have most successfully resisted change and reform. Most of them have been rated by inspectors as unfit for human habitation. Old and unsanitary buildings, poorly qualified and constantly changing personnel, intermingling of all types of prisoners—sick and well, old and young, hardened criminals and petty offenders—in overcrowded cell-blocks and "tanks," and the almost complete absence of even the most rudimentary rehabilitative programs constitute a scandalous state of affairs which will not be eliminated until the public is aroused to the point where it backs the efforts of the many sheriffs and jailers who are trying to correct bad conditions and practices, and insists that the others do so or be replaced.

Developments of major importance during the past 35 years, and continuing in the present era, are the diversification of adult correctional institutions to meet the varying needs of individual prisoners, and more effective emphasis on rehabilitation through individualized training and treatment within the institutions. The increased use of group methods—group counseling and therapy, the therapeutic community concept, and so on—may appear to run counter to the individualized approach. In actuality, however these methods do not; a group program is often the most effective, economical way of dealing with individual problems and needs.

The primary diversification of institutions has been on the basis of degrees of custody. It is now recognized that only a minority of prisoners need to be confined in maximum security prisons, and that even in institutions of this type supervision by qualified personnel is more effective as a custodial measure than the old reliance on heavy stone or concrete and steel. An individual's need of maximum security, moreover, does not negate the need of training and treatment, which have their proper place in even the most secure prison.

The number of medium-security institutions and minimum-security camps, farms and other facilities has increased steadily over the past three decades. None of the new institutions constructed by the two most rapidly expanding systems in the country, the Federal and California's, since their expansion began in the 1930's and 1940's respectively was of the maximum security type until the U.S. Bureau of Prisons opened its new 658-man penitentiary at Marion, Illinois, in 1963, following the closing down of Alcatraz Island. Other correctional systems have followed the same trend toward medium and minimum security facilities. Efficient classification programs and adequate staffing of institutions by qualified personnel have proved the keys to successful use of lessened custody.

Types of prisoners who would have been confined fifty years ago in a mass treatment, maximum security, walled prison may be found now in several kinds of minimum and medium security institutions or units, and in a variety of facilities organized and operated to serve a special function or to care for a special category of prisoners. Although we still use the term "prison" as a generic term for convenience, we speak today of correctional rather than penal institutions. Current correctional philosophy calls for individualized as opposed to mass treatment to the fullest practicable extent, even in maximum security institutions, with rehabilitation as a fundamental aim of the institution.

Rehabilitation is no longer a vague, haphazard and loosely defined process. The essential elements of a well-rounded correctional program of individualized training and treatment in an institution for adult offenders . . . include the following: scientific classification and program-planning on the basis of complete case histories, examinations, tests and studies of the individual prisoners; adequate medical services, having corrective as well as curative treatment as their aim, and making full use of psychiatry; psychological services, properly related to the problems of education, work assignment, discipline and preparation for parole; individual and group therapy and counseling, and application of the therapeutic community concept, under the direction of psychiatrists, psychologists, or other trained therapists and counselors; casework services, reaching families as well as prisoners; employment at tasks comparable in variety, type and pace to the work of the world outside, and especially tasks with vocational training value; academic and vocational education, in accordance with the individual's needs, interests, and capabilities; library services, designed to provide wholesome recreation and indirect education; directed recreation, both indoors and outdoors, so organized as to promote good morale and sound mental and physical health; a religious program so conducted as to affect the spiritual life of the individual as well as that of the whole group; discipline that aims at the development of self-control and preparation for free life, not merely conformity to institutional rules; adequate buildings and equipment for the varied program and activities of the institution; and, above all, adequate and competent personnel, carefully selected, well trained, and serving under such conditions as to promote a high degree of morale and efficiency.

Today, with few exceptions, correctional administrators subscribe to the philosophy of rehabilitation as opposed to the old punitive philosophy, although many of them lack the funds and personnel, and some the vision and ability, to translate their beliefs into actual programs.

3   *State Correctional Institutions for Adults*

THE PRESIDENT'S COMMISSION
ON LAW ENFORCEMENT AND
ADMINISTRATION OF JUSTICE*

For purposes of this survey, adult correctional institutions are understood to be those facilities operated by the 50 States, Puerto Rico, and the District of Columbia which receive felons sentenced by the criminal courts.

I. INTRODUCTION

Even so simple a definition as the one above is not easily applied to 52 correctional systems as diverse as those found in the United States.

Generally, a felony is regarded as an offense punishable by imprisonment in excess of 1 year, but many criminal codes define the term differently. For this and other reasons, some institutions covered by this part of the survey receive both misdemeanants and felons.

Some States have separate facilities for the juvenile delinquent and the adult felon; in others, the same facility receives both. This survey includes those institutions which receive juveniles if they also routinely accept offenders sentenced by the adult criminal courts. Thus, the age floor for some institutions is 15; for others, it is 16, 18, or 21. The offenses represented can vary from truancy to murder.

The term "correctional institution" is comparatively new in penology

* From *Task Force Report: Corrections,* The President's Commission on Law Enforcement and Administration of Justice (Washington, D.C.: U.S. Government Printing Office, 1967), pp. 177–184.

and is not universally descriptive of the institutions surveyed. Many of the institutions are called prisons, penitentiaries, reformatories, industrial institutions, prison farms, conservation camps, forestry camps, etc. They vary from the highly sophisticated to the exceedingly primitive.

A. History of Incarceration

In the long history of man, imprisonment of the convicted offender is a relatively recent practice. Until less than two centuries ago, most convicted offenders were fined, mutilated, banished, tortured, or killed. Prisons and jails existed only as places where persons were held pending sentence or ransom, and as protection for creditors against debtors. Preludes to imprisonment for crime may be seen in the institutions where violators of the church's canons did penance, and in the galleys used, at one time or another by many seafaring nations, for confinement and hard labor.

In the last half of the 18th century, social theorists—among them, Montesquieu, Beccaria, Rousseau, and Blackstone—rejected the system of brutal punishments on grounds of humanity, convenience, and commonsense. Out of the ferment they generated, there evolved a new theory of criminal punishment which, as formulated by William Paley in 1785, advocated reform of the criminal through a regime of solitary imprisonment. The theory held that confining the criminal in a separate compartment, where he is secluded from "the society of his fellow-prisoners, in which society the worse are sure to corrupt the better . . . is calculated to raise up in him reflections on the folly of his choice and to expose his mind to such bitter and continued penitence as may produce a lasting alteration in the principles of his conduct."[13]

In 1787 a small group of Americans, including Benjamin Franklin and Dr. Benjamin Rush, organized the Philadelphia Society for Alleviating the Miseries of Public Prisons; a year later, in the first of many memorials issued to the legislature, the society declared its belief that "solitary confinement to hard labor and total abstinence" would prove the most effective means of reforming criminals.[14] Impressed with the argument in favor of hard labor in prison, which satisfied the desire for profit as well as the demand of piety, the Pennsylvania General Assembly, in 1790, enacted legislation providing solitary confinement to hard labor. The course of penal history was changed; the penitentiary system was born.

The new institutions in Pennsylvania and New York were built and operated according to this concept of hard labor in solitary confinement, but in a short time the officials of the prison at Auburn, N.Y., deciding that solitary confinement was beyond the strength of man, shifted to the practice of congregate confinement. Prisoners were confined to solitary cells at night but, during the day, worked together under a rule of silence. The congregate or Auburn system was copied, in one form or another, in many States. An important reason for its popularity was that congregate labor was more efficient and productive, a significant consideration during these early years of the industrial revolution.

In 1831, De Beaumont and De Tocqueville noted that the States were disunited, except in matters affecting their common national interests. "They preserve their individual independence, and each of them is sovereign master to rule itself according to its own pleasure. By the side of one State, the penitentiaries of which might serve as a model, we find another whose jails present the example of everything which ought to be avoided."[15] These words, written 135 years ago, need not even be paraphrased to describe accurately the uneven quality of prisons in the United States today.

B. Contact With Other Correctional Services

The area of service covered by the adult correctional institution does not have clearly defined boundaries; as a result, it is subject to occasional border disputes. During the early days of the penitentiary, its function was to receive and hold almost all convicted felons; the few exceptions were those sentenced to execution, to the whipping post, or to a fine. Soon houses of refuge were established for young offenders, and over the years the child has usually been separated from the adult. The line of separation is not uniform throughout the Nation; in some States, young children convicted of serious crimes may be committed to the adult institution. In many States intermediate institutions receive both juveniles and adults. Thus, the border between the juvenile and the adult is blurred.

The extent to which probation is used varies widely, from about 80 percent of felony convictions in at least one state to less than 30 percent in several States. (A similar variation exists between counties in the same State.) Where adult probation services are well developed, the commitment rates to correctional institutions are low.

States vary also in the percentage of prisoners paroled and the average amount of time served before parole is granted—variables which similarly affect the population count in the institution.

In some States the borders separating State from county jurisdiction are poorly defined. In one State at the time of the survey, over 2,000 prisoners were serving sentences in excess of 2 years in county jails and local institutions.

The border between correctional institution and mental health facility fluctuates from State to State, and sometimes even within the same State. In certain States, institutions for defective delinquents are operated by a correctional agency; in others, they are operated by some other agency. In some States, the correctional agencies have units for the emotionally disturbed and psychotic prisoners; in other States, such persons are transferred to facilities operated by the mental health authority; and in some States the emotionally disturbed are retained in special wings, units, or facilities of the correctional agency while the psychotic are committed to the mental health agency.

The line between services of the correctional institution and its brother agencies is further obscured by furloughs, halfway houses, and work release programs. Some correctional authorities argue that furlough should be a function of the institution; others maintain that it is a parole function. Some institutions are establishing experimental halfway houses; many officials feel that these, too, should be a part of the parole service.

II. SURVEY FINDINGS

A. The Institution Workload

During 1965, over 125,000 persons were received in adult correctional institutions in the United States. Of this number almost 80,000 were felons. In 1955–65, the number of felons received annually increased, but the commitment rate compared with the general population decreased.[16] Inasmuch as the number of crimes, the number of arrests, and the number of convictions all have increased, the decrease in commitments per 100,000 of population apparently reflects an increase in the use of sentences other than imprisonment in a number of States.

Statistics obtained from the States for this survey indicate that, in 1966, 201,220 persons were confined in the State institutions. However, this figure includes a number of misdemeanants as well as felons.

The length of stay of inmates in State correctional institutions varies according to the State's sentencing laws, the practices of its courts, its parole laws, and the practice of its releasing authority. The survey shows that the average length of stay ranges from less than 6 months in one State to as much as 5 years in several States (see table 1). In 12 states the average is less than 18 months; in 15 states it is more than 30 months.

TABLE 1

Average Length of Stay in Adult Institutions, by Number of States

Average length of stay	Number of States	Average length of stay	Number of States
Less than 6 months	1	37 to 48 months	2
7 to 12 months	2	49 to 60 months	3
13 to 18 months	9	Unknown	3
19 to 24 months	14		—
25 to 30 months	8	Total	52
31 to 36 months	10		

The average length of stay of inmates has many implications for institutional size, program development, personnel requirements, and cost of operation. One State, which still sends its felons to Federal institutions, spent only $379,000 last year, while another State's bill was over $62 million. These figures do not include capital construction. The cost of operating 358 State correctional institutions in the 52 jurisdictions totaled $384,980,648 in 1965.

More than 46,000 employees guard, feed, and attempt to rehabilitate the 200,000 inmates. One large State employs over 6,700 persons in these tasks, while one of the smaller States employs only 23. One medium-size State with a fairly large prisoner population (2,000) employs only 34 staff persons, using armed inmates to enforce security.

B. Organization

Where each institution is a separate entity, with its board or warden reporting directly to the Governor, it is difficult to organize an integrated institutional system providing diversity of custody and treatment. That was the prevailing pattern in the first third of this century.

In 1945, there were still 8 States (in the total then of 48) in which each adult correctional institution was separately administered; today only 3 have this arrangement.

In 1945, State boards with no other functions provided central administration for adult correctional institutions in 13 States; today the same situation obtains, although some of them have changed their name from prison board to department of correction.

In 1945, adult correctional institutions in 27 States were administered by an agency having additional functions; today this is the plan in 34 States and Puerto Rico.

Standards call for the administration of State correctional institutions to be vested in a separate State department of correction or its equivalent. This implies that the department would also have other correctional functions.

Only 16 States even partially meet this standard. However, there are several States in which a multipurpose correctional agency in a State department enjoys considerable autonomy even though it does not have separate status.

C. Institutional Patterns

1. Physical Plant

When the Quakers built the famous Eastern State Penitentiary in 1829, they understood that plant and program planning should be hand-in-glove, and they built their institution at Cherry Hill to fit their program, even though the result was America's most costly public building of its day. By 1870 the penologists had an entirely different concept of reform, but, though they made great program innovations, they continued to be tied architecturally to the philosophy of the older era. Much of today's institutional programing is circumscribed by outmoded architecture, or by prisons built with only economy, isolation, or security in mind. The result, in many instances, is that the program fits the structure, rather than the other way around.

Though it is axiomatic that a good warden can run a good prison in an old red barn, a good plant helps. Recent institutional design has stressed function and small self-contained program units.

The 52 jurisdictions have, exclusive of satellites, 358 State correctional institutions for adults (see table 2). The total rated capacity is 213,584; the average daily population is 201,220 (94 percent of capacity). Thirty-five of the institutions house only women. In several States a single institution receives both men and women but separates them in different buildings; sometimes, in these instances, the women's building is off the grounds of the main institution. Two States send their female prisoners to the women's institution of an adjacent State. Alaska and Hawaii continue to use the Federal Bureau of Prisons for their few female prisoners. A few

TABLE 2
Number of Institutions Serving Special Population Groups

Major population	Number of institutions	Major population	Number of institutions
Male felons	114	Reception centers and other	
Females	35	special units	26
Youthful offenders	41	Unreported	12
Misdemeanants	34		
Mixed	96	Total	358

States contract with counties for the care of all or some of their women prisoners.

Of the 358 institutions, 55 are the maximum security type; 124 are medium security; 103, minimum security; and 68 mixed. The security classification of eight was not reported.

Including satellite facilities of core institutions, the total number of correctional units is 398. Of these, 170 may be classified as prisons, penitentiaries, or major correctional institutions; 55 are categorized as reformatories, industrial schools, or vocational institutions; 76 are ranches, camps, or farms; 72 are road camps (in 3 Southern States); 8 are facilities for the ill, the psychotic, or the defective; 7 are reception centers; 5 are special purpose units; 5 are unclassified. During the past decade there has been a considerable increase in the use of reduced custody facilities of all types.

Of the original institutions still in use, 61 were opened before 1900; 25 of these are now more than 100 years old. Of the dormitories or cell blocks now in use, 31 percent are more than 50 years old; 29 percent are between 25 and 50 years old; 20 percent are between 10 and 24 years old; 20 percent are less than 10 years old. In the process of construction now are 44 cell blocks or dormitories, to house 5,676 persons; 63 additional units designed to serve over 17,000 prisoners have been authorized but are not yet under construction. Not all of the new units being constructed or in the planning stage will add to the present capacity; some are being built to replace archaic facilities.

2. Personnel

(A) NUMBER AND RATIO. Personnel standards recommended the following:

1. Taking into account the type of population, the rate of turnover, and the mission of the institution, minimum workload standards for

institutional casework should provide for 30 cases per month for case-workers assigned exclusively to the reception process, and 150 inmates per counselor in general institution programs.

2. Clinical services (psychiatric, psychological, and counseling) for a general institution population of 600 inmates require a minimum of 1 psychiatrist, 3 clinical psychologists, and 3 specialized counselors.

3. Under professional leadership and consultation, programs of group counseling conducted by lay personnel of the institution should be part of the clinical services of the institution.

4. There should be at least 1 professionally qualified vocational counselor having a workload of 40 cases per month, or 1 counselor to every 30 inmates.

The 358 correctional facilities in the 52 jurisdictions employ 46,680 persons—approximately 1 for every 5 inmates. Custodial personnel make up the largest number, 30,809 (66 percent). Over 13,000 (28 percent) have administrative, clerical, maintenance, culinary, or industrial duties. There are 306 physicians, psychiatrists, and dentists: 327 graduate and practical nurses; and 327 other paramedical personnel. Only 1,124 (2.4 percent) of all correctional employees are psychologists, social workers, or counselors. An additional 1,654 (3.5 percent) are vocational or academic teachers, and 359 (.8 percent) are chaplains. Thus, only 3,137 persons (6.7 percent of all employees) carry primary responsibilities for treatment functions. On the whole, 13 jurisdictions have a ratio of professional staff members (psychiatrist, psychologist, social worker, and counselor) to inmates of less than 1:100. One State has a ratio of 1:55; on the other hand, 11 States have professional staff-inmate ratios not better than 1:500, and 2 have ratios of about 1:2,000. The national average is 1:179.

Many more persons are employed in custodial than in treatment positions. The average officer-inmate ratio for the Nation is 1:7, with a range from 1:3 in a New England State to 1:200 in a State using armed inmate guards.

The ratio of all employees to inmate averages 1:4, it ranges from 1:2 to 1:59.

(B) CIVIL SERVICE. Standards call for merit system coverage for all institutional employees.

In practice, civil service does not apply to superintendents in 54 percent of the States, to professional employees in 28 percent, and to custodial officers in 26 percent (see table 3). A merit system for institutional employees does not exist in 13 States (none of which is considered to be in the vanguard of institutional achievement).

TABLE 3
Number of States Covered by Civil Service or Merit System, by Position

Position	Number of States
Superintendent	23
Professional worker	36
Custodial worker	37

(C) SALARIES. Starting salaries in correctional institutions range from a low of $1,500 for custodial officers in one jurisdiction to $18,000 for superintendents in a large State. For superintendents the median beginning salary is between $10,000 and $11,000, with a range from $3,001 to $18,000. For counselors the median beginning salary is between $5,000 and $6,000, with a range from $3,001 to $10,000. For teachers the median is the same as the counselors'; the range is from $3,001 to $9,000. For guards the median is between $4,000 and $5,000; the range is from $1,500

TABLE 4
Beginning Salaries of State Adult Institutional Personnel, by Number of Agencies

	Superin-tendent	Counselor	Teacher	Custodial officer
Under $1,500	0	0	0	0
$1,500 to $2,400	0	0	0	1
$2,401 to $3,000	0	0	0	1
$3,001 to $4,000	1	3	3	22
$4,001 to $5,000	0	6	16	13
$5,001 to $6,000	1	18	23	12
$6,001 to $7,000	2	8	3	0
$7,001 to $8,000	4	4	2	0
$8,001 to $9,000	6	0	1	1
$9,001 to $10,000	5	1	0	0
$10,001 to $11,000	12	0	0	0
$11,001 to $12,000	3	0	0	0
$12,001 to $13,000	7	0	0	0
$13,001 to $14,000	4	0	0	0
$14,001 to $15,000	3	0	0	0
$15,001 to $16,000	1	0	0	0
$16,001 to $17,000	0	0	0	0
$17,000 to $18,000	1	0	0	0
Over $18,000	0	0	0	0
Total	50	40	48	50

to $9,000 (see table 4). Many institutions report difficulties in securing competent help at these salaries. Correctional administrators say it is especially difficult to attract qualified professional personnel to rural areas, while good custodial personnel are hard to come by in high-income urban locations.

(D) EDUCATIONAL REQUIREMENTS.   Only 24 percent of all jurisdictions require the superintendent to have a college degree; 48 percent have no minimum educational requirements whatever (see table 5). In three States an applicant who could not qualify for the guard position because he lacked a high school diploma would not be disqualified for the superintendency.

Qualifications for the professional positions vary, and the meaning of the position title itself is not uniform throughout the States. In 28 percent of all jurisdictions, one can be a "professional worker" without having graduated from high school. In at least one jurisdiction the mail clerk is called a social worker.

TABLE 5
Educational Requirements

Position	Percentage of States requiring qualifications			
	None	*High school graduate*	*College graduate*	*Graduate degree*
Superintendent	48	28	24	
Custodial officer	41	59		

(E) INSERVICE TRAINING.   The following specifications are found in standards on inservice training:

1. At the correctional department level, and in each large institution, full-time staff should be assigned to the responsibility of establishing and directing a personnel training program.

2. Inservice training programs should include both basic training for new employees and continuous inservice training to improve knowledge and skills.

3. Training of custodial personnel should be considered of sufficient importance to warrant the budgeting of funds for 52 hours of training annually.

A member of the survey team commented: "Even with the suggested millennium of competitive salaries and an adequate supply of professional manpower, we will fall short of our performance expectations without a definite allocation of resources and additional employee training, which should approximate the practicing psychiatrist's periodic need to undergo therapy conducted by a colleague. Staff in a correctional institution need some reinforcing therapy, not only to improve their performance in dealing with inmate behavioral problems, but to maintain their own values and perspective against the erosion of the inmate culture."

In 24 percent of all jurisdictions, no inservice training is provided; of those jurisdictions where it is, only 26 percent schedule as much as 30 hours per year.

3. Program

To describe program activities found in 358 institutions located in 52 jurisdictions is not a simple task. As one surveyor put it: "The programs in this State look great on paper, but . . . ." However, some conclusions can be stated with assurance on the basis of on-site visits by surveyors, observations of authorities who have recently written on the subject, and the survey data on budgets, personnel, and plants, all three of which affect program activity.

A State that has only 34 institutional employees, none of whom is a professional, has little in common with one employing either a teacher, a caseworker, a psychologist, a psychiatrist, or a chaplain for every 21 inmates. A universe of programing difference separates a State that confines a daily average of only 80 persons from one that normally maintains a population of over 24,000. Programing is one thing in a Rocky Mountain State having only one institution, a maximum security prison; it is a vastly different thing in a southeastern State that operates 80 or 90 small facilities spread throughout its numerous counties. No single pattern can describe the average institutional program for the entire Nation.

In varying degrees and with vastly different mixes, all jurisdictions provide for custody, discipline, health and medical services, nutrition, classification, counseling, education, recreation, religious work, and visiting. Many also encourage a variety of optional and special interest activities.

(A) CUSTODY AND CONTROL. Most institutional programs are shaped to meet the requirements of custody and control. Custody and control are the nucleus, the paramount consideration of the entire institutional apparatus. That is why two-thirds of all adult institutional employees are engaged in custodial tasks. This emphasis on custody and control is "universally prescribed by law, custom, and public opinion. Although at times such a concept may seem at variance with attempts to introduce rehabilitative services, it is doubtful that any . . . program which ignores this reality will long endure."[17]

Control has a safeguarding as well as a repressive function. "Most inmates will admit and even require the keepers to assume this function. They understand that the metal detector which uncovers a file intended for an escape attempt will also detect a knife intended for the unsuspecting back of a friend. Inmates will privately express their relief at the construction of a segregation wing which protects them from the depredations of men who are outlaws even in the prison world. Much as they complain of the disciplinary court which punishes them for their infractions, they are grateful for the swift and stern justice meted out to inmates who loot their cells. In short, these men realize, sometimes dimly, sometimes keenly, that a control system which is lax enough to permit thievery and intimidation must eventually result in a deterioration and vicious circle."[18]

(B) DISCIPLINE. Task force standards call for disciplinary measures to be determined and controlled by the governing body of the correctional system.

Although the survey did not attempt to measure the types of disciplinary methods being used, the institutions were asked whether corporal punishment was permitted. "Corporal punishment," says the standard, "should never be used under any circumstances. Physical force may be used only when necessary to protect one's self or others from injury, to prevent escape, and to prevent serious injury to property. Officers should not be permitted to carry clubs." Most institutions are able to conform to the standard in spite of provocation from some inmates whose behavior at times is beyond description. Some institutions try to comply but fail in stressful situations. Three institutions indicated that corporal punishment is permitted and used as a necessary measure of control. These same institutions offer few constructive activities, and the privileges are so meager that the prisoner can be deprived of little except his blood.

(C) CLASSIFICATION. The standards call for diversification by age, sex, custodial requirements, types of inmates, and program needs, and for at least annual review of the custody classification of each prisoner. Classification, in the prison world, is an organized and coordinated way of continuously evaluating the inmate and assigning him to appropriate placements and activities within the institutional system. A properly operating classification procedure, equipped with a sufficient number of program options in housing, work, and treatment, can provide the inmate with more significant safeguards than those traditionally offered by stone walls and raw custodial power. For example, work options and diversification in housing can protect the youthful novice from the influences of those to whom crime has become a way of life. It can surround the inveterate escape artist or predatory mugger by expensive security features while the co-operative and stable offender tills the soil and sleeps in low-cost barracks. Thus, classification enables a system to have as much or as little control as required, and it substitutes intelligent discrimination for unmodulated regimentation. The needs of both the system and the inmate are served.

In many States the development of classification procedures has turned the task of custody and control to new directions. Of the 52 jurisdictions, 47 (92 percent) report some kind of classification system. Some are exceedingly sophisticated, possess considerable clinical resources, involve the participation of key decisionmakers, offer broad alternatives, and pervade the entire institutional process from admission to parole. Others do not amount to much.

(D) WORK. William Paley, whose "Principles of Moral and Political Philosophy" helped to establish the penitentiary system, thought that hard labor would have a salutary effect on prisoners because "aversion to labor is the cause from which half of the vices of low life deduce their origin and continuance."[19] Since the earliest days of the correctional institution, work has been an important part of its life; it may well be the most important single aspect of the program.

Up to the end of the 19th century hard labor was part and parcel of imprisonment. Inmates were engaged in production for the open market, and States were able to realize considerable income from prison labor. Some of the contractual arrangements between the States and private lessees resulted in situations akin to slave labor. Gradually, as labor unions and industry alike opposed the competition from prison labor, the States prohibited the sale of prison-made goods on the open market. The Hawes-Cooper Act (1934) and the Ashurst-Sumner Act (1935) excluded prison-made goods from interstate commerce. As a result, State use laws were enacted, limiting the sale and distribution of prison-made goods to tax-supported and nonprofit activities. This sheltered-market system neutralized some of the labor-industry opposition but resulted in a demoralizing reduction of prison employment. Few scenes are more discouraging and contradictory than a prison yard full of men leading a life of indolence while waiting for release to a life of work.

Although the reaction to prison labor restrictions in many States has been constructive and imaginative, taking such forms as work-release programs and a marked increase in the number of conservation and farming activities, the problems of idleness—the meaningless work assignments, the swollen maintenance crews, etc.—remain perplexing concerns of correctional management. The task of motivating the inmate to choose work rather than the alternative—the idle list or the isolation cell—is equally perplexing.

One approach—cash payment—is normal for our society. Federal Prison Industries, Inc., a creation of the Federal Bureau of Prisons, pays wages ranging from $10 to $75 per month; the average in 1960 was $31.36.[20] The States are generally less generous. A 1957 study in 33 states reported a daily rate of payment ranging from $0.04 to $1.30; the average was $0.34 a day.[21] At least 10 States provide reduction in sentence as a form of payment for work.

(E) VOCATIONAL AND ACADEMIC TRAINING.   Enthusiasm for vocational training in the institution has waxed and waned since 1870, when the elements of the program were first formulated by Zebulon Brockway, the first superintendent of the Elmira Reformatory in New York. A few years ago it was at a low point, with wardens limiting the vocational training function to teaching a man how to "adjust to the job he finds himself in, his boss, and his fellow workers."

Interest in vocational training is now once again on the rise. Institutions in several States have exceedingly fine programs. One of the new stimuli to development of such programs is a current sociological theory: Society must offer the opportunity, but the man must be prepared to seize it. Another is the furtherance of the incentives and motivations mentioned above. A recent study of the Federal prison system observed that "learning a trade or in other ways preparing for a better job opportunity outside of prison was the first interest of most inmates at every prison studied."[22]

Especially important are the new funds available through the Manpower Development and Training Act, the war on poverty, and the vocational rehabilitation program. The survey revealed exciting new vocational training efforts, some of them in States not heretofore noted for progress in penology, financed in part by one or more of these sources. One of the most imaginative programs reported is being conducted for a State's correction department by a large electronic corporation using both State and Federal funds.

Some effort at vocational training was reported by 70 percent of all institutions during the survey. Collectively they employ 761 vocational teachers.

Academic education is offered by 88 percent of the institutions, which employ 893 academic teachers, 1 for every 225 inmates. A large number of inmates also serve as teachers, and there is considerable volunteer effort by interested citizens. In some States the academic educational effort is highlighted by dignified graduation exercises complete with caps and gowns, important speakers, and, most important of all, proud relatives.

Many new kinds of educational programs are reported. A few institutions give intensive courses in social adjustment which are attended by a majority of the inmates. Most offer correspondence courses, some at the college level. In a State in the South a cooperative program involves the State's department of education, its division of vocational training, and the correctional agency; one of the small correctional institutions is completely saturated by this intensive educational effort. Under a Federal grant, a large State in the Southwest has hired 21 remedial education specialists for an attack on illiteracy. Some States have developed extensive literacy programs under title II-B of the Economic Opportunity Act; others are exploring the implications of the Federal Elementary and Secondary Education Act. Federal money streams are beginning to water some of correction's deserts.

(F) INMATE COUNSELING.   The standards suggest 1 counselor per 150 inmates, and 1 psychiatrist, 3 clinical psychologists, and 3 caseworkers per 600 inmates.

Every jurisdiction reports some kind of counseling program, be it by psychiatrists, psychologists, sociologists, social workers, teachers, counselors, chaplains, or guards. Some States make a most considerable individual or group counseling effort; in other States, if one can judge the quality from the number and training of the staff involved, the effort amounts to very little. State correctional institutions employ a total of 1,124 social workers, psychologists, psychiatrists, and counselors. Ten States having only 43 percent of the Nation's prison population employ 67 percent of these specialists. On the other hand, 10 other States with 21,000 prisoners (11 percent of the Nation's prison population) employ only 24 behavioral specialists (1 for each 458 inmates). Three of the States confining 15,000 prisoners, report employing no such personnel.

Many States are reporting new trends in counseling, including a growing dissatisfaction with formal and highly structured efforts. The specialists are increasingly moving into the dormitories and cell blocks to confront the inmate. Many highly trained professionals are being withdrawn from traditional psychotherapeutic efforts to direct, supervise, and consult with subprofessionals and nonprofessionals, who are performing the direct treatment task—either group or individual—in increasing numbers. Some States are involving their great reservoir of treatment potential—the custodial, administrative, and industrial employees—in saturation counseling efforts. In other States, of course, like the three mentioned in the paragraph above, the institutional administration gives no thought to inmate counseling.

(G) BRIDGES TO THE COMMUNITY.   In an effort to break up the abysmal isolation of the correctional institution, many jurisdictions are attempting to involve the outside world in institutional programs. Alcoholics Anonymous, Narcotics Anonymous, Dale Carnegie, the Jaycees, the Bad Check Association, Synanon, Opportunities, Inc. (in which businessmen find jobs for inmates), community theaters, athletic clubs, and many other groups are all regularly welcome in many institutions.

Visiting for families and friends has been considerably liberalized in many States. Facilities for visiting have been improved, and the open and contact form of visit is more common. Even an ancient maximum-security bastille in an Appalachian State now has an excellent open visiting room in place of the old reinforced glass and concrete barrier. One State cites, as its most imaginative rehabilitation activity, its arrangements for conjugal visits.[23]

In one State the legislature has approved a statute requiring its revolutionary new correctional treatment and research center to be built in the largest city so that the university there, with its many social, medical, and psychiatric resources, can be thoroughly integrated into the correctional effort.

Five States report the availability of halfway houses in their systems.

(H) INSTITUTIONAL INFORMATION.   Committee standards call for establishment, in the department of correction, of (a) a central unit responsible for the systematic collection, interpretation, and publication of statistical data on the prison system, its population, operations, and programs; and (b) a central unit responsible for planning research and evaluating correctional programs.

Thirty-six of the 52 jurisdictions have some kind of central statistical and research unit, and some of them have begun to collect and utilize data concerning the institutional process. A few of the larger States are using electronic data processing equipment in the effort, and the output of these machines is finding its way into the decisionmaking process. Significant research, however, is still quite rare and is almost exclusively in the hands of nongovernmental groups. In California, the nonprofit Institute for the Study of Crime and Delinquency has the staff and flexibility to utilize research funds available from private foundations and Federal granting agencies such as the National Institute of Mental Health. In Pennsylvania, the American Foundation is channeling considerable sums into its Studies in Corrections, an agency headed by a former deputy director of the Federal Bureau of Prisons. Universities, through their traditional departments and, recently, via their new correctional centers, have become more attentive to research problems in correctional institutions. By the summer of 1966, 274 current research projects having adult correctional institutions as their locale were registered in the Information Center of the National Council on Crime and Delinquency.

A recent study makes five practical research suggestions of interest to institutional administrators:

1. Maximum determination and communication of correctional needs require compilation of the most complete post-release information that any correctional agency now has within its own facilities, or can readily obtain, on the offenders recently released from its custody or still under its supervision.

2. Evaluation of correctional program effectiveness can be most conclusive and persuasive if the presentation of postrelease data is focused on the responsibilities which the correctional agency must meet.

3. Economic problems of releases can be remedied if these problems are known and if their solution is given much higher priority in correctional operation than has been the practice heretofore.

4. Facts on failure of treatment must be flaunted, not hidden, if improvements are to be procured.

5. Improvements in correctional operations suggested by research findings will be most readily supported if introduced as piecemeal innovations, and if an evaluation program is part of the innovation proposal.[24]

4   *Juvenile Institutions*

THE PRESIDENT'S COMMISSION ON LAW ENFORCEMENT AND ADMINISTRATION OF JUSTICE*

A juvenile training facility is normally part of a system separate from other State and local juvenile correctional services, which usually include, at a minimum, the courts, juvenile probation, and supervision (aftercare) of those released from the training facility. Together these services provide resources for the differential treatment required for juvenile offenders committing offenses from various levels of motivation.

I. INTRODUCTION

A. Purpose Served by Training Facilities

The role of the training school is to provide a specialized program for children who must be held to be treated. Accordingly, such facilities should normally house more hardened or unstable youngsters than should be placed, for example, under probation supervision.

The juvenile institutional program is basically a preparation and trial period for the ultimate test of returning to community life. Once return has been effected, the ultimate success of the facility's efforts is highly dependent on good aftercare services. These are needed to strengthen

* From *Task Force Report: Corrections,* The President's Commission on Law Enforcement and Administration of Justice (Washington, D.C.: U.S. Government Printing Office, 1967), pp. 141–149.

changes started in the institution; their value can be proved only in the normal conditions of community life.

B. Historical Development

The training school originated as a State activity early in American history.[25] So far as can be determined, the first public training institutions exclusively for juveniles were established in Massachusetts, New York, and Maine. The Lyman School for Boys opened in Westborough, Mass., in 1846. Then came the New York State Agricultural and Industrial School in 1849 and the Maine Boys Training Center in 1853. By 1870, Connecticut, Indiana, Maryland, Nevada, New Hampshire, New Jersey, Ohio, and Vermont had also set up separate juvenile training facilities; by 1900, 36 States had done so. They appear now in every State, including Alaska, which opened a youth conservation camp at Wasilla in 1960, approximately 2 years after achieving statehood.

Consistent with their historical development, training programs by and large are administered by the State.

C. Working Philosophies

The term "school of industry" or "reformatory" often designated the early juvenile training facilities, thus reflecting the relatively simple philosophies upon which their development was based. Their reform programs sought chiefly to teach the difference between right and wrong. Teaching methods were primarily on a precept level, tending to emphasize correct behavior, formal education, and, where possible, the teaching of a trade so that the trainee would have the skills to follow the "right."

To a large extent these elements continue to bulwark many programs, but the efficacy of the old methods has been increasingly questioned, and working philosophies now are moving in new directions, primarily for two reasons.

First, although statistics vary from school to school and can be differently interpreted, most experts agree that about half of the persons released from juvenile training facilities can be expected to be reincarcerated.[26]

Second, they agree that if treatment is to produce lasting change, it must (regardless of technique) touch upon the personal reasons for delinquency. Like most people, juveniles caught in the "wrong" usually

find it more comfortable to justify themselves as "right" than to ackɪ owl-
edge responsibility for being wrong and seeking to change. For the
delinquent this means that, from the view he has of himself, he does not
act out of "evil" but out of a "good" which makes sense and can be
justified. Delinquent behavior may be a satisfying experience to a
youngster, especially if it meets his emotional needs. The approach,
therefore, cannot be merely an appeal for a change in behavior that is
offensive to the school; it must be concerned with what the behavior
means to the youngster himself. Therefore, according to this view, the
function of a training facility is to help a minor look honestly at his own
attitudes and see to what degree they create difficulties in the sense that
"as ye sow so shall ye reap." Having seen this, a minor then has a personal
reference point for change that is connected with his own perception of
"good"; he can arrive at personally responsible behavior because he feels
this personal connection.

Evidence of the practicality of this viewpoint is found in observations
common among training school youngsters themselves, who are quite
capable of pointing out those in their group who are "really doing good"
and those who are "just playing it cool." If the training school makes
conformity the hallmark of progress, it teaches duplicity because, in so
doing, it is suggesting that the real problem to be met is not "genuine
change of feelings" but only change of "appearances," simply doing
whatever the outer situation demands to "get by." The implications of
this for further involvement in trouble are clear.

II. SURVEY FINDINGS

The survey findings are organized around three factors that significantly affect the operation of juvenile training facilities—(1) the presence of
working philosophies that are consistent with what makes change possible; (2) a use of juvenile institutions by the courts and related groups
that allows a program focused on change to operate; and (3) the presence
of personnel, physical facilities, administrative controls, and other resources tailored to the job of producing change.

A. Working Philosophy

A good working philosophy clearly relates the institution's activities to
its purpose and to the problems it must meet in serving this purpose.

Such a relationship between purpose and program is clearly outlined in the operations of some facilities. As a general matter, however, the absence of a clear working philosophy that ties programs to the achievement of more responsible attitudes is a significant weakness crucial to the problem of improving services.

Lack of understanding concerning the practicality of newer philosophies is a major problem. The difficulty of securing their acceptance is clearly illustrated by developments in the issue of discipline. For some years standards have declared that "corporal punishment should not be tolerated in any form in a training school program." The misbehaving youngster should see, to the greatest degree possible, the reason for a rule and its meaning for the particular brand of difficulty he encounters on the "outs." In this way discipline can become an avenue to new behavior having the force of personal meaning. The use of force shifts the emphasis away from the youngster and onto the smooth running of the institution. For someone with antagonistic attitudes, hitching behavior to the good of something he dislikes can be expected to have little lasting effect.

Thus, apart from the issue of whether physical abuse results, use of corporal punishment can reasonably be taken as a rough statistical indicator of the degree to which treatment viewpoints are actually operating. The survey found that corporal punishment is authorized in juvenile institutions in 10 States.

Another indicator of working philosophy is found in an institution's answer to the question, "How much security?" The institution's need to develop the youngster's self-control often collides with the public's concern over escapes. Caught between the two, the administrator may set up a system of tight management which, he rationalizes, is for the youngsters' "own good." Thus the juvenile is used to serve the institution instead of the other way around.

A solution can be achieved by public and professional education. Though public expectations toward training facilities are often unrealistic, they must be met by the administrator if he wants to hold his job. Therefore, maximum efficiency—doing the best that current knowledge will allow—cannot be reached until this blurring effect is looked at honestly. If training facilities are to change youngsters, they must be allowed to operate out of philosophies consistent with this purpose. The public needs to learn that treatment approaches which allow "breathing room" are not naive but are, on the contrary, extremely practical. Properly conceived, they are directed at getting the trainee to assume more responsibility for his life rather than assigning it later to the police.

B. Uses Being Made of Training Schools

In theory, training schools are specialized facilities for changing children relatively hardened in delinquency. In practice, as the survey shows, they house a nonselective population and are primarily used in ways which make the serving of their theoretical best purpose, that of "change," beside the point.

This is not to say that other purposes being served by the typical training facility are not important in themselves. Rather, the point is whether they can best be served by a training facility, and, if they cannot, the effect of this extraneousness on the facility's prime reason for existence, the basic job for which it is intended. The extent to which its ability to do this job is diminished becomes clear from the following list of its "other" expedient purposes:

> Use as a detention or holding facility for youngsters awaiting completion of other plans for placement.
>
> Providing basic housing for youngsters whose primary need is a foster home or residential housing.
>
> Housing large numbers of youngsters whose involvement in trouble is primarily situational rather than deep-seated and who could be handled more efficiently under community supervision.
>
> Caring for mentally retarded youngsters committed to the training school because there is no room in a mental retardation facility or because no such institution exists.
>
> Providing care for youngsters with severe psychiatric problems who are committed to the training school because of no juvenile residential treatment program.
>
> Use of girls' facilities to provide maternity services.

The problem of varied intake is further complicated by differences in court commitment philosophies, each of which is a working view of "the best purpose a training facility should ideally serve." In summary, the effects of the diverse elements cited contribute to training facilities wherein no one is best served and most are served in default.

Variations in use of training schools are found among the states as a whole, as well as among the counties of a single State, and further show that many reference points other than "change" are the determiners of practice. If juvenile institutions were actually working in allegiance to a common "best use," statistics which reflect practice would have some uniformity of meaning. That this is not true is revealed by some of the statistical sketches below. For example, length-of-stay statistics do not now reflect differences in time needed to effect "change." If they did, one system's length of stay could be compared with another's, as a guideline for the efficacy of a given program. Rather, the data show that length of stay reflects some extraneous factor such as "overcrowding," or a population whose primary need is "housing," or children awaiting unavailable placements, or children who, though better suited to a probation program, must be held "long enough" to avoid court or community problems.

C. Resources to Produce Change

1. Capacity

The survey covers 220 State-operated juvenile institutional facilities in all States, Puerto Rico, and the District of Columbia.[27] These facilities, constituting 86 percent of the juvenile training capacity in the United States, had a total capacity of 42,423 in 1965 and a total average daily population of 42,389, which was 10.7 percent more than the population reported to the Children's Bureau in 1964 by 245 State and local facilities.[28]

The overcrowding suggested by daily population figures is not uniform. In 17 jurisdictions, in programs housing total average daily populations of 7,199 children (17 percent of the total), the average daily population is more than 10 percent below each system's capacity. Conversely, in 11 States, in programs housing 9,165 children (22 percent of the total reported by all 52 jurisdictions), the average daily population is 10 percent or more above their respective systems' capacities.

In many States the capacity of State and locally run training facilities is extended through use of private facilities. In some instances these are publicly subsidized, but control of the program remains in private hands. During the survey, 31 States reported using private facilities for the placement of delinquents. An estimate of the use of private facilities was not possible in eight of these States. The 23 States submitting estimates reported they had placed 6,307 youngsters in private facilities in 1965.

Concern about the increasing numbers of delinquents being housed in training facilities is growing. Only eight States at present have no plans for new construction which would increase the capacity of their institutional programs. Construction under way in 17 States will add space for 4,164 youngsters at a cost of $41,164,000. Thirty-one States report that they have $70,090,000 of construction authorized for an additional capacity of 7,090. Projecting still further ahead, 21 States report plans for additional capacity of 6,606 by 1975 at an anticipated cost of $66,060,000.

Thus, new construction, under way or authorized, will increase the present capacity (42,423 in State-run facilities) by 27 percent. By 1975, planned new construction will have increased present capacity by slightly over 42 percent.

2. Program

(A) DIVERSIFICATION.   In contrast to the diversified program "balance" recommended by the standard, juvenile training facilities in most States present limited diversity of programs. Six of the larger jurisdictions now have nine or more facilities, but 8 States have only one facility serving juveniles and 14 States have only two facilities—a boys' school and a girls' school, a pattern that characterized State juvenile institutional systems for many years (see table 1).

TABLE 1
Distribution of Training Schools, by States

Number of jurisdictions	Number of facilities	Total facilities
6	9 or more	69
18	4 to 8	97
6	3	18
14	2	28
8	1	8
52		220

In States which have expanded their facilities further, the most numerous separate new programs are small camps for boys and reception centers (see table 2). The camp is one of the fastest growing developments in the institutional field; 49 camps have been established in 20 States, with Illinois alone operating 10 of them. Ten States now have a total of 14 separate reception programs.

The rapid growth of camp programs has been attributed to low cost of

TABLE 2
State-Operated Juvenile Institutions, by Type and Number

Type	Number	Type	Number
Boys institution	82	Residential center	4
Girls institution	56	Vocational center	1
Co-ed institution	13	Day treatment center	1
Camp	49		
Reception center	14	Total	220

operation, often half that of a training school in the same State, and to a good success rate, which in turn has been attributed to size and selection of population. Many of the camps have a capacity of 50 or less; standards call for capacities of 40 to 50.

(B) AVERAGE STAY. The length of stay for children committed to State training facilities ranges from 4 to 24 months; the median length of stay is 9 months. The number of children at the extremes of the range is relatively small (see table 3). Five State systems, housing 3 percent of the total, report an average length of stay of 6 months or less; eight State systems, housing 8 percent of the total, report average lengths of stay of more than 12 months. The remainder of the State systems—three-fourths of the total, housing nine-tenths of the institutional population—have an average length of stay of 6 months to a year.

Reception centers which serve primarily placement diagnostic purposes and do not include a treatment program for segments of their population report a surprisingly uniform average length of stay, ranging from 28 to 45 days.

TABLE 3

Average Length of Stay in State-Operated Juvenile Institutions, by Number of States

Average length of stay (months)	Number of jurisdictions	Average length of stay (months)	Number of jurisdictions
4–6	5	13–15	5
7–9	22	16–18	2
10–12	17	19–24	1

(C) ACTUAL AVAILABILITY OF SERVICE. Services that look the same "on paper" are revealed by the survey to differ widely in quality. For example, 96 percent of the facilities contacted report the provision of medical services, and 94 percent report that dental services are provided. In fact, however, examination of operating practice in each jurisdiction shows major differences in the quality of these services. Where medical and dental services represent an especially expensive drain on hardpressed budgets, as is true in many programs, the decision that treatment is "needed" may be reached less quickly than where services are routinely available and "paid for." Thus quality differences are born.

Similar differences between what is available "on paper" and what is available "in fact" are to be found among other services offered by training facilities (see table 4). The survey data indicate that nearly all programs (95 percent) provide recreational services; 88 percent, educational programs; 86 percent, casework, and 79 percent, counseling services; and 75 percent, psychological, and 71 percent, psychiatric services. The question of concern, however, is not their provision "on paper" but their adequacy for the problems being faced. From this viewpoint, with the possible exception of education, improvement of all types of services seems badly needed. Support for this view is based on the existing ratios of treatment personnel to training school population.

TABLE 4
Services Available in State-Operated Juvenile Institutions,
by Number of Institutions

Service	Number of institutions (total: 220)	Percentage
Medical	211	96
Recreation	208	95
Dental	206	94
Education	193	88
Casework	190	86
Social work service	173	79
Psychological	165	75
Psychiatric	156	71

(D) COSTS.   Regardless of the adequacy of services, the cost of care in a training facility is high. The 52 jurisdictions report a total operating cost of $144,596,618 to care for an average daily population of 42,389 youngsters. This means an average per capita operating expenditure of $3,411. The national average, however conceals considerable variation in costs among the States. Forty-two jurisdictions operate training facility systems without a separate reception and diagnostic center, at an average per capita cost ranging from $871 to $7,890. Within this group, 6 States operate juvenile institutional systems for average per capita costs falling below $1,600 per year; 8 report average costs between $1,600 and $3,000; 13 report costs between $3,000 and $4,500; and 13 report average annual per capita costs above $4,500.

The inclusion of a reception and diagnostic center as part of a diversified juvenile institutional system helps to individualize institutional placements. Ten jurisdictions have set up programs consistent with the idea of specialized facilities, and another 10 are on the verge of doing so. This trend makes especially significant the costs experienced in States with separate reception programs. Among the 10 that operate such systems, per capita costs range from $1,757 to $5,723. Average per capita cost is less than $2,000 in three of these States; from $2,000 to $2,500 in two States; from $3,900 to $4,500 in three States; and $4,877 and $5,723 in the two remaining States.

3. Staff

The impact of a program upon children is largely determined by adequacy of staff, both quantitatively and qualitatively.

In 1965, State-run juvenile facilities employed 21,247 staff in programs housing an average daily population of 42,389 trainees.

(A) TREATMENT PERSONNEL. Of the total number employed, 1,154 were treatment personnel—psychiatrists, psychologists, and social case-workers.

The standard calls for a minimum of 1 full-time psychiatrist for 150 children. On the basis of the average daily population of 42,389 in 1965, the number of psychiatrists required is 282.

The survey data show that the equivalent of 46 psychiatrists served the 220 State-operated facilities. More than half of them are found in only 5 States, with 1 State having the equivalent psychiatric time of 10 out of the total of 46 psychiatrists. Each of 37 States has less than the equivalent of 1 full-time psychiatrist available to its juvenile institution population. Only 4 States have enough psychiatric service available to satisfy the required 1:150 ratio.

To meet the requirements nationally, juvenile institutions need a total of 236 more psychiatrists than they now have.

The standard calls for a minimum of 1 full-time psychologist for 150 children. On the basis of the average daily population, the number of psychologists required is 282.

The survey data show that the equivalent of 182 psychologists work in the State-run juvenile facilities. However, as with psychiatrists, psychologists are found to be unequally distributed among the States: 106 (almost 60 percent of the total) are found in 9 States. Each of 21 States had the equivalent of not more than 1 psychologist. Only 12 States come up to the standard ratio.

To meet the requirements nationally, juvenile institution systems need a total of 100 more psychologists than they now have.

The standard declares that under ordinary conditions, a full-time caseworker in a juvenile institution should be assigned not more than 30 children. On the basis of the average daily population, the number of caseworkers required is 1,413.

The survey data show, in the 220 institutions, a total of 926 case-workers, or 66 percent of the number required. To meet the requirements nationally, juvenile institution systems need a total of 487 more caseworkers than they now have.

Because the lack or absence of clinical personnel in many programs made comprehensive assessment uncertain, the survey established a general treatment potential index by stating the number of psychiatrists, psychologists, and caseworkers found in a system, combined in one category called professional personnel, in proportion to the number of trainees in the system. Since no single ratio was available as a national standard for such an index, the existing standards applicable to psychiatrists (1:150), psychologists (1:150), and caseworkers (1:30) were combined, making a total of 7 professional personnel per 150 trainees, or a ratio of 1:21.43 as a guideline.

The range of indexes for 50 States is from 1:30 to 1:522.[29] The average index is 1:64; the median is 1:33. In all, 14 State systems have treatment ratios better than the 1:21 suggested. Among the 38 jurisdictions with ratios poorer than this guideline, 22 have ratios of 1:42.9 (double the suggested guideline) or more.

(B) TEACHERS.   The standard calls for a teacher-pupil ratio not exceeding 1:15.

Standards bearing on teacher ratios in training facilities are difficult to apply to survey data. Where public school systems assume a portion of the training system's academic burden, their teachers were not counted as institutional employees for purposes of the survey.

There were 2,495 teachers in the 220 institutions, an overall teacher-pupil ratio of 1:17. In 24 States, the teacher-pupil ratio is better than the 1:15 standard cited, and in 36 States it is better than 1:20. Moreover, in the remaining States several jurisdictions have ratios that are high because of the reasons cited above.

The general picture given by the survey data is consistent with experienced observation: The established standard for training facilities is met to a far greater degree in teaching than it is in the casework or psychological counseling function. The reason is probably that, in many facilities, academic teaching has been the traditional mainstay of programing; also, the teaching role is better understood, and training for teachers is well established. In those facilities where there aren't enough teachers, the problem is more likely to be budget than an insufficient supply of trained teachers. Even where salaries are competitive the training school is handicapped in recruiting the good teacher because its working conditions are usually less attractive than the public school's.

(c) CHAPLAINS. Standards call for chaplains on each staff in a number sufficient to serve the major religious faiths represented in the institution. A fair application of this standard to statistics is difficult; no clear criteria exist whereby adequate chaplaincy service may be determined. Here, probably more than in any other aspect of institutional program, a standard on adequate number should be viewed as an emerging guideline to be modified according to specific operating conditions. Review of survey data makes possible a valuable commonsense appraisal of the overall level of chaplaincy services. It shows a clear general need for more chaplains in most systems.

The 220 State institutions are served by 158 chaplains. Further, 32 State systems have less than the equivalent of 1 chaplain per facility; of these, 18 have less than half-time services per facility, and 12 have no chaplaincy service staffing at all. The overall chaplain-trainee ratio is 1:268. The ratios in 40 jurisdictions having chaplains range from 1:23 to 1:258. In 26 State systems the ratio is above 1:150—which is particularly significant in light of the standard of 150 recommended for institution capacity.

(d) MERIT SYSTEM COVERAGE. Standards call for placing all training school personnel under a merit or civil service system.

While the majority of State training facility staffs are covered under a merit system, the superintendents still remain outside such protection in 30 States (see table 5). With only two exceptions, States covering professional staff under a merit plan also cover supervisory and cottage staff in this manner.

TABLE 5
Percentage of 52 Jurisdictions Providing
Civil Service or Merit System

Position	Coverage (percent)	No coverage (percent)
Superintendent	42.3	57.7
Professional workers	63.5	36.5
Cottage staff	59.6	40.4

(e) SALARIES. In general, salaries in merit-covered systems are higher than in nonmerit systems for comparable positions. Table 6 shows comparative salaries for some positions. Table 7 shows beginning salaries according to position and the number of institutions paying that salary.

(F) WORKWEEK.   Prevailing practice in juvenile institutional facilities is approaching the recommended standard of a 40-hour workweek. In 16 States the workweek is more than 40 hours, and in 7 of these States, it is more than 50 hours.

TABLE 6
Minimum Starting Salaries for Merit System States and
Nonmerit System States

Position	Minimum starting salary	Merit States average	Nonmerit States average
Superintendent	From $5,000 to $15,000	$9,446	$9,473
Caseworker	From $3,240 to $9,000	5,824	5,109
Academic teacher	From $2,400 to $8,640	5,395	4,552
Vocational teacher	From $3,600 to $8,640	5,302	4,752
Cottage staff	From $1,600 to $8,592	3,912	3,199

TABLE 7
Beginning Salaries of Juvenile Institutional Personnel,
by Number of Agencies

	Psychi- atrist	Super- intend- ent	Psy- chol- ogist	Case- worker	Aca- demic teacher	Voca- tional teacher	Cot- tage staff
Under $1,500	0	0	0	0	0	0	0
$1,501–$2,400	0	0	0	0	1	0	3
$2,401–$3,000	1	0	0	0	1	0	6
$3,001–$4,000	0	0	0	3	2	3	24
$4,001–$5,000	1	1	0	6	14	15	12
$5,001–$6,000	0	3	1	14	22	18	4
$6,001–$7,000	0	2	8	19	5	6	1
$7,001–$8,000	1	4	12	4	2	1	0
$8,001–$9,000	0	8	4	1	1	1	1
$9,001–$10,000	0	11	2	0	0	0	0
$10,001–$11,000	1	7	5	0	0	0	0
$11,001–$12,000	1	8	0	0	0	0	0
$12,001–$13,000	6	3	0	0	0	0	0
$13,001–$14,000	1	3	0	0	0	0	0
$14,001–$15,000	1	1	0	0	0	0	0
$15,001–$16,000	2	0	0	0	0	0	0
$16,001–$17,000	2	0	0	0	0	0	0
$17,001–$18,000	0	0	0	0	0	0	0
Over $18,000	2	0	0	0	0	0	0
Total	19	51	32	47	48	44	51

(G) EDUCATIONAL QUALIFICATIONS. The standard calls for the superintendent to have completed graduate training in the behavioral sciences or related fields of child development.

The survey found substantial variation among systems on educational requirements for the position (see table 8). Twelve jurisdictions require the superintendent to have a graduate degree; 28 require a college background; 10 have no formally established educational requirements—but this does not necessarily mean that trained persons are not sought. A number of systems recruit by trying to get the best person possible without formulating the requirements.

The standard calls for the caseworker to have graudated from an accredited school of social work.

Only three jurisdictions have failed to establish requirements for this position. Thirty-six require a college background; 11 require, in addition, a graduate degree.

The cottage staff in charge of the living unit, where most of the minor's time is spent, is the backbone of the training facility program. The key to effectiveness for this classification is ability to relate to children, emotional maturity, and flexibility in adapting to new situations.

TABLE 8
Educational Requirements, by Number of States

Position	None	High school graduate	College graduate	Graduate degree
Superintendent	10		28	12
Caseworker	3		36	11
Cottage staff	25	25		

No standard for this position has been offered. The traditional standard has been a high school education. Particularly in more sophisticated systems, graduation from college would be the preferred qualification.[30]

Under present salary schedules for the cottage staff position, college graduates, or even persons having not more than a high school education (as required in 25 States) are virtually unattainable. Salaries are so low that establishing educational requirements is beside the point; as shown in table 8, 25 States set no requirement for the position. One State reports that some of its cottage staff are on public welfare.

4. Housing

Much of the Nation's training facility plant is old but being improved. In many States patched-onto use of the first old reform school is still evident, but sharp increases in the population of these facilities have produced, along with problems, some benefits, including mainly the development of smaller living units.

(A) FACILITY SIZE.   The standard recommending that a juvenile institution be limited to 150 children is based on experience which shows that the smaller the facility the more likely it is to enhance the impact of program. "The treatment atmosphere tends to break down in institutions where the population rises above [150]" because of "such therapeutic dangers as rigidity and formality necessary to help a large organization function."[31]

Despite the advantages cited for the smaller institution, the trend has been in the other direction. The great bulk of the juvenile institutional population is now housed in facilities considerably larger than the prescribed standard. The principal concession to the standard is an occasional attempt to break down large institutions into several small administrative units in the hope that each will take on the climate of a small separate entity.

(B) LIVING-UNIT SIZE.   Standards generally call for the living unit to have a maximum capacity of 20 where groupings are homogeneous; the size for a heterogeneous group, or a group of severely disturbed children, should be from 12 to 16.[32] Girls should have private rooms.

Standards pertaining to size should not be applied arbitrarily; their spirit is more important than the letter. The existence of many excellent living-unit programs in living units that do not meet the accepted size standard shows that ingenuity of staffing, effective group techniques, and sincerity of effort are important, and that the lack of understanding implied by mechanical application of the standard probably guarantees a poor program.

This is merely a cautionary note; it does not impair the validity of the standard. Large living units require compensating staff and program efforts to produce results equivalent to those expected and more easily achieved in the small unit. The degree to which massnesss can be compensated for is limited.

The importance of the standard calling for a maximum capacity of 20 is just beginning to be realize. Of the 1,344 living units in State-run juvenile institutions only 24 percent have a capacity of 20 or less. In 68 percent of them, the capacity is from 21 to 50; in 8 percent, it is 50 or more.

In general, living-unit size is related to period of construction. Typically, the smaller units are relatively new. About 34 percent of all living units are 10 years of age or less; 16 percent are 50 years old or more.

While the standard is not met by most living units, its importance is increasingly being recognized. Survey data on living units under construction, authorized, and projected show that, in all 3 categories, over 90 percent of the units will have a capacity of 30 or less. A capacity of 20 or less is found in 55 percent of present construction, 63 percent of authorized construction, and 45 percent of projected construction (see table 9).

TABLE 9
Capacity of New Living Units in State Juvenile Training Schools,
by Number of Units

Capacity of unit	Units under construction		Units author-ized [1]		Units pro-jected		Total Units	
	Num-ber	Per-cent	Num-ber	Per-cent	Num-ber	Per-cent	Num-ber	Per-cent
Single room			22	8.2			22	3.2
2 to 10	2	1.5	17	6.3			19	2.8
11 to 15	2	1.5	3	1.1	18	6.5	23	3.4
16 to 20	70	51.9	126	47.0	107	38.8	303	44.6
21 to 30	49	36.3	76	28.4	127	46.0	252	37.1
31 to 40	6	4.4	11	4.1	10	3.6	27	4.0
41 to 50	2	1.5	2	.8			4	.6
51 to 100	4	2.9	7	2.6	1	.4	12	1.8
100 to 200			1	.4	3	1.1	4	.6
Over 200			[2] 3	1.1	[3] 10	3.6	13	1.9
Total	135	100	268	100	276	100	679	100

[1] Does not include a $13,900,000 allocation for 2 institutions and 2 camps.
[2] Includes 1 at 375 and 2 at 400.
[3] Includes 10 at 250.

(C) LOCATION. The institution should be separated from a metropolitan area by a buffer zone, but not of so great dimensions that the institution is virtually inaccessible. Isolation aggravates problems of staff recruitment and housing and reduces use of services offered by related agencies. Training schools have often been established in an isolated section of the State by a legislature concerned largely with bolstering the surrounding community's economy. The lack of foresight in the decision is brought home forcefully a few years later when the institution's location is shown to make its program expensive to operate and difficult to staff.

Reasonable access to a university allows for use of its faculty in staff development, research, consultation, and recruitment.

Of the 29 jurisdictions reporting bad location of 1 or more facilities, 46 percent cite it as a reason for difficulty in recruiting professional staff; 15 percent cite it as a deterrent to visits by parents.

5. *Administrative Resources*

Administration of a program consistent with the purpose of change is affected by issues of (*a*) the source of direction, (*b*) custody and release, (*c*) inspection and subsidy, and (*d*) quality of research and information.

(A) CENTRALIZED DIRECTION.   Some control over the types and numbers of children going to a given facility is necessary for development of an individualized program. Selection of the facility in which a youngster is to be placed, particularly in States having diversified programs, should preferably rest with the parent agency, if one has been established. (Direction of activities important to a program within the institution— for example, the academic school service—should rest chiefly with the institutional administrator.)

The survey data show that the direction of training facility programs is increasingly being centralized to produce better coordination with related agencies and more specialized use of facilities. Centralization is resulting in common use of a parent agency to administer institutional programs. In only three States do juvenile institutions now completely administer their own programs as agencies. In 46 jurisdictions the institutions work under some type of parent agency, which, in 21 States, has only correctional responsibilities. Other common administrative arrangements place juvenile facility operation under a State department of public welfare (in 14 States) and under a State board of institutions (in 6 States).

(B) CUSTODY AND RELEASE.   The standard declares that legal custody of a child committed to an institution should be vested in the parent agency rather than the institution.

Consistent with the trend toward centralized direction, more control is being vested in the parent agency, which assumes legal custody upon commitment in 31 jurisdictions. Legal custody during commitment is vested in the institution in 13 States and in the court in 3 States.

Similarly, administrative control of release is the more common pattern. In 31 States the release decision is made either within the facility or by its controlling parent agency. In 9 States the decision is made by a parole board. In 10 States the court is involved to a varying degree in the release decision: in 5 of these States the court grants all releases; in 1 or 2 others it has the power to control release only in certain types of cases; and in the remainder it shares responsibility for the release with the institution.

(C) INSPECTION AND SUBSIDY. The standard calls for the parent State agency to have inspection and subsidy authority over local delinquency treatment programs.

The survey data show that, of the 16 States that have locally run facilities, 4 set standards on personnel qualifications in local institutions and 2 of the 4 set standards on program content and details of new construction. Seven of these 16 States also subsidize the local programs to some degree. Subsidy forms include partial assumption of operating costs, various formulas for subsidizing construction, and the provision of consultation and training services.

(D) RESEARCH AND INFORMATION. Programs, like people, must know what they are doing to do it well. To do an institutional job well calls for statistics and research that can help solve day-to-day program-management problems and provide a guideline for evaluating the parolees' degree of success in staying out of trouble. The information gathered for these purposes is also a resource for better public understanding of institutional problems. The standard recommends that the central parent agency be responsible for research, consultation, and collection of statistics concerning juvenile populations and programs.

Thirty-eight of the 52 jurisdictions have a central source for the collection and dissemination of statistics (see table 10), which evince, unfortunately, no agreement on the purposes for which they have been gathered. Much of the data collected has no reference to problems of

TABLE 10
State Agencies Responsible for Collection of Statistics

Type of agency	Number of States	Type of agency	Number of States
Correction	14	Bureau of research	2
Department of public welfare	9	Not reported	4
Youth authority	4		—
Department of institutions	3	Total	38
Board of control	2		

operational importance. Few States have information on subsequent adjustment of juvenile parolees.

6. New Programs

The press of mounting delinquency problems in recent years has stimulated the development of numerous kinds of programs significant to the juvenile institutional field. Three of the most significant of these new types are described briefly below:

(A) COMMUNITY-BASED TREATMENT SERVICES.   As the name implies, these services include various methods of handling juveniles in a community setting as alternatives to commitment or for reducing the number of commitments. They are of special interest because of their relative economy compared with institutional commitment and because of the advantages of treatment in a setting as normal or "close to home" as possible.

The principal vehicles include intensified and selective probation and parole caseloads offering special counseling and community help plus "in and out" and trial furloughs; group homes and agency-operated residential treatment programs; "day care" in specialized institutional programs that return youngsters home at night and on weekends; regional detention centers with diagnostic service intended to reduce "dumping" into institutions; special "closed" local facilities with intensive counseling; and family involvement.

(B) GROUP TREATMENT.   Group treatment techniques offer essentially the advantage of economy over one-to-one counseling relationships, plus treatment advantages gained from insights on behavior through viewpoints pressed from several sources. In the institutional setting they have included families of the trainees. Their common goal is acceptance of responsibility rather than satisfaction with shallow conformity.

(C) DIVERSIFICATION.   Development in this direction is represented by the growth of small camp programs, halfway houses, group-treatment centers, reception and screening centers, vocational training centers, and special short-term programs.

5 *Local Adult Correctional Institutions and Jails*

THE PRESIDENT'S COMMISSION
ON LAW ENFORCEMENT AND
ADMINISTRATION OF JUSTICE*

In the vast majority of city and county jails and local short-term institutions, no significant progress has been made in the past 50 years.

I. INTRODUCTION

In the second decade of this century, Louis Robinson wrote:

> From many points of view, the jail is the most important of all our institutions of imprisonment. The enormous number of jails is alone sufficient . . . to make [one] realize that the jail is, after all, the typical prison in the United States. . . . From two-thirds to three-fourths of all convicted criminals serve out their sentence in jails. But this is not all. The jail is, with small exception, the almost universal detention house for untried prisoners. The great majority, therefore, of penitentiary and reformatory prisoners have been kept for a period varying from a few days to many months within the confines of a county or municipal jail. Then, too, there is the class, not at all unimportant in number, of individuals, who, having finally established their innocence, have been set free after spending some time in the jail awaiting trial. Important witnesses also are detained in jail, and it is used at times for still other purposes, even serving occasionally as a temporary asylum for the insane. The part, therefore, which the jail plays in our scheme of punishment cannot be overestimated. Whether for good or for evil, nearly every criminal that has been apprehended is subjected to its influence.[33]

* From *Task Force Report: Corrections,* The President's Commission on Law Enforcement and Administration of Justice (Washington, D.C.: U.S. Government Printing Office, 1967), pp. 162–168.

71

Now, in the seventh decade, this statement by Robinson and his comments on filth, neglect, and maladministration still accurately describe the role and status of jails and short-term institutions in the United States.

These institutions have a long history. As a place of detention for accused persons, the jail traces its lineage back to Biblical times. The workhouse was conceived and developed in the latter half of the 16th century to deal with unemployment, vagrancy, petty thievery, prostitution, and disorderly conduct. So successful was it in clearing the streets and public places of the economically depressed and the socially offensive that Parliament ordained establishment of such an institution for minor offenders in every county in England. The innovation of this type of imprisonment spread during the 17th century to Holland, Belgium, and Germany, and, eventually, to America.

Successful reclamation of vagrants, prostitutes, and disorderly persons through programs of constructive work and training in the houses of correction, combined with concern for the basic dignity inherent in every human being, began to evolve into a new penology in which the focus was on penitence and reform. Punishment as an end in itself was replaced by punishment as a means of deterrence and reform. In the 20th century, the dominant trend in penological thinking—but not, for the most part, in the jail itself—has been toward substitution of constructive treatment programs for mere custody as more promising and more effective controls over offenders.

The deeper the offender has to be plunged into the correctional process and the longer he has to be held under punitive (though humane) restraints, the more difficult is the road back to the point of social restoration. It is logical, then, to conclude that the correctional process ought to concentrate its greatest efforts at those points along the criminal justice continuum where the largest numbers of offenders are involved and the hope of avoiding social segregation is greatest. In a sense, the intensity of the treatment process should be in inverse ratio to the degree of custodial care required. On the correctional continuum, jails are at the beginning of the penal or institutional segment. They are, in fact, the reception units for a greater variety and number of offenders than will be found in any other segment of the correctional process, and it is at this point that the greatest opportunity is offered to make sound decisions on the offender's next step in the correctional process. Indeed, the availability of qualified services at this point could result in promptly removing many from the correctional process who have been swept in unnoticed and undetected and who are more in need of protective, medical, and mental care from welfare and health agencies than they are in need of custodial care in penal and correctional institutions. In a broad sense, the jails and local correctional institutions are reception centers for the major institutions; in effect, they are mausoleums more than first-aid emergency rooms.

II. SURVEY FINDINGS

The survey data are concentrated, by design, on those jails and institutions (including farms, camps, etc.) where a convicted offender may serve 30 days or longer. In the sample counties, 215 facilities were found which meet this condition. It is difficult to consider them only as sentence institutions because most of them also receive and hold persons awaiting trial and prisoners serving sentences of less than 30 days, but they are viewed here mainly in this light. Some observations on their function as places of detention for untried offenders are made at the end.

A. Number and Type

Table 1 gives a national estimate of the number of local correctional institutions and jails in 1966. In addition to this State-by-State count, more detailed information was secured from the 250 counties in the survey sample concerning types of facilities, number of prisoners, etc. The 215 local institutions which receive inmates for 30 days or longer in the sample counties are classified as shown in table 2. The term "jails" adheres characteristically to the county level of government; the designations "correctional institutions, camps, and farms" have been adopted principally by larger municipalities and State-controlled short-term confinement facilities. Thus, it may be noted that the percentages for institutions by type in the 250-county sample are extraordinarily close to the national percentages in table 1.

TABLE 1
Local Institutions and Jails, by Type of Jurisdiction

Type of institution	Number	Percent
County institutions	2,547	73.3
City institutions	762	22.0
City-county combined	149	4.3
Other	15	4
Total	3,473	100.0

TABLE 2
Number of Local Institutions and Jails, by Type

Type	Number	Percent
Jail	158	73.5
Correctional institution	26	12.1
Camp	18	8.4
Farm	9	4.0
Combination or other	4	2.0
Total	215	100.0

The number of persons held in 1 year for service of a sentence (distinct from the number held under pretrial detention) is 1,016,748; the average daily population serving sentence is 141,303.

B. Population Characteristics

1. Types of Offenders

The law generally classifies violators according to the seriousness of the offense of which they are convicted. Two broad categories have been developed—felons and misdemeanants. "The distinction between misdemeanors and felonies is, in general, a distinction between less serious and more serious crimes; but it does not always hold. The line between a theft that is a misdemeanor and a theft that is a felony is drawn by the value of the property, a distinction which may be totally irrelevant in determining the sentence."[34] The inaccurate popular conception is that only misdemeanant offenders are committed to local institutions and that felons are sent to State prisons.

Of the 215 institutions studied, 49.6 percent admitted felony cases for service of sentence; 50.4 percent excluded felony cases. (It would be interesting to know how many prisoners serving misdemeanor sentences in the institutions which exclude felony cases are actually serious offenders who happened this time to get caught for a lesser offense or who committed a felony that was subsequently reduced to a misdemeanor.)

Every criminology textbook written within the past 40 years includes a graphic description of the physical and moral decay that grips the majority of jails across the Nation. The indiscriminate mixing of all types of prisoners—the sick and the well, the old and the young, hardened criminals and petty offenders, the mentally defective, the psychotic, the vagrants and alcoholics, the habitual recidivists serving life sentences in short installments—has been recognized for years but, with few exceptions, has remained unchanged. "Fully 50 percent of all commitments . . . are for drunkenness or other offenses directly related to alcohol. Multiple commitments are the rule and not the exception—10, 20, and even 50 commitments of one alcoholic are commonplace."[35] Record-keeping procedures make it impossible to determine how many persons account for over 1 million commitments a year, but it is safe to estimate that the number of persons is considerably lower than the number of commitments. It is also evident—even though the percentages cannot be computed—that the vast majority of those presently confined in these institutions will return after release for subsequent short terms or will graduate to major institutions as they become more criminally sophisticated.

2. Length of Sentence

The maximum sentence which may be served in jail is 12 months in most States; the range is from less than 6 months to life, as shown in table 3. The statutory limitation on terms which may be served in local institutions other than jails is somewhat similar (see table 4). Even in States where a maximum of 1 or 2 years is fixed, the legal limits are circumvented by use of consecutive sentences.

3. Age

In most States, commitment of persons less than 16 years old to jails and local adult institutions is now prohibited by statute. Such commitments are legal in 14 States, and 11 States still have offenders under 16 in these institutions. In 4 States no minimum commitment age is set, in 1 State it is 7 years, and in the others it is 12, 13, 14, or 15. In several instances, children aged 10, 12, 15, or 17 can be legally committed to these institutions for life.

C. Cost

The total annual national estimate of operating expenditures (capital outlay costs excluded) for prisoners serving sentence is $147,794,214 (38 percent as much as the comparable cost of all State institutions). For an

TABLE 3
Maximum Jail Sentence, by Number of States

Maximum legal sentence	Number of States	Maximum legal sentence	Number of States
Less than 6 months	3	Over 60 months	2
9 months	1	Does not apply	6
12 months	30	Unknown	5
24 months	2		—
27 months	1	Total	51
30 months	1		

TABLE 4
Maximum Legal Sentence in Local Institutions Other Than Jails,
by Number of States

Maximum legal sentence	Number of States	Maximum legal sentence	Number of States
Less than 6 months	4	30 months	1
12 months	20	Over 60 months	3
15 months	1	Does not apply	14
18 months	1	Unknown	4
24 months	2		—
27 months	1	Total	51

average daily population of 141,303 prisoners, this means an average annual per capita cost of $1,046 and a daily per capita cost of $2.87 (55 percent of the comparable costs in State institutions).

D. Personnel

1. Number

The national estimate of the number of positions totals 19,195, an employee-inmate ratio of 1:7. The types of positions and the number for each are shown in table 5.

Of these 19,195 positions, only 501 (less than 3 percent) are identifiable as professional (social workers, psychologists and psychiatrists, and teachers). The 3,701 labeled "other" can be assumed to be engaged in tasks classified as administrative, clerical, supervisory, vocational, medi-

TABLE 5
Positions in Jails and Local Adult Institutions, by Number

	Number	*Ratio*
Social workers	167	1:846
Psychologists	33	1:4282
Psychiatrists	58	1:2436
Academic teachers	106	1:1333
Vocational teachers	137	1:1031
Custodial officers	14,993	1:9
Other	3,701	1:38
Total	19,195	1:7

cal, and culinary. Custodial officers constitute 78 percent of all employees.

2. Qualifications

Although specific standards for personnel in institutions primarily serving misdemeanant offenders are not formulated by the special committee, the general standards for personnel may be applied. These call for educational qualifications appropriate for the positions, civil service or merit system coverage, and adequate salaries.

The administration of most county jails is under the control of the sheriff, who has law enforcement and other responsibilities quite extraneous to and often considered more important than correctional functions. Numerous administrative, professional, and practical disadvantages flow from combining custodial and treatment responsibilities for offenders in agencies whose personnel are in the political arena (in most counties the sheriff is an elected officer) and to whom the community looks more specifically for the investigation, arrest, and prosecution of offenders rather than their reformation. There are unquestionably some progressive and interested sheriffs, unwilling to be mere custodians, who have developed sound correctional treatment programs. But generally, changing the sheriff (in many instances, every 2 years) results in changing the jail personnel: no worthwhile program can be built on such shifting sands.

(A) EDUCATIONAL QUALIFICATIONS AND CIVIL SERVICE. The minimum educational requirements for the principal administrator, the social worker, and the custodial officer are quite revealing. For the position of superintendent, warden, or head jailer, 53 percent of the institutions studied called for no specific minimum educational background; 39 percent required a high school education, and only 8 percent a college education. Of these positions, 56 percent were not under civil service or merit system coverage (see tables 6 and 7).

The educational requirements for the custodial officer closely resemble the superintendent's: No minimum requirement in 53 percent of the counties, a high school education in 46 percent, and college education in 1 percent. The merit system coverage for custodial officers is exactly the same as for superintendents—44 percent have it; 56 percent do not.

TABLE 6
Minimum Educational Requirement, by Percentage of Institutions

| Position | Minimum requirement, percent | | | |
	None	High school	College	Postgraduate
Superintendent	53	39	8	
Custodial officer	53	46	1	
Social worker	9	41	44	6

TABLE 7
Civil Service or Merit System Coverage, by Percentage of Personnel

Position	Coverage	No coverage
	Percent	Percent
Superintendent, jailer, or warden	44	56
Custodial officer	44	56
Professional positions	86	14

The picture changes radically in the social worker positions. For these, only 9 percent of the counties have no minimum requirements; 41 percent ask for high school graduation; 44 percent, for college; 6 percent, for postgraduate work. Likewise, 86 percent of these workers have civil service coverage and only 14 percent do not.

The difference in these percentages means that county and local institutions that do not have merit system coverage are also the ones that rarely have social workers.

In a generally progressive and economically sound Eastern State, regular personnel in all local institutions have merit system coverage under examinations prepared and conducted by the State civil service commission. However, about 50 percent of the staff are classified as temporary employees because they do not meet the requirements set up by the merit system—a situation that must be tolerated because wage scales are too low to attract qualified staff.

(B) SALARIES. The survey showed that, in the sample institutions, the salary of the superintendent or head administrator ranged from under $1,500 to more than $18,000 a year, with a median salary range of $7,000-$8,000; the salary of a custodial officer in these institutions ranged from under $1,500 to $9,000 a year, with a median range of $4,000-$5,000 (see table 8).

Low salaries, low qualifications, and lack of good merit system coverage go hand in hand. The areas where improvement can be noted are those which first adopt civil service coverage and then move on to organization of unions or employee associations which gradually exert pressure and achieve salary upgrading. In spite of the discomfort that such organization may cause some administrators, the successful efforts of labor in obtaining salary increments can be utilized by the progressive administrator to obtain and retain better-qualified personnel.

(C) INSERVICE TRAINING. Since most persons employed as custodial officers are not equipped for performance of their duties by previous experience or training, a formal, continuous inservice training program is essential. It should consist of sessions on custodial procedures and techniques, classification and treatment policies and procedures, and similar subjects.

The survey showed that only 38 percent of the facilities offer any sort of inservice training and that, in most instances, it consisted of little more than training in the use of firearms, supervision of correspondence, and an occasional staff conference.

E. Physical Plant

The national estimate of the total rated capacity of all facilities in this portion of the survey is 192,197 beds. Thus we have approximately 36 percent more living space than is needed to accommodate the estimated daily population of 141,303. Yet we hear constantly of overcrowded jails and short-term institutions (and overcrowded they are in the metropolitan and urban centers). Some of the empty cells are in places where they are not needed, others are vacant because they are unfit for human occupancy.

One New England State, for example, reports four jails having a total

TABLE 8
**Beginning Salaries of Local Adult Institutional Personnel,
by Number of Agencies**

	Superintendent or jailer	*Custodial officer*
	Percent	Percent
Under $1,500	.6	1.2
$1,500 to $2,400	.6	2.9
$2,401 to $3,000	1.8	6.3
$3,001 to $4,000	4.2	8.0
$4,001 to $5,000	10.8	33.3
$5,001 to $6,000	10.8	25.3
$6,001 to $7,000	12.6	16.6
$7,001 to $8,000	11.4	5.8
$8,001 to $9,000	16.2	.6
$9,001 to $10,000	9.0	
$10,001 to $11,000	7.2	
$11,001 to $12,000	10.2	
$12,001 to $13,000	1.2	
$13,001 to $14,000	.6	
$14,001 to $15,000		
$15,001 to $16,000		
$16,001 to $17,000		
$17,001 to $18,000	.6	
Over $18,000	1.8	
Total	100	100

of 899 cells without sanitary facilities. The construction of many existing local institutions predated inside plumbing and electricity; they still have slop buckets, bullpens, and unshaded electric bulbs dangling from exposed fixtures. A New England State has three jails that were built 160 years ago; a State in the Midwest reports that many of its local jails are 100 years old.

TABLE 9

Age of Short-Term Institutions, by Percentage

Age	*Percentage*
Less than 10 years old	24
10 to 24 years	11
25 to 50 years	30
Over 50 years	35

The age of all institutions for short-term prisoners is shown in table 9.

The national estimate of new construction for short-term prisoners and for untried prisoners (with possible use for sentenced prisoners also) shows a total of about 47,000 beds (see table 10).

TABLE 10

New Construction of Short-Term and Detention Institutions

	Capacity			
	Under construction	*Authorized*	*Planned for construction by 1975*	*Total*
For short-term prisoners	3,196	2,683	9,982	15,861
For untried prisoners	4,240	9,824	17,247	31,311

F. State Supervision and Assistance

In Connecticut, Rhode Island, Delaware, and Puerto Rico, the local jails are no longer autonomous; they are operated as State institutions. In several other States (e.g., Maine, Massachusetts, and North Carolina) short-term misdemeanant offenders are committed to the houses of correction, farms, and road camps; the county jails, usually operated by sheriffs and other law enforcement officials, are used only for persons detained for trial.

Committee standards call for the State governments to be responsible for the quality of correctional programs and systems operated by local jurisdictions. An important role for the State in this regard is standard setting.

Twelve States set standards for local institutions and 19 set jail standards for personnel, construction, salaries, health, etc. Eleven States inspect local institutions and 19 inspect local jails. Two States subsidize local institutions; six subsidize local jails.

Over 60 percent of the States accept no responsibility for standards in local institutions and jails. No such percentage can be found for State government inactivity in other fields of local human welfare—e.g., child care, public housing, nursing, hospital services, etc. Frequently the reason for this absence of interest is not the State's unwillingness to get into the jail and local institution picture but rather the resistance of local patronage interests to State interference. Even in those States that authorize and even legislate inspection and consultation services, the caliber and efficacy of the services are questionable. Elaborate and detailed reports of visits are written, filed, and generally forgotten; no attempt is made to enforce the standards.

G. Programs

Inmate work programs, other than janitorial and institutional maintenance tasks, are small in number and poorly organized, equipped, and supervised. The goods they produce are generally expensive and inferior, and the vocational or trade training is not constructive.

Insofar as behavorial change programs are concerned, the picture is still more dismal; see table 11 for the frequency of imaginative or unusual rehabilitation programs reported in the 215 institutions studied.

TABLE 11
Rehabilitation Programs for Short-Term Prisoners,
by Percentage of 215 Institutions

Program	Number of institutions	Percentage
Work release	24	11
Educational	22	10
Group counseling	19	9
Alcoholics	15	7
Other	44	20
None	140	65
Unknown	3	1

Little is being done for the inmates principally because the personnel and the institutions lack the necessary qualifications and services. Yet a few pilot programs show that greater investments at this point on the correctional continuum can produce substantial savings in manpower and money. A small but growing number of conscientious, qualified, and determined jail and workhouse administrators are developing community support and originating pilot and demonstration programs which show that correctional treatment can be successfully initiated and furthered within the time limits of short-term institutional commitments. The four institutions discussed below are examples of this progress.

1. ST. PAUL, MINN. The workhouse receives misdemeanants, gross misdemeanants, and some felons; the maximum sentence is 1 year; the

average sentence is 28 days; the average daily population is under 200 men and 15 women, about 80 percent of whom have had prior short-term sentences.

During the past 8 years, program operation has expanded considerably through the addition of professional staff and volunteers. All inmates are assigned to either work or school programs.

Work assignments include truck and livestock farming, and maintenance work for other institutions (painting, carpentry, laundry, etc.).

The educational program, using inmate teachers, started 5 years ago; unsatisfactory results led to hiring a part-time school teacher, who is paid from the inmate canteen fund. A recently obtained $44,000 foundation grant will pay for a regular teacher in special education, books, and equipment. Ninety-seven inmates have obtained high school diplomas; some of them have continued with extension courses given by the University of Minnesota.

Inmates on the work release program pay $3 a day for room and board and furnish their own transportation; men earning substandard wages or attending school are not charged. The work releasees pay the institution approximately $25,000 a year for room and board. Under provisions of the Economic Opportunity Act, interviewing, counseling, and aptitude and vocational testing services are available to men under 21 years of age on work release.

Since the work-or-school program started, more than 93 percent of the prisoners selected by the institution for work or school release have not returned to the institution on a subsequent commitment.

An Alcoholics Anonymous counselor (paid by the canteen fund) conducts four AA meetings a week.

Professional and lay volunteers from the community assist in all the programs.

2. WESTCHESTER COUNTY, N.Y. The county has two adjacent, but separate, short-term institutions. One, the county penitentiary, houses men sentenced for periods up to 1 year. The other, the county jail, houses men and women awaiting sentence, and also women serving short sentences.

The penitentiary program (farming, carpentry, tailoring, Alcoholics Anonymous meetings) was supplemented some years ago by a program of basic education set up by the NCCD Westchester Citizens Committee.[36] This was followed by a pilot project for women in the jail, where there had been no activities program at all.

The women (average population, 20) ranged in age from 17 to 70, and were committed mostly for alcoholism, shoplifting, forgery, narcotics, abortion, and disorderly conduct; the average length of stay was 60 to 90 days. The objective of the project was to demonstrate how citizen volunteers could effectively serve to enrich the activities program in a short-term institution. Forty-one volunteers with a variety of professional backgrounds but without any prior experience working with offenders were recruited and trained in the special requirements governing work in a correctional institution. Courses in needlecraft, typing and shorthand, personal grooming, nursing, and arts and crafts were organized. The overall results showed that citizen volunteers can enrich the activities program in a short-term correctional institution. It also provided an example of how public agencies and community services can cooperate in this field.[37] All of this presumes, of course, a cooperative institutional management.

3. MULTNOMAH COUNTY (PORTLAND), OREG. The county correctional institution, a minimum security facility was opened on December 1, 1963. Per capita operating cost is about $4 a day for an average population of 80 inmates. The institution receives persons serving more than 60 days; the average length of sentence served is 180 days.

The operating staff consists of a counselor, a cook, and eight custodial officers who, assisted by a part-time chaplain, are frequently involved in counseling in one form or another in their daily contact with the inmates. The counselor, a trained clinical psychologist, chairs the classification committee and selects special cases for psychotherapy. Volunteer student tutors from a local college teach courses primarily for the illiterate but also give help to those seeking general education or specific instruction anywhere from grade school to college levels. Medical services, including corrective surgery and dentistry, are available through the county hospital. Selection of inmates suitable for work release is made by the institution, not by the court. Cooperative agreements have been reached with State and Federal authorities to accept prisoners from their penitentiaries and assume full authority and supervision of these men under the work release program.

In the 2 1/2 years since the Multnomah County Correctional Institution received its first inmates, the recidivism rate of the more than 500 prisoners released—including vagrants, skid row alcoholics, and "installment plan" lifers—has been less than 20 percent; only 16 inmates (3.2 percent) have walked away.

4. SAN DIEGO COUNTY, CALIF. Recognizing the futility of mass treatment, San Diego County has established five honor camps to which

inmates are sent after classification at the county jail. Three have minimum custody and a capacity of 96 inmates; another, also minimum custody, has a capacity of 20; the fifth has medium custody and a capacity of 51. The aim is redirection of the inmate through constructive work and therapeutic counseling. Grouping is based on inmate treatment needs. Individual and group counseling sessions, informal educational programs, and work projects involving forestry work, firefighting, firebreak construction, road building, roadside clearance, etc., keep inmates constructively occupied. Recreation programs stress participation rather than watching. Family visiting under relaxed but supervised conditions strengthens the inmate's ties with home and community.

In 1964, with supplementary financial support from the National Institute of Mental Health, Crofton House was opened in San Diego. Approximately 20 men, assigned from the total honor camp population, live in the halfway house, go out to work under a work release program, and, by living in the community, gain the experience of how to live socially acceptable lives and also enable the community to understand more clearly the problems of criminality. The house is managed by a husband-wife team but is maintained by the inmate residents.

H. Pretrial Jail Detention

As stated above, the emphasis in this part of the survey was on the use of jails and local institutions for convicted offenders serving 30 days or more. In practice, of course, most of these institutions are also used for the detention of persons awaiting trial.

1. The local jail should be used only for persons awaiting trial (and perhaps, for practical reasons, persons sentenced to terms of less than 30 days).

Persons accused of crime who are kept in custody pending trial, because of the nature of the alleged offense or their inability to make bail, require a program radically different from the type that is appropriate for the convicted offender. Of the present charge the accused, no matter what his prior record may be, is still legally not guilty and cannot, under the Constitution, be subjected to punishment or to any measure of restraint and restriction greater than is necessary to produce him in court when his case is called. Program for him should permit him all reasonable means to prepare his defense and to maintain the status of a person accused but not convicted. It ought to be a separate and distinct function from the management and care of the sentenced prisoner. Failure to take the distinction seriously "is equivalent to expecting a community general hospital, without specialized staff and facilities, to undertake the inpatient treatment of physical handicaps, tuberculosis, mental illness, drug addiction, alcoholism, and all the infectious and degenerative diseases, in addition to the common illnesses appropriately dealt with in a general hospital."[38]

2. The number of persons held in jail awaiting trial can be sharply reduced.

Jails across the country are crowded with accused persons who remain in custody for substantial periods simply because they cannot afford to post even nominal bail. "The bail system has, almost from its inception, been the subject of dissatisfaction. Every serious study since the 1920's has exposed defects in its administration. Yet, proof of the need for reforms has produced little in the way of fundamental change. Committing magistrates misunderstand or misapply the criteria for pretrial release; bail determinations are made on the basis of skimpy and unverified facts; the final decision as to whether a defendant is to be kept in jail usually rests in the hands of the professional bondsman; and a substantial number of defendants, accused but not convicted, are denied release because they are poor."[39]

Not the least of the many reasons for delayed justice and delayed disposition is the lack of a "statistical monitoring system within the existing court structure [which] would enable the exercise of essential controls over the time required for the successive steps in the judicial process."[40]

Persons detained awaiting trial must be kept physically close to the courts and all persons and agencies concerned with the disposition. If the jail is to be raised from the level of a mere warehouse to the status of a purposeful detention center, there must be a well-organized and effective liaison process involving the agencies having an active interest in untried prisoners. The jail should have day-to-day knowledge of all changes in the prosecution process and should have qualified staff in sufficient quantity to recognize and promptly resolve any roadblocks to disposition. Pretrial release on recognizance or nominal bail of all eligibles should be so organized that those defendants for whom pretrial incarceration is not necessary can be released at the preliminary hearing. These procedures will require personnel and money for new functions. But some of these costs ultimately will be offset by reduction of man-days served. Additional savings will result from decreases in capital expenditures for new jail facilities and in welfare subsidies to dependents of persons who need not be detained.

3. Specialized programs should be conducted at jails even for the untried and for prisoners sentenced to less than 30 days.

Quite aside from the question of the untried defendant's guilt, undetermined in the pretrial period, 90 percent or more of the group—according to experienced jail administrators, particularly in the more populated jurisdictions—come from multiproblem families and are overwhelmed, not only in jail but even when free, with economic, health, family, educational, and religious problems which they cannot resolve and which make them antisocial, unsocial, and asocial. "Justice delayed is justice denied" has a corollary: "Correctional treatment too long postponed does not correct." The jail holding only untried prisoners and those committed for less than 30 days could, if properly staffed, be made a most effective clinic for the voluntary treatment (through counseling and referral) of thousands of persons who, because their root problems go undiagnosed and unattended, now keep coming back to jail.

6   Our Sick Jails

RICHARD A. McGEE*

Thoughtful practitioners and scholars alike have condemned this old derelict of local government for decades on end, but the common jail lives on with pathetically little change. Even when a new one comes into being, smelling of fresh paint and civic righteousness, it usually gets worse and worse until it also joins the ranks of what President Nixon's Task Force on Prisoner Rehabilitation calls "the most glaringly inadequate institution on the American correctional scene."[41]

Nearly fifty years ago, Fishman called these institutions "Crucibles of Crime".[42]

President Johnson's Commission on Law Enforcement and Criminal Justice, in its report on *Corrections,* points out with commendable diligence a bare handful of "Programs of Promise" out of 3,473 local jails in the country.[43]

Richard Velde, Associate Administrator of the Law Enforcement Assistance Administration, made this statement recently:

> Jails are festering sores in the criminal justice system. There are no model jails anywhere; we know, we tried to find them. Almost nowhere are there rehabilitative programs operated in conjunction with jails. It's harsh to say, but the truth is that jail personnel are the most uneducated, untrained and poorly paid of all personnel in the criminal justice system—and furthermore, there aren't enough of them.
>
> The result is what you would expect, only worse. Jails are, without question, brutal, filthy, cesspools of crime—institutions which serve to brutalize and embitter men to prevent them from returning to a useful role in society.[44]

*From *Federal Probation* XXXV, 1 (March 1971):3-8. Reprinted by permission of Richard A. McGee.

Sheriff Michael H. Canlis, President of the National Sheriffs' Association, said as recently as October 1970:

> It has been said that most (jails) are only human warehouses. We must ask ourselves, is merely keeping our prisoners secure, enough?
> If we content ourselves with maintaining nothing more than a human warehouse, we are not only perpetuating the so-called failure of an element in the system of criminal justice, but we might, to some degree, be responsible for a contribution for some of the increases in crime.[45]

I personally opened the Rikers Island Penitentiary in New York City as its first warden, and later, as Deputy Commissioner and for a time Acting Commissioner of the New York City Department of Correction, was responsible for the administration of all of New York City's local lockups, detention prisons and misdemeanant institutions. Since then I have inspected scores of local jails.

Only a few months ago, at the request of the San Francisco Crime Committee, I visited the jails of that proud city. The committee has made its report and I shall not add to it here except to say that some of the conditions observed in San Francisco's new Hall of Justice Jail were shocking even to so jaded an eye as mine.

In fairness, however, it must be added that in San Francisco, as in numerous other jurisdictions, it is virtually impossible to fix responsibility for the glaring and obvious inadequacies because control of the resources of the local government are so fragmented that when the chips are down the "buck" is usually on someone else's desk. Then when the heat is off, the "buck" gets lost and nothing much happens until the next scandal hits the headlines.

But let us set aside the scandals, the instances of mismanagement and local political indian-wrestling. Surely we don't need another century of indictments to convince us that the local city and county jails as now organized and managed simply must be replaced by a more rational system.

So, what can be done?

First, let us discuss the larger problem, of which the jail is only the most visible part—visible because it is a physical place peopled by public offenders and public employees.

The total problem is not the jail alone, but the whole agglomeration of public services involved in the *management* of *law offenders* after *arrest*.

The management problem involves all the parts of the criminal justice system—police, courts, prosecutors, defense attorneys, detention jails, probation services, and parole at the local level; and then there is the state government's correctional system; and overlapping these, the federal system. The total so-called "system" must deal with the whole gamut of illegal acts, from minor traffic infractions to the most heinous of felonious crimes. The persons who commit the offenses include every imaginable kind of human being in the society—murderers, drunk drivers, prostitutes, thieves, forgers, mental cases, alcoholics, drug addicts, muggers, juveniles out of control, rioters, beggars—everybody is eligible if he gives cause to be arrested.

As a practical matter, however, we find the local jail being occupied principally by drunks, addicts and petty thieves. And as for the women, if the prostitutes were eliminated from the jail populations, most of the women's quarters would be virtually empty most of the time.

Based on a very rough estimate, about 7 per cent of the three million persons, more or less, who pass through these jails each year are charged with or convicted of felonies, and 93 per cent are misdemeanants. It can be seen readily enough that the problem of jail administration, aside from holding a few felons awaiting disposition by the courts, is that of managing a miscellaneous array of persons charged with or convicted of offenses of a relatively minor nature. Only a very few of these are incarcerated for periods of six months to one year. A study of two large counties in California revealed that about one-third of the sentenced prisoners on a given day were serving terms of 30 days or less, one-third one month to three months, and one-third over 90 days up to and including one year.[46]

The question is often posed, what can be accomplished toward treating, managing or rehabilitating persons who receive sentences of 30 days or less. As has been pointed out, this only accounts for about one-third of misdemeanants who are sentenced. The same question might be asked about those who receive sentences of 30 to 90 days, who constitute another one-third. The group that we might well be most concerned about is the third that receives sentences of three months to one year. What, also, of the substantial number of untried defendants presumed innocent under our law who may wait in jail for periods of three months to a year or more while the judicial machinery unwinds, leading to the day when the judge can finally render his decision. In some metropolitan jurisdictions 60 per cent or more of the daily jail population is made up of persons who are unsentenced. The warehousing practice is bad enough for the unsentenced, but it has no validity whatsoever for those serving sentences. One month in jail may not seem long either to the judge or the sheriff, but to the prisoner it may be the longest 720 hours in his life, and just one of those hours could include the most damaging experience in his lifetime. Contrariwise, short stays in jail are a way of life for thousands of deteriorated middle-aged alcoholics and petty offenders. A 1963 study of some seven thousand inmates in five New York county penitentiaries showed that over 20 per cent were serving a term which was their tenth or more.

The remedies for the deficiencies and abuses of the common jail are many. Some are relatively easy to find and can be applied by simple shifts in procedures. Others will require substantial changes in law and in administrative organization.

Among the procedural changes available, some of which are already in use in many jurisdictions, are:

1. The use of citations instead of jail booking for selected cases at the time of apprehension.

2. Release on "Own Recognizance" by the court at the time of arraignment by many of those unable to post money bail as a guaranty of appearance in court when ordered to do so.

3. Adoption of a policy by the courts of giving priority in court disposition to those in jail as opposed to those awaiting trial while out on bail.

4. The use of short form or "quicky" presentence probation reports in misdemeanor cases, so that the judge may have information about each defendant which might have relevance to his decision to choose among such alternative dispositions as suspended sentence, supervised probation, fine, and length and type of jail sentence.

5. Provision for payment of fines on the installment plan in cases wherein the defendant is employed but does not have enough ready cash on the day when sentence is pronounced.

6. The use of work-furlough releases for employable and reasonably reliable jail inmates.

7. The use of parole and post-institutional supervision for most jail inmates and especially for men with families who receive jail sentences of more than 60 days.

8. Development of detoxification and rehabilitation programs outside the jail system for chronic alcoholics.

There is nothing either startling or new or illegal in the above list of procedural practices. What is really startling to any taxpayer who is concerned about the effectiveness of his dollar is that the number of jurisdictions which exploit *all* of these practices to the fullest are almost non-existent.

Assuming the same number of officers and the same degree of police vigilance and efficiency now existing, and assuming that the above practices were fully utilized, it is probable that the *daily populations of the nation's local jails could be cut by as much as fifty per cent without risk to the public safety.* Then, it is fair to ask, why isn't it being done?

The reasons are not difficult to find. Some are so obvious they need only to be mentioned without elaboration. Others are more elusive.

ADMINISTRATIVE PROBLEMS

The most apparent reason for inefficiency and ineptitude in jail management lies in the governmental organizational structure in which the jails are embedded. According to the President's Commission on Law Enforcement and Administration of Justice, there were at the last count (1965), 3,473 local jails in this country. These were projected to have by 1975 an average daily population of 178,000. If this population were evenly distributed, each jail would have each day only 51 inmates. The fact, of course, is that hundreds of jails are mere lockups for a dozen or so and many of these are completely empty part of the time. In addition to the city and county jails there are thousands of police lockups in our towns and hamlets which are little more than cages. On the opposite end of the size distribution, we see great metropolitan facilities like those in Chicago, Los Angeles and New York City, which number their inmates in the thousands. They are uniformly overcrowded, impersonal, un-dermanned, and under-programmed.

Seven hundred sixty-two, or 22 per cent of all local jails are a part of city government, and with rare exceptions these are operated by the municipal police. Except for inertia and vested interest, there is no logical reason for the municipal police to run any jail where offenders are confined for more than 48 or 72 hours to permit delivery in court and transfer to a county or regional jail. This is especially obvious in a place like Sacramento, California, where the county detention jail and the police jail are located on the same city block, or in San Francisco, where the sheriff's jail and the city police jail are on the sixth and fifth floors respectively of the Hall of Justice.

The most common practice is for local jails to be a part of county government and to be operated by the county sheriff. Twenty-five hundred and forty-seven, or 73.3 per cent of all local jails are so managed. A few jurisdictions, like New York City and Denver, Colorado, have city-county governments, with the jails operated by an administrator appointed by the mayor or the board of supervisors. At the 1965 count, there were 149 such jails or city prisons and only fifteen were operated by state governments.

A revealing survey of the jails of Illinois was made recently by the Center for Studies in Criminal Justice, the Law School, University of Chicago.[47] Of the 160 jails studied, 101 were county operated and 59 were city jails. Even worse, of the 13 very large jails, four were city and nine county. In California, as of September 26, 1968, there were 27,325 prisoners in local jails and camps. Of these, 2,151, or about 8½ per cent, were in city operated facilities. This percentage had dropped from about 22 per cent in 1960.

Municipal police forces have trouble enough enforcing the law and keeping the peace in the cities without expecting them also to be either expert or very much interested in managing local jails with all the challenges presented by their diverse inhabitants and the ever present potentialities for crisis and scandal inherent even in the best of them.

It appears, then, that there is substantial movement away from the practice of placing the jail management function under the city police. This begins to tidy up the administrative picture somewhat, but moves only a short step toward more rational and efficient systems of pre-adjudication, detention and correctional programs provided by local government.

There is no real agreement in concept or practice at this time as to how services for corrections at the local levels of government are best organized and managed. In Vermont and Connecticut, the jails are under state jurisdiction. In New York City, with its "Home Rule" Charter, there is no county sheriff and the city's detention jails and institutions for sentenced misdemeanants are administered by a Department of Correction, headed by a Commissioner appointed by the Mayor. In San Diego County, California, the sheriff runs the jail for pre-trial detention and a separate Department of County Camps headed by an administrator appointed by the County Board of Supervisors operates the facilities for most of the sentenced misdemeanants.

Other patterns involve regional jail districts comprised of two or more counties, or contractual relations between adjoining jurisdictions, in which one county serves another for some kinds of prisoners on a cost reimbursement basis.

Most of these joint operations are fraught with very real problems of transportation, funding for building construction, and petty political friction.

In the preceding discussion of local jails, we have been speaking exclusively about such institutions for the care and confinement of adult men and women. These appear to have developed historically largely as unwanted appendages of agencies charged with the jurisdiction's police power. However, with the movement of population to the cities, county sheriffs have been losing more and more of their direct enforcement functions to the city police. As a result, the county jails have tended to become a larger share of each sheriff's patronage empire, and hence a function he is less willing to relinquish. The prison systems of the state governments have been used traditionally mostly for the more serious and more persistent convicted felons. In some states they may also accept sentenced misdemeanants of certain classes, especially women. But even with nearly 200,000 prisoners in state prisons, the lion's share of the day-to-day prisoner traffic is still in the local jails.

Parallel with this development in the adult offender field, we have seen different patterns in the delivery systems of services for juvenile offenders. Just as confinement and treatment programs for adults have tended to grow out of the police function, the juvenile services have emerged from the judicial function. This is because probation services originated in the courts. Detention halls and probation supervision for wards of the juvenile courts are more often than not adjuncts of the judicial rather than the executive branch of local government.

In spite of the division of the management of detention facilities for adults and juveniles between the sheriffs and the probation departments in most counties, probation services for both adult and juvenile offenders are combined in the local probation department in most jurisdictions. Here again we find every conceivable kind of variation of organization, of policy development, of control over employees, and of financial support.

A few examples support this point: In California, each county has a probation department within the court system, serving both juveniles and adults, except in two counties. In Los Angeles County, the head of this largest county probation department in the State is appointed by and reports to the board of supervisors, not to the courts. Stranger still, in some counties he is appointed by the judge of the juvenile court, even though there are usually more adults than juveniles in the total case load. In Wisconsin, probation and parole services are in the State Division of Correction except in Milwaukee. In Washington State, adult probation is combined with the state parole system and is under the State Division of Institutions, but juvenile probation is under the juvenile courts, with some state financial aid provided. New York State has just created a unified state department of probation, but with typical illogic, has separated it from the State Department of Correction.

Viewed by anyone outside the correctional field who is possessed of the most elementary sense of administrative order and common logic, the ways in which we in this country organize our resources to deal with millions of law breakers, from the point of arrest on, must look as if it were designed by a madman with the advice of Public Enemy No. 1.

The time must come soon for concerned and responsible public officials to review this organizational "weed patch" with a view of making some sense out of it—sense to the taxpayer even if not to all the vested interests, ideological hangups, traditions and political bickering over power and sources of money.

That so little movement has taken place in the last century might make the problem seem hopeless if it were not for some contemporary developments. Without elaboration out of scale with the scope of this article, some of these are worth mentioning.

The first is a growing concern about the nation's unbalanced tax structure. We argue that crime and the treatment of offenders is essentially a local problem, but the tax bases of the cities and counties grow weaker and weaker in comparison with those of state governments and the federal government. We must either find ways to feed state and federal moneys back to the local units of government or the higher levels of government must assume more of the burden for rendering direct services. "Correctional" services have always been at the end of the parade—behind health, hospitals, welfare, transportation, and education in these fiscal adjustments. Weak though recent efforts toward state subsidies and federal aid in this field have been, there are encouraging signs that our political leaders are beginning to recognize the problem.

Another hopeful sign is the increasing number of states which are developing stronger state departments of corrections, headed by competent administrators. This, coupled with stronger career services and better educated professionals at the journeyman and middle-management levels, cannot help but bring more pressure from within toward sounder organization and better performance.

It is also encouraging to note the interest shown last year by President Nixon in the appointment of a White House Task Force on Prisoner Rehabilitation, the statements of concern by Chief Justice Burger, and the American Bar Association's recent establishment of a Commission on Correctional Facilities and Services.

The anxiety of the average citizen about the crime and delinquency problem generally must inevitably put the whole system on its mettle. All the participants in the administration of criminal justice are creatures of government. They must begin to produce, or perish.

If we would attempt to think logically about some portion of the "Justice System", such as the jails, we ought to come to some conclusions as to how to divide the total task among mutually supportive entities in the system without doing violence to our constitutional law and our established form of government.

We must start out, then, by calling to mind our doctrine of the separation of powers among the judicial, executive, and legislative branches. First, let us consider the role of the judiciary with particular reference to developments in the supervision of convicted persons placed on probation. It seemed sensible enough for the trial court judge in a one man court with one or two probation officers, to appoint these persons as functionaries of his office to make pre-sentence investigations and to report to him from time to time on how a handful of probationers were doing. But now, with most of our population concentrated in great metropolitan complexes, this arrangement is as archaic as a one cow dairy. In Los Angeles County, for example, the Probation Department has some four thousand employees, administers an annual budget of $53,000,000, runs 30 detention facilities for juveniles, and supervises a case load of adults and juveniles of 41,000 persons.

The decision to grant or revoke probation is and should no doubt continue to be a judicial function, but the operation by the probation department is as clearly an executive function as is the city police department or the operation of the state prison system. Accordingly, except in those rural counties with one man courts, we must conclude that the administration of probation should be an executive function and a unit of state or county government. Except for the historical development of the services, there is no more logic in having the judge administer the probation service than there is for him to run the jails and prisons to which he commits defendants. If it is logical for the courts to administer large correctional (probation) programs, why then should we not suggest that the jails for adult offenders are as rational a component of court administration as detention halls for juveniles?

Looking at the question in another way, one might inquire why the sheriff or other police official should not administer the probation services with just as much logic as supports the notion that he is best fitted to manage the jails. If we persist in mixing the judicial roles of the courts with functions which are clearly executive, we may be running the risk of raising constitutional questions of jurisdiction.

The President's Commission on Law Enforcement and Administration of Justice, commenting on this issue, says:

> Most jails continue to be operated by law enforcement officials. The basic police mission of apprehending offenders usually leaves little time, commitment, or expertise for the development of rehabilitative programs, although notable exceptions demonstrate that jails can indeed be settings for correctional treatment. Many law enforcement officials, particularly those administering large and professionalized forces, have advocated transfer of jails to correctional control.

The most compelling reason for making this change is the opportunity it offers to integrate the jails with the total corrections network, to upgrade them, and to use them in close coordination with both institution and community-based correctional services. As long as jails are operated by law enforcement officials, no matter how enlightened, it will be more difficult to transform them into correctional centers. As a major step toward reform, jails should be placed under the control of correctional authorities who are able to develop the needed program services. The trend should be away from the isolated jail and toward an integrated but diversified system of correctional facilities.[48]

A dispassionate view of the best possible way to organize the criminal justice system cannot but lead to the conclusion that there are *three* major groups of functions, each requiring different emphasis, different attitudes, and different professional training and occupational skills. In skeletal outline, they are as follows:

The Police
—Direct prevention and peace keeping
—Detection and apprehension

The Courts, including Prosecution and Defense
—Application of the law
—Judgmental disposition

The Correctional Agencies
—Pre-sentence investigation and community supervision of probationers and parolees
—Management and control of defendants awaiting adjudication (jails and juvenile halls)
—Management of residential facilities and programs for all committed offenders (jails, prisons, correctional schools and halfway houses)

If the above is a rational division of functions, it is clear that each political jurisdiction, be it a state or a county or a regional district within a state, should establish the equivalent of a department of corrections, which would be responsible for the management of all offenders under its jurisdiction, whether accused or convicted, and whether incarcerated or under community supervision.

This would mean: First, that the courts should relinquish administrative direction of probation services.

Second, that jails and camps for adult offenders must be removed from the administrative direction of police agencies.

Third, that in jurisdictions (usually counties) with too small a population to operate efficiently, they must either combine into regional districts or turn the functions over to state government.

Fourth, that the unrealistic administrative dichotomy between youth and adult correctional programs existing in many local jurisdictions be discontinued.

Fifth, that to encourage these changes and to ensure equality of treatment throughout the system, both the state governments and the federal government must provide financial assistance based upon adherence to decent standards.

"Equal Justice Under Law" are noble words engraved in marble over the entrance to the Supreme Court Building in the Nation's capitol. If we really believe in this great democratic concept, we can hardly continue to tolerate the spectacle of a mental case charged with disorderly conduct sitting naked on the concrete floor of a bare isolation cell in a local jail while in another jurisdiction he would be in a hospital.

It is equally incongruous for a minion of organized crime charged with felonious assault to be walking the streets free on bail while scores of minor but indigent offenders sit idly in overcrowded jails awaiting court disposition.

Finally, it is not enough to say that the local jail as we know it is a failure—it is a scandal! All the palliatives and all the uncoordinated efforts at patching up the present system will continue to fail. Basic reorganization of the whole structure for managing offenders at the local levels of government is required. NOTHING LESS WILL DO!

7   *The Federal Prison System*

U. S. BUREAU OF PRISONS*

HISTORY OF FEDERAL PRISONS

Congress created the Bureau of Prisons in 1930. Before the federal prison system was established, rehabilitation of federal offenders was virtually an impossibility. Administrators of the seven federal prisons then in existence functioned independently, with relative autonomy. Funds were appropriated separately by Congress to each institution. Over 12,000 offenders were confined in the federal prisons, rendering the institutions little more than "human warehouses." An equal number of federal prisoners were held in state and local institutions. . . .

Federal prison personnel numbered about 650 in the late 1920's, entirely too few to staff the institutions adequately. New guards were simply shown to their posts; training was unknown. Regimentation of the staff was almost as pervasive as that of the inmates.

THE FEDERAL BUREAU OF PRISONS IS ESTABLISHED

In 1929 a Congressional Committee was established to study conditions in federal prisons and to recommend remedial legislation. On May 14, 1930, President Hoover signed an Act of Congress creating the United States Bureau of Prisons. The Act directed that the Bureau develop the

* From U.S. Bureau of Prisons, Annual Report—1969 (Washington, D.C.: U.S. Government Printing Office, 1969).

99

federal prisons into an integrated system of classified institutions providing a program of custody and treatment based on the individual needs of the offender.

Congress directed the U.S. Public Health Service to furnish medical personnel and services to all the institutions. It placed the fledgling U.S. Probation Service in the Bureau's organization. (The Probation Service was transferred later to the jurisdiction of the U.S. Courts.) An independent three-man Board of Parole was established, replacing the old system of institution boards. Also, the new legislation provided a program of diversified industrial employment within the institutions. . . .

The U.S. Bureau of Prisons now operates an integrated system of 35 facilities covering eight correctional categories:

Youth and juvenile institutions
Young adult institutions
Adult penitentiaries
Adult correctional institutions
Short-term camps
Female institutions
Community treatment centers
A medical treatment center, used for treatment of inmates with medical or psychiatric problems.

Inmates are assigned to institutions on the basis of a number of factors, including age, length of sentence, prior criminal history, treatment needs, legal residence and family ties. A heavy concentration of academic and vocational instruction is provided in facilities for younger offenders, while those for older, recidivistic inmates center on industrial training.

Over the years the increase in the number of federal criminal statutes, plus the rising crime rate, have generated varying rates of growth in the population of federal prisons. At the close of the fiscal year, June 30, 1969, persons confined in federal prisons numbered 20,555. . . . The median age for those committed was 28.3. Nearly 3,500 offenders were convicted of assaultive offenses, such as robbery, kidnapping and homicide. An additional 1,400 offenders were committed for violation of narcotic laws. The number of minor liquor law and immigration law violators has declined in recent years. . . .

PLANNING TREATMENT PROGRAMS

In all federal institutions programs for the rehabilitation of the offender are initiated in the first few weeks following his commitment. During this time he lives in a separate unit and receives a thorough diagnostic study of his requirements for education, vocational training, and treatment of physical or psychiatric problems. An institutional treatment program is developed as a result of these findings and progressive goals are set for the inmate.

In almost all of the federal institutions, planning and management of inmates' programs are in the hands of "treatment teams." This is a small group of staff specialists who are responsible for developing institutional programs and guiding the progress of a designated caseload of inmates. The "team" method differs from the traditional method of classification by a central committee and makes possible far greater insight into the problems and needs of the individual offender. The result is better use of institutional and other resources and more effective treatment for the inmate. . . .

EDUCATION AND TRAINING

The institutions provide complete educational and vocational training facilities. Tests show that the intelligence level of federal offenders follow the same distribution curve as the national population. However, their educational achievement lags five years behind the national average. In many cases the deficiency is related to poor adjustment to the traditional education process. The Federal Prison System has shifted away from conventional classroom methods and towards instruction specifically tailored to the inmate's needs. Innovative approaches are used, including learning laboratories, team teaching and other up-to-date educational tools and techniques. The use of programmed material has been expanded in every institution. Before long, the complete high school equivalency curriculum will be available to all inmates in programmed instruction form. . . .

A number of federal inmates who have the potential to benefit from higher education are taking college courses. Usually the courses are given at the institutions under the auspices of a local college, as at the U.S. Penitentiary, Leavenworth, Kansas, which is affiliated with the Highland (Kansas) Junior College. Through the study-release program, other inmates can attend on-campus classes at local community colleges. . . .

FEDERAL PRISON INDUSTRIES, INC.

The Bureau's vocational training program is financed primarily by profits from Federal Prison Industries, Inc. This government-owned corporation is operated as an integral part of the Bureau of Prisons. Its Board of Directors is appointed by the President and includes representatives of industry, labor, agriculture, the public, and the Defense and Justice Departments.

Over 25 percent of the inmates in the Federal Prison System are employed full time in approximately 50 Industries' enterprises. Services and products, sold only to other federal agencies, range from key punch operations at the Federal Reformatory for Women, Alderson, West Virginia, to assembly of electronic cables for the space program by inmate workers at the U.S. Penitentiary, McNeil Island, Washington.

In 1969, for the second consecutive year, Federal Prison Industries, Inc. declared a record $5 million dividend to the U.S. Treasury. This payment brings to $77 million the amount the Corporation has paid to the Treasury since the first dividend was declared in 1946. . . .

Following a recent study of all institutional operations, the Corporation has been closing those activities that have minimal training value and replacing them with operations providing skills with better employment potential. As a result, occupations such as needle trades are being discontinued and skills in the new technologies are stressed. An illustration is the computer operator and programmer course given at the U.S. Penitentiary, Leavenworth, Kansas. Private employers are hiring inmates graduating from the course as quickly as they are released.

The Bureau of Prisons has been encouraging private business and industry to become involved in correctional education and training. An example of industry response is the Lockheed Corporation, which was given a contract to develop an aircraft structural assembly training program at the Federal Correctional Institution, Lompoc, California. Inmates who successfully complete the training find work in the aerospace industry at varying skill levels.

In addition to preparing the inmate for return to the community by giving him marketable skills, Federal Prison Industries, Inc. also helps him find a job. The agency finances the work of 27 Employment Placement Officers based in major metropolitan areas throughout the country. In the past year, these officers assisted 5,500 releasees and probationers in finding employment.

HEALTH SERVICES

A corps of 270 medical professionals and technicians gives inmates in federal institutions health care equivalent to that found in most communities. Operating under the Division of Health Services, the institution medical complement this past year included 63 medical doctors (20 of them psychiatrists,) 18 psychologists, and 33 dentists. Almost all of the professional staff are commissioned officers in the Public Health Service, who spend at least one two-year tour of duty at the federal prisons.

The Medical Center for Federal Prisoners at Springfield, Missouri has facilities for performing major surgery and for providing specialized medical and psychiatric care. It accommodates a daily average of 750 inmate-patients.

The Medical Center also conducts a "Physician's Assistant" training program. In this comprehensive 12-month course, medical technical assistants in federal and other correctional agencies can learn or brush up on the latest diagnostic and treatment techniques. The course has substantially increased the capacity of paraprofessionals to perform routine medical and administrative tasks, freeing the institution physician for direct patient care.

In addition to training civilian staff, the Health Services Division provides specialized training for inmates. An outstanding example is the Central Dental Laboratory, a Federal Prison Industries, Inc. enterprise at the U.S. Penitentiary, Lewisburg, Pennsylvania. In the course of a year, 45 inmate technicians trained at the Laboratory made over 3,000 dentures for federal inmates. A 90 percent success rate is reported for graduates of the training program, whose services are in high demand by private laboratories.

Female offenders are being successfully trained as dental assistants and hygienists at the Federal Reformatory for Women, Alderson, West Virginia and the Women's Division of the Federal Correctional Institution, Terminal Island, California.

In 1968 the Bureau's first special treatment center for federal offenders who are narcotic addicts was opened at the Federal Correctional Institution, Danbury, Connecticut. Two more units were opened in fiscal year 1969, one at Alderson and the other at Terminal Island. A fourth unit was opened in January of 1970 at the Federal Correctional Institution, Milan, Michigan. . . .

RELIGIOUS SERVICES

Almost all of the federal institutions have full-time Protestant and Catholic chaplains who carry on an active religious program. The religious needs of Jewish inmates and other groups are served by local clergy on a part-time basis. The chaplains work closely with institution staffs and are involved in the treatment programs. Frequently, through establishing his own personal rapport with an inmate, a chaplain can persuade the individual to accept the help the staff is trying to give him.

All of the institutions have non-denominational chapels where inmates can attend services. In some instances, inmates, particularly young offenders, may be given permission to accompany a responsible citizen to religious services in the community. . . .

COMMUNITY-BASED TREATMENT

The Federal Prison System has introduced a number of innovations to help offenders make a successful transition from institution to community life.

A good illustration is the work-release program under which inmates work at jobs in the community during the daytime and return to the institution at night. More than 6,000 men and women have participated in work-release since it was established in the Federal Prison System with passage of the Federal Prisoners Rehabilitation Act of 1965. Earnings of these inmates have now reached $5,750,000. From their salaries in over three and a half years, work-releasees have paid the institutions $639,000 for room and board, paid $902,500 in taxes, sent $843,200 home to help support their dependants, and accumulated savings of $1,623,400 to be used on release.

Through study-release, also authorized under the Rehabilitation Act, increasing numbers of inmates are attending academic and vocational schools in the community. Furloughs, another provision of the Act, were granted last year to more than 750 inmates, who made unescorted trips on emergency home visits, to seek jobs and for other approved purposes.

A particularly valuable transitional operation has been the Bureau of Prisons' Community Treatment Center program. Begun in 1961 with three residential centers, the program has expanded today to eight Centers, located in Chicago, New York, Los Angeles, Kansas City, Detroit, Atlanta, Houston and Oakland. Each of the facilities is designed to accommodate 25 offenders up to the age of 35 who are within 90 days of their release.

Staff counselors provide center residents with a supervised environment, help them find jobs, and give them guidance and support. Family problems and special difficulties, such as drug addiction or alcoholism, get professional attention. During the past year, the centers accommodated over 1,200 inmates. Included, for the first time, were female offenders, who were housed at the New York City Center.

The residential facilities also serve as a diagnostic resource to Federal Courts. This service is provided where the Court requests more information before taking final action on a case.

An inmate's chances for post-release success are improved, the Bureau has found, if his transition from the institution to the community is made in familiar surroundings. Accordingly, the Federal Prison System has contracted with 21 local residential and work-release centers to provide housing and other services to federal inmates who will be released in their area.

The residential program available to federal offenders now also will include the state-wide facilities of North Carolina, as a result of a contract negotiated this past year with the state's Department of Corrections. This is the Bureau's first statewide contract; others are expected to follow.

TECHNICAL ASSISTANCE

For many years state and local correctional agencies have come to the Federal Bureau of Prisons for advice on how to improve their programs and operations. The Bureau's informal practice of giving technical assistance when requested received official sanction in a law enacted in 1968 by the 90th Congress. During the last year Bureau central office and field staff responded to requests from more than 25 states and hundreds of local communities. Assistance ranged from improving the food service in local jails to comprehensive planning for entire states.

The Bureau's technical assistance program has been merged with the Law Enforcement Assistance Administration (LEAA). This is a sister agency in the Department of Justice, responsible for administration of the Omnibus Crime Control and Safe Streets Act. Bureau of Prisons personnel assist LEAA in developing programs and activities designed to improve criminal justice systems throughout the nation. . . .

In addition to its consultation service, the Bureau conducts training classes and publishes correctional guides. The section most continuously and directly involved in furnishing technical assistance has been the Community Representatives staff. This unit has the responsibility of inspecting approximately 800 jails and other nonfederal facilities to determine their suitability for boarding the 3,900 federal prisoners who annually are held for brief periods in non-federal institutions.

The inspection staff is being expanded through use of institution-based employees. These district inspectors will be used on a part-time basis to inspect jails in nearby areas. As the 10 full-time inspectors travel about the country, they frequently hold training classes in jail operations for local institution personnel. A jailer's correspondence course conducted by the section has gained widespread popularity. Last year its enrollment reached 3,000. A new course soon will be available offering college-caliber instruction in different levels of jail operation and management.

Guidelines on detention centers and residential centers were published and distributed by the Bureau of Prisons this past year. Another publication to be issued shortly will cover jail planning. Persons working in or interested in corrections also can receive the "Community Exchange," the Bureau's newsletter reporting on new programs and activities in the correctional field.

PERSONNEL

Employee development is built into the program of every institution and is comprehensive in its scope. In fiscal year 1969 over 144,000 hours of training were given employees throughout the system. Training ranged from expanding technical knowledge to developing new skills.

In the past year, the U.S. Penitentiary at Atlanta, Georgia, had considerable success with an experimental Industrial Relations counseling unit. Using a new training technique, the institution then trained a pilot group of officers as correctional counselors. A later study showed that after training, the officers functioned as well as professionally trained counselors. Twelve employees have been trained and promoted to newly established full-time correctional counselor positions at the institution.

Because of the specialized nature of corrections, the development of potential managers is a continuing concern of the Bureau of Prisons. In the past year, a number of employees participated in advanced academic and technical training. To develop a high-level managerial staff with broad perspectives, the Bureau encourages its employees to acquire a variety of institutional experiences. Among the top administrators and their deputies in the system today are former caseworkers, correctional officers, educators, and in one instance, a farm manager.

CONCLUSION

While the federal system's efforts to change offenders have been greatly expanded in recent years, the Bureau of Prisons and corrections in general still have a long way to go in the struggle against recidivism.

According to recent studies, some forty percent of those who are released from confinement later return to prison. The rates are even higher among persons under 20 years of age. It is abundantly clear that traditional penal institutions not only have failed to change behavior but all too frequently tend to confirm offenders in their criminality.

President Richard M. Nixon has said that "A nation as resourceful as ours should not tolerate a record of such futility in its correctional institutions." To bring about immediate and widespread reform, the President has issued a directive to improve the Federal corrections system so it can serve as a model for state and local reforms. The President's 13-point program, which will be coordinated and supervised by the Attorney General, will provide information, technical aid and funds to help states and localities make needed improvements in their correctional systems.

It must be noted that the fight against recidivism can be waged successfully only when all of the nation's resources are involved. In outlining his reform program, the President cautioned that the successful solution of the crime crisis "will require the best efforts of the government at every level and the full cooperation of our citizens in every community. One of the areas where citizen cooperation is most needed is in the rehabilitation of the convicted criminal . . . Unions, civic groups, service clubs, labor organizations, churches and employers in all fields can do a great deal to fight crime by extending a fair chance to those who want to leave their criminal records behind them and become full and productive members of society."

LOCATIONS OF BUREAU OF PRISONS INSTITUTIONS & COMMUNITY CENTERS

Juvenile and Youth Institutions

Ashland, Ky.
Englewood, Colo.
Morgantown, W. Va.

Young Adult Institutions

El Reno, Okla.

Lompoc, Calif.
Milan, Mich.
Petersburg, Va.
Seagoville, Tex.
Tallahassee, Fla.

Adult Penitentiaries

Atlanta, Ga.
Leavenworth, Kans.
Lewisburg, Pa.
Marion, Ill.
McNeil Island, Wash.
Terre Haute, Ind.

Adult Correctional Institutions

Danbury, Conn.
La Tuna, Tex.
Sandstone, Minn.
Terminal Island, Calif.
Texarkana, Tex.

Short Term Institutions

Allenwood, Pa.
Eglin, Fla.
Florence, Ariz.
McNeil Island, Wash.
Montgomery, Ala.
New York, N.Y.
Safford, Ariz.

Female Institutions

Alderson, W. Va.
Terminal Island, Calif. (Women's Division)

Community Treatment Centers

Atlanta, Ga.
Chicago, Ill.
Detroit, Mich.
Houston, Tex.
Kansas City, Kans.
Los Angeles, Calif.
New York, N.Y.
Oakland, Calif.

Medical Treatment Center

Springfield, Mo.

8   *Correctional Philosophy and Architecture**

HOWARD B. GILL*

The *Handbook of Correctional Institution Design and Construction* published by the Federal Bureau of Prisons states, "No other single factor has so retarded the development and success of rehabilitative programs as has the lag in correctional architecture."[49] On the other hand, Austin MacCormick has said, "modern penology can be conducted in a barn."[50] Unfortunately practically no penal programs in the United States are conducted in barns. More often such programs are being undertaken in what I have called massive, medieval, monastic, monolithic, monumental, monkey-cage monstrosities. Such structures without doubt reflect a philosophy now 100 years out of date, but they still dominate the over-all climate of many of our prisons and hence the penal philosophy which struggles to emerge in spite of them. It is this conflict which has resulted in a schizophrenic type of split personality in the current penal philosophy of the United States. How did we get this way? And what can we do about it?

HISTORICAL TRENDS IN UNITED STATES PENAL PHILOSOPHY

Penal Philosophy—1787

Modern penal philosophy had its beginning in the United States when a small band of Quakers and Free-thinkers met at the home of Benjamin

* From *Journal of Criminal Law, Criminology and Police Science* 53, 3 (1962): 312–322. Reprinted by permission of author and publisher.

110

Franklin in 1787 and listened to a paper by Dr. Benjamin Rush, father of American psychiatry. Dr. Rush called for a new program for the treatment of criminals. In his paper he proposed the establishment of a prison which would include in its program (a) classification of prisoners for housing, (b) a rational system of prison labor, (c) indeterminate periods of punishment, and (d) individualized treatment of convicts according to whether crimes arose from passion, habit, or temptation.[51]

While the principal recommendation made by Dr. Rush, namely the treatment of offenders not according to the crimes committed but rather according to the problems underlying the crimes, was not put into effect until approximately 150 years later, the more obvious recommendation that "doing time" should replace capital and corporal punishment was in 1790 written into American penal philosophy for all time. And it was written in the remodeling of the Walnut Street Jail in Philadelphia by architect-builders who sought to carry out the philosophy of these early prison reformers. Indeed among the best evidences we possess today of what this philosophy meant in practice are the plans of this and other early American prisons as they have come down to us. Thus did architects and architecture begin to mould and fashion penal philosophy.

However, within 30 years the faint-hearted, beset by the problems which still plague us today—overcrowding, idleness, political influence, poor personnel, and the unsuitability of prison structure—were ready to throw the whole thing overboard and return to the simpler and swifter methods of dealing with criminals which had previously prevailed. The penitentiary program was saved in 1820 by a stalwart prison warden and two architects.

Penal Philosophy—Circa 1830

The warden was Elam Lynds, who established the famous Auburn System of prison discipline at the State prison in Auburn, New York, and who was aided and abetted by his architect-builder John Cray. The other architect was John Haviland, who helped dream up and establish the Pennsylvania System at Eastern Penitentiary, Philadelphia. The penal philosophy behind these two systems was that offenders not only should "do time" as penance for their misdeeds, but also that they should do time under a strict discipline of non-communication in surroundings which were "fearsome and forbidding."

Elam Lynds expressed the core of his philosophy when he "contended that reformation of the criminal could not possibly be effected, until the spirit of the criminal was broken."[52] And this his system proceeded to do in ways which persisted long after Lynds has passed from the scene.

In both the Auburn and the Pennsylvania systems, prison architecture played a leading role. In the Auburn System, prisoners were housed in "inside cells" and worked together in congregate work-shops under the silent rule. In the Pennsylvania System, prisoners were housed in "outside cells" where they worked and lived in solitary confinement. Thus within 40 years of the inauguration of a new penal philosophy in America, architects and architecture began to play a lead role in determining and in implementing that philosophy. In spite of many succeeding developments and modifications, this penal philosophy persisted for over 100 years and still continues to play a part in current penal thought.

What did this "prison discipline" (or penal philosophy) stand for? How has it been modified over the years? To what extent does it persist today? What will take its place? To answer these questions will be the purpose of this paper.

"Prison Discipline"—1830-1930

Modified though it was by the introduction of religion, education, industrial training, medical care, recreation, and parole, as late as 1925 this prison discipline represented a harsh, cruel, and futile philosophy, as Barnes and Teeters have pointed out.[53] Its chief tenets were hard and punitive labor, deprivation of all but the bare essentials of existence, monotony of the most debilitating sort, uniformity, degradation, corporal punishment, non-communication with normal society, no interpersonal relations with non-criminals, subservience to petty rules, no responsibility, isolation and self-absorption, mass living and movement, reform by exhortation. If this seems like a pretty grim description, one has only to recall the clichés of these years, some of which are still current, to realize to what extent these were the bases for the accepted penal philosophy in the United States from 1830-1930. Typical of such clichés are such catch phrases as, "We treat all prisoners alike," "No fraternization," "Do your own time," "No prisoner is going to tell me how to run my prison." The very housing of offenders in cage-like structures is itself an aspect of this penal philosophy.

Such a penal philosophy denied every essential need in the human personality including love, independence and interdependence, imagination and truth, achievement, identity, intimacy and the need to belong, creativity and integration. Indeed this philosophy we now know emphasized every pathology in the human personality—rejection, doubt, guilt, inferiority, diffusion, self-absorption, apathy, and despair. Not only did it avoid developing normal personalities, it actually produced pathological personalities. Men came out of prison worse than when they entered.

Such was the prison discipline of Elam Lynds and his successors for 100 years.

The Beginnings of a Modern Penal Philosophy

In 1916 a movement started at old Auburn Prison in New York by Thomas Mott Osborn brought the first rift in this armor. He dared to show the world that prisoners knew more about what was going on in prisons than the guards did, and moreover that the contribution of prisoners was essential to the effective management of prisons. He was crucified for such heresy, but he broke the back of the old guard. Moreover by bringing groups of prisoners into discussion with staff members regarding prisoners' problems, he anticipated a movement which is of prime importance in today's penal philosophy.

Almost at the same time (1916-1918) at Sing Sing, New York, Dr. Bernard Glueck began the individual study of prisoners. He was followed by Dr. W. T. Root at Western Penitentiary, Pittsburgh. Then came the organization of such studies by W. J. Ellis and others in New Jersey under a system which we know as "Classification." Massachusetts adopted the system in 1930, and the Federal Bureau of Prisons in 1934. This system of Classification destroyed once and for all another basic tenet of the old prison discipline, namely, "All prisoners should be treated alike," for once given case histories of offenders, treatment must be individualized.

MODERN PENAL PHILOSOPHY—A TRANSITION STATE

These then were the beginnings of a new penal philosophy—a philosophy which we are still trying to translate into programs, personnel, and architecture. Slowly these two basic concepts are changing the character of prison discipline. I say "slowly changing" because we must recognize the present as a transition state which contains much of both old and new, if we are to plan for the future, especially in the construction of penal institutions which will persist long after we are gone.

What are the characteristics of this transition state? And what is the penal philosophy which will emerge from it?

The outstanding characteristics of any transition state are anxiety and confusion. Penal philosophy is today in a state of anxiety and confusion. There is one thing for which we must give the Old Guard credit—they knew what they meant by prison discipline. They had a penal philosophy which was definite and easy to understand. I have outlined its harsh concepts. Any prison employee who did not abide by it was guilty of a serious breach of the prison discipline, and was treated accordingly. I am not so sure that we have as yet substituted a penal philosophy as well recognized as the old prison discipline. We have a number of conflicting philosophies at present.

The Custodial Prison

One penal philosophy still in vogue is founded in the past and attempts to carry on the philosophy of Elam Lynds. It has regard for only one basic concept, security, and beyond that only grudgingly modifies the harsh terms of penal servitude. These are still "Custodial Prisons." They are fighting a losing battle.

The Progressive Prison

Another group has superimposed upon the old discipline a philosophy of treatment which substitutes programs of medical care, industrial training, education, religion, social work, and recreation for the monotony of hard labor and the deprivation and degradation of the old prison. Radios and rodeos, entertainment and college courses, some vocational training, bright and shining hospitals, eager social and religious workers, libraries—all these abound. The demand is always for more and more such services—larger appropriations and larger staffs. The result is called "rehabilitation," but unfortunately the recidivism rate remains fairly constant at 60-65 per cent. Some of the toughest prison wardens in America are running "Sweet Jails." These are the so-called "Progressive Prisons."

The Progressive Prison holds the center of the stage today, and it presents a very attractive kind of humanitarianism in the treatment of offenders. It represents a natural swing of the pendulum away from the harsh cruelty of the old penology, and it somehow fills the vacuum caused by the decline in prison industries due to the opposition of free labor and capital to the sale of prison products on the open market. It is one of the characteristics of the transition state, but it is not the ultimate answer to the problems of corrections and should be examined critically by both penologists and their architects.

While the Progressive Prison presents a fine facade, it does not go to the heart of the correctional problem—criminality. It is not the purpose of the prison to become a great medical clinic, a substitute for public education, a profit-making industrial factory, or a recreational and social center for convicts. The success of a prison is not to be measured by its medical, surgical, or psychiatric services, by the number of school graduates it may produce, by the amount and value of its prison products, or by the number and diversity of its recreational and social activities. Neither will the establishment of "programs" for individual prisoners avail simply by outlining a list of activities for such prisoners which have little or nothing to do with their criminal problems.

The Professional Prison

A third, small but growing, group of prison workers are recognizing the need for a more precise professional approach in penal philosophy. It is to some of the intimations of this philosophy that I want to call your attention, because this may be the penal philosophy which the institutions we are building today will be called upon to serve. I have called this a professional penal philosophy as distinguished from the custodial or the progressive penal philosophy.

A PROFESSIONAL PENAL PHILOSOPHY FOR THE FUTURE

As I see it, this professional penal philosophy is built around five simple concepts:

(1) That security must be assured in order that it may be assumed—and kept in its proper place.

(2) That prisoners are classified primarily into four groups—New, Intractable, Tractable, and Defective.

(3) That for Tractable (or treatable) prisoners the first concern is

problem-solving before programs, and the second concern is the *accultur-ation* of such prisoners to the society to which they will return. (For the New and the Intractable and the Defective, there are other concerns, but we shall not consider these at this time.)

(4) That correctional staffs will operate in five areas: 1—Executive, 2—Administrative, including fiscal and clerical, 3—Professional, 4—Security, and 5—Treatment.

(5) That prison architecture must meet all four of these concepts.

The Philosophy of Security

I shall mention only seven basic points relating to the philosophy of security. There are more, but these will illustrate the trend.

(1) Security is the primary business of the prison; but not its ultimate goal. Having assured security, it may then be assumed and the main business of the prison—reform—got on with.

(2) Security deals with three basic elements—escape, contraband, and disorder. Hence maximum, medium, and minimum risks deal not only with escape, but also with contraband and disorder. Equal in importance to the escape risk are the dope pedlar, the addict, the "alkie," the "kite" artist, the disturber, the agitator, the conniver, the politician, the stool pigeon, the wolf, and the punk. Hence open-mesh fences, while some-times sufficient to prevent escape, are not adequate protection against the introduction of contraband or adequate for control of disturbances. The so-called bad psychological effect of walls on prisoners is a myth of Progressive Penology. Wire fences are characteristic of concentration camps; walls are characteristic of gardens and privacy. It is not necessary that walls be obnoxious; it is essential that they be adequate.

(3) Maximum, medium, and minimum refer exclusively to security and should not be confused with treatment classifications. The acting-out prisoner or the escape artist may be the most hopeful prospect for reform because he has character—bad character maybe, but character neverthe-less. The moron who does not have brains enough to escape has the least potential for reform. He may be rated minimum in security but certainly neither best nor better for treatment. Hence the correlation of max-imum, medium, and minimum with bad, better, best is a myth—but unfortunately a very popular one in many texts and with some architects.[54] The hopeful, treatable prisoner may be a maximum, a medium, or a minimum security risk, similarly with the intractable or defective pris-oner. The new prisoner is automatically a maximum security risk.

(4) Security is a speciality just as case-work for treatment is a specialty

and should be so regarded in the administration of prison guards, methods, equipment, and architecture. It should not be confused with or combined with treatment. Security is best served when a special corps of prison guards is trained in security policies and practice as the police of the prison community. They will man the gates, the walls, and the towers, patrol and search the grounds and buildings, and be responsible for the initial reception, the final discharge, and the transportation of prisoners. They will not fraternize with prisoners, but at all times be firm, stern, and authoritarian. They will be interested in treatment only as a general policy of the institution.

(5) The place of the security force should be recognized as primary, and neither incidental to nor dominating the operation of the prison. It should be a division *co-ordinate* with the administrative, the professional, and the treatment divisions of the organization.

(6) The security force can operate most effectively from a control center outside the prison enclosure, with auxiliary stations at strategic points within the prison proper. Such control center will house the arsenal, the central telephone switchboard, the central key board, all emergency utilities, inspection of all mail and all persons or packages entering or leaving the prison, offices and training facilities for the guard force, all plans affecting escapes, contraband, or disorder, and quarters for the stand-by guard force.

(7) "Divide and rule" is a sound security principle and supplements the small group principle of treatment. It is applicable in security planning, especially to housing prisoners in as many and as small groups as possible and to providing recreation for prisoners in as many different and separate areas as possible.

Specifically how these seven principles may be applied to prison architecture is subject-matter for a whole text in itself and cannot be included in this paper.

The Philosophy of Prisoner Types

With regard to prisoner personnel, once having determined security, it is good philosophy not to deal with prisoners according to the crimes which they have committed or the activities which the institution offers, however various these may be. If it may be assumed that all new prisoners will be put in a class by themselves for observation, our first concern then will be whether a prisoner is amenable to treatment or not, that is whether he is tractable (wanting and capable of treatment), intractable (not wanting treatment), or defective (limited or incapable of treatment).

Obviously a prisoner who wants treatment and is capable of responding to it will require a different sort of staff, program, and architecture than those who do not want or are extremely limited or incapable of treatment. The tractable prisoner may be 17 or 70, but he will ordinarily cooperate with the staff, respond to mutual trust, and be capable of living under fairly normal conditions in his daily activities. Such prisoners represent perhaps half of the offenders in our state and federal prisons today.

In contrast, those prisoners who want to "do their own time," who either do not desire to change or are not capable of change, require another type of handling. Some are hostile, hardened, professional thugs, hoodlums, racketeers, swindlers, sex deviates, who will not cooperate with the prison staffs, who cannot be trusted, and who cannot be kept confined except under abnormal measures of restraint. These are the intractables or the untreatable. They may not be disturbers or escape risks. They may just want to be left alone. They are sometimes described as "good prisoners."

However, the philosophy governing the lives of such prisoners is rule by fear, force, and deprivation. Therefore, within the bounds of decency, this is the philosophy which must be met with fear, force, and deprivation. One fights fire with fire. Perhaps this is what Elam Lynds had in mind when in accord with the light of his day he called for "breaking the spirit of the criminal." Today we call it shock therapy.

Other prisoners are mentally ill or so low-grade as to be defective. To mix either intractables or defectives with tractable prisoners is obviously poor penal philosophy. Yet most of our state prisons have been built on this kind of hodgepodge intermingling.

It seems only sound philosophy to suppose then at least four types of prisons for these four types of prisoners: the new, the intractable, the tractable, and the defective offender. In other words, a professional penal philosophy proposes to be selective in its treatment. It frankly proposes to "take the best apples out of the barrel first"—and if some rotten ones get left on the scrap heap, that is just too bad.

Architectural Considerations re Prisoner Types

If we accept as basic these four types of prisoners, we shall postulate four distinct types of penal institutions: a reception center or section for new prisoners, very simple custodial type of institution for the intractables, a normal type of institution with treatment facilities for the tractables, and a specialized partly custodial, partly hospital, and partly educational type of institution for the defectives.

Since each of these four types will contain among them maximum, medium, and minimum risks, provisions for all three types of risk must be made in each institution.

The reception center will contain facilities for orientation, diagnosis, classification, and planning. It may be expedient in the average state to plan the reception center in conjunction with the institution for the intractables. Since all new prisoners should be kept under maximum security and since a large percentage of the intractables will also require maximum security, the two groups may be housed in the different sections of the same institution. This will also make available to the intractables the advantages of the professional staff assigned to new prisoners if and when they desire. The door should always be left open.

Since "treatment" is not yet possible with the intractables, the barest minimum of facilities for decent confinement is sufficient—both architecturally and otherwise. This does not imply the use of monkey-cages or mass living. On the contrary it calls for simple, secure living quarters, including dining facilities in small groups for ease of control, and sufficient work and recreational facilities for diverse small groups to keep prisoners healthy.

However, since most states have inherited a number of penal institutions which may be classed as custodial and will probably not abandon them, the problem here involves chiefly how such institutions may be remodelled to serve as reception centers and as places for confinement of the intractable according to professional penal philosophy. This is beyond the scope of the present inquiry and will not be pursued further.

The type of institution for tractable prisoners represented by a professional penal philosophy is called the community prison—sometimes the therapeutic community. It may be noted in many of the newer state correctional institutions such as in California, Connecticut, District of Columbia, Massachusetts, Michigan, Missouri, and Wisconsin and in some countries in Europe. This type of institution will be considered further under Treatment of Prisoners.

The Philosophy of Treatment

As a result of the establishment of the Classification System and its Classification Board, the Progressive Prison has developed treatment for all prisoners—intractable, tractable, and defective—around a single concept, namely "programs." Such programs are usually only a reflection of the facilities for medical care, industries, education, recreation, religion, and social work available in each particular institution. As has been forcefully pointed out by such authorities as Dr. Ralph Brancale of New Jersey, such "programs" have frequently little or no relationship to prisoners' problems.[55]

It is the philosophy of the Professional Prison, first, that *problem-solving* must *precede* programs, and in fact problem-solving must *determine* the program for the most part; and, second, that only those programs are justified which help solve problems and/or which will acculturate prisoners to the society to which they will return. Now this is revolutionary philosophy for it will change the entire nature of correctional institutions for tractable prisoners.

Programs are institution-oriented. Problem-solving is client-oriented, to borrow a phrase from our friends in social psychology; in psychiatry, it is sometimes called sector-therapy. At once we sense a complete shift in emphasis. Under "programs," all prisoners receive the "full treatment," i.e., they go through a system which is ideally so complex that it has fallen of its own weight. The zeal of our system has eaten us up. Under "problem-solving" the prisoner with a $50 problem gets $50 worth of treatment. Most prisoners are not $50,000 cases, yet the Classification System proposes to give every prisoner the time and attention of at least that amount of professional service. It has proved tremendously expensive in personnel and facilities, so much as to become utterly unrealistic.

On the face of it, the philosophy of problem-solving looks equally elaborate, for it will require all the professional skills now employed in the Classification System. But it will have these differences: (1) it will enable the same professional staff to cover a much larger clientele, and (2) it will go to the heart of each problem instead of skirting all around it in a vague, indefinite manner. One is "bird-shot penology"; the other is "bull's eye penology."

Architectural Considerations re Treatment

Architecturally, the effect should be to reduce the demand for elaborate medical, industrial, educational, recreational, and other facilities which have become so popular under program philosophy. While problem-solving has many facets, the goal of this penal philosophy is to reach and solve as quickly as possible the significant problems related to criminality, leaving other areas of activity to those best suited to deal with them. This penal philosophy assumes the position that crime is a symptom of a maladjustment—situational, medical, psychological, antisocial, or custodial—and that the job of the prison is to resolve the specific maladjustment as far as possible, and *only that.* This philosophy applies the scientific principle of parsimony; it does as little as is *necessary* to achieve its goal—the reduction of criminality. The effect on prison planning should be obvious.

Yet this professional philosophy will not neglect medical care, industry, education, recreation, or religion. It proposes that prisons should seek to acculturate prisoners to the society to which they will return, and in so doing it will take the bombast out of progressive penology by trimming these activities down to normal. Except for problem-solving related to criminality, there is no reason why prisoners should be given more elaborate hospital care, or greater vocational, and educational, and recreational advantages than the average citizen. However, the most startling result of the philosophy of acculturation will be seen in its effect on the daily living conditions and the participation in them by tractable prisoners.

To return tractable prisoners to a society in which men live in small family groups, in ordinary dwellings, under normal conditions affecting their basic needs of nourishment, work, play, and other human relationships, we need to accustom them to the advantages of such living by confining them under similar conditions. This is the concept of the community prison—sometimes called the therapeutic community. It is as far removed from monkey-cage cells or mass living as black is from white. It calls for a complete reorientation of our thinking about prison architecture. Imagine what this would do to a 500-man cell block, or a dining-room seating 1000 inmates, or a single recreation yard where the same 1000 prisoners mill around in aimless confusion or stupidly watch a few performers, or to the prison rule that denies prisoners the opportunity to participate in any responsibility for the activities which make up their daily life. But before tackling prison architecture, we shall need to examine the effect of this new philosophy on staff personnel.

The Philosophy of Staff Personnel

The philosophy I am proposing for staff personnel is based on a five-fold classification: Executive, administrative, professional, security, and treatment. (See Chart I.) The executive group will include the warden and his immediate associates, or deputy wardens, and the heads of departments. The warden runs the front office and with his staff sets the policies; the associate warden runs the office "inside" and directs the operation of the prison routine carrying out the policies adopted. The administrative group will comprise the fiscal, clerical, personnel adminis-

CHART I

FIVE ESSENTIALS IN A CORRECTIONAL AGENCY*

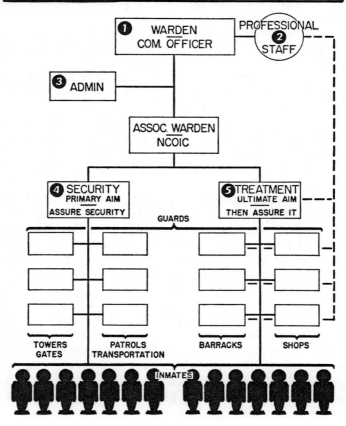

tration, purchasing, store-keeping, and routine maintenance functions of the institution. The professional group will include the physician, psychiatrist, psychologists, dentist, nurses, teachers, vocational, avocational and recreational instructors, librarian, industries manager and all his technical personnel, chaplains, social workers, and other specialists. The security force will include those primarily responsible for the prevention of escape, the introduction of contraband, and the control of disturbances—i.e., the police force of the prison community. The treatment staff will include all those guards who are in personal contact with the prisoners either in the living quarters or at work or play, and their supervisors.

These are not startlingly new concepts of staff organization, but may I point out certain principles of organization which differ from current custodial or progressive philosophy.

It is now the general practice in progressive prisons to have two deputies; one in charge of security and one in charge of treatment. The deputy in charge of security controls the entire guard force, handles the general operational routine of the prison, and is in authority over prisoners. The deputy in charge of treatment has charge of certain professional activities including classification, education and training, religious services, and recreation, but usually medical care and industries are left under the direct control of the warden. The deputy for treatment and his staff have advisory powers only. Hence we see the unfortunate situation where the deputy for treatment has responsibility for treatment but no power to make it effective. This has been the cause of one of the most serious conflicts in progressive prisons—the conflict between custody and treatment. It is my philosophy that this conflict can be resolved and security and treatment given their proper setting by observing three changes in current practice:

(1) The Deputy in Charge of Security will be responsible only for the three basic problems of escape, contraband, and disorder and will limit the contact with prisoners of his guard force to these functions. He is no longer in charge of the general operation of the prison or its over-all routine.

(2) The Deputy in Charge of Treatment will be responsible for the daily operation of the prison and for carrying out the recommendations of the professional staff in the contact with prisoners of his guard force.

(3) The entire professional staff will derive its authority directly from the warden and have advisory powers only. Similarly with the administrative staff.

The Philosophy of Prison Architecture

Finally we come to prison architecture. (See Chart II.) What effect will this professional penal philosophy in security, prisoner personnel, treatment, and staff personnel have on prison architecture?

CHART II
TYPES OF PRISON STRUCTURE*

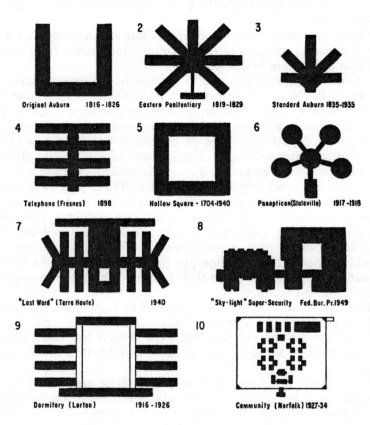

Original Auburn   1816-1826   Eastern Penitentiary   1819-1829   Standard Auburn 1835-1935

Telephone (Fresnes)   1898   Hollow Square - 1704-1940   Panopticon(Stateville)   1917-1918

"Last Word" (Terre Haute)   1940   "Sky-light" Super-Security   Fed.Bur.Pr.1949

Dormitory (Lorton)   1916-1926   Community (Norfolk) 1927-34

Maximum Security Prisons for Intractables

As regards prisons for the intractable, there are in existence in federal and state prison systems enough maximum security facilities now to care for all intractable prisoners for some time to come. The Federal Bureau of Prisons alone has approximately 5000 such cells, which is 20 per cent of their total population, a figure set by some authorities as sufficient for intractables in any system.[56] Even in states where some remodeling of existing prisons may be necessary, this should suffice to care for the intractables without further construction.

Let me illustrate. Under the direction of political Commissioners of Correction who knew little or nothing about corrections, the Commonwealth of Massachusetts within the past ten years replaced the old Charlestown prison with a new "Super-security Prison" of the sky-light[57] type at South Walpole, Massachusetts. It is known as the "concrete horror" and is condemned most roundly by the officers employed to run it, for reasons which we need not detail here. In 1878 a new state prison was opened in Massachusetts at Concord, but was taken over for a reformatory. It has always been a state prison and still is. In fact when riots recently occurred at Walpole, the worst prisoners were transferred to Concord for safe-keeping. Had Massachusetts remodelled the Concord institution for its intractable prisoners and used the $10,000,000 spent on the Walpole prison to construct additional facilities for tractable prisoners, professional penology would have been advanced and the future served. As it is, $10,000,000 has been spent extravagantly on an institution which is almost as out-of-date as the disgrace at Charlestown which it replaced.

In addition to the anachronism at Walpole, one has only to mention the state prisons at Greenhaven, New York, Graterford, Pennsylvania, Jackson, Michigan, or Stateville, Illinois to understand why a reexamination of prison architecture is needed.[58] Other examples of more recent construction of this unfortunate type of prison may be found in a pamphlet entitled *Recent Prison Construction 1950-1960* issued by the Federal Bureau of Prisons.[59]

Prison administrators, federal or state, and their architects who propose to add more cellular facilities of the maximum security type may be liable to the charge of extravagant and unnecessary expenditure of public funds, and may find on completion of such facilities that they are already from 60 to 100 years out of date. Moreover they will enjoy the dubious distinction of having wished on posterity for many years to come additional monolithic monstrosities in penal architecture. This is worse than the "lag" referred to by the federal handbook on construction already quoted since it will be positive action of a sort which will perpetuate a past no one wishes to impose on future generations. The time has come to call a halt to this type of prison construction.

Institutions for the Defective Delinquent

Institutions for the defective fall into a class which combines many aspects of the prison, the hospital, and the training school following the best practices in all three. The Medical Center of the Federal Bureau of

Prisons at Springfield, Missouri,[60] the Medical Facility at Vacaville, California, the Institution for Defective Delinquents, Wilkes-Barre, Pennsylvania,[61] and the John Howard Pavillion of St. Elizabeths Hospital, Washington, D.C., are notable examples. We shall not discuss these here.

Correctional Institutions for Tractable Prisoners

When we consider the type of correctional institution which will fit the needs of tractable offenders and which will be in line with the professional penal philosophy outlined herewith, we are confronted with a variety of excellent examples in the United States. Several institutions for women may be mentioned including State Industrial Home for Women, Muncy, Pennsylvania (1913), the Federal Institution for Women at Alderson, West Virginia (1927), and a somewhat similar federal institution originally built for women at Seagoville, Texas (1940). (Once a "give-a-way" institution as far as the men were concerned, the Seagoville institution for a time became synonymous with the latest philosophy of prison building for tractable male prisoners.) Massachusetts built such an institution for men at Norfolk (1927-1934). New Jersey opened one at Annandale in 1929; Missouri at Algoa Farms (1932), and California at Chino (1941).[62]

More recently (1950-1960) institutions for the more hopeful type of prisoner (tractable) have been opened or are under construction at Corona, California, Enfield, Connecticut, Lorton, D.C., Ionia, Michigan, Moberley, Missouri, and Fox Lake, Wisconsin.[63] These institutions have promise of providing the facilities for a penal philosophy which fits the second half of the 20th Century.

There are too many details involved in such institution plans and programs to present here. However, some outstanding characteristics may be found in common in all of them.

(1) The over-all atmosphere which is conveyed by personnel, program, and architecture is one of normal living under normal conditions where mutual trust and respect, cooperation and willingness have replaced the old prison discipline. However, the new prison discipline as a way of life distinguished from mere obedience to rules and regulations has still to be defined and made clear. This will come in due time.

(2) The small group principle is reflected in housing, dining, recreation, and all important activities. The "institution family" attempts to approximate the family unit in outside society which is the norm.

(3) Prisoners are expected to participate with the staff in the duties and

responsibilities of running the institution, with the staff always in control. This joint undertaking provides the everyday atmosphere of a society built on sound democratic principles. Advisory committees and councils made up of prisoners who work with staff members do much to develop and enrich prison life, and build social responsibility.

(4) Security, while primary, is not the dominant or the ultimate goal.

(5) There still exists some confusion as to the relationship of security and treatment, as to the authority and obligations of the professional staff, and as to whether "programs" or problem-solving is paramount. One thing is outstanding, acculturation to normal, responsible living has taken over.

(6) Evidence of the emphasis on both acculturation and problem-solving is shown in the architecture. Housing units contain individual rooms in simple one or two story buildings with seldom more than 50 prisoners to a unit. Group recreation is provided for each unit. Multiple dining-rooms follow out the small group principles. Group meetings and discussions are provided for. A large variety of contacts with the normal world outside brings the "good life" into the institution. Facilities for individual counseling on the part of both guards-in-contact and front-office professionals are included in the over-all plan. Supervising each group are "guards-in-contact" who work closely with the professional staff to carry out their recommendations for treatment.

(7) From Europe, word comes that the philosophy of normalcy has been extended to establish some institutions where the prisoners "live in" but "work out" in the community.[64] Others permit conjugal visits both in the institution and outside.[65]

Such correctional institutions for tractable prisoners are called therapeutic communities or community prisons. These experiments today are significant; they will form the penal philosophy of tomorrow. For to paraphrase Truman Kelley:

> Philosophers are never dismayed; for in markings near about, they discern the contours of the land and glimpse the portals of the future.

9   *Patterns of Correction*

GARRETT HEYNS*

Even though there has been an unmistakable trend, in recent years, toward integration of correctional institutions and agencies, the process of development has assumed many different forms, and not all states have progressed equally far. The result is that there are many "patterns of correction."

Initially a state's involvement in correction was limited to prisons. There was no other correctional agency. Each prison carried out its functions without any official relationship to another—if indeed the state had more than one such institution or other agency interested in correction. Each was considered mostly a local establishment and had its own board of trustees, appointed by the governor. Each board appointed its warden and was concerned exclusively with its own institution's policy and administration.

The next step came when a state's correctional system expanded through the addition of more penal institutions, or perhaps some of a special type, such as a reformatory, and of other agencies, such as parole. At this point the need was felt for a better type of administration which would make possible greater coordination within the system. Institutional boards had proved unsatisfactory: either they paid scant attention to such few duties as they had or they became too involved in administration or patronage. Their primary weakness was that they impeded efforts at coordination. This situation led to the formation of central boards with more comprehensive responsibilities and wider authority.

* From *Crime and Delinquency* 13, 3 (July 1967): 421–431. Reprinted by permission of the National Council on Crime and Delinquency and Mrs. Garrett Heyns.

Many states today administer their systems through boards, variously named (boards of control, boards of correction, etc.) and differing as to their area of concern. Some are in charge solely of adult institutions; others supervise training schools and, in a few instances, probation and parole. Some boards also have charge of other state institutions, such as those for the mentally ill and retarded. In a few boards, membership is ex-officio; in others, members are appointed by the governor to serve at his pleasure or for a term of years. Board members may work part-time and be paid per diem while in attendance at meetings or engaged in official business, or they may serve full-time and be salaried. Thus, there is little uniformity, except for the fact that control is vested in several persons rather than in a single executive.

The degree of integration which seems so highly desirable was not achieved through the board type of administration. Greater efficiency of administration and fuller integration could be secured by combining all institutions and agencies in one department under a single administrator. Each of the various entities (probation, institution, parole) with which a person comes into contact—whether he be juvenile or adult, from the time his case is adjudicated until his discharge—is part of the correctional process. There is, therefore, logic to placing them in one department, thus providing for coordination, exchange of information, and a continuous program of treatment.

This has been accomplished in many states, at least to some extent, through placing correction in an already existing larger state department, or through establishing a separate, independent organization. Thus, the development reaches its latest stage: the integration into one organization of many, if not all, correctional activities, under one administrative head.

With few exceptions, the states have developed units which provide for some degree of coordination and integration. However, if desirable integration calls for an independent department of correction concerned with the administration of probation, institutions, and parole, both juvenile and adult, and with the supervision of local institutions, one finds that the evolutionary process is far from complete. The states have not progressed uniformly; some states are still in the early stages of development and, even in those that have developed independent units, structure differs widely.

There are, however, groups of states with clearly identifiable types of administrative controls. Starting with these, we may begin to classify the various correctional systems into three major categories, though there is some overlapping among the groups and some marked differences within each group: (1) those that use boards to manage their correctional programs; (2) those that have placed correction in some larger, existing department; (3) those that administer correction in an independent department. The first and second categories are again subdivided.[66]

I. BOARDS OR COMMISSIONS

A. Board for an Individual Institution or Agency

1. ARIZONA.   The Parole Board supervises adult parole. The board of directors for juvenile institutions controls juvenile institutions and parole. The state prison is supervised by the superintendent of the prison.

2. ARKANSAS.   Each correctional institution has its own board. Adult probation and parole are administered by the Board of Pardons, Paroles, and Probation. Juvenile probation and parole are the concern of the Department of Public Welfare.

3. CONNECTICUT.   Independent boards or commissions govern juvenile institutions, adult correctional institutions, parole, and adult probation. The state has a central jail administration under the State Jail Administrator.

4. MISSISSIPPI.   The institutions are under independent boards. Adult probation and parole are under the Probation and Parole Board. Juvenile parole is supervised by the Department of Public Welfare.

5. NEW HAMPSHIRE.   The state prison and the juvenile institution have their own independent boards. Adult parole is under a Board of Parole.

6. NEW MEXICO.   A board of directors controls the penitentiary. Juvenile institutions have independent boards. The Board of Probation and Parole administers adult probation and parole.

B. Board Concerned with More than One Area of Correction

1. IDAHO.   Each of the three members of the full-time Board of Correction has a special function: the chairman is warden of the penitentiary; the vice-chairman is director of rehabilitation; the secretary

is director of parole and probation. This board is involved only with adult offenders. The Board of Education supervises juvenile institutions.

2. OKLAHOMA. The three-member Board of Public Affairs supervises the penitentiary and the reformatory. The Board of Parole and Probation is the paroling authority and is in charge of field services. Juvenile institutions and aftercare are in the Department of Public Welfare.

3. TEXAS. A Department of Corrections under a Board of Corrections has charge of adult correctional institutions. The board of Pardons and Paroles is the paroling authority and supervises parolees. The Youth Council supervises juvenile correctional institutions and aftercare.

4. UTAH. A seven-member Board of Corrections governs the prison, adult probation, parole supervision, and the Board of Pardons and Paroles. The Department of Public Welfare has supervision of juvenile institutions and aftercare.

C. Ex-officio Board

1. FLORIDA. The Board of Commissioners of State Institutions is composed of the governor, the secretary of state, the attorney general, the state treasurer, the comptroller, the commissioner of agriculture, and the superintendent of public instruction. The Division of Corrections supervises the adult correctional institutions; the Division of Child Training Schools supervises juvenile institutions and aftercare. The Probation and Parole Commission, which is not a part of the Board of Commissioners of State Institutions, is the paroling authority and is in charge of adult parole and probation field services.

2. NEVADA. The Prison Commission, consisting of the governor, the secretary of state, and the state treasurer, has charge of the state prison. The Board of Parole Commissioners has charge of parole and field services. The governor, the justices of the Supreme Court, and the attorney general constitute the Board of Pardon Commissioners. Juvenile institutions are administered by the Department of Public Welfare.

3. OREGON. The Board of Control, consisting of the governor, the secretary of state, and the state treasurer, supervises all state institutions.

The Division of Corrections of the Board of Control oversees juvenile institutions, aftercare, and adult institutions. The Board of Parole and Probation is not under the Division of Corrections.

4. WYOMING. The governor, the secretary of state, the state treasurer, the state auditor, and the superintendent of public instruction constitute the Board of Charities and Reform, which supervises the penitentiary, other state institutions, and probation and parole and also sits as the Board of Pardons.

D. Board Concerned with Other Functions in Addition to Correction

1. NEW JERSEY. The Board of Control regulates the administration of the Department of Institutions and Agencies, which supervises all state institutions. The Division of Correction and Parole, in the Department, is in charge of both juvenile and adult institutions. The Parole Board is in the Division of Correction.

2. NORTH DAKOTA. The Board of Administration has charge of all state institutions; another board has charge of adult probation and parole.

3. SOUTH DAKOTA. The Board of Charities and Correction has control of all state institutions. Juvenile aftercare and adult probation and parole come under the Board of Pardons and Paroles.

4. IOWA. The director of the Division of Corrections is appointed by the three-member full-time Board of Control. The Division supervises juvenile and adult correctional institutions as well as juvenile community (field) services. Adult probation and parole and field services come under the Board of Parole (which is not part of the Board of Control).

II. LARGER STATE DEPARTMENT

A. Department of Welfare

1. ALASKA. The Youth and Adult Authority, a division of the Department of Health and Welfare, supervises juvenile detention, probation,

institutions, and aftercare; misdemeanant and adult probation; and local and state adult institutions. The Board of Parole is also placed in the Authority. Alaska is one of two states (the other is Rhode Island) that have effected complete integration of all correctional activities in one administrative unit, under a full-time director.

2. HAWAII. The Correction Division in the Department of Social Services has supervision of juvenile institutions and aftercare and also adult institutions. The adult parole program is under the Board of Paroles and Pardons, which is also within the Department of Social Services.

3. RHODE ISLAND. The Division of Correctional Services in the Department of Social Welfare has a scope of authority similar to that held by the Youth and Adult Authority in Alaska.

4. VIRGINIA. The Division of Youth Services in the Department of Welfare and Institutions has control over juvenile institutions; it includes the Bureau of Juvenile Probation and Detention. The Division of Corrections is in charge of the adult institutions. The Parole Board functions as part of the Department of Welfare and Institutions. The Department has authority to establish minimum standards for jails and to enforce its rulings in the courts.

5. WISCONSIN. The Division of Corrections in the Department of Public Welfare is responsible for the operation of institutions for adult offenders and juvenile delinquents. The Division also provides probation services to all courts of criminal jurisdiction (outside of Milwaukee County) and supervises all adult offenders released on parole and juveniles released to aftercare supervision. The director serves as chairman of the seven-man parole board; the other six members serve full-time under civil service.

B. Department of Institutions[67]

1. COLORADO. The Division of Corrections has charge of the adult correctional institutions; the Division of Youth Service is in charge of juvenile institutions and juvenile aftercare. The Division of Adult Parole supervises adult parolees and probationers. The paroling authority is the Board of Parole, which is not in the Department of Institutions.

2. Louisiana.   The Department of Institutions supervises juvenile institutions and adult probation, adult institutions, and parole. Juvenile probation and aftercare are supervised by the Department of Public Welfare.

3. Montana.   The Department of Institutions controls juvenile and adult parole and institutions. Adult probation and parole are the concern of the Board of Pardons. Juvenile probation and aftercare are supervised locally.

4. Nebraska.   Juvenile and adult institutions and parole are controlled by the Department of Corrections in the office of the director of Public Institutions. Other correctional functions are under local control.

5. Vermont.   The Department of Institutions includes juvenile and adult institutions and adult probation and parole. Juvenile probation is in the Department of Social Welfare. The Division of Probation and Parole is in the Department of Institutions, which is the paroling authority and supervises field services.

6. Washington.   The Division of Adult Correction includes the adult institutions; the Division of Juvenile Rehabilitation has charge of juvenile institutions and aftercare. Both divisions are in the Department of Institutions. Juvenile probation is under local control. The Board of Prison Terms and Paroles is the paroling authority and directs probation and parole field services.

7. West Virginia.   The office of the Commissioner of Public Institutions includes a Division of Corrections, under a director, which has charge of juvenile and adult institutions and the administrative and supervisory functions of the Board of Probation and Parole. Granting of adult parole is the function of this Board; the director of the Division of Corrections has authority to place juveniles on parole. The Department of Public Welfare has charge of juvenile and adult probation and parole field services.

C. Department of Public Safety

Illinois.   This department includes adult institutions and parole. Juvenile institutions and aftercare are under the Youth Commission. Other correctional functions are under local control.

D. Department of Justice

PENNSYLVANIA. The Department's Bureau of Correction has charge of adult institutions. The adult Board of Parole is also in the Department of Justice. Juvenile institutions are under the Department of Public Welfare. Other correctional functions are under local control.

E. Department of Mental Health and Correction

1. MAINE. All correctional functions, except supervision of local institutions, come under this department. The Bureau of Corrections has charge of adult institutions, juvenile institutions, and aftercare. The Probation and Parole Board is included in the department.

2. OHIO. The department is called Mental Hygiene and Correction. The Division of Correction has charge of adult institutions. The adult parole authority is in this division; it has the paroling function, is in charge of parole supervision, and includes a probation services section. Juvenile institutions and parole come under the Youth Commission. Other correctional activities are locally controlled.

III. INDEPENDENT DEPARTMENTS

1. ALABAMA. The Board of Corrections has replaced the former Department of Corrections and is in charge of adult institutions. Adult probation and parole are under the Board of Pardons and Paroles. Juvenile institutions are under separate boards. Juvenile probation and parole are the responsibility of the Department of Pensions and Security and of local authorities. Juvenile detention and local adult institutions are controlled locally.

2. CALIFORNIA. The Youth and Adult Corrections Agency includes the Department of Corrections, the Department of the Youth Authority, the Adult Authority, and the Women's Board of Terms and Paroles. Juvenile detention, juvenile probation, and local adult institutions are administered by local authorities

3. DELAWARE. The Board of Correction is the general policy-making authority but is not the administrative head of the Department of

Correction. The commissioner supervises adult correctional institutions and the operation of probation and parole field services. The Probation and Parole Commission is not within the Department of Correction. Juvenile detention, institutions, and aftercare come under the Youth Services Commission.

4. GEORGIA. A part-time Board of Corrections, which appoints a director as executive officer, controls the state penal system. Adult parole is the concern of the Parole Board. Adult probation is under the Board of Probation and local authorities. Neither of these boards is under the Board of Corrections. Juvenile detention, probation, institutions, and aftercare are all in the Department of Family and Child Services.

5. INDIANA. The Department of Correction, which controls adult and juvenile institutions, has four divisions: parole, probation, farm and industries, and classification and treatment. There is a full-time parole board for adult institutions and the Boys' School. Part-time boards supervise the women's prison and the Girls' School.

6. KANSAS. The Office of the Director of Penal Institutions supervises prisons. The Board of Probation and Parole has charge of adult probation and parole. Juvenile institutions and aftercare are under the Department of Social Welfare. Detention, juvenile probation, and jails are controlled locally.

7. KENTUCKY. Included in the Department of Corrections are the Division of Probation and Parole, in charge of field services, and the Division of Institutions, in charge of the adult institutions. The Parole Board is for administrative services only. Juvenile institutions and probation and aftercare are in the Department of Child Welfare.

8. MARYLAND. The Department of Correction has charge of adult institutions. Juvenile institutions and juvenile detention are under the Department of Public Welfare. Juvenile and adult probation and parole are under the Board of Parole and Probation, although local authorities are also involved in juvenile detention, probation, and aftercare.

9. MASSACHUSETTS. The Department of Correction supervises adult institutions. The Parole Board is in the Department "but not subject to its jurisdiction." Adult and juvenile probation are under the Probation Commission. Juvenile institutions and aftercare are the concern of the Youth Service Board.

10. MICHIGAN. The Department of Corrections has jurisdiction over adult institutions and parole and probation field services, through appropriate divisions. The Parole Board is in the Department. Juvenile institutions and aftercare are under the Department of Social Services. Juvenile probation and detention and jails are under local control, although the Department has certain responsibilities with regard to jails.

11. MINNESOTA. The Division of Adult Corrections in the Department of Corrections has charge of adult institutions and adult parole services. The Division of Youth Conservation supervises the institutions for juvenile delinquents; it is also the paroling authority for juveniles and is in charge of aftercare. The Adult Corrections Commission is the paroling authority for adult offenders; the Division of Field Services supervises adult probationers and parolees.

12. MISSOURI. The Department of Corrections has control over adult institutions; its Parole Board is the paroling authority and supervises probation and parole field services. Juvenile institutions and parole are under a Board of Training Schools in the Department.

13. NEW YORK. The Department of Correction is concerned solely with adult institutions. The Board of Parole is the paroling authority; the Division of Parole in the Executive Department has supervision over parolees. The Division of Social Welfare is in charge of juvenile institutions and aftercare. Other correctional functions, such as jails and probation, are locally administered.

14. NORTH CAROLINA. The Prison Department is concerned only with supervision of the adult institutions. The Board of Juvenile Correction has charge of juvenile institutions. The Board of Parole is the paroling authority and is in charge of field services. Adult probation is under the Probation Commission. Other correctional activities are under local authorities.

15. SOUTH CAROLINA. The Department of Corrections is concerned with adult institutions only. The Probation, Parole and Pardon Board has control over parole and probation and field services. Juvenile institutions and parole are supervised by the Board of Juvenile Correction.

16. TENNESSEE. The Department of Correction has charge of adult and juvenile institutions, the latter being supervised by its Youth Services Division, which also has charge of juvenile probation and aftercare. The

adult Pardons, Parole and Probation Board, with the commissioner of the Department as chairman, is concerned with adult parole and probation and parole field services.

DISCUSSION

It is evident that these groups are not equally efficient. The "local board" type of control, which makes no provision for coordination, deserves the lowest efficiency rating. Members are likely to be busy men who have no time for their official duties; they may, at least initially, have little interest in or knowledge of correctional problems; and, as a rule, they meet too infrequently to permit close attention to business. The tendency is either to interfere too much in day-to-day operations or to leave everything to the head of the institution or agency—which may, under the circumstances, be a bit of a blessing. Some of the states which use this type of control have very limited systems and are so poor that a more elaborate organization would be too expensive and unnecessary. However, no one doubts the need for coordination of correctional activities, and to acquire it to some degree would require very little additional money.

The ex-officio boards are subject to substantially the same criticisms. The likelihood of having members with an interest in correctional programs is even less than in appointive boards. Certainly such interest is not likely to be a factor in the election. Moreover, men highly placed in government are too busy with the duties of their own office to have much time left for correction. If they happen to be of different parties, political differences may have repercussions throughout the system. There are also many objections which regularly attach to plural executive administrations.

Other types of organization, under boards, are preferable to local boards. Their involvement with more than one institution, or with other correctional activities as well, makes for a greater degree of knowledge and coordination. As a rule, the broader the coverage, the better. Whenever the chairman of the board acts as chief administrator, such possibility is enhanced. In some states the legal provision for bipartisan boards reduces the possibility of political interference in the management of board affairs. However, it is true here, as it is in other fields, that a committee makes a very poor administrative device. Intimate knowledge of correctional activities, as well as professional leadership, is often lacking in such boards. Individual interference in management is not unlikely. Advisory boards have their value, but administrative boards are another matter.

Placing correction in a larger, existing department is a step forward. This type of organization has its appeal for states where the number of institutions and agencies is not large enough to warrant establishing an independent department. It is interesting to note that the two states that have achieved the greatest degree of integration of correction (Alaska and Rhode Island) have placed correction in the welfare departments. Seven states have correction in the department of institutions. Correction in Colorado and Montana was so organized fairly recently.

Including correction in an existing larger department makes for more efficient administration. Including correction in the department as a separate division or divisions covering most of the field has many advantages and serves as well as an independent department of correction. The development of a good program may be jeopardized, however, if the chief administrator of the larger department is primarily interested in another of its functions. This may result in less administrative time spent on correction and less effort to secure the necessary appropriations. This situation may weaken the centralization of correctional authority and encourage a tendency by the institutions to become autonomous, thus thwarting coordination. Much depends on personalities within the organization. If capable directors of the division are secured, such dangers are lessened. Adequate salaries must, of course, be provided, or capable men will not be attracted to the subordinate positions.

For populous states with extensive correctional systems, the preferable form of correctional administration seems to be the separate, independent department under a single executive. The administrator is almost certain to be familiar with the problems of correction and is under no temptation to ignore these interests because of other functions. It is possible to include divisions dealing with the chief areas in the field and for the head of each of these to be a specialist who knows the program, thus assuring professional leadership and the greatest degree of coordination, exchange of information, and mutual assistance. Sixteen of the states now have a separate department, but it is evident that most of them have a long way to go before they can be said to have truly integrated systems of correction. In addition, there is considerable difference of opinion as to which areas should be included in such a department.

There is, for instance, no consensus as to the inclusion of the adult paroling authority and parole field services. All agree that in making its decisions, the parole board should be autonomous and, if placed in the department of correction, should not be subordinated to the director of the department. The contention is that the inclusion of the board would secure greater coordination in matters of mutual interest and less "passing the buck" in the matter of parole failures. This arrangement has been carried out successfully in several states, such as California, Michigan, and Wisconsin.

Disagreement centers chiefly on the question of the best location of supervision of parolees. On the one hand, it is argued that time in institutions and time on parole are parts of the same sentence, and that, since parole is a continuation of the rehabilitation process begun in the institution and it is the duty of the institutional treatment staff to prepare for parole, the highest degree of coordination is desirable and can best be secured by placing parole supervision and the institutional program under the same administration.

There are those, however, who argue that the authority which grants parole and sets the conditions should have the staff to see that these conditions are met; that under such arrangement the authority is in the best position to evaluate the success of its services. However this question is resolved, there is no doubt that efficiency demands the closest possible coordination between the paroling authority and the department of correction.

A similar disagreement concerns the question of including juvenile correctional services in the same department with adult institutions, probation, and parole. One viewpoint is that the two should not be combined in the same organizational structure because of differences in the approach to the juvenile offender, a different treatment philosophy, and different staff training needs; and that the association of the juvenile with the adult offender may have a deleterious effect upon the public attitude toward the juvenile and may adversely affect the juvenile himself. On the other hand, it is argued that many juveniles pass into the adult institutions and, therefore, that the same questions are asked and many of the same techniques used and, because of this, the adult staff should know what is being done in the juvenile agencies—something which can best be accomplished if the two fields are under the same general administration. Such separation as is desirable can be provided for through the organization of different divisions—one for juveniles and one for adults within the same department. Those jurisdictions which have this arrangement seem quite successfully to have overcome the objections of those who advocate separate organizational structures.

Integrating probation with institutions and parole in one department also presents problems. The granting of probation is regarded as a function of the court and is therefore a local concern, whereas the supervision of correctional institutions and parole is a state responsibility. So here we have the traditional dilemma of local autonomy versus state control, and the tendency of local organization to guard its authority and power. There appears to be no demand that the power to grant probation should be removed from the courts. Supervision of the probationer is something else. Under the local court, it is plagued by a variety of weaknesses. Many courts, particularly in rural areas, are not sufficiently well staffed to do a good job of supervision. Frequently staff is not well trained because the salary scale is too low to attract persons equipped for the task. The pay offered is often below the state scale for similar duties and responsibilities. The judge is frequently too busy to pay attention to supervision of those whom he has placed on probation. A step toward remedying this situation would be to have the court continue its function of granting probation and to permit the appropriate state agency to exercise supervision. This would bring about integration of probation with other correctional activities.

To an outsider the various devices conceived for the control of our correction systems must be bewildering. He will wonder whether he should regard our efforts as demonstrations of ingenuity or as monuments to stupidity. Although we would prefer that he see them as steps toward a goal—the organization that will work most efficiently toward restoring the offender to useful citizenship—our time is almost up. We have more than enough evidence that some of the existing types of controls are archaic and that others are far from being as efficient as we would like them to be. Our citizenry is aghast at the increasing number of offenders and at the rising cost of handling them. If our correctional systems are to be factors in reducing crime, we shall have to make them more efficient. True there are other problems—such as manpower—which we must solve in our quest for greater effectiveness. But we are here discussing organization. Leaders in all states, therefore, should be putting thought and effort into improving the administration of their correctional systems.

The Correctional
Institution
as a Community

Introduction

The social experiences of inmates who must live with each other may determine the impact of a correctional institution on its residents to a greater extent than all purposes, guidelines, procedures or programs which a government can ordain. Locking up hundreds or thousands of people together for months or years may affect their behavior after their release in ways that are not anticipated if one looks only at the formal aspects of institutional management.

The readings presented here describe some variations of institutional life, their causes and consequences. Theoretical guidelines for identifying and explaining such variations are outlined by Clarence Schrag, a distinguished sociologist at the University of Washington, who has also worked—at different times—as a guard and as a director of that state's prisons. He sets forth "foundations for a theory of correction" which focus attention on the communication channels, the shared expectations, and the reciprocal, complementary or symbiotic relationships that develop among prison staff and inmates. These generate an unofficial system of authority and obligation somewhat independent of the official administrative hierarchy. Four major patterns of inmate adaption are delineated and explained in terms of the inmate's socio-cultural experiences, both in and out of prison.

A more intimate view of prison experience from the convicts' perspective is presented by John Irwin. It is based on unusually extensive contacts with many inmates and ex-inmates of California prisons. Irwin describes the varied inside affiliations and outside identifications maintained during imprisonment, the differences among inmates in motivation for various

145

types of achievement, the segmentation of inmates by prison program innovations, and as a result of all these features, a great diversity of adaptations to imprisonment.

Professor Elmer H. Johnson of Southern Illinois University's Center for Study of Crime, Delinquency and Correction, formerly Assistant Director of North Carolina prisons, explains why a few inmates come to be widely denounced by the others as "rats", the slang term for informants. His analysis is particularly applicable to the most repressive traditional prisons. On the basis of extensive interviews with inmates, two major types of "rat" are differentiated according to whether or not they were assimilated into the inmate social world. Three sub-types are examined within each of these major categories. The designation of some inmates as "rats" is seen by Johnson as having social functions for most inmates and for staff. This labeling, he asserts, occurs even when there is no evidence that those labeled were informants.

Gordon Trasler writes from experience in British prisons, but his analysis of "the social relations of persistent offenders" seems applicable everywhere. The need for intimate relationships with others, he points out, develops in early childhood; when such relationships are not found in one setting they are sought elsewhere. The offender's experience, he explains, makes him look primarily to his peer group for social support when his criminal and penal activities make him increasingly inept in relating to others. The promotion of such self-segregation gives penal institutions major handicaps in trying to rehabilitate offenders. Therefore, drastic changes are recommended to augment inmate relationships with persons in the outside community.

Women's prisons are explored in the work of two sociology professors, David Ward and Gene Kassebaum. With assistance of female researchers they studied intensively such an institution in California. They describe in detail the reception process, a feature of all correctional institutions. In this initial experience inmates are stripped of many symbols of their former statuses and are made to feel distinctly inferior and untrusted. The separation from family as a consequence of imprisonment is shown to be an especially severe deprivation for most women. Women prisoners, on the whole, are described as much more limited in criminal and penal experience than male prisoners; hence the inmate code of "doing one's own time" and not informing to staff is less prevalent among them than in men's prisons. What was distinctive, however, and has also been noted by investigators elsewhere, is the greater propensity of women than men in prison to develop homosexual pseudo-family relationships as an adaptation to the pains of imprisonment.

A perspective on "the social meaning of prison homosexuality" is provided by John H. Gagnon and William Simon. For several years they helped to continue the research on sexual behavior pioneered at Indiana University by the late Alfred C. Kinsey. As long as prisons are one-sex institutions, they point out, all efforts to achieve the conformity of their inmates to prescribed norms in social relationships probably fail in one very important area—in relationships with the opposite sex. They find, however, that the particular form and extent of sexual maladjustment promoted by imprisonment varies greatly according to the age, sex, and prior sexual and nonsexual experience of those imprisoned. Furthermore, the homosexual activity in prisons can only be understood if seen as an effort to offset deprivation suffered by the prisoners in seeking to fulfill their total social needs, rather than as simply a search for sexual release.

Bernard Berk directs attention to the important question of the effect of changes in style of institution management on the inmate's experience of the institution community. Consistent with other studies, he found that custodially-oriented management generates an informal organization of inmates which is resistant to staff goals, while treatment-oriented management generates an informal organization supportive of staff goals. These contrasts among institutions in the orientation of inmates to staff were greater among inmate leaders than among the rest of the inmates, and varied directly with the involvement of prisoners in the informal inmate organization. This suggests the crucial importance of inmate relationships as a determinant of correctional institution achievements, by their opposition or support, even though institution management seldom refer to these informal relationships as a major element in their correctional enterprises.

Thomas P. Wilson extends Berk's analysis by showing that it is not only the goals of management which determine inmate communication patterns and attitudes with respect to staff, but also the manner in which management disseminates its objectives. Where the inmate's treatment program is prescribed entirely by management, with "privileges" or penalties dispensed according to the inmate's conformity to these prescriptions, the inmate is more often alienated or opportunistic with respect to the program than when he participates in decisions on his program for rehabilitation.

In concluding this section on correctional institutions, Daniel Glaser and John R. Stratton address the problem of measuring inmate change in prison. The predominant approach has been to identify types of adaptation to prison life, but these typologies, whether formulated by the investigator or borrowed from inmate slang, are idealizations. They point to relevant dimensions of inmate variation, but the types fit easily only the extreme cases on these dimensions and cannot reliably be applied to a cross-section of prisoners. Sequential measurement of a panel of inmates at different times in their prison experience, or measuring groups of prisoners presumably differing only in the duration of their prior confinement, reveals a variety of attitude changes during the course of imprisonment. For measuring the consequences of prison experience a more relevant method is *ex post facto* comparison, to correlate the behavior of inmates after release with the conditions and duration of their confinement. Such study has only been done thus far with crude differentiation of prisoners and prison programs. Highly relevant to such analysis of the impact of prisons on prisoners is the next section of this book, on specific programs in correctional institutions.

10 Some Foundations for a Theory of Correction

CLARENCE SCHRAG*

THE CORRECTIONAL COMMUNITY

Cultural Determinants of Correctional Policy

Problems of criminality and activities of criminals have attained such prominence in contemporary social life that nearly all persons have some conception of the methods or techniques of crime, the supposed causes of crime, and tactics of crime control. Common conceptions of criminality exert an important influence on the activities of correctional administrators because administrators regard themselves as representatives of the broader community in their dealings with criminals. Moreover, they are so regarded by the members of the broader community. Correctional officials, in other words, carry a public trust, and their duties and responsibilities are defined for them in terms of conventional beliefs concerning criminal behavior. Thus, the objectives and policies of correctional institutions are largely reflections of beliefs and values that are indigenous to the broader community.

If their objectives deviate very far from those of the broader community, correctional officials encounter various forms of public opposition. Consequently, the assessment of changes or trends in public expectations is an inevitable and important task for the correctional official. To the extent that social conventions are supportive of confused or contradic-

* From *The Prison: Studies in Institutional Organization and Change* edited by Donald R. Cressey. Copyright © 1961 by Holt, Rinehart and Winston, Inc. Reprinted by permission of the author and publisher.

149

tory correctional objectives, it may be expected that prison policies will reflect these confusions and contradictions.

According to available evidence, the foremost responsibilities assigned to prison officials are maintenance of custodial security and protection of society against convicted offenders. Therapy comes next. "You can't treat the prisoners if you can't keep them," and similar mottoes indicate the relative values ordinarily attached to treatment and custody. Among the goals that receive weaker public endorsements, although they are strongly invoked in special cases and in times of crisis, are deterrence of potential offenders and reinforcement of cultural norms and values.

While the relative importance attached to different correctional objectives may vary somewhat in different segments of the community, the protective functions of correctional institutions are usually given the highest rankings, followed by the therapeutic or restorative functions, and finally the integrative functions. Moreover, staff members of correctional institutions, in general, follow the same order of rankings, the primary exception being that top-level administrative officials who have been indoctrinated in modern treatment philosophy tend to place a higher premium on therapy.

Like the goals and objectives of correctional institutions, the policies of such organizations are greatly influenced by conventional assumptions concerning criminal behavior. Correctional programs are founded on a public conception of the criminal as a person who habitually engages in deliberative misconduct. In fact, the conception of malicious intent is an essential ingredient of criminal conduct as defined by statute. Furthermore, persons who are regarded as being incapable of willful wrongdoing, namely, children and the insane, do not ordinarily come under the purview of criminal law or under the correctional policies that are presumably designed for deliberative offenders.

Although the above conception of criminal behavior may be gradually changing under the impact of contemporary explanations of human conduct, it seems clear that the bulk of opinion and the weight of official and legal doctrine are still largely in support of the traditional notion that the criminal knows the difference between right and wrong, that he makes a rational and considered decision against the moral order, and that his choice is subject to voluntary control. Criminals and prisoners, in other words, are believed to be capable of conformity but disposed to play the role of the rebel. Prisoners consequently are expected to exhibit antisocial attitudes and to be resistive and unruly in their contacts with correctional authorities. To the degree that prisoner roles are conditioned by the traditional assumptions mentioned, these assumptions may be expected to strengthen the staff-inmate conflicts and the negativistic attitudes of prisoners that have been so frequently noted in correctional research.

The role of the prison official, as perceived in the broader community, also reflects the influence of the assumptions mentioned above. In effect, inmates are absolved of any responsibility for prison programs and policies; and officials are held fully accountable for the attainment of correctional objectives, the maintenance of plant and equipment, the protection of inmate health and welfare, and the enforcement of inmate conformity and obedience.

The focus of traditional prison policies is the enforcement of compliance and obedience despite the expected opposition of the inmates. Strict surveillance and punitive actions are deemed necessary to show the prisoner that society is stronger than he is. Force and restraints, according to the view that seems dominant in the broader community, should only be used when necessary to maintain control; but they should always be available in sufficient degree to insure the maintenance of control. Thus, correctional institutions are frequently viewed as autonomous societies having police powers sufficient for the prompt detection of any rule violations and for rigorous enforcement of official rules and regulations.

The prison world, as seen from a conventional perspective, is a world of conflict between forces of good and of evil. Prisoners are expected to exercise their antisocial propensities if they can get away with it. Officers are, or are expected to be, the sentinels of the good society who carry the full authority of the official community in their relations with the inmate caste. Their first objective is to obtain by means of external constraints the compliance that prisoners are disinclined to display voluntarily.

Significantly, the traditional view of the prison is also the view of most staff members and inmates. Striking similarities can be noted in the previously mentioned assumptions and in the way staff members and inmates perceive their own social roles and the roles of each other.

To illustrate, staff members and inmates were questioned concerning various possible solutions to problematic situations that frequently arise in correctional institutions. In addition to stating their own preferred solutions to the problems, officers and inmates indicated the solutions that they thought would be adopted by most officers and by most inmates. Then the observed preferences of the two groups were compared with their anticipated preferences.

Responses to the questionnaires clearly show that the role of the inmate is quite uniformly perceived as an "antisocial" role, whereas the role of the officer is just as consistently perceived as an "authoritarian" role. That is, both staff members and inmates regularly overestimate the number of antisocial solutions to prison problems that are actually chosen by the inmates. Likewise, both staff members and inmates, in attempting to anticipate the solutions that are chosen with greatest frequency by staff members, consistently assign to prison officials a higher degree of authoritarianism than is warranted by their actual choices. Moreover, differences in the role of the inmate as perceived by officers and by the inmates themselves are relatively minor. The same thing holds for the role of the officer.

The conclusion suggested is that staff members and inmates share perceptual distortions in such a manner that they see the differences in their assigned roles as being greatly exaggerated. These distortions tend to reinforce the traditions of conflict between the two groups. Furthermore, the distortions are in complete accord with the conventional view of the prison as a world of conflict. It may consequently be assumed that the distortions reflect the influence of cultural factors upon the cognitive behavior of staff members and inmates. The cultural expectation of staff-inmate conflict impregnates the perceptions of the members of the prison community, and in this way it may function as a self-fulfilling prophecy.

The strategies for "reforming," "rehabilitating," "treating," or "correcting" criminals in institutions also are greatly influenced by the assumptions of persons in the broader society, and these assumptions have been importantly revised during the course of correctional history. Early efforts were to be aimed at "breaking the will" of the offender. Current conceptions of treatment place greater emphasis upon the inculcation of useful habits, such as thriftiness and industriousness, and the acquisition of social and occupational skills. Thus, the treatment function of the prison is to make available to inmates a variety of facilities, including programs of academic and vocational training, medical care, religious instruction, counseling, and parole planning, to mention only the standard treatment devices.

But the assumption that it is entirely up to the inmate to take advantage of treatment opportunities if he is so inclined is still an important feature of treatment philosophy. Behavior is still regarded as primarily a matter of personal volition. Reorganization of attitudes and modification of affective attachments to objects and persons in the social environment are generally viewed as personal issues over which prison policies have little control. The possibility of redefining the roles and changing the social positions of inmates by means of administrative procedures receives relatively little consideration, although some efforts along these lines are being initiated through various forms of group therapy. . . .

Administrative Organization of the Prison

The structure of prison administration is organized around conventional definitions of correctional objectives and conventional assumptions concerning criminal behavior. More specifically, the administrative structure of the prison is comprised of a hierarchy of offices or staff positions, each of which implies certain duties and responsibilities, and a chain of command linking the various offices in a rationally predetermined manner. The immediate objective of this structure is the attainment of uniform compliance to a set of official rules and regulations that designates the behavior expected of staff members and inmates.

The articulation of authority patterns and staff positions provides a powerful and intricately balanced mechanism for manufacturing policy decisions. Everyday observations of inmate behavior are reported from the lower levels of command up the ladder to higher levels, where the numerous reports are collated and official decisions are made. Then directives and supportive information, sanctioned by top-level administrators, flow back down the ladder in a unilateral sequence, from division chief to supervisor to officer and, in turn, to the inmates. Hence, the typical communication pattern in the close-custody prison is for reports of a first-hand factual nature to move upward in the chain of command and for policies, directives, and interpretations of factual materials to move down the ranks of employees.

Despite the clear logic of its structure, there may be significant defects in the system of unilateral authority relations. First, the system assumes that officers are fully committed to the objectives and policies announced by the chief administrator. Secondly, it assumes that the administrative machinery of the prison embodies the power and authority of the broader community in dealing with the inmates. Thirdly, it assumes that inmates occupy a caste-like status that deprives them of any influence in the determination of policy. None of these assumptions is very realistic if judged in terms of social activities that are normally observed in the prison community. Let us briefly examine these assumptions in the order mentioned.

ALIENATION OF THE OFFICER.   Instead of insuring agreement between rank-and-file officers and top-level administrators, the unilateral flow of authority and communication may tend to produce a considerable barrier between the low-ranking officer's world of everyday experience and the picture of that world as it is viewed from the top levels of command.

Frequently persons in highest authority are far removed from the scene of contact between staff members and inmates where the relative worthiness of alternative policies is most clearly revealed. Administrative decisions regarding specific situations are based chiefly on facts reported by subordinates. Therefore, administrative judgments are sometimes jeopardized by the distortions of fact that tend to occur when reports are repeatedly reviewed, digested, and passed upward through the ranks of the administrative hierarchy. In addition, the highest authorities may be among the last persons to learn about the impact of their decisions upon the relations between staff members and inmates. Generally, the higher the rank of the administrative officer, the greater his dependence on reports of the observations of others and the less direct the sources of his information.

Again, the officers who are most immediately affected by correctional policies are the ones who play the least part in policy formation. The task of low-ranking officers is to carry out orders, not to evaluate them. Feedback, such as criticism of directives received, is minimized, and in some institutions no official procedure for such reverse flow of communication is available. When reverse flow of critical comment is tolerated, it is often restricted to informal relations among trusted associates and is not treated as a matter of policy. Failure of unilateral communication to exploit the possibilities of feedback encourages the development of unofficial channels for the diffusion of messages. This may seriously interfere with the operation of the formal machinery of administration.

Official communication, based on the unilateral design, seems to be at a distinct disadvantage when competing with the mutual give-and-take that characterizes unofficial relations among officers or between officers and inmates. Two factors are of special significance in this connection. First, official directives generally assume the form of unqualified and universal imperatives. This results from the tendency for rationalizations, justifications, and elaborations to get lost or misinterpreted as the directives filter down the ranks of the administrative hierarchy. Secondly, for every official directive that is issued there is likely to be an unofficial interpretation which results from comments and discussions occurring outside the official channels of communication. For subordinate officials, it is perhaps the unofficial version that has the more comprehensible meaning and fits the directive into the over-all plan of prison administration. If this is the case, the unilateral system of communication, instead of eliminating the influence of hearsay and rumor, may tend to make unofficial messages an essential part of the officer's conception of prison policy.

Allegiance to the official administration may be less important to the subordinate officer than are his many involvements in the unofficial conventions of the prison community. His knowledge of the official program is sometimes limited to the specific rules and regulations that are his immediate concern. His information about prison affairs comes primarily from sources other than those that are officially prescribed. For example, over half of the subordinate officers in a state prison were unaware of the existence of a certain group therapy program that had been in operation for more than nine months. And the majority of those officers who knew about the program stated that they had learned of it from inmates or fellow officers rather than from their superiors.

In many institutions, the status of subordinate officers is essentially connected with their lack of official information, their limited influence, and their minimal participation in matters of administrative policy. Attitudes of detachment and feelings of powerlessness or meaninglessness with respect to the official program are also commonly noted. Objective factors related to the status of subordinate officers tend to reinforce their feelings of powerlessness, and vice versa. The result is that officers of the lower ranks frequently are alienated from the official program. This is reflected, for example, in the negative correlation that is observed between the length of service of low-ranking officers and the degree of their confidence in prison treatment programs.

THE ILLUSION OF UNLIMITED AUTHORITY. Because of the primacy of custodial functions, the greatest concern of prison administrators is the constant threat of prisoner escapes and uprisings. Major techniques for the control of inmate rebellions are, first, the show of force and, secondly, appeals to the inmates based on the notion that the prison's administration embodies the power and authority of the political state.

However, neither technique seems to be nearly as effective in organizing the routine activities of the prison community as are the unofficial alliances between staff members and inmates. Routine activities of the prison are largely governed by a system of symbiotic social relations that is designed to eliminate the necessity of force except in emergencies. This symbiotic system is based on certain fundamental weaknesses in the official structure of prison administration.

First of all, the repeated use of force is often self-defeating. Its cost is excessive in terms of manpower and material resources. It is detrimental to inmate moral and interest in staff-inmate harmony. Force begets force in the sense that officers who are employed in the continued use of force are thereby deprived of the major social means for obtaining voluntary inmate cooperation. This is largely the reason for the traditional separation of custodial and therapeutic functions in the close-custody prison.

A more crucial reason for restraint in the employment of force is that public opinion generally denies the necessity of its continued use in correctional institutions. Withdrawal of public support from correctional administrations that are founded on repetitive displays of official violence has occurred with increasing frequency during the course of our penal history. For example, the use of force in the recent wave of prison riots almost always resulted in public inquiries into the complaints of the rioting prisoners. These inquiries clearly revealed that public opinion was by no means unanimous in its support of prison policies, a situation that was apparently anticipated by the riot leaders and may have contributed to their rebellions.

While social conventions hold administrators responsible for the conduct of prison inmates, they also assume that strict surveillance and rigorous enforcement of appropriate penalties should make major displays of violence a rare occurrence. Consequently, most prison administrators, in order to maintain their official positions, must utilize devices other than violence in gaining inmate conformity and obedience. Force, then, is increasingly regarded as a device to be used as a last resort in case of emergency. Its public justification is sometimes threatened by the conventional belief that efficient prison administration should make its use unnecessary.

For the above reasons, the appeal to authority is a far more prevalent mechanism of official control. However, the functions of authority in the prison community are also subject to common misunderstanding. Authority is based on the assumption that persons in subordinate positions will voluntarily submit to the dictates of their superiors. But authority is effective only if subordinates share the social perspectives of their superiors. Our discussion of alienation has already suggested that officers occupying different ranks in the administrative hierarchy do not necessarily share similar views of the official program.

It is sometimes naively assumed that an officer's instruction to an inmate carries the full sanction of the prison's administration and that the officer's failure to enforce his order is evidence of the "corruption" of his authority. This is not necessarily the case. It would be far more realistic frankly to admit that the officer's control over an inmate depends primarily on his skills of persuasion and leadership.

Consider, for example, the alternative procedures that are available to an officer in the event that an inmate refuses to obey his command. First, he might resort to physical force. Generally, there are official regulations that restrict the use of force except in cases of attempted escape or threatened bodily injury. These regulations are designed to prevent unnecessary use of force. Therefore, if the officer uses force, he must justify his actions to his superiors in the same way that his superiors need to justify violence in the face of public opinion. His superiors are likely to hold the common opinion that effective leadership and preventative methods should make force unnecessary. Repeated involvement in violence against inmates is consequently likely to result in termination of the officer's employment by the institution.

Again, the officer may use the more common procedure of reporting inmate misconduct to his superiors. Penalties against the inmate may then be determined by a disciplinary committee. However, should the committee receive an extraordinary number of complaints or reports from a given officer, this too may be interpreted as evidence of incompetence on the part of the officer. Inmates, of course, are fully aware of the role they play in the official evaluation of an officer's services. Thus continued employment of a given officer depends largely upon the degree of voluntary cooperation that he can win from the inmates. Skill in interpersonal relations is more important in this situation than is the "corruption" of highly restricted authority, and the idea that officials have unlimited authority is simply not consistent with the essential evidence.

THE FICTION OF OFFICIAL AUTONOMY.   Another defect of the unilateral system of communication and authority is the assumption that prison policies are autonomous and uninfluenced by inmate pressures. Official policy views the prisoner as being habitually antisocial and inclined to violate regulations if he can get away with it. Further, policy holds that the only defensible role for the officer to play is to enforce all rules to the letter and "let the chips fall where they may." Since the inmates are not involved in the formulation of policy, their only opportunity for influencing the administration of the institution is in the area of policy enforcement. Therefore, if the rules are enforced without deviation, complete domination over the inmates presumably can be gained.

For instance, rules aimed at curbing food pilferage may define as contraband all items of prison fare that are found in any place other than the mess-hall. As a consequence, any inmate found in possession of unauthorized food is officially presumed to be guilty of theft or somehow involved in the food racket. Excuses don't count.

Similar presumptions of guilt operate with respect to other rules and regulations. The apparent purpose of the presumptions is to base the decision of guilt upon objective factors and to eliminate problems of judgment concerning extenuating circumstances. In this way it is believed that the possibility of inmate influence in the dispensation of prison justice will be minimized.

However, undeviating enforcement of all rules can involve an officer in the repeated employment of force and/or the issuance of innumerable rule-infraction reports. The practical effect, in either case, may be to create official doubts concerning the officer's competence, as has already been mentioned. Furthermore, the officer may have full knowledge of extenuating circumstances in certain cases and may therefore disagree with the official presumption of guilt. If the officer takes into consideration the alleviating conditions and gives the inmate a "break," he is in danger of official reprimand. In addition, toleration of rule infractions in the face of a policy of complete enforcement makes the officer vulnerable to charges of collusion with the inmates. This is precisely the point at which conniving inmates seek to "get something on" the officer, to be held against him later in more important situations and progressively to bring him under inmate domination.

The traditional policy of complete rule enforcement breaks down because it does not allow room for individual judgment concerning the circumstances related to rule violations. It places the officer in a fine dilemma. As a practical matter the officer can neither enforce all rules to the letter nor can he admit that he tolerates certain rule violations. This is why many correctional institutions, including some close-custody prisons, are developing mechanisms for taking into account the circumstances related to rule violations. However, all of these mechanisms, so far as can be ascertained, involve distinctive modifications of the unilateral system of communication; they either give the officer considerable discretion in reporting violations, a procedure that is euphemistically called "counseling," or they provide for the inmate an official opportunity to defend his actions.

Nevertheless, insistence upon unilateral relations among staff members and between staff members and inmates, rather than paucity of treatment facilities, is the feature most characteristic of the traditional close-custody prison. Restrictions against feedback and participation in policy formation, of course, are extended to the inmate population. However, such restrictions apparently run counter to some of the assumptions underlying modern therapeutic techniques. Modern methods of group therapy and guided participation in programming activities, for example, encourage the inmate to evaluate and perhaps initially to criticize the behavior standards that he is expected eventually to adopt as his own. Frank expression of skepticism and freedom of discussion, instead of insuring rejection of social norms, are believed to improve the inmate's understanding of social controls and to further the development of self-imposed discipline.

If the above analysis of defects in traditional prison policies is valid, then it seems clear that the unilateral organization of the close-custody prison may place severe limitations upon the treatment potential of our prisons and may provide a greater barrier against the resocialization of the offender than do the bars and walls that attract such adverse comment. How to modify traditional policy so as to integrate the roles of inmates and officers within a more efficient official organization continues to be one of the most difficult problems of prison administration.

Some Aspects of Prisoner Society

Juxtaposed with the official organization of the prison is an unofficial social system originating within the institution and regulating inmate conduct with respect to focal issues, such as length of sentence, relations among prisoners, contacts with staff members and other civilians, food, sex, and health, among others. The unofficial system, contrary to administrative rules and regulations, does not demand uniformity of behavior. Rather, it recognizes alternative roles that inmates may play with respect to each of the focal issues.

In various subtle ways the unofficial social system encourages reciprocal, complementary, or symbiotic relationships among inmates and between inmates and officers. Behavior prescriptions are based on interlocking role alternatives that are organized around the focal issues. Alternative roles are allocated among the inmates so as to maintain a fairly stable social equilibrium within the society of prisoners. To illustrate, consider some of the alternative roles that are organized around the procurement of illicit foods. Codes of conduct pertaining to food pilferage differ for "scores" (spontaneous or unplanned thefts) and "routes" (highly organized thefts). An inmate who "scores for food" may consume it or share it with friends, perhaps for past or expected favors, but he is not expected to sell it. Food obtained through organized theft is ordinarily sold in the illicit food racket.

Sale of pilfered food is regulated by an intricate division of labor and responsibility based on a network of symbiotic roles. Designated inmates are assigned the job of obtaining the food and delivering it to distributors.

Distributors, in turn, may sell on credit to trusted inmate customers. Or the food may be sold on a cash basis to inmates from whom knowledge of procurement techniques is carefully concealed. Roles affiliated with the food racket are further delineated in terms of the kinds and quantities of foods stolen; in terms of the food sources, such as the officer's mess or the inmate's mess, for example; and, finally, in terms of the methods of distribution and exchange.

Only those inmates who are involved in the food racket, of course, need to know the details of the system. Designation of role incumbents is handled informally, chiefly by mutual agreement among the persons concerned. But once a role has been assumed, it places upon the incumbent fairly precise requirements regarding his relations with others who participate in the racket, and with nonparticipating inmates and staff members as well. Furthermore, the amount of knowledge and skill required of an inmate depends upon the degree of his involvement in the racket. The food racket may be so well organized, however, that if all persons involved in it know and fulfill their assignments, the pilferage system can operate with an efficiency that is alarming and costly to the prison's administration.

Maintenance of a *sub rosa* organization such as the food racket requires that inmates be capable of assessing the probable behavior and the loyalty attachments of their fellows. Roles and statuses must generally be appropriate to the skills and interests of the persons involved. Errors made by the inmates in the assignment of roles ordinarily work to the advantage of the prison's administration and its officials. In order to minimize such errors, a fairly elaborate system of role allocations is set into operation not only with respect to food pilferage but in all areas of behavior related to the focal issues.

Allocation of roles is based on evidence regarding the affective orientations of the inmates, the accuracy and consistency of their perceptions of role requirements, and the degree of agreement between their perceived role requirements and their performance. Role allocations not only reflect the assessments and expectations of fellow inmates relative to the person in question, but they also in a large measure determine this person's opportunities for future social contacts and his access to information and to other social resources.

Evidence relevant to role assignments is obtained from observations made during initiation ceremonies and from a variety of contrived testing situations that accompany the introduction of an inmate into the prisoner community. The process of role allocation commonly proceeds in a standardized sequence of events. First, a degree of consensus is attained regarding the inmate's relative loyalties to the administration and to his fellow prisoners. Attempts are made to determine whether a given inmate generally evaluates situations according to the codes of prisoner society or according to the dictates of the officials. Then, the inmate's knowledge of prisoner roles and his skill in dealing with problematic situations are carefully examined. Knowledge of prisoner society indicates a given inmate's potential for aiding or obstructing the goals and strategies of his fellow prisoners. Finally, the consistency, reliability, and integrity of the inmate's behavior are investigated in a variety of contrived situations. Within six months, or so, after the inmate's admission into the institution, his major roles in the prisoner community seem to have been pretty well established. Role assignments, of course, are sometimes modified through a continuous re-evaluation of the inmate's performance, but the frequency of such modifications is usually not great enough to disturb the social equilibrium.

In addition to exercising great care in the allocation of roles, especially in areas involving high risk of detection by the officials, inmate society sets up expectations of mutual care and protection among the prisoners. These expectations, of course, conflict with the official suggestion to "do your own time," and they provide a basis for strong inmate morale in the face of persistent staff opposition. Roles played by prisoners with respect to forbidden activities create sets of mutual obligations that define conceptions of loyalty and protect organized rackets from interference by nonparticipating inmates or staff members. The rule that an inmate should not do anything to interfere with another's participation in forbidden activities is apparently the strongest commandment in the prisoner's code of conduct.

For example, inmates engaged in the food racket, in order to maintain a climate favorable to the continuation of this enterprise, may be expected to support and protect various other forbidden activities. Inmates who profit from such support or nonintervention are required to reciprocate in like manner. A system of largely unspoken but finely graded reciprocities of this kind tends to integrate prisoner society in its opposition to the prison's official administration.

But the system of inmate reciprocities, like the official system of unilateral communications, is vulnerable in crucial ways to outside interference. Deviations from the system, although they may be largely concealed from many of the inmates, are as much the rule as the exception. One problem is competititon among inmates who are striving for higher status and authority within the society of prisoners. Again, the system is far less autonomous than the inmates would like to believe, and whenever it is disrupted by official intervention, there is great difficulty in determining exactly what went wrong. Finally, many of the inmates refrain from full involvement in the system; they may feel an allegiance to the official codes or they may be greatly influenced by official rewards and punishments. All of this lessens the effectiveness of the social controls that are primarily accessible to the prisoners.

The result is that neither the official system nor the society of prisoners can long retain dominance in the prison community. Symbiotic relationships tend to develop in such a way that, although the integrity of the two systems may be retained on the surface, the behavior of an inmate or a staff member in almost any given case is determined by intersecting influences that cannot be realistically accredited solely to either system. It is to this topic that we now turn our attention.

PATTERNS OF INMATE ADAPTATION

Sets of role alternatives, as previously indicated, reflect the organization of inmate behavior with regard to given focal issues. The conception of a social system, however, signifies a higher level of organization than that dealing with specific issues. Society, as an abstract concept, implies that the role alternatives assumed by given individuals with respect to various issues are interrelated in a more or less systematic manner. Thus, the pragmatic problem related to the concept of the social system is for research to determine the empirical regularities, if any, among sets of role alternatives. We call such regularities role configurations.

Major Role Configurations

Role configuration implies that a particular alternative regarding a given focal issue will be empirically connected with a certain alternative related to a second issue. A straightforward empirical procedure for identifying configurations of role alternatives would be to list all logically possible combinations of alternatives and then determine the frequencies with which the combinations occur. This procedure is unrealistic, of course, because the combinations rapidly reach staggering proportions and the relevant observational data are not available. An alternative procedure is to focus attention on the role configurations that are implied in the prison's symbolic system, including its argot, proverbs, legends and beliefs.

Prison argot makes many sharp distinctions between alternatives, which define the separate roles organized around a given issue, and configurations, which specify sets of alternatives that are perceived as being interrelated. "Merchant" for example, denotes the salesman role in a variety of situations, whereas "food peddler" identifies a single role alternative. The "merchant" configuration cuts across a number of focal issues. It is involved in a variety of *sub rosa* organizations and consequently arouses stronger inmate support or opposition. The term, as it seems to be used in prison, does not merely label a given role alternative, but implies that several alternatives are empirically connected.

It is immediately apparent, however, that inmates may erroneously perceive a particular set of role alternatives as being interrelated. Therefore, a distinction should be made between perceived relationships and confirmed or empirically verified relationships among role alternatives. Likewise, it is necessary to distinguish between normative statements, or behavior *prescriptions, and statements about overt performance, or behavior *descriptions. Since these distinctions are not ordinarily made in the use of prison language, great caution must be observed in relying upon the prison's symbolic system as a guide in the identification of role configurations.

Keeping in mind the perceived-confirmed and the prescribed-performed dichotomies mentioned above, a number of cross-tabulations were made of roles that are supposed to be interrelated according to prison argot, proverbs and legends. Several configurations were found that cut across a number of issues within the prison community. Most important, in our opinion, is a set of configurations that deals primarily with issues involving social relations among inmates, contacts with staff members, and access to the civilian world. The set includes four major configurations, to which are attached the prison labels "square John," "right guy," "con politician," and "outlaw."

Briefly, inmates who fall within the "square John" configuration consistently define role requirements in terms of the prison's official social system. By contrast, "right guys" just as regularly perceive requirements according to the norms of prisoner society. "Con politicians" shift their frame of reference from staff norms to inmate norms with great alacrity. "Outlaws," deficient in aptitude for identification, are in a perpetual anarchistic rebellion against both normative systems and against affective involvements in general.

Whereas the above argot labels refer to specific sets of interconnected role alternatives, our interest is in developing a typological system relating these role configurations to other social or cultural aspects of the prison community. In order to emphasize this distinction, a shift from argot labels to a more neutral terminology seems advisable. Consequently, the terms *prosocial, antisocial, pseudosocial,* and *asocial,* will hereafter be used in lieu of the argot labels in the respective order in which they have appeared. These role configurations, in the interest of brevity, will be called, collectively, social types.

Career Variables

To investigate the assumption that there are distinctive variations in the careers of the various social types, groups of inmates belonging to different types were interviewed and their case-histories were carefully examined. Clear distinctions were noted in the criminal records of the social types, their family and community experiences, and their attitudes towards crime and society. Major findings are summarized below.

Prosocial inmates are most frequently convicted of violent crimes against the person, such as homicide and assault, or naïve property offenses, chiefly forgery. Few have prior arrests, and their criminal careers are initiated relatively late in life. Their offenses are situational. That is, the offenses reflect extraordinary social pressures frequently involving real or imagined misbehavior on the part of a spouse or of close friends.

While in prison, prosocial inmates maintain strong ties with family and civilian associates, and they are sympathetic and cooperative toward prison officials. Generally supportive of established authority, they believe in the efficacy of punishment, show strong guilt for their offenses, and expect to pay for their crimes in order to renew civilian life with a clean slate. Naïve about illegal techniques and strategies, they have little knowledge of, or contact with, organized crime.

Antisocial inmates are highly recidivistic, their careers frequently progressing through stages of truancy, expressive theft with other gang members, instrumental theft involving contacts with "fences" and other organized criminals, and culminating in patterns of unsophisticated crimes, such as robbery, assault, and burglary.

Coming chiefly from families having other delinquent members and living in underprivileged urban areas, antisocial inmates frequently earn a livelihood via contacts with organized crime, but do not often rise to positions of power in this field. Rebellion against conventional norms has continuity in their careers and is noted in their educational, occupational, and marital adjustments. Close ties with the parental family were commonly seen, however.

In prison, the antisocial offenders continue their close association with criminalistic elements and their rebellion against civil authorities. Their philosophy of life, as reflected in the slogans "only suckers work," "all politicians are crooks," and "big shots and real criminals never get caught," alleviates their sense of guilt and solidifies inmate opposition against the prison's administration.

Pseudosocial inmates are involved primarily in subtle, sophisticated, profit-motivated offenses, such as embezzlement, fraud, and forgery. Relatively few have juvenile records, and onset of criminality often occurs after a position of respectability has already been attained in the civilian community.

Family and community backgrounds are frequently middle-class, but evidence of inconsistent parental discipline and other family disharmony is the most striking feature of their preinstitutional careers. Apparently, pseudosocial offenders acquire their facility in role-playing at an early age, and they are frequently described as having a pleasant, ingratiating manner. Educational and occupational records are far superior to those of antisocial offenders.

In prison, pseudosocial inmates display chameleonic skill in shifting their allegiances from staff members to inmates, and vice versa, according to the exigencies of the moment. Pragmatic and instrumentally oriented, they exploit to their own advantage the conflicts and inconsistencies inherent in the prison's social structures. Although they are recognized to be unreliable, their strategic position between the two social systems makes them the mediators in staff-inmate conflicts and results in rewards, such as relatively short sentences, desirable prison assignments, and reduced custody, among others.

Asocial inmates commit a variety of offenses against persons and property, frequently using bizarre methods without clear motive or reason. Recidivism is extremely high, and there is early evidence of severe behavior disorders, although age at first arrest varies considerably.

Paramount among findings regarding social backgrounds is the seemingly universal evidence of early rejection. Asocial offenders are frequently reared in institutions, shifted around various foster homes, or are otherwise lacking reasonable care and attention from their parents. Social abilities and skills in the use of social symbols are greatly retarded. The careers of asocial offenders are marked by high egocentrism and an inability to profit from past mistakes or to plan for the future. These persons often exhibit an apparent distrust and fear of personal ties of any kind. Their problems are solved by direct and immediate aggression.

In prison, asocial inmates are the undisciplined troublemakers who are chiefly involved in riots, escape plots, and assaults on both inmates and officers. Nevertheless, their lack of capacity for cooperative enterprise means that most of their rebellions are destined for failure.

Several tentative conclusions can be drawn from the above findings. Generally, antisocial offenders are reared in an environment consistently oriented toward illegitimate social norms. Asocial and pseudosocial offenders exhibit defective normative perceptions growing out of early parental rejection and patterns of inconsistent discipline, respectively. They suffer severe personal frustrations at an early age and acquire distinctive adaptation techniques. Prosocial offenders, although utilizing legitimate normative standards, seem unable to cope with intense social pressures or unique personal problems. That persons with such varied problems of adjustment should play distinctively different roles in the prison community does not seem surprising.

Cognitive and Affective Orientations

It will be remembered that staff members and inmates uniformly perceive sharp and consistent distinctions between role requirements that are defined conventionally and those defined in terms of the prisoner social system. The concept of criminal subculture, at least so far as staff and inmate perceptions are concerned, does have specifiable pragmatic meaning as a set of behavior prescriptions. Consequently, criminal subculture, as a deviant or an illegitimate normative system, may be useful in revealing additional distinguishing characteristics among our social types.

Speculation concerning the life organizations of individual offenders and their knowledge of, and attachments to, cultural standards leads to the expectation of systematic variations in the frames of reference employed by the various social types. That is, some types are expected to utilize legitimate norms and others illegitimate norms as frames of reference. Moreover, variations in cognitive and affective orientations toward the two normative systems, unless our speculations lead us astray, should be highly associated with the patterns of personal and social traits that were noted previously.

More specifically, prosocial offenders appear to evaluate problematic situations with reference to legitimate norms, to have greater cognitive understanding of legitimate role requirements than of illegitimate requirements, and generally to apply legitimate norms in specific situations regardless of the personal discomfiture that might result. Conversely, it is expected that antisocial offenders will consistently employ deviant or illegitimate norms as standards of reference, to exhibit detailed cognitive knowledge of illegitimate role requirements, and likewise to display their allegiance to these norms irrespective of the impact on personal goals or objectives. Their general opposition to legitimate means of achievement is expressed figuratively in the motto, "only suckers work." The two types, then, are alike in emphasizing collective values, such as loyalty, mutual aid, and group solidarity, but they differ in the normative systems used as standards of judgment.

Pseudosocial offenders, by contrast, are capable of shifting their normative perspectives according to the availability of instrumental rewards. They stress personal achievements rather than collective goals, exploitative strategies rather than conventional procedures, and affective neutrality rather than strong identifications with persons or social conventions. Their cognitive knowledge and role-playing skills extend to the deviant realm as well as to the conventional one. Above all, to be bound by social conventions or moral commitments is for them a sign of weakness.

Asocial offenders are similarly detached from social conventions and moral commitments. However, in their case, detachment reflects ignorance of role requirements and deficiency in role-playing ability rather than emancipation. Moreover, their conceptions of the illegitimate system appear to be as much distorted as their conceptions of legitimate norms. They are generally incapable of developing affective ties either with prisoners or with officials. Thus, their behavior is ordinarily impulsive and motivated by expressive functions; only rarely does it reveal the deliberative and instrumental characteristics so commonly noted among the pseudosocial inmates.

Information obtained by presenting to staff members and inmates alternative solutions to common prison problems has already been mentioned. The solutions chosen by members of the different social types seem to agree with the above arguments. For example, staff members and prosocial inmates tend to choose the same solutions, while pseudosocial offenders choose solutions representative of both conventional and deviant prescriptions. Antisocial offenders are fairly consistent in following the choice-pattern dictated by the illegitimate normative system. Asocial offenders make the greatest number of irregular choices.

Evidence regarding cognitive knowledge possessed by the social types has been difficult to obtain. However, tests or argot vocabularies suggest that, at the time of admission to the institution, antisocial offenders have the best knowledge of prison lingo. Pseudosocial offenders, though, appear to learn more rapidly and they may eventually attain a higher degree of proficiency. Asocial inmates, perhaps surprisingly, have a less adequate vocabulary, so far as labels for prisoner roles are concerned, than do the prosocial inmates; and both of these groups, of course, have vocabularies inferior to those of the antisocial or pseudosocial inmates. Further empirical investigation is needed, however, to demonstrate important anticipated differences in cognitive knowledge among the social types.

In summary, the social types reveal systematic differences in their cognitive and affective orientations toward the legitimate and illegitimate normative systems that are found in the close-custody prison, especially with respect to their attitudes regarding expressive (group-integrating) and instrumental (goal-achievement) norms. Some of the observed differences are indicated in Table 1, where (X) represents high knowledge or affective support for the norm, and (—) represents limited knowledge or affective rejection.

TABLE 1
Cognitive and Affective Attachments Of Social Types

	Legitimate Norms		Illegitimate Norms	
Social type	Cognitive knowledge	Affective attachment	Cognitive knowledge	Affective attachment
Prosocial	X	X	—	—
Antisocial	—	—	X	X
Pseudosocial	X	—	X	—
Asocial	—	—	—	—

Social Contact and Participation

Normative orientations of prison inmates are importantly related to their patterns of social participation. In general, inmates are selectively responsive to those segments of their society that reinforce their own standards of judgment and provide continuity of experience. Persons having similar beliefs and values are sought out and their friendships are cultivated. Encounters with shocking or markedly dissimilar points of view are avoided, if possible. The same factors operate in contacts with staff members. Consequently, members of the various social types, since they are characterized by distinctly different normative orientations, may be expected to exhibit distinctive variations in their patterns of contact and participation within the prison community.

A reasonable expectation, for example, is that prosocial offenders will have extensive contacts with staff members, while their contacts with inmates are restricted largely to other members of the prosocial type. Conversely, antisocial offenders may be expected to have extensive contacts among the inmates, but minimal relations with the staff. Prosocial offenders may have a wider range of contacts involving both staff and inmates, while the asocial inmates may be restricted to fewer relations in either category. The expected patterns are listed in Table 2, assuming that contacts are dichotomized in terms of high and low frequencies, and that the relatively highest frequency of contact for a given social type is marked (X).

TABLE 2
Participation Pattern of Social Types

Social type	High staff / high inmate	High staff / low inmate	Low staff / high inmate	Low staff / low inmate
Prosocial	—	X	—	—
Antisocial	—	—	X	—
Pseudosocial	X	—	—	—
Asocial	—	—	—	X

Direct evidence regarding inmate participation patterns is not yet available. Indirect evidence was obtained, however, by asking a sample of inmates to report the relative amount of their contacts with staff members and other inmates as compared with the contacts of the average inmate. The reported patterns are consistent with those hypothesized, except for the prosocial inmates who reported a somewhat higher amount of inmate contacts than was expected.

Amount of contact, however, may have less social significance than the quality of the relationships, such as friendship, animosity, or leader-follower patterns. Evidence pertinent to the quality of interaction comes from a sociometric study in which inmates reported the names of their closest prisoner friends. Friendship choices were classified according to the social type of the respondent and of the person chosen. Major findings are that members of every social type except one select their friends most frequently from their own type. The single exception is again the prosocial offender, who expresses a slight preference for pseudosocial friends over his choice of prosocial friends. In addition, both prosocial and pseudosocial inmates receive fewer choices than would be expected if friendship were independent of social type; whereas antisocial inmates and, to a lesser extent, asocial inmates receive more than their proportionate numbers of choices.

The same study obtained the names of inmates designated as leaders. Most striking among the findings is the high frequency with which asocial inmates are identified as leaders. Even the prosocial and pseudosocial types, despite their sharp cognitive and affective differences as compared with asocial inmates, frequently select asocial inmates as leaders.

The rationale behind such choices may be revealed in a comment made by one of the respondents to the effect that, "One thing clear is that the outlaws aren't going to make any deals with anybody." Evidently the fears and suspicions aroused by members of the other social types result in leadership status for inmates who are incapable of any high degree of mutual effort. Presumably, then, the higher the tensions and anxieties within the prisoner community, the greater the leadership potential of the asocial type.

Thus it appears that while pseudosocial and perhaps prosocial inmates may have a wider range of contacts, the social climate of the close-custody prison provides for the antisocial and asocial inmates a higher social status and involves them more frequently in patterns of friendship and positions of leadership.

Degrees of participation in staff-sponsored activities and treatment programs likewise show consistent variations among the social types. Greatest participation in such organized activities, as expected, involves the prosocial offenders, followed in order by the pseudosocial, antisocial, and asocial types. Also, prosocial inmates, to a far greater extent than the others, engage in programs aimed specifically at therapy, while the pseudosocial and antisocial offenders display primary interest in recreation and other expressive functions. The relatively staff-centered orientation of the prosocial inmates is clearly revealed in the data.

Communication patterns mediate the intrapersonal processes of the inmates and their resulting self-conceptions. For example, various dimensions of self-conception are shown to vary according to the inmate's duration of confinement, his pre-institutional criminal record, his normative orientation, and his social position within the prison community. Included among the self-concept dimensions that show the above relationships are the inmate's perception of his own status in prisoner society, perception of the degree of his sophistication regarding criminal activities, and the amount of support he perceives as coming from persons in the civilian environment. These relationships, when measured by brief questionnaires, are not very strong, but they are consistently in the expected direction.

Even among juvenile delinquents, there is evidence, derived from responses to an adjective check-list, that the prosocial delinquent defines the correctional institution and the broader community as supportive agencies. In addition, he conceives of himself as a person who, although generally conventional in his conduct, has made a mistake that requires official attention. By contrast, antisocial delinquents perceive correctional institutions and civilian society as restrictive and antagonistic organizations. They conceive of themselves, in a sense, as leaders of the loyal opposition. Here, then, is another area in which further research is strongly indicated.

Patterns of contact and participation, as has been noted, are good indicators of inmate goals and interests. But they also regulate access to the means of goal achievement. They serve as integrative or divisive social forces that mold the individual according to the group's image of him or contrive his expulsion from the group. In consequence, the prosocial offender, for example, has a relatively clear path to conventional or legitimate behavior. He is divested of loyalty obligations toward the inmates, is ill advised concerning the illicit machinations of prisoner society, and in many other subtle ways is deprived of access to the means of goal achievement within the illegitimate social system. However, the ubiquitous pressures of the illegitimate system and the inevitable frustrations produced by his prisoner status make it increasingly difficult for him to maintain his prosocial orientation with the passage of time. Perhaps these are some of the main reasons for the positive correlation that has been observed between the parole violation rates of prosocial offenders and the duration of their confinement.

Participation patterns, then, by regulating access to social means and resources, apparently achieve some modification of inmate normative orientations and behavior standards. The reverse is also true. That is, inmates can sometimes produce changes in prison culture. Generally, prosocial offenders are cultural conservators for whom the stability of even a somewhat oppressive order is preferable to the uncertainties of social revision or experimentation. Pseudosocial inmates, in contrast, are the great innovators. Their exploitative interests, varied resources, and affective neutrality make them the natural catalysts of social invention and change. Antisocial prisoners are rebels who have a cause, namely, the subversion of established authority. Again, the nihilist role is played by asocial inmates, whose language is force, and who are frequently assigned the role of leader in riots, escapes, and similar rebellious activities.

The combined impact of the major role configurations and their related normative systems and participation patterns is to produce the social equilibrium that is commonly observed in the prison community, a fluid and moving equilibrium that enables the society of prisoners to make fairly easy adaptations to the many shocks and strains occasioned by changes in correctional personnel or policies or by other factors over which the inmates exercise relatively little direct control. Equilibrium implies some balance in the way the social types are interrelated, and the evidence outlined above suggests that among the more important balancing mechanisms are factors in the preinstitutional careers of the inmates, their normative orientations, and their patterns of social participation within the prison community.

11 The Prison Experience: The Convict World

JOHN IRWIN*

PRISON-ADAPTIVE MODES

Many studies of prison behavior have approached the task of explaining the convict social organization by posing the hypothetical question—how do convicts adapt to prison? It was felt that this was a relevant question because the prison is a situation of deprivation and degradation, and, therefore, presents extraordinary adaptive problems. Two adaptive styles were recognized: (1) an individual style—withdrawal and/or isolation, and (2) a collective style—participation in a convict social system which, through its solidarity, regulation of activities, distribution of goods and prestige, and apparent opposition to the world of the administration, helps the individual withstand the "pains of imprisonment."

I would like to suggest that these studies have overlooked important alternate styles. First let us return to the question that theoretically every convict must ask himself: How shall I do my time? or, What shall I do in prison? First, we assume by this question that the convict is able to cope with the situation. This is not always true; some fail to cope with prison and commit suicide or sink into psychosis. Those who do cope can be divided into those who identify with and therefore adapt to a broader world than that of the prison, and those who orient themselves primarily to the prison world. This difference in orientation is often quite subtle but

* From John Irwin, *The Felon* (Englewood Cliffs, N.J.: Prentice-Hall, Inc., 1970), pp. 67–85. Copyright © 1970 by Prentice-Hall. Reprinted by permission of the author and publisher.

173

always important. In some instances, it is the basis for forming very important choices, choices which may have important consequences for the felon's long term career. For example, Piri Thomas, a convict, was forced to make up his mind whether to participate in a riot or refrain:

> I stood there watching and weighing, trying to decide whether or not I was a con first and an outsider second. I had been doing time inside yet living every mental minute I could outside; now I had to choose one or the other. I stood there in the middle of the yard. Cons passed me by, some going west to join the boppers, others going east to neutral ground. The call of rep tore within me, while the feeling of being a punk washed over me like a yellow banner. I had to make a decision. *I am a con. These damn cons are my people . . . What do you mean, your people? Your people are outside the cells, home, in the streets. No! That ain't so . . . Look at them go toward the west wall. Why in hell am I taking so long in making up my mind? Man, there goes Papo and Zu-Zu, and Mick the Boxer; even Ruben is there.*[1]

This identification also influences the criteria for assigning and earning prestige—criteria relative to things in the outside world or things which tend to exist only in the prison world, such as status in a prison social system or success with prison homosexuals. Furthermore, it will influence the long term strategies he forms and attempts to follow during his prison sentence.

It is useful to further divide those who maintain their basic orientation to the outside into (1) those who for the most part wish to maintain their life patterns and their identities—even if they intend to refrain from most law breaking activities—and (2) those who desire to make significant changes in life patterns and identities and see prison as a chance to do this.

The mode of adaptation of those convicts who tend to make a world out of prison will be called "jailing." To "jail" is to cut yourself off from the outside world and to attempt to construct a life within prison. The adaptation of those who still keep their commitment to the outside life and see prison as a suspension of that life but who do not want to make any significant changes in their life patterns will be called "doing time." One "does time" by trying to maximize his comfort and luxuries and minimize his discomfort and conflict and to get out as soon as possible. The adaptation made by those who, looking to their future life on the outside, try to effect changes in their life patterns and identities will be called "gleaning."[2] In "gleaning," one sets out to "better himself" or "improve himself" and takes advantage of the resources that exist in prison to do this.

Not all convicts can be classified neatly by these three adaptive styles.

Some vacillate from one to another, and others appear to be following two or three of them simultaneously. Still others, for instance the non-copers mentioned above, cannot be characterized by any of the three. However, many prison careers fit very closely into one of these patterns, and the great majority can be classified roughly by one of the styles.

Doing Time

When you go in, now your trial is over, you got your time and everything and now you head for the joint. They furnish your clothing, your toothbrush, your toothpaste, they give you a package of tobacco, they put you up in the morning to get breakfast. In other words, everything is furnished. Now you stay in there two years, five years, ten years, whatever you stay in there, what difference does it make? After a year or so you've been . . . after six months, you've become accustomed to the general routine. Everything is furnished. If you get a stomachache, you go to the doctor; if you can't see out of your cheaters, you go to the optician. It don't cost you nothing.[3]

As the above statement by a thief indicates, many convicts conceive of the prison experience as a temporary break in their outside career, one which they take in their stride. They come to prison and "do their time." They attempt to pass through this experience with the least amount of suffering and the greatest amount of comfort. They (1) avoid trouble, (2) find activities which occupy their time, (3) secure a few luxuries, (4) with the exception of a few complete isolates, form friendships with small groups of other convicts, and (5) do what they think is necessary to get out as soon as possible.[4]

To avoid trouble the convict adheres to the convict code—especially the maxims of "do your own time" and "don't snitch," and stays away from "lowriders"—those convicts engaged in hijacking and violent disputes. In some prisons which have a high incidence of violence—knifings, assaults, and murders—this can appear to be very difficult even to the convicts themselves. One convict reported his first impression of Soledad:

The first day I got to Soledad I was walking from the fish tank to the mess hall and this guy comes running down the hall past me, yelling, with a knife sticking out of his back. Man, I was petrified. I thought, what the fuck kind of place is this? (Interview, Soledad Prison, June 1966)

Piri Thomas decided to avoid trouble for a while, but commented on the difficulty in doing this:

The decision to cool myself made the next two years the hardest I had done because it meant being a smoothie and staying out of trouble, which in prison is difficult, for any of a thousand cons might start trouble with you for any real or fancied reason, and if you didn't face up to the trouble, you ran the risk of being branded as having no heart. And heart was all I had left.[5]

However, except for rare, "abnormal" incidents, convicts tend not to bother others who are "doing their own number." One convict made the following comments on avoiding trouble in prison:

If a new guy comes here and just settles down and minds his business, nobody'll fuck with him, unless he runs into some nut. Everyone sees a guy is trying to do his own time and they leave him alone. Those guys that get messed over are usually asking for it. If you stay away from the lowriders and the punks and don't get into debt or snitch on somebody you won't have no trouble here. (Interview, San Quentin, July 1966)

To occupy their time, "time-doers" work, read, work on hobbies, play cards, chess, and dominoes, engage in sports, go to movies, watch TV, participate in some group activities, such as drama groups, gavel clubs, and slot car clubs, and while away hours "tripping" with friends. They seek extra luxuries through their job. Certain jobs in prison, such as jobs in the kitchen, in the officers' and guards' dining room, in the boiler room, the officers' and guards' barber shop, and the fire house, offer various luxuries—extra things to eat, a radio, privacy, additional shows, and more freedom. Or time-doers purchase luxuries legally or illegally available in the prison market. If they have money on the books, if they have a job which pays a small salary, or if they earn money at a hobby, they can draw up to twenty dollars a month which may be spent for foodstuffs, coffee, cocoa, stationery, toiletries, tobacco, and cigarettes. Or using cigarettes as currency they may purchase food from the kitchen, drugs, books, cell furnishings, clothes, hot plates, stingers, and other contraband items. If they do not have legal access to funds, they may "scuffle"; that is, sell some commodity which they produce—such as belt buckles or other handicraft items—or some commodity which is accesible to them through their job—such as food items from the kitchen. "Scuffling," however, necessitates becoming enmeshed in the convict social system and increases the chances of "trouble," such as conflicts over unpaid debts, hijacking by others, and "beefs"—disciplinary actions for rule infractions. Getting into trouble is contrary to the basic tenets of "doing time," so time-doers usually avoid scuffling.

The friendships formed by time-doers vary from casual acquaintanceships with persons who accidentally cell nearby or work together, to close friendship groups who "go all the way" for each other—share material goods, defend each other against others, and maintain silence about each other's activities. These varying friendship patterns are related closely to their criminal identities.

Finally, time-doers try to get out as soon as possible. First they do this by staying out of trouble, "cleaning up their hands." They avoid activities and persons that would put them in danger of receiving disciplinary actions, or "beefs." And in recent years with the increasing emphasis on treatment, they "program." To program is to follow, at least tokenly, a treatment plan which has been outlined by the treatment staff, recommended by the board, or devised by the convict himself. It is generally believed that to be released on parole as early as possible one must "get a program." A program involves attending school, vocational training, group counseling, church, Alcoholics Anonymous, or any other special program that is introduced under the treatment policy of the prison.

All convicts are more apt to choose "doing time," but some approach this style in a slightly different manner. For instance, doing time is characteristic of the thief in prison. He shapes this mode of adaptation and establishes it as a major mode of adaptation in prison. The convict code, which is fashioned from the criminal code, is the foundation for this style. The thief has learned how to do his time long before he comes to prison. Prison, he learns when he takes on the dimensions of the criminal subculture, is part of criminal life, a calculated risk, and when it comes he is ready for it.

> Long before the thief has come to prison, his subculture has defined proper prison conduct as behavior rationally calculated to "do time" in the easiest possible way. This means that he wants a prison life containing the best possible combination of a maximum amount of leisure time and maximum number of privileges. Accordingly, the privileges sought by the thief are different from the privileges sought by the man oriented to prison itself. The thief wants things that will make prison life a little easier—extra food, a maximum amount of recreation time, a good radio, a little peace.[6]

The thief knows how to avoid trouble; he keeps away from "dingbats," "lowriders," "hoosiers," "square johns," and "stool pigeons," and obeys the convict code. He also knows not to buck the authorities; he keeps his record clean and does what is necessary to get out—even programs.

He occasionally forms friendships with other criminals, such as dope fiends, heads, and possibly disorganized criminals, but less often with square johns. Formerly he confined his friendship to other thieves with whom he formed very tight-knit groups. For example Jack Black, a thief in the last century, describes his assimilation into the "Johnson family" in prison:

> Shorty was one of the patricians of the prison, a "box man," doing time for bank burglary. "I'll put you in with the right people, kid. You're folks yourself or you wouldn't have been with Smiler."
>
> I had no friends in the place. But the fact that I had been with Smiler, that I had kept my mouth shut, and that Shorty had come forward to help me, gave me a certain fixed status in the prison that nothing could shake but some act of my own. I was naturally pleased to find myself taken up by the "best people," as Shorty and his friends called themselves, and accepted as one of them.
>
> Shorty now took me into the prison where we found the head trusty who was one of the "best people" himself, a thoroughgoing bum from the road. The term "bum" is not used here in any cheap or disparaging sense. In those days it meant any kind of a traveling thief. It has long since fallen into disuse. The yegg of today was the bum of twenty years ago.
>
> "This party," said Shorty, "is one of the 'Johnson' family." (The bums called themselves "Johnsons" probably because they were so numerous.) "He's good people and I want to get him fixed up for a cell with the right folks."[7]

Clemmer described two *primary* groups out of the fourteen groups he located, and both of these were groups of thieves.[8]

Presently in California prisons thieves' numbers have diminished. This and the general loosening of the convict solidarity have tended to drive the thief into the background of prison life. He generally confines his friendships to one or two others, usually other thieves or criminals who are "all right"; otherwise he withdraws from participation with others. He often feels out of place amid the changes that have come about. One thief looking back upon fifteen years in California prisons states:

> As far as I'm concerned their main purpose has been in taking the convict code away from him. But what they fail to do is when they strip him from these rules is replace it with something. They turn these guys into a bunch of snivelers and they write letters on each other and they don't have any rules to live by. (Interview, Folsom Prison, July 1966)

Another thief interviewed also indicated his dislocation in the present prison social world:

> The new kinds in prison are wild. They have no respect for rules or other persons. I just want to get out of here and give it all up. I can't take coming back to prison again, not with the kind of convicts they are getting now. (Interview, Soledad Prison, June 1966)

Like the majority of convicts, the dope fiend and the head usually just "do time." When they do, they don't vary greatly from the thief, except that they tend to associate with other dope fiends or heads, although they too will associate with other criminals. They tend to form very close bonds with one, two, or three other dope fiends or heads and maintain a casual friendship with a large circle of dope fiends, heads, and other criminals. Like the thief, the dope fiend and the head tend not to establish ties with squares.

The hustler in doing time differs from the other criminals in that he does not show a propensity to form very tight-knit groups. Hustling values, which emphasize manipulation and invidiousness, seem to prevent this. The hustler maintains a very large group of casual friends. Though this group does not show strong bonds of loyalty and mutual aid, they share many activities such as cards, sports, dominoes, and "jiving"—casual talk.

Square johns do their time quite differently than the criminals. The square john finds life in prison repugnant and tries to isolate himself as much as possible from the convict world. He does not believe in the convict code, but he usually learns to display a token commitment to it for his own safety. A square john indicated his forced obedience to the convict code:

> Several times I saw things going on that I didn't like. One time a couple of guys were working over another guy and I wanted to step in, but I couldn't. Had to just keep moving as if I didn't see it. (Interview, Soledad Prison, June 1966)

He usually keeps busy with some job assignment, a hobby, cards, chess, or various forms of group programs, such as drama groups. He forms friendships with one or two other squares and avoids the criminals. But even with other squares there is resistance to forming *close* ties. Square johns are very often sensitive about their "problems," and they are apt to feel repugnance toward themselves and other persons with problems. Besides, the square usually wants to be accepted by conventional people and not by other "stigmatized" outcasts like himself. So, many square johns do their time isolated from other inmates. Malcolm Braly in his novel *On the Yard* has captured the ideal-typical square john in prison:

> Watson had finally spoken. Formerly a mild-mannered and mother-smothered high school teacher, he had killed his two small sons, attempted to kill his wife, cut his own throat, then poisoned himself, all because his wife had refused a reconciliation with the remark, "John, the truth is you bore me."
>
> Watson stood with culture, the Republic, and motherhood, and at least once each meeting he made a point of reaffirming his position before launching into his chronic criticism of the manner in which his own case had been, was and

would be handled. " . . . and I've been confined almost two years now and I see no point in further imprisonment, further therapy, no point whatsoever since there's absolutely no possibility I'll do the same thing again . . ."

"That's right," Red said softly. "He's run out of kids."

And Zeke whispered, "I just wish he'd taken the poison *before* he cut his throat."

Watson ignored the whispering, if he heard it at all, and went on, clearly speaking only to Erlenmeyer. "Surely, Doctor, as a college man yourself you must realize that the opportunities for a meaningful cultural exchange are sorely limited in an institution of this nature. Of course, I attend the General Semantics Club and I'm taking the course Oral McKeon is giving in Oriental religions, but these are such tiny oases in this desert of sweatsuits and domino games, and I can't understand why everyone is just thrown together without reference to their backgrounds, or the nature of their offense. Thieves, dope addicts, even sex maniacs—"

Zeke threw his hands up in mock alarm. "Where'd you see a sex maniac?"

"I don't think it cause for facetiousness," Watson said coldly. "Just yesterday I found occasion to step into the toilet off the big yard and one of the sweepers was standing there masturbating into the urinal."

"That's horrible," Zeke said. "What'd you do?"

"I left, of course."

"Naturally. It violates the basic ideals of Scouting."[9]

The lower-class man, though he doesn't share the square john's repugnance towards criminals or the convict code, usually does not wish to associate closely with thieves, dope fiends, heads, and disorganized criminals. In his life outside he has encountered and avoided these persons for many years and usually keeps on avoiding them inside. He usually seeks a job to occupy himself. His actual stay in prison is typically very short, since he is either released very early and/or he is classified at minimum custody and sent to a forestry camp or one of the minimum-custody institutions, where he has increased freedom and privileges.

Jailing

Some convicts who do not retain or who never acquired any commitment to outside social worlds, tend to make a world out of prison.[10] These are the men who

seek positions of power, influence and sources of information, whether these men are called "shots," "politicians," "merchants," "hoods," "toughs," "gorillas," or something else. A job as secretary to the Captain or Warden, for example, gives an aspiring prisoner information and consequent power, and enables him to influence the assignment or regulation of other inmates. In the same way, a job which allows the incumbent to participate in a racket, such as clerk in the kitchen storeroom where he can steal and sell food, is highly desirable to a man oriented to the convict subculture. With a steady income of cigarettes, ordinarily the prisoner's medium of exchange, he may assert a great deal of influence and purchase those things which are symbols of status among persons oriented to the convict subculture. Even if there is not a well-developed medium of exchange, he can barter goods acquired in his position for equally-desirable goods possessed by other convicts. These include information and such things as specially-starched, pressed, and tailored prison clothing, fancy belts, belt buckles or billfolds, special shoes, or any other type of dress which will set him apart and will indicate that he has both the influence to get the goods and the influence necessary to keep them and display them despite prison rules which outlaw doing so. In California, special items of clothing, and clothing that is neatly laundered, are called "bonaroos" (a corruption of *bonnet rouge,* by means of which French prison trustees were once distinguished from the common run of prisoners), and to a lesser degree even the persons who wear such clothing are called "bonaroos."[11]

Just as doing time is the characteristic style of the thief, so "jailing" is the characteristic style of the state-raised youth. This identity terminates on the first or second prison term, or certainly by the time the youth reaches thirty. The state-raised youth must assume a new identity, and the one he most often chooses, the one which his experience has prepared him for, is that of the "convict." The prison world is the only world with which he is familiar. He was raised in a world where "punks" and "queens" have replaced women, "bonaroos" are the only fashionable clothing, and cigarettes are money. This is a world where disputes are settled with a pipe or a knife, and the individual must form tight cliques for protection. His senses are attuned to iron doors banging, locks turning, shakedowns, and long lines of blue-clad convicts. He knows how to survive, in fact prosper, in this world, how to get a cell change and a good work assignment, how to score for nutmeg, cough syrup, or other narcotics. More important, he knows hundreds of youths like himself who grew up in the youth prisons and are now in the adult prisons. For example, Claude Brown describes a friend who fell into the patterns of jailing:

"Yeah, Sonny. The time I did in Woodburn, the times I did on the Rock, that was college, man. Believe me, it was college. I did four years in Woodburn. And I guess I've done a total of about two years on the Rock in about the last six years. Every time I went there, I learned a little more. When I go to jail now, Sonny, I live, man. I'm right at home. That's the good part about it. If you look at it, Sonny, a cat like me is just cut out to be in jail.

"It could never hurt me, 'cause I never had what the good folks call a home and all that kind of shit to begin with. So when I went to jail, the first time I went away, when I went to Warwick, I made my own home. It was all right. Shit, I learned how to live. Now when I go back to the joint, anywhere I go, I know some people. If I go to any of the jails in New York, or if I go to a slam in Jersey, even, I still run into a lot of cats I know. It's almost like a family."

I said, "Yeah, Reno, it's good that a cat can be so happy in jail. I guess all it takes to be happy in anything is knowin' how to walk with your lot, whatever it is, in life."[12]

The state-raised youth often assumes a role in the prison social system, the system of roles, values, and norms described by Schrag, Sykes, and others. This does not mean that he immediately rises to power in the prison system. Some of the convicts have occupied their positions for many years and cannot tolerate the threat of every new bunch of reform-school graduates. The state-raised youth who has just graduated to adult prison must start at the bottom; but he knows the routine, and in a year or so he occupies a key position himself. One reason he can readily rise is that in youth prison he very often develops skills, such as clerical and maintenance skills, that are valuable to the prison administration.

Many state-raised youths, however, do not tolerate the slow ascent in the prison social system and become "lowriders." They form small cliques and rob cells, hijack other convicts, carry on feuds with other cliques, and engage in various rackets. Though these "outlaws" are feared and hated by all other convicts, their orientation is to the convict world, and they are definitely part of the convict social system.

Dope fiends and hustlers slip into jailing more often than thieves, due mainly to the congruities between their old activities and some of the patterns of jailing. For instance, a central activity of jailing is "wheeling and dealing," the major economic activity of prison. All prison resources—dope, food, books, money, sexual favors, bonaroos, cell changes, jobs, dental and hospital care, hot plates, stingers, cell furnishings, rings, and buckles—are always available for purchase with cigarettes. It is possible to live in varying degrees of luxury, and luxury has a double reward in prison as it does in the outside society: first, there is the reward of consumption itself, and second there is the reward of increased prestige in the prison social system because of the display of opulence.

This prison life style requires more cigarettes than can be obtained legally; consequently, one wheels and deals. There are three main forms of wheeling and dealing for cigarettes: (1) gambling (cards, dice and betting on sporting events); (2) selling some commodity or service, which is usually made possible by a particular job assignment; and (3) lending cigarettes for interest—two for three. These activities have a familiar ring to both the hustler and the dope fiend, who have hustled money or dope on the outside. They very often become intricately involved in the prison economic life and in this way necessarily involved in the prison social system. The hustler does this because he feels at home in this routine, because he wants to keep in practice, or because he must present a good front—even in prison. To present a good front one must be a success at wheeling and dealing.

The dope fiend, in addition to having an affinity for wheeling and dealing, may become involved in the prison economic life in securing drugs. There are a variety of drugs available for purchase with cigarettes or money (and money can be purchased with cigarettes). Drugs are expensive, however, and to purchase them with any regularity one either has money smuggled in from the outside or he wheels and deals. And to wheel and deal one must maintain connections for securing drugs, for earning money, and for protection. This enmeshes the individual in the system of prison roles, values, and norms. Though he maintains a basic commitment to his drug subculture which supersedes his commitment to the prison culture and though he tends to form close ties only with other dope fiends, through his wheeling and dealing for drugs he becomes an intricate part of the prison social system.

The head jails more often than the thief. One reason for this is that the head, especially the "weed head" tends to worship luxuries and comforts and is fastidious in his dress. Obtaining small luxuries, comforts, and "bonaroo" clothing usually necessitates enmeshing himself in the "convict" system. Furthermore, the head is often vulnerable to the dynamics of narrow, cliquish, and invidious social systems, such as the "convict" system, because many of the outside head social systems are of this type.

The thief, or any identity for that matter, *may* slowly lose his orientation to the outside community, take on the convict categories, and thereby fall into jailing. This occurs when the individual has spent a great deal of time in prison and/or returned to the outside community and discovered that he no longer fits in the outside world. It is difficult to maintain a real commitment to a social world without firsthand experience with it for long periods of time.

The square john and the lower-class man find the activities of the "convicts" petty, repugnant, or dangerous, and virtually never jail.

Gleaning

With the rapidly growing educational, vocational training, and treatment opportunities, and with the erosion of convict solidarity, an increasing number of convicts choose to radically change their life styles and follow a sometimes carefully devised plan to "better themselves," "improve their mind," or "find themselves" while in prison.[13] One convict describes his motives and plans for changing his life style:

> I got tired of losing. I had been losing all my life. I decided that I wanted to win for a while. So I got on a different kick. I knew that I had to learn something so I went to school, got my high school diploma. I cut myself off from my old YA buddies and started hanging around with some intelligent guys who minded their own business. We read a lot, a couple of us paint. We play a little bridge and talk, a lot of time about what we are going to do when we get out. (Interview, Soledad Prison, June 1966)

Gleaning may start on a small scale, perhaps as an attempt to overcome educational or intellectual inferiorities. For instance, Malcolm X, feeling inadequate in talking to certain convicts, starts to read:

> It had really begun back in the Charlestown Prison, when Bimbi first made me feel envy of his stock of knowledge. Bimbi had always taken charge of any conversation he was in, and I had tried to emulate him. But every book I picked up had few sentences which didn't contain anywhere from one to nearly all of the words that might as well have been in Chinese. When I just skipped those words, of course, I really ended up with little idea of what the book said. So I have come to the Norfolk Prison Colony still going through only book-reading motions. Pretty soon, I would have quit even these motions, unless I had received the motivation that I did.[14]

The initial, perfunctory steps into gleaning often spring the trap. Gleaning activities have an intrinsic attraction and often instill motivation which was originally lacking. Malcolm X reports how once he began to read, the world of knowledge opened up to him:

> No university would ask any student to devour literature as I did when this new world opened to me, of being able to read and *understand*.[15]

In trying to "improve himself," "improve his mind," or "find himself," the convict gleans from every source available in prison. The chief source is books: he reads philosophy, history, art, science, and fiction. Often after getting started he devours a sizable portion of world literature. Malcom X describes his voracious reading habits:

> I read more in my room than in the library itself. An inmate who was known to read a lot could check out more than the permitted maximum number of books. I preferred reading in the total isolation of my own room.
> When I had progressed to really serious reading, every night at about ten P.M. I would be outraged with the "lights out." It always seemed to catch me right in the middle of something engrossing.

Fortunately, right outside my door was a corridor light that cast a glow into my room. The glow was enough to read by, once my eyes adjusted to it. So when "lights out" came, I would sit on the floor where I could continue reading in that glow.[16]

Besides this informal education, he often pursues formal education. The convict may complete grammar school and high school in the prison educational facilities. He may enroll in college courses through University of California (which will be paid for by the Department of Corrections), or through other correspondence schools (which he must pay for himself). More recently, he may take courses in various prison college programs.

He learns trades through the vocational training programs or prison job assignments. Sometimes he augments these by studying trade books, correspondence courses, or journals. He studies painting, writing, music, acting, and other creative arts. There are some facilities for these pursuits sponsored by the prison administration, but these are limited. This type of gleaning is done mostly through correspondence, through reading, or through individual efforts in the cell.

He tries to improve himself in other ways. He works on his social skills and his physical appearance—has his tattoos removed, has surgery on physical defects, has dental work done, and builds up his body "pushing iron."

He shys away from former friends or persons with his criminal identity who are not gleaners and forms new associations with other gleaners. These are usually gleaners who have chosen a similar style of gleaning, and with whom he shares many interests and activities, but they may also be those who are generally trying to improve themselves, although they are doing so in different ways.

Gleaning is a style more characteristic of the hustler, the dope fiend, and the state-raised youth than of the thief. When the former glean, though they tend to associate less with their deviant friends who are doing time or jailing, they are not out of the influence of these groups, or free from the influence of their old subculture values. The style of gleaning they choose and the future life for which they prepare themselves must be acceptable to the old reference group and somewhat congruent with their deviant values. The life they prepare for should be prestigious in the eyes of their old associates. It must be "doing good" and cannot be "a slave's life."

The state-raised youth who gleans probably has the greatest difficulty cutting himself off from his former group because the state-raised values emphasize loyalty to one's buddies:

I don't spend much time with my old YA [Youth Authority] partners and when I do we don't get along. They want me to do something that I won't do or they start getting on my back about my plans. One time they were riding me pretty bad and I had to pull them up. (Interview, Soledad Prison, June 1966)

He also has the greatest difficulty in making any realistic plans for the future. He has limited experience with the outside, and his models of "making it" usually come from the mass media—magazines, books, movies, and TV.

The dope fiend and the head, when they glean, tend to avoid practical fields and choose styles which promise glamor, excitement, or color. Most conventional paths with which they are familiar seem especially dull and repugnant. In exploring ways of making it they must find some way to avoid the humdrum life which they rejected long ago. Many turn to legitimate deviant identities such as "intellectual outsiders," "bohemians," or "mystics." Often they study one of the creative arts, the social sciences, or philosophy with no particular career in mind.

The hustler, who values skills of articulation and maintained a good "front" in his deviant life, often prepares for a field where these skills will serve him, such as preaching or political activism.

The square john and the lower-class man, since they seldom seek to radically change their identity, do not glean in the true sense, but they do often seek to improve themselves. The square john usually does this by attacking his problem. He is satisfied with his reference world—the conventional society—but he recognizes that to return to it successfully he must cope with that flaw in his makeup which led to his incarceration. There are three common ways he attacks this problem: (1) he joins self help groups such as Alcoholics Anonymous, (2) he seeks the help of experts (psychiatrists, psychologists or sociologists) and attends the therapy programs, or (3) he turns to religion.

The lower-class man is usually an older person who does not desire or deem it possible to carve out a radically new style of life. He may, however, see the prison experience as a chance to improve himself by increasing his education and his vocational skills.

The thief tends to be older and his commitment to his identity is usually strong, so it is not likely that he will explore other life styles or identities. This does not mean that he is committed for all time to a life of crime. Certain alternate conclusions to a criminal career are included in the definitions of a proper thief's life. For instance, a thief may retire when he becomes older, has served a great deal of time, or has made a "nice score." When he retires he may work at some well-paying trade or run a small business, and in prison he may prepare himself for either of these acceptable conclusions to a criminal career.

DISORGANIZED CRIMINAL

In the preceding discussion of prison adaptive modes, the "disorganized criminal" was purposely omitted. It is felt that his prison adaptation must be considered separately from the other identities.

The disorganized criminal is human putty in the prison social world. He may be shaped to fit any category. He has weaker commitments to values or conceptions of self that would prevent him from organizing any course of action in prison. He is the most responsive to prison programs, to differential association, and to other forces which are out of his control. He may become part of the prison social system, do his time, or glean. If they will tolerate him, he may associate with thieves, dope fiends, convicts, squares, heads, or other disorganized criminals. To some extent these associations are formed in a random fashion. He befriends persons with whom he works, cells next to, and encounters regularly through the prison routine. He tends not to seek out particular categories, as is the case with the other identities. He does not feel any restraints in initiating associations, however, as do the square john and the lower-class man.

The friendships he forms are very important to any changes that occur in this person. Since he tends to have a cleaner slate in terms of identity, he is more susceptible to differential association. He often takes on the identity and the prison adaptive mode of the group with which he comes into contact. If he does acquire a new identity, however, such as one of the deviant identities that exist in prison, his commitment to it is still tentative at most. The deviant identities, except for that of the convict, exist in the context of an exterior world, and the more subtle cues, the responses, the meanings which are essential parts of this world cannot be experienced in prison. It is doubtful, therefore, that any durable commitment could be acquired in prison. In the meantime, he may be shaken from this identity, and he may continue to vacillate from social world to social world, or to wander bewildered in a maze of conflicting world views as he has done in the past.

RACE AND ETHNICITY

Another variable which is becoming increasingly important in the formation of cleavages and identity changes in the convict world is that of race and ethnicity. For quite some time in California prisons, hostility and distance between three segments of the populations—white, Negroes and Mexicans—have increased. For several years the Negroes have assumed a more militant and ethnocentric posture, and recently the Mexicans—already ethnocentric and aggressive—have followed with a more organized, militant stance. Correspondingly, there is a growing trend among these two segments to establish, reestablish or enhance racial-ethnic pride and identity. Many "Blacks" and "Chicanos" are supplanting their criminal identity with a racial-ethnic one. This movement started with the Blacks.[17] A black California convict gives his recently acquired views toward whites:

> All these years, man, I been stealing and coming to the joint. I never stopped to think why I was doing it. I thought that all I wanted was money and stuff. Ya know, man, now I can see why I thought the way I did. I been getting fucked all my life and never realized it. The white man has been telling me that I should want his stuff. But he didn't give me no way to get it. Now I ain't going for his shit anymore. I'm a Black man. I'm going to get out of here and see what I can do for my people. I'm going to do what I have to do to get those white motherfuckers off my people's back. (Interview, San Quentin, March 1968)

Chicanos in prison have maintained considerable insulation from both whites and Blacks—especially Blacks—towards whom they have harbored considerable hostility. They possess a strong ethnic-racial identity which underpins their more specialized felonious one—which has usually been that of a dope fiend or lower-class man. This subcultural identity and actual group unity in prison has been based on their Mexican culture— especially two important dimensions of Mexican culture. The first is their strong commitment to the concept of "machismo"—which is roughly translated manhood. The second is their use of Spanish and Calo (Spanish slang) which has separated them from other segments. Besides these two traits there are many other ethnic subcultural characteristics which promote unity among Chicanos. For instance, they tend to be stoic and intolerant of "snitches" and "snivelers" and feel that Anglos and Blacks are more often snitches and snivelers. Furthermore they respect friendship to the extreme, in fact to the extreme of killing or dying for friendship.

Until recently this has meant that Chicanos constituted the most cohesive segment in California prisons. In prison, where they intermingle with whites and Negroes, they have felt considerable distance from these segments and have maintained their identification with Mexican culture. However, there have been and still are some divisions in this broad category. For instance, various neighborhood cliques of Chicanos often carry on violent disputes with each other which last for years. Furthermore, Los Angeles or California cliques wage disputes with El Paso or

Texas cliques. Many stabbings and killings have resulted from confrontations between different Chicano groups. Nevertheless, underpinning these different group affiliations and the various criminal identities there has been a strong identification with Mexican culture.

Recently the Chicanos, following the footsteps of the Negroes in prison and the footsteps of certain militant Mexican-American groups outside (e.g., MAPA and the Delano strikers) have started organizing cultural-activist groups in prison (such as Empleo) and shaping a new identity built upon their Mexican ancestry and their position of disadvantage in the white society. As they move in this direction they are cultivating some friendship with the Negroes, towards whom they now feel more affinity.

This racial-ethnic militance and identification will more than likely become increasingly important in the prison social world. There is already some indication that the identity of the Black National and that of the Chicano is becoming superordinate to the criminal identities of many Negroes and Mexican-Americans or at least is having an impact on their criminal identities.

> A dude don't necessarily have to become a Muslim or a Black National now to get with Black Power. He may still be laying to get out there and do some pimping or shoot some dope. But he knows he's a brother and when the shit is down we can count on him. And maybe he is going to carry himself a little differently, you know, like now you see more and more dudes—oh, they're still pimps, but they got naturals now. (Interview, San Quentin, April 1968)

The reassertion or discovery of the racial-ethnic identity is sometimes related to gleaning in prison. Frequently, the leaders of Blacks or Chicanos, for example, Malcolm X and Eldridge Cleaver, have arrived at their subcultural activism and militant stance through gleaning. Often, becoming identified with this movement will precipitate a gleaning course. However, this is not necessarily the case. These two phenomena are not completely overlapping among the Negro and Chicano.

The nationalistic movement is beginning to have a general impact on the total prison world—especially at San Quentin. The Blacks and Chicanos, as they focus on the whites as their oppressors, seem to be excluding white prisoners from this category and are, in fact, developing some sympathy for them as a minority group which itself is being oppressed by the white establishment and the white police. As an indication of this recent change, one convict comments on the present food-serving practices of Muslim convicts:

> It used to be that whenever a Muslim was serving something (and this was a lot of the time man, because there's a lot of those dudes in the kitchen), well, you

know, you wouldn't expect to get much of a serving. Now, the cats just pile it on to whites and blacks. Like he is giving all the state's stuff away to show his contempt. So I think it is getting better between the suedes and us. (Interview, San Quentin, April 1968)

THE CONVICT IDENTITY

Over and beyond the particular criminal identity or the racial-ethnic identity he acquires or maintains in prison and over and beyond the changes in his direction which are produced by his prison strategy, to some degree the felon acquires the perspective of the "convict."

There are several gradations and levels of this perspective and attendant identity. First is the taken-for-granted perspective, which he acquires in spite of any conscious efforts to avoid it. This perspective is acquired simply by being in prison and engaging in prison routines for months or years. Even square johns who consciously attempt to pass through the prison experience without acquiring any of the beliefs and values of the criminals, do to some extent acquire certain meanings, certain taken-for-granted interpretations and responses which will shape, influence, or distort reality for them after release.

Beyond the taken-for-granted perspective which all convicts acquire, most convicts are influenced by a pervasive but rather uncohesive convict "code." To some extent most of them, especially those who identify with a criminal system, are consciously committed to the major dictum of this code—"do your own time." As was pointed out earlier, the basic meaning of this precept is the obligation to tolerate the behavior of others unless it is directly affecting your physical self or your possessions. If another's behavior surpasses these limits, then the problem must be solved by the person himself; that is, *not* by calling for help from the officials.

The convict code isn't any different than stuff we all learned as kids. You know, nobody likes a stool pigeon. Well, here in the joint you got all kinds of guys living jammed together, two to a cell. You got nuts walking the yard, you got every kind of dingbat in the world here. Well, we got to have some rules among ourselves. The rule is "do your own number." In other words, keep off your neighbors' toes. Like if a guy next to me is making brew in his cell, well, this is none of my business. I got no business running to the man and telling him that Joe Blow is making brew in his cell. Unless Joe Blow is fucking over me, then I can't say nothing. And when he is fucking over me, then I got to stop him myself. If I can't then I deserve to get fucked over. (Interview, San Quentin, May 1968)

Commitment to the convict code or the identity of the convict is to a high degree a lifetime commitment to do your own time; that is, to live and let live, and when you feel that someone is not letting you live, to either take it, leave, or stop him yourself, but never call for help from official agencies of control.

At another level, the convict perspective consists of a more cohesive and sophisticated value and belief system. This is the perspective of the elite of the convict world—the "regular." A "regular" (or, as he has been variously called, "people," "folks," "solid," a "right guy," or "all right") possesses many of the traits of the thief's culture. He can be counted on when needed by other regulars. He is also not a "hoosier"; that is, he has some finesse, is capable, is levelheaded, has "guts" and "timing." The following description of a simple bungled transaction exemplifies this trait:

> Man, you should have seen the hoosier when the play came down. I thought that that motherfucker was all right. He surprised me. He had the stuff and was about to hand it to me when a sergeant and another bull came through the door from the outside. Well, there wasn't nothing to worry about. Is all he had to do was go on like there was nothin' unusual and hand me the stuff and they would have never suspected nothing. But he got so fucking nervous and started fumbling around. You know, he handed me the sack and then pulled it back until they got hip that some play was taking place. Well you know what happened. The play was ranked and we both ended up in the slammer. (Field notes, San Quentin, February 1968)

The final level of the perspective of the convict is that of the "old con." This is a degree of identification reached after serving a great deal of time, so much time that all outside-based identities have dissipated and the only meaningful world is that of the prison. The old con has become totally immersed in the prison world. This identification is often the result of years of jailing, but it can result from merely serving too much time. It was mentioned previously that even thieves after spending many years may fall into jailing, even though time-doing is their usual pattern. After serving a very long sentence or several long sentences with no extended period between, any criminal will tend to take on the identity of the "old con."

The old con tends to carve out a narrow but orderly existence in prison. He has learned to secure many luxuries and learned to be satisfied with the prison forms of pleasure—e.g., homosexual activities, cards, dominoes, handball, hobbies, and reading. He usually obtains jobs which afford him considerable privileges and leisure time. He often knows many of the prison administrators—the warden, the associate wardens, the captain, and the lieutenants, whom he has known since they were officers and lesser officials.

Often he becomes less active in the prison social world. He retires and becomes relatively docile or apathetic. At times he grows petty and treacherous. There is some feeling that old cons can't be trusted because their "head has become soft" or they have "lost their guts," and are potential "stool pigeons."

The convict identity is very important to the future career of the felon. In the first instance, the acquiring of the taken-for-granted perspective will at least obstruct the releasee's attempts to reorient himself on the outside. More important, the other levels of the identity, if they have been acquired, will continue to influence choices for years afterward. The convict perspective, though it may become submerged after extended outside experiences, will remain operative in its latency state and will often obtrude into civilian life contexts.

The identity of the old con—the perspective, the values and beliefs, and other personality attributes which are acquired after the years of doing time, such as advanced age, adjustment to prison routines, and complete loss of skills required to carry on the normal activities of civilians—will usually make living on the outside impossible. The old con is very often suited for nothing except dereliction on the outside or death in prison.

12 Sociology of Confinement: Assimilation and the Prison "Rat"

ELMER H. JOHNSON*

Through physical and social psychological isolation from free society, confinement creates a prison community which requires the new inmate to adjust to unfamiliar traditions, values, and social relationships. The role of prisoner "rat" can be seen as a product of this assimilative process.

This paper is based on a study of fifty inmates denounced by fellow prisoners as "rats" during the years 1958 and 1959 in a state-wide prisoner population averaging 11,000. These fifty were referred to the Central Classification Committee, the "supreme court" of the state-wide classification system, on the basis of an official's description of the case as one involving actual threats to the inmate.

The "rat" usually is seen as a turncoat against the inmate code who exchanges information for personal advantages. Although this definition covers the majority of "rats," it does not include all situations blanketed under the empirical use of the term by inmates. The communication of information to officials is not the only prohibited behavior which qualifies an inmate as a "rat" in the eyes of his peers. For example, refusal to join in action against officials can have similar effect.

There is the further problem that the inmate definition of a fellow as a "rat" involves more than the simple matter of prohibited behavior by the subject. Sometimes the informer is not labelled as a "rat." Sometimes, the non-informer is labelled a "rat" even though accusers concede his innocence. Part of the answer to this apparent inconsistency lies in the

* From *Journal of Criminal Law, Criminology and Police Science* 51, 5 (1961): 528–533. Reprinted by permission of author and publisher.

193

relationship between the personal characteristics of the subject inmate
and the social expectations of his peers.

These characteristics are involved in two ways. First, they function in
a manner similar to victim proneness wherein certain individuals uncon-
sciously invite theft, rape, and other crimes against themselves. [18] The
sociology of confinement creates a climate of inmate suspicion whereby
the possession of certain personal characteristics deviating from inmate
expectations render an inmate prone to being judged a "rat." These
characteristics range from middle class qualities similar to those of certain
prison employees to qualities of the dependent personality vulnerable to
pressure of others, including officials. On the other hand, other inmates
are able to preserve links with officials without alienating fellow prisoners
because their overt behavior and personal characteristics coincide with
inmate expectations. Secondly, the personal characteristics of the subject
inmate affect the quality of his response to the experience of being
assigned the "rat" role.

Obviously, the "rat" serves the prison's formal organization as a
communication link with the inmate informal groups. Moreover, as a
target for aggression, he serves two major functions for the inmate
informal groups. First, the aggression integrates these groups by drama-
tizing loyalty to their code, by dissuading potential transgressors through
demonstration of the power of inmate sanctions, and by strengthening
in-group ties through opposition to an enemy previously within the
group. Secondly, the "rat" serves as a "drain" for "free-floating" aggression of prisoners stemming from the restraints and social deprivations of
regimented confinement. This is similar to the process of "displacement"
described by Allport. [19] The "rat" is a substitute target for releasing
pent-up tensions.

The "rat" is particularly useful for these purposes because prison
officials are uncertain in their attitude toward him. In fact, the officials
share some of the distaste for the traitorous member of the opposition,
even when he asserts loyalty to the officials' own values. His dependability
and reliability as an ally are questioned, but the possibility should not be
ignored that the official finds the "rat" a useful target for his own hostility
and irritation arising from the effects of the sociology of confinement on
the keeper.

The aggressive prisoner uses the "rat" to vent hostilities in a manner
drawing at least tacit approval of his peers and unlikely to invite
retaliation from officials if institutional order is preserved. Thus, the
extremely anti-social prisoner can enjoy the role of inmate champion,
rather than the penalties given the self-seeker, if his aggression is directed
against the "rat."

The "rat" is defined by inmates in terms of his non-assimilability within the prisoner groups according to inmate norms. A prisoner's assimilability involves his acceptability by the inmates and his acceptance, at least overtly, of the values and traditions of the inmate informal groups. Therefore, "assimilation" as a concept is appropriate at this discussion.

ASSIMILATION AND THE "RAT"

Clemmer uses the concept in the sense of a more or less unconscious process during which a person, or group of persons, learns enough of the culture of a social unit in which he is placed to make him characteristic of that unit. He presents "prisonization" as an adaptation of this concept to the taking on by the inmate "in a greater or less degree of the folkways, mores, customs and general culture of the penitentiary." He describes the general patterns of many newcomers' integration into prison life from initial external accommodation toward internalized assimilation of the values and attitudes characteristic of the prisoner culture.[20]

The effects of confinement press the newcomer toward affiliation with prisoner culture. Confinement subjects him to a repressive environment wherein protection of free society and maintanance of institutional order take precedence over his individualized goals. Confinement involves the compulsory nature of his admission to this abnormal community, the restriction on his spacial mobility, and assignment to him of a subordinate and restricted social role. Inmates share the experience of rejection by outside society, with its consequential feelings of guilt, remorse, resentment, or hostility.[21]

Sharing with other inmates the experiences of confinement, the newcomer is encouraged to affiliate with informal, congeniality groups of prisoners bound by conduct codes, a communication system, and a structure defining rights and obligations. Through the emotional support of colleagues sharing the feelings of rejection and repression, the affiliation promises him a degree of protection against the blocking by official restrictions of his immediate wish-fulfillment. It appears reasonable to assume that a high proportion of the new prisoners enter this group life. Clemmer estimates some sixty per cent do so.

A clue to the nature of this group life lies in the characteristics of its leaders. Schrag found them to have served more years in prison, to have longer sentences remaining, to be more frequently charged with violent crimes, to be more likely to have been diagnosed officially as homosexual, psychoneurotic, or psychopathic, and to have had a significantly greater number of serious rule infractions.[22] It would appear that the preferred personality characteristics stem from values emphasizing reaction against authority and presumed competency in various deviancy roles. However, beyond such values personified by preferred behavioral and personality models, Clemmer has noted that the inmate leader must have a reputation for reliable action according to prisoner values and must be "right." The latter was defined as "being faithful, trustworthy; opposed to tale bearing or 'snitching.'"[23]

Inmate groups define the "rat" for ostracism, and perhaps as a target for active aggression, because of violations of the inmate code in a manner deemed serious. It is not necessary always that such violations have been committed provided the subject has a reputation for not being "right" or if his personality characteristics open him to suspicion of special vulnerability for "rat" behavior.

Our study found the fifty "rats" to fall in two general categories: (a) Assimilated "Rats"—those who had been assimilated within the prisoner informal groups and had been accused of violating the inmate code; (b) Unassimilated "Rats"—those who had not been assimilated within these groups and nevertheless had been threatened because of alleged violations of the inmate code. Therefore, all "rats" had been found wanting relative to a code even if the subject had not accepted the code or had not been found acceptable for assimilation into inmate informal groups.

ALTERNATIVES TO PRISON ASSIMILATION

If the rehabilitation purposes of a correctional institution are to be achieved, this assimilation process must be challenged by a relatively homogeneous "official culture" to which the newcomer is to be assimilated through mutual effort of prisoner and official. Some aspects of this matter are treated in another paper.[24]

The custodial technology and concentration of power in officials would appear, at first glance, to give the formal organization complete control over inmates necessary for such assimilation. Even casual examination erases this impression. Sykes documents the failure of custodians to maintain institutional order in their skirmishes with the inmates individually and in informal groups. He points out the lack of essential ingredients for effecting compliance by the rules: The sense of duty as a motive for compliance and an effective, consistent system of rewards and punishments.[25]

The lack of a consistent set of organizational goals is a further handicap. Disillusionment with strictly punitive objectives has failed to

bring philosophical unity among those who man the correctional bureaucracy. The prison is a hybrid among social institutions, a shot-gun
marriage of dissimilar institutions: The army at war in terms of custody,
the factory in terms of prison industries, and the school or hospital in
terms of rehabilitation. This groups within a prison bureaucracy dissimilar professional personality types, each personifying dissimilar value
systems and each assigning dissimilar roles to the inmate.

To affiliate with this formal organization, the new inmate must
overlook, or be unaware of, this philosophical disunity among his
keepers. He must evaluate himself in terms of the role assigned, *i.e.*, as
one who must be guarded and regarded with custodial suspicion, or one
whose major deficiencies require rehabilitation, or one whose function is
to work efficiently with minimum personal rewards. Furthermore, he
must accept the restrictions and social stigma of confinement as a
prerequisite.

The newcomer must express with care any affiliation with the formal
organization in order to avoid inmate definition as an agent of officials.
He must be at least tolerated by those with whom he lives in close
physical proximity. If enmity of fellows is aroused, his assignment to the
"rat" role can cause officials to suspect his motives in defining himself as a
proper candidate for rehabilitation programs or as an ally of the custodial
meriting special consideration and protection.

A third general alternative for the newcomer is alliance with a faction
created as a form of accommodation between some inmates and some
members of the lowest level of the status hierarchy of the formal
organization. Harper describes these factions.[26] Von Mering and King
discuss the traditional custodial role which lends itself to this form of
accommodation.[27] Here formal organizational goals of a progressive
correctional system are subverted in subtle fashion. Membership within
these factions usually subjects the inmate to the role of dependent
personality in his relationships with officials. Rehabilitation objectives
may be served, but the opposite is just as likely. This alternative is a form
of accommodation for purposes of reducing conflict and of achieving a
measure of security for individuals, rather than learning of the culture of
a social unit. Therefore, this does not qualify as assimilation.

The same assessment can be made of a fourth general alternative for
the newcomer. He may avoid commitment to any grouping by assuming
the role of a social isolate. If marked and habitual isolation from all social
groups was not characteristic of the inmate's earlier life, this requires
unusual self-reliance and moral independence when incarceration is
prolonged. Clemmer's discussion of the "Semisolitary Man" and the
"Complete Solitary Man" is pertinent.[28]

VARIETIES OF "RATS"

Assimilated "Rats" were found to include three subtypes: Quislings, Cornered "Rats," and Accommodated "Rats." Quislings are considered by their fellows to have accepted a formal or informal role within the official organization for personal gain in a manner which threatens the achievement of inmate informal group goals or the achievement of inmate-approved personal goals of other individual prisoners. This may involve a formal role whose essential function within the official organization requires open opposition to inmate-approved values. An example would be the formal role of "Dog Boy" found in Southern prison systems for bloodhound handling on prisoner escape chases. Other formal roles, such as inmate clerk, places the inmate within the formal organization where he may serve as a communication link between officials and inmates. However, he may remain neutral as a social isolate or he may prefer his formal role to serve the ends of inmate informal groups. He may be subject to definition as a Quisling when he supplements this formal role with the informal role of regular informant for officials.

Cornered "Rats" and Accommodated "Rats" make up the remainder of the Assimilated "Rats." They differ only in the quality of their response to the experience of being defined as outcasts by their fellows. Usually all Assimilated "Rats" become outcasts on the basis of some specific incident which reverses their previous acceptance among inmate informal groups. The Cornered "Rat" reacts to this experience with extreme anxiety, inviting further inmate threats because of his unusual qualification as a target for aggression and, thereby, increasing the seriousness of his plight. In contrast, the Accommodated "Rat" employs his wit and/or physical strength to attempt control over his new situation for creating a new equilibrium in his interrelationships with other inmates. He strives to postpone or prevent overt conflict, at least mitigating inmate opposition. Sometimes he solicits officials for sanctuary if these efforts fail. One such inmate wrote an official:

> I have been labelled an informer. I am aware of my present status and have made every effort to amend it. I have cooperated with officials in every way. Word has been sent to my camp by one of the prisoners who was at the camp where I was attacked. I am to appear before the Grand Jury against the two prisoners who attacked me. It won't be long before the same thing happens again. I am at the end of my rope. I am partially crippled in my right leg. I am not able to fight any more. The only recourse I have is the official side, so I would appreciate your intercession. I have turned to the officials after all these

years. I can't go back to the convict side. I am trusting you to find me a place comparatively safe. I admit my past has been pretty bad but from where I stand now I can't go back.

Unassimilated "Rats" also have three subtypes: Unsocialized, Mentally Maladjusted, and Flaccid "Rats." The lack of assimilation to the inmate culture does not necessarily indicate either a high rehabilitation potential or the absence of criminal personality qualities. The lack of assimilation may stem from a general inability to integrate themselves within any social grouping or accept social norms requiring at least minimal consideration for the interests and values of peers. When these inabilities are combined with a specific incident which causes the inmate to be defined in the informal inmate groups to be an enemy, the "rat" role becomes pertinent.

The Mentally Maladjusted subtype has an unusual degree of persecutory ideation which would not appear substantiated by facts. It is not necessary that the degree of this ideation qualify the subject as a psychotic. His habitual suspicion of others deludes him into the assumption that he has been labelled a "rat." Since confinement creates an environment pregnant with suspicion and because he lacks skills in interpersonal relationships, the subject already has been defined by inmates as a marginal individual. Therefore, his delusion and protestations of innocence against a role to which he actually has not been assigned is likely to be interpreted as "rat" behavior.

A dependent personality, the Flaccid "Rat" is characterized by lack of firmness and elasticity of personality, requiring guidance and support of others to afford goals and resources for attaining them. Inmates call him the "Sorry Rat." Confinement thrusts him into a social situation magnifying the effect of his weakness. Unable to choose sides in any value conflict, he is vulnerable particularly to pressures, tossed helplessly between contending forces because of his inability to accept firm allegiance to any group. He is selected out from the dependent personalities in the inmate population on the basis of some specific incident or because of his clumsy efforts to gain emotional support from officials. His personal weaknesses already have caused his peers and officials to define him as an appropriate candidate for the informer role. An incident finds him ripe for definition as a "rat." Resembling the Cornered "Rat" in his quickness to fear and his reluctance to retaliate, he is particularly appropriate to serve as a "drain" for "free-floating aggression."

The Unsocialized subtype has personal-social characteristics which alienate him from inmate informal groups. Sykes discusses the "Center Man" as the inmate who too blatantly takes "on the opinions, attitudes, and beliefs of the custodians."[29] It is from this segment of Clemmer's "ungrouped" prisoners that the Unsocialized "Rat" is selected on the basis of an incident which sparks latent inmate enmity. The subtype may violate the inmate code through ignorance of prison life, because a high proportion of them are first offenders. In other cases, the vocabulary, recreational interests, and personal tastes of a middle class prisoner may arouse ethnocentric prejudices of prisoners who stem largely from lower socio-economic strata. If the prisoner lacks flexibility in adjustment to new circumstances, he may indicate aloofness from, and distain for, his peers and their values. Superior formal education or vocational exper-ience may give the prisoner an advantage in competing for strategic formal roles with the prison's formal structure. In the performance of such roles, the prisoner may indicate his preference for certain officials with similar social class qualities as against his fellow inmates. On the other hand, his personal maladjustment may cause him to rebel against institutional authority but in a manner which indicates his distain for fellow prisoners and their values. Again, as a personality already found by inmates to be marginal, he is particularly vulnerable to definition as a "rat" if an incident places him in serious conflict with inmate values. The following letter from an inmate describes the effects of such an incident on a bad check writer ignorant of the patterns of prison life:

> This is first time in my life to be in any trouble or any prison. I was stupid to the ways of prison life. I did not feel very good one day. A convict told me he could get me something for $1.50 so I would feel better. I never heard of a whammy nose inhaler before. So stupid me, I boldly carried it in my pocket. I found out how the whammies were getting in. The officials wanted to know where I got mine. I broke down and cried and told everything. Convicts call this a rat. But I was doing my duty. In doing so, I know I prevented three convicts from overpowering a guard to escape. . . . I also told of a convict planning to rob a grocery store when he was released. I wasn't trying to get by with anything under the watchful eyes of this prison system. . . . I have learned my lesson well and never no more will I commit a crime. I am truly ashamed for the disgrace I brought on myself and my family.

Although infractions suffer from the unreliability characteristic of most criminal statistical attributes, the infraction records of the fifty "rats" are summarized in Table 1 to offer a crude index of their response to their assigned role. To eliminate the extraneous influence of variations in the length of the period of confinement, annual infraction rates are pre-sented in Table 2.

We hypothesize that assignment to the role of "rat" causes an inmate to court official protection through reduction of behavior likely to incur

TABLE 1

Type of "Rats" Reported in One State-Wide Prison System by Type
of Infractions Before and After Being So Defined, 1958–1959

Type of "Rat"	General Type of Infraction of Prison Rules			
	Before being called "Rat"		After being called "Rat"	
	Disci-plinary	Cus-todial	Disci-plinary	Cus-todial
Assimilated (23)	43	56	9	12
Cornered (9)	20	16	7	11
Quislings (9)	18	25	2	1
Accommodated (5)	5	15	—	—
Unassimilated (27)	59	31	16	3
Flaccid (8)	24	11	9	2
Mentally Maladjusted (7)	14	6	4	—
Unsocialized (12)	21	14	3	1

Statistic in parentheses is number of inmates so classified.

When the "disciplinary" columns are combined and the "custodial" columns also are combined, a chi-square value of 19.68 is obtained. This is significant at less than the 1 per cent level.

punishment. Therefore, the infraction rate should be less after such assignment than previous to it. Table 2 supports this hypothesis. The smallest decline is for Cornered and Flaccid "rat." This might be explained by the probability that the anxiety-ridden prisoner would solicit punitive segregation as a refuge.

Differentiation between "disciplinary" and "custodial" infractions appears to support the view that Assimilated "Rats" differ from Unassimilated "Rats" in their reaction to the social environment of confinement. "Disciplinary" infractions are defined as non-violent violations of work, moral, and other behavioral norms deemed by officials to be essential to orderly life within an authoritarian community. "Custodial" infractions involve violence, escapes, and other direct assaults on institutional security. Assimilated "Rats" had a proportionately greater share of "custodial" infractions as one might expect of the "prisonwise" inmate. Unassimilated "Rats" reflected their inferior success in adjusting to the regimented environment with their emphasis on "disciplinary" infractions.

TABLE 2
Number of Infractions per Year Before and
After Definition as "Rat" by Type of "Rat"

Type of "Rat"	Total Infrac-tions per Year	Number of Infractions per Year		
		Before being called "Rat"	After being called "Rat"	Percent de-crease
Assimilated	1.15	1.21	.73	39.7
Cornered	1.45	1.61	1.21	24.8
Quislings	1.08	1.23	.40	67.5
Accommodated	.65	.82	.00	100.0
Unassimilated	1.23	1.66	.56	66.3
Flaccid	1.85	2.30	1.14	50.4
Mentally Maladjusted	.98	1.58	.34	78.5
Unsocialized	1.00	1.33	.32	75.9

The total number of infractions committed during the period by prisoners in each category is divided by the number of years the prisoners were confined during the period either before or after they were recognized by officials to have been defined by the prisoners as "rats."

Confinement thrusts the prisoner into a situation characterized by the conflict between two major value systems. In theory, the values of the formal organization support resocialization of the inmate and press him toward "good citizenship." The values of the inmate informal organization center around opposition to the objectives of the formal organization and gaining of personal objectives. Through confinement, isolation from outside society subjects the inmate to this value clash in unfamiliar situations. Although the new prisoner is likely to be deficient in the maturity and self-insights required for effective decision-making, the conditions created by confinement require that he take a personal stand of fundamental importance in determining the ultimate significance of his imprisonment. The existence of the "rat" indicates the risks involved in avoiding or reversing this decision. Furthermore, the "rat" as a product of the assimilation process illustrates the cost to the individual prisoner of the sociology of confinement.

13 *The Social Relations*
of Persistent Offenders

GORDON TRASLER*

Those who have investigated groups of habitual criminals have frequently remarked upon the tenuous and unstable nature of their relations with others. It is to be expected that repeated imprisonment will have some effect upon a man's social ties; but the evidence suggests that a lack of satisfactory friendships with people of either sex is characteristic of those destined to become persistent offenders, even before the first brush with the police. Various explanations have been advanced to account for this; perhaps the most influential is the contention that there is a causal connexion between inability to form friendships and criminality. It is suggested, for example, that the criminal act is itself a response to anxiety, depression, or irrational guilt generated by the frustrations and the loneliness which the offender has encountered in his attempts to make satisfactory contacts with others.[30] It is hard to conceive of any way in which such hypotheses could be tested. On the other hand there is no doubt that the belief that criminality is the result of inadequacy in personal relationships has become an important part of the thinking of those whose task it is to organize penal institutions. Various systems of training and counselling have been introduced which rely to some degree upon the assumption that to extend the offender's opportunities and capacities for inter-personal contacts is likely to be beneficial—not merely in the limited sense that it will make life in prison more bearable for him

* From *The Sociological Review,* Monograph No. 9, "Sociological Studies in the British Penal Services," edited by Paul Halmos (Keele, Great Britain: University of Keele, January 1965), pp. 87–97. Reprinted by permission of the author and publisher.

and for those who have to guard him, but valuable as a correctional measure, reducing the probable frequency of his subsequent convictions. These developments raise several theoretical questions which will be examined in this paper. It will be contended that the connexion between inadequacy in inter-personal relations and criminality is neither simple, nor directly causal. This is not, however, an exercise in criminological theory, but an essay in penology; it will be shown that such knowledge as we possess concerning these matters has implications for the organization of correctional institutions.

THE SOCIALIZATION PROCESS

We may conveniently distinguish three processes of learning which begin (but are not completed) during the first two or three years of a child's life. These are the establishment of patterns of dependency, the acquisition of the elementary skills of inter-personal relations, and training in social values. There is currently some controversy about the origins of affectional needs; it is not certain whether they are primary characteristics of the species, or whether they should properly be regarded as secondary drives which have been acquired through the repeated association of human contacts with the satisfaction of physical needs. What is not in dispute, however, is the fact that children learn to gain satisfaction from (i.e., to become dependent upon) their parents, and that generalization to other adult figures, to siblings, and later to age peers, is normally closely controlled by the complex system of rôle-relationships which forms the structure of the family and its immediate social setting. Whether or not the need for dependency is learned, particular patterns or styles of dependency certainly are.

The satisfactions which the child derives from these early relationships have an important role to play in encouraging him to develop and to practise a great many skills. Some of these are the basic tools of inter-personal communication. He learns to recognize the meaning of various facial expressions, gestures and intonations of voice: he gains some control over his own emotional reactions—to be patient, to adjust his behaviour to that of other people, and in a rudimentary way to be tactful. These quite subtle and precise skills and perceptual discriminations are shaped by the reinforcement (both positive and negative) which he receives from his parents' reactions to his behaviour: basic social competence, like the more advanced facility of language, is learned because it elicits satisfactions in the form of the approval of others.

There is an essential sequence in this early social learning—the child must learn to recognize expressions before he can acquire skill in responding to them; the learning of appropriate gestures and of speech is contingent upon the discovery that communication with the mother is satisfying. It is also a necessary basis for the development of the more sophisticated skills which adolescents and adults need in their contacts with others, and which are particularly vital in the most intimate affectional relations.[31]

The process that is sometimes called 'ethical learning'—that is, the acquisition of those basic moral attitudes and inhibitions which normally control social behaviour—is also motivated by the child's early dependency upon his parents, but in a rather different fashion. There is good reason to believe that this is primarily a matter of associative conditioning; not a matter of reward, but the attachment of feelings of anxiety or guilt to certain types of behaviour and to the motives which give rise to them. Actions, such as pilfering or aggressiveness, which are regularly accompanied by parental disapproval (and the emotional upset which this arouses in the child) become fraught with anxiety, so that in time he develops a positive aversion which effectively deters him from behaving in these ways again. Parents may express their disapproval by physical punishment, by verbal rebuke, or simply through their natural reactions of disgust or disappointment: in any event it seems to be the temporary suspension of a relationship upon which the child has come to rely that effects the training, rather than the particular form of response they select. Although it is conventional to distinguish 'love-oriented' methods of child training from 'punishment-based' procedures, the difference is probably of little importance; what *is* significant is that all ethical training depends upon the prior existence of a bond of affection between the child and his parents in which he has learned to find satisfaction and reassurance.[32]

It is unnecessary, then, to search for a causal connexion between criminality and inadequacy in relationships with others. Both may result from the partial failure of learning processes which rely for their effectiveness upon the bond of dependency which normally develops between the young child and his parents.

DIFFERENTIAL PATTERNS OF DEPENDENCY

Sociological studies of child rearing indicate that the period of his life during which the infant is wholly dependent upon his parents for affectional support varies greatly. In some socio-economic groups it extends almost to the time of starting school, whereas in other classes and neighbourhoods children begin to make friendships with age-peers at the age of three, or even earlier. The causes of these variations appear to be several; there are substantial subcultural differences in styles of child management and in the conception of what constitutes proper supervision of infants, and there is no doubt that the physical characteristics of the household and the street in which the child is brought up set the limits to the duration of the phase of maximum dependency upon his parents, and to its exclusiveness.[33]

The timing of this extension of the child's social contacts and the rapidity with which it proceeds are of considerable significance. The phase of total dependence upon the parents provides optimal conditions for social training; temporary withdrawal of their approval is an immensely powerful sanction against which the child has no defence. As he establishes other social relations beyond the family group he becomes gradually less vulnerable to their disapproval—he has alternative sources of reassurance which he can draw upon when he is out of favour.

In those social groups in which the period of total dependency is comparatively brief, children generally transfer a large part of their emotional investments to the peer group—usually the neighbourhood play group. They become heavily dependent upon its collective goodwill, and highly sensitive to its disapproval. By this means the peer group may become a powerful agent of social training, assuming to some degree the authority which the parents have relinquished. On the other hand, the content of the social training which results may be different; the values of the peer group may conflict, in some respects, with those of the parents of its members.

Where the period of total dependence upon the parents is considerably longer (as it is in many middle-class families) the sequence of events is rather different. Because the child does not make substantial relationships with others of his own age until he is comparatively mature, he is less likely to become heavily dependent upon the peer group. The major part of his moral training, and the learning of basic social skills, is completed within the family circle; by the time that he extends his social contacts beyond the family he is already becoming independent, and has less need of support and reassurance.

Such differences in early social experiences have various long-term consequences, of which two are particularly relevant to the present discussion. The first concerns characteristic styles of dependency. Children who have been weaned relatively early from exclusive dependence upon their parents, and encouraged to seek many of their social satisfactions from their age-peers in neighbourhood play groups, will grow up relatively sensitive to group pressures and criticisms; while those who have derived virtually all their affectional support from their parents during the most vulnerable years of early childhood will be disposed to respond most readily to parent-like figures of authority, and will be less sensitive to group pressures.[34]

Secondly, it has been shown that the duration and exclusiveness of the young child's dependency upon his parents are positively correlated with rapidity and effectiveness of ethical training; by implication, those individuals who become criminals because they have been inadequately socialized are likely, *ceteris paribus,* to have been reared in families and neighbourhoods in which children are encouraged to extend their social contacts and attachments beyond the immediate family into the peer group relatively early. This is, of course, consistent with the observation that a high proportion of convicted offenders are apparently recruited from those social strata in which these conditions obtain.[35]

THE PRISONER SOCIETY

As several careful studies of prisons have shown,[36] the nature of the system of rules, status-relations and conventional attitudes which together comprise the structure of the inmate group is partly determined by the external function of the institution as a symbol of Society's rejection of criminals. His forfeiture of citizen status is sharply demonstrated to the individual offender by the manner in which he is admitted—deprivation of clothing and possessions, being numbered, inspected, weighed and documented—which has the effect of emphasizing his isolation and loss of personal identity. These procedures are reminiscent of the initiation of a military recruit or a new boy in a boarding school; for the prisoner, however, they represent not admission into a new status, but a deprivation of personal identity which he must continue to endure for the full term of his sentence. The society which has rejected him is represented within the prison by the uniformed staff and the 'superior officers', all of whom have homes and families and status in the outside world. Their custodial roles and their immense authority vis-à-vis individual prisoners are conferred by the State; in exercising them they furnish constant reminders of the social degradation to which prisoners have been subjected.

In these circumstances the primary function of the inmate society is to provide self-esteem and status for its members. It follows, for reasons that have been analysed by Cohen in his study of adolescent gangs,[37] that the fundamental characteristic of the inmate culture is the explicit and emphatic rejection of the authority and standards of the external society and—to the extent that they fulfil their roles as official representatives—of the custodial staff.[38] It is necessary that its values should be explicitly different; that admission to the inmate group and the opportunity to compete for status within it should entail outright rejection of the criteria by which Society, through the proxy of judges and prison officers, censures the lawbreaker. The social distance which separates the inmate group from the custodial staff of a penal institution is thus a necessary consequence of the fact of imprisonment itself; it may be accentuated by the expression of hostile or contemptuous attitudes on either side, but it is not generated by them.

The inmate society is capable of exerting intense pressure upon its individual members. For the prisoner, cut off from his family, his workmates, and from virtually all his other social affiliations, it is the only available reference group. The alternative to membership of the inmate society, and subscription to its values, is total isolation—a condition which few men are able to tolerate for long. This is a fact which has grave implications for those who wish to use penal institutions as agents for the re-socialization of offenders. It is often suggested that the sovereign authority of the prison culture can be effectively diluted by encouraging the development of personal relationships between individual inmates and prison officers. But this is no solution. Membership of the inmate society specifically entails, as we have seen, rejection of the 'official' value-system; it follows that friendships with individual members of the custodial staff will be restricted to areas of mutual interest to which official values do not relate. Social contacts centered upon a common hobby, a sporting interest, or allegiance to the same home town have always been tolerated, even in the most repressive prisons, because they present no threat to the central value system of the inmate culture. Attempts to extend the basis of such contacts by individual counselling, in order that they may be used to modify primary social attitudes, will inevitably be firmly resisted by the prison society; any individual prisoner who may be persuaded to engage in a constructive relationship of this type must forfeit his rights as a member of the inmate group.

There is, however, another possibility; one might attempt not merely to augment the prison culture, but to supplant it—to substitute a network of personal relationships between officers and inmates for the closed society of the inmate group. This involves, as a first step, a radical redefinition of the roles of governors, custodial officers, and even administrative staff; this is difficult, but it can be achieved. However, there are further difficulties. The abruptness with which a newly-imprisoned man loses his social roots gives rise to a strong centripetal effect in any institution which receives offenders immediately after sentence; this tends to foster the growth of a strong, introverted, defensive inmate group despite all attempts by the staff to establish a more open web of relationships. Here, too, the differences in styles of socialization to which reference was made earlier are of particular importance. A high proportion of offenders, as we have seen, have learned to look to the peer group for support and the satisfaction of emotional needs. For them two-person, quasi-parental relationships with persons in authority are inherently less satisfying. In prison they have a marked tendency to conform to the inmate subculture and to regard the prisoner society as their sole reference group. In these circumstances it is clearly futile to attempt to displace the inmate society; it may, on the other hand, be possible to exert some moderating influence upon its values by systematically infiltrating the group itself. This appears to be one of the goals in the most drastic variant of group counselling, in which the groups are coextensive with the population of the institution—inmates and custodians—and the structure of relations within them is to some degree integrated into the network of authority and communication of the institution as a whole. This is clearly a formidable undertaking, and one which demands considerable courage and flexibility of mind in the prison staff and administrators. But it is not easy to envisage any other solution to the problem of curtailing the destructive effects of the inmate culture upon those individuals who are especially responsive to group pressures.

Fortunately this is not true of all offenders; some, on the contrary, have been brought up in such a manner that they are normally disposed to rely upon two-person relationships in preference to dependence upon the peer group. Integration into the inmate society is for these men the unattractive alternative to total isolation; they may readily be persuaded to transfer their allegiance to members of the prison staff, if opportunities for such relationships are provided. (This state of affairs entails certain hazards of its own; these are unfortunately beyond the scope of the present discussion.)[39] Individual differences in styles of dependency are relevant to decisions about the allocation of offenders; there are obvious reasons for endeavouring to ensure that the population of any institution is reasonably homogeneous in this respect.

IMPRISONMENT AND SOCIAL SKILLS

It is an inevitable consequence of membership of a small, relatively stable community—and especially of one so effectively cut off from the external world as a prison—that the individual is called upon to employ a much smaller range of social skills than he needs in a more normal social environment. The pattern of life and work in a prison is simple and unvarying; once he has become accustomed to the routine, a prisoner can anticipate the slow sequence of events—the meals, the march to the workshop, exercise, the locking and unlocking of cells, 'slopping out'— which makes each day almost indistinguishable from the last and the next. The range of social responses which he is required to make is similarly restricted and predictable. In most institutions contacts between inmates and custodial staff are few, transient and superficial; they conform more or less closely to stereotyped modes of interaction which are part of the traditions of prison life. Orders, comments, requests and even jokes follow a familiar pattern; the inmate is not expected to show initiative in contacts with officers. Comparable conditions obtain in relations between prisoners. The hierarchy of status, the codes of loyalty and conduct, the styles of address and response that constitute the structure of the inmate society are clear-cut, unchanging, and readily learned. While he remains in prison the individual seldom has recourse to the more subtle social skills; tact, insight, and accurate judgment of the attitudes and reactions of other people, so necessary to men and women in the ordinary world, are rarely needed. After prolonged or repeated imprisonment, a man's social reactions become blunted; he is clumsier, less perceptive, and much less confident in his dealings with others.

At the same time his relationships with his family and friends generally become attenuated and unreal. It is true that he is entitled to receive visits and letters; but visits are usually brief, artificial, stilted contacts with a wife in her best clothes, determined to present a brave face for the sake of her husband's morale, and often disconcerted by the humiliating conditions in which such meetings must take place. Letters are even less useful as a means of sustaining affectionate relationships. Few prisoners are skilled in the use of written language; the knowledge that whatever they write will be read in the censor's office inhibits both the prisoner and his correspondent.

In these circumstances it is not surprising that many prisoners at the beginning of their sentences endure great anxiety about their wives and families. The infidelity of women is a constant topic of conversation; a man who hears malicious gossip about his wife is in an unenviable predicament. He cannot go to discover the facts for himself, and he is usually reluctant to seek the help of the welfare officer. His only contact with the outside world is his wife; when he does see her, the cheerful manner and smart clothes which she has assumed for his sake do little to dispel the suspicion that she is not finding his absence hard to endure. The leisured, empty prison day gives many opportunities to brood upon worries of this kind; they are apt to grow into major personal crises. The outcome is occasionally an outburst of unruly behaviour—an assault, or the smashing of cell furniture; but usually the prisoner resolves the problem by withdrawing his emotional investment from a relationship that has become intolerably hazardous. He gradually ceases to care about his wife or his family, so insulating himself against further uncertainty.

These are depressing reflections for those who are concerned with the resettlement of discharged prisoners. Even without these handicaps, a man is confronted upon his release with problems which constitute a searching test of his skill in inter-personal relations. He may have to establish new patterns of intimacy with his wife and his children in a family group which has inevitably re-formed in his absence; this demands tact, restraint, and a sensitive understanding of the attitudes and needs of others. These are not problems which all discharged prisoners have to face; some are unmarried, and a great many more have lost their wives somewhere along the road that led to prison. But the task of finding and settling into a job, the unusual experience of having to seek out friends and to sustain a relationship that is spontaneous (not imposed, like contacts with cellmates or acquaintances in the exercise yard)—these are encountered by every prisoner at the end of his sentence, and they are very strange and very difficult to a man who has just emerged from the undemanding environment of a penal institution. To tackle these problems successfully requires a considerable measure of competence and assurance in relations with others—qualities which are scarce enough in criminals, particularly in those who have spent a substantial period in prison.

CONCLUSION

Our discussion indicates that confining men in penal institutions has several consequences which are inconsistent with the intention that they should be resocialized and ultimately resettled in the community. These inconsistencies are sharpened by the fact that offenders, as a class, are unrepresentative of the general population in two respects: (1) they tend to be particularly responsive to group pressures and to look mainly to the peer-group for social support, and (2) they tend to lack competence and skill in relationships with others. We have seen that these facts foster the development of an influential inmate group within the penal institution, the values of which are necessarily at variance with those of the wider society. Finally, it has been argued that imprisonment has a corrosive effect upon social skills, which are of critical importance in resettlement after release from prison; although it is unlikely that inadequacy in inter-personal relations can be counted as a cause of criminality, it may well be a cause of recidivism.

It is hard to see how the intrinsic disadvantages of institutions as correctional devices could be remedied. The characteristics of the inmate culture are largely determined by the fact of imprisonment itself; it seems unrealistic to suppose that they could be substantially modified by any of the methods that are at present being tried. Nor does there seem to be any practicable way of reducing the dependence of the individual prisoner upon the inmate group. There are various steps which might be taken to combat the erosion of social skills during long periods of imprisonment. Of these, perhaps the most urgent is greatly to increase the amount of meaningful contact between prisoners and their wives and families: improved conditions for visiting, home leave, relaxation of the censorship, and more adequately staffed welfare departments ought to be regarded not as amenities, but as necessities of social hygiene. It is possible to envisage changes in the organization of institutions that might provide for a greater diversity of patterns of social interaction for inmates, giving opportunities for the exercise and development of social skills which are not at present demanded.

But these are subsidiary matters. The real question at issue is whether, in the light of contemporary knowledge, we are justified in attempting to use closed institutions as devices for retraining those offenders whose criminality is a consequence of inadequate socialization. The arguments advanced in this paper suggest that we are not.

14   Women in Prison

DAVID A. WARD AND
GENE G. KASSEBAUM*

The removal of deviant members from the community for various periods of time has long been a technique of social control. The use of civil banishment, exile, penal colonies, and jails has an ancient history. In modern times, the radical decline in the use of capital punishment, and the expansion of the prison system have been accompanied by the gradual development of the concept of rehabilitation, in addition to retribution, as the underlying rationale for incarceration. As the ideology of rehabilitation has grown, the physical rigors of the earlier prisons have been modified and humanized. Severe deprivations of diet and activities, the imposition of unusually hard labor, and physical abuse have diminished. The physical plants and programs have become more adequate to the human needs of the inmate population.

Yet prisons they remain, for in addition to direct deprivation of certain material comforts and personal belongings, the restrictions on personal freedom, and the separation from family and friends, imprisonment entails the social and psychological deprivations and injuries which have been described in a number of recent studies.[40] The "pains of imprisonment," as Sykes has referred to them, include the problems resulting from status degradation, changing roles, ego damage, and feelings of guilt, anxiety, fear, and embarrassment.

The development of an informal inmate organization is now seen as a

* From David A. Ward and Gene G. Kassebaum, *Women's Prison* (Chicago: Aldine Publishing Company, 1965), pp. 1, 2, 10–15, 53–54, 74–79; copyright © 1965 by David A. Ward and Gene G. Kassebaum. Reprinted by permission of the author and publisher.

reaction to these deprivations and restrictions.[41] Since inmates are supposed to be deprived and restricted as a part of penal confinement their attempts to militate against the pains of imprisonment constitute resistance to the efforts of the staff to control the environment. As the typically deleterious effects of patient or inmate informal organization on staff programing have been made explicit by research, attempts have been initiated by the administration to intervene between individual inmate and organized inmate resistance. These efforts to manipulate institutional environments are variously referred to as "therapeutic communities" and "environmental therapy" and they are articulated in programs such as group counseling, group psychotherapy, and community living.[42] While our concern here is not with these attempts to "rehabilitate" criminal populations, we are concerned with explicating the character of the pains of imprisonment which women prisoners experience and with examining the adaptations made to these deprivations. There are certain aspects of confinement in Frontera that are the same as those reported in other total institutions and other features that are peculiar to women prisoners and to this prison. . . .

The role of citizen can be taken away through an official process, but there is no similar process by which the role of prisoner is done away with upon readmission to the free world.

The implications of these new designations, is, as Garfinkel has pointed out, that other, former identities are seen as accidental or illusory and that the person is now what she really was all along.[43] It is to this process of stripping civilian identities from new prisoners that we now turn.

THE RECEPTION PROCESS

New arrivals at Frontera undergo a process of admission similar in many respects to that in other institutions.[44] They are questioned for personal and legal information and then told which of their personal belongings they may retain. Many articles must be held until release or sent to one's family. It is symbolic of what Goffman calls "role dispossession" that engagement rings and some wedding rings are taken away.[45] (The reason given for not allowing valuable rings to be kept is that they may be used as a medium of exchange.) The implications of imprisonment become apparent when type of underwear becomes a matter of custodial interest. Inmates may keep their own underwear only when it is: 1. pastel in color—and specifically not navy blue, purple, brown or black, "because of escape."[46] (Although one wonders whether many women would try to escape clad in their under-clothes.) Red underwear may not be kept. It is reputed to be "a symbol of homosexuality." 2. It must be unpadded "to prevent narcotics from being smuggled in."

In addition to its physical setting, Frontera may be distinguished in other ways from those prisons for men which also house all types of offenders including life-termers. One obvious difference is the number and variety of articles that women can bring in or have sent to them: coats, jackets, raincoats (all "no quilting, padding or fur"), sweaters ("no turtle neck, V-neck or tight slipover"), gowns or pajamas, bathrobes ("no quilting or padding"), shoes ("low heels, bedroom, thongs, tennis"), "simple" costume jewelry (earrings, necklaces, scatter pins, bracelets), non-electric clocks, dark glasses, unopened cigarettes, suitcases ("no larger than 18 x 26"), unfinished knitting and light hand-sewing material, tooth brushes, hair rollers, etc. Clothing is provided for those without these articles and all inmates are issued six dresses which are the standard garb of the population. In addition, inmates may spend up to $22.00 per month in the canteen on a variety of items such as candy, several kinds of cookies, cheese, instant coffee, cocoa, jelly, potato chips, crackers, peanut butter, face cream, talcum, hand lotion, deodorant, lipstick, makeup, shampoo, eyebrow pencils, hair brushes, nail polish, and hair nets.

Thus the more complete deprivation of personal possessions that occurs in prisons for men does not take place at Frontera. The pains of the admission experience are perhaps mitigated slightly by permitting the women to have these items.

After being fingerprinted and photographed, the inmate takes a supervised bath. Reception officers have pointed out that this is an embarrassing experience for many women because circumstances of privacy do not prevail. The bathroom has no door and a staff member supervises the bathing process to insure cleanliness. Following this comes the most embarrassing admission experience, a rectal and vaginal examination by a nurse in a room with other women present—an examination not for medical reasons, but for the discovery of contraband. Upon completing these activities new arrivals are issued temporary clothing and are sent to the reception cottage. . . .[47]

SEPARATION FROM FAMILY AS THE MOST SEVERE DEPRIVATION FOR WOMEN IN PRISON

There is one sense in which it seems warranted to view imprisonment as more severe for women than men. It is usually the case that women are regarded as more closely linked to the care and upbringing of children than are men. The separation of mother and child is countenanced only under extraordinary conditions.

When a woman is separated from her children because of penal confinement, the custody of the child may be taken from the father and assigned to other relatives. Should the father be impossible to locate, in prison himself, or adjudged not responsible, the child may be placed in a private agency or become a ward of the state. The confined mother's concern is not only with separation from her children but also with how they will be cared for while the husband works; moreover, the husband may look for another female to take over the maternal role. The distinction between male and female prisoners here is that the father in prison is presuming that his wife will, despite economic hardship, continue to play her role as mother. The mother in prison, however, is asking her husband to assume primary responsibility for the care and supervision of children when his primary role in the family is that of breadwinner.

Dispossession of the mother role also removes an important personal emotional object from the inmate. The most direct manifestation of this uniquely female deprivation is observed in the case of women who are pregnant when they are received at the prison. They bear the child in the prison maternity ward, but within a week to ten days, the child is taken from the prison and placed, pending release of the mother: (1) with an approved family member, (2) in a foster home under the supervision of the welfare department, or (3) in a foster home in the county in which the prison is located.

The separation from children is acutely felt at Frontera where fifty-nine percent of the women have minor children and sixty-eight percent are mothers. . . .[48]

CRIMINAL MATURITY AS RELATED TO ENDORSEMENT OF THE INMATE CODE

Sixteen percent of our sample strongly endorsed the model of the inmate code, but the normative views of our sample of female prisoners as a whole seem similar to those we would expect of a group of inmates whose limited criminal and penal experience would characterize them as criminally "immature." This immaturity makes more understandable the widespread practices of Frontera inmates in snitching and acting like staff. The inmate who supports a code which specifies what can and cannot be divulged to staff has some way to establish limits on the kinds of conversation in which one can engage with staff. With no specific prohibitions made clear, many inmates at Frontera have no idea as to whether the information given to a staff member, in order to be regarded as a good (i.e., cooperative) inmate, is likely to be harmful to another inmate. Under these conditions inmates can reveal information with less likelihood of feeling guilty over betraying others.[49] While there is support of the inmate code by right guy types in the female prison community, our data indicate that this "hero of the inmate social system" is in the minority and does not, by any means, represent the approved role model for the majority of female prisoners. The fact that the women do not endorse more strongly norms which characterize male prisoner ideology and, in particular, that they do not feel bound to maintain group solidarity by no-ratting rules, thus has important implications for inmate roles. The lack of importance attributed to the ideals of inmate loyalty and solidarity means that less importance is given to the right guy type of role and at the same time less criticism is directed toward stool pigeons and center men types.

There are also few merchants at Frontera. Our interviews turned up no evidence of any extensive merchandising of either extra supplies of approved items or contraband. While the small number of merchants can perhaps be partially accounted for by the wide variety of goods and personal belongings available to inmates, it is also based on the inability to organize illicit merchandising of goods due to the abundance of inmate informers.

The free flow of conversation and information between inmates and staff and the exclusion of inmates from work assignments in the offices of upper echelon staff, prompted few inmates to assume the role of politician. Would-be politicians found little response to their suggestions for organizing inmate interests or opposition among the general inmate population.

Finally, there were virtually no women who were *toughs* or *gorillas* in the sense of employing physical force or violence to get what they want.[50] In short, the only roles similar to those of male prisoners which are prevalent among the women are the roles which deny support to the inmate code—the snitch and the related center man role type, and the *square john* or prosocial type of prisoner. . . .

THE HOMOSEXUAL ADAPTATION TO IMPRISONMENT

A homosexual love affair may be viewed as an attempted compensation for the mortification of the self suffered during imprisonment. During a period when personal worth is most severely questioned, sexual involvement implies that the inmate is worth something, because another person cares about her and pays attention to her. Homosexuality also alleviates depersonalization. In prison, the inmate is stripped of identifying and distinctive qualities, capabilities, and symbols until she comes to resemble all others around her, but through an intimate relationship she is again found personally distinctive. The process of status degradation is diverted as positive characteristics of the inmate are noticed by others. Normative guidance is provided for the new inmate. Anomie and the consequent anxiety about how to do time, how to get along, and how to get out is alleviated when a constant and trusted source of information and advice is available. The suitor provides this service; the homosexual relationship is the medium of exchange.

There is no traditional convict code at Frontera, but many of the maxims which constitute an important part of the folklore of the female prisoner community are intended to justify and encourage the homosexual adaptation to new inmates. Some of these are: "You can't make it unless you have someone." and "Everyone is doing it so if you don't you are either a prude or crazy." The implication is that social acceptance by other inmates depends on admitting that turning out is justified because it makes doing time bearable. Other statements apply to the content of the homosexual experience: "Once you have a woman you'll never want a man," "You get easily addicted to homosexuality," "The *femme* [feminine homosexual role player] will never leave the woman who *turns her out* [introduces her to homosexuality]." Some potential candidates for homosexual involvement are identified in the claim that "strippers and models are likely to be homosexual." However, despite statements about the aftereffects of homosexual involvement, it is evident that this adaption is most frequently seen as temporary and prompted only by the prison experience. Those women who turn out in prison define themselves as *bisexual,* and they expect to return to heterosexual relationships upon release.

Distinctions are made in inmate argot between those who are introduced to homosexuality in prisons, the *jail-house turnouts,* and those who were homosexual before they got to prison and expect to continue in the *gay* life after release, the *true homosexuals.* Further role differentiation is based, as is the case with heterosexual affairs, on a division of labor with one partner playing the masculine or *butch* role, and the other the feminine or *femme* role. The principal means of inmate role differentiation at Frontera then, is in terms of sexual role—homosexual or heterosexual; jailhouse turnout or true homosexual; butch or femme.[51]

The culture and social structure of prisons for men seem to reflect a wider variety of pains of imprisonment than is the case in the women's prison. There are homosexuals in male prisons and norms surrounding homosexuality, but there are other important concerns and these are articulated in the roles of *merchant, politician, tough,* and *right guy.*

The overriding need of a majority of female prisoners is to establish an affectional relationship which brings in prison, as it does in the community, love, interpersonal support, security and social status. This need promotes homosexuality as the predominant compensatory response to the pains of imprisonment.

OTHER ADAPTATIONS TO IMPRISONMENT

There are other modes of adaptation utilized at Frontera. For some inmates, the pains of imprisonment are mitigated by psychological withdrawal:

> This can take the form of renouncing the goals, the drives, or the needs which are frustrated, either consciously or unconsciously, leaving the prisoner immune in apathy or seeking the gratifications of sublimation. Or it can take the form of a withdrawal into fantasy based on fondled memories of the past or imaginary dramas of life after release.[52]

Other inmates actively rebel and become chronic rule violators who fight with staff and fellow inmates (so-called troublemakers and malcontents).[53] There are some inmates at Frontera who are continually in trouble, but it is our impression that most of them fall into two principal categories—severely emotionally disturbed individuals and homosexuals, particularly young homosexuals, who use the violation of institutional rules to impress partners or to react to interventions by the staff in their affairs.

Another adaptation is what Goffman has called "colonization," the acceptance of institutional life as being a satisfactory existence.[54] These are the people who are commonly referred to as "having found a home." Generally, they do not want to bother or to be bothered by staff or inmates or by institutional programs as they perform the ritual of doing time. Some, as we have noted earlier, come to identify with the staff to the extent that they consider fellow inmates with a disdain they believe they share with staff. They make efforts to identify with the staff by informing on the conniving and rule-breaking activities of inmates. These are the women described earlier who correspond to the male prisoner type called the *center man.*

Inmates may utilize more than one adaptation at any given time or at various stages of their confinement.[55] Our data suggest that more inmates at Frontera resort to homosexuality than to psychological withdrawal, rebellion, colonization, or any other type of adaptation. During the initial phase of assuming a homosexual role, the behavior of some women may be an effort at rebellion, but in the long run, prison homosexuality or bisexuality is an effort to satisfy a variety of other needs. The greatest vulnerability to homosexual overtures at Frontera seems to come at the beginning of a sentence when the problems of adjustment to imprisonment are greatest. The process of turning out thus seems to represent socialization of the new inmates into practices which provide support, guidance, and emotional satisfactions during a period when these are lacking. The most important implication of this adaptation for the social organization of the inmate community is that, structurally, the women's prison may be viewed as a non-cohesive aggregate of homosexual dyads and friendship cliques. Unlike the male prisoner community, where individual needs may be met by supporting to one degree or another the tenets of the inmate code, the needs of female prisoners are most often met by another individual. When inmates at Frontera talk about loyalty, sharing, trust, and friendship, they are talking about these qualities in terms of a homosexual partner or close friend, not the inmate community.[56]

15 The Social Meaning of Prison Homosexuality

JOHN H. GAGNON AND WILLIAM SIMON*

The last half century has seen marked, if uneven, progress in most areas of prison management and perhaps even more marked progress in the creation of a new ideology of prison management. However, despite evidence of progress, there still remains a major area of behavior with which prison systems have been unable to cope. This is the problem of sexual adjustment that occurs in all institutions where one sex is deprived of social or sexual access to the other. It is in the area of sexuality that the prison is perhaps more limited than it is in other areas of activity, partially because of its very single-sex nature and partially because the society rarely provides clear guidelines for sexual behavior even outside the penal institution.

In the midst of the confusion about sexual standards and sexual behavior, the prison exists as the major single-sex institution in the society that has (unlike the mental hospital and other closed institutions) within its walls a population that is physically and, for the most part, psychologically, intact and is, at the same time, sexually experienced. The prison administrator is faced with a fundamental dilemma: He is aware of the sexual needs of the population that he is charged with holding and retraining, but he is also aware that he is not going to get much support or even a sympathetic hearing from the larger society if he focuses upon the problem of the sexual adjustment of his population.

* From *Federal Probation*, XXXII (March 1968): 23–29. Reprinted by permission of the author and publisher.

SOME MAJOR CONSIDERATIONS

There are two major areas that require clarification before one can proceed to discuss the actual patterns of sexual adjustment among prison populations. The first is an unfortunate tendency to view the sexual adjustment of prisoners as arising exclusively from the contexts of prison life. It is frequently assumed that any group of people who were incarcerated for any period of time would react sexually in the same way as those who are presently in prison. This is a major oversimplification brought about primarily because of a lack of information about the prior sexual and nonsexual lives of those who are imprisoned and the way in which this prior experience conditions a person's responses not only to sexual deprivation, but also to a general loss of liberty.

The second element that is important to specify is the range of sexual responses that are available to those imprisoned. With the exception of the small number of prisons that allow conjugal visits, there are only three forms of sexual behavior that are generally available to a prison population (except for animal contact for those males on prison farms). These are nocturnal sex dreams, self-masturbation, and sexual contact with other inmates of the same sex. The meaning, amount, and the character of these adjustments will be strongly dependent on the meaning that these same behaviors had for the inmate before he or she was incarcerated. Thus, the problem for the inmate is not merely the release of sexual tension, but the social and psychological meaning that such release has and the motives and beliefs that it expresses for him. The source of this set of values does not reside in the prison experience, but outside the prison in the community at large. Thus, the prison provides a situation to which prior sexual and social styles and motives must be adapted and shaped.

There are two major dimensions on which most sexual activity is based. One is that of age, with the primary break occurring between adolescence and adulthood. The other, perhaps of greater significance, is the differential meaning of sexuality to the two sexes. Thus, the striking differences between the sexual orientations of men and women noted in the Kinsey volumes offer the best starting point for a discussion of sex in prison.[57] The discussion that follows focuses on the responses of adult male and female inmates to the prison experience, with only passing reference to institutions for adolescents as they represent continuities to the adult institutions.

MALE RESPONSES TO IMPRISONMENT

Male prison populations are not random selections from the larger society and do not reflect the usual distributions of the population in terms of education, income, ethnicity, occupation, social class, and general life style. The men who make up the bulk of the imprisoned populations tend to be drawn from deprived sections of the society or from families imbedded in what we have now come to call the culture of poverty. As a consequence, the sexual experiences of these men and the meaning that sex has for them differs in significant ways from other portions of the population that are less likely to be imprisoned.

A number of dimensions of these differences may be found in the work of Kinsey and his colleagues in which they report the substantial differences to be found in the sexual activity and attitudes of men who have differing amounts of education.[58] These findings are further amplified in the volume, *Sex Offenders,* where a comparison of imprisoned men and men of the same social origins without delinquent histories showed that the men with prison histories generally have wider sexual experience of all kinds than do men leading conventional and nondelinquent lives.[59] These variables suggest that at least the modal male prison population enters institutions with differing commitments to sexuality than would a middle-class or working-class population. We can therefore suggest that the response of these latter groups to institutionalization will differ as well.

Prior Sexual Adjustment a Factor

Drawing on what we know about the dimensions of the prior sexual adjustments of men who go to prison, our first major sense of the experience is actually how little sexual activity of any sort occurs within the prison.[60] Thus, even after the shock of imprisonment has worn off (and often for the recidivist this occurs quickly), there is no sudden burst of sexual activity of any type. Confirming these impressions is the low order of complaint one hears about sexual deprivation, even when prisoners are presenting a list of grievances after a riot or outbreak of some sort. Part of this is surely due to the closeness of custody in the institution and the fact that men move and live in close proximity, and, except for certain moments of the day, there is very little privacy—not so much from the custodial staff as from the inmates.

However, another cause of this reduction is that sexual activity is potentiated by or channeled through an existing set of social frameworks that do not exist in prison. The man in prison finds himself without the appropriate stimuli which suggest opportunities for sexual activity or situations that are appropriate for such activity. Without the existence of these social cues, the biological imperative of sexual arousal is never even elicited.[61] The absence of females, the sheer sensory monotony of the prison environment, the absence of those social situations that call for sexual responses (being out on the town, going drinking, etc.) serve as effective inhibitors of sexual responsiveness. The most successful aphrodisiacs seem to be an absence of anxiety, the presence of available sexual cues, an adequate diet, and plenty of rest. Of these, only the latter two are commonly in the prison environment and in some cases only the last is.

The other source of sexual cues is fantasy, those remembered or desired sexual experiences that commonly serve as the basis for masturbation. However, as a result of the social origins of the bulk of the prison population, there is a major taboo against masturbation and a paucity of complex fantasies that would sustain a commitment to sexual experience.[62] Thus, unlike the middle-class male who learns and rehearses sexual styles in the context of masturbation, the usual prisoner is drawn from a population in which sexual experience is concrete and not symbolic; in which there is a taboo on masturbation; and, finally, in which much of heterosexual experience is structured around the need to have sexual encounters that validate his masculinity among other men. In this environment it might be said that men have sex in order to be able to talk about it.

The Kinsey evidence is that even among lower-class men who do masturbate there is often no conscious fantasy accompanying the behavior, and it serves primarily as a mechanical release of felt physical tension. This is quite unlike the middle-class situation in which masturbation occurs at relatively high rates accompanied by fantasies of sexual experience. These fantasies then begin to facilitate further masturbation and a continuing commitment to this sexual outlet. This adjustment rarely happens in the lower-class environment and, along with the sensory poverty of the prison environment, accounts for the ease with which strong commitments to sexuality are abandoned. Thus, prisoners may complain about sexual deprivation in terms such as "I would really like to have a piece" but often this is a continuation of lower-class male talk about sex, not a passionately felt drive that will eventuate in sexual activity.

Male Homosexuality More Than Outcome of Sexual Desire or Need for Physical Release

Since most prisoners do not seem to feel an overwhelming sexual need, male homosexuality in this context must be seen as something more complex than merely the outcome of sexual desire or the need for physical release. There are varying estimates of the number of males who have homosexual contact during their periods of imprisonment, but the range is probably somewhere between 30 and 45 percent, depending upon the intensity of custody in the institution, the social origins of the population, and the duration of the individual sentence.[63] It seems quite clear that the frequency of homosexual contact is usually quite low, even among cellmates; and in no sense does it approach the rates of heterosexual or homosexual behavior of these same prisoners on the outside, except possibly for those prisoners who come into the institutions with well-developed homosexual commitments and who become the "passive" partners in homosexual liaisons. In some prisons, usually those with a very low order of custody inside the walls, high rates of homosexual behavior may be achieved; however, these are not the prevalent conditions in most prison systems.

It must be pointed out that homosexuality in prison is quite a different phenomenon than homosexual experience in the outside community. Thus, the image of homosexuality as consisting of masculine-seeming men who are always "active" and feminine men who are always "passive" in the sexual performance derives primarily from both journalists and scientists observing homosexuality in prisons and then extending their observations unchecked to the outside world.[64]

Homosexuality in the prison context is partly a parody of heterosexuality, with the very sexual activity suggesting masculine and feminine role components. We now know that this is a basic oversimplification not only of homosexuality in general, but heterosexuality as well. It is, however, in the prison environment where this parody is most likely to occur, for the crucial variable is that many of the men who take part in the homosexual performances conceive of themselves, and wish others to conceive of them, as purely heterosexual.

Thus those prisoners known in prison parlance as "jockers" or "wolves" think of themselves as heterosexual; and, as long as there is no reciprocity in the sexual performance (aiding in the ejaculation of the other male) or the penis is not inserted in their mouth or anus, other inmates will continue to conceive of them in the same way. Thus the homosexual world of the prison is roughly divisible into aggressive "active" males (jockers, wolves) and "passive" males. The latter group commonly includes males who are heterosexual on the outside but who are coerced, either by fear or debt, to be homosexual (usually labeled "punks") and males who have already well-developed preferences for males from their outside experience and who enter prison as homosexuals.[65] The relationships of these males is usually highly stylized both socially and sexually, the aggressor providing protection, a measure of affection and perhaps gifts (in the case of older inmates), and the passive inmate providing sexual access, affection, and other pseudo-feminine services. In the cases of long-term inmates these relationships may be conceived of as pseudo-marriages, resulting sometimes in a greater degree of sexual reciprocity; however, such reciprocity results in a decline in other inmates' estimates of the aggressive male's masculinity.

Search for Meaningful Relationships

The sources of this homosexual activity for the predominantly heterosexual and aggressive male seem to be twofold. One element is certainly a search for meaningful emotional relationships that have some durability and which serve as a minimal substitute for affective relationships that they normally have on the outside. This is not unlike the chance homosexual contact between men during combat or in other situations of all-male communities under circumstances of fear and crisis. It represents an attempt to counter the effort of the prison to atomize the inmate community in order to reduce the potential for collusion, which could result either in conniving for goods and services or in attempting escape. One of the collective responses to this attempt is the development of a resistant inmate community, and at the individual level one of the responses is the establishment of homosexual liaisons.

A second motivation underlying many of these relationships transcends the level of affectional need and essentially becomes a source for the continued validation of masculinity needs and a symbol of resistance to the prison environment. The male whose primary source of masculine validation in the outside community has been his sexual success (rather than work, family, etc.) and who has conceived of himself as aggressive and controlling in his responses to his world finds himself in prison deprived of these central supports for his own masculinity. In reaction to this he enters into homosexual relationships in which he can be conceived as the masculine, controlling partner and which for him and for other males in the system validate continued claims to masculine status.

A complicating factor here is that some men suffer a profound psychological crisis when the supports for their masculine identity are removed. In these cases both severe homosexual panics or falling into "passive" homosexual roles are likely to result.

In general, these homosexual relationships are developed not through force, though there is evidence of homosexual rape, especially in poorly controlled detention institutions where the powerful threat of imprisonment to masculinity is first felt, in penal institutions that are inadequately controlled, and in juvenile institutions where the sexual impulse is less well-ordered and tends to be confused with aggression by the adolescent male. In most cases the "passive" partner drifts into the relationship through falling into debt, being afraid of the environment, and feeling that he requires protection, or because he already has a well-developed commitment to homosexuality that he cannot or does not want to conceal. Once an inmate has fallen into this role it is extremely difficult to shift out of it, and, if a current relationship breaks up, there will be pressure to form a new one. Even in a reincarceration there will be a memory of his role from prior institutionalization and there will be pressure to continue. It is as if the prison required as one of its role types the "passive" homosexual, and, if a number of them are removed, there is pressure to restore to equilibrium the relationship between those playing aggressive-masculine roles and those playing passive-feminine roles.

Problems Facing the Prison Administrator

This conceptualization of the pattern of homosexuality in the prison for men suggests a number of problems that face the prison administrator in dealing with sexuality. It means that as long as the prison is an environment which is largely devoid of situations where legitimate affectional ties can be established there will be a tendency for the formation of homosexual relationships, especially among those men serving long sentences who have concomitantly lost contact with meaningful persons in the free community. If in addition the prison does not allow legitimate attempts of the inmates to control their own lives and does not give an opportunity for expressions of masculinity and self-assertion that are meaningful among men at this social level, there will be homosexual relationships created to fulfill this need. The proposal for conjugal visits does not meet this problem, in part because it is available for only the very small number of inmates who have intact families. There is little evidence that the society will tolerate sexual relationships for prisoners when these relationships are not sheltered under the umbrella of a marriage.

What is clear is that the prison is not a seething volcano of sexual passions, and that as a matter of fact most males survive the deprivation of the sexual outlet and usually even survive transitory homosexual commitments to return to relatively conventional heterosexual lives on the outside.

What the sexual problem in the male prison does represent is a series of land mines, some for the administration, more for the inmates. In the case of the inmates, men get into relationships which have some potential for shaping their future commitments to sexuality; relationships which leave them open to exploitation; and, especially for those who take the passive role, the possibility of distortion of their self-conceptions. Further, there is some tendency for these relationships to create problems of sexual jealousy. When a relationship deteriorates or when a transfer of affection takes place, there is a distinct possibility of violence. The violence that does occur often is extreme, and at this point becomes a serious matter for prison management.

The dilemma for the prison manager is that often he is not aware of the relationships until they erupt into violence. Attempts at intervention in this process through getting inmates to aid in the identification of those involved may result in serious scapegoating of these persons out of the sexual anxieties of the other prisoners. The segregation of these prisoners has also been attempted. However, one major difficulty with this measure seems to be that when the most obvious homosexuals are removed from the situation there is a tendency to co-opt other persons to take their place. This tendency is also noted when the aggressive male is removed, though the policy has usually been to remove only those men who are conventionally obvious, that is, who are excessively effeminate.

Probably the only long-term solution is to adopt the policy of home visits at intervals during incarceration and to provide alternative modes of self-expression for those social and psychological needs which, because of the current structure of the male prison, result in homosexuality.

FEMALE RESPONSES TO IMPRISONMENT

As we have noted before, the major dimension which differentiates between the sexual adjustment of persons in the larger society is gender; that is, men and women differ fundamentally in their sexual commitments. While this is obvious, the consequences for the differential sexual adaptation of the males and females in prison are not.

By and large, there is in society a bias against committing females to prison, especially when any alternative is available. Thus the women's prison often has within it women who have either committed major crimes (most commonly homicide) or had long careers in crime and who have been strongly recidivistic. Thus in a certain sense the female institution is composed of some women who have had no prior link to delinquent life-styles and a larger number who had long-term ties with such a life.

Women have Fewer Problems than Men in Managing Sexual Deprivation.

However, the sexual adjustment of these women to imprisonment is strongly linked to the general goals to which most women are socialized in the larger society. Probably the most significant difference between men and women in this regard is that women are socialized in the language of love before they learn about sex, while men are socialized in the language of sex before they learn about love. The consequence of this is that women commonly show considerably fewer problems managing sexual deprivation than do men, and while there is little evidence, one might expect that the frequencies of any sexually ameliorative behaviors, such as masturbation and homosexuality, are considerably less frequent for women than for men in prison. There is considerable evidence that such behaviors are less frequent among women in the free society than among men, and one should not be surprised that such continuity would be found inside the prison. In addition, women seem to tolerate the absence of overt sexual activity far better than do men, and thus the rates of overt sexual behavior in the female institutions should be considerably lower than those found in male institutions.

Women Tend to Establish Family Systems.

The typical response of women to the depersonalizing and alienating environment of the penal institution differs substantially from that of males. Nearly universally in juvenile institutions, and in some observed cases in institutions for adult females, female prisoners appear to form ·

into pseudofamilies with articulated roles of husband and wife, and then, especially in juvenile institutions, extend the family to include father, mother, and children, and aunts, uncles, and cousins.[66] These family systems seem to arise from three sources. One source is a process of compensation; the majority of females in these institutions are from severely disordered homes, and the creation of the pseudofamily often compensates for this lack. A second source results from the socialization of women who, unlike males who form gangs in self-defense, tend to form families, the basic institution in the society in which they have stable and legitimate roles. Finally there is the fact that the pseudofamily operates to stabilize relationships in the institution and to establish orders of dominance and submission, the primary model for which women have in family relationships with fathers, husbands, and children. Since all social systems require some form of articulation which is hierarchical in nature, it is not odd that women model their experience on the institution that they know best in the outside community. There is some evidence that the pseudofamily is not as prevalent in institutions with older females, and it is possible to speculate that in these institutions dyadic friendship patterns are more frequent and may be more similar to those in male institutions.

Inside the context of these familial structures there is the potential for and the acting out of overt homosexual contacts. In the two most recent studies of female prisons there are varying estimates of the number of women who are involved in homosexual practices, but this variation is probably a function of differing definitions, with one limiting the estimate to overt physical contact (yielding a rate of about one-half) and the other probably referring to the proportion of the population who are currently involved in roles in pseudofamily structures (yielding a rate of about 85 percent).[67]

Deprivation of Emotionally Satisfying, Stable, Predictable Relationships with Males

A minor part of the overt female homosexual contacts may arise from deprivation of sexuality, but the primary source is the deprivation of the emotionally satisfying relationships with members of the opposite sex and the desire to create the basis for a community of relationships that are stable and predictable. The overt homosexuality derives somewhat from the conventional sexual content role definitions of husband and wife, but also partially from the fact that a certain proportion of females who come into these institutions may well have experience with lesbian relationships through experience with prostitution in the free community. This is not to say that female homosexuals become prostitutes, but rather that among prostitutes homosexual relationships are sought because of the degraded conditions of contacts with men. The processes of induction into homosexual activity in the women's prison is often based on the same principles that one observes in male institutions as part of a search for affection and stability in personal relationships. The homosexual relationship offers protection from the exigencies of the environment and the physical homosexual contacts are less sought for the physical release that they afford than for the validation of emotionally binding and significant relationships.

CONCLUSION

From the arguments posed above it is suggested that what is occurring in the prison situation for both males and females is not a problem of sexual release, but rather the use of sexual relationships in the service of creating a community of relationships for satisfying needs for which the prison fails to provide in any other form. For the male prisoner homosexuality serves as a source of affection, a source of the validation of masculinity, or a source of protection from the problems of institutional life.

In a like manner, the females tend to create family structures in an attempt to ward off the alienating and disorganizing experience of imprisonment; the homosexual relationships are merely part of the binding forces of these relationships.

The problem for the prison administrator then becomes considerably more complex than merely the suppression of sexual activity—it becomes a problem of providing those activities for which the homosexual contacts are serving as substitutes. The inmates are acting out their needs for self-expression, control over their own behavior, affection, and stability of human relationships. The homosexual relationship provides one of the few powerful ways of expressing and gratifying these needs. Unless these needs are met in some other way, there is little opportunity for adequate control of homosexual activity in the prison environment. It might be hypothesized that any attempt to become more coercive and controlling of inmate behavior in order to reduce homosexual contacts may result not in a decrease in activity, but perhaps in an increase. By increasing coercion one increases the pressure to divide inmates from one another, and one decreases their capacity for self-expression and self-control. As the pressure builds there may well be a tendency for homosexual relationships to increase in importance to the inmate population as a reaction to the intensity of the pressure.

Imprisonment and the concomitant sexual deprivation of inmates obviously has some serious consequences, at least during imprisonment, and has a minor potential for complicating postinstitutional life. Little systematic research exists that links the prior nonprison experience of the prisoner, both sexual and nonsexual; methods of institutional management; and the consequences of the interaction of these two elements for the inmate's future functioning. The fact that many inmates adjust easily to the climate of deprivation in the prison may be a measure of their pathology and inability to get along in the outside community rather than a measure of healthy functioning. Just because we manage to make people conform to a climate of deprivation, both sexual and nonsexual, is no reason that we should.

16 Organizational Goals and Inmate Organization

BERNARD B. BERK*

While sociological interest in informal organization dates back to the time of Cooley, there has been little exploration of the relationships between formal and informal organization. Earlier research efforts have been more concerned with documenting the existence of informal organization and demonstrating that it had an impact upon organizational functioning than in trying to establish relationships between it and the organizational context. Different conclusions have been reached in regard to its contribution to the formal organization's ability to achieve its goals, with Roethlisberger and Dixon highlighting its subversive aspect in limiting productivity in economic organizations, while Shils and Janowitz suggest it can facilitate the goals of military organizations by developing social cohesion.[68] Reconciling these findings rests upon the notion that organizations with different goals, structures, and contexts should produce different patterns of informal organization, and informal organization would also have different effects upon the functioning of such diverse types of organizations. What is needed is specification of relationships between the parameters of formal and informal organization and identification of those aspects of organizations which generate oppositional informal organization. By limiting this investigation to one particular type of organization and by examining variation in one of its parameters—its goals—it is hoped some clarification of the problems may emerge.

* From *American Journal of Sociology*, 71, 5, (March 1966): 522–534. Copyright © 1966 by the University of Chicago Press. Reprinted by permission of the University of Chicago Press and the author.

233

Specifically, this paper examines relationships between organizational goals and informal organization in a variety of correctional institutional settings. The study had major objectives. First, we sought to replicate Grusky's study of the consequences of treatment goals for the informal organization of prison inmates.[69] Second, we were concerned with extending existing formulations concerning the relationship between the formal and informal structure of total institutions and, in particular, the conditions which generate informal organizations that are fundamentally opposed to the existing administration.

DESCRIPTION OF RESEARCH SITES

The three institutions selected for study were minimum-security prisons which differed in their emphasis of treatment goals. The criteria used to determine the extent to which treatment goals were dominant were: (1) the presence of a full time counselor or of treatment personnel; (2) the existence of a rehabilitative program; and (3) the active implementation of educational, vocational, or other auxiliary-type programs. The three prisons (to be called Benign, Partial, and Lock) were ranked on a continuum ranging from a strong treatment orientation to a strong custodial orientation.[70]

Camp Benign ranked as the most treatment-oriented institution, as all three criteria were present. In addition, it was the smallest, containing only ninety-seven inmates. This prison was characterized by considerable staff-inmate interaction, maximal opportunities for counseling and guidance, and a sincere effort directed at changing the inmate.[71] Camp Partial was slightly larger (127 inmates) and had both a full-time counselor and a limited educational program. However, it did not have an official treatment program. Treatment techniques employed in this institution tended to be subverted to custodial ends, such as securing inmate conformity. Camp Lock, which had 157 inmates, was the most custodially oriented institution, the sole rehabilitative program being an Alcoholics Anonymous group. Its primary goal was containment, and there was little official pretense or concern about treatment or rehabilitation. The officials sought to run an institution which attracted as little attention as possible from the community.

THE FINDINGS

Inmate Attitudes

The first area investigated was the differences in attitudes of inmates of the treatment and custodial prisons. Numerous observers have asserted that the relationship between guards and inmates in custodial institutions is characterized by hostility, mistrust, suspicion, and fear, promulgated by both the official dictates of the prison and the informal norms among the inmates.[72] Grusky, Vinter and Janowitz, and others have argued that a positive and co-operative type of staff-inmate relationship is a prerequisite for and a consequence of treatment goals. This is due primarily to accepting attitudes on the part of the staff, the over-all replacement of formal controls by more informal ones, and the general reduction of inmate deprivations.

Grusky found support for the hypothesis that more positive attitudes among inmates are found in treatment, rather than in custodial institutions. By comparing attitudinal responses of inmates in three institutions, each situated in a different position along the treatment-custodial continuum, we were able to test this same hypothesis more carefully than could be done in the original case study.

As in the original study, inmate attitudes in three areas were examined: attitudes toward the prison, staff, and treatment program. Table 1 demonstrates a positive relationship between favorable inmate response toward the prison and the degree of development of its treatment goals. Where about six out of ten of Benign's inmates were positively oriented toward the prison (63 per cent), not quite five of ten of Partial's inmates (48 per cent) and less than four of ten of the inmates at Lock (39 per cent), the most custodially oriented prison of the three, had positive feelings toward their institutions. A similar pattern is revealed concerning attitudes toward the staff. At Benign, 44 per cent of the men had favorable attitudes toward the staff, whereas only 29 per cent at Partial and 23 per cent at Lock were as positively oriented toward the staff. The third area of inmate attitudes investigated were those toward existing programs. These attitudes were also found, as expected, to be related to the goals of the prison. At Benign, 89 per cent of the men felt that the program had helped them, as compared with 82 per cent of the men at Partial, and 75 per cent of the men at Lock who expressed similar views. Attitudes toward the programs were the most positive and reflected, in part, the salience of the program which, in turn, was due to the official support for treatment goals. In short, Grusky's original hypothesis was strongly confirmed.[73] Significant differences were found between the prison which was most custodially oriented and the one most treatment-oriented.

The Effects of Socialization

In order to give a sharper test to the proposition, the length of

TABLE 1
Inmate Attitudes toward the Prison, Staff, and Program

	Benign (per cent)	Partial (per cent)	Lock (per cent)
Attitudes toward the prison:[a]			
Favorable (scale types I–II)	63.1	48.2	39.1
Attitudes toward the staff:[b]			
Favorable (scale types I–II)	44.3	29.2	23.4
Attitudes toward the program:[c]			
Favorable (item response "yes")	88.8	81.9	74.8
N=	(95)	(124)	(138)

[a]For a description of scale, see O. Grusky, "Treatment Goals and Organizational Behavior" (unpublished Ph.D. dissertation [University of Michigan, 1958]), p. 141. The coefficients of reproducibility for this scale were Benign .91, Partial .90, and Lock .93. The coefficients of scalability were .54, .77, and .81, respectively. A difference of over 12.5 per cent between the camps is significant at the .05 level by a difference-of-proportions test.

[b]The coefficients of reproducibility for this scale were Benign .88, Partial .91, and Lock .92; for scalability, they were .53, .75, and .77, respectively.

[c]Only a single item, "Do you feel (the program) has helped you in any way?" was available. No answer: Benign 2, Partial 3, Lock 19.

residence in the institution was held constant. In this manner, the consequences of official socialization could be examined. It would be expected that the longer the inmate was exposed to the values and programs of the prison, the more likely he would be influenced by them; that is, inmates who have spent a long time in the prison should most clearly reflect the impact of the prison on their attitudes, and those who have been there only a short time should be least affected.

The data presented in Figure 1 show a strong relationship between attitude toward the staff and length of time spent in the prison. Inmates who had spent longer time in the custodially oriented prison were more likely to hold negative attitudes than those who had only been there a few months, whereas the reverse was true at the treatment-oriented prison where inmates who had spent a long time in the prison were more likely to hold positive attitudes than negative ones.[74] When those inmates at Benign who had spent fewer than three months in the prison were compared with those who had spent more than eight months there, we found that only about one of three (35 per cent) of the former, as contrasted with about half (56 per cent) of the latter, fell into the most

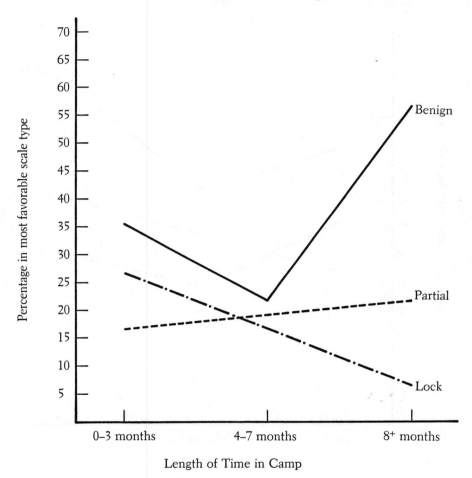

FIG. 1.–Relationship of attitudes toward staff to length of time spent in prison. The *N*'s from which percentages were based for the 0–3 month period were: Benign 26, Partial 33, and Lock 55. For the 4–7 month period, they were 36, 35, and 44, respectively. And for the 8+ month period, they were 30, 59, and 35.

favorable scale type. At Camp Lock the reverse was found true. The proportion of positive responses dropped sharply from 27 per cent of the inmates who had been there less than three months to less than 9 per cent of those who had been there eight or more months. Camp Partial exhibited a mild positive influence, reflecting its intermediate position.[75]

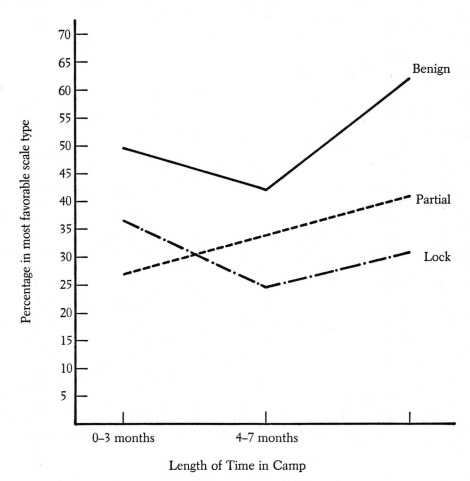

FIG. 2.—Relationship of attitudes toward prison and length of time spent in prison. The *N*'s from which percentages were based are the same as for Fig. 1.

In Figure 2, the same general relationship is revealed with respect to attitudes toward the prison, but not quite as clearly. The proportion of inmates at Lock who were favorably oriented decreased slightly from 36 per cent of those whose stay was short-term to 31 per cent of those having a longer-term stay in the prison. In contrast, the percentage of favorable responses increased at Benign from 50 per cent of those having less than three months' experience to 64 per cent of those who had eight or more months in prison. However, in both prisons, inmates with four-seven months' experience were most negative.[76]

Influence of Other Variables

Before any conclusions could be drawn from these findings, it was necessary to control for other relevant variables, since an important obstacle to studies of this nature is that inmates are not usually randomly assigned to treatment institutions. This was true of this study as well, in that inmates at Benign were younger and likely to have been less serious offenders. However, this type of selectivity does not appear to have accounted for the results obtained in this study. *Age:* Initially, it might have been argued that the older age of the inmates at Lock and Partial would be sufficient to account for the more negative attitudes found there. Our findings, on the contrary, show age to be inversely related to negative attitude at both Lock and Benign, with the younger inmates in both camps more likely to hold negative attitudes. No difference was found at Partial. Furthermore, young inmates were more positive at Benign than their counterparts at Lock. The same was true for older inmates. This would suggest that selectivity in regard to age would operate against the hypothesis. *Type of offender:* It similarly could have been argued that inmates at Partial and Lock were more experienced and hardened criminals, well indoctrinated in the ways of crime and would, therefore, exhibit more negative attitudes. We may ask, first, whether this is true and, second, if so, is this factor large enough to account for the differences obtained between the prisons? Again, the findings show, in contradiction to what is commonly believed, that the more serious offenders, by a variety of measures, did not have more negative attitudes. On the contrary, these two variables were generally unrelated. In the few cases where differences were found, they were small and variable. Furthermore, the direction of this relationship was reversed in the treatment institution, where the more serious offenders were more likely to hold more positive attitudes than the less serious offenders. And, finally, when comparable groups of types of offenders were compared in the various camps, they were more positive in their attitudes at Benign than at Lock.[77]

It would appear (see Table 2) that the selectivity in regard to age and type of offender would not be sufficient to account for the differences obtained in this study, and certainly could not account for the differences between Partial and Lock, since there was little difference in the types of inmates sent to those two camps. It should be pointed out, however, that inmates at Benign were more positive during the early period than inmates at the other camps, which may have been partly due to a selectivity, or may have resulted from the camp having had an initial positive impact on inmate attitudes. In any case, whatever differences existed in the nature of the inmates in the organization initially as a result of differential recruitment procedures, inmates became more positive over time in the treatment institution and more negative in the custodial one, reflecting the differential impact of the organization upon its members.

By these tests, then, it appears that, regardless of any selectivity in input, the differences between prisons were responsible for attitudinal differences.

TABLE 2
Inmate Attitudes toward the Prison by Age and Type of Offender
(Per Cent in Most Favorable Scale Type)

	Benign (per cent)	N	Partial (per cent)	N	Lock (per cent)	N
Age:						
25 years and under	47.6	(86)	36.3	(11)	11.1	(18)
26+	77.7	(9)	35.4	(111)	35.9	(114)
Number of prison sentences:						
1	48.6	(70)	37.1	(62)	34.2	(76)
2 or more	56.0	(25)	35.1	(61)	29.3	(58)
Number of charged crimes:						
1–3	45.9	(61)	31.9	(47)	35.5	(45)
4+	65.3	(26)	39.6	(63)	33.3	(70)
Seriousness of crimes:*						
Less serious crimes	50.0	(18)	47.5	(59)	30.8	(39)
More serious crimes	50.0	(74)	34.7	(59)	31.6	(76)

*When more than one crime was charged, the most serious was coded. Serious crimes were regarded as murder, rape, and assault. The less serious crimes consisted in robbery, burglary, larceny, etc.

Informal Organization

These attitudinal differences between prisons reflected major differences in the nature of the informal organization among prison inmates.

Support for this assertion is reflected in the finding that attitudes of inmates were related to the degree of their involvement in the inmate subculture. Attitudes appeared to be acquired as a result of informal socialization and participation in prison subculture, and reflected those informal standards held by its members.

Involvement and participation in the subculture was measured by the number of friendship choices the inmate received from other inmates. Three types of inmates were distinguished: the uninvolved or isolate who received no choices, the moderately involved who received from one to three choices, and the highly involved who received four or more friendship choices. Table 3 shows that at Benign isolates were the most negative and highly involved inmates the most positive in their attitudes toward the prison. At Lock, the reverse was true with the highly involved inmates the most negative and the uninvolved inmates the most positive in their attitudes. At Partial, negative attitudes were related to both high and low involvement in the subculture. It is not immediately clear why moderately involved inmates at Partial were more positive than isolates. In all three prisons, however, favorableness of attitude was related to degree of involvement with the informal organization.[78]

TABLE 3

Degree of Involvement in Informal System and Attitudes toward the Prison*
(Per Cent in Most Favorable Scale Type)

	Benign (per cent)	N	Partial (per cent)	N	Lock (per cent)	N
Isolates (received no choices)	33.3	(15)	32.4	(37)	33.3	(75)
Moderately involved (received 1-3 choices)	50.6	(63)	38.5	(78)	30.2	(59)
Highly involved (received 4+ choices)	64.6	(17)	25.0	(12)	20.0	(5)

* Involvement measured by the number of friendship choices received by the inmate.

Informal Leadership

Further evidence of the impact of custodial and treatment goals on informal organization among prison inmates was found in the kinds of attitudes held by informal leaders in the various prisons.

Both Schrag's[79] and Grusky's studies dealt with the relationship between leaders and organizational goals. Schrag asserted that leaders were uniformly selected from among the most negative inmates. In contrast, Grusky hypothesized that orientation of the leader would vary with the type of total institution; specifically, informal leaders in treat-

TABLE 4
Leadership and Attitudes toward Prison
(Per Cent in Most Favorable Scale Type)

	Benign (per cent)	N	Partial (per cent)	N	Lock (per cent)	N
Leaders	61.3	(31)	47.5	(50)	23.3	(37)
Non-leaders	45.3	(66)	35.5	(77)	34.3	(97)

TABLE 5
Leadership and Attitudes Toward Program*
(Per Cent Favorable)

	Benign (per cent)	N	Partial (per cent)	N	Lock (per cent)	N
Leaders	74.2	(31)	47.6	(50)	39.3	(37)
Non-leaders	62.5	(66)	48.0	(77)	63.5	(97)

*The particular item asked if they thought the programs in the camp were a good idea.

ment institutions were seen as more likely to be co-operative than their counterparts in custodially oriented prisons.

Consistent with Grusky's hypothesis, leaders at Benign were more positive in their attitudes than were leaders at Partial who, in turn, were more positive than those at Lock.[80] However, this might have been true for any sample of inmates, because inmates were, as a whole, more positive at Benign than at Lock. By comparing the leaders with the non-leaders within each prison, a more precise test of this relationship was obtained. Tables 4 and 5 show leaders were more positive than the non-leaders at Benign, while the reverse was true at Lock where the leaders were more negative than the non-leaders. This relationship was found to hold both for attitudes toward the prison and the institution's programs.

OBSERVATIONS ABOUT INFORMAL ORGANIZATION

The Function of Informal Organization in Total Institutions

Having replicated Grusky's study and substantiated the hypothesis, we sought to develop a fuller explanation of the findings. Inmate attitude reflect the nature of inmate subculture and informal organization which, in turn, is conditioned by formal organizational characteristics, such as the formal structure and the official objectives.

Informal organization develops in prison because: (1) inmates are isolated from society; (2) institutionalization generates common problems of adjustment[81] which require co-operation for their solution while simultaneously providing a situation with opportunity for effective inter-action with others similarly situated;[82] and (3) inmates are members of a formal organization which, by its very nature as a system of action, can never fully anticipate or co-ordinate all behavior through the formal system alone; hence, informal organization serves to close the gaps of the formal organization.

Two kinds of informal organization have been identified in the prisons studied—one supportive of the official structure and the other in opposition to it. We submit that the goal of treatment encourages the development of the former, and the goal of custody the latter.

Inmate subcultures develop as solutions to the problems and deprivations experienced by inmates in the prison situation. They would, therefore, differ in their form and content as the nature of the problems experienced by inmates, particularly those created by the institutional experience itself, differ. The two different types of informal organization developed because the inmate subsystem performed contrasting functions in the treatment and custodial institutions.

Two reasons may be suggested to explain the character of the inmate subculture in the custodial institution; first, the problems faced by inmates tend to be more severe there; in addition, inmates perceive the custodial institution itself to be responsible for their problems. As a result, they band together in opposition to the prison and its administration, which they see as the source of their frustrations.[83] Consequently, inmate subcultures tend to become more and more dominated by the values of professional criminals which already emphasize a strict demarcation between the guards and inmates, since these groups are seen as fundamentally in opposition to one another.

The emergence of this subculture compounds an already difficult problem—a central concern, in fact, of the custodial institution—that of maintaining social control within the prison. Since techniques for insuring conformity are inadequate, guards resort to various methods of accommodation and bargain for conformity with the means available to them.[84] One method, as Sykes points out, is to "buy compliance at the cost of tolerating deviance." In return for the guards overlooking selected infractions of the rules, inmates are expected to comply with the rest. In this fashion, inmates begin to regulate their own behavior and, in so doing, begin to fulfill, in part, the formal organization's task of maintaining internal order. The more effectively they are able to exert control over their behavior, the more advantageous is their bargaining position vis-à-vis the guards—a process which itself has a further consolidating effect upon inmate subculture. In this manner, inmates are able to gain some degree of freedom from the demands and pressures of the formal organization, thereby increasing the relative amount of control they can exercise over the conditions of their existence.[85] This newly gained mastery over their environmental conditions is, however, illusory. It would appear that they have merely traded their previous situation and its attendant deprivations for subjugation to an even more despotic ruling group—other inmates who have less compunctions and fewer limitations about the use of force and violence to gain compliance with their ends. Thus, in reality, freedom is usually only temporary, as inmate leaders quickly replace the official demands for conformity with new demands for conformity to new rules which sustain their dominance.

In contrast to this picture of informal organization in custodial institutions, we can view the development of informal organization in treatment institutions. While inmate organization can also be found in treatment institutions, it does not generally take on an oppositional character. It does not simply because many of the psychological deprivations of imprisonment have been reduced, and a shift in patterns of control has occurred. Inmates are treated with more respect by the organization and, as a result, the institution is not perceived by inmates to be totally against them or antithetical to their interests. In addition, the treatment institution is more flexible in regard to its rules, and treatment needs of inmates are considered in its demands for conformity. Furthermore, in its attempt to regulate behavior, formal methods of controls are replaced by more informal ones, thus reducing resentment and hostility. This leads to a greater tolerance in the range of inmate conformity and, concomitantly, "control" becomes less important in the hierarchy of organization objectives. Accordingly, there is little pay-off from the administration for inmates' regulation of their own behavior.

Selected aspects of the formal organization's structure also have an impact on informal organization. Particularly in total institutions, the formal authority structure serves as a model for the informal. The custodially oriented prison, which is usually highly centralized, tends to produce a similar type of informal inmate leadership; for such an adaptation serves, on the one hand, to strengthen official control and administration of the prison and, on the other, to stabilize inmate relations by focusing attention on the deprivations inflicted by the authorities. Because inmate subculture there is dominated by criminal values emphasizing a strict demarcation between guards and inmates, informal leadership must thereby justify itself by securing special concessions from the oppressors, the "screws," in return for which the leaders prevent their men from stepping too far out of line. The typical inmate in such a situation is confronted with few alternatives and usually accepts the values and the leadership as it is presented to him, thereby perpetuating the subculture.

The inmate subsystems are seen as performing different functions within their respective institutions which, as we have seen, are directly linked to the goals of the prison. In the custodial prison, even though oppositional and subversive to the organization, it also functioned to assist it in the maintenance of internal order by regulating inmate behavior, though this is usually at the cost of the "corruption of the formal authority system." In contrast, control of inmate behavior was not a primary function of informal organization in the treatment institution. Informal organization there was more compatible with the formal organization and was more oriented toward meeting the particular needs of inmates and integrating and co-ordinating their behavior.

The functioning of informal leaders was, in turn, directly linked to the functions performed by the inmate subsystem, and, as a consequence, the informal leaders' main task in the custodial prison was one of exercising control over the behavior of other inmates. In order to effectively implement this end, the informal leadership employed the same techniques as the formal organization and developed a highly consolidated and centralized power structure. And, like the formal organization, it also relied upon coercion and force, rather than on consensus or co-operation, to insure conformity.

In contrast, the informal leaders in the treatment institution, because the treatment goal allowed for a broader range of inmate adaptation, performed a variety of functions depending on the particular needs of the inmates, and functioned more as co-ordinators and integrators of behavior rather than as controllers, as they did in the custodial prison. Not only did the informal leaders play very different roles in the two types of prisons, but techniques of leadership differed as well, since the inmate subsystem in the treatment institution tended to be based more upon consensus and co-operation than was true of the custodial prison.

These speculations led to a new hypothesis about the structure and functioning of informal leadership in the different types of prisons. As we have pointed out, one of the techniques for maintaining order in the custodial prison was the *centralization of control* by informal leadership.

Because this function was less important for the inmate subsystem in the treatment institution, it was hypothesized that the more treatment-oriented the prison, the less centralized the informal leadership structure would be and the proportionately greater number of inmates who would emerge as top leaders.

The data supported this hypothesis. At Benign, 9.3 per cent of the inmates were chosen as top leaders (that is, received nine or more choices), while at Partial 6.3 per cent were chosen, compared with only 1.3 per cent of the inmates at Lock. When inmates were asked: "Who were leaders?" similar results were obtained. Forty-three per cent of the inmates at Benign were named, compared with 38 per cent at Partial and 23 per cent at Lock.[86] Both measures indicated greater concentration of power and centralization of control in the custodial prison.

A second technique, adopted by inmate leaders in the custodial prison to control inmate behavior, was the use of coercion to secure conformity and to maintain power. This led to a hypothesis dealing with types of persons likely to rise to positions of leadership or influence in the two types of prisons. Because *control* was an important function of the inmate leaders in the custodial prison, individuals disposed toward such behavior would be more likely to rise to positions of leadership there than would be true of treatment prisons where a more charismatic, socioemotional, or consensus-oriented type of leader would be expected to develop. Therefore, it was hypothesized that leaders in the custodial institution would be more authoritarian, reflecting their "tough-minded" orientation toward the use of power, and would be "less well liked," due to their reliance upon coercion and emphasis upon control than leaders in treatment institutions. Support for this hypothesis comes from the finding that leaders were selected from the most authoritarian inmates at Lock, whereas the reverse was true at Benign, where leaders were selected from the least authoritarian inmates.[87] Not only was the leadership structure more decentralized at Benign, but the leadership positions were occupied there, as well, by less authoritarian persons. Furthermore, leaders at Benign were less authoritarian than those at Partial who, in turn, were less authoritarian than the leaders found at Lock. No difference in authoritarianism was found between the general population of inmates at the three prisons. In addition to their being less authoritarian, the leaders at Benign were liked better, friendlier, and more approachable by other inmates than was true of the leaders at Lock.[88] This style of leadership is reflected in the findings that leaders at Benign were more likely to be chosen by other inmates as "well liked," a "best buddy," and as someone with whom they could discuss their personal problems, than was true of the leaders at Camp Lock. Camp Partial once again was found to exhibit an intermediate position with regard to its leaders.

SUMMARY AND CONCLUSIONS

The purpose of this study was twofold: (1) to replicate a study conducted by Grusky; and (2) to examine the consequences of treatment and custodial goals upon the inmate subsystem within correctional institutions, with particular emphasis on the conditions generating oppositional informal organization. Three areas of concern were inmate attitudes, the effect of socialization, and the development of informal leadership.

1. The findings on the whole supported Grusky's major hypothesis: Inmates were more positive in their attitudes toward the institution, staff, and programs in the treatment institution than those in the custodial one. Furthermore, they became more positive or negative with the length of time they spent in the prison, depending upon the type of organizational goal, thereby suggesting that it was the prison experience which was primarily responsible for the development of negative attitudes.

2. Differences between prisons were found to be related to differences in inmate organization. Two facts suggested this: First, attitudes were found to be related to degree of involvement with inmate organization, and second, leaders' attitudes were found to vary systematically with the prison's goals, being more positive in the treatment institution and more negative in the custodial one.

3. The informal leadership structure was also found to be more centralized in the custodial institution in an attempt to maintain more effective control over inmate behavior. The informal leaders among the inmates played different roles, depending upon organizational goals and contexts; and these roles were directly linked to the function of the inmate subculture within the prison. Leaders in the custodial prison were also found to be more authoritarian and less well liked than leaders in the treatment prison, reflecting the differences in their roles.

The goal of "custody," with its concomitant centralized- and formal-authority structure and increased deprivations for inmates, contributed significantly to the development of the hostile informal organization in the custodial prison. The disenfranchisement of inmates from possible rewards of the institution encouraged the development of negative attitudes and a hostile informal leadership.

17   *Patterns of Management and Adaptations to Organizational Roles: A Study of Prison Inmates*

THOMAS P. WILSON*

Much of the research and speculation on behavior in organizations concludes that individuals who are treated with respect and given autonomy by their superiors have better relations with superiors and peers and also perform better in their assigned tasks than do individuals who are closely and arbitrarily supervised.[89] However, though it appears that supportive management styles do generate improved relations with superiors and close relations among peers, there is some evidence that such management is not consistently associated with high performance.[90] This suggests that the mechanisms by which management practices in organizations affect subordinates are not adequately understood. The present paper attempts to add some clarification through an investigation of prison inmates' adaptations to "bureaucratic" and "participative" patterns of institutional management.

Previous studies of correctional and psychiatric institutions have shown that flexible and supportive management patterns are associated with comparatively good relations between inmates and staff and with close relations among inmates. Early institutional studies dealt mainly with custodial institutions, characterized by authoritarian and arbitrary supervisory practices, and generally inmates were found to be antagonistic to staff.[91] In these institutions, order and control appeared to depend on inmate power structures maintained by covert and often unwitting collusion between staff and an inmate elite, and the "inmate code" was

* From *American Journal of Sociology*, 74, 2 (1968): 146–157. Copyright © 1968 by the University of Chicago Press. Reprinted by permission of the University of Chicago Press and the author.

seen as playing an important part in sustaining inmate solidarity in opposition to staff, mitigating the effects of distrust and hostility among inmates, and legitimating the privileged access of the elite to interaction with staff.[92] In contrast, recent research in correctional[93] and mental institutions[94] indicates that this kind of inmate organization is less prominent in treatment-oriented institutions. For example, Street, Vinter, and Perrow compared inmates in several juvenile correctional institutions and found a tendency for inmates in the treatment-oriented institutions to get along better with staff and to have closer relations with fellow inmates. They suggest that official goals emphasizing treatment lead to humanitarian and flexible management practices, while custodial goals lead to authoritarian and rigid patterns of control, and they propose that the former generate more positive relations than do the latter.[95]

While this interpretation is consistent with conclusions from research in other kinds of organizations, the problem remains of understanding how participative types of management lead to improved relations between subordinates and superiors and to closer relations among subordinates. Moreover, the seemingly inconsistent effects of management practices on task performance remain to be explained.

An important contribution to these problems is Goffman's observation that the role prescribed for an individual in an organization not only specifies certain patterns of behavior as required of him but also serves as an implicit definition of what sort of person he is and that a member must adapt to this organizational assumption of what he is.[96] Thus, an individual can be viewed as acquiring a set of attitudes toward himself in relation to others in the organization that both enables him to interact viably with others and makes it possible for him to live with himself.[97] Such a complex of attitudes may be termed the individual's *adaptation* to his organizational role.[98] Although the problem of adaptation exists for the members of any organization, it is particularly acute for inmates, since institutional role prescriptions tend to apply to every activity of inmates throughout the day and night and often are inconsistent with an individual's conception of himself as an autonomous person with goals, needs, beliefs, and abilities of value.[99]

For the purpose of this study, adaptations will be classified in terms of the relation between the individual's own personal goals, together with the means he employs to pursue them, and the organizational structure. Thus, three types of adaptation will be identified: *co-operative,* in which the personal goals pursued by the individual coincide with the goals others expect him to pursue as part of his role; *opportunistic,* in which goals are not shared, but the individual relies on organizational activities as means to achieve his own ends; and *alienated,* in which goals are not shared nor is the organization used as an opportunity for the pursuit of of goals.[100]

A second important concept is that of an organization as a hierarchical structure of decision making, in which an individual at one level is responsible for decisions affecting those subordinate to him. From the point of view of the subordinate, then, it is possible to distinguish between those decisions for which he himself is directly responsible and those decisions made by his superior that affect him.[101] The critical point is that the latter decisions strongly affect the nature of the situation to which the subordinate must adapt. Consequently, the way in which he is involved in these decisions should markedly affect his type of adaptation.

Patterns of management, then, can be classified in terms of how superiors involve their subordinates in decisions, and the two such patterns of concern here can be called bureaucratic and participative. The essential characteristic of bureaucratic management is that decisions affecting subordinates are made by the superior applying rules that both establish the categories in terms of which situations are defined and specify the alternative courses of action. In contrast, participative management consists of the superior involving subordinates in decisions affecting them by having them participate in defining the nature of the situations about which decisions have to be made and in identifying the possible courses of action.[102]

The hypothesis can now be advanced that co-operative adaptations are associated with participative management, since participative practices provide mechanisms for bringing about congruence between superiors' and subordinates' definitions of situations and, moreover, place high value on such consensus, whereas bureaucratic practices do not. Further, the attitudes toward self and others comprising adaptations should influence subordinates' behavior toward superiors and peers. Consequently, as a second general hypothesis, adaptations should operate as an intervening variable between patterns of management and subordinates' relations with superiors and peers. Thus, the common finding that participative styles of management are associated with improved relations between subordinates and superiors and close relations among subordinates should be explained in part by the effects of management practices on subordinates' adaptations.

METHODS

An opportunity to investigate the effects of management patterns and adaptations on subordinates' relations with others was provided by a demonstration project in a correctional institution.[103] Three housing units in the institution were studied, two of which were administered bureaucratically while the third was operated by the demonstration project using participative management practices.

Although the institution was ideologically committed to treatment and offered numerous treatment programs, these, as well as the routines of daily living, were administered by complex systems of rules. To provide an incentive for comformity and to simplify supervision, the housing units of about 180 men each were divided into "honor" and "non-honor" units. New inmates were placed in non-honor units with relatively few privileges and close supervision, and they were permitted to move to honor units, with more privileges and less supervision, only after accumulating seniority in terms of time without disciplinary infractions. Moreover, they remained in an honor unit only as long as they stayed out of disciplinary trouble. A non-honor and an honor unit were selected randomly for study.

The third unit studied, called C Unit, was operated by the demonstration project for the purpose of experimenting with new approaches to treatment within the institution. In doing this, the project established a participative pattern of management within C Unit, in which inmates became involved in decisions about problems of living within the unit and about the program of the project. The C Unit population of 130 men at any one time was drawn randomly from a pool of inmates in the institution, but the eligible pool itself was not completely representative of the institution.[104]

The major source of data is an interview survey conducted in the three units after the project had been in operation for about sixteen months.[105] In addition, participant observation over the year and a half preceding the survey provided information about the nature of the project and institution, and institutional files were used to obtain background data on the inmates in the survey samples.

The main independent variable, pattern of management, is indicated by an inmate's housing unit: the non-honor unit was bureaucratic with low privileges; the honor unit was bureaucratic with high privileges; and C Unit was, to a far greater extent than the rest of the institution, participative and had about the same privileges as honor units. The index of type of adaptation was constructed by combining questions reflecting an inmate's attitudes toward each of up to seven staff members to whom he was related.[106] Inmate behavior toward staff was studied using questions pertaining to communication with staff about three matters important in the daily lives of inmates: personal worries; rules and procedures; and annoying behavior of other inmates.[107] Inmates indicating they talked to staff about two or three of these topics were classified as "high" on the index of communication with staff, while those indicating one and none were classified as "medium" and "low," respectively. Finally, two indicators were used to describe relations among inmates. First, inmates were divided into those who wanted half or more of their inmate associates as friends after release and those wanting less than half of their associates as friends.[108] Second, inmates were asked if they talked with other inmates about their own personal problems.[109] Those inmates who both wanted half or more of their associates as friends and talked with others about personal problems were classified as having "close" relations with their peers.

FINDINGS

Participative and bureaucratic management practices are strongly associated with co-operative and opportunistic adaptations, respectively, as can be seen in Table 1. Inmates in C Unit were far more likely to have co-operative adaptations than were inmates in the bureaucratic housing units. It will be noted, in addition, that the low-privilege unit had a higher proportion of inmates with alienated adaptations than did the high-privilege unit, giving rise to an ordinal relation between housing unit and type of adaptation. This probably reflects the selection process by which inmates gained access to honor units, since alienated adaptations are more likely to result in non-conforming behavior, and thus exclusion from the honor units, than are opportunistic adaptations.

When background characteristics are introduced as control variables, the relation between pattern of management and type of adaptation is unaffected. This, together with the fact that C Unit did not differ markedly from the other units in the distribution of any of the background characteristics, suggests that the findings cannot be explained by possible lack of representativeness in the C Unit selection procedures.

The Effects of Exposure

As with other background factors, when the amount of time inmates had spent in their respective units is held constant, the association between pattern of management and type of adaptation is unaffected.[110] Time in unit, however, can also be used as an index of exposure to a particular pattern of management, and Table 2 is organized to facilitate examination of the effects of exposure to each pattern. Looking first at

TABLE 1
Type of Adaptation, by Management Pattern
(Percentages)

Type of adaptation	Management Pattern		
	Bureaucratic		*Participative (C Unit)*
	Low privilege	*High privilege*	
Co-operative	5	13	40
Opportunistic	53	62	52
Alienated	42	25	8
Total	100	100	100
Base	(57)	(60)	(120)

NOTE.—$r = 0.39$; $d_{yx} = 0.39$.

the bureaucratic-low-privilege unit, one can see that the proportion of opportunistic adaptations tends to increase with increased exposure. Since most of these inmates were new to the institution, it appears that opportunistic adaptations developed among new arrivals as the length of their stay increased. This interpretation is supported when time in the institution is added as an additional control variable, although the number of cases is too small to warrant presentation.

In the bureaucratic-high-privilege unit, it appears that inmates who had been in the unit for a short time were very likely to have opportunistic adaptations, but as time in the unit increases, the proportion of opportunistic adaptations declines regularly, and the shift tends to be toward alienated adaptations. This suggests that during their initial period in the institution, inmates acquired opportunistic adaptations, and these became most prominent when they moved to honor units. However, as inmates remained in a particular unit, the pattern of living became routinized and, in effect, opportunities for continued pursuit of personal goals declined, with the result that opportunistic adaptations became less rewarding and thus less frequent. This interpretation presupposes that the critical factor is time spent in the same housing unit rather than the total length of stay in the institution, which implies that inmates with a short time in the unit should be very likely to have opportunistic adaptations, irrespective of how long they have been in the institution. This appears to be the case, for among inmates in the bureaucratic-high-

TABLE 2
Type of Adaptation, by Time in Unit And
Management Pattern
(Percentages)

Type of adaptation	Months in Housing Unit[a]			
	0–3	4–6	7–12	13 or More
Bureaucratic—Low Privilege				
Co-operative	8	0	[0]	[0]
Opportunistic	47	62	[3]	[1]
Alienated	45	38	[1]	[1]
Total	100	100		
Base	(38)	(13)	(4)	(2)
Bureaucratic—High Privilege				
Co-operative	13	7	25	7
Opportunistic	80	67	56	43
Alienated	7	26	19	50
Total	100	100	100	100
Base	(15)	(15)	(16)	(14)
Participative (C Unit)				
Co-operative	27	39	62	45
Opportunistic	59	58	33	45
Alienated	14	3	5	10
Total	100	100	100	100
Base	(41)	(36)	(21)	(22)

[a]Item: "How long have you been in —— Unit?"

privilege unit for six months or less, the percentages with opportunistic adaptations are 75 for inmates in the institution six months or less and 70 for inmates in the institution for seven or more months (percentage bases of 20 and 10, respectively).

Finally, in C Unit, co-operative adaptations increase steadily with exposure to participative management, up to about one year. The decline after this point may be attributable to inmates having exhausted the opportunities of the C Unit program as in the bureaucratic-high-privilege unit, although it is worth noting that the shift is toward opportunistic rather than alienated adaptations. When time in the institution is introduced as an additional factor (see Table 3), it appears that exposure to participative management is more likely to lead to co-operative adaptations if inmates have spent little time in the institution than if they have been in the institution for a long while before coming to C Unit. Inmates who had been in the institution for a long period before entering C Unit had been exposed to the bureaucratic patterns of the institution and should have tended to acquire opportunistic or perhaps alienated adaptations. It appears that developing co-operative adaptations is inhibited by such previous experience.

These findings indicate that co-operative and opportunistic adaptations are associated with exposure to participative and bureaucratic management patterns. Moreover, the inhibiting effect of previous exposure to bureaucratic patterns on acquisition of co-operative adaptations suggests that the attitudes comprising adaptations to organizational roles are not superficial responses to the immediate situation, but instead involve more stable characteristics of the individual. Thus the first hypothesis is supported.

TABLE 3

Percentage Co-operative among Inmates in C Unit for Six Months or Less, by Time in Institution and Time in Unit

Months in institution	Months in C Unit (Participative Management)		
	0–3	*4–6*	*Percentage difference*
0–6	29 (24)	45 (20)	+16
7 or more	24 (17)	31 (16)	+ 7

Inmate Communication to Staff

As anticipated from previous studies, inmates living under participative management practices in C Unit were more likely to communicate with staff than were inmates in the two bureaucratic units (see Table 4). However, the central question here is the extent to which the effects of management practices on inmate behavior toward staff are exerted through inmates' adaptations. If type of adaptation acts as an intervening variable, then first of all, the tendency toward higher communication with staff in C Unit should be reduced when type of adaptation is held constant. There is some suggestion of this, particularly in the high-communication category, but C Unit inmates still remain less likely than others to be low. In addition, if type of adaptation intervenes between pattern of management and communication to staff, then an association should exist between adaptations and communication when pattern of management is controlled. This also appears to be the case, as can be seen by inspecting the differences among types of adaptation within the columns of Table 4, and as is reflected in the values of Kendall's -b for the relation between adaptation and communication within each unit: these are 0.27, 0.40, and 0.15 for C Unit, the high-privilege unit, and the low-privilege unit, respectively. Finally, the association between pattern of management and type of adaptation found in Table 1 ($\tau=0.39$) is unaffected when communication is held constant: the values of τ are 0.39, 0.32, and 0.35 for high, medium, and low levels of communication, respectively.[111] There is, then, some evidence that inmates' adaptations play a part in the mechanism by which pattern of management affects inmate communication to staff.

Closeness of Relations Among Inmates

Turning now to relations among inmates, one can see in Table 5 (top line) that C Unit inmates were somewhat more likely than others to have close relations with their peers, which is the direction of finding anticipated from previous studies. However, when type of adaptation is controlled, it is evident that the higher proportion of inmates with close relations in C Unit results from the high proportion with co-operative adaptations in that unit. In addition, closeness appears to be related to type of adaptation, except in the low-privilege unit. Finally, when closeness is held constant, the original relation between pattern of management and type of adaptation remains: the values of τ are 0.52 and 0.33 for inmates with and without close relations, respectively. These findings, while not as strong as for communication with staff, indicate that type of adaptation plays a part in the processes by which pattern of management affects relations among inmates.

Although the relation between participative management and close relations among inmates, in the top line of Table 5, is in the anticipated direction, it is not particularly strong. The relatively small difference of 8

TABLE 4
**Communication to Staff, by Management Pattern and
Type of Adaptation (Percentages)**

Communica-tion index	Management Pattern		
	Bureaucratic		Participative (C Unit)
	Low privilege	High privilege	
	All Types of Adaptation		
High	26	18	38
Medium	18	30	30
Low	56	52	32
Total	100	100	100
Base	(57)	(60)	(120)
	Co-operative		
High	[1]	[5]	52
Medium	[1]	[3]	29
Low	[1]	[0]	19
Total			100
Base	(3)	(8)	(48)
	Opportunistic		
High	33	14	31
Medium	13	32	29
Low	54	54	40
Total	100	100	100
Base	(30)	(37)	(62)
	Alienated		
High	17	7	10
Medium	21	20	40
Low	62	73	50
Total	100	100	100
Base	(24)	(15)	(10)

TABLE 5
Percentage with Close Relations, by Management
Pattern and Type of Adaptation

Type of adaptation	Management Pattern		
	Bureaucratic		Participative (C Unit)
	Low privilege	High privilege	
All types of adaptation	25	30	38
	(57)	(60)	(120)
Co-operative	[0]	[3]	52
	(3)	(8)	(48)
Opportunistic	27	35	29
	(30)	(37)	(62)
Alienated	25	13	20
	(24)	(15)	(10)

per cent between the bureaucratic-high-privilege and the participative units can be attributed to an "anomalously high" rate in the bureaucratic-high-privilege unit of 30 per cent instead of around 25 per cent. An explanation for this anomaly is suggested by a detailed examination of the components of the "closeness" index: wanting half or more of one's associates as friends and talking to other inmates about personal problems.

It can be seen in the top line of Table 6 that inmates in C Unit were the most likely to want their associates as friends, and there is some tendency for this pattern to disappear when type of adaptation is held constant. However, the striking finding is that inmates in the bureaucratic-high-privilege unit were persistently the least likely to establish friendships with other inmates. In contrast, an opposite pattern appears in Table 6, Part B: inmates in the bureaucratic-high-privilege unit were the most likely to talk with others about personal problems, and this is particularly so among inmates with opportunistic adaptations. Moreover, this latter finding holds when wanting associates as friends is held constant as well (see Table 7, Parts A and B).

It appears, then, that inmates in the bureaucratic-high-privilege unit were the least likely to form friendships but at the same time frequently talked to other inmates about personal problems, especially if they had opportunistic adaptations. A suggestion as to what might be going on can be found in the character of the honor units in this institution. It will be recalled that inmates gained access to, and remained in, honor units only by conforming very strictly to the complex system of impersonal rules established by the staff. Although the same rules applied in the non-honor units, the effective pressure to conform was less, since the sanction of loss of currently enjoyed honor-status privileges was absent. In the participative unit, on the other hand, the demand for conformity to staff expectations was high, but these expectations were not so often a unilateral imposition by staff but instead frequently were legitimated by

TABLE 6
Components of Closeness Index, by Pattern
of Management and Type of Adaptation

| Type of adaptation | Management Pattern | | |
| | Bureaucratic | | Participative (C Unit) |
	Low privilege	High privilege	
	A. Percentage wanting half or more of associates as friends		
All types of adaptation	60 (57)	52 (60)	70 (120)
Co-operative	[2] (3)	[6] (8)	75 (48)
Opportunistic	60 (30)	51 (37)	68 (62)
Alienated	58 (24)	40 (15)	60 (10)
	B. Percentage talking with other inmates about personal problems		
All types of adaptation	30 (57)	50 (60)	43 (120)
Co-operative	[1] (3)	[3] (8)	58 (48)
Opportunistic	27 (30)	60 (37)	37 (62)
Alienated	33 (24)	33 (15)	20 (10)

TABLE 7
Percentage Talking to Other Inmates about Personal Problems,
by Friendship Level and Pattern of Management

Want half or more of associates as friends	Management Pattern		
	Bureaucratic		*Participative (C Unit)*
	Low privilege	*High privilege*	
A. *All types of Adaptation*			
Yes	41 (34)	58 (31)	54 (84)
No	13 (23)	41 (29)	19 (36)
B. *Opportunistic Adaptations Only**			
Yes	44 (18)	68 (19)	43 (42)
No	0 (12)	50 (18)	20 (20)

*Cell frequencies for the other types of adaptation are too small to warrant presentation.

joint deliberation over issues viewed as important by the inmates themselves.

It can be conjectured, then, that inmates in the high-privilege unit, particularly those with opportunistic adaptations, were under considerably greater pressure to conform to externally imposed rules than were the inmates in the other two units. Apparently, successful adjustment to this pressure diminished inmates' capacity to form friendships with each other and, at the same time, led to high levels of personal tension[112] requiring some kind of management that avoided violating the rules, such as talking with other inmates about personal worries.

The consequence of this for the relation between closeness and pattern of management in the top line of Table 5 is direct. Suppose that there were no tendency for inmates in the high-privilege unit to talk more often about personal problems. Then in Table 7, Part B, the percentage talking about personal problems for inmates in the high-privilege unit who wanted half or more of their associates as friends would be about 44 instead of 68. If this "corrected" figure is used, then the percentage with close relations in that unit as a whole drops from 30 to 22 and the top line of Table 5 would read 25, 22 38, and the percentages for inmates with opportunistic adaptations would become 27, 22, 29. Thus, the anomaly in Table 5 can be interpreted as resulting from the effects of high pressure to conform to bureaucratic rules on inmates with opportunistic adaptations.

DISCUSSION

The present study is consistent with previous research in finding tendencies for inmates to have better relations with staff and closer relations with peers under participative management than under bureaucratic supervision. In addition, there is some support for the hypothesis that these effects of management practices are exerted in part through the adaptations of subordinates to their organizational roles. Adaptations, apparently, are affected by the way the individuals are involved in decisions affecting them, which in turn affect their relations with others. However, it also appears to be necessary to take other factors into account; for example, in the present case, the effects of high pressure to conform to bureaucratic rules seem to be important, and, in theory, earlier socializing experiences should be significant as well.[113] In the light of these findings, it may be proposed that a central social-psychological mechanism affecting behavior in organizations is the complex of attitudes an individual develops toward himself in relation to others in the organization.

Finally, it should be noted that the data of this study do not speak to one of the major problems raised at the outset, namely, the uncertain relation between management practices and task performance by subordinates. However, the model developed here does suggest a hypothesis. Patterns of management refer to the way subordinates are involved in decisions affecting them that are made by their superiors. It may be suggested, however, that a central factor influencing subordinates' task performance is the nature of the decisions for which they themselves are responsible. At one extreme, a subordinate's role may be highly routinized, requiring virtually no decisions having significant consequences for the activities of the organization. In this case, the subordinate's adaptation is less important in determining the effectiveness of his role performance than such factors as the rewards and punishments his superiors can employ, the norms of his peer group, and his personal expectations about these matters derived from past experience, since external conformity is in large part sufficient for adequate performance of routines. At the other extreme, a subordinate may be called upon to exercise continuously a high degree of discretion in order for the activities of the organization to be successful. In this case, the subordinate's type of adaptation can be very important, for if he is pursuing personal goals incongruent with those of the organization, the effectiveness of his performance in terms of organizational goals will be impaired. Thus, the importance of patterns of management in affecting subordinates' task performance should depend in large part on the kinds of decisions subordinates have to make, and consequently no simple general relation between patterns of management and performance can be anticipated. In particular, it may be suggested that participative management practices will have little effect unless subordinates have, or are given, responsibility for exercising discretion.

These considerations point to the importance of differences among organizations in terms of structures of decision making, which, as Perrow has argued, are strongly affected by the technologies of organizational activities.[114] This suggests, in turn, that in order to place the present discussion within the framework developed by Perrow, the hierarchal model of decision making with which this paper began should be replaced by a model in which decision making is differentiated both laterally and hierarchically, and the notion of pattern of management should be generalized to include the way individuals are involved in decisions affecting them that are made not only by superiors but by colleagues and by individuals in other lines of authority as well. With these modifications, the concept of adaptation provides an explicit link between social-psychological concepts and the structural concept of organizational role.

18 Measuring Inmate Change in Prison

DANIEL GLASER AND
JOHN R. STRATTON*

That inmates change in prison has always been assumed. Clemmer coined the word "prisonization" to designate such change, but he did not define it precisely.[115] Parole and the indeterminate sentence are predicated, in part, on the assumption that change can be discerned while a man is in prison; that is one reason why it is contended that the optimum time to release the inmate can be determined more adequately after he has been confined than at the time of sentencing. Similarly, designation of an appropriate institution and an optimum program for an inmate involves, in part, some assumptions that one can predict if or how the man will change while confined.

As Garrity points out . . . the approach to this problem most strongly suggested by sociological literature is to assume that all prisoners become criminally oriented during imprisonment. Prisons have been called "training schools for crime." It has been pointed out that if offenders are thrown into contact primarily with other offenders and are isolated from sources of support for anti-criminal values, one should expect them to become increasingly criminal in their attitudes. This development is fostered also by the fact that it is necessary for the prisoner to rationalize his being in prison; the status degradation which he experiences in the process of arrest, trial, and incarceration, along with the breaking of family and friendship ties by incarceration, may

* From *The Prison: Studies in Institutional Organization and Change* (New York: Holt, Rinehart and Winston, 1961), pp. 381–392. Reprinted by permission of the author and publisher.

263

leave him with a powerful need to enhance his own self-esteem. One form of rationalization is what has been called "rejecting the rejectors," that is, the offender's blaming noncriminal persons for his difficulty. It has been asserted that inmate contact with other prisoners facilitates their sharing of such self-justification in criminality, and that this profoundly impairs their acceptance of prison rehabilitation programs.

While generalizations implying the above are often used in arguments deploring our penal institutions, those involved in correctional work argue that prison can have positive as well as negative consequences for the promotion of conformity to noncriminal behavior norms. It is pointed out that prison provides opportunities to learn occupational skills for those individuals who have had no means of earning a legitimate livelihood at other than unskilled labor. The "success stories" of every warden seem predominantly to concern hardened criminals who became successful mechanics, printers, barbers, or other tradesmen. Academic training is available in many institutions, and some inmates retarded in school on the outside progress in prison through courses ranging from the three Rs to advanced college work. Available recreational time in prison also promotes the development of reading and other conventional leisure-time interests that may carry over to the outside. Prison personnel also point out that in prison men learn to comply with authority, and those who at first have difficulty staying out of fights eventually learn to get along with other men. Inmates with physical defects have these corrected and most leave prison in better physical condition than they entered it. Even some relationships of the offenders with conventional persons outside the prison, such as parents, sometimes seem to improve during the forced separation resulting from imprisonment. Also, ties with criminal peers in and out of prison, which compete with conventional influences, sometimes sharply deteriorate and prove disappointing to an offender while he is confined. It is possible that for many prisoners, sociologists make a profound error in treating prison membership groups as positive reference groups.

Statements like those cited in the foregoing paragraphs can be tossed back and forth, with illustrations from isolated cases, but with very little precise knowledge of the extent of their validity or invalidity. Treatment programs and procedures are suggested, implemented, and revised more on the basis of impressions from striking cases than on the basis of systematic evidence. Before the effectiveness and efficiency of various prison and release programs can be assessed, it will be necessary to obtain some measure of their consequences. This means one must determine if they produce change, and if so, what kind of change they produce, how they produce it, and in whom.

This chapter will discuss some of the ways in which theory and research may approach the task of measuring inmate change in prison. It will summarize the results of some relevant research already completed, and will indicate the form in which results are likely to appear from other research still underway.

ANALYSIS OF INMATE ROLES

What would appear to be a frame of reference for determining inmate change in prison is suggested by the various attempts to differentiate distinct social types among inmates. Presumably each type represents a unique pattern of thinking, acting and feeling to which certain inmates gradually are habituated. If this presumption were completely valid, the research task might consist primarily of identifying these types. Several major limitations, however, have prevented the delineation of inmate social types from sufficing for the measurement of inmate change in prison.

One early limitation was ambiguity in conceptualizing social types. Clemmer, in his pioneer study, employed only three categories for differentiating an entire inmate population: the "elite," the "middle class" and the "hoosier." It is clear from his discussion that these are broad and arbitrarily divided prestige strata, rather than unique role behavior patterns. Thus, in an unsystematic manner, he distinguishes some role patterns within his broad categories, such as the "politicians" among the elite.[116]

Schrag was more concerned with using inmate-recognized behavior patterns as his criteria for designation of types. His "right guy," "politician," "outlaw" and "square John" are distinguishable from each other by unique constellations of values and habits. His residual group, the "dings," are not homogeneous, but they are fairly distinct from the four basic categories.[117]

Classifiers of inmate social types since Schrag, have recognized his major categories but have described a few other types by focusing on some more specific behavioral dimensions. Thus Morris Caldwell, who departs from Schrag's more pure use of the inmates' own language, designates inmate muscle-development enthusiasts as "Spartans," and he also distinguishes "religionists," "leather-workers" and "moon-shiners."[118]

Sykes, in his major work, stresses reliance on prisoner argot for the differentiation of distinct inmate behavior roles, and presents a diverse catalogue, on many behavioral dimensions. Thus inmates are differentiated with respect to homosexuality as "wolves," "fags," or "punks," and they are differentiated by the extent and form of their non-sexual aggression towards others as "ball-busters," "hipsters," "toughs" and "gorillas."[119]

The vagueness of theoretical orientation exhibited by Clemmer and Caldwell in distinguishing social types is relatively absent in Schrag and Sykes. Both of the latter have their conceptual foundations in the analysis of social types by the late Samuel M. Strong and his mentor, the late Louis Wirth. Social types were believed by these theorists to be classifications of role patterns by aspects more significant than those which an outside observer might ascribe, for "social types stand for what the members who live in these various social worlds believe to be critical and important."[120] It is in an effort to capture the inmates' own role differentiations that Schrag and Sykes deliberately cling to the inmates' own designation of these types, and Sykes calls them "argot roles."

A limitation of the social type concept, however, is that these types tend to refer to extreme, rather than average or prevailing, roles in a group. As Strong puts it, social types

> . . . are constructs which the group arrives at by selecting or abstracting accentuated forms of conduct displayed by some of its members and having specific connotations in terms of the interests, concerns, and dispositions of the group. . . . An exaggerated form of conduct . . . catches the attention of the people, who categorize it . . . e.g., the 'social climber'.[121]

What these social-type analysts seem to have uncovered, but which they apparently did not recognize, is what might be called a "poor man's" or non-academic version of Weber's "ideal type." Like the ideal type, the social type is an abstraction from actual behavior. It selects out for special attention some distinguishing features of behavior which have a strategic function in a social system. It portrays certain role occupants in this system as though they were more consistent in their behavior than all or most persons in these roles are. It then is possible to analyze the causes and consequences of their behavior in the social system by deduction from the attributes ascribed to the pure types. This was done by Weber in analyzing bureaucracy in terms of a "bureaucrat" ideal type; it was done by Sykes, Schrag, and notably by Cloward, in analyzing the prison social system in terms of politicians, merchants, and other inmate types.[122] It is done by all of us in analyzing our daily social life with such social type categories as "eager-beaver," "glad-hander" and "four-flusher"; these exaggerate the behavior of any specific individual, but they give us a sense of comprehending a social reality which would be confused and meaningless unless subjected to some such abstraction and distortion process.

In the experience of the senior writer, in attempting to classify inmates by social typologies, it was easy to find consensus in naming major types, and in identifying inmates who epitomize each type. However, it is noteworthy that inmates usually disagree extensively if asked to type every single person in any particular unit. Furthermore, few inmates will accept an allegation that they fit closely any specific type. It becomes apparent that each type is seen as something of an exaggeration. Also, a majority of types convey derogatory connotation, the most notable exception to this being "right guy." However, should any specific individual claim to be, or be described by others as, a "right guy," a few minutes probing will indicate that even the "right guy" is an idealized— rather than a typical—figure. Focus on any specific individual elicits references to the manner or time in which his behavior has deviated from the "right guy" standard to that of a politician, merchant, square, or other type, even when "on the whole" he is accepted as a "right guy."

The evolution of empirical concepts in social science often starts with classification of cases into discrete types with respect to some variable, then progresses to ranking or measuring each case on the variable, so that more fine discriminations can be made. Only crude beginnings of the latter operation are available in the measurement of that inmate behavior which is presumed to change in prison. Two distinct approaches may be discerned in efforts to deal with this problem. The first method is to compare direct expressions of attitude procured from offenders who are at different stages in a correctional career. We shall call this the "sequential measurement" technique. A more indirect approach is to compare the post-release behavior of offenders as a means of assessing the extent to which their behavior in prison indicated that they were enduringly changed, or as an index of the effects of different periods of exposure to imprisonment. We shall call this the "ex post facto comparison" technique.

SEQUENTIAL MEASUREMENT

By "sequential measurement" studies we encompass both those in which the same subjects are seen at different times and those in which comparisons are made between groups of subjects at different stages in correctional experience who are believed to have been identical when first committed.

Fiedler and Bass recently reported a comparison of the responses of various groups of offenders who were asked to rate themselves, and others in their group, on pairs of opposite adjectives like "friendly" and "unfriendly," or "cooperative" and "uncooperative," using six-point scales between the opposites. Adding these into a "self-esteem score" by the number of points on the scale selected in the direction of the favorable adjective in each pair, these authors found that non-confined offenders rated themselves less favorably than a control group of non-offenders, but that confined offenders rated themselves significantly more favorably than did non-confined offenders, although not as favorably as the non-offenders. This same pattern of contrast was found among juveniles in public schools and state training schools, and among military personnel in a regular unit and a disciplinary center.

Both a sociological and a psychological explanation are offered by Fiedler and Bass for their findings. The sociological explanation is that with confinement offenders change their reference groups increasingly to their fellow offenders, by comparison with whom they may regard themselves more favorably than they could prior to confinement, when they more often compared themselves with non-offenders. The psychological explanation is that confinement, as punishment, reduces feelings of guilt, that is, that self-esteem is enhanced by expiation. Both explanations for the findings are speculative, and the findings themselves merit review by panel studies involving successive contacts with the same subjects.[123]

Wheeler studied conformity to conventional norms in inmates of a Washington reformatory by rating each inmate on the extent to which he agreed with the reformatory staff in his responses to questions on the propriety of the behavior of various characters described in anecdotes. These anecdotes reported hypothetical value conflict situations in prison life. As one aspect of this study, Wheeler compared inmates at three stages of prison experience: those in the first six months of confinement, those who had served six months and had at least six months to serve, and those with less than six months left to serve.

We shall limit our reference to Wheeler's findings to two noteworthy features. In the first place, he observed a U-shaped curve, in which conformity to conventional norms was higher at the beginning and at the end of imprisonment than in the middle. This was explained as reflecting progressive change from outsider to fellow inmate reference groups until the last stages of imprisonment, when reference is redirected to outside persons. This explanation was supported by findings that the U-shaped change was least pronounced for those inmates reporting least contact with other inmates.

Wheeler's second finding was that, despite the U-shaped curve, there was a general trend for inmates to move away from conformity to conventional norms with each increment of prison experience. He found that both first termers and recidivists exhibit the U-shaped pattern, but the recidivists start and finish with lower conformity than the first offenders.[124]

Metaphorically, Wheeler's data suggest that offenders follow a spiral pattern of cyclical movement from conventional to criminal norms, progressively drifting more criminal. Criminality increases with each return to crime, and during much of imprisonment. However, with each return to the conventional world from prison, most offenders become somewhat more conforming to conventional norms, for a while at least. Always there is some possibility of this spiral movement being interrupted by their achieving security, either in the criminal or in the conventional world.

Cloward, in reinterviewing military prisoners every six weeks from commitment to their twenty-fourth week of confinement, noted what he called a strain toward passivity with respect to administration-fostered goals and means, and a strain toward isolation from other inmates. The latter is associated with what he calls "pluralistic ignorance," in that each inmate keeps other inmates ignorant of the extent to which he actually is pursuing conventional goals, by "putting up a front" of greater conformity to inmate norms of opposition to such goals.[125] The latter phenomenon may be responsible for much masking of the upswing in the U-shaped curve indicated in Wheeler's data.

In the four-year research program in the Federal Correctional System directed by Glaser, which at this writing is not half completed, measures of inmate change are sought using a panel approach similar to that of Wheeler. Inmates in five Federal prisons are compared at various stages of sentence completion—after their first week in prison, after six months' incarceration, between the first and last year of expected confinement, and within three months of release. While the findings still are in the first stage of analysis, some preliminary tabulations may be of interest.

When responses to the question "Do you think your sentence was fair," were plotted over the time, the resulting profile indicated that approximately 60 percent of the inmates interviewed within a week of their admission to prison felt that their sentence was fair. However, there was a significant increase in the proportion calling their sentence very unfair as one moved from those interviewed in their first four days in prison to those seen in their fifth, sixth or seventh day. Little further change in this attitude was indicated during the first six months of incarceration, but the proportion calling their sentence "fair" dropped to 36 percent by the middle of the sentences. Yet the proportion of inmates interviewed within 90 days of release who described their sentence as fair was 70 percent. The resulting profile is similar to Wheeler's U-shaped curve. It suggests that inmates focus on inmate reference groups very rapidly at first, and continuously during most of their imprisonment, but as release time approaches, most of them assume the perspectives of non-prison reference groups.

Two other indications of this U-shaped curve revealed thus far in the Federal prison panel study may merit mention at this time. First, interest in participating in religious activity was high among inmates on admission, it declined sharply after the first six months, but it rose sharply in the last three months. Also, three-quarters of the inmates ranked learning a trade or improving their academic education high among their interests when they were first received in prison, this proportion decreased significantly during the next six months of confinement, then it rose significantly for inmates in the middle of their sentence. In interpreting these trends, it is hard to disentangle actual reference to outside groups from anticipations that pursuit of conventional interests in prison will facilitate favorable parole consideration.

Some suggestion of reference group influence is provided by other findings. The proportion of inmates who expected post-release assistance mainly from parents or siblings was constant during most of the confinement, but increased slightly near release. The proportion who expected help mainly from their wives decreased as imprisonment progressed, reflecting an increasing proportion of marriages breaking during the husband's confinement. Looking at the other side of the coin, the proportion of inmates who report that their close relatives will "make trouble for them" on release decreases somewhat as release time approaches.

Additional support for a reference group explanation for the U-shaped changes reported during Federal imprisonment is provided by inmate accounts of their orientations to fellow inmates. In the early phases of their incarceration, most inmates in our sample report that they try to stay to themselves as much as possible or to limit their interaction to a few inmate friends. In the middle of their sentence they more frequently report trying to have as many inmate friends as possible. In the last few months, however, they report more of the early pattern of having only limited interaction with other inmates.

Further analysis of the Federal panel data will cover a variety of other interview items and will include separate tabulations for offenders of different criminal record and other background characteristics. We have not yet completed coding and tabulating a considerable body of narrative material, and we are still working on analysis of over a thousand reports by inmates of what they did and what they talked about, hour by hour, in the 24 hours preceding each of our panel interviews.

EX POST FACTO COMPARISON

Most parole prediction studies have investigated duration of time confined as a possible predictor of post-release behavior. They have invariably found that, taken alone, it is a poor predictor compared to others as readily available. Most findings suggest that the releasees least likely to return to crime are those with the most brief and those with the longest prison confinement. This curvilinear relationship seems to be an artifact of the relationship between criminal record and time served: those with the least prior criminality are released soonest, except for those who have committed murder, who are confined longest, and who also are less often professional criminals than are prisoners in the middle range of time served.

Most parole prediction studies also investigate the relationship to post-release behavior of any manifestation of behavior change during imprisonment which is recorded in prison files. These inquiries also have been relatively fruitless, especially when compared with efforts to relate pre-prison behavior to post-release record. This probably reflects, in part, a lesser influence on post-release behavior of change during any particular imprisonment, as compared with influences of the total life prior to a specific imprisonment. However, the major deficiency probably is the inadequate records available on behavior during imprisonment, the only regularly recorded item being known rule infractions.

While most efforts to correlate such prison behavior records with post-release data have indicated little relationship, our preliminary analysis of file data on a sample of 1956 Federal penitentiary releasees reveals markedly higher post-release success for those whose rule infractions were low or declined towards release, and for those for whom an improvement in over-all "adjustment" was reported by prison officials. This was the best of fifty predictors tested specifically on those penitentiary inmates who had no prior arrests or had a gap of five or more years in their arrest record at some time in the free community. The failure of prison punishment to predict parole outcome very accurately for offenders with much prior confinement may be interpreted as due to the fact that the most criminally oriented inmates are well adjusted to confinement. However, our Federal penitentiary data suggest that development of an ability to conform to prison rules usefully distinguishes the most non-recidivistic of those inmates who, collectively, have the least prior criminal record.

Donald L. Garrity pioneered in the most useful adaptation of parole prediction procedures to measurement of change during imprisonment. After classifying Washington state prisoners by file data presumed to provide very crude indices of Schrag's social types, he tabulated each type's parole violation rate for different periods of confinement. Those presumed to be "square Johns" (no prior record, conformity to prison rules, and constructive use of prison time) had parole violation rates which, though always low, increased with time served. Those believed most resembling the "right guy" (early and persistent criminality, little conventional family influence, and little schooling) had violation rates which, though always high, decreased with time served. For inmates of this "right guy" category in the reformatory, violation rate decreased for increasing duration of time served until the end of the fifth year, then increased; in the penitentiary, violation rates for this category of inmates were lowest if they were released between the tenth and twentieth years of confinement.

Garrity's cases were too few to have much significance for fine time-distinctions in the separate presumed social type differentiations. However, summarizing the trends over all types, he concluded that the greater the amount of stability prior to incarceration, the more an increase in duration of incarceration was associated with an increase in post-release failure, but the greater the instability before prison, the more continued imprisonment was associated with increased post-release success.[126]

Our preliminary analysis of post-release outcome for a small sample of 1956 Federal penitentiary releasees supports Garrity's conclusions. For the most successful major releasee group (those with no prior arrest or a gap of five or more years in their arrest record), 100 percent were successful of 13 released within a year after imprisonment, 96 percent were successful of 28 released during the second year, and only 77 percent were successful of 35 confined over two years. The least successful major releasee categories were those who were not able to avoid arrest for a period as long as five years in the free community, and who had two or more years of imprisonment prior to the commitment from which they were released. The success rates for this group increased with time served from 38 percent for those released in their first year of confinement to 48 percent for those released after serving over two years. Information has not yet been available on enough cases in such research to permit fine differentiations by type of offender, by prison program, or by time served. However, the consistency of findings thus far suggests that more work with this ex post facto comparison procedure can be very productive of valid and useful generalizations on inmate changes during imprisonment.

SUMMARY AND CONCLUSIONS

Practical application of sociological knowledge to judicial and correctional decisions depends greatly on ability to measure inmate change in prison. Differentiation of prisoner behavior on the basis of inmate social types has directed attention to polar patterns, but prisoners display some attributes of several patterns. This suggests the need for differentiating inmates by finer gradations of crucial variables.

Two approaches to discernment of change on specific variables were described. The first is sequential measurement of characteristics of inmates at different stages in correctional experience. The second ex post facto correlation of post-release behavior with length of exposure to imprisonment, or with manifestations of behavior recorded during imprisonment. Research on both of these methods still is highly limited, but results already are of considerable interest and suggest great promise in further efforts.

Specific Programs in Correctional Institutions

Introduction

The significance of the prison system, if not its effectiveness, has always been assumed. Prisons must make some impression upon the prevalence and incidence of crime. If the system does not help with rehabilitation and reintegration of the offender, then the fact that so many persons are incarcerated must deter those who might otherwise commit crimes.

Very few of the assumptions or beliefs which might be held about the penal system can be defended by data or hard evidence. Some think that few offenders get away with it for very long—that while few crimes can be traced through the various parts of the machinery of justice to end in some form of penal or correctional process, offenders who continue to commit crimes may in general expect to spend some time in institutions. Others doubt that this is true. Those who doubt the effectiveness of the measures in these terms often defend the penal processes on other grounds, namely that it is not the size of the group of convicted offenders nor its unrepresentativeness which is significant, but rather that society defends its value systems by the symbolic action of the criminal justice machinery. We thus may move from the "numbers game" to the "dramatic/symbolic" defense of the procedures.

If the latter argument is supported, it would seem to follow that it was not the mere fact of the 'drama' but the *visibility* of the measures taken. Justice must be *seen* to be done. Hence we would expect research to concentrate not upon actual actions, but upon the publicity received by those actions, and the possible effects of these processes. But again, there

277

is little research and no hard data to support this assumption. Whether we advocate the 'dramatic/symbolic' or the 'factual' defense of the processes of the criminal justice machinery, we have little to inform us regarding outcomes.

The implications for action of the two widely different forms of attempts to justify the actions of society through the medium of the criminal justice machinery differ widely. There can hardly be a research design for a form of social action or policy change which is consistent with both of these viewpoints. If we take the latter view, or if we are skeptical of the importance of the results the correctional establishment delivers when we take the "numbers game" view, then the variation in the length of time an offender is insulated from society is not important in terms of the total problem of crime. It would seem that the separation of these two viewpoints should be the starting point for research.

It may be that the objective factors of the prison, such as the size of the incarcerated population, are not relevant; rather it may be the subjective impact—the matter of the "drama" or "image" raised earlier—that is pertinent. There are, after all, few poets, composers or artists, but the few are extremely important for our culture. Is the role of the prison and the prisoner of similar importance? Is the prison system significant only in terms of its symbolism?

We have not succeeded in measuring the significance of the symbolism of our penal institutions. We must assume that it is very considerable since that is the only way we are able to attribute any degree of rationality to the actions society takes through the medium of the criminal justice system.

Most imprisoned offenders are at some time released. If *none* were ever released what would be the saving to society in terms of crime? Again we have no estimates. The cost of detention could be calculated and it is very unlikely that any political party could raise enough taxation to implement such a policy. In the past it was ensured that the criminal, once detected, had no opportunity to commit further crimes—he was hanged or otherwise disposed of. Yet we know that criminal activity continued. How is it that such a radical policy did not work?

The only known way definitely to prevent recidivism is still the death penalty. Only the death penalty makes further crime (as indeed any other activity) by that person impossible. If today, by some super, ideal social work or other means we were able to prevent all further recidivism, what would be the impact upon the total of criminal behavior? We might be expected to know this, but we do not. We are, in fact, little better informed in this area of knowledge than was primitive man!

We have become so involved with detailed aspects of the processes of crime control and offender treatment that major questions have receded from our view. We see process as equally subject to research and to moral statements and we swallow the really big assumptions of our total policy without a single doubt.

But perhaps process is the only thing with which it is profitable for us to be concerned. We cannot agree wholly with the extreme liberals, and we are equally inhibited by the policies of the extreme conservatives. We tread warily with our research around the middle ground. This middle ground is represented here with papers reporting modifications to the prison system. No one advocates an entirely different system, beginning, let us say, with the abolition of all prisons. Why does a prisonless society seem unthinkable?

If man had not invented the penal system, including its prisons and the death penalty, what else might he have invented to deal with the difficulties of running a society where offenders attack other's persons and property? No very different system seems to be imaginable. This, it is suggested, is because the issues emerge from essentially moral concepts. When we say, typically, that we cannot support fully the extreme philosophies, we are stating a moral and often political position, and the moral position restricts our scientific imagination. We do not seek information which could place our moral or political stance in jeopardy: indeed we do not know how to look for such information.

Progress can only begin from where we are now. We can hope for a more rapid process, and we can stimulate evolutionary processes. Perhaps we are right to consider process in this way. Revolutions have not had much creditable effect on any penal systems. If we try to jump too far ahead we are liable to fall back rather than to make progress. The goal is not an ideal system, but a system which is continuously adapting to the new views of old problems which can be taken from our new perspectives. And the new perspectives are a function of our creative imagination. If we cannot dare to put into practice, at least we should dare to imagine, and be extremely daring in our imagination.

The first two articles in this section are the works of committees of prison officials and their academic consultants. One is a set of rules for handling prisoners agreed upon by an International Penal and Penitentiary Commission, and the other a prescription for classification of prison inmates drafted by a committee of the American Correctional Association. The distinctive problems and principles relevant to education and discipline in prisons are reviewed in the articles by Daniel Glaser. Prison industry problems are discussed with sophistication by Elmer H. Johnson. Like Glaser, he is a university sociologist with extensive work and research experience in prisons. Inmate self government and pre-release programs for prisoners are surveyed by J. E. Baker, a career correctional official formerly in the federal and New Mexico prison systems and currently Deputy Commissioner of Kentucky's Department of Corrections.

The selections which follow represent a sample of articles which have appeared in recent years describing variations of process in the penal system. The old may think these too innovative, the young too traditional. They represent the most imaginative innovations described in the sources we examined.

19 Standard Minimum Rules for the Treatment of Prisoners

INTERNATIONAL COMMISSION OF JURISTS*

PRELIMINARY OBSERVATIONS†

1. The following rules are not intended to describe in detail a model system of penal institutions. They seek only, on the basis of the general consensus of contemporary thought and the essential elements of the most adequate systems of today, to set out what is generally accepted as being good principle and practice in the treatment of prisoners and the management of institutions.

2. In view of the great variety of legal, social, economic and geographical conditions of the world, it is evident that not all of the rules are capable of application in all places and at all times. They should, however, serve to stimulate a constant endeavour to overcome practical difficulties in the way of their application, in the knowledge that they represent, as a whole, the minimum conditions which are accepted as suitable by the United Nations.

3. On the other hand, the rules cover a field in which thought is constantly developing. They are not intended to preclude experiment and practices, provided these are in harmony with the principles and seek to further the purposes which derive from the text of the rules as a whole.

* From a report submitted by the International Commission of Jurists to United Nations, Fourth United Nations Congress on the Prevention of Crime and the Treatment of Offenders. 17-26 August, 1970, Kyoto, Japan.

†Editors' Note: Paragraph numbers are partially out of sequence due to pending revisions in the minimum Rules for Treatment of Prisoners.

It will always be justifiable for the central prison administration to authorize departures from the rules in this spirit.

4.   (1) Part I of the rules covers the general management of institutions, and is applicable to all categories of prisoners, criminal or civil, untried or convicted, including prisoners subject to "security measures" or corrective measures ordered by the judge.

(2)   Part II contains rules applicable only to the special categories dealt with in each section. Nevertheless, the rules under section A, applicable to prisoners under sentence, shall be equally applicable to categories of prisoners dealt with in sections B, C and D, provided they do not conflict with the rules governing those categories and are for their benefit.

5.   (1) The rules do not seek to regulate the management of institutions set aside for young persons such as Borstal institutions or correctional schools, but in general Part I would be equally applicable in such institutions.

(2)   The category of young prisoners should include at least all young persons who come within the jurisdiction of juvenile courts. As a rule, such young persons should not be sentenced to imprisonment.

PART I.   RULES OF GENERAL APPLICATION

Basic Principle

6.   (1) The following rules should be applied impartially. There shall be no discrimination on grounds of race, colour, sex, language, religion, political or other opinion, national or social origin, property, birth or other status.

(2)   On the other hand, it is necessary to respect the religious beliefs and moral precepts of the group to which a prisoner belongs.

Register

7.   (1) In every place where persons are imprisoned there shall be kept a bound registration book with numbered pages in which shall be entered in respect of each prisoner received:

(a) Information concerning his identity;

(b) The reasons for his commitment and the authority therefor;

(c) The day and hour of his admission and release

(2) No person shall be received in an institution without a valid commitment order of which the details shall have been previously entered in the register.

Retention of Prisoners' Property

43.   (1) All money, valuables, clothing and other effects belonging to a prisoner which under the regulations of the institution he is not allowed to retain shall on his admission to the institution be placed in safe custody. An inventory thereof shall be signed by the prisoner. Steps shall be taken to keep them in good condition.

(2) On the release of the prisoner all such articles and money shall be returned to him except in so far as he has been authorized to spend money or send any such property out of the institution, or it has been found necessary on hygienic grounds to destroy any article of clothing. The prisoner shall sign a receipt for the articles and money returned to him.

(3) Any money or effects received for a prisoner from outside shall be treated in the same way.

(4) If a prisoner brings in any drugs or medicine, the medical officer shall decide what use shall be made of them.

Separation of Categories

8.   The different categories of prisoners shall be kept in separate institutions or parts of institutions taking account of their sex, age, criminal record, the legal reason for their detention and the necessities of their treatment. Thus,

    (a) Men and women shall so far as possible be detained in separate institutions; in an institution which receives both men and women the whole of the premises allocated to women shall be entirely separate;

    (b) Untried prisoners shall be kept separate from convicted prisoners;

    (c) Persons imprisoned for debt and other civil prisoners shall be kept separate from persons imprisoned by reason of a criminal offence;

    (d) Young prisoners shall be kept separate from adults.

Accommodation

9.   (1) Where sleeping accommodation is in individual cells or rooms, each prisoner shall occupy by night a cell or room by himself. If for

special reasons, such as temporary overcrowding, it becomes necessary for the central prison administration to make an exception to this rule, it is not desirable to have two prisoners in a cell or room.

(2) Where dormitories are used, they shall be occupied by prisoners carefully selected as being suitable to associate with one another in those conditions. There shall be regular supervision by night, in keeping with the nature of the institution.

10.   All accommodation provided for the use of prisoners and in particular all sleeping accommodation shall meet all requirements of health, due regard being paid to climatic conditions and particularly to cubic content of air, minimum floor space, lighting, heating and ventilation.

11.   In all places where prisoners are required to live or work,

   (a) The windows shall be large enough to enable the prisoners to read or work by natural light, and shall be so constructed that they can allow the entrance of fresh air whether or not there is artificial ventilation;

   (b) Artificial light shall be provided sufficient for the prisoners to read or work without injury to eyesight.

   See above Rule 9(1)

19.   Every prisoner shall, in accordance with local or national standards, be provided with a separate bed, and with separate and sufficient bedding which shall be clean when issued, kept in good order and changed often enough to ensure its cleanliness.

12.   The sanitary installations shall be adequate to enable every prisoner to comply with the needs of nature when necessary and in a clean and decent manner.

13.   Adequate bathing and shower installations shall be provided so that every prisoner may be enabled and required to have a bath or shower, at a temperature suitable to the climate, as frequently as necessary for general hygiene according to season and geographical region, but at least once a week in a temperate climate.

14.   All parts of an institution regularly used by prisoners shall be properly maintained and kept scrupulously clean at all times.

Personal Hygiene

15.   Prisoners shall be required to keep their persons clean, and to this end they shall be provided with water and with such toilet articles as are necessary for health and cleanliness.

16.   In order that prisoners may maintain a good appearance compatible

with their self-respect, facilities shall be provided for the proper care of the hair and beard, and men shall be enabled to shave regularly.

Clothing and Bedding

17.   (1) Every prisoner who is not allowed to wear his own clothing shall be provided with an outfit of clothing suitable for the climate and adequate to keep him in good health. Such clothing shall in no manner be degrading or humiliating.

(2) All clothing shall be clean and kept in proper condition. Underclothing shall be changed and washed as often as necessary for the maintenance of hygiene.

(3) In exceptional circumstances, whenever a prisoner is removed outside the institution for an authorized purpose he shall be allowed to wear his own clothing or other inconspicuous clothing.

18.   If prisoners are allowed to wear their own clothing, arrangements shall be made on their admission to the institution to ensure that it shall be clean and fit for use.

Exercise and Sport

21.   (1) Every prisoner who is not employed in out-door work shall have at least one hour of suitable exercise in the open air daily if the weather permits.

(2) Young prisoners and others of suitable age and physique, shall receive physical and recreational training during the period of exercise. To this end space, installations and equipment should be provided.

Food

20.   (1) Every prisoner shall be provided by the administration at the usual hours with food of nutritional value adequate for health and strength, of wholesome quality and well prepared and served.

(2) Drinking water shall be available to every prisoner whenever he needs it.

Medical Services

22.   (1) At every institution there shall be available the services of at least one qualified officer who should have some knowledge of psychiatry. The medical services should be organized in close relationship to the

general health administration of the community or nation. They shall include a psychiatric service for the diagnosis and, in proper cases, the treatment of states of mental abnormality.

(2) Sick prisoners who require specialist treatment shall be transferred to specialized institutions or to civil hospitals. Where hospital facilities are provided in an institution, their equipment, furnishings and pharmaceutical supplies shall be proper for the medical care and treatment of sick prisoners, and there shall be a staff of suitably trained officers.

(3) The services of a qualified dental officer shall be available to every prisoner.

23.   (1) In women's institutions there shall be special accommodation for all necessary pre-natal and post-natal care and treatment. Arrangements shall be made wherever practicable for children to be born in a hospital outside the institution. If a child is born in prison, this fact shall not be mentioned in the birth certificate.

(2) Where nursing infants are allowed to remain in the institutions with their mothers, provision shall be made for a nursery staffed by qualified persons, where the infants shall be placed when they are not in the care of their mothers.

24.   The medical officer shall see and examine every prisoner as soon as possible after his admission and thereafter as necessary, with a view particularly to the discovery of physical or mental illness and the taking of all necessary measures; the segregation of prisoners suspected of infectious or contagious conditions; the noting of physical or mental defects which might hamper rehabilitation, and the determination of the physical capacity of every prisoner for work.

25.   (1) The medical officer shall have the care of the physical and mental health of the prisoners and should daily see all sick prisoners, all who complain of illness, and any prisoner to whom his attention is specially directed.

(2) The medical officer shall report to the director whenever he considers that a prisoner's physical or mental health has been or will be injuriously affected by continued imprisonment or by any condition of imprisonment.

26.   (1) The medical officer shall regularly inspect and advise the director upon:

(a) The quantity, quality, preparation and service of food;
(b) The hygiene and cleanliness of the institution and the prisoners;
(c) The sanitation, heating, lighting and ventilation of the institution;

(d) The suitability and cleanliness of the prisoners' clothing and bedding;

(e) The observance of the rules concerning physical education and sports, in cases where there is no technical personnel in charge of these activities.

(2) The director shall take into consideration the reports and advice that the medical officer submits according to rules 25 (2) and 26 and, in case he concurs with the recommendations made, shall take immediate steps to give effect to those recommendations; if they are not within his competence or if he does not concur with them, he shall immediately submit his own report and the advice of the medical officer to higher authority.

Discipline and Punishment

27. Discipline and order shall be maintained with firmness, but with no more restriction than is necessary for safe custody and well-ordered community life.

28. (1) No prisoner shall be employed, in the service of the institution, in any disciplinary capacity.

(2) This rule shall not, however, impede the proper functioning of systems based on self-government, under which specified social, educational or sports activities or responsibilities are entrusted, under supervision, to prisoners who are formed into groups for the purposes of treatment.

29. The following shall always be determined by the law or by the regulation of the competent administrative authority:

(a) Conduct constituting a disciplinary offence,

(b) The types and duration of punishment which may be inflicted;

(c) The authority competent to impose such punishment.

37. Prisoners shall be allowed under necessary supervision to communicate with their family and reputable friends at regular intervals, both by correspondence and by receiving visits.

Notification of Death, Illness, Transfer, etc.

44. (1) Upon the death or serious illness of, or serious injury to a prisoner, or his removal to an institution for the treatment of mental affections, the director shall at once inform the spouse, if the prisoner is married, or the nearest relative and shall in any event inform any other person previously designated by the prisoner.

(2) A prisoner shall be informed at once of the death or serious illness of any near relative. In case of the critical illness of a near relative, the prisoner should be authorized, whenever circumstances allow, to go to his bedside either under escort or alone.

(3) Every prisoner shall have the right to inform at once his family of his imprisonment or his transfer to another institution.

38.   (1) Prisoners who are foreign nationals shall be allowed reasonable facilities to communicate with the diplomatic and consular representatives of the State to which they belong.

(2) Prisoners who are nationals of States without diplomatic or consular representation in the country and refugees or stateless persons shall be allowed similar facilities to communicate with the diplomatic representative of the State which takes charge of their interests or any national or international authority whose task it is to protect such persons.

39.   Prisoners shall be kept informed regularly of the more important items of news by the reading of newspapers, periodicals or special institutional publications, by hearing wireless transmissions, by lectures or by any similar means as authorized or controlled by the administration.

Books

40.   Every institution shall have a library for the use of all categories of prisoners, adequately stocked with both recreational and instructional books, and prisoners shall be encouraged to make full use of it.

Religion

41.   (1) If the institution contains a sufficient number of prisoners of the same religion, a qualified representative of that religion shall be appointed or approved. If the number of prisoners justifies it and conditions permit, the arrangement should be on a full-time basis.

(2) A qualified representative appointed or approved under paragraph (1) shall be allowed to hold regular services and to pay pastoral visits in private to prisoners of his religion at proper times.

(3) Access to a qualified representative of any religion shall not be refused to any prisoner. On the other hand, if any prisoner should object to a visit of any religious representative, his attitude shall be fully respected.

42.   So far as practicable, every prisoner shall be allowed to satisfy the

needs of his religious life by attending the services provided in the institution and having in his possession the books of religious observance and instruction of his denomination.

Instruments of Restraint

33. Instruments of restraint, such as handcuffs, chains, irons and strait-jackets, shall never be applied as a punishment. Furthermore, chains or irons shall not be used as restraints. Other instruments of restraint shall not be used except in the following circumstances:

  (a) As a precaution against escape during a transfer, provided that they shall be removed when the prisoner appears before a judicial or administrative authority;
  (b) On medical grounds by direction of the medical officer;
  (c) By order of the director, if other methods of control fail, in order to prevent a prisoner from injuring himself or others or from damaging property; in such instances the director shall at once consult the medical officer and report to the higher administrative authority.

34. The patterns and manner of use of instruments of restraint shall be decided by the central prison administration. Such instruments must not be applied for any longer time than is strictly necessary.

30. (1) No prisoner shall be punished except in accordance with the terms of such law or regulation, and never twice for the same offence.

  (2) No prisoner shall be punished unless he has been informed of the offence alleged against him and given a proper opportunity of presenting his defence. The competent authority shall conduct a thorough examination of the case.

  (3) Where necessary and practicable the prisoner shall be allowed to make his defence through an interpreter.

31. Corporal punishment, punishment by placing in a dark cell, and all cruel, inhuman or degrading punishments shall be completely prohibited as punishments for disciplinary offences.

32. (1) Punishment by close confinement or reduction of diet shall never be inflicted unless the medical officer has examined the prisoner and certified in writing that he is fit to sustain it.

  (2) The same shall apply to any other punishment that may be prejudicial to the physical or mental health of a prisoner. In no case may such punishment be contrary to or depart from the principle stated in rule 31.

  (3) The medical officer shall visit daily prisoners undergoing such

punishments and shall advise the director if he considers the termination or alteration of the punishment necessary on grounds of physical or mental health.

Removal of Prisoners

45. (1) When prisoners are being removed to or from an institution, they shall be exposed to public view as little as possible, and proper safeguards shall be adopted to protect them from insult, curiosity and publicity in any form.

(2) The transport of prisoners in conveyances with inadequate ventilation or light, or in any way which would subject them to unnecessary physical hardship, shall be prohibited.

(3) The transport of prisoners shall be carried out at the expense of the administration and equal conditions shall obtain for all of them.

Information to and Complaints by Prisoners

35. (1) Every prisoner on admission shall be provided with written information about the regulations governing the treatment of prisoners of his category, the disciplinary requirements of the institution, the authorized methods of seeking information and making complaints, and all such other matters as are necessary to enable him to understand both his rights and his obligations and to adapt himself to the life of the institution.

(2) If a prisoner is illiterate, the aforesaid information shall be conveyed to him orally.

36. (1) Every prisoner shall have the opportunity each week day of making requests or complaints to the director of the institution or the officer authorized to represent him.

(2) It shall be possible to make requests or complaints to the inspector of prisons during his inspection. The prisoner shall have the opportunity to talk to the inspector or to any other inspecting officer without the director or any other members of the staff being present.

(3) Every prisoner shall be allowed to make a request or complaint, without censorship as to substance but in proper form, to the central prison administration, the judicial authority or other proper authorities through approved channels.

(4) Unless it is evidently frivolous or groundless, every request or complaint shall be promptly dealt with and replied to without undue delay.

Institutional Personnel

45. (1) The prison administration shall provide for the careful selection of every grade of the personnel, since it is on their integrity, humanity, professional capacity and personal suitability for the work that the proper administration of the institutions depends.

(2) The prison administration shall constantly seek to awaken and maintain in the minds both of the personnel and of the public the conviction that this work is a social service of great importance, and to this end all appropriate means of informing the public should be used.

(3) To secure the foregoing ends, personnel shall be appointed on a full-time basis as professional prison officers and have civil service status with security of tenure subject only to good conduct, efficiency and physical fitness. Salaries shall be adequate to attract and retain suitable men and women; employment benefits and conditions of service shall be favourable in view of the exacting nature of the work.

47. (1) The personnel shall possess an adequate standard of education and intelligence.

(2) Before entering on duty, the personnel shall be given a course of training in their general and specific duties and be required to pass theoretical and practical tests.

(3) After entering on duty and during their career, the personnel shall maintain and improve their knowledge and professional capacity by attending courses of in-service training to be organized at suitable intervals.

48. All members of the personnel shall at all times so conduct themselves and perform their duties as to influence the prisoners for good by their examples and to command their respect.

49. (1) So far as possible the personnel shall include a sufficient number of specialists such as psychiatrists, psychologists, social workers, teachers and trade instructors.

(2) The services of social workers, teachers and trade instructors shall be secured on a permanent basis, without thereby excluding part-time or voluntary workers.

50. (1) The director of an institution should be adequately qualified for his task by character, administrative ability, suitable training and experience.

(2) He shall devote his entire time to his official duties and shall not be appointed on a part-time basis.

(3) He shall reside on the premises of the institution or in its immediate vicinity.

(4) When two or more institutions are under the authority of one director, he shall visit each of them at frequent intervals. A responsible resident official shall be in charge of each of these institutions.

51. (1) The director, his deputy, and the majority of the other personnel of the institution shall be able to speak the language of the greatest number of prisoners, or a language understood by the greatest number of them.

(2) Whenever necessary, the services of an interpreter shall be used.

52. (1) In institutions which are large enough to require the services of one or more full-time medical officers, at least one of them shall reside on the premises of the institution or in its immediate vicinity.

(2) In other institutions the medical officer shall visit daily and shall reside near enough to be able to attend without delay in cases of urgency.

53. (1) In an institution for both men and women, the part of the institution set aside for women shall be under the authority of a responsible woman officer who shall have the custody of the keys of all that part of the institution.

(2) No male member of the staff shall enter the part of the institution set aside for women unless accompanied by a woman officer.

(3) Women prisoners shall be attended and supervised only by women officers. This does not, however, preclude male members of the staff, particularly doctors and teachers, from carrying out their professional duties in institutions or parts of institutions set aside for women.

54. (1) Officers of the institutions shall not, in their relations with the prisoners, use force except in self-defence or in cases of attempted escape, or active or passive physical resistance to an order based on law or regulations. Officers who have recourse to force must use no more than is strictly necessary and must report the incident immediately to the director of the institution.

(2) Prison officers shall be given special physical training to enable them to restrain aggressive prisoners.

(3) Except in special circumstances, staff performing duties which bring them into direct contact with prisoners should not be armed. Furthermore, staff should in no circumstances be provided with arms unless they have been trained in their use.

Inspection

55. There shall be a regular inspection of penal institutions and services by qualified and experienced inspectors appointed by a competent authority. Their task shall be in particular to ensure that these institutions are administered in accordance with existing laws and regulations

and with a view to bringing about the objectives of penal and correctional services.

PART II.   RULES APPLICABLE TO SPECIAL CATEGORIES

A.   Prisoners Under Sentence

Guiding Principles

56.   The guiding principles hereafter are intended to show the spirit in which penal institutions should be administered and the purposes at which they should aim, in accordance with the declaration made under Preliminary Observation 1 of the present text.

57.   Imprisonment and other measures which result in cutting off an offender from the outside world are afflictive by the very fact of taking from the person the right of self-determination by depriving him of his liberty. Therefore the prison system shall not, except as incidental to justifiable segregation or the maintenance of discipline, aggravate the suffering inherent in such a situation.

58.   The purpose and justification of a sentence of imprisonment or a similar measure deprivative of liberty is ultimately to protect society against crime. This end can only be achieved if the period of imprisonment is used to ensure, so far as possible, that upon his return to society the offender is not only willing but able to lead a law-abiding and self-supporting life.

59.   To this end, the institution should utilize all the remedial, educational, moral, spiritual and other forces and forms of assistance which are appropriate and available, and should seek to apply them according to the individual treatment needs of the prisoners.

60.   (1) The régime of the institution should seek to minimize any differences between prison life and life at liberty which tend to lessen the responsibility of the prisoners or the respect due to their dignity as human beings.

(2) Before the completion of the sentence, it is desirable that the necessary steps be taken to ensure for the prisoner a gradual return to life in society. This aim may be achieved, depending on the case, by a pre-release régime organized in the same institution or in another appropriate institution, or by release on trial under some kind of supervision which must not be entrusted to the police but should be combined with effective social aid.

61.   The treatment of prisoners should emphasize not their exclusion from the community, but their continuing part in it. Community agencies should, therefore, be enlisted wherever possible to assist the staff of the institution in the task of social rehabilitation of the prisoners. There should be in connection with every institution social workers charged with the duty of maintaining and improving all desirable relations of a prisoner with his family and with valuable social agencies. Steps should be taken to safeguard, to the maximum extent compatible with the law and the sentence, the rights relating to civil interests, social security rights and other social benefits of prisoners.

62.   The medical services of the institution shall seek to detect and shall treat any physical or mental illnesses or defects which may hamper a prisoner's rehabilitation. All necessary medical, surgical and psychiatric services shall be provided to that end.

63.   (1) The fulfilment of these principles requires individualization of treatment and for this purpose a flexible system of classifying prisoners in groups; it is therefore desirable that such groups should be distributed in separate institutions suitable for the treatment of each group.

     (2) These institutions need not provide the same degree of security for every group. It is desirable to provide varying degrees of security according to the needs of different groups. Open institutions, by the very fact that they provide no physical security against escape but rely on the self-discipline of the inmates, provide the conditions most favourable to rehabilitation for carefully selected prisoners.

     (3) It is desirable that the number of prisoners in closed institutions should not be so large that the individualization of treatment is hindered. In some countries it is considered that the population of such institutions should not exceed five hundred. In open institutions the population should be as small as possible.

     (4) On the other hand, it is undesirable to maintain prisons which are so small that proper facilities cannot be provided.

64.   The duty of society does not end with a prisoner's release. There should, therefore, be governmental or private agencies capable of lending the released prisoner efficient after-care directed towards the lessening of prejudice against him and towards his social rehabilitation.

Treatment

65.   The treatment of persons sentenced to imprisonment or a similar measure shall have as its purpose, so far as the length of the sentence permits, to establish in them the will to lead law-abiding and self-supporting lives after their release and to fit them to do so. The treatment

shall be such as will encourage their self-respect and develop their sense of responsibility.

66.   (1) To these ends, all appropriate means shall be used, including religious care in the countries where this is possible, education, vocational guidance and training, social casework, employment counselling, physical development and strengthening of moral character, in accordance with the individual needs of each prisoner, taking account of his social and criminal history, his physical and mental capacities and aptitudes, his personal temperament, the length of his sentence and his prospects after release.

(2) For every prisoner with a sentence of suitable length, the director shall receive, as soon as possible after his admission, full reports on all the matters referred to in the foregoing paragraph. Such reports shall always include a report by a medical officer, wherever possible qualified in psychiatry, on the physical and mental condition of the prisoner.

(3) The reports and other relevant documents shall be placed in an individual file. This file shall be kept up to date and classified in such a way that it can be consulted by the responsible personnel whenever the need arises.

Classification and Individualization

67.   The purposes of classification shall be:
   (a) To separate from others those prisoners who, by reason of their criminal records or bad characters, are likely to exercise a bad influence;
   (b) To divide the prisoners into classes in order to facilitate their treatment with a view to their social rehabilitation.

68.   So far as possible separate institutions or separate sections of an institution shall be used for the treatment of the different classes of prisoners.

69.   As soon as possible after admission and after a study of the personality of each prisoner with a sentence of suitable length, a programme of treatment shall be prepared for him in the light of the knowledge obtained about his individual needs, his capacities and dispositions.

Privileges

70.   Systems of privileges appropriate for the different classes of prisoners and the different methods of treatment shall be established at every

institution, in order to encourage good conduct, develop a sense of responsibility and secure the interest and cooperation of the prisoners in their treatment.

Work

71.　(1) Prison labour must not be of an afflictive nature.

(2) All prisoners under sentence shall be required to work, subject to their physical and mental fitness as determined by the medical officer.

(3) Sufficient work of a useful nature shall be provided to keep prisoners actively employed for a normal working day.

(4) So far as possible the work provided shall be such as will maintain or increase the prisoners' ability to earn an honest living after release.

(5) Vocational training in useful trades shall be provided for prisoners able to profit thereby and especially for young prisoners.

(6) Within the limits compatible with proper vocational selection and with the requirements of institutional administration and discipline, the prisoners shall be able to choose the type of work they wish to perform.

72.　(1) The organization and methods of work in the institutions shall resemble as closely as possible those of similar work outside institutions, so as to prepare prisoners for the conditions of normal occupational life.

(2) The interests of the prisoners and of their vocational training, however, must not be subordinated to the purpose of making a financial profit from an industry in the institution.

73.　(1) Preferably institutional industries and farms should be operated directly by the administration and not by private contractors.

(2) Where prisoners are employed in work not controlled by the administration, they shall always be under the supervision of the institution's personnel. Unless the work is for other departments of the government the full normal wages for such work shall be paid to the administration by the persons to whom the labour is supplied, account being taken of the output of the prisoners.

74.　(1) The precautions laid down to protect the safety and health of free workmen shall be equally observed in institutions.

(2) Provision shall be made to indemnify prisoners against industrial injury, including occupational disease, on terms not less favourable than those extended by law to free workmen.

75.　(1) The maximum daily and weekly working hours of the prisoners shall be fixed by law or by administrative regulation, taking into account local rules or custom in regard to the employment of free workmen.

(2) The hours so fixed shall leave one rest day a week and sufficient time for education and other activities required as part of the treatment and rehabilitation of the prisoners.

76. (1) There shall be a system of equitable remuneration of the work of prisoners.

(2) Under the system prisoners shall be allowed to spend at least a part of their earnings on approved articles for their own use and to send a part of their earnings to their family.

(3) The system should also provide that a part of the earnings should be set aside by the administration so as to constitute a savings fund to be handed over to the prisoner on his release.

Education and Recreation

77. (1) Provision shall be made for the further education of all prisoners capable of profiting thereby, including religious instruction in the countries where this is possible. The education of illiterates and young prisoners shall be compulsory and special attention shall be paid to it by the administration.

(2) So far as practicable, the education of prisoners shall be integrated with the educational system of the country so that after their release they may continue their education without difficulty.

78. Recreational and cultural activities shall be provided in all institutions for the benefit of the mental and physical health of prisoners.

Social Relations and After-Care

79. Special attention shall be paid to the maintenance and improvement of such relations between a prisoner and his family as are desirable in the best interests of both.

80. From the beginning of a prisoner's sentence consideration shall be given to his future after release and he shall be encouraged and assisted to maintain or establish such relations with persons or agencies outside the institution as may promote the best interests of his family and his own social rehabilitation.

81. (1) Services and agencies, governmental or otherwise, which assist released prisoners to reestablish themselves in society shall ensure, so far as is possible and necessary, that released prisoners be provided with

appropriate documents and identification papers, have suitable homes and work to go to, are suitably and adequately clothed having regard to the climate and season, and have sufficient means to reach their destination and maintain themselves in the period immediately following their release.

(2) The approved representatives of such agencies shall have all necessary access to the institution and to prisoners and shall be taken into consultation as to the future of a prisoner from the beginning of his sentence.

(3) It is desirable that the activities of such agencies shall be centralized or coordinated as far as possible in order to secure the best use of their efforts.

B. Insane and Mentally Abnormal Prisoners

82. (1) Persons who are found to be insane shall not be detained in prisons and arrangements shall be made to remove them to mental institutions as soon as possible.

(2) Prisoners who suffer from other mental diseases or abnormalities shall be observed and treated in specialized institutions under medical management.

(3) During their stay in a prison, such prisoners shall be placed under the special supervision of a medical officer.

(4) The medical or psychiatric service of the penal institutions shall provide for the psychiatric treatment of all other prisoners who are in need of such treatment.

83. It is desirable that steps should be taken, by arrangement with the appropriate agencies, to ensure if necessary the continuation of psychiatric treatment after release and the provision of social-psychiatric after-care.

C. Prisoners Under Arrest or Awaiting Trial

84. (1) Persons arrested or imprisoned by reason of a criminal charge against them, who are detained either in police custody or in prison custody (jail) but have not yet been tried and sentenced, will be referred to as "untried prisoners" hereinafter in these rules.

(2) Unconvicted prisoners are presumed to be innocent and shall be treated as such.

(3) Without prejudice to legal rules for the protection of individual

liberty or prescribing the procedure to be observed in respect of untried prisoners, these prisoners shall benefit by a special régime which is described in the following rules in its essential requirements only.

85.   (1) Untried prisoners shall be kept separate from convicted prisoners.

    (2) Young untried prisoners shall be kept separate from adults and shall in principle be detained in separate institutions.

86.   Untried prisoners shall sleep singly in separate rooms, with the reservation of different local custom in respect of the climate

87.   Within the limits compatible with the good order of the institution, untried prisoners may, if they so desire, have their food procured at their own expense from the outside, either through the administration or through their family or friends. Otherwise, the administration shall provide their food.

88.   (1) An untried prisoner shall be allowed to wear his own clothing if it is clean and suitable.

    (2) If he wears prison dress, it shall be different from that supplied to convicted prisoners.

89.   An untried prisoner shall always be offered opportunity to work, but shall not be required to work. If he chooses to work, he shall be paid for it.

90.   An untried prisoner shall be allowed to procure at his own expense or at the expense of a third party such books, newspapers, writing materials and other means of occupation as are compatible with the interests of the administration of justice and the security and good order of the institution.

91.   An untried prisoner shall be allowed to be visited and treated by his own doctor or dentist if there is reasonable ground for his application and he is able to pay any expenses incurred.

92.   An untried prisoner shall be allowed to inform immediately his family of his detention and shall be given all reasonable facilities for communicating with his family and friends, and for receiving visits from them, subject only to such restrictions and supervision as are necessary in the interests of the administration of justice and of the security and good order of the institution.

93.   For the purposes of his defence, an untried prisoner shall be allowed to apply for free legal aid where such aid is available, and to receive visits from his legal adviser with a view to his defence and to prepare and hand to him confidential instructions. For these purposes, he shall if he so desires be supplied with writing material. Interviews between the prisoner and his legal adviser may be within sight but not within the hearing of a police or institutional official.

D.   Civil Prisoners

94.   In countries where the law permits imprisonment for debt or by order of a court under any other non-criminal process, persons so imprisoned shall not be subjected to any greater restriction or severity than is necessary to ensure safe custody and good order. Their treatment shall be not less favourable than that of untried prisoners, with the reservation, however, that they may possibly be required to work

20   *Classification*

AMERICAN CORRECTIONAL ASSOCIATION*

The factors which contribute to the making of delinquents and criminals are many and complex. Usually, they involve destructive earlier human relationships, especially in the home. The techniques and services utilized in correctional treatment have also come to be varied and general. Correctional treatment means, in this connection, everything in an institution that affects individual growth, especially the interpersonal relationships among the staff and inmates which may compose a constructive human environment in the prison. Because specific "cures" for any of the different kinds of criminality are as yet unknown, no one technique or service can be said to function effectively as curative in and of itself. A therapeutic atmosphere in the institution provides a basic condition for many kinds of treatment found in correctional work.

Some organized procedures are obviously necessary to insure the best possible kind of integration, coordination, and continuity of diagnosis, individualized program planning, and the general conduct of care and treatment as applied first in the institution and continued later in the community. *Classification* is the term used to designate these organized procedures.

> Classification . . . contributes to a smoothly, efficiently operated correctional program by the pooling of all relevant information concerning the offender, by devising a program for the individual based upon that information,

* From the *Manual of Correctional Standards*, (Washington, D.C.: American Correctional Association, 1966), pp. 351–365. Copyright © 1966, by the American Correctional Association. Reprinted by permission of the American Correctional Association.

and by keeping that program realistically in line with the individual's require-ments. It furnishes an orderly method to the institution administrator by which the varied needs and requirements of each inmate may be followed through from commitment to discharge. Through its diagnostic and coordinating functions, classification not only contributes to the objective of rehabilitation, but also to custody, discipline, work assignments, officer and inmate morale and the effective use of training opportunities. Through the data it develops, it assists in long-range planning and development, both in the correctional system as a whole and in the individual institution.[1]

The alternative to classification is the continuation of the "guess and by golly" system which plagued prison operation through history. Rehabil-itation of the offender is difficult and complex in the extreme. Only an approach which accepts this fact has hope of success.

ESSENTIAL FEATURES OF CLASSIFICATION

1. The Classification Process

The classification process consists of organized procedures by which diagnosis, treatment-planning, and the carrying out of the component parts of the general treatment program are coordinated and focused *on the individual* in prison and on parole.

2. The Reception Program

The reception program includes the instruction or orientation of the newly-received inmate regarding the institutional and parole programs during his stay in reception facility while the initial diagnostic case studies are being made.

3. The Admission Summary

The admission summary consists of the compilation, first, of informa-tion from all phases of the diagnostic study during the reception period; and, second, of the listing of recommendations issuing from this diagno-sis for the treatment of each individual. The admission summary is the cornerstone upon which a cumulative case history is developed, as information about the inmate is added to it systematically during his time in prison and on parole.

4. The Records Office

A records office, conveniently located and well organized, is essential for the classification program. The cumulative case histories are the primary sources of information about the inmates' programs and all other aspects of their cases.

5. The Institutional Classification Committee

The institutional classification committee consists of personnel representing all institutional departments having contact with individual inmates. They meet together as a whole or in subgroups to consider and to direct the care and treatment program of each individual inmate.

6. The Initial Classification Meeting

The initial classification meeting occurs shortly after an inmate's assignment to an institution. All diagnostic factors available in the case are studied, and a realistic program of custodial care and constructive treatment is formulated.

7. Reclassification

Reclassification meetings are held at regular intervals, and whenever a major change in an inmate's program appears indicated. Such reviews of an individual's case help insure continuity in the treatment program and expedite necessary program revisions to meet the changing needs of the inmate.

8. Classification Procedures Immediately Prior to Parole or Release

Prior to a parole hearing, the classification committee may prepare a special summary or preparole report which represents the coordinated staff thinking about an inmate's adjustment and readiness for release so important in the deliberations of a paroling authority. It may also include relevant suggestions as to the most satisfactory treatment program for the individual after release on parole.

DISCUSSION OF THE ESSENTIAL FEATURES OF CLASSIFICATION

1. The Classification Process

The primary objective of classification as a systematic process is the development and administration of an integrated and realistic program of treatment for the individual, with procedures for changing the program when indicated. This primary objective is attained through five general approaches: (a) The analysis of the individual's problems through the use of every available diagnostic technique, including social investigation, medical, psychological, psychiatric examinations, educational, vocational, religious, and recreational studies. The observations of custodial officers offer data of value. (b) A treatment and training program is evolved in staff conference during or after the inmate's personal appearance before them, based upon these analyses and a frank discussion of its purposes with the inmate. (c) The program decided upon must be placed into operation. (d) It may be revised when indicated. Classification, a dynamic process, cannot be effective unless program modifications are made in accordance with the changing needs of the individual inmate. (e) What is done for the inmate in the institution needs to be correlated with his program on parole.

Classification, therefore, is neither specific training nor general treatment, but rather the process through which the resources of the correctional institution can be applied effectively to the individual case. Classification is more than labeling inmates in categories or types, or the segregation of similar groups of offenders in separate institutions. Yet the classification program becomes more effective when separate, specialized facilities are available for the treatment of different types of offenders. Classification may be conceived of as the process of pooling all relevant knowledge about the inmate so that important decisions and activities affecting him may be better coordinated. It serves also as the means of directing toward him the individualized and group treatment he needs.

Classification is part of the program of the correctional system as a whole. Upon the basis of classification findings, the planning of the correctional system is assisted through knowledge of what types of programs and institutions are needed. Every state correctional department should employ a high-ranking member of the staff to be responsible for supervising classification in the correctional system as a whole, and for coordinating the institutional program with parole planning and treatment. Standards should be set for the system-wide classification program with provision for necessary variations in details in the several facilities.

For the operation of a classification program, adequate facilities, the necessary diagnostic and treatment personnel and the understanding and cooperation of management personnel are essential. However, the principles of classification may be applied even when personnel and facilities are minimal. A classification program is, therefore, not entirely dependent upon a full staff of professional personnel, well-trained management people, and extensive treatment facilities, although the program can be more effective to the extent that these conditions exist. The correctional system with little by way of professional staff or facilities, if it still attempts to apply the principles of classification, may achieve thereby a more effective use of its resources in individualized treatment.

2. The Reception Program

No time may be more important to the prisoner, in determining his later attitudes and patterns of behavior, than when he enters the institution. He may entertain the layman's concept of the prison as a place of punishment. He may be in the throes of emotions, such as guilt, anxiety, resentment, self-pity, depression, remorse, and hostility. Few prisoners bring with them any reality-based understanding of the correctional program or any real hope of profiting from this experience. Most have erroneous preconceptions gained from other prisoners while in jail awaiting trial and commitment. The reception period immediately following admission to prison is, therefore, of great significance. Intimate and skilled counseling is especially necessary to help the inmate start his efforts to gain insight into his situation and to accept what he, himself, must do about it.

A. Advantages of a Separate Reception Process

The segregation of new inmates for medical or custodial reasons is provided. Some authorities believe that the medical quarantine period need be no longer than five days. The total period of separate housing for inmate orientation and case study varies in practice from four to eight weeks. It is desirable that the reception or admission-orientation unit have its own facilities for interviews, group testing, educational classes, discussion groups, and recreation. A period of segregation insures that the new inmate will be readily available for diagnostic studies. An orientation program for inmates may be carried out advantageously. In this situation orientation means informing the inmate not only regarding the details of everyday life in prison, but also the broader purposes of treatment in the institution and thereafter on parole. To the man who has never before been in prison, there is much he needs to know, not only about prison regulations, practices and organization, but also about the treatment and training opportunities available. To the man who has been confined previously, his past institutional experiences may have established uncooperative attitudes which must be changed before he will accept assistance or enter into a constructive program.

In most jurisdictions, inmates are still committed by the courts directly to a particular institution, for example, to one of the state prisons or the state reformatory. It is far more desirable to provide by law that offenders be committed by the courts to the state correctional system and the custody of the Director or Commissioner of Corrections, or the equivalent official or board. This central authority should then be empowered to determine the institution to which the individual will be committed. Upon the basis of the admission classification study it can be determined to what particular type of program and institution the inmate properly belongs. When this is done, it may be said that the classification procedure in a state or federal correctional system begins when the offender is committed to prison.

B. Staff Role in Reception Processing

If resources permit, specialized staff conduct the diagnostic-classification process. The staff soon becomes skilled in the case-conference method and in the preparation of brief, yet comprehensive, case summaries. Moreover, opportunity is given in the reception unit for careful observation of the newly-received prisoners by correctional officers and other staff members. The staff may recognize and plan for those inmates who are likely to present institutional problems by virtue of mental illness or defectiveness or acted-out hostility toward authority. Likewise, those who may try to escape may be noted as would be true also of others who need to be handled carefully by virtue of some special features of their cases, such as newspaper notoriety or political implications. Inmates with special problems such as these may be recognized and recommendations for their disposition prepared in accordance with the policies and procedures of the prison system.

To accomplish the important objectives of orientation mentioned above, staff members from the various departments meet with groups of inmates and not only give them information, but also through discussion encourage the new men to raise the innumerable questions which are in their minds. Inmate speakers, representing organizations like Alcoholics Anonymous, may also assist in the program. Orientation is most effective if spaced throughout the period of classification study. Some correctional systems provide initial group psychotherapy or group counseling during this period.

Other techniques currently being used include guided tours through the institution, motion pictures and slides showing the institutional activities, facilities and programs, and distribution of brochures describing the institutional programs as well as its rules and regulations. Such "rule books" should contain clear, concise statements as to the "does" as well as the "don'ts." They should be informative and explanatory in tone rather than harsh and threatening, true guidelines for conduct rather than detailed listing of all the possible infractions. Group discussion of "the rules" is a valuable means of increasing understanding of them and may at the same time elicit information about individual inmate's difficulties in conforming.

C. Inmate Activity Program During the Reception Period

There is great need for a well-organized activity program during the reception period. Most persons committed to correctional institutions have already spent considerable time in idleness in jail awaiting trial, sentence, and commitment. Further idleness during the reception period tends to increase tensions and hostilities. The reception program should provide reading material, regular recreational activities, including exercise periods, religious services, and special work assignments either in the reception unit or outside it. The reception inmate should be kept separate from the general population at all times.

3. The Admission Summary

The compilation of the results of the diagnostic study has been called commonly the admission summary. It forms the first document of the cumulative case history. The admission summary should consist of the following: (1) account of the legal aspects of the case. In addition to citations from the summaries of the reports of law enforcement, judicial, and other officials, this may contain an explanation by the inmate of how he got into trouble; (2) summary of the man's earlier criminal history. If he has previously been in a juvenile or an adult correctional institution, reports from these places contain information regarding his program therein and related facts about his attitudes and behavior; (3) social history, or the man's biography as a person, based upon the probation report or field investigation, staff interviews, tests, examinations, and other staff observations. This may also be provided or amplified by his family or friends, former employers, and others who may assist through interviews or answers to questionnaires; (4) physical condition; (5) vocational interests, competence and experience; (6) educational status; (7) religious background and interest; (8) recreational interest; (9) psychological characteristics evaluated by the psychiatrist and the psychologist; (10) behavior in the reception center, reported by the custodial staff; and (11) initial reaction to group psychotherapy or group counseling, or other forms of treatment. From the above interview and counseling situations, data are obtained from the inmate's standpoint, that is, the man's own story, as well as from other persons. The admission summary becomes a practical document when the final page is devoted to a listing of recommendations in the above areas of diagnostic study for the inmate's institutional and parole program.

Most correctional systems have found it advisable to prepare a master stencil of the admission summary from which additional copies may be made through a duplicating process. Copies are required not only for the classification committee but also after the reception period for the central office of the prison system, and still later for the parole agency. Requests for copies of the case history may also come from other institutions or appropriate community agencies.

A. Selective Reception Processing Schedules

Complete reception processing as outlined in the above sections may not always be necessary for every incoming inmate. Men very recently released from prison, for whom an adequate cumulative case summary is available, may receive a briefer processing. This may be particularly true for parole violators as well as recidivists where the reason for return to prison is simply an extension of already well-documented behavior. In such cases, the reception staff may bring the case up to date with a brief re-admission statement containing a summary of the man's activities while in the community and a brief evaluation of the reasons for his return to prison. Caution must be observed, however, so that men who have committed a serious or bizarre offense or who have suffered a serious emotional upset during their period of freedom are referred for the appropriate, complete diagnostic evaluation.

4. The Records Office

The effectiveness of the classification program depends upon coordination of efforts among all departments of the institution in a mutually consistent and supportive program of care and treatment. So that all employees may be informed regarding the program, the cumulative case histories of all inmates should be maintained in one conveniently located place, the records office. Unnecessary duplication of record keeping should be reduced thereby to a minimum. The records office needs to be equipped with chairs and desks so that anyone desiring to study an inmate's case there should be able to do so conveniently. Case folders may be checked out to staff members who may use them elsewhere, for example, in interviews or classification committee meetings. *Under no circumstances should inmates have access to these case records or to parole records.*

From the time the inmate enters the institution until his release, memoranda, reports, criminal records, the admission summary, progress reports, and other data concerning his background, conduct and any correspondence in his behalf, are filed in his individual case folder. The inmate's central file may contain the following, preferably placed in a standard order of filing:

a) Copy of the cumulative case summary.
b) All legal documents including warrants, "holds," certified copies of indictments, commitments, or judgments.
c) Probation officer's report and other diagnostic summaries from other agencies.
d) Up-to-date progress reports in the areas of work assignments, vocational training, education, psychiatric and medical treatment.
e) Record of disciplinary infractions, including actions taken and facts relating to the infraction.
f) Any correspondence relating to the inmate.
g) Identification material including a recent picture and fingerprints.
h) A record of all classification transactions, including transfers from one institution to another, changes in custody, etc.
i) Cumulative case summaries of crime partners.

So that the inmate central file may be as up-to-date as possible, many of the briefer reports can be submitted in "chrono" form so that they may be available at any time. Subsequently these brief progress reports will be incorporated into periodic summary reports at the time of reclassification or just prior to parole hearings.

The cumulative case histories filed in the individual case folder in the records office must be confidential. The prisoner will not talk freely to the psychiatrist, the chaplain or other staff members, if he knows that written reports of these interviews will be filed where such information will be accessible to other prisoners. Moreover, persons in law enforcement departments or social agencies may decline to submit reports unless they are assured of the confidentiality thereof.

Along with the above arrangements, the need must be recognized for employees to be trained in the efficient reading and study of the case history. This is done best by actual, first-hand demonstrations of their use by the institution's staff of experienced caseworkers. Such instruction should include an emphasis upon the importance of confidentiality. Instruction should also be given in the preparation of reports and the need to avoid duplication by repeating what is already stated in the record.

The organization of the individual case folder and the housing of all such records are of great importance in the program of classification. No meetings of the classification committee should be held without the case folders of the inmates whose cases are to be considered being immediately available. Reports of actions at such meetings should be summarized after each case is discussed for inclusion in the inmate's case history. The use of a recording device has proved to be a helpful and efficient method for immediately recording the outcomes of case discussions.

5. The Institutional Classification Committee

The key element of the classification process is the classification committee, or, as it is sometimes called, the classification board. Because of its functions in coordinating the activities concerning the inmate in the institution, the classification committee should be composed of those staff members who most represent the diagnostic, treatment, and security responsibilities of the institution. These are usually department heads or their designees. The membership will vary as between institutions, depending upon size and the extent to which diagnostic, training and treatment services have been developed. In the more adequately staffed institutions, the committee may include the warden or superintendent, as chairman, (usually ex officio) and as alternate chairman, an associate or deputy warden in charge of classification and treatment activities. The presence of the warden or superintendent emphasizes the importance of the classification committee functions, and in institutions where classification is not yet thoroughly "sold" insures that committee actions carry his full support and authority. In larger institutions, it is usually impossible for the warden or superintendent to attend all classification committee meetings or to devote the time effective classification demands. In these cases, the chairman is usually an associate warden (treatment) or a supervisor of classification. In addition, any of the following may be included, the supervisor of education, the vocational supervisor or counselor, the industries supervisor, the chaplains, the chief medical officer, the psychiatrist, the psychologist, and the correctional officer in charge of the admission unit. For effective and economical service in the large prison, the committee may be subdivided into smaller working units. This trend toward smaller committees is believed by many to be most desirable, especially for purposes of reclassification. Some even believe the classification process should be completely decentralized and placed in the hands of individual caseworkers. The committee, then, would serve as a classification and treatment council where principles and policies, rather than individual cases, can be discussed.

The institution supervisor of classification is responsible for the development of procedures which will permit smooth and efficient operation of the program. He schedules cases for the meetings, notifies committee members of the dates when reports are required, and supervises their assembly into the various classification reports. He reviews the material submitted, noting discrepancies, incompleteness and repetition, and takes the steps necessary to eliminate deficiencies and maintain classification standards at a high level. Finally, he has the important responsibility of seeing that the recommendations are referred to the proper persons and to check thereafter to note whether or not they have been carried out. In the parole agency, there is a simplified form of the classification process. The study of the man's case is carried on largely by the field parole agent alone or sometimes with a supervisor present.

6. The Initial Classification Meeting

The purpose of the initial classification meeting held after the reception period is to develop a program for and with the inmate which will be realistically directed toward his rehabilitation. At initial classification, it is necessary to coordinate the diagnostic material prepared by the staff, to weigh the various factors contributing to his delinquent behavior, and to evaluate his potentialities and limitations. This is accomplished through the staff conference method.

In the presentation of cases at the initial classification meeting, some institutions require that each member of the committee orally summarize the section of the report which relates to his department. In others, the admission summary is presented briefly by the supervisor of classification or by the social worker or psychologist or other staff member who is best informed about the case. Elsewhere, each member may be asked to summarize a number of cases. If possible, presentations should be prepared in advance, with the main findings and relevant information of each case stressed. Following presentation, the committee should discuss the case fully and agree upon a tentative program before the inmate is brought into the room.

The inmate should participate in the planning of his own program since one which is imposed upon him will not be as well accepted as one in whose development he feels he has had a part. The time during his personal appearance should be conducted so as to put the inmate immediately at ease. The way has been prepared for inmate participation by discussions of the inmate's future during interviews held during the reception period. At the meeting, he is free to express his frank opinion of the values of the proposed program as he views it. In some cases, conflicts and misunderstandings may be assuaged by interpreting to him the meaning and purpose of his program, and, when indicated, adjusting it according to his own expressed needs.

Committee recommendations should cover all important aspects of the inmate's institutional life. Some recommendations at initial classification will be tentative and dependent upon further information and observation. The first decision to be made by the classification committee, if a reception center is not available in the prison system, may be the inmate's assignment to a suitable institution. Such recommendations will be limited by the number and variety of institutions in the correctional system and the statutory provisions permitting transfers. In the main, transfers are made (a) to place the inmate in an institution better suited to his training and treatment needs; (b) to separate recidivists and vicious offenders from the unsophisticated; (c) to place inmates who are in need of special medical or psychiatric treatment in institutions affording the appropriate facilities; (d) to separate informers from persons against whom they have informed; and (e) to separate an inmate from a co-defendant or an associate who has an adverse influence on him. Also, transfers may be made on occasion to adjust populations by relieving overcrowding or for other administrative reasons.

The second consideration is the degree of custody required for the inmate. It is obvious that mental defectives, known homosexuals, escape risks and others likely to present management problems need to be classified custodially so as to try to protect them from exploitation and the institution from avoidable management problems.

A third phase of classification concerns work assignments. Recommendations are based upon physical condition, the inmate's mental and mechanical aptitudes, his past work history, occupational interests, his needs and opportunities upon release, and last but not least, the jobs and the training available within the institution. If possible, work assignments are made on a training basis. In order to insure that a specific program of vocational training not be changed without committee action, work assignments should be classified into two groups. The first group consists of jobs which may be changed only on recommendation of the classification committeee, such as vocational training and specific occupational or industrial assignments. The second groups consist of those which may be changed by the administrative officer in charge of work assignments. Ordinarily, inmates assigned at institutional convenience to general labor or maintenance may be changed from one of these assignments to another without committee action.

The fourth area, recommendation relating to the academic program, must be realistic and coordinated with the rest of the program, especially work and vocational assignments. Academic placements will, of course, depend upon the policies and facilities of the institution together with the inmate's mental ability, educational record and his interests. This is another phase of the program which rests exclusively with the committee. No single officer should have the authority to remove an inmate from such an assignment. Many other types of recommendations may be mentioned briefly. Medical and psychiatric recommendations are considered in themselves as well as in connection with assignments to other aspects of the program. Social service recommendations may include requests for additional information or the desirability of arrangements with community agencies to provide assistance and other social services to the inmate's family during his confinement. Provision for regular casework contacts with the inmate or his family may also be outlined in collaboration with local private and public agencies.

The recommendations of the chaplain may include attendance at church services, enrollment in religious-education classes, and religious counseling. Provisions for church services and a program of religious education classes add much to the institutional climate and to the treatment program. It is in the area of personal religious counseling, however, that the chaplain may make his greatest contribution to the individualized treatment.

A good recreational program may raise the general institutional morale and reduce the amount of time devoted by inmates to the discussion of criminal activities. Socially acceptable avocational interests may be suggested for the use of leisure time.

In some institutions, the classification committee also determines where the inmate shall be quartered. It is becoming increasingly recognized that the living quarters and associations of the inmate in the housing unit may vitally affect his adjustment and participation in a constructive program.

Other recommendations may be made in individual cases; for example, an emotionally unstable or depressed individual may require special psychiatric attention. An alcoholic may benefit by Alcoholics Anonymous, drug addicts by similar special programs. When professional clinical staff is insufficient, employees who have demonstrated abilities to deal effectively with persons with special problems may be given counseling responsibilities for them.

Where time allows, the classification committee at initial classification would do well to summarize and record, at the close of its deliberations on the case, data about three features of his case which present the inmate as a person to be treated. First would be the factors believed to have been important in causing or contributing to the inmate's criminal behavior. Second would be important aspects of the individualized plan of treatment with the reasons therefor. Third would be a review of assets and liabilities in the case, with an estimate of the probable outcome of the treatment plan. This is sometimes called the client's treatability. If a brief, clearly presented summary of the thoughts of the staff about the inmate were furnished to the personnel, especially those in day-to-day contact with the inmate, with suggestions and precautions as to counseling and supervision, a notable advance might occur in the correctional program.

7. Reclassification

The study and observation of an inmate must be a continuous process if a program of treatment is to be kept realistic and effective. First must be the assurance that the program not only is placed into operation, but also changed when circumstances warrant. Routinely scheduled reclassifica tion is necessary to make possible the continued integration of the individual's program with all the institutional departments involved. Because human personality is dynamic and changing, reclassification is necessary to guarantee that there will be neither forgotten men in prison nor "dead end" placements. The inmate's efforts and accomplishments are officially recognized by reclassification committees. At these times the committee recommends desirable changes in his program.

An inmate's case should be brought up for reclassification whenever any significant change in his program seems necessary. Custodial and other personnel should be encouraged to refer matters requiring attention to the office of the institutional supervisor of classification. In individual cases, some institutional committees may set a time for the first reclassification at the initial classification meeting; others hold to a uniform requirement that reclassification occur at least once a year or at some other interval. In some jurisdictions, particularly those handling young offenders, progress reports are required much more frequently.

The institutional supervisor of classification is responsible for scheduling and notifying members of the committee of the reclassification agenda. Division heads may be required to submit any new and pertinent information about the inmates involved. The progress reports of school, work and quarters officers, who are in daily contact with the inmate, may be especially valuable.

The full classification committee should, if possible, constitute the reclassification committee. In the larger institutions, because of the number of cases involved, the classification committee may be divided into two or more subcommittees. Some feel this is not a healthy practice for it tends to focus on single program changes without considering the inmate's total program balance. The sub-committee would, however, represent the various departments primarily concerned with the decisions. The supervisor of classification or other employees may present a digest of cases to the committee at the reclassification meeting. The actions of the committee or any sub-committee are recorded as progress reports and added to the cumulative case records.

8. Classification Procedures Immediately Prior to Parole or Release

Just prior to an inmate's appearance before the parole authority, a progress report should be prepared in order that the paroling authority may have a complete and up-to-date history of his activities within the institution and such other information pertinent to his readiness for release. Where there is good communication between the institution and the paroling authority, some believe direct parole recommendations should be made by the classification committee. After his appearance before the paroling authority, the classification committee should review the case in the light of the authority's action. At this time, especially if parole has been denied, it is imperative that the staff or a staff member discuss with the inmate the meaning of the action.

A serious handicap in the over-all correctional program has been the insufficient mutual understanding and cooperation of institutional and parole officials. Usually these two divisions of the correctional system have been in separate governmental agencies. Consequently, in some jurisdictions, communication has not been adequate. In other jurisdictions, fortunately, the relevant parts of the cumulative case history are sent to those actively supervising the inmate on parole. Whatever the administrative relationships between prison and parole officials, the need is apparent for continuity of the treatment program which has been started in the institution. The classification material should be available to the parole officer who should use it as basic data for planning his supervision of the inmate in the community.[2] In this connection, and similar to what the reception program does in the way of institutional orientation, a good classification program would require institutions to conduct pre-release training programs. These should be the joint responsibility of the institutional and parole officials. The class sessions should include at least one conducted by a field parole agent and, if possible, one to which the parole agent brings one or more successful parolees. Other sessions would be the responsibility of the institutional staff, who, in some jurisdictions, use group counseling, printed material and demonstrations to supplement class instruction. The better pre-release programs have utilized the services of public spirited citizens in the community to discuss informally with inmates a wide range of subjects, including what the employer expects of the employee, union activities and regulations, employment resources, services of community agencies, etc.

When men violate their parole and are returned to prison, the institution officials should receive adequate information about their attitudes and behavior in the community, a statement or the official reason for revocation, and what seem to have been the factors in their failure. The reports of the field parole agents and their statement about the man's parole violation become part of the man's cumulative case record when the violator is returned to the institution. The readmission summary, prepared for initial classification of the parole violator shortly after his return to prison, might draw heavily on these reports in evolving plans for the new institutional program for the parole violator. In some correctional systems, parole violators are processed in the reception unit. In others, they are segregated and treated differently from the newly received inmates. In any case, the institutional and community treatment programs should be reviewed in the light of the violation on parole to determine, if possible, the reasons for failure and to find guidelines for a revised program.

SUMMARY

In general, classification contributes to an efficiently operated correctional program from reception to discharge from parole. This it does by the cumulative recording of all relevant information concerning the individual offender, by continuous development and revision of the program for the individual based upon this information, and by trying to keep the program realistically in line with the individual's welfare. Classification furnishes an orderly method by which the varied needs of each prisoner may be followed through from commitment to discharge from parole. Through its diagnostic and coordinating functions, it not only contributes to the objective of rehabilitation, but also to more efficient institutional management and morale and more effectively directed supervision on parole.

Informal discussions, during classification meetings or thereafter, of questions of policy or procedure raised by staff members, are important for the advancement of the correctional program. Suggestions from these discussions may assist in the long-range planning of needed local or system-wide facilities and in developing policies and procedures, both in the individual institution and in the correctional system as a whole.

21 The Effectiveness of Correctional Education

DANIEL GLASER*

Nobody knows conclusively and precisely the effectiveness of correctional education. Statistics vary from one study to the next. When one defines "success" for research purposes as the absence of post-release felony convictions or parole violations, some studies indicate that inmates who were in prison school succeed more than those who were not, while other studies have the opposite finding.[3] Analysis usually indicates that these results are due largely to the selection of inmates for prison school, rather than due just to the effects of the school.

Despite these sources of contradictory findings in gross comparisons of releasees, there is some evidence of a favorable impact from correctional education. If one compares only inmates of similar age and criminality, and only those confined for long terms, those in prison school for an appreciable portion of their term have higher post-release success rates than those in prison school only briefly or not at all. Furthermore, inmates who advance their grade level while in prison have higher success rates than those who do not. Even these findings may be accounted for partly by the selection of students for school, or by the initial attributes of those who advance in grade level as compared with those who do not, rather than being purely effects of the schooling. We can only become highly confident in the conclusiveness of research on prison education if many more prisoners are considered eligible for a prison school program than are assigned to it, and if those assigned are

* From *American Journal of Correction*, 28, 2 (March–April 1966): 4–9. Reprinted by permission of the American Correctional Association.

selected by a purely random process, the remainder serving as a control group. However, this controlled experiment approach to research on prison education is only part of the last of four needs distinctive of prison school programs which I wish to discuss, in considering how we can increase the effectiveness of correctional education.

BROADENING THE CHALLENGE

The first requirement for more successful education with the types of pupil predominant in prison is to increase the challenge of prison education. There should be a broader range in correctional pedagogy between that which frustrates the potential student, because he fears he will fail at it, and that which dulls his interest, because he finds it boring. This challenge area is narrow, for many students, and difficult to locate. We have some clues as to the cause of this narrowness from recent studies of so-called "culturally deprived" school populations. There also are clues, from recent experiments with special education methods, as to how education can be made more challenging.

One conclusion that is emerging from a variety of sociological studies is that the educability and the delinquency of youth are not just functions of his home, not just the heredity or the cultural environment provided by his parents. Instead, they reflect his neighborhood. The average income of a neighborhood within a large city is closely related to the average school performance in the neighborhood, and even to the prevailing attitude toward schooling there, and to the delinquency rates. Within any neighborhood the children of parents of different income do not differ in delinquency and in school achievement as much as over-all rates for neighborhoods differ according to the average income of each neighborhood.[4] Thus, youth reflect the school conditions of their neighborhoods, in addition to their individual school problems, although correctional education has tended to focus on the individual attributes.

The differences between schools from neighborhoods of diverse income are illuminated dramatically by the data presented in Patricia C. Sexton's book, *Education and Income.*[5] This New York University professor, and wife of an Assistant Director of the U.S. Office of Economic Opportunity, classified school districts in a large metropolis according to the average family income reported for their areas by the U.S. Census. In districts where the average family income was below $3,000 per year, the income range which the Office of Economic Opportunity employs as a working definition of "poverty," the average achievement test score in the fourth grade was 3.5, while in school districts where family income averaged $9,000 or more per year, the average test score was 4.8. For eighth grade classes, the average test score in the povertous districts was 6.8, while in the richer districts it was 8.7.[6] The further one advanced in the school level, the farther behind was the achievement in the poorer districts. These are the differences in composite scores on the Iowa Achievement Tests; the differences were somewhat greater than this in the scores on reading ability, and not as great in tests on arithmetic.

Reading ability deficiency seems to be the key problem, for it is this deficiency which increasingly differentiates those who complete high school from those who drop out, as well as those who progress in college from those who never enter, or who enter but fail to remain long. As Mrs. Sexton says: "lower-income students are poor readers very often because their parents cannot or do not read to them at home, because they do not have books in their homes, and because even if they had books, their environment would not be conducive to reading. They are poor readers because they usually do not use public libraries, have never been taught to use them, have never been properly encouraged by libraries to enter and make themselves at home." On the average, a tenement flat with residents totaling two or more people per room, with small rooms and a loud television set, with no books or magazines, and with illiterate adults, is less conducive to a student's realization of his reading potential than is a home with more rooms that residents, and with magazines, books, and educated adults.

It is well established that deficiences in reading ability, and in accompanying verbal fluency, are reflected in intelligence test performance. Remedial reading instruction and motivation to do well tend to raise I.Q. scores, yet the myth that these scores reflect only inherent ability often has the vicious effect of barring some students from the remedial reading classes which might raise their intelligence test performance. Compounding these difficulties further are other problems which statistically distinguish schools in low-income neighborhoods: these schools receive a disproportionate share of the least educated and experienced teachers; they are the most overcrowded and the most poorly equipped of the city schools; they have the most frequent use of punitive discipline and the least extensive distribution of special awards for superior scholarship. In Mrs. Sexton's study it was even found that these schools in the lowest income neighborhoods had taken less advantage of the opportunity to secure free lunches for students, from surplus foods, than had schools in neighborhoods of somewhat greater income. In summary, the schools in the districts of lowest income level tend to be administered in a manner which is least responsive to the distinctive needs of these districts.

The psychological effects of the child's total experience in low-income neighborhoods, as compared with experience in high-income neighborhoods, is indicated by the responses which fifth grade students in these two types of setting gave to a questionnaire on perspectives towards daily social living. To the question, "Do you often think that nobody likes you?," 62 per cent of the fifth-graders in low-income areas said "Yes," as compared with only 19 per cent of those in high-income locations. Only 4 per cent of the students in higher-income settings responded affirmatively to the question, "Do you have just a few friends?," as compared with 42 per cent of the lower-income students. To the question, "Are people often so unkind or unfair that it makes you feel bad?," 62 per cent of the lower-income fifth-graders said "Yes," as contrasted with only 15 per cent of those from families of higher income. The affirmative responses to the question, "Do people often act so badly that you have to be mean or nasty to them?," were 46 per cent in the poorer settings and only 8 per cent in the richer districts. And just one more of many additional examples that could be cited: 46 per cent of the low status background children, as compared to 15 per cent of those from high status, answered "Yes" to the question, "Is it hard to make people remember how well you can do things?"[7]

What we see is that students in the schools of poorer neighborhoods, who predominate in our correctional populations, tend to have a background from early childhood of feeling that others are hostile and unappreciative toward them, and that they have to be hostile in response. These characteristics tend to be most pronounced among our prisoners, since they so frequently were the most maladjusted even in schools which in entirety tended to be much less conducive to academic pursuits than were schools in average or higher-income areas. With increased public awareness of this cumulative problem in students from so-called "culturally deprived" settings, there has been widespread experimentation with special methods of instruction to give such students a sense of acceptance and success in their schooling. The problem is to make studying a more rewarding and exciting activity for them.

Perhaps the best-known approach to this problem is that of programmed learning. By breaking instruction into bits, in well-planned sequences, programmed texts or teaching machines start students with learning tasks that they can master with ease. The programs also permit students to advance to more difficult tasks only when they have mastered the prerequisite learning. Thus students from the backgrounds which distinguish the correctional population have much more experience with success when studying by programmed methods, than most of them encounter with conventional teaching and studying procedures. It is especially significant in prison to have each individual progress at his own rate, because prisoners come to the school at all times of the year, and with a great variety of prior curriculum exposure and mastery. If all are given the same lessons at the same time, even in classes that have been grouped as well as possible by prior school record or by test scores, parts of each lesson will be frustrating to some students and boring to others. The best students will learn well by any teaching method, but poor students, or students that are easily distraught with schooling, tend to do distinctly better with programmed instruction than with conventional pedagogy. That is why conventional aptitude tests are less accurate predictors of subsequent achievement with programmed instruction than with ordinary teaching.

While programmed instruction is a major resource for increasing the challenge in our prison schools, it will not solve all of our problems here. Some academic and vocational subjects are not so readily taught by programmed methods, or, at least, have not yet been subjected to good programming. More important, there is a second major need in school programs for correctional populations which programs alone do not solve. This is the need to alter the social experience which offenders have associated with schooling.

CHANGING THE SCHOOL'S SOCIAL RELATIONSHIPS

As we have seen, the typical prison school student needs distinctly individualized pedagogy if he is to experience a continuous challenge and reward in his studies, but he has a background of regimented mass education in crowded schools. His personal relationships to teachers have frequently been characterized by conflict. By contrast, his most rewarding social experience has often been among peers who share his problems, and who extol his hostility to school authorities. He has learned to expect to feel that he has failed, and to fear derision, if he copes with a school learning problem in a social setting. With this background, it often is difficult to get studying by a prisoner energetically initiated and maintained in a prison school, even with programmed devices or other optimum lesson material.

One of the needs of the student who has felt persistent failure in school is a need to feel that he is regarded as personally important, and to feel that he is well liked. Much has been written of the need to make reading matter for slum children have some relevance to their life experience, but this is more than a matter of the illustrations and of the plots of the stories. In special schools for youngsters for whom learning to read has been a painful experience, to be resisted, one successful technique is to have a teacher provide a period of individual instruction in which she sits at a typewriter and types out a story that the student tells her. The story may be about himself, about what he has done that day, or anything that he wishes to make up. The teacher types it in approximately the boy's own words, perhaps improving the grammar and sentence structure slightly, and possibly abbreviating it somewhat. This now is given to the student as his reading lesson; he is likely to be interested in it, since it deals with the most fascinating subject for most of us, ourselves. In this fashion not only does rapid progress in reading ability frequently occur, but it can change attitudes toward reading. This can spread to other reading and to writing by the student, on his own, when the teacher is not available. In addition, the story-typing exercises may provide a useful vehicle for a counseling relationship between the teacher and the student, for the teacher who is skillful with questions and other reactions to the stories may thereby influence the student's thinking about himself.

While staff time for one-to-one instruction of this sort is limited, a small amount sometimes goes a long way. Also, it frequently is possible to augment staff by having students help each other. I am not referring to inmate teachers in the usual sense of handling a class, but to mutual aid by fellow students in the same class. A pleasing game may be created where one student writes or types what another dictates, especially when priority in the writing role is a reward for those who are slightly superior in the learning. This obviously has limitations, but the general principle of having people learn by teaching others in the same class can be adapted to many situations where a more personal tutorial relationship is needed than staff alone can provide. In scattered after-school study centers established in the last few years to cope with the problems of slum schooling, students from the same neighborhood are hired as "homework helpers."

Being from the same background and close to the same age—preferably slightly older—may make an inmate distinctly acceptable as a tutor for those prison pupils who would be uneasy with a staff member as tutor. At Draper Prison, in Alabama, where impressive achievements with programmed learning are reported they have established an inmate Service Corps in the prison school consisting of the more advanced students, who spend part of their school time as tutors for the less advanced. College student interns also are reported to be a good teaching resource at Draper.[8]

KEEPING CORRECTIONAL EDUCATION HONEST

One unfortunate solution to problems of conflict and inadequacy in some slum schools has been to make the education fraudulent. Peace sometimes is achieved in such schools at the expense of education, for there often is consensus of pupils and teachers that both teaching and learning should be minimum effort activities. So-called "social promotion" from kindergarten to high school has allegedly been encouraged in slum schools by large city school administrators as a way of avoiding pressures for equal educational services in minority group ghettos.

Many prison school pupils come from this kind of school background. They are not retarded in grade completed, but are revealed by test to have an educational achievement grossly below that for the grade in which they were last registered. They are used to school being a place where one "gets by" without real effort, and regardless of whether or not learning occurs. They come from a background of boredom in school to a situation where schooling, if it were suddenly to be as demanding as their prior grade warrants, would be most frustrating. Realization of this deficiency can be most humiliating, and resistance to school will be evoked if they are placed in a grade well below that which they thought they had achieved. Yet studies which begin at the point where their knowledge stops may be essential. Resulting ego shock can be reduced by avoidance of grade designation; to falsify grade levels by exaggerating them is to assure future ego shock from failure.

Some prison schools play the social promotion game or, at least, maintain the atmosphere of social promotion slum schools. These are places where the teachers merely serve time, along with their students. By not caring whether or not the students learn, or even whether the classroom discussions are perpetually bull sessions irrelevant to the subject-matter of the course, some prison education directors make their lives extremely soft. The inmates who have found such a school an easy way to do time will see to it that the school looks like a constructive enterprise: they will keep it orderly, and will help the Supervisor of Education make impressive charts on inmate participation in school. He may get promoted for this, and become the type of warden who merely serves time, while the inmates do not achieve a significant rate of progress. It may be that prison schools of this sort accounted for our finding, in some federal prisons, that inmates not in school had better post-release records than those in school; inmates out of school and in prison industry may have worked at a pace that prepared them better for outside employment conditions than did such added abilities as they learned in the school.

Other kinds of corruption in prison schooling are stimulated by the fact that most correctional systems, appropriately, let their inmates know that participation in prison school will be rewarded. The main reward, an uncertain one, is that schooling may impress the parole board favorably. Although the validity of this belief varies, it usually is cultivated assiduously by prison staff. More dependable rewards may result from the fact that completion of a certain grade, or procurement of a diploma, is made prerequisite for admission to the most popular skilled trade courses or work assignments. The federal minimum security prison at Seagoville, Texas, requires involvement in self-improvement activities such as schooling in order for an inmate to be assigned to any paying job, such as one in prison industries, or to receive Industrial or Meritorious Service good time. All of these incentive systems motivate the prisoner to use his time constructively, but they also motivate many inmates to try to convey a fraudulent impression of school achievement.

On the whole, I suspect there is no more cheating in prison schooling than in many universities, where files of old examinations and term papers are the major character-building contribution of some fraternities. But one depravity does not justify another. In prison the cheating takes many forms. Copies are made of correspondence course lessons, and are sold for cigarettes or other commissary goods. Sometimes a bright inmate will complete a whole course for another inmate for a carton or two. Clerks in the prison school, and inmate teachers, can be pressured or bribed to falsify records of course completion or, minimally, to check examination papers before they are graded officially.

Wherever this sort of thing can occur, we are dealing with a lazy prison school administration. If staff will insist on supervising all final or other key examinations themselves, if they will base course credit primarily on such examinations, and if they will keep the records of major examinations and course completions entirely and continuously under their control, inaccessible to any inmate, a report on an inmate's educational achievement in prison will be dependable. Wherever inmates are involved in key examination supervision, or have access to key school records, corruption in prison education is not just an ever-present danger—it probably is a usually-present reality for some fraction of the inmates.

RESEARCH: THE KEY TO PROGRESS

Research is the bookkeeping of corrections. Unfortunately, many correctional enterprises operate without such bookkeeping. When this happens, like businesses without bookkeeping, they may soon be bankrupt. However, unlike business, corrections can provide a steady salary for its employees even when it is bankrupt.

While research is worthwhile in any school, it is not always as essential as it is in prison schools. Most schools can learn the answers to their questions by studying the published reports of research done elsewhere, in schools or with pupils comparable to theirs. In correctional education there is not enough research literature available to meet the needs of prison schools. In addition, each correctional system has unique features in sentencing and parole policies, and in the communities it serves, which make some of the knowledge it needs apply only to it. Procurement of this knowledge requires two kinds of research.

The first research need is follow-up data, on a routine basis, regarding the utilization of prison schooling in post-release life, and regarding its correlation with non-recidivism. Unfortunately, crime control in the United States is generally administered by completely autonomous agencies, each of which serves a successive stage of what should be a continuous process, but each of which is insufficiently concerned with agencies dealing with other stages. Parole supervision agents should routinely determine whether a parolee is working, and what kind of work he is doing. They could routinely record this on forms, on which they could also note the parolee's response to inquiry on what prison training he is using at his job. If these forms were sent back to prison, there would be a basis for evaluating the practical impact of much specific training, as well as correlating the relationships between prison education participation or progress and post-release self-sufficiency.

Where almost all correctional institution releasees serve an appreciable period of parole or conditional release supervision, the record of post-release criminality can be procured from parole supervision records, and can then be correlated with the prison education record. Where many releasees do not receive parole, or a follow-up is desired on criminality beyond the parole period, we still are faced with the claim of the Justice Department that they cannot procure clerical help to provide post-release fingerprint report data for correctional evaluation research. However, a partially satisfactory substitute is the record on releasees returned to prison within the same state during a particular post-release period, supplemented by the record on inquiries from those states which routinely request information on prior prison record when they incarcerate someone who previously served time elsewhere.

The second type of research need was hinted at earlier. This is experimental research. It is invaluable both for measuring the effectiveness of a new correctional education enterprise, and to procure financial support for new enterprises.

If we secure for an educational program twice as many applicants or nominees as the program can handle, then select people for the program and for a control group by a purely random method, we can have much confidence that the difference between the subsequent record of any appreciable number in the program and those in the control group is a consequence of the program. There is no other procedure nearly as dependable, but it requires that separation of the treatment from the control group involves a purely random process, such as tossing a coin, using a table of random numbers, or separating by odd and even prison registry number. When this is done for an appreciable number of cases, we can be confident that any personality factors or other attributes apart from the educational program which affect subsequent records, are as frequent in the experimental group as in the control group. When officials interfere with the purely random assignment of inmates to experimental and control groups, we have reason to suspect the validity of the research findings.

Of course, if a controlled experiment shows a program to be beneficial, or if it shows it to be ineffective or even harmful, it is still appropriate that research probe further. Experimental research is more conclusive than other research, but its findings still are not absolute and final. Sometimes the impact of a program comes from some unintended feature of it, rather than from the apparent features; it may be due only to the unusual personalities of the officials which the program employs, or to the unusual enthusiasm or caution distinguishing the administration of a new program. Only as we repeat experiments, in different settings and circumstances, and the results are consistent, can we gain extreme certainty about the validity of its findings. Of course, this is also true of experimental research in medicine and other fields; it is especially relevant in corrections, however, because of the many complexities which can confound the impact of correctional programs.

A final note on experimental research is that it provides an outstanding sales argument. Where support for a new program is not readily forth-coming, because of doubts as to whether it is worthwhile, this resistance will generally be reduced markedly should one propose that the program be introduced only on a controlled experimental basis. If favorable results then are yielded by the experiment, the administrator has a much stronger sales argument than he previously had. If the experimental findings do not confirm expectations regarding the program, it will be just as well that the program was introduced on a limited scale at first. The administrator can then cite this valuable knowledge in proposing that the experiment now be conducted with a different program, either completely different or a modification of the program that failed. Legislators usually are sufficiently familiar with science to realize that this is the only way in which knowledge in corrections can be made more precise and cumulative. Are correctional administrators this well informed?

CONCLUSION

Four needs of correctional education have been indicated: (1) to broaden its challenge for those who have been frustrated or bored in previous schooling; (2) to change the social relationships which its students associate with schooling; (3) to become honest or to remain honest; and (4) to conduct research. Some ways of meeting these needs were suggested. As these needs are met, all four of them, effectiveness in correctional education should become more clearly evident.

22   *Disciplinary Action and Counseling*

DANIEL GLASER*

PROCEDURES IN DISCIPLINE

The prison staff's policies regarding discipline may have far-reaching effects on staff members' relationships to inmates and, hence, on other prison programs. Discipline involves issues on which there is much staff disagreement and uncertainty. The immediate concern in discipline is with procuring conformity of inmates to the behavior patterns required of them for smooth functioning of the institution, but the *Manual of Correctional Standards* of the American Correctional Association asserts further:

> Discipline . . . looks beyond the limits of the inmate's term of confinement. It must seek to insure carry-over value by inculcating standards which the inmate will maintain after release. It is not merely the person's ability to conform to institutional rules and regulations, but his ability and desire to conform to accepted standards for individual and community life in free society. Discipline must . . . develop in the inmate personal responsibility to that social community to which he will return.[9]

One of the first issues that arises in connection with disciplinary policy is whether or not penalties should be determined by the type of infraction or by the behavioral patterns and circumstances peculiar to the inmate who commits the infraction. Modern criminal and correctional law holds that confinement should vary according to the characteristics of the

* From *The Effectiveness of a Prison and Parole System* by Daniel Glaser, copyright © 1964, by The Bobbs-Merrill Company, Inc., pp. 116–129. Reprinted by permission of the publisher.

329

offender; probation, the indeterminate sentence, judicial discretion in sentencing, and parole serve as alternative, complementary, or supplementary devices for achieving such variation. In applying these devices in the spirit of the so-called "new penology," the nature of a man's offense is only one of many pieces of information considered in attempting to achieve an understanding of the offender as a person.

Despite this trend, it is still widely contended that within the social world of the prison, the effective motivating of all inmates in order to achieve conformity to institution rules requires that similar penalties be imposed on all who commit similar rule infractions. Nevertheless, in spite of this principle, federal prisons hold with the modern trend, and penalties are not closely dependent upon the infraction. They are initially uncertain, and are determined largely by the offender's total record and by his attitude while in disciplinary status.

The disciplinary agency in a federal prison is called the "adjustment committee." It was formerly called the "disciplinary court," and though this designation sometimes recurs in prison parlance, it is frowned upon by senior staff members. The committee is usually presided over by the associate warden for custody and has two additional members: one is either the associate warden for treatment or the chief of classification and parole, and the other, the senior custodial captain or lieutenant. A prison psychiatrist or other medical officer may be asked to participate as an adviser in some cases. When the committee believes that an inmate's conduct warrants his removal to a segregation cell, he is sent there not for a given number of days but for an indeterminate period of time during which officers representing the committee are able to talk to him several times each day, a physician may check him, and the chaplain usually visits him. These visitors are consulted by the members of the adjustment committee, and the man will be released from segregation when it is believed that his "attitude" warrants this action.

The duration of disciplinary segregation is much briefer in federal prisons than in most state prisons; the median period in federal prisons seems to be two or three days. Also, although many state prisons serve a restricted diet to men in disciplinary confinement and deny them reading and writing matter, men in segregation in federal prisons now receive the regular inmate food (but without seconds); they may have a Bible, and they may write and send letters, but not receive them. Like other prisons, the federal prisons also have a few completely stripped and closed "isolation" cells to be used for inmates extremely noisy, abusive, or suicidal. These are located among the regular open cells which are normally used for disciplinary segregation. Such isolation cells are usually empty.

If an inmate, when not being dealt with for a specific rule infraction, is considered seriously disturbed, assaultive, homicidal, or suicidal, or seems to be in extreme fear of attack from other inmates, he may be placed in a nondisciplinary maximum-custody unit. This is often called "administrative segregation." It exists in almost all prisons. Such units resemble the regular disciplinary section of a prison in that the men are kept almost continuously confined in cells and have their meals brought to them. Unlike the men in disciplinary segregation, men in these units may have personal possessions in the cells and may obtain study material and some types of art and game material. There may be variations in the extent to which the inmates are restricted to their cells, but usually they are taken from the cells individually and are always accompanied by a custodial officer. In large prison systems inmates believed to require a long term of such surveillance are transferred to the institution designed primarily for maximum custody (in the federal prison this was formerly Alcatraz, but it is now the federal prison at Marion, Illinois), where they can eat, work, and play in small groups within closed sections of the prison.

A number of lesser penalties are used more frequently than segregation in most federal disciplinary practice. The inmate may be temporarily restricted to quarters without being transferred to the segregation unit, he may be barred from a particular activity temporarily, he may be warned, or he may be asked to apologize to an injured party. In addition, the "good time" deducted from a sentence for conforming behavior during confinement and other rewards he may have earned are withheld if the prisoner misbehaves. Very serious misconduct may even result in revocation of previously granted good time. In general, time off for good behavior is much less automatic and secure in federal prisons than in many state prisons (indeed, no inmate receives more than 180 days of good time unconditionally; and all good time may be canceled for postrelease misbehavior and have to be served again). Finally, where an infraction in prison constitutes a clear felony, especially an assault to kill or to do bodily harm, the prisoner is taken into the court in whose district the prison lies where he may receive a new sentence.

HYPOTHESES UNDERLYING DISCIPLINARY POLICY

The relationship of disciplinary policies to inmate-staff relationships is an area in which conflicting hypotheses may reasonably be formulated. For example, one point of view can be summarized by the hypothesis: Disciplinary penalties which are determined by the offense rather than the offender, and interpreted "by the book" rather than with flexibility, create shared expectations in staff and inmates as to what penalty is mandatory; the person guilty of the offense, therefore, knows the penalty is prescribed by agencies beyond the control of the officers confronted with his offense, so he does not become hostile toward the staff because of it. This implies that when the offender commits an infraction he knows what penalty to expect if he is caught, and he feels that the staff is obliged to impose this penalty on him should they catch him, regardless of how friendly they may feel toward him.

Some years ago I presented what I thought was a fairly strong argument for the foregoing definite penalty hypothesis.[10] Examples of its success in reducing specific types of infraction have been cited. At one state institution for "young and improvable" offenders, a penalty of seven days of isolation always was imposed on every inmate involved in a fight, unless he not only did not start it, but made every possible effort to retreat from it and not fight back, or unless other clearly extenuating factors were present. More severe penalties were imposed for anyone clearly established as the initiator of the fight and for anyone using any kind of weapons. It was evident that most new inmates with a history of ready fighting got into fights only once or twice, then learned to avoid them. Inmates remarked that they learned to walk away from provocations in prison which they previously would have reacted to by immediate fighting. In terms of psychological learning theory, old habits seemed to be extinguished and new conforming behavior reinforced by this punishment and by the rewards of "extra privileges" and favorable assignments.

Despite this kind of support for the definite penalty hypothesis, the arguments of federal officials and readily available observations in federal prisons provide a strong case for two quite opposite hypotheses. One hypothesis stresses flexibility of rules. It asserts that objectionable behavior by men in prison is so diverse that no set of rules could encompass it without being long, complex, and difficult to apply, or so arbitrary that it would arouse resentment by dealing similarly with highly diverse acts. It follows that strain in inmate-staff relationships is minimized by a policy of flexible rules interpreted to fit each case which takes into account primarily the effect of each penalty on the future behavior of the offender. The other hypothesis asserts that the administration of disciplinary penalties is most effective if it: minimizes alienation of the rule-violating inmate from staff and maximizes his alienation from inmate supporters of his infraction; promotes in him a clear regret over having committed the infraction; but provides him with a perception of clearly available opportunities to pursue a course of behavior which will restore him to good standing in the prison and give him a more favorable self-conception than he had as a rule violator.

It has become particularly evident in federal experience that an incapacitating penalty such as solitary confinement in idleness rapidly loses effectiveness as it is prolonged. The first one to three days of such an experience seems to have a greater impact than any subsequent day. Even the first day or so seems useful only in influencing the inmate's communication to the staff. For most infractions serious enough to warrant segregation, a few hours of segregation, or an overnight stay in the case of infractions occurring in the evening, is sufficient to permit the staff to complete its investigation of the infraction and of the offender's attitude. By talking with the inmate during this period staff members are usually able to evoke in him a willingness to cooperate in a somewhat restricted program, but one which will enable him to earn back at least as satisfactory a prison status as he had previously. If this type of response is not awakened, the inmate is likely to be transferred to a close-custody institution or to be held for some time in a maximum-custody unit.

When prison staff personnel perform both counseling and disciplinary functions, it is impossible for the latter not to affect the former function. An impersonal view of punishment by those punished seems to exist, if at all, only when a person is punished by nature rather than by another human being. For this reason, a deliberate effort to integrate discipline with counseling is appropriate. It follows, therefore, from the concept of rehabilitation as a change which occurs in a man's inner values, that discipline rehabilitates inmates providing that the rules become internalized as their personal opinions. Also, habits are best extinguished if they are not merely punished, but if alternative behavior is reinforced by reward.

Clearly the two hypotheses, on flexible-rules and on constructive-penalty, depend upon the existence of a prison staff of high calibre. Flexible handling of disciplinary infractions requires keen judgment and an ability to suppress hostile impulses and prejudices. An impressive feature of the best federal prison discipline (not found at all federal prisons) is the imperturbability of the staff after a major individual infraction such as an escape has occurred. Instead of an hysterical tightening of the whole institution for some days taking place, and the establishment of new restrictions on everyone, a reaction which would occur in most prisons, the best federal prison officers quietly and efficiently execute an appropriate "escape plan." The plan varies with the place of the escape and the time it is discovered, but usually one officer notifies police officials and the FBI, another prepares extra photographs and fingerprints for these agencies, a third calls aside likely informants for interrogation as to the course and probably destination of the escapee, and others make appropriate patrols of the institution grounds and surroundings. There are few escapes per year, almost all are "walkaways" from outside jobs, and the escapees generally are caught in a day or two. Often most of the prison is unaware of the escape until they learn of it through news media, usually after the escapee is captured. Escapes are reviewed locally and in Washington, and sometimes at the national meetings of federal wardens that are held every few years. However, remedies which would have prevented a particular escape but would grossly limit prison programs and impair inmate-staff relationships are invariably rejected.

Essentially, one might say that the flexible-rules and constructive-penalty hypotheses call for a government of men, not laws, in the prison, which might seem against the American governmental tradition. However, it is appropriate to deviate partially from this tradition in a prison which achieves its primary goal, that of rehabilitating offenders, through relationships between staff and inmates. With a good staff it is possible to achieve a consensus among most staff members and inmates as to what handling of infractions is fair and constructive, even when the handling is flexible. Of course, any American prison staff still has some limits to its behavior set by both statutory law and administrative regulation. The issue is how much latitude these laws and regulations should allow.

The ideal of a "government by laws, not men" developed in a period of rebellion against the abuses of tyranny. Prison staffs have the power to be tyrannical, and where they lack the qualification and training to use this power wisely, a government by rigid laws may be most appropriate. In other words, the very specific regulation of discipline by rules suggested in the definite-penalty hypothesis might be preferable in a prison with a staff incapable of handling its authority with the wisdom which is demanded by the flexible-rules and constructive-penalty hypotheses. Indeed, in a prison operating under a punitive tradition with poorly selected, sadistic, or relatively untrained or improperly trained personnel, introduction of the flexible disciplinary policy suggested by the flexible-rules hypothesis could be disastrous. However, when staffs exist such as those in federal prisons and in some of the best state prisons, flexible disciplinary policy will enhance prison order and augment the rehabilitative influence of inmate-staff relationships.

It is probable that the flexible approach is more advantageous than a rigid-rule policy in dealing with major infractions which traditionally receive automatic and severe penalties. Nuisance infractions involving little serious threat to prison order, such as those from careless habits in putting away equipment or clothing or doing work incorrectly, might be administered under the fixed rules of the definite-penalty hypothesis without seriously violating constructive-penalty objectives. This assumes that the penalties imposed would not be such as to alienate the offender from the staff if imposed uniformly, and that the infractions are not likely to receive appreciable inmate support.

It should be stressed that order in a prison is a collective event reflecting the overall patterns of relationship between staff and inmates as well as intra-staff and intra-inmate relationships.

SPECIAL COUNSELING PROGRAMS IN PRISON

The Manual of Correctional Standards of the American Correctional Association asserts:

> . . . Counseling, as the term is coming to be used in working with offenders, encompasses the personal and group relationships undertaken by staff with voluntary participation by inmates or parolees. It has as its goals either the immediate solution to a specific personal problem, or a long-range effort to develop increased self-understanding and maturity within the offender. . . .
>
> Counseling, casework and clinical services are to be seen as a continuous part of the total correctional program . . . in the institutional system, from reception through parole and discharge.[11]

In federal prisons counseling is considered one of the caseworker's major responsibilities. In practice, time pressures for preparation of his reports and correspondence on which other officials rely often cause report-writing to take precedence over counseling. Teachers, work supervisors, custodial staff, and all others dealing with inmates are also expected to do a certain amount of counseling whenever the need and opportunity arise. In federal prisons, as in most other prisons, inmates may send a note to any staff member requesting an interview, but many are reluctant to undertake this deliberate message writing. Indeed, in prison argot, such a request is called a "cop out," the same label used for the admission of an offense to police or to the court, which suggests that prisoners seeking interviews may be suspected of being informers. Nevertheless, interview requests are often numerous, and frequently inmates must wait a long time before an interview can be scheduled by the staff member they wish to see. An interesting development in several federal prisons is an "open door" period, generally during the noon hour, when caseworkers and some staff members remain available in their offices for a visit without appointment or formal request by any inmate not in maximum custody.

Three large research projects, concentrated in California, have been exclusively concerned with counseling in which extra personnel or new tasks for old personnel have been introduced. These projects are: the PICO (Pilot Intensive Counseling) project of the California Youth Authority; the California Study of Correctional Effectiveness at the University of California at Los Angeles; the IT (Intensive Treatment) project of the California Department of Corrections. In addition, several smaller counseling research programs are being conducted by these California agencies and by others.

The Pilot Intensive Counseling Organization, or "PICO," started in 1955 with inmates committed as Youth Authority wards to the Deuel Vocational Institution, an adult prison operated by the Department of Corrections. About 1,600 youth had been involved in this experiment by 1961. At admission the youths were classified by clinical judgment as either amenable or nonamenable to treatment by individual counseling. Then, independently of this classification, half of all of the cases were randomly selected as control groups and placed in units with no special counseling staff, while half entered treatment units for which individual psycho-therapy was provided by social caseworkers with a caseload of approximately 25 per therapist.

Postrelease results of the experiment show dramatically less return to prison for the individually counseled amenable cases than for the amenable cases in the control group. However, those persons classified as nonamenable reacted quite differently; there was a somewhat higher failure rate for those in the intensive counseling program than for those placed in the control units.

The public saves police, court, and jail costs when a man is not returned to prison; it also enjoys the more important saving to society of fewer crimes committed by those treated; and for the offenders and those who love them there is the benefit of less subsequent anguish. It should be recalled that the savings were demonstrated for only half of the cases studied—those classified initially as amenable to treatment; a slight loss, rather than a savings, resulted from counseling with the cases classified as nonamenable. The experiment was confined to older youth offenders, with a median age of about twenty, so it is conceivable that findings might be quite different with other age groups. Subsequent phases of the research involve specifying the differences between those who are amenable to individual counseling treatment and those who are not, so that even greater profit from counseling may be discernible in the future by sharper definition of those most likely to benefit from it.[12]

The California Department of Corrections has invested a tremendous amount of time and effort in promoting improved inmate-staff communication within its institutions. Long before it had much research, "group counseling" was introduced in the adult institutions. Line custodial staff and work supervisors, as well as teachers and other specialists, were involved in regular meetings with small groups of inmates to guide them in discussions of inmate problems.[13] In the major prisons and in Sacramento, full-time nonresearch staff are now employed solely in coordinating these efforts.

There seems to be no doubt that the opportunity to "ventilate" feelings in these programs has, on the whole, improved relationships between staff and inmates as well as helped inmates to get along with each other in the institution. Doubtless this has been a major factor in the virtual absence of riots in this large correctional system, a calm which is especially striking because overcrowding and inmate idleness is more prevalent in California prisons than in prisons of some other states or in federal prisons. Whether improved communication in the institutions also reduces the extent to which inmates return to crime upon release is another matter.

In 1958 the California Study of Correctional Effectiveness was established in the School of Social Welfare of the University of California at Los Angeles financed by grants from the National Institutes of Health. During the 1958-60 period this project's staff made an extensive study of the history of correctional reform in California, observed group counseling practice, interviewed correctional staff members at many levels of authority, and prepared a long questionnaire on staff perception and evaluation of group counseling and other correctional issues.

The questionnaire responses showed that 35 per cent of California's Department of Corrections employees in 1959 were then leading an inmate counseling group or had previously done so. This 35 per cent consisted of 27 per cent of the line correctional officers, 55 per cent of the custody administrators, 57 per cent of the educators and researchers, 74 per cent of the chaplains, and 86 per cent of the mental health personnel. About half of the employees endorsed the opinion that group counseling brings about personality changes in offenders and reduces prison-rule infractions; only about a quarter thought it reduced recidivism; and nine per cent thought it had no proven effects. Indeed, when asked to pick one of four specified correctional activities which makes the greatest impact on an offender's reformation, 51 per cent of the employees picked "advice and help from the parole officer," 27 per cent picked "punishment and surveillance aspects of parole," 9 per cent picked group counseling, and 6 per cent picked psychotherapy.

Partial explanation for the extent of California staff participation in group counseling may be provided by the finding that about a third of them believe this participation helps an employee's chances of promotion. The participation of about half the California prisoners in these groups may also be explained, in part, by its contributing to their chances for an earlier parole; at any rate, 48 per cent of the staff thought that this participation helped inmates obtain an early parole. These factors, of course, need not prevent the program's promoting inmate tractability and even reformation; promotion and parole certainly were not the only motives in staff and inmate participation in group counseling.

The California Department of Corrections "therapeutic communities" consist of dormitories of about 80 inmates who work and live apart from the rest of the prisoners. Each inmate is in one large and one small group counseling meeting per day. Parole officers visit these sessions on a regular schedule to initiate some of the contacts which are planned to be continued after the inmate's release. Psychotherapists lead the groups, and special research operations are under way to follow up these cases in order to determine the effectiveness of this treatment for various types of offenders.

In the California institutions there is great variation in staff leadership activity in these discussions. Conversations with staff members reveal a large diversity of opinion as to their most appropriate role. Some hold that the leader should discourage inmates from talking about anything but their immediate problems of living together in the prison; at a unit under a psychologist with this view, the inmates were concerned that those in one end of a dormitory tended not to talk much to the newly received inmates at the other end. Other psychologists, by questions, lead the inmates to analyze their own and each other's personality and to discuss their relationships to parents and siblings. Still other leaders give hardly any direction, and the discussion will often sound like ordinary conversations of inmates in other prisons—the most delinquent seem to be the most articulate; the youths extolling past "kicks" from drugs, drinking, and girls, and penitentiary inmates bemoaning persecution of ex-cons by the police. The least staff-directed groups seem to focus most on the future, and the less conventional inmates in these groups rationalize reversion to a criminal or disorderly way of life. The meetings formalize in this situation and cause the staff to become the audience to conversations that otherwise would occur only among inmates.

There seems to be, therefore, a great need for experimentation with group-treatment programs in prison to evaluate these variations in the direction given these groups. This variation may be much more important than the factors thus far studied, such as size, frequency, and staffing of group meetings. The research in California concluded that the only inmates in group counselling who had somewhat lower parole violation rates were those inmates who had remained in the same counselling group for a long time and had had no change in the staff member leading the group. This conclusion suggests that the relationship that develops between the inmate and the staff member, rather than just the relationship of the inmate to other inmates in the group, may be that factor which changes his postrelease perspectives.[14]

23   Inmate Self-Government

J. E. BAKER*

In penology there yet persists the dream of finding a specific for the treatment of the myriad ills consigned to prisons by society. Historically the most intriguing attempts to create such a specific are those concerned with inmate self-government.

Of all concepts in corrections, inmate self-government is most likely to arouse partisan feelings. Other issues arising from time to time have been debated and resolved in orderly fashion by an incorporation in practice or at least an acceptance in principle. This has not been the case for self-government plans. The pros and cons of the matter as expressed today are essentially the same as those several decades ago. The static quality of the debate is interesting and significant for several reasons. First, it indicates little thoughtful examination of the inmate self-government concept and a paucity of fresh thinking. Reasons for or against self-government apparently stem from the psychological truism that [we observe and remember selectively in accordance with our developed expectancies] Such selectivity tends to affirm the correctness of the expectancy.

Second, it appears that attitudes toward self-government are based primarily on accounts of such arrangements as advocated or practiced many years ago. Apparently, there has been no organized attempt to apply recent theoretical studies of institutional social processes or the results of experimentation in inmate social organization to the concept of self-government.

* From *Journal of Criminal Law, Criminology and Police Science*, 55, 1 (1964): 39–47. Reprinted by permission of the author and publisher.

Third, advocates of self-government tend to regard it as a method or model of treatment which can be applied across the board to all inmates in all institutions.

Fourth, in contrast to other concepts which have intermittently appeared on the correctional scene, there apparently has been no real application of scientific principles in determining the efficacy and efficiency of self-government.

There appear to be very few neutral or uncommitted persons on this subject. Opinions are quite definite and can be summarized as follows:

Positive: Inmate self-government or inmate council systems are a part of the "new penology," hence are therapeutic in nature. Since we are nothing if we are not therapeutic, then we are "for" self-government. We know self-government will work if insidious forces do not undermine it.

Negative: The entire history of self-government proves how unsound it is. It never lasted anywhere. That is proof enough of its unworthiness. If inmates were smart enough to govern themselves they would not be in prison in the first place.

As can be readily seen, nothing in the position of either camp is in the nature of a reason. In either point of view we recognize familiar stereotypes not defensible on an intellectual basis.

In an attempt to provide a better perspective on inmate self-government, we have examined past experiments and experiences and have solicited the views of present correctional institution administrators. Our summaries and discussions are concerned with suggestions as to the reasons for the rigidity of opinions about the concept of self-government through inmate councils. In addition, we offer some views on the prospects for these groups in correctional institution practice.

No claim of completeness is made for the historical review of self-government experiences. Undoubtedly there have been other experiences about which no accounts have been published or which have not come to our attention. However, the review is a representative sampling of self-government experiments in correctional institution history.

In addition we sent a questionnaire to 52 penitentiary and penitentiary-type institutions in all regions of the United States. Recipients were asked to give certain information as to the administration of their advisory councils if they "have or have had" such a group.

PAST EXPERIMENTS AND EXPERIENCES

The earliest reference we found to an inmate self-government system in American penal institutions is that of the *Walnut Street Jail,* Philadelphia, in 1793. Our information is meager, mentioning only that the prisoners established rules to provide harmonious living with each other. As an example, a regulation pertaining to cleanliness was cited. It provided that no man should spit elsewhere than in the chimney. Punishment for violations was exclusion from the society of fellow prisoners. It is stated this was found to be sufficient.[15]

At the *New York House of Refuge* in 1824, a reformatory for delinquent children, the first Superintendent, Joseph Curtis, introduced a modified form of self-government. Rule violators or those charged by others with committing an offense were tried by a jury of boys. The Superintendent was the Judge. If the accused was found guilty the number of lashes to be given was announced by the foreman of the jury and administered by the Superintendent.[16] The system had no other features of consequence. Curtis was Superintendent for approximately one year. The system terminated at his departure.

Another reformatory for delinquent children, the *Boston House of Reformation,* established in 1826, was the setting for an early experiment which was broader in scope and lasted throughout the several years tenure of its originator. A young Episcopal minister, the Reverend E. M. P. Wells, became Superintendent of the institution in 1828 and promptly attracted considerable attention by his rather intensive education programming. Inmates were given a voting participation in the administration of the school. Corporal punishments were entirely excluded. Monitors were appointed from among the youngsters at the beginning of each month, and the head monitor presided over the institution in the absence of the officers.[17]

While his contemporaries had some reservations about his program, there was a consensus as to the outstanding nature and ability of Wells himself. Disagreement with the Boston Common Council after an official inspection visit in 1832 led to his resignation soon thereafter.

In his autobiography published in 1912, Zebulon R. Brockway reports that while he was Superintendent of the *Detroit House of Corrections* during the 1860's, he experimented with engaging prisoners in monitorial and mechanical supervision and in educating their fellow prisoners.[18] He claims this was ennobling to the prisoners so assigned. While we would not seriously doubt Mr. Brockway's claim of a self-government group during the 1860's, it does seem rather odd that he had never previously mentioned it.

The Mutual Aid League organized at the *Michigan Penitentiary* in 1888, under Warden Hiram F. Hatch, is the earliest contemporarily reported record of any inmate self-government system among adult prisoners.[19] The set of principles involved in this arrangement anticipated by many years those widely publicized three decades later in Osborne's Mutual Welfare League. In an unsupervised meeting an inmate committee drew up a constitution, naming the organization *The Mutual Aid League of the M.S.P.* This constitution set forth the usual ideals of self-government and group advancement. Meetings were held monthly with the Warden as presiding officer. Reports indicate he attended meetings "without guards." Warden Hatch received considerable criticism from contemporaries, which he answered by referring to a favorable record in the maintenance of prison discipline.[20]

The story of *The George Junior Republic* founded in 1896 by William Reuben George (1866-1936) is a familiar one and needs no recounting here except its mention as a rather early experience in institutional self-government. In 1908 the National Association of Junior Republics was organized and continues to the present. For this study, the George Junior Republic has special importance, since two of the later strong advocates for inmate self-government in penal institutions were associates of the founder. They were Thomas Mott Osborne, Member, Board of Directors, and Calvin Derick, General Superintendent.

Calvin Derick utilized the pioneering work of George when appointed Superintendent of the *Ione Reformatory in California* in 1912. He outlined and formulated a program using inmate self-government as the keystone of its arch. It is significant to note that the Ione experiment represents the first acknowledgement and endorsement of inmate self-government by any state. At the inauguration of the second president of the self-government group, Governor Hiram Johnson of California went to the school and placed the stamp of his official approval upon the experiment.[21]

The purported sole purpose of this system of self-government was to furnish a medium in which the boys might develop a civilization of their own with as many degrees and gradations as necessary to meet their needs and interests, the ideal being to come as close as possible to standards of civilization.

In his annual report for 1915, Frank Moore, Superintendent of the *State Reformatory, Rahway, New Jersey,* explains the failure of a self-government plan begun in 1914 and abandoned at the end of the year: "[A]fter giving the question sober consideration the inmates of the Reformatory felt that it was better for them that the institution should return to the original plan of being governed by the appointed authority of the institution and hence the council disbanded."[22]

In December, 1913, *The Mutual Welfare League* was founded at New

York State's Auburn Prison by Thomas Mott Osborne. The stated purpose and objective of this inmate self-government group was to alter concepts of confinement then practiced routinely in the majority of penal institutions.

It was Osborne's contention, based on his experience with the George Junior Republic, that self-government was the practical remedy for the evils of the prison system. After a voluntary one week term of confinement at Auburn Prison he developed, with inmate assistance, the methods of implementing a self-government plan in an institution for adult offenders. A cardinal principle was that prisoners must work out their own plan, rather than have an outside plan presented to them. Osborne noted: "This was real, vital democracy; this was solving the problem in the genuine American spirit."[23]

It is significant to note that Warden Rattigan, of Auburn, with the approval of the New York State Superintendent of Prisons, proposed to hand over all infractions of discipline to the League except in five instances: assault on an officer, deadly assault upon another inmate, refusal to work, strike, and attempt to escape.

Prisoner cooperation was the foundation of the League. Its operations were based on the premise that the prison could be treated as a community. Tannenbaum espouses this by his comment: "Prisoners possessed among themselves a public opinion that if properly harnessed could be made effective in the enforcement of public policy and the development of public morale, which would make discipline both easier upon the warden and more effective with the men."[24]

Osborne became Warden of *Sing Sing Prison* on December 1, 1914. He immediately organized a Mutual Welfare League which has been described by Wines as follows:

> The real instruments of self-government at Sing Sing were the committees. It was these that effectively expressed the wishes of the prisoners and took the initiative in getting things done. The Warden's day was filled with appointments with committee chairmen who wanted assistance or advice. The chairmen quickly came to realize that a great deal of power lay in their hands if they knew how to wield it. Not only were they trustees of the wishes of their fellow-inmates, but the prison officials came to regard them as responsible makers of institution policy. Some of them became adept in the art of getting what they wanted without appearing to ask for much. Aside from the specific things they accomplished, their activity was beneficial in two ways: (1) It taught them some of the difficulties of administration, thus enabling them to pass that knowledge back to their constituents; and (2) It enabled the prison authorities, by means of

the understanding thus promoted, to rely upon cooperation where before they would have received only suspicion and distrust.[25]

Later, Osborne organized a League while serving as Commandant of the Naval Prison, Portsmouth, New Hampshire.

At the *State Reformatory, Cheshire, Connecticut,* a self-government experiment was begun in 1915 and abandoned in the following spring. While we have no adequate description of its operation, Mr. Charles H. Johnson, Superintendent during the last eight months of the self-government regime, made the following report:

> The reason for the dissatisfaction in the organization was that it lent itself readily to so much misrule and dishonesty that the inmates were tired of it. . . . It was finally decided at a gathering of the inmates that the management of the institution should be placed with the Superintendent and the officers appointed by law.[26]

In 1927 Howard B. Gill, Superintendent, *State Prison Colony, Norfolk, Massachusetts,* inaugurated a program of individual directional inmate treatment called the Norfolk Plan. This approach utilized balanced programs in the following broad areas: (1) inmate classification, (2) group system of housing and supervision, (3) community organization on a basis of joint-responsibility, and (4) individual programs for treatment.[27]

Based upon a classification of prisoners into groups of fewer than 50 men the development of a complete program for the period of confinement was directed by a House-Officer acting as a resident caseworker. Such an officer lived with the inmates for 24 hour periods on an alternate schedule.

The third phase of the Plan, an inmate organization known as the Council, occurred as a direct outgrowth of the group system of housing and supervision. Together with the staff, the Council constituted the community government of the institution.

In an address before the Conference on the Treatment of Criminal Delinquency at Cambridge, Massachusetts, December 4, 1930, Gill reported as follows:

> . . . This is not to be confused with the strictly penal administration of the Colony which is in the hands of the Superintendent and his assistants. Also in contrast to inmate organizations in some institutions which are founded on the principle of self-government in the hands of inmates only, this community organization operates on the principle of joint responsibility in which *both* officers and inmates take part.

. . . In general the plan has worked, although it is neither an 'honor system' nor 'self-government,' because it is founded frankly on a basis of results for both Staff and men. . . . Neither officers nor men give up their independence or their responsibilities, and each continually checks the other to insure square dealing; but both agree that cooperation works better than opposition where men must work and eat and live together, whatever the circumstances.[28]

Summary

Two features of these past experiments stand out, both containing the seeds of self-destruction—inmates functioning as disciplinarians, and the dependence of the systems on a lone individual for sponsorship.

Discipline is a part of the treatment process which must be retained in toto by prison personnel. Its proper administration requires a degree of objectivity which is not to be found in the object itself. This feature of the past experiments calls for an altruism psychologically not possible in the faulty ego structure of the socially disadvantaged and damaged person.

Involvement in the disciplinary process appears to have been a point of departure for these systems. One need not ponder long the question as to why. Examine only briefly the accounts of the early prisons, and the stark naked brutality of disciplinary practices assaults your senses. Revolting as they are to us today, these were the accepted methods of dealing with deviancy. The untrained personnel of the old prisons were ill equipped to handle discipline problems. To the originators of the early experiments apparently this was the area in most urgent need of change. Also, this was an area offering the best prospects for effecting a positive change. All the administrator need do was to reassign the responsibility for discipline from staff to inmates. This he could not do in other functional areas without a complete breakdown of operation. For this reason, it is believed, the self-government idea became equated with the handling of disciplinary matters.

Only at Gill's Norfolk State Prison Colony was staff support enlisted. It is apparent that it was not wanted by the other experimenters. Those employees affected by self-government were often placed in situations subordinating them to inmates. Little comment is necessary regarding the administrative crassness of this arrangement. Modern management recognizes the need for interpretive communication in advance of the implementation of an innovation. The presence of untrained and incompetent personnel intensifies that need. We can speculate as to the many positive changes which might have resulted had administrators of yesteryear focused their efforts on staff development.

SELF-GOVERNMENT SURVEY

Forty-four responses were received to a questionnaire sent to 52 penitentiaries to gather information about self-government or inmate council groups and asking the opinion of recipients as to the value of such groups. The replies are rather illuminating, particularly those of a negative nature.

The responses to questions regarding the operation of existing councils, of which seven were reported, are as follows:

Formal Administration of Councils: Of the seven reported existing Advisory Councils, five operate under a Constitution and By-Laws.

Staff Sponsors: Three councils are under the sponsorship of the Warden or Superintendent, and two have the Associate Warden for Treatment as sponsor. There is no designated staff sponsor for the remaining two groups.

Membership Qualification: Conduct record and length of time served or remaining to be served are mentioned by five respondents. One reports the exclusion of maximum and close custody men. Another indicates the only qualification is assignment to a job in the area represented.

Method of Selection: All are elected by ballot vote, subject to approval of the administration, except one group.

Preparation of Agenda for Meetings: In five instances the Council prepares its own agenda, in two of which the further approval of the Warden is required. Agenda for the two remaining groups is made by the Council Chairman. One of these is assisted by the Council Secretary.

Council Meetings: Four councils meet monthly, one semi-monthly, one weekly, and one meets as the need arises.

Participation in Activities: The question asked was: *Does the group have any voice or function in planning and/or carrying out institutional activities or activities involving outside persons,* with a subsequent listing of the activities mentioned in Table I. This table also gives the number of institutions replying affirmatively with reference to the various activities.

In addition, one institution reports a recreation committee separate from the council; one has a sub-committee on developing plans for a general recreation program, and another has a sub-committee taking an active interest in general rules development and other specific prison activities. Still another report states that the council may submit to the Superintendent some change or addition to any inmate program not purely administrative or disciplinary in nature.

Advantages of Council Membership: To the question: *Are there any material advantages to an inmate as a member of the group,* only two

TABLE 1
Activities in Which Groups Participate

Activities	No. of Institutions
Recreational programs	4
Entertainment programs	5
Holiday programs	5
Blood bank	3
Tours or visits by service clubs, student groups, industrial representation groups	1
Other: Eye bank 1, Postage fund 1, Charity drives 2, Sanitation drives 1, Safety drives 1, Self-improvement 1, Talent shows 1, TV-Radio-Movies 1, and Curio program 1.	

responses were affirmative and were qualified by: *Only his social development,* and *gives him status in the eyes of the inmates but no material advantage from the viewpoint of the administration.*

Council Membership as Individual Treatment: All responses were negative to the question: *Is there a conscious or planned use of group membership as a part of the development plan for a particular individual inmate?*

Evaluation of Council: The last question, in three parts, was designed to elicit the respondent's estimates of the value of his experience with an advisory council arrangement:

a. *If you presently do not have a group but did in the past, for what reason was it discontinued?*

b. *Did you feel it was successful or unsuccessful?*

c. *Please give reasons for your answer to (b).*

Two institutions having existing councils replied to this question as follows:

Success varies with its membership. Sometimes [the council] is constructive, sometimes just carping and fault finding. The strongarm inmate or the cutie is likely to become a leader in this type of activity and enforce the wishes of a few on the many.

. . . considered to be helpful . . . to bring to attention of administration certain complaints from the inmate body . . . on matters that may easily be taken care of by the administration. The group has no authority and its suggestions are accepted as nothing more. . . .

Other respondents reporting on previous experiences with Advisory Councils:

They are of absolutely no value in an institution. Of the many years I watched them operate, I do not know of any constructive suggestion they ever made.

We do not have any inmate self-government group or Inmate Council. I experimented with one back about 1939 or 1940 and it was a failure and more harm than good. When a prisoner is adjusted enough to advise how to run the prison he doesn't belong here. He should be released.

In one institution which had undergone a critical period in the 1952 riots:

Shortly after . . . a group of inmates supposedly representative of the inmate body, functioned for a while as an Inmate Council for the purpose of establishing a better understanding between inmates and the administration for improving conditions and operation of the institution. Inmates selected members of this group by ballot. Members selected were of the aggressive, hard core criminal type of individual and it was not long before they were using their position to manipulate in favor of their friends and themselves. It is the consensus here that inmate self-government groups do not help for better administration, or rehabilitation in a maximum security institution.

One penitentiary reports a now defunct committee of inmates which met with the Treatment Associate Warden each month in a school classroom to plan the institutional publications.

One Warden reported previous favorable experience in another prison system. After receiving his present appointment this Warden permitted election of an Inmate Committee, subject to his confirmation. "However, this venture was unsuccessful . . . inmates used this position for their own personal gain. I let the committee die of its own accord. At the present time, I do not plan to have another such committee."

Another institution found that in attempting to use an inmate advisory committee on food, "the inmate's idea of proper feeding far exceeded what our budget would permit."

One Warden reported favorably on a council he had at another institution and felt was successful. It proved to be a good sounding board concerning inmate morale, and its very operation was a factor in maintaining morale at a high level. He plans a similar organization at his present institution when "I feel we are ready."

Other comments were:

I have seen inmate councils in other institutions and they have proven disastrous.

I personally, as a Warden at this institution, have never had contact with a group of this nature; however, I have seen several groups of this nature in operation when I have been in other positions at other institutions. . . . It would take a great deal to change my personal opinion as to the benefit of having a group of this nature operating within a penal institution.

I happen to be on the side who thinks there is no value in inmate councils. Through the years there have been many rehabilitative programs that have placed more control in the inmate's hands and each one of these programs have proved disastrous. . . . One of these rehabilitative programs caused the riot (in 1952). It is going on nine years now that we have the place under control. Custody is in first place . . . before you can teach you have to have attention. We have had no trouble during this period, so you can see why I am not in favor of inmate councils.

With the exception of the first, the following comments imply a definite point of view in spite of no actual experience with self-government groups.

. . . no experience with the so-called inmate self-government group. This does not mean that I am necessarily opposed to such groups. . . . We accomplish, perhaps, some of the alleged benefits of self-government through our guidance program and the constant individual guidance activity between staff members and inmates which occurs here.

We do not have any self-government groups. To date, I am not convinced that such groups are justified within a penitentiary such as ours.

. . . members of our inmate body are not permitted to organize such groups.

No inmate is granted privilege or assignment having authority over others.

We have never had an inmate self-government unit in operation in this institution and from the information I have verbally experienced from some wardens, I am of the opinion that we do not wish to have one.

About 40 years ago there was one and it did not work out well. . . . I understand that as time went on it became involved in the administration of the institution. We found it was most unsuccessful.

Many years ago, probably 25 or 30, the Inmate Council used their privilege to meet in the evening within a cell block to plan and execute an escape attempt. One of the guards was severely beaten. That episode ended the Council.

Summary

It is interesting to note that of 44 responding institutions only 13 report experience with inmate self-government or advisory council groups. Six respondents who have never had direct experience with such groups expressed a negative view based usually on the negative experience of others.

Geographically, of seven existing councils six are located in Western institutions and one in a New England State facility. Five of the six previous councils were located in the Eastern and Mid-Eastern States; one in the Southeast.

The chief executive officer of the seven institutions is directly involved in discussions with the council. While other staff members attend meetings in four institutions, in only two of these are they reported as alternates to the executive.

Councils are reported as being active principally in intra-mural interest programs such as recreation and entertainment. Participation in activities designed to encourage social identification is slight.

Reportedly there is no advantage to council membership. However, there were only two responses to a question concerning this. Probably the five instances of silence are more significant, reflecting, perhaps, a line of thought that council membership is its own reward. The visibility of this altruistic view is beclouded somewhat in view of there being no reported instances of council membership as a part of the development plan for an individual. Correctional administrators endorse various forms of compensation for participation in other programs, principally those involving work. Perhaps thought should be given to providing some compensation for members where the council is frankly used as an administrative adjunct. The writer hopes that this suggestion, so implicit in the question "Are there any material advantages to an inmate as a member of the group?" was not met with silence because it was regarded as either threatening or ridiculous.

Two factors contributing to a favorable evaluation of experience with a council were given as:

1. Success is dependent upon the identification of council members.

2. The functions of the council are well understood by all concerned so that no question exists regarding its functional scope and purpose. Constitutions and by-laws are a means of insuring this understanding.

The reasons advanced by those whose evaluation of their experience with a council was negative were inversely identical:

1. Aggressive types of inmates elected to the council attempted to use their positions for personal gain.

2. The purpose, procedure, and scope of the council were not similarly viewed by inmates and staff.

Oppositions to the concept of inmate self-government or advisory council groups form a cluster of considerations offensive to some correctional administrators. These may be summarized as:

1. Inmates should not be permitted to give advice regarding operation of the institution.

2. Inmates should not be placed in positions of ascendance over other inmates.

3. Inmates should not be placed in positions advantageous to personal gain.

DISCUSSION

The self-government concept grew out of the harshness of the old prison regime. It was an attempt to provide a framework within which the inmate could exercise some freedom of expression and choice. It was unique to the prevalent social patterns of the periods in which we find it briefly emerging. There was little knowledge of and concern for the law-abiding citizen's condition. The principles of industrial management espousing the welfare of the individual were unknown. Prison administration as a science was at best in an embryonic stage. Humane treatment of offenders was the concern of only a dedicated few, virtually none of whom was in actual correctional practice. We find references to this or that person as being a "humane warden." Apparently this was a novel situation.

Treatment as we envision and practice it today did not exist. Life in the old prison was a deadly monotony under a stern and often brutal autocracy. There are few accounts of career administrators and fewer accounts of occupational mobility. The guard remained a guard. Supervisory custodial personnel were usually hired at that level. Wardens and their deputies were appointed as a part of a political patronage system. Unfortunately, some of these features currently exist, but not to the same degree.

Those correctional workers who consider their experience with inmate councils to be successful realize that the councils are not designed to assist "in running the place." They know that while it is desirable to instill a sense of responsibility in the inmate, they must not confuse that aspect of resocialization with their duty to retain and exercise all functions of management. These functions cannot be abrogated or delegated.

For too long many fictions concerning inmate self-government have gone unchallenged in correctional literature. Probably one of the most absurd is the notion that such systems reduce operational costs. O. F. Lewis made this statement: "And just as in most modern days (1922) it has been found that participation of the prisoners in their own government has in the main resulted in decreased necessity for watchfulness by guards, so in the Walnut Street Prison. In 1794 the Duc de la Rochefoucauld-Liancourt discovered that 280 convicts were governed by only 4 officers, the women prisoners being under the control of a woman."[29] This is evidently supposed to be a case for self-government, adding to the "proof" that self-government is also good from the economical standpoint. Actually, all it tells us is what every correctional administrator of any worth already knows—custodial detention is a relatively simple and economical matter. There was no program other than custodial containment at Walnut Street. In one modern Midwestern penitentiary, with a current average population of 1400, no more than 30 of the custodial complement of 150 would be needed to effect security functions alone, provided such personnel worked 12 hours daily, seven days each week, as did the keepers at Walnut Street in 1794.

We know that these systems of inmate self-government could not have succeeded under the most favorable circumstances. Such systems would be unworkable even in the most enlightened of modern correctional institutions. As administered, most of the past experiments in inmate self-government were inadequately structured and implemented arrangements superimposed on an untrained staff by individuals whose zeal far exceeded their correctional management ability. All of the self-government systems reviewed depended on a central figure and rapidly expired when that person departed. Apparently little, if any, effort was made to indoctrinate the staff and lead them to an acceptance of this concept of managing prisoners.

It is quite apparent that each of the originators of these systems was a person in advance of his time, an innovator and experimenter, dynamic and creative, impatient with current conditions. None had a trained or professional staff recruited and developed under a merit system. There were no personnel development programs. Salaries were low, hours were long, tenure was insecure, and employee benefits were unheard of. All of these circumstances add up to extreme conditions. Little wonder then that the proponents of the various systems of inmate self-government justified their stand with such extreme statements as "Which is better (for inmate development) the autocratic system or the self-government system?"

CONCLUSION

In 1960 the Warden's Association of America went on record as being in opposition to the idea of inmate self-government. Our study of literature which penetrates United States correctional history 169 years, and the survey responses of 44 penitentiary administrators reveal similar negative attitudes which we believe grew primarily from an erroneous equation of self-government with discipline by inmates.

Self-government was used by its early advocates as a means of promoting the goals of improved prison conditions, public acceptance of the released offender, and the reduction of criminal behavior. Today we see these goals being realized through personnel development, programs to acquaint the public with modern correctional methods, and inmate classification and individual treatment.

On the current scene there are no longer inmate self-government systems as proposed and attempted in the early experiments and experiences we have described. The features of these systems most acceptable to prison administrators have been retained under an arrangement known as the inmate advisory council. Dickson, Fenton, and Holzschuh[30] have pointed out that the advisory council represents one of the most satisfactory devices for encouraging the inmates of a prison to think constructively about their own institutional environment and provides a means by which inmates may share the responsibility with the staff of making the prison a better place in which to live.

Many administrators regard the advisory council as simply a device for the communication of inmate complaints to the administration. This narrow view has produced the term "gimme groups."

Successfully used, the council has a two-way function. It is an agency for communicating to inmates the responsibilities which the administration expects of them and to present a picture of the administrative problems in the areas with which inmates are concerned—notably food. By showing them the budget and soliciting their suggestions as to how a better job might be done with available resources, a structure is created which provides for and encourages thoughtful, constructive feedback. This approach involves the same psychological principles basic to management efforts to provide employee job satisfaction—call it morale if you wish.

It is significant to note that no institution responding to our survey questionnaire indicated a conscious or planned use of group membership as a part of the development plan for a particular individual inmate. It would appear that this use is one of the principal features of the rationale for inmate advisory councils, yet is the least explored area of all. For instance, a properly operated council offers an excellent vehicle for the harnessing and direction of the abundant energies and usually high abilities of many offenders not amenable to conventional treatment forms. Some men need an experience of working for the welfare of others. Others require ego-satisfying assignments in which they can escape the feeling of being engulfed in the crowd.

Perhaps correctional administrators would be well advised to look again at the modern counterpart of self-government, the inmate advisory council. They should consider it in its proper perspective as a part of social education for inmates, and as a morale-raising device for the entire institution through its facilitation of two-way communication between staff and inmates.

24 *Prison Industry*

ELMER H. JOHNSON*

Inconsistency of goals and the masking of genuine motives under the guise of prisoner "rehabilitation" are particularly marked in the history of prison industries.

On one hand, it has been argued that the prisoner should work to pay for his keep and ease the burden of supporting the criminal placed on taxpayers who were his prey. A similar attitude has been applied to the insane and mentally defective, but recent decades have left the prisoner as the prime target. A second argument has been that "hard labor while wearing stripes" is an efficient means of deterring future crime or of balancing the scales of retribution by imposing work as punishment. A third argument is that prison labor instills habits of industry. The imposition of menial drudgery has been defended as "therapeutic" in this superficial sense. A fourth argument defines habits of industry and marketable job skills as essential ingredients in preparing the released prisoner for social-psychological integration into a free society in which job status is the basis of responsible social participation.

On the other hand, correctional institutions face many impediments in realizing any of these purposes. Under the *principle of less eligibility,* the inmate is considered less worthy of satisfactory employment and training than the worst-paid noncriminal. This principle was supplanted by what Mannheim calls the *principle of nonsuperiority;* namely, the earlier principle was slightly liberalized to contend that the condition of the

From Elmer H. Johnson, *Crime, Correction and Society* (Homewood, Ill.: The Dorsey Press), pp. 558–566. Reprinted by permission of the author and publisher.

criminal should not be superior to that of the worst-paid noncriminal. Consequently, the restriction of prison industry was stimulated by a psychological perspective conflicting with the pure economics of reducing prison operational costs.[31]

CONFLICT AMONG GOALS

The several objectives frequently conflict with one another. Labor as a punitive device stigmatizes labor for nonpunitive purposes. It strengthens inmate resentment against the prison and its officials, complicating vocational training, which requires instructor-student rapport. Conversely, employment for the sake of vocational training aborts the deterrent effect of punitive labor. Efforts to maximize economic return from industries require emphasis on output, rather than on correction of faulty attitudes of the prisoner-worker. Work pace must not be interrupted to counsel prisoners or to afford the personalized instruction necessary for on-the-job training. Industrial foremen usually are selected for their qualifications in meeting output quotas, rather than for their instructional skills. Maximum output usually demands concentration on a few products to exploit the possibilities of minimizing per unit costs. Cost factors favor the use of power machinery which reduces the economic advantage of prison labor and reduces the contribution of prison industries in overcoming prisoner idleness. The increased volume of output raises the issue of competition with free labor. In keeping with the objectives of individualized treatment, vocational training requires a wide variety of products to extend the range of skills taught. On the other hand, because the prisoners generally are either unskilled or semiskilled, the industrial manager is limited in the range of products appropriate for his labor force.

Wardens agree that the most difficult prison to administer is the one in which prisoners languish in idleness. Absence of work leads to moral and physical degradation and corrupts institutional order. However, aimless drudgery is of little advantage. Consequently, official statements of industrial goals recognize rehabilitation of prisoners to varying degrees. As Grunhut has noted, the attainment of rehabilitation through labor is supposed to be through *training FOR work* and *training BY work*.[32] Work has the virtue of relieving boredom. Under the concept of training by work, it is assumed that habits developed through regular employment will persist automatically. In contrast, training for work would employ this more superficial and immediate motivation to work as the first stage of a more sophisticated process of stimulating the prisoner's interest in employment on a long-term basis. Inmate employment becomes only one facet of a multifaceted effort to change the prisoner's attitudes and values. Wages and consideration of the inmate's individual qualities in job assignment can be inducements to promote work motivation.

EVOLUTION OF LABOR SYSTEMS

Systems of prison industries have been based on the so-called "sheltered market" and on the open market. Generally, contemporary prison industries employ the "state-use" and "public works and ways" systems for a sheltered market. The four open-market systems are lease, contract, piece-price, and state account. These four systems are chiefly of historical interest.

The *state-use system* produces goods and renders services for agencies of the state and their political subdivision. *Public works and ways* involves road construction and repair, reforestation, soil-erosion control, and the like. The *lease system* turned care and custody over to an entrepreneur for a stipulated fee. Under the *contract system,* the state retained control of inmates but sold their labor to an entrepreneur at a daily per capita fee. The entrepreneur furnished the raw materials and paid the prison a stipulated fee for each unit of finished product under the *piece-price* arrangement. The state became the manufacturer under the *state account system* and sold its products on the open market.[33]

Sources of Opposition

When reformers sought to develop prison labor programs for purposes other than punishment, they encountered hostility from organized free labor and from some businessmen and industrialists. The development of group cohesiveness has been a major problem for organized labor in the United States where workers have been prone to identify themselves with the lower middle class. The workers have lacked the spontaneous class solidarity upon which European unions were based psychologically. Selig Perlman describes the experimentation which culminated in the job-conscious unionism of the American Federation of Labor about 1890. Recognizing the strength of property rights in American society, unionism adapted the concept of property rights to claim the union's right to control jobs. Job opportunity was viewed as limited. The worker's adherence to the union was won through establishing "rights" in the jobs for the individual and for the work group through agreements regulating priority and seniority in employment.[34] Since organized labor regards as exclusively its own the rights so painfully acquired, labor unions have been sensitive to the extension of job rights to nonmembers. Under the principle of less eligibility, the prison inmate was regarded as an inappropriate competitor for the jobs of free labor.

Labor unions and employer's associations have found a common cause in protesting the "competition" of prison labor. As early as 1801, a New York law required boots and shoes to be labeled with the words "State Prison."[35] The prosperous contract industries attracted major opposition in the northern industrial states in the 1880's. There were a series of investigations into the contract and lease systems in 11 states during the 1870's and 1880's. Manufacturers in certain industries organized a National Anti-Contract Association in 1886.[36] In 1887 contracting of federal criminals was made illegal. Brockway proposed the piece-price system as an alternative to counter the growing opposition to the contract system.

From Lease to State-Use

During the 1830-70 period, the lease and contract systems provided employment and the funds to establish the American penitentiary, but the zeal to make prisons self-supporting had killed the idea that prisoners should be denied opportunities to communicate with each other.. Some prisons had been turned over to economic exploiters, jeopardizing security and treatment. The priority of profit making tended to jeopardize parole of skilled prisoners, control of contraband, and the warden's authority. To keep production costs down, the contractor tended to discourage absenteeism necessary for inmate participation in rehabilitation programs. Mass production of a limited variety of articles was favored over the diversity appropriate for vocational training on an individualized basis. Competition with free industry was direct. Just as many prisons were freeing themselves of the objectionable features of the contract and lease systems and achieving steady employment, the opponents of prison industry succeeded in barring sale of prison-made goods on the open market.[37] As one major exception to the general trend, Minnesota established a model state account system in the early 1890's when it took over production and marketing of farm machinery and bindery twine from contractors.[38] The political power of Minnesota farmers and the absence of production of farm machinery in the state explains the continued sale of prison-made farm machinery on the open market, a rare phenomenon today.

The state-use plan was suggested in 1887 and was endorsed in 1900 by the United States Industrial Commission.[39] Legislation struck at the interstate commerce in prison-made goods, with the result that the state-use and public works and ways systems have become paramount. The Hawes-Cooper Act of 1929 deprived the goods of their interstate character and made them subject to state law. The Ashurst-Summers Act of 1935 prohibited transportation of goods into states forbidding their entry and required the labeling of prison-made goods shipped in interstate commerce. In the face of mass unemployment during the depression, every state had passed legislation by 1940 to take advantage of this opportunity to ban prison-made goods of other states.[40]

GOALS OF WORK PROGRAMS

Two divergent trends have shaped prison labor programs. One trend reflects the attitude that prison labor should be looked upon as different from labor in general. In keeping with the punitive ideology, the prisoner is thought of as part of the abnormal world of repressive confinement. Labor is seen as a punishment and as an obligation imposed on the prisoner. The prisoner's "hard labor" is deprived of the dignity and incentives of labor in general. His work becomes an activity which isolates him from the rest of society. The deterrence and rehabilitative rationalizations for punishment prescribe hard work at lowest levels of skill. Even with the rise of humanitarian concern for the lot of the prisoner, the opportunity to work was advocated in the spirit of charity to help the prisoner avoid the moral and physical degradation of idleness; even the humanitarians did not seek to end the differentiation between labor behind bars and labor in the community.

The second trend has been toward improvement of prison labor conditions and increased concern that prison employment should play a part in rehabilitation of character. The aim is to prepare the inmate for a constructive life after release, and prison labor is viewed as an activity intended to reduce the alienation of the offender from society. Vocational instruction is used to develop occupational skills and work motivation. The tasks are related to the inmate's self-interest. The rhythm of work and the conditions of employment are as similar as possible to those in the free world.

A third approach is utilitarian in that some administrators consider prison labor as something to be used to help balance the prison budget. The increasing acceptance of the state-use system is an adjustment of prison administration to the pressure by critics of prison competition with free labor. Being able to cite reduction of governmental costs through prison industries is an additional factor in meeting criticism. However, when given undue priority, the utilitarian approach can negate rehabilitative efforts as the price for budget balancing.

Lopez-Rey argues that within certain limitations prisoners should share the fundamental human rights to work and to earn equal pay for equal work. The limitations stem from the juridical situation of the prisoner which denies him the right to select his work, to refuse a certain task without justification, and to change his place of work. Aside from these limitations, Lopez-Rey would organize prison labor to be as similar to free labor as circumstances would permit. He would bring private industry into the prison to provide the equipment and wage scales of free labor. He argues prisoner self-respect and self-responsibility would emerge as basic elements in rehabilitation of prisoners. Therefore, he contends, many of the existing psychological and psychiatric services would become unnecessary.[41]

Labor and Rehabilitation

Usually there are four activities related to training and employment of inmates. First, the maintenance activities are concerned with the feeding and clothing of prisoners, with providing heat, power, light and other operational requirements of the institution. Second, farms reduce the food costs and afford employment. Third, the industrial department provides employment, possible opportunities for on-the-job training, and a means of reducing the costs to the taxpayer of prison operations and of government in general. Fourth, the educational department contributes to improvement of work skills to promote postrelease employment and to upgrade the quality of prison industrial production.

In merging labor and rehabilitation purposes, a prime problem is to overcome conflicts among the four activities. Ideally, prison industries would be provided well-trained and motivated workers through prisoner classification and vocational training programs which would wed job requirements with inmate self-interest. Unfortunately, most prisons do not integrate vocational training, inmate vocational interests, and choice of industrial specialities to coincide with a vocational training program consistent with the job market for released offenders. Even for the adequate workers among the prisoners, industries must compete in the face of higher priority usually given maintenance activities.

Industrial supervisors have been habituated to using excessive numbers of prisoners because their quality as workers usually depresses productivity. This habit is reinforced by another major problem. Releases on parole or completion of sentence create a high rate of turnover, especially for prisoners most likely to be efficient workers because their characteristics are consistent with early release.

In too many instances prison-made goods are inferior in design and workmanship to the products of private enterprise. The state-use industries have not been able to capture a significant share of the market offered by other governmental institutions because of quality inferiorities and because of the stigma attached to prison-made goods. This failure has contributed to the small scale of industrial operations—too small to support standards of cost reduction and continuity of production essential to giving the inmate familiarity with work situations in the free community.

As a whole, prisoners have inadequate educational attainment, vocational skills, and work habits. To use the bulk of them for anything above unskilled labor, vocational and academic training is required to prepare them for industrial tasks. This preparation consumes a portion of the sentence, reducing the period when a skilled worker will be available for full-time work assignment.

To make prison industrial work a real asset to vocational training, plants must be modernized by eliminating useless jobs, by insisting that each shop be operated on the basis of present-day methods, by emphasizing quality of products, by stressing the goal that men be helped to develop themselves, by holding job training to rigid standards, by recognizing that some inmates are incapable of training, and by emphasizing the recognition of individual differences.[42]

If his labor is to contribute to production goals and his own long-term interest, the industrial program must motivate the prisoner, encourage development of good work habits, and fit him to tasks appropriate to his intelligence, educational potential, age, and ability. To achieve these difficult objectives, Springsted advocates training of industrial supervisors in orientation of new workers, constructive handling of grievances, and recurrent problems for counseling.[43]

It is difficult to strike a proper balance between vocational training for prisoner rehabilitation and the achievement of high production for its own sake. However, even if prisoner rehabilitation were the only aim, the administration would encounter difficult problems: Should an inmate scheduled for early release be given priority in assignment to a wage-paying task so that he may gain funds to support himself and his dependents on the outside? What kinds of work should be given to the physically handicapped? What limitations should there be on the prisoner's expenditure of his earnings? Should a long-term prisoner be permitted to become so wedded to a particular job that he loses interest in other prison programs more in keeping with his needs?[44]

Trade advisory committees and councils provide the means for organized labor and management to participate in vocational and industrial training programs of prisons. A *trade advisory committee* may be set up for each vocational area, whereas a *trade advisory council* represents all trade training within a correctional institution. California has used this plan to obtain expert advice on training standards, procedures, equipment, trainee evaluation, postrelease placement, and instructor requirements. Increased support of prison industries by union and management has been an additional advantage.[45]

Wages for Prisoners

When labor is forced and unrewarded, there is little incentive for diligence and development of skill. As an incentive and reward, money is as effective within an institution as it is in the free society. It is part of the American cultural norms shaping the personality that the offender brings into the institution. Therefore, money is a familiar incentive to him, one that will continue to operate after he is released. Money has great exchange power because the individual can convert it into the specific reward he values most among purchased goods and services. By using money, the institution skirts the difficult problem of fitting a reward to the interests of each inmate. Money serves as a bridge between self-interest and the ability to cooperate with others within a social organization.

The inmate should bear the financial burden of supporting his dependents, rather than adding them to the public welfare programs. He would have a "nest egg" to support himself during the crucial early period of release before he finds employment. With funds available to ease the released prisoner's adjustment, disintegration of families would be prevented. The inmate's sense of responsibility for his family would be nurtured during his confinement. Wages symbolize the state's interest in the inmate's personal welfare.[46] Lack of money contributes to inmate subterfuge, disorder, and labor inefficiency. Leavenworth Penitentiary has rewarded prisoner-workers with a "paid vacation" after two years of good conduct. Wages were continued during a period of absence from work. Improved worker moral and job tenure were reported.[47]

Objections have been raised against inmate wages. Deprivation of earning capacity is viewed as part of punishment. Easing of the lot of the prisoner's family would reduce the deterrent effect of imprisonment. The cost of prison operations already is too great without the additional expense of paying wages.[48] To pay wages to convicted criminals has been opposed as a travesty on social justice when thousands of honest citizens are unable to find employment.[49]

In a national survey, 20 states, the District of Columbia, and the Federal Bureau of Prisons reported payment of wages to from 90 to 100 percent of their inmates. In five states, no more than 10 percent earn money. Six states did not permit inmate earnings in prison. Of 33 states supplying such information in another survey, wages ranged from 4 cents a day to a high of $1.30 a day.[50]

SUMMARY

In a society emphasizing work as the major status determinant, prison industry has important potentialities for making the correctional institution a means of rehabilitation. The trend toward opening new forms of communication with the free community holds promise for reducing the serious discrepancy between the prison and the outside society as universes of social experience. However, if the trend is to have significant results, issues related to prison labor must be resolved. We have reviewed those issues.

25 *Preparing Prisoners for Their Return to the Community*

J. E. BAKER*

It had been known for a long time that the highest percentage of postprison failures occurs within 6 months after release, with the greater number taking place during the first 60 days. But it was not until the early forties that penal and correctional institutions realized that something must be done to help inmates bridge the gap between the prison community and life in free society. The concept of prerelease preparation was thus added to the machinery of corrections.

Much experimentation followed in attempts to formulate workable procedures to help prepare prisoners for their return to the community. From these efforts evolved three principles now recognized as essential in establishing a realistic program of prerelease preparation:

(1) To make available to prerelease inmates information and assistance deemed pertinent in release planning.

(2) To provide each prerelease inmate the opportunity, in a non-threatening situation, to discuss problems and anxieties relating to his release and future social adjustment.

(3) To provide a system of evaluating the effectiveness of release planning procedures.

It is not our purpose to explore the effectiveness of prerelease preparation in terms of reduced recidivism rates. Rather, we present a narration and analysis of one program based on the three principles cited and highlight some of the significant feelings and attitudes of inmates as they

* From *Federal Probation*, XXX (June 1966): 43–50. Reprinted by permission of author and publisher.

approach release and 6 months following release. The program described here is that at the U.S. Penitentiary, Lewisburg, Pennsylvania, while the author was assigned there as chief of classification and parole.

UNDERLYING PHILOSOPHY OF THE PROGRAM

The program was not fully outlined in advance of its implementation. The approach was experimental in nature with flexibility and adaptability to the specific needs of individual inmates taken into account in determining the potential value of any proposed activity within the program.

A part of the program's approach was taken from the basic premises of the Alcoholics Anonymous. To the prerelease inmate was presented this proposition: You accept that release to the community will pose problems of varying kind and degree; you have a sincere desire to avoid further delinquency; you are resolved that you do not wish to undergo again the experience of confinement; you wish to begin the basis of a sound future. Having acknowledged these things, you want help from others. Prerelease planning can be a part of the answer to your needs. The remainder of the answer lies within you in your own capacities and your sincere willingness to utilize them for your self-betterment.

Throughout the program emphasis was placed on the individual's responsibility for his future. Group meetings were designed to furnish information and to stimulate thinking about future plans, both immediate and long-range.

Although casework personnel were charged with the administration and supervision of the program, staff participation was not limited to them.

The chaplains, safety supervisor, vocational supervisor, and business office employees also took part as discussion leaders. The Federal Probation Service cooperated by having probation officers meet with groups of prerelease inmates. In addition, persons from the community such as bankers, insurance agents, clergymen, and employment officers gave generously of their time and talents.

CONTENT AND PROCEDURES OF THE PROGRAM

As it developed, the prerelease program eventually provided intensive preparation in three categories: mandatory considerations, planning and resources, and emotional factors, each comprised as follows:

Mandatory Considerations

(1) Legal aspects
   (a) Statutory provisions concerning mandatory release and parole
   (b) Civil rights and responsibilities
   (c) Release to other custody
(2) Administrative aspects
   (a) Rules of supervision
   (b) Role of the U.S. probation officer
   (c) Destination determination
   (d) Clearance procedures

Planning and Resources

(1) Employment information and counseling
   (a) Job responsibilities
   (b) State Bureau of Employment services
   (c) Bureau of Prisons Employment Placement Service
(2) Financial planning
   (a) Gratuity allowance
   (b) Disposition of personal funds
   (c) Discharge clothing
   (d) Transportation
(3) Community resources
   (a) The clergy
   (b) Banking
   (c) Insurance
   (d) Alcoholic rehabilitation

Emotional Factors

(1) Common social problems
   (a) Race relations
   (b) Highway safety
   (c) Credit-installment buying
(2) Attitudinal problems
   (a) A series of discussion groups providing opportunity for a review
       of possible readjustment problems

All men within approximately 90 days of their release date were eligible
for participation in the program. All meetings were held during the day.

Attendance was required at certain meetings and was optional at others. Attendance was required at the following meetings.

General Session

This was an introductory meeting to discuss the purpose and scope of the prerelease program and to provide information essential to preparing for release.

Detainer Meeting

Participants were those men with warrants on file calling for their release to other custody. Information was given regarding assistance available from the staff in furnishing data to detaining authorities concerning the inmate's institutional adjustment and future plans.

Meeting with the Probation Officer

Every other month representatives of the probation staff conducted a discussion on supervision. This gave the prerelease inmate an opportunity to discuss his problems with an experienced field officer. Applicants scheduled for the next meeting of the U.S. Board of Parole had the option of attending this meeting, as did those men who had no supervision to follow.

Meeting Relating to Supervision Requirements

Each month a caseworker conducted a discussion of supervision requirements. Each of the conditions of release was read and interpreted. Samples of reporting forms were circulated and a demonstration given as to their proper completion. (Only men with supervision to follow were required to attend.)

Meeting to Discuss Social Problems

There are certain problems and issues of our society common to all persons and affecting the welfare of all. It was believed that men about to re-enter society would profit from reminders concerning traffic safety, race relations, and credit-installment buying.

Final Sign-Out

During the last 2 days of his stay in the institution each man being released under supervision was interviewed for the purpose of answering any last-minute questions he might have regarding the conditions of release. At that time he signed his release certificate.

Attendance at the following meetings was optional.

Discussion of State Employment Services

On alternate months a representative of the State Employment Service interpreted and discussed the functions of his office. Provision was made for registration of the prerelease inmate and referral to the area of his release.

Meeting on Occupational Adjustment

Each month a vocational supervisor conducted a discussion on relationships with peers and supervisor, ways and means to improve work habits, and the highly important topic of proper attitudes as they relate to job stability.

Discussion of Employment Placement Services

Although no group meetings were conducted by him, a representative of the Bureau of Prisons Employment Placement Service interviewed men in prerelease status. This Service provides job placement for those who apply. Its functions were explained to prerelease inmates at the general session. The representative visited the institution quarterly to interview interested applicants and determine the most feasible approach to job placement.

Community Resources Series

It was believed to be important that men soon to return to society should learn or be reminded of the many resources available in most communities. A series of three meetings, each on an alternate 3-month schedule, was conducted by community representatives of religion, banking, and insurance.

Meeting to Discuss Alcoholism

Arrangements were made with the State Division of Alcoholic Studies and Rehabilitation to conduct meetings every other month. Speakers provided information regarding the concern of responsible officials for the problem of alcoholism and the resources available for assistance to the individual.

Special Discussion Groups

It was believed that special emphasis should be given in certain socioeconomic areas in an effort to encourage participants to free themselves from dependence on the thinking of others, often a serious readjustment problem for men who have been confined for considerable time. It was the consensus of the staff that social education discussion groups offered the best media for successful accomplishment. Each group met three times, once each month. Any man within 6 months of his release date and applicants scheduled for the next meeting of the Board of Parole were eligible to attend. The caseworkers acted as leaders, their areas of discussion being: "Living With Others," "Effective Community Living," "Current Trends," and "Human Relations."

Haberdashery Prevue

The discharge clothing room had been converted to resemble a haberdashery in which all clothing items were displayed in glassed counters or on racks. Each article had an assigned point value. Each prerelease inmate was allotted 330 points with which to "purchase" his clothing. In order that he might see the items available and have time to examine their cut and quality to insure his making the best possible use of the points allowed him, any eligible man who wished was permitted to make a prevue tour of the haberdashery in the company of other prerelease inmates. These tours were arranged and conducted by the clerical staff of the casework office.

PROGRAM AIDS

Prior to the general session already mentioned, each prerelease inmate was sent a copy of a *Prerelease Handbook,* with an introduction page explaining its content and purpose:

> This booklet is for the information and use of men nearing the time of leaving the institution. It explains the program of the institution designed to assist in the solution of release planning problems and the program of the United States Board of Parole concerning supervision. In addition, it points out some of the important obligations which many men will have after release.

In addition to facsimile reproductions of the statement of release conditions found on the reverse side of both the parole and mandatory release certificates, each booklet contained four detachable interview request forms. These were pre-addressed to the caseworker and bore the large imprint "This Is a Prerelease Request." Caseworkers could readily single out these requests for priority handling.

A staff guidebook entitled *A Prerelease Program* was distributed to all participating staff members. It contained a schedule of meetings with an outline of program content. This made it possible for all concerned to familiarize themselves with the material to be presented in each meeting as well as the methods of presentation that had proved most effective.

To establish liaison with the U.S. probation officers who would supervise the released inmate, each probation office in the northeastern, eastern, and southeastern districts was furnished a copy of the guide book. By reference to the program content and a summary of the individual's release orientation the probation officer could readily determine the nature and extent of release preparation.

The aforementioned summary of release orientation was a prerelease program participation record form showing the program meetings attended. A space was provided for comments about special interests or specific attitudes of the released inmate.

Booklets and pamphlets obtained through commercial and government sources were made available in the institution library and through the group discussion leaders. These contained information regarding the employment outlook in several occupational areas; wage surveys conducted periodically in various locations; information on the establishment and operation of small businesses; labor market information; and tips on obtaining and holding employment.

A liberal use was made of sound motion pictures, filmstrips, tape recordings, color slides, and posters.

DETERMINING MAJOR CONCERNS

To provide the staff with leads as to the major concerns of the prerelease inmate a questionnaire was found to be the most feasible method. A questionnaire was designed to obtain insight into the prerelease inmate's attitude toward chances for successful social adjustment, immediate postrelease problems, anticipated readjustment problems, and analysis of prison experience.

It was believed that if the prerelease program was to be made a part of the treatment process, there should be some provision for determining its effectiveness. More will be said of this later.

After its purpose was explained, as well as that of the 6-month followup study, the questionnaire was distributed at the close of the first meeting. Its completion was discretionary. The discussion leader told those willing to complete it to take it to their housing unit and return it within a few days in an envelope provided.

Voluntary discussions were another means of eliciting leads to the major concerns. These groups will be commented upon in some detail later.

RESPONSES OF INMATES PRIOR TO RELEASE

Responses shattered the traditional belief of many correctional workers that inmates with no postrelease supervision have little interest in release preparation. Nonsupervision releases completed 45 percent of all questionnaires accepted for completion.

A summary analysis of responses revealed the average prerelease inmate to be principally interested in finding a job and having money to meet release needs. He also had a strong wish for assistance from the institution. As he viewed the situation 90 days prior to his release, his principal and immediate postrelease interest was to "settle down and stay out of trouble." His anticipated major problems were finding adequate employment and/or financial assistance. He had no real fear of nonacceptance by his family but did express some uncertainty. He anticipated some difficulty with former friends but nothing of consequence. From society at large he expressed the hope for acceptance. He had no antagonism toward the institution, expressing the feeling that the confinement experience was an expensive lesson, usually deserved.

This picture of the attitudes and feelings of the average prerelease inmate were in contrast to traditional views held by correctional workers. As previously mentioned, there was no appreciable difference in the interest manifested in release planning by supervision and nonsupervision cases. While principal prerelease interests were compatible with traditional beliefs, immediate postrelease plans were not, as we have been led to believe, to "have a ball," but rather to "settle down and stay out of trouble." Since this response was made by almost all, the staff believed that a further exploration of the emotional content of such a response would be of value.

Several group meetings, limited to 15 participants each meeting, were arranged for those who have given "settling down and staying out of trouble" as an immediate postrelease interest. Your writer and the then associate warden for treatment conducted most of the meetings. Films depicting how to overcome personal handicaps and problems were used. While relatively few sessions produced spontaneous discussion, those which did occur were meaningful in terms of revealing significant attitudes and feelings. These can be classified under two major categories: acceptance by others and feelings of being disadvantaged. An examination of each reveals some important attitudes which should be taken into account in dealing with inmates nearing release.

These group sessions clearly indicated that the prerelease questionnaire has only a limited value in eliciting information regarding anxieties concerning release. Much material was produced in the group setting which was not mentioned or had not been requested on the written form.

Acceptance by Others

Concern about acceptance was a very strong feeling frequently expressed. Individuals speculated on the desirability of changing residence or not returning directly to family or friends. Such fears and attitudes were voluntarily expressed as: "I wish I could be sure of what other people will expect of me"; "The cops won't give you a chance"; "The probation officer better not come snooping around my house." Other feelings involved threats to pride as expressed through fears of loss of economic and social status, and reluctance to accept help from others. A frequently asked question was, "Should I tell an employer that I'm an ex-convict when I apply for a job?" In many instances the attitude that an "ex-con can't get a decent job anyway" doomed any attempted interpretation.

Feeling of Being Disadvantaged

Although less frequently expressed, feelings of being disadvantaged seemed to be fairly common. Some inmates expressed fear of loss of initiative as a result of confinement. They pointed out that in society a person must compete with others for the necessities and luxuries of life, whereas in the prison these items, such as they might be, are furnished with a minimum of effort by the recipient.

Other feelings related to the need to "catch up" after release. The participants felt that valuable time had been lost in prison and that they would find their contemporaries well established in their jobs and in possession of material goods. In contrast, the released inmate would have only the clothes given him on release and a few dollars "to tide me over." When these feelings were being aired, released inmates with prior experience readily recalled intense feelings of inferiority and impatience to achieve what others had required.

RESPONSES OF INMATES AFTER RELEASE

As mentioned previously, it was believed there should be some provision for determining the effectiveness of the prerelease program. While there are many sources for obtaining information, such as the family and the probation officer, it was decided to limit the followup contacts to the released inmates.

The period studied was the first 6 months following release, believed to be the most critical in terms of social and occupational adjustments. A questionnaire was sent 6 months after release to those who had indicated a willingness to reply. Designed to complement the prerelease questionnaire previously described, the postrelease questionnaire was constructed to elicit the respondents' views on the effects and benefits of supervision, occupational adjustment, significance of the prison experience in their social adjustment, and to evaluate the prerelease program itself.

Effects and Benefits of Supervision

Eighty percent of the respondents who had been or were still under supervision reported that the probation officer was of assistance in obtaining employment, providing advice and help with general readjustment, and in resolving family problems.

Answers to questions regarding the parole advisor revealed frequent contact, usually on a weekly basis, occurring most often in the advisor's home. Other places of contact were at the released inmate's home, the advisor's place of business, an AA clubroom, and church. Assistance rendered by the advisor was characterized as being helpful as a counselor, in obtaining employment, and in controlling "bad habits."

Occupational Adjustment

Of the 83 respondents, 55 had jobs at release. Sixteen obtained jobs later. Of the 55 who had jobs on release, only 22 percent were on the same job 6 months later. The other 78 percent had left their employment at periods ranging from immediately after release to 5 months, the majority of severances occurring within 90 days postrelease. The principle reasons for severance were reported as finding a better liked or a higher paying position or being laid off.

Of the 71 who were employed at the time of reply, 87 percent stated they liked their job and intended to stay on. Only 38 percent had not yet told the employer of their prison record. Half of these gave as a reason for withholding the information, "They didn't ask"; the remainder felt that loss of job would result from revelation.

Of all respondents, both employed and unemployed, only 23 percent reported difficulty in finding employment because of their prison record.

Significance of Prison Experience in Social Adjustment

Questions in this category were designed to determine difficulties the released inmate experienced with family members and others as a result of having been in prison. As shown in Table 1, 24 men reported instances of rejection.

TABLE 1
Rejection by Relatives and Friends as Reported
by 24 Inmates following Release from Prison

Number reporting rejection*	Relationship of person rejecting inmate			
	Relatives	Former friends	Business associates	Church members
5		x		
2			x	
2				x
11	x	x		
2	x	x	x	
1	x	x	x	x
1		x		

* 57 reported no instance of rejection

Responses to a question regarding the most difficult problem faced immediately after release were predominantly (70 percent) in the areas of finding employment, adequate finances, and in becoming acclimated to free society.

Evaluation of Prerelease Program

The purpose of the questions in this category was to elicit attitudes toward participation in the program and to determine what features—positive or negative—were best remembered.

Two-thirds of the respondents believed the prerelease program was of help primarily in the areas of adjusting and advice provided by the staff. Best remembered was the opportunity to meet as a group with others facing release and the provision for open discussions of common problems. Only a minority recalled the increased privileges in correspondence and visits. The major criticism expressed was that group meetings were not long enough. To the question, "What did you like most about the prerelease program," we believe it worth reporting a waggish, yet majestic, reply: "Being released!" It is recognized that those respondents still under supervision might be reluctant to say anything against the program.

Miscellaneous Inquiries

Other inquiries were made to assess the prison experience as viewed 6 months after freedom, and to encourage respondents to include any comments or suggestions they might have.

To the inquiry, "What do you feel now was the most important thing you learned during the time you were serving your federal sentence," the responses centered primarily around the value of having learned a trade, academic improvement, and increased skills in interpersonal relationships and in controlling personal behavior.

Thanks were expressed to the institution staff for assistance rendered. Staff members most frequently mentioned were line employees, usually job foremen.

COMPARISON OF PRERELEASE AND POSTRELEASE RESPONSES

Some of the postrelease inquiries were designed to correspond with those in the prerelease questionnaire. A comparison of the responses provided an opportunity to examine a person's attitudes and feelings in several areas 90 days prior to release and 6 months after his return to the community. Since studies have shown that persons under stress magnify certain problems and concerns, it was believed that such a comparison would substantiate, or deny, that problems which loom large when viewed during imprisonment are not necessarily major areas of postrelease concern or do not exist at all. Further, it was believed that such information would be of value in the interpretations that could be made based on actual cases of men who had experienced the prerelease program.

The following question was asked prior to release: "What do you feel you have profited by during the time you have served?" And this related question was asked after release: "What do you feel, now, was the most important thing you learned during the time you served your federal sentence?" The responses are shown in Table 2.

TABLE 2

Benefits Derived from Imprisonment as Reported by 83 Inmates prior to Release and following Release from Prison

Nature of benefit derived	Prerelease response	Postrelease response
Learning a trade	16	17
Education	14	12
How to get along with others	10	9
Crime does not pay	9	13
Obedience	3	4
That it pays to be courteous and honest	2	2
That I cannot do as I please	2	2
Patience	2	4
Religious reawakening	2	0
Not to trust women	1	1
Derived no benefit	7	3
No response	15	16

It is interesting to compare responses to the prerelease inquiry, "What do you feel is the biggest problem facing you after release," with responses to the postrelease question, "What was the most difficult problem you faced immediately after release?"

It is noted that in 29 instances the anticipated major problem was not the same as the actual major postrelease problem reported. In 7 instances the respondent had indicated no anticipated problem. However, each of them reported having had various problems; in 3 instances this related to employment.

Of those anticipating problems, 2 reported having no problem after release. Seven anticipated an employment problem and in all instances this proved to be so. Of the 7 who anticipated a financial problem, none reported it as the actual problem. Six indicated employment as the actual problem after release, and one cited readjustment to civilian life.

In addition, respondents were asked to indicate whether the postrelease problem still prevailed at the time of reply. There were 22 affirmative answers, 29 replied that the problem had been resolved, and 32 did not respond. The preponderant difficulty, both anticipated and actual, related to employment.

The remaining comparisons fall within those questions designed to determine the significance of the prison experience in social readjustment. To the prerelease question, "Do you have any worries about how your family will treat you when you get home," 74 answered No and 6 said Yes. Three did not reply. However, 14 men reported postrelease rejection by relatives.

A similar question regarding friends indicated only 4 responses anticipating difficulties. Postrelease replies revealed that difficulty was actually encountered in only 3 of these instances. However, there were 20 instances of released inmates being shunned by former friends.

CONCLUSION

We do not know to what extent the postrelease adjustment is the result of institutional training and experience, prerelease preparation, supervision by the probation officer, acceptance by and encouragement from the family, a break in finding the right job, or any combination of a host of other variables. However, on the basis of our study we can point up some factors which may be of value in formulating a prerelease program.

A prerelease program should provide for a period of evaluation in which the experiences of the inmate and the specialized knowledge of the staff may be examined in a final effort to point the way to realistic solutions of the myriad problems facing the man about to be released. Additionally, opportunity should be given the prerelease inmate to verbalize his feelings and thoughts about his problems. These provisions fulfill the first two principles of prerelease planning.

While no claim is made as to the efficacy of the followup study, it did point up the need for some rethinking as to how staff effort might effect better release planning. To this extent it fulfilled the third principle of prerelease planning.

Special privileges such as extra visiting time and extra correspondence are welcomed, but are by no means essential to an effective prerelease program. Some practitioners believe that separate or special housing should be provided for prerelease inmates. Unless all men participating in the program can be so housed, the use of such units seems inadvisable.

In 78 percent of the cases in which there was definite employment at release, severance had occurred usually within 90 days. Further, 85 percent of respondents were employed 6 months following release. These two facts lead to an interesting speculation regarding job assistance efforts. While the value of a job-in-hand at time of release cannot be debated, it might be a more judicious use of staff effort to focus on equipping the individual to hold a job. When a prerelease inmate verbalizes an apprehension regarding getting postrelease employment, there is usually conjured the spectre of employer prejudice and adverse public opinion. Experience and reason tell us that neither of these is a major obstacle to obtaining a job. Witness the fact that two-thirds of employed respondents had told their employers of their prison record.

In view of the foregoing we submit that such an apprehension can be interpreted in most instances as an admission of a social lack—the inability, due to insufficient knowledge, to not only get a job, but more importantly, a fear of not knowing how to hold it. This has significance for institutional training efforts, as it indicates a need for increased emphasis on job-relationships with peers and supervisors, as well as on job-finding methods. This brings us face to face with a characteristic common to prison inmates—a low frustration tolerance with the corollary of limited perseverance in the face of almost any obstacle.

The foregoing is further borne out by some interesting facts. Whenever a released inmate was referred to a state employment service, a union, or a prospective employer through the Bureau of Prisons Employment Placement Service, a letter of introduction was always given him. Fifty percent made the initial contact, but when a job was not immediately available few reported back for further interview.

From our discussions with men who had had the experience, we found that the letter of introduction served to allay fears of making the initial step; its presence instilled confidence, assuring that an open door awaited them. However, when the contact did not produce results there was a tendency to revert to former patterns of behavior with a consequent failure to follow through.

Prerelease programming is a part of the institution's overall correctional effort. It cannot be isolated from other treatment activities. Ideally, the thrust of institutional programming should be in the direction of release planning, commencing with admission classification. The desirability of this is quickly evidenced when a prerelease program is initiated. Almost immediately the inadequacies of conventional correctional programs are exposed.

It is not believed that prerelease programs are necessary for all releasees. To apply such programs across the board to all men would be wasteful of time and effort. Participants should be carefully selected by the casework staff on the basis of individual need, potential, and expressed wish to profit from the experience. This presupposes a general program and an institutional atmosphere which motivates and encourages men toward self-improvement efforts.

While the group approach is beneficial in several ways—not the least being conservation of staff time—it must always be regarded only as supplemental to individual planning with each prerelease inmate. The role of the staff can be at best no more than supportive and the measure of success no greater than the individual's sincerest efforts.

Fusion
of Institutional and
Community Programs

Introduction

Progress in the operation of correctional institutions differs from progress in many other types of organization. In contrast to other agencies, the correctional institution advances in its development as it reduces its separate existence. An integration of institution and community correctional services is increasingly sought, as achievement of rehabilitation is a meaningless claim if it can be made only during a prisoner's confinement rather than after his release.

Such extension of correctional service into the post-release community is most feasible for an institution serving only the county or metropolis in which it is located. The largest institutions of this type are jails. Mark S. Richmond and George W. Aderhold of the U.S. Bureau of Prisons provide a survey of alternatives to jail confinement and of extensions of jail programs into the community. They begin with pretrial programs, which vary from diversion to medical agencies or release on recognizance to voluntary pretrial correctional services for detainees. Post-conviction measures they describe include greater use of probation for misdemeanants. For those with jail sentences they recommend work release, halfway houses, and the introduction of vocational training and even of paid employment for jail prisoners, linked with post-release employment. Methods of organizing such enterprises and systems for administering them are discussed in detail by these practical and experienced authors.

A more detailed survey of special community programs that provide alternatives to institutionalization is presented in the *Task Force Report: Corrections,* issued by the President's Commission on Law Enforcement and Administration of Justice. Their numerous specific examples, con-

383

ceivably relevant to every type of correctional institution, include guided group interaction programs, prerelease guidance centers, intensive community treatment operations, parole from the institution reception center, and residential treatment programs operated in family-type apartments or houses in the community.

Ultimately, the extension of correctional institutions into the community means not only the provision of government services outside traditional institutions, but the involvement of non-criminal community residents in correctional programs, wherever these programs may be located. Vincent O'Leary of the School of Criminal Justice of the State University of New York at Albany, whose career includes direction of parole services for the states of Washington and Texas, and directing training and research in correctional innovation on a nationwide basis, outlines four directions for such citizen involvement: (1) working directly in service to offenders; (2) recruiting public support for correctional programs; (3) expanding opportunities for correctional clientele in economic and other institutions of the community; (4) providing intimate friendship and social support for offenders released into the community. The different types of citizen that must be recruited and the problems to be anticipated in each of these four types of citizen enterprise are discussed in detail.

In concluding this section, Daniel Glaser presents his vision of the prison of the future. With the goals of evoking in offenders identification with non-criminal persons in the community, and enhancing their prospects of success in legitimate pursuits, he calls for prisons that are small, diverse, and located in the communities from which their inmates come. These should give inmates paid employment related to post-release job opportunities, and be linked with rehabilitation organizations in the community. They should strategically mix diverse types of inmates, and be informal in staff-inmate relationships. That this vision is not unrealistically utopian is evident, since the preceding articles in this part of the book describe forerunners of such ideal prisons in various types of institution-community fusing enterprises, already in existence.

26 *New Roles for Jails*

MARK S. RICHMOND AND
GEORGE W. ADERHOLD*

CURRENT CONCEPTS OF CORRECTIONS

The conceptual framework of correctional practice has undergone many changes over the years. Of the many principles and theoretical considerations from which traditional programs and services are being reexamined and upon which new approaches are being made, the following have particular significance for the local institution:

• "The general underlying premise for new directions in corrections is that crime and delinquency are symptoms of failures and disorganization of the community as well as of individual offenders. . . . . The task of corrections therefore includes building or rebuilding solid ties between offender and community, integrating or reintegrating the offender into community life . . . . This requires not only efforts directed toward changing the individual offender, which has been almost the exclusive focus of rehabilitation, but also mobilization and change of the community and its institutions . . . . "[1]

• The focus of corrections is intervention in delinquent and criminal careers, through management and control of crises and programs designed to overcome handicapping deficiencies.

• The deeper an offender has to be plunged into correctional processes and the longer he has to be locked up, however humanely, the greater the

* From *New Roles for Jails*, U.S. Bureau of Prisons (Washington, D.C.: Department of Justice, June 1969), pp. 1–26.

385

cost and the more difficult the road back to the point of socialization that will permit successful reintegration in the community.

• A person's needs for control or for help are not necessarily related to his legal status.

These principles are being applied in various ways, both at pre-trial stages and after conviction. The following innovations could have great impact on the operation of local community correctional centers.

PRETRIAL PROGRAMS

Early Diversion

One idea—scarcely tried—having great promise for the future is the diversion of certain types of medical and social problems out of the correctional system. Recent court decisions that alcoholism is a disease, not a crime, will cause a major reduction of jail commitments. It is estimated that at least one-half of all misdemeanant arrests are for drunkeness or offenses related to the use of alcohol. A diversion system could keep off criminal court calendars and out of jails drug users, homeless men and other socially incompetent people whose offenses hurt themselves but not society. Other lesser offenders could be diverted from prosecution by voluntarily accepting help before trial in programs similar to the Manhattan Employment Project now being conducted on an experimental basis by the VERA Institute of Justice in New York.

Pretrial Liberty

It has been pointed out repeatedly that the system which permits accused persons with money to be free awaiting trial while those without resources have to stay in jail is one of the great blots on our notions of equal justice. Every accused person, rich or poor, is presumed to be innocent until proven guilty. Legally, the only assurance that properly can be demanded of an accused person is that he will be present for trial.

Experiments a few years ago, also by the VERA Institute, established that persons with solid community ties through job, family and friends can give their promises to appear in court without bond and can be expected to answer when their cases are called. In fact, experience to date suggests that fewer persons who are released on their own recognizance abscond than those on regular bail. The information needed to allow a judge to decide whether to trust a defendant's word can be collected and verified by relatively untrained interviewers in a matter of hours. Release on recognizance is coming into wide use and favor across the nation.

In a number of jurisdictions experiments are underway to extend further the scope of pretrial liberty through selective use of summons in place of arrest for certain offenses. To the accused this could mean complete avoidance of the question of bail, elimination of the waiting period before arraignment for this determination to be made and freedom from the stigma of arrest if acquitted.

Experiments are being made also with "partial" detention for selected persons. Essentially, this is a procedure which permits the accused to work at his regular job but requires his confinement in jail during non-working hours, at night or during weekends.

Services to the Pretrial Defendant

Just as it would be the purpose of an intake unit to screen out of the criminal justice system those persons whose problems of management and control can be met adequately without court intervention, so those who are admitted to the criminal justice system may have similar needs. From preliminary surveys, it is apparent that these tend to cluster in the following areas: family problems, occupational problems, legal problems and medical or psychiatric problems.

It has long been evident that a program could be provided which encompasses a range of services extending from arrest, through trial and sentencing. The design of such a program may take various forms and it will require the support and cooperation of many community agencies and services to bring it into being.

POST-CONVICTION PROCEDURES

Probably the greatest impact on jails and their operations are coming from the introduction of non-traditional post-conviction procedures. From time immemorial a fine or a sentence to jail have been the principal dispositions for the lesser offender. In the vernacular, these have been called "30 days or 30 dollars." As a matter of fact, it often makes very little difference which the court selects, since a large proportion of defendants have no money for a fine and go to jail anyway.

Greater Use of Probation

Strangely enough, probation, which is used in more than 50% of all convictions throughout the United States, is used very little in misdemeanant courts. In some of the larger misdemeanant jurisdictions probation is used in less than 2% of all dispositions. The reason for this seems to be that judges want a presentence report before imposing probation and the conventional presentence investigation requires more time and trained personnel than the lower courts have.

The idea has now been advanced that the procedures first used by VERA to select good risks for release on recognizance can be adapted to selecting good risks for probation. Intelligent high school graduates and college undergraduates can be taught how to utilize specially devised interview forms and to conduct verifications of a few significant items that will enable recommendations to reach the court within a day. Coupling this kind of procedure with the utilization of selected volunteers in providing probation supervision (already demonstrated in a few jurisdictions) could increase the number of misdemeanants placed on probation and result in a corresponding decrease in jail commitments.

Extending the Limits of Confinement

Increasing numbers of jurisdictions are passing enabling legislation that have the effect of extending the limits of confinement from traditional jails and prisons. Legislation of this kind permits the development of work release or work-furlough programs. While most such programs are work oriented, a number of correctional agencies are able to utilize "work release" provisions of the statutes to include the education and vocational training of selected prisoners in the community. In some jurisdictions the law permits the granting of furloughs or unescorted trips outside the institution for such specific purposes as visiting a dying relative, attending the funeral of a relative, obtaining needed medical services not otherwise available or personally contacting prospective employers.

"Halfway Houses" represent another variation of the principle of extending the limits of traditional confinement. Recognizing that the real opportunities for successful reintegration of offenders lie in the community, some offenders need correctional experiences which can provide: (a) motivation for acquiring a conventional role in a non-delinquent setting; (b) realistic opportunities for testing this role; and (c) rewarding experiences which will tie them to the new role. Community residential centers in which carefully conceived programs are skillfully administered are in a unique position to meet a particular range of correctional needs.

Changes such as the foregoing do not mean that local jails eventually will be going out of business. Quite the contrary. Jails are needed not only for the safekeeping of those who require it but as community correctional centers with capabilities of providing a broader range of services.

For example, while probation departments will continue to bear major responsibility for giving the courts information about offenders, there are many cases in which this information should be augmented by more detailed study and observation than probation departments can conduct. In such cases the local institution can serve as a diagnostic and classification center—mobilizing from the community the professional and technical services required.

The local institution could marshal the medical resources that would enable it to give supporting services to alcoholic detoxification centers.

Educational and vocational training resources can be tapped for the development of in-house programs, where these are necessary, or to which selected prisoners may be given access under "study release" procedures.

In one state it has been proposed that felons convicted of property offenses who may be candidates for an early parole be sent back to the jail in their own community to serve their sentences in a setting that will acquaint them with the situations they will face when released. This rationale need not be limited to property offenders.

These trends and future possibilities will have an obvious bearing on the planning of new local facilities. Clearly, it is not enough to determine that the rate of population increase in a given community has been so much over the last ten years, and, therefore, so many more jail cells will be needed over the next ten years.

The changes sketched here do suggest that there is a new promise that the jail can be transformed into a significant contributor in the continuum of correctional services. In the past, as the Corrections Task Force of the President's Crime Commission has pointed out, change has been inhibited by two considerations; the first has been a feeling of futility about the investment of resources in the correction of the misdemeanant. The minor offender, it has been argued, has such a short sentence that little can be accomplished in the time available. A second problem has been the cost of services. . . .

There are an increasing number of non-correctional resources in most communities which can and should be mobilized in the effort to create a broad-gauged program for the reintegration of the misdemeanant into the community. The exploitation of these services and resources substantially eliminates the need for large outlays for new and independent services within the jail. Planners who make a careful analysis of the possible contributions of the community mental health services; the local employment placement services; the vocational rehabilitation agency; the public education system; the department of public health; the welfare department as well as the range of private voluntary agencies will uncover many resources which can appropriately be applied. The assessment of resources should not overlook the possible direct involvement of business and industry in providing training opportunities, both within the institution and in the community—especially when such training is short-term and will contribute directly to the solution of significant labor shortages. For example, in one community, a manufacturer of electronic equipment faced a critical need for workers trained in electro-soldering. In cooperation with institutional officials, a plan was worked out for the industry to establish a training unit within the institution. The costs both of the necessary equipment and the training personnel were borne by the industry, and the trainees, after a reasonably short period of instruction, were placed on work-release jobs in the community and eventually on full-time jobs in the industry in which they were trained.

Admittedly the conversion of the jail into an effective local correctional center cannot be accomplished without some cost to the taxpayer, but until such a reorientation of the jail is accomplished, it will continue to function as a human warehouse. In the long run, strengthening the capacity of the local correctional center should result in real cost savings as well as a reduction in crime. . . .

Programs and Services in the Community

From the discussions of preceding pages, it is clear that very few correctional agencies can realistically aspire to all of the resources that would be needed to conduct a broad range of programs and services. By now, it should be equally clear that such an attempt should be avoided where possible.

To illustrate: what would be involved in a proposal to provide complete diagnostic services to the courts as well as for classification purposes in scheduling correctional treatment programs? If these services were to be performed at a jail or correctional center, a few rooms set aside for interviews, tests and examinations are the least that would be required. Depending upon the range of functions to be performed on site and the numbers of people to be processed the needs might be much greater, such as space for supporting clerical services, a waiting room, a staff conference room, even an infirmary. The variables from which planning choices will have to be made are: (a) what functions for what numbers of people can be performed on an "out-patient" basis and what functions under what conditions must be performed on an "in-patient" basis; (b) among both "in-patient" and "out-patient" groups, what services must be provided on site and what can be provided in other facilities; (c) what services can be provided by resident staff and what will be needed from other sources.

For example, a program plan might be as follows: (1) the local jail will draw upon city medical services for unusual diagnostic problems, major surgical procedures and in-patient care and treatment of serious mental illness; (2) the clinical services provided at the jail will be available, as needed, to all persons committed; (3) diagnostic services may be extended on an out-patient basis to selected sentenced prisoners, probationers and parolees, as well as to pre-sentenced persons. (Persons requiring in-patient care, whether at the jail infirmary or elsewhere, usually are those who are self-destructive, physically ill, medically unstabilized—such as a diabetic—or in need of psychiatric study under controlled conditions.)

Depending upon local circumstances, professional staff may be recruited on a part-time basis or special services may be purchased, as needed, under contract from local professional resources. Another agency may provide diagnostic and treatment teams as an extension of its own program. In Massachusetts, for example, the Department of Mental Health has a Division of Legal Medicine which provides diagnostic and clinical services to the courts and correctional agencies both on an in-patient and out-patient basis.

It may not be necessary that clinical facilities, such as described in the example above, be a part of the local institution. In some jurisdictions, the services needed may be provided by a local hospital, an existing mental health clinic, or some combination of community services offered by other agencies. In Massachusetts, court clinics function effectively when attached to probation departments. Limited office space is furnished in the court buildings and referrals to special facilities are made as needed. In several jurisdictions, after care programs include clinical services which may consist of no more than conveniently located office space for professional staff who have access to the special facilities that may be needed.

ADMINISTRATION AND MANAGEMENT

In the national profile of corrections, nine service organizations are identified: juvenile detention, juvenile probation, juvenile institutions, juvenile aftercare, misdemeanant probation, adult probation, local adult institutions and jails, adult institutions and parole [2] The survey conducted for the President's Crime Commission found only one state (Alaska) in which all nine correctional services are organized into a single department. In two states, seven functions are administered by a single correctional agency. Conversely, in five states each juvenile institution is administered by a separate board and in three states this is the administrative pattern for each adult institution. Between these extremes, only six states have a single correctional agency that administers more than three of the nine functions.

In a number of states, correctional services are administered by departments that have other responsibilities such as welfare, mental health, hospitals and public safety. In all, there are 41 state departments whose primary function is not corrections but which administer several correctional services. This does not necessarily mean that the services are consolidated since seldom is more than one correctional service placed under one correctional administrator.

The situation with respect to the administration of local adult institutions and jails is infinitely more complicated. Only in Connecticut, Delaware and Rhode Island are they state-administered. In most jurisdictions, these institutions function autonomously and their relationships to other correctional institutions and programs, if not entirely remote, lack the kind of integration that would enable total coordinated correctional effort.

Local Administration

Typically jail management is the responsibility of elected local officials. Unlike schools, hospitals and mental health programs, where the need for competent, trained and full-time leadership has long been recognized, the administration of local correctional facilities is more often than not one of the many responsibilities of the sheriff. He in turn must rely upon subordinates who ordinarily have had no preparation for the management of a correctional facility. There is an obvious need for a better administrative framework of continuity if the development and management of realistic and practical jail programs is to be assured.

Beyond this, it is the exceptional jail that has or can acquire the necessary money, personnel and facilities with which to do a more effective job. The increasingly high costs of operating any correctional institution present nearly insurmountable problems for cities and counties whose authority to tax is limited. When coupled with lack of popular support that derives from common rejective attitudes toward offenders as a class agencies which deal with such persons are disadvantaged in the development of effective programs. In these circumstances personnel training and opportunities for a career in jail work continue to be the exception rather than the rule.

State Administration

The elusiveness of workable direct solutions to these problems has provided the rationale for several alternatives. As noted above, the alternative of state operation has appeared so far in only three states. While state administration has the theoretical advantage of drawing upon greater resources, standardizing operating procedures and consolidating supportive services, there is as yet no empirical evidence that greater effectiveness has been achieved. In two of the three states the experience is quite limited and no systematic effort has been made that would permit this kind of evaluation. Until very recently, in one state, the administration of jails has been separate and distinct from the administration of all other correctional institutions. Nowhere has the attempt yet been made to integrate fully all of the functions performed by state and local government agencies presently operating in the area of corrections.

A number of states have made the compromise of providing state inspection of local institutions and jails. Some state inspection laws require compliance with minimum standards relating to safety, security, health, sanitation and humane treatment. In other states the inspection service is advisory only. While states with enforcement authority may have the power to discontinue the operation of institutions that fail to meet minimum standards, the reality of political life insures that this rarely occurs.

Collaborative Administration

Various kinds of collaboration offer other choices. The "metro" form of government in which the administrative functions of a city and county merge is one. Instead of perpetuating the separate operation of "city" jails and "county" jails, these institutions are managed under a single authority. Increasing numbers of planning groups are considering the feasibility of regional institutions and jails that would provide essential services to a given geographic area regardless of city and county jurisdictional lines. Resistance to this idea comes from implicit threats to local authority. The arguments against this notion have a familiar ring. As with regional schools, questions are raised about the equitable sharing of costs, where ultimate authority will lie and problems of transportation.

Collaboration is also found in the form of subsidy. This may be in the nature of personnel training which a state provides local staff. It may be in furnishing technical assistance for planning and program development. It may appear in the form of direct programs and services provided by other agencies. Increasing use is being made of contractual arrangements between correctional agencies under which specific local services are purchased. An example of this is seen in plans that are being formulated in one metropolitan area to provide broad-range correctional programs and services to all local offenders regardless of the court jurisdiction from which they come. Under this plan, the state and Federal governments will contract with the local correctional agency at daily per capita rates for the care and correctional treatment of the offenders for whom they are responsible.

It is quite likely that local or state planning groups can do little or nothing about solving immediate problems of political and jurisdictional limits that are imposed upon local correctional programs. However, from painstaking examination of the issues involved and from an understanding of the capabilities and mechanisms needed for the eventual delivery of comprehensive, coordinated correctional services, planners can provide a blueprint for the attainment of long-range goals. In so doing they will choose among alternatives and identify priorities with which intermediate and compatible steps can be taken.

ISSUES IN FACILITIES DESIGN

At some stage in planning a new facility the architect is brought in. Generally, the earlier this can occur the better. It will be the architect's eventual responsibility to produce the design of the facility and to develop the construction plans and specifications. Since these are produced from a program of architectural requirements that have been agreed upon by all parties concerned, the architect's early involvement—even as an observer—in the choices that are made among program alternatives will result in better functional design and reduce subsequent delays and costs of effecting changes that can be avoided.

Planners who have had little or no experience working with an architect should recognize that he is a planning specialist. It should be expected that, whether he may be experienced in designing correctional facilities, he will apply his knowledge and skills to the problems and needs at hand rather than rely on stereotypes of other structures. Since program planners and managers are not always as certain as they should be of the programs desired and the specific functions involved, the architect may find himself confronted with an information vacuum. To fill this vacuum, consciously or not, he may resort to stereotype design blocks or usurp the responsibilities of others for planning the programs for which the facility is to be built.

FACTORS IN RELATING FACILITIES TO FUNCTIONS

Location

From a program standpoint, the institution should be as close to the centers of business, industry, schools, medical facilities, welfare service agencies and the courts as circumstances permit and accessible to public transportation. Not only will this facilitate the use of such resources, but problems of staffing are simplified when there are not tiring or complicated daily trips to and from the job. For selected prisoners who are to participate in programs of work release, study release, clinical services or other community activities, transportation problems can contribute heavily to program failures.

The choice of location must also be based on economic and design considerations. Building sites in the inner city are scarce, expensive and affected by zoning ordinances. The separation of functions in a large or multi-programmed facility can be achieved by high rise adaptation in contrast to the lateral spread that is possible where land is more plentiful, as in out-lying areas. The initial capital outlay for an inner city facility undoubtedly would be substantially greater and it is likely that more compromises would have to be allowed in functional design. The construction costs of a facility in an outlying area could be substantially less but operating costs might be higher because of transportation and the additional man-days required for escort duty.

A systematic analysis of alternate sites should be made using modern tools of economic evaluation of different costs over varying time spreads.

Size

Not only have local institutions not functioned as integral parts of a larger correctional system, but in the correctional field, unlike others, there are no universally accepted standards for optimum size. The survey conducted for the President's Crime Commission recommended that "ideally, a homogeneous population of less than 100 (but not exceeding 200) offers the best milieu for treatment and maintenance."[3] The Crime Commission itself said that the model institution should be "relatively small." It has long been established that from a program standpoint the larger the institution population the more its members—both staff and inmates—lose their identity and individuality. Conversely, the per capita cost of operating a fully programmed institution that is too small would be prohibitive.

The size of a proposed institution can only be determined from estimates of the rate of commitment and the length of stay. The facts, figures and choice of alternatives that are used in arriving at estimates constitute the real problem for planners. The absence of firm hand-holds make this a most difficult and uncertain task. Moreover, it can be ancitipated that when expanded correctional resources are available, judges will be more prone to commit locally many who otherwise would be imprisoned in state facilities. This has happened in one populous county which acquired a well-staffed probation department, excellent mental health services, a good honor camp and a significant work release program in recent years. Despite the fact that between 8,000 and 9,000 people are processed through the local jail each year and at any given time about 1,500 adults are being supervised by the probation department, the local courts commit fewer than 50 persons annually to the state department of corrections.

Cells versus Dormitories

A basic question in correctional institution design is security for whom and for how many. This question usually arises first in connection with housing. Unfortunately, there are few guidelines and little concensus among correctional administrators as to what the ratio of cells to dormitory space should be. In part, this can be determined by the kind of institution that is proposed. Cells are especially advisable for institutions handling maximum security types of offenders, while open institutions and minimum security camps can have a high proportion of dormitory space. Since jails and detention centers confine people whose security and supervisory requirements are virtually unknown upon arrival, a fairly. high proportion of single cells or rooms is in order.

One of the factors which will have a strong influence upon the ratio of cells to dormitory space will be the extent to which the institution has staff to gather information essential for the classification of prisoners. When such basic data about offenders are available, the management of the population is facilitated and housing assignments can be made in the light of the security problems which individual or groups of offenders present.

To plan for them is not so simple. The construction costs of cells or rooms are considerably greater than dormitory space because they require more square footage, plumbing, wiring and fixtures. The door fronts, alone, of maximum security cells can cost as much as $1,000 each. The traditional over-emphasis on security has produced over-built institutions in which cells are costly to build and to maintain. The inflexibility of such institutions also limits the development and expansion of correctional programs.

Functional Grouping

It goes without saying that both in the interest of construction economy and operational efficiency the design should attempt to locate functions closely when there is a high incidence of activity relationship. To accomplish this, the specific functions that are involved in the various programs and services must be analyzed in terms of how they are performed, when, by whom and where. There are many examples of the difficult questions that must be decided.

Assume, for instance, that the admission procedure calls for a complete physical examination of each new prisoner, including a full chest X-ray. Should examining rooms and an X-ray machine be provided in the receiving section or, since these exist in the infirmary plan, should newly committed prisoners be taken to the infirmary for initial physical examinations? To provide these accommodations in the receiving section would mean additional space and the acquisition costs of duplicated equipment. To use infirmary facilities would require an excessive amount of traffic in an area which normally holds non-patient traffic to a minimum and might require additional staffing to provide escort service between the infirmary and the receiving section. If neither of these choices is acceptable, what are the possibilities of locating the infirmary and receiving section close together so that common functions between the two programs can be shared?

Again, assuming that casework services are to be provided, where should the offices be located? The function of interviewing prisoners might argue that offices or interview rooms be provided in those locations where most of the prisoners are: in the housing units, the infirmary and the receiving and discharge unit. But, does it matter that the space provided for interviewing is used only a few hours a day, possibly on certain days of the week and that much of the interviewing may be performed by non-resident staff or by females? Where should interviews be held with members of the family, lawyers and other non-prisoners? Casework services also involve much use of the telephone, dictation and transcription of correspondence and reports, use of official records and conferences with other members of the staff, as well as with representatives of outside agencies. The design problems of relating interdependent functions in a correctional institution are complicated by the need to reconcile factors of accessibility and security which may be incompatible.

Flexibility

The two most distinguishing characteristics of older prisons and jails are their massive structural security and lack of flexibility. Both are wasteful of scarce funds applied to excessive construction costs and higher than necessary operating expenses. The management of these institutions over many years has demonstrated that effective control of prisoners involves far more than total reliance on physical barriers. Not only are the types of prisoners and the purposes of their confinement undergoing constant change, but methods of dealing with them are continually changing as well. New techniques, programs and services present new requirements.

Security is obtained in many ways: by technological advances in communications, such as audio and visual monitoring systems; by more effective interpersonal relationships between staff and inmates; by better diagnosis and classification; by greater involvement of prisoners in goal-oriented correctional programs that are geared to achievement.

In theory, structural security can be achieved in either of two ways. Principle reliance can be placed on perimeter security, such as may be achieved by armed towers and sophisticated fence or wall alarm systems. With this design the compound area can be fairly open and permit great freedom of movement. Relatively little security is achieved by internal structures. Conversely, reliance can be placed on the structural security of the facility units themselves. This design intends a minimum of controlled movement between units and, therefore, less need for perimeter security. In this circumstance, inmate participation in program is generally limited to that which can occur within the respective units. But programs and services are so diverse and individual needs for supervision and control are so varied that neither of these designs, in their pure form, is appropriate for most institutions.

One of the more common ways of avoiding either extreme is to develop a design based on "zone control" which has both structural and operational implications. There are a number of activities in an institution which are 24-hour operations and which, therefore, require the greatest security and supervision. Included among these are the housing units, infirmary, control center and main lobby or front gate. Some activities, like food service, may operate from 12 to 16 hours a day. Others will operate from, say 8:00 am to 4:30 pm five days a week, while still others will occur for only three or four hours during the early evening. By grouping the facilities in accordance with the schedule of usage and by providing convenient access to them, portions of the institution not in use during intervals of time can be sectioned off.

Carrying this concept a step further, it will be seen that great flexibility can be assured certain sections of the institution by providing free-span areas in which partitions can be placed for various purposes. At minimum cost these can be relocated to meet changing program and operational needs. Distinctions will need to be made among the partitions as to their relative permanence and the particular purposes they serve, e.g., as sound barriers or to provide some degree of internal security. . . .

CONCLUSION

By now it is fully apparent that the problems and tasks of planning a Community Correctional Center are many and profound, but these are not all substantive. In these times, both from the standpoint of strategy and the usefulness of the planning effort, it can be argued that such a project should not be undertaken independently of the comprehensive criminal justice planning conducted under the Safe Streets and Omnibus Crime Control Act or of related planning projects sponsored by many other local, state and Federal agencies. However badly a new jail may be needed, it will never function effectively by itself.

Viewed in broader perspective, the local institution is but one component of corrections in the universe of criminal justice which also includes police, prosecution and the courts. In order to assess the feasibility of change, planning groups may find it useful to organize possible alternatives into three categories aimed at:

1. Improved operations within the criminal justice system.
2. Mobilization of resources outside the criminal justice system.
3. Increased equity in the administration of justice.

The first category includes more efficient procedures to promote faster flow of people through the system, methods of upgrading personnel, reorganization and new information systems and management methods. Although there are a number of obstacles inhibiting change in these areas, it is unlikely that these changes will achieve their intended objectives unless they are treated as parts of a larger approach toward organizational development and renewal. New procedures and tools require organizational change and change in the attitudes and skills of personnel utilizing them.

The other two categories call for new involvements outside the criminal justice system, but many outside resources already are inadequate to the tasks they are being asked to perform. Moreover, outside agencies tend to reject involvement with offenders because of the dangers, offender proneness to failure and the second-rate status of the criminal justice system. Effective collaboration with outside resources will require both that the organizations and individuals involved redefine "crime" in the context of their own functions and that the criminal justice system be given a visibility and place of central importance which, for the most part, it now lacks.

27 *Special Community Programs: Alternatives to Institutionalization*

THE PRESIDENT'S COMMISSION ON LAW ENFORCEMENT AND ADMINISTRATION OF JUSTICE*

In recent years a number of experimental community programs have been set up in various parts of the country, differing substantially in content and structure but all offering greater supervision and guidance than the traditional probation and parole programs. The new programs take many forms, ranging from the more familiar foster homes and group homes to halfway houses, "guided group interaction" programs, and intensive community treatment. As such, they offer a set of alternatives between regular probation supervision and incarceration, providing more guidance than probation services commonly offer without the various disruptive effects of total confinement. They also greatly enrich the alternatives available in parole supervision. The advent of these programs in the postwar decades and their recent growth in numbers and prominence are perhaps the most promising developments in corrections today.

These programs are by and large less costly, often far less costly, than incarceration in an institution. Evaluation has indicated that they are usually at least as effective in reducing recidivism and in some cases significantly more so. They therefore represent an important means for coping with the mounting volume of offenders that will be pouring into corrections in the next decade. Although population forecasts indicate that the number of adult criminals who will be incarcerated in the next 10 years will increase only slightly, the projections for juveniles on the basis

* From *Task Force Report: Corrections,* The President's Commission on Law Enforcement and Administration of Justice (Washington, D.C.: U S. Government Printing Office, 1967), pp. 38–44.

of present trends are alarming. As noted in chapter 4, it is estimated that by 1975 the number of juveniles who would be confined would increase by 70 percent; whereas in 1965, there were about 44,000 juveniles in State and Federal correctional institutions, by 1975 this number would reach about 74,000. Such an increase would place a burden on the correctional system that increased community programing could go far to alleviate.

Among the special community programs at least five types are important enough to warrant special discussion: guided group interaction programs; foster homes and group homes; prerelease guidance centers; intensive treatment programs; and reception center parole. These programs are reviewed here as examples of approaches that are capable of, and deserve, widespread application in a variety of modifications.

GUIDED GROUP INTERACTION PROGRAMS

Underlying one of the newer programs for treating the young delinquent in the community is the premise that juvenile delinquency is commonly a group experience and that therefore efforts to change delinquent behavior should focus primarily on a group like that within which the individual operates. A number of group counseling methods have been employed but the method called guided group interaction has been used most extensively in those programs which involved a research component.

The general strategy of guided group interaction calls for involving the offenders in frequent, prolonged, and intensive discussions of the behavior of individuals in the group and the motivations underlying it. Concentrating on participants' current experiences and problems, the approach attempts to develop a group "culture" that encourages those involved to assume responsibility for helping and controlling each other. The theory is that the offender-participants will be more responsive to the influence of their fellow offenders, their peers, than to the admonitions of staff, and less likely to succeed in hoodwinking and manipulating each other.

As the culture develops and the group begins to act responsibly, the group leader, a staff member, seeks to encourage a broader sharing of power between the offenders and the staff. At first, group decisions will be limited to routine matters, such as the schedule of the day, but over time they may extend to disciplinary measures against a group member or even to decisions concerning readiness for release from the program.

Highfields

The Highfields project in New Jersey was the pioneer effort in guided group interaction.[4] Initiated in 1950, it has been duplicated in communities and also in institutions and used with both juveniles and adults. Highfields limits its population to 20 boys aged 16 and 17, who are assigned directly to it from the juvenile court. Boys with former commitments to correctional schools are not accepted, nor are deeply disturbed or mentally retarded youths. The goal is to effect rehabilitation within 3 to 4 months, about half the average period of incarceration in the State training school.

The youths are housed in the old Lindbergh mansion. They work during the day at a mental institution immediately adjacent to their residence. In the evening they participate in the group counseling sessions. On Saturdays, they clean up the residence. Saturday afternoon is free, and Sunday is reserved for receiving visitors and going to religious services. Formal rules are few.

Early efforts to evaluate the effects of the project on recidivism, as compared with those of the State reformatory, are still the subject of academic dispute. However, it is clear that Highfields was at least as effective as the reformatory, perhaps more effective, and that it accomplished its results in a much shorter period of time at greatly reduced monthly costs.

Pinehills and Other Developments

Important variations on the Highfields project developed at Essexfields, also in New Jersey, and at Pinehills in Provo, Utah. As at Highfields, program content at Essexfields and Pinehills centered around gainful employment in the community, school, and daily group meetings. The most significant difference was that, in the Essexfields and Pinehills experiments, the offenders continued to live at home.

The regimen at both Essexfields and Pinehills was rigorous. At Pinehills, for example, all boys were employed by the city. They put in a full day's work on the city streets, on the golf course, in the cemetery, wherever they were needed. They were paid 50 cents an hour. During the late afternoon, after the day's work was finished, all boys returned to the program headquarters where they met in daily group sessions. About 7 p.m. they were free to return home. They were also free on Sundays.[5]

In the daily group sessions all group members, not just adult staff, were responsible for defining problems and finding solutions to them. By making the program operations to some extent the work of all involved, both offenders and staff, it was possible to make a better estimate of just how much responsibility for his own life a given offender could take.

The fact that these guided group interaction programs are located in the community means that the problems with which the group struggles are those that confront them daily in contacts with their families, friends, teachers, and employers. This is one great strength of a community program over an institutional program. The artificiality of institutional life is avoided, and concentration can be placed upon the issues with which every offender eventually has to deal.

The Pinehills experiment was one of the first to set up an experimental design by which to assess the effectiveness of the project. Offenders assigned to the program were compared with two control groups: One group which was placed on probation, and another which was committed to a training school. The initial design was such that all three groups could be drawn randomly from a common population of persistent offenders living in the same county. Although there was some difficulty in exactly maintaining the research design, the data appear significant. The results, as measured in terms of recidivism, are shown in table 1.

TABLE 1
Effectiveness of Three Programs for Juvenile
Delinquents, Utah, 1964, as Measured
by Percentages of Releasees Not Arrested
Within 6 Months of Release

Program	Percentage of releasees not arrested within 6 months	
	All boys assigned to program	*All boys completing program*
Pinehills (experimental)	73	84
Probation (controls)	73	77
State school (controls)	42	42

Other variations of guided group interaction projects have been developed in the Parkland project in Louisville, Ky., in the GUIDE (Girls Unit for Intensive Daytime Education) program in Richmond, Calif., and in another girls' program in San Mateo, Calif. All three of these projects entail the daily gathering of the group in a center for participation in a combination of educational activities, craft projects, center development and beautification, and group and individual counseling. The Parkland project took its name from its location in two portable classrooms on the grounds of the Parkland Junior High School. In addition to morning classes in the school, the program entails afternoon work in and about the Louisville Zoo and terminates with group counseling sessions and dinner.

Contributions of Guided Group Programs

These projects, like Highfields, represent an authentic departure from traditional community programs for delinquents. The Highfields type of program is unique in that the group process itself shapes the culture and social system of the total program. The key element seems to be the amount of decision-making authority permitted the group, which has considerably more authority to decide than in traditional group therapy programs. J. Robert Weber, who made a study of promising programs for delinquents, said of the Highfields type of program:

> If one asks a youth in most conventional institutions, "How do you get out?" one invariably hears some version of, "Be good. Do what you are told. Behave yourself." If one asks a youth in a group treatment program, "How do you get out?" one hears, "I have to help myself with my problems," or "When my group thinks I have been helped." This implies a basic difference in the social system of the organization, including staff roles and functions.[6]

In the large institution, Weber concluded, the youth perceives getting out in terms of the problem of meeting the institutional need for conformity. In the group treatment program the youth sees getting out in terms of his solution to his own problems, or how that is perceived by other youths in the group

FOSTER HOMES AND GROUP HOMES

Foster-home placement has long been one of the most commonly used alternatives to institutionalization for juvenile probationers. The National Survey of Corrections reported that 42 percent of the 233 probation departments surveyed utilized this resource. A sizeable proportion of juvenile aftercare programs also make foster placements a routine part of their work.

The utilization of foster homes or group homes in lieu of institutional confinement has several obvious advantages, provided the offender does not require the controls of an institution. Such placements keep the offender in the community where he must eventually work out his future. They carry less stigma and less sense of criminal identity, and they are far less expensive than incarceration.

Weber reported in 1966:

> Discussions with State administrators would seem to indicate that foster care is in an eclipse. Reception center staffs report disillusionment with foster care for delinquents. Yet a look at actual placement practices of the State agencies and local courts indicates an unabated use of foster care.[7]

The opinions encountered by Weber may be a reflection of the long and controversial history of foster-home placement for delinquents. The decision to sever family ties, even temporarily, is a hard one to make for the youth who might otherwise be placed on probation at home. And more difficult juveniles who might be sent to institutions are often beyond the capacity of the usual foster home to manage. It is obvious, however, that many delinquent youngsters come from badly deteriorated family situations and that such conditions are significant, perhaps critical, factors in generating delinquent behavior. When the delinquency-inducing impact of a slum neighborhood is added to a destructive family setting, placement of the delinquent away from home becomes increasingly necessary.

A number of States have begun to develop group homes as a variant to traditional foster-home care for youths who need a somewhat more institutional setting or cannot adjust to family life. The Youth Commission of Minnesota, for example, reported using seven group homes under arrangements with the home operator or with an intermediate agency. A nominal retaining fee was paid for each bed licensed; and, when a youth actually was placed in the home, the rate of pay was increased.[8]

The Wisconsin Division of Corrections in 1966 was operating an even more ambitious program. Thirty-three homes for boys or girls were in use under a payment plan similar to that employed in Minnesota. With four to eight adolescents in each home, the total population handled was equivalent to that of at least one institution, but operating costs were one-third to one-fourth less.[9]

In both States the adolescents placed in group homes were those who had been received on court commitment as candidates for institutional placement. In Wisconsin, approximately one-fourth of the group had been released from institutions for placement in a foster home. Other jurisdictions are experimenting with the group-home technique. Michigan, for example, reported a plan to use larger homes operated by State employees for parolees from their institutions.[10]

There is some doubt about the wisdom of committing offenders to State agencies for placement in foster homes or group homes, when this function could as readily be performed by the courts through associated probation and welfare services. It is far less expensive for a local court to commit a youth to the State, even though that commitment entails some additional stigmatization, than to undertake the development and operation of local resources of the same kind. This problem derives from the fragmented administrative structure of American corrections, and could be overcome by a carefully planned program of subsidies from State to local governments. Such a plan was developed in California in 1965. Under its terms subsidies are given to those county probation departments which are successful in reducing commitments to State institutions by the development of improved community-based programs.

HALFWAY PROGRAMS: THE PRERELEASE GUIDANCE CENTER

In corrections as in related fields, the "halfway house" is an increasingly familiar program. Initially, such programs were conceived for offenders "halfway out" of institutions, as a means of easing the stresses involved in transition from rigid control to freedom in the community. The prerelease guidance centers of the Federal Bureau of Prisons are the best-known halfway-out programs in the United States. Recently the halfway house has come to be viewed as a potential alternative to institutionalization, and thus a program for those "half-way in" between probation and institutional control.

Federal Prerelease Guidance Centers

The first prerelease guidance centers of the Federal Bureau of Prisons were opened in 1961 in New York, Chicago, and Los Angeles, and others were established subsequently in Detroit, Washington, and Kansas City. Each center accommodates about 20 Federal prisoners who are transferred to it several months before their expected parole date. Thus they complete their terms in the community but under careful control.

Some of the centers are located in what were large, single-family houses; some occupy a small section or scattered rooms in a YMCA hotel; and one is located in a building once operated as a small home for needy boys. All are in neighborhoods with mixed land usage, racial integration, and nearby transportation.

Offenders transferred to these centers wear civilian clothes. They generally move from prison to the centers by public transportation without escort. For a day or two they are restricted to the building, although they may receive visitors there. In the YMCA's they eat in a public cafeteria in the building and use the public recreation areas, taking out YMCA memberships. Following a day or two of orientation and counseling, they go out to look for jobs. After they are on a job, they are gradually given more extensive leaves for recreational purposes and for visits with their families. As their parole date approaches, some may even be permitted to move out of the center, although they are still required to return to the center for conferences several times a week.

These centers are staffed in large part by persons rotated from regular institution staff who are highly oriented to counseling. One full-time employee is an employment counseling specialist. Several others, such as college students in the behavioral sciences, are employed on a part-time basis and provide the only staff coverage during the late night hours and part of the weekend. In addition to individual counseling, there are several group sessions a week. Federal probation officers, who will supervise the offenders when they go on parole, participate in the center's counseling activities. By the time a resident is ready to begin his parole, almost all of his individual counseling has been assumed by his parole supervision officer.

A major function of these temporary release programs has been to augment the information available to correctional staff. This information includes both diagnostic data on the individuals temporarily released and information on the assets and deficiencies of correctional programs and personnel. In addition, they provide optimum circumstances for counseling, since the counseling can deal with immediate realities as they are encountered, rather than with the abstract and hypothetical visions of the past and the future or the purely institutional problems to which counseling in institutions is largely restricted.

Inmate misbehavior while on work release or in prerelease guidance centers is not a rare thing, particularly for youthful offenders. Although a majority adjust quite satisfactorily, some get drunk, some get involved in fights and auto accidents when out with old or new friends, and some are late in returning to the center. An appreciable number of the youth have difficulty in holding jobs, some fail to go to work or to school when they are supposed to be there, a few abscond, and a few get involved in further crime. The important point is that they would be doing these things in any case, and probably more extensively, if they had been released more completely on their own through parole or discharge. Under the latter circumstances, however, correctional staff would know of the releasee's difficulties, if at all, not nearly so promptly as is possible with temporary release measures.

When an individual returns from a temporary release to home, work, or school, his experience can be discussed with him by staff, to try to assess his probable adjustment and to note incipient problems. Many difficulties can be anticipated in this way. The inmate's anxieties can be relieved by discussion, and discussion may also help him develop realistic plans for coping with prospective problems. When persistent or serious misbehavior occurs, sanctions are available to staff, ranging from restriction of further leaves or temporary incarceration to renewed institutionalization, with a recommendation to the parole board that the date of parole be deferred.

A number of offenders on work release, live in prerelease guidance centers. Some of them attend school part- or full-time, in addition to or instead of working; this sometimes is called "study release." It is particularly appropriate for juvenile and youthful offenders and is highly developed at several State establishments resembling the Federal prerelease guidance centers.

State Prerelease Centers

The Kentucky Department of Corrections, under a grant from the Office of Economic Opportunity, has a series of vocational training courses in its State reformatory which are identical with courses established at several centers in the State under the Department of Labor. Prerelease guidance centers were established near these centers in three cities, so that reformatory inmates could continue their institution courses in the community, where as trainees they receive a small stipend, in addition to highly developed job placement services.

The Federal Bureau of Prisons assisted in establishing these centers and sends Federal inmates from these cities to the centers. Conversely, State correctional agencies share in the operation of the Federal prerelease guidance centers in Detroit and Kansas City, assigning some State inmates there, and the District of Columbia Department of Corrections plays a major role in the operation of the center in Washington. This State-Federal collaboration could well serve as a model for many types of correctional undertaking.

INTENSIVE COMMUNITY TREATMENT

Perhaps the best known of the country's efforts at controlled experimentation in the correctional field is the California Youth Authority's Community Treatment Project, now in its sixth year. Operating within a rigorous evaluative design, it offers an excellent illustration of the profitable partnership which can develop when carefully devised program innovations are combined with sound research.

The subjects of the project consist of boys and girls committed to the Youth Authority from two adjacent counties, Sacramento and San Joaquin. While under study in a reception center, each new group is subjected to a screening process which excludes some 25 percent of the boys and 5 to 10 percent of the girls because of the serious nature of their offenses, the presence of mental abnormality, or strenuous community objections to their direct release. The remaining youngsters are then either assigned randomly to the community project—in which case they form part of the experimental group—or are channeled routinely into an institution and eventually paroled.

An interview by a member of the research staff provides the basis for classification of the offender subgroups. This categorization is made in terms of the maturity of the youth, as reflected in his relationships with others, in the manner in which he perceives the world, and in the way he goes about gaining satisfaction of his needs. A variety of standardized tests seeks to measure the extent of his identification with delinquent values as well as his general personality characteristics.

The program provided for the experimental group offers singly or in combination most of the techniques of treatment and control which are in use in corrections today: individual counseling, group counseling, group therapy, family therapy, involvement in various other group activities, and school tutoring services by a certificated teacher with long experience in working with delinquents. The goal is to develop a treatment plan which is tailored to the needs of each type of offender. The resulting plan is then implemented at a level of high intensity, made possible by the availability of carefully selected and experienced staff on a ratio of 1 staff member for each 12 youths.

A program center serves as the hub of activity; it houses the staff and provides a recreation area, classrooms, and a musicroom. A limited outdoor sports activities area also is available. In the late afternoon and some evenings, the center resembles a small settlement house operation as the wards come in after school for counseling, tutoring, and recreational activity.

An unusual and controversial feature of the experiment is the frequent use of short-term detention at the agency's reception center to assure compliance with program requirements and to "set limits" on the behavior of the participants. The detention may vary from a few hours to a few days.

Results have been measured in several ways. A repetition of the psychological test battery seeks to determine what movement has occurred in the socialization of the individual offender. The responses of the various categories of youth have revealed greater success with some than with others, and may eventually provide a more reliable indicator of who should be institutionalized. Finally, the "failure rate," as measured by the proportion who are later institutionalized because they have committed additional offenses, is carefully compared with similar information on members of the control group who have been institutionalized and then returned to the community under regular parole supervision.

The latest report of the project activity available to the Commission revealed that checks of parolees, at the end of 15 months of parole exposure, showed that 28 percent of the experimental group had been subject to revocation of parole, as compared to 52 percent of the control group which was afforded regular institution and parole handling.[11]

After several years of pilot work, the California Youth Authority decided in 1964 to extend the community treatment format to the Watts area of Los Angeles and to a neighborhood in west Oakland. Both are high-delinquency areas; both are heavily Negro in population. Essentially duplications of the original experiment, the two new program units do not have a research component. Instead of random assignment of the subject, the youths committed from a given area are screened by project staff for direct release from the reception center.

In the absence of a control group, the success of the program has been measured by comparing the failure rate of the youth assigned to it with equivalent statewide rates for youths of the same middle to older adolescent age range. At the end of 15 months of parole exposure, 39 percent of project wards had been subject to parole revocation as compared to a statewide revocation rate of 48 percent for youths of the same age bracket.

The Los Angeles and Oakland adaptations of the original demonstration were initiated, in part, to alleviate acute population pressures in the institutions. With caseloads of 15 youths per officer, the $150 per month cost per boy is three to four times as much as that of regular parole. But it is less than half the average monthly cost of institutionalizing an offender. These experiments are now handling a group that is larger than the capacity of one of the new institutions that the Youth Authority is building. Thus they obviate the investment of $6 to $8 million.[12]

RECEPTION CENTER PAROLE AND SHORT-TERM TREATMENT PROGRAMS

Diagnostic parole is a program whereby all commitments from the juvenile court are referred to a reception center where they can be screened for eligibility for parole, either immediately or after a short period of treatment. This program has reached significant proportions in an increasing number of States.

While most State systems have long had some informal arrangements for returning a few cases to the community at an early date, more organized procedures developed almost simultaneously in New York, Washington, Kentucky, and California in the early 1960's. These programs were conceived in part as a response to acute population pressures in overcrowded institutions. The seemingly successful results have led to a substantial increase in the volume of cases diverted from the training school to short, intensive treatment programs followed by parole in the community.

In New York the screening is undertaken by special aftercare staff while the youngsters are in New York City's Youth House awaiting delivery to the State school system. The youths selected to return to the community are those who are thought to be amenable to conventional casework procedures. Those selected are placed in an intensive casework program. The apparent success of the original unit in New York City has led to an expansion of the program and to the practice of returning still other youngsters to the community after the intake studies carried on in the State schools.

Washington, another State with a central reception center for juvenile offenders, is also screening those committed. A significant percentage of cases are assigned to immediate placement in foster homes or other community-based programs, including four halfway houses.

The California Youth Authority apparently is making the greatest use of the reception center release procedure. Currently some 20 percent of the boys and 35 percent of the girls processed are being released to regular parole or to foster-home placement at the termination of reception period. This is typically a month long, but in some instances release may be postponed for another 30 to 90 days.[13]

The California Youth Authority's Marshall Program represents an interesting variation in the practices discussed above. The program was initiated 3 years ago as a device for easing population pressures in the institutions. It provides for the selection of cases by the clinical staff and the project director for a 3-month intensive treatment program at the reception center at Norwalk.

Based on "therapeutic community" concepts, the project involves the youths in a half-day work program in institution operation and maintenance, some specialized education classes, and daily group counseling. Active participation is rewarded by progressively longer and more frequent home furloughs. Parents provide the transportation, and furloughs are scheduled so that parents can participate in group counseling activities as they return their sons to the center. Parental involvement is seen as a significant program component.

While the performance of the project graduates has not been subjected to comparison with a control group, agency research staff have sought to match the subjects with youths possessed of the same characteristics who have been processed through the regular institution programs. With 15 months of parole exposure time, 44 percent of the Marshall youths, as against 47 percent of the matched group, were subject to parole revocation. Moreover, the relatively short program period of 3 months, as compared against the average stay of 8 to 9 months in the State schools, means a significant saving of public funds.[14]

The success of reception center parole has been encouraging. Other States will undoubtedly develop reception centers that feature sophisticated screening techniques and intensive treatment for those offenders who are deemed most susceptible. To date, parole from reception centers has been confined to the juvenile field. However, there is no inherent reason why this approach should not be taken with adults, and hopefully it will be so used in the near future.

PROSPECTS FOR DEVELOPING ALTERNATIVE PROGRAMS

This chapter has described some of the most promising programs in the correctional field. Unfortunately, however, only a few correctional agencies are developing any of them. The great bulk of correctional programs in this country today still consists of either traditional supervision in the community under probation or parole or confinement in institutions. And further, the newer alternatives to institutionalization are not even known to many correctional personnel.

Comprehensive Programing

Such programs can be developed with effective leadership. The State of New York, for example, has established a particularly comprehensive set of programs as alternatives to incarceration of juveniles.[15] The Division for Youth was launched initially as an agency for dispersing funds to local jurisdictions for general delinquency-prevention and character-building programs. In 1962 it initiated an imaginative effort to modify the conventional probation-incarceration sequence. Operating as an independent entity in State government, it has provided a series of community programs for youthful offenders who might otherwise have been committed to either State training schools or the prison system. Approximately three-fourths of its intake comes through referrals or commitments from the juvenile and criminal courts. The others are referred from other agencies or come in on their own initiative.

The agency has developed three distinct program forms. For the more sophisticated delinquent there are a number of installations that replicate the Highfields model. Work during the day at some State facility is followed by daily group counseling sessions in a nearby residence that houses 20 to 25 older adolescents. Other program elements are minimal and are left largely to the residents' ingenuity. For the more immature and dependent youngster, a small forestry camp operation provides a combination of work, academic instruction, and group counseling.

Finally, for the youth who is not too committed to delinquency and who possesses some stability and maturity, there are residential centers in the cities of the State. These take two organizational forms. The earlier projects were located in houses that would accommodate 20 to 25 youths. Recently the division has experimented with the use of large apartments in conventional apartment houses. The pattern calls for a cluster of three units, each housing seven or eight wards and house parents. A program director supervises and divides his time among the three operations. The organized program is minimal, although the group counseling pattern prevails on a daily basis. Primarily, jobs or schooling are sought within the communities adjacent to the centers.

The Division for Youth is providing some postrelease supervision, although it would not be described as a strong aspect of this innovative effort. An interesting feature is the employment of graduates of the program in modified staff roles in both the residential and postrelease phases of the operation.

The division's research arm, only recently organized, is attempting some objective evaluation of operational effectiveness. An analysis of the postrelease performance of all youthful graduates after 7$^1/_2$ months of exposure to the community indicated that 13 percent had been convicted of further offenses, and only 8 percent reconfined. While the nature of this operation precludes the establishment of a control group and thus prevents the creation of a yardstick against which performance can be measured, the "failure" rate appears impressively low as compared with performance of typical State school releasees.

Problems to be Confronted

Extensive development of alternatives to institutions requires that several problems be solved, and solved simultaneously. First is the need to make administrators and legislators aware of these programs and thus create conditions favorable for developing them. Demonstration projects which duplicate successful alternatives to institutionalization will have to be set up in various parts of the country. Such a process would require changes in the funding policies of many Federal and private agencies, which usually will support only a new type of program and not a duplication of one already proved successful. Such duplication is essential if correctional personnel and citizens are to become aware of the potentials of alternatives to institutions.

A second major problem is the familiar one of manpower. Most of these programs require skills which many correctional personnel do not have. Several centers should be established at sites of successful programs of all kinds, to train workers in the skills involved. This proposal would have particular application to training personnel for the special community programs described here.

The variety among correctional administrative structures in the country makes it difficult to determine how the new community programs could best be administered. The limited history of the prototypes indicates that the State itself will have to play a major and continuing role in order to coordinate services.

In some jurisdictions, the State may well operate virtually all of the alternative programs; in others, only part of them. For example, it is anticipated that the State will usually operate community programs for parolees. For probationers the situation is different, since a number of counties will continue to operate probation services. Where the State does not operate all community programs, it should at least supply leadership and subsidies in order to promote their development.

Whatever the administrative arrangement, it is essential that all elements of corrections should be involved. Special community programs must be perceived by all parts of the correctional apparatus as legitimate and integral parts of the system. There is a great tendency for each part of the system to push forward with its own existing programs. For example, institutional managers are apt to urge new institutions rather than looking at the possibility of alternative programs. Failure to involve important elements of· the correctional community can jeopardize not only the creation of new community programs but the survival of those which prove successful. The Pinehills project in Provo, Utah, described earlier in this chapter as exciting both in its operation and in its research design, does not exist today. This project and other successful ones were not picked up by a correctional agency once the initial grant moneys were exhausted. It is clear that new community programs must be integrated into the main line of corrections if they are to succeed and survive.

It is also essential that representatives of allied service agencies, such as welfare and mental health, be involved in planning for community programs. Correctional foster-home placements, for example, are closely involved with such placements by welfare agencies, and consideration must be given to the needs of both systems. Many of the specialized community programs in corrections will lay demands on the same resources as mental health agencies. It is essential that corrections and the mental health field work out accommodations, so that there is a functional relationship.

Finally, one of the most critical problems in developing new community programs is to secure the involvement and participation of the community itself. Too often, promising programs such as halfway houses have failed simply because the community was not prepared to tolerate them. Thus it is essential that the public be brought into planning early and that correctional managers make intense efforts to insure citizen understanding and support.

28 Some Directions for Citizen Involvement in Corrections

VINCENT O'LEARY [*]

The notion that the citizen can play a vital role in corrections is as old as the field itself.[16] One only has to recall the tremendously significant part played by religious groups in American corrections or to review the programs of the John Howard Association, the Osborne Association, and prisoners' aid societies through the years.[17]

But even with these contributions, it is fair to say that corrections and its clientele were, and still are, largely isolated from the community. As the National Crime Commission recently said: "Corrections is not only hard to see; traditionally, society has been reluctant to look at it." [18] And the growth of a professional service in corrections may have actually heightened its isolation. Government programs, for example, virtually replaced the large number of citizens who provided supplementary or direct parole supervision in a considerable part of the United States prior to World War II. Desirable as this professionalization may have been, it resulted in a loss of intimate knowledge and sense of responsibility by persons outside the correctional establishment.

Since the latter part of the 1950's, there has been an emphasis on reversing these trends, on bringing the citizen more directly into correctional affairs. The President's Committee on Juvenile Delinquency and Youth Crime, particularly, was instrumental in pressing for the enlistment of citizen groups in delinquency-prevention activities. This emphasis sprang directly from that Committee's adoption, and relatively

* From *The Annals of the American Academy of Political and Social Science,* 381 (January 1969): 99–108. Reprinted by permission of author and publisher.

417

consistent application, of a theoretical position which contended that the essential task in delinquency-prevention and control was the reordering of society's opportunity system, particularly in education and employment. Though it actually gave little direct attention to the traditional correctional services—probation, parole, or institutions—the Committee's programs had a carry-over effect and accentuated their need for more citizen support.

This emphasis on citizen involvement has been paralleled by a growing willingness by citizens to make a personal commitment to correctional programs. Recently, the National Council on Crime and Delinquency (NCCD) embarked on a large-scale effort to enlist citizens in work on the problems of criminal justice. The response was substantial, with a significant number of persons indicating specific interests in correctional services. This experience has been repeated elsewhere by groups such as halfway-house associations.[19]

Despite the growing awareness of the need to build citizen interest, few correctional programs appear prepared to engage in utilizing citizens successfully. In a survey of the twenty largest states, NCCD's staff found only limited utilization of citizens in correctional programs. Apparently, many more of them could be enlisted in correctional enterprises than are now being used. Possible explanations of this disparity can be traced to the history of corrections and to the nature of its bureaucracy and its ideology. In each of these, powerful forces can be identified which militate against an intimate participation by citizens.

Even those correctional agencies which have successfully tempered these forces often find difficulty in mounting effective programs. Usually, the chief reason is a failure to allocate the staff and financial resources required to carry them out. Another important source of failure is the lack of recognition of the varied roles which citizens might play. Each role appeals to a different kind of person. Each rests on different assumptions about the function to be served. Each requires a specific strategy for recruitment and training, and for obtaining the maximum contribution of each person. Failure to recognize these differences almost inevitably produces, for citizens in the programs, low motivation, low productivity, and low continuance and, for the correctional managers, frustration and disillusionment. An examination of four key citizen roles in corrections will help to point up the differing attractions and requirements of each role. Such a review will also illustrate the forces in the correctional system which tends to support or oppose them.

The roles are not mutually exclusive; the same person could play several simultaneously. They are quite distinct, however, and require quite different behaviors on the part of corrections if they are to be successfully engaged.

THE CORRECTIONAL VOLUNTEER

The first and most common role for the citizen in corrections is as a volunteer willing to assume responsibility, more or less formalized, for working directly with offenders. In fact, an important source of the growing perceived need for increased citizen participation is the inability of corrections to provide the manpower needed for the level of services increasingly demanded of it. Organizations such as the United States Children's Bureau, as an illustration, have consistently pointed out a tremendous shortage of probation officers in the United States. The idea of citizens providing this service on a voluntary basis was an obvious response to this continuing problem. It was an idea which has been seized upon by several agencies.

One of the most outstanding programs of this kind is sponsored by the University of Colorado. College students and other citizens are enlisted to work as assistant probation officers and in a wide variety of other activities.[20] Another outstanding program is in the Municipal Court of Royal Oak, Michigan, where probation services are largely dependent upon a staff of volunteers. The program has been so successful, that it has been adopted by the Methodist Church, and large numbers of citizens are now being recruited for probation-officer duties in misdemeanant courts.[21]

Programs like these could be vastly expanded.[22] The National Crime Commission made a strong plea for employing more citizens to reduce correctional manpower shortages. It maintained that "current demonstrations of the vitality of the volunteer in corrections argue strongly that he can be a strong ally in correctional programming."[23] A task force of the Joint Commission on Correctional Manpower and Training is working to develop ways to remove obstacles to the use of volunteers. One explanation offered for the reluctance of corrections to use volunteers is the professional strivings within the field. The argument is made that nonprofessionals are seen as diminishing the status of an agency and are therefore resisted.[24]

Another explanation can be found in the way in which correctional organizations typically function. Like most public organizations, correctional agencies tend to develop patterns of behavior aimed at sustaining the agency which may have little relation to external program objectives.[25]

Alternative approaches to tasks tend to be evaluated by their efficiency in protecting the organization's welfare and minimizing the required expenditure of energy.

Such cross-currents must be understood if an agency is to use volunteers successfully. The introduction of volunteers can mean an expenditure of organizational energy on activities which may not "build the agency." The volunteer in corrections tends to be less sensitive to such needs and to make demands directed toward goals other than those of system-maintenance. Parole officers, for example, often will contend that they have great difficulty in dealing with volunteers because they "refuse to understand the necessity of observing the administrative regulations of the parole department and only think about the parolee."

Volunteer programs are too often encouraged in which the volunteer is actually granted little power or given tasks which largely tend to support latent organizational needs. Thus, volunteer programs ostensibly aimed at providing a needed service to inmates may do little more than foster institutional stability and harmony. Administrators can easily support volunteer activities such as these, but ultimately will pay the price in the quality of persons that they are able to attract. A higher order of administrative skill, and dedication to goals larger than the agency's welfare, are needed if creative and able volunteers are to be recruited and held.

The effective development of a volunteer program requires, foremost, a clear decision by correctional managers that they have an important function to serve in corrections. It requires a willingness to invest volunteers with the power to use their skills and resources. It requires a commitment of staff time and funds to develop an adequate program of recruitment, screening, training, and supervision. It requires training for all agency staff who will be expected to deal with volunteers.

THE SOCIAL PERSUADER

Another citizen-participant role is characterized by the person of influence in the dominant social system who is willing to persuade others to support corrections and its programs. This type of strength is especially valuable in bidding for legislative support. It is critical in mobilizing assistance to expand programs of community-based corrections. Opportunities for offenders are also dependent upon the extent to which corrections is able to enlist powerfully placed persuaders to intervene in the community's social structure.

The National Crime Commission made this type of citizen activity an important concern. It is recommended that regional planning and liaison councils be set up to consider the effectiveness of correctional apparatus in various areas, to review future plans and projects, and to make recommendations for change.[26] Public involvement is needed to shape workable programs; more important, it is needed if they are to be fostered and achieved.

A recent survey by the Harris Poll tellingly revealed how little public involvement there has been in correctional affairs and the resultant gap between its programs and public understanding of them.[27] Increased efforts toward public education may help to narrow the gap, but they cannot substitute for citizens who have a direct stake in an agency's program. A few correctional departments have developed citizen advisory boards; a few sponsor events such as an annual conference for community leaders; almost none have a systematic, formalized, and well-developed program of substantial involvement of key citizens.

This lack may be explained by several reasons—the traditional isolation of corrections, a lack of aggressive leadership, or an acute absence of resources. It could be argued that another factor of major significance has been the resistance of corrections to sharing power over its program with those outside the system. That sharing is the price which must be paid for the involvement of persons of influence.

There is little reason to expect that corrections will be exempt from a generalized reaction against governmental bureaucracy. There has been a significant change in the perception of the nature of government since the 1930's. Then, the predominant idea was to free its experts and to provide them with resources so that they could perform their task efficiently. There has been a growing disenchantment with this view. As Frank Remington points out, we now find a considerable effort to restrict the power of the government expert and to hold him much more accountable for his actions.[28]

This thrust toward a decentralization of governmental actions and power is becoming common cause for the liberal as well as the conservative.[29] Governmental agencies of all kinds are under increasing pressure for direct participation by citizens in shaping their policies. Corrections, too, must learn how to share responsibility with the citizen.

It may find this more difficult than do other agencies because of its long tradition of isolation and because of its authoritarian strain. The talented correctional administrator, however, will discover—and some have already discovered—the administrative techniques and the organizational models which permit direct participation by citizens. Most of all,

422 Fusion of Institutional and Community Programs

administrators will need to develop the habit of sharing information freely with citizens in the planning as well as the implementation stages of policy. At present, correctional administrators tend to share information only when a program is finally shaped and there is a need to sell it.

Perhaps the most dramatic effort aimed toward enlisting citizens to promote correctional change is the program of the National Council on Crime and Delinquency. Begun in 1954 with a grant from the Ford Foundation, its citizen-action program has grown until today there are citizen councils in twenty states. Typically, these programs have enlisted a relatively small group of persons with influence in a state. Each council is provided with a full-time consultant and the program resources of a national agency. From this base, a variety of programs has been developed.

Cause-and-effect claims are always perilous, but a conservative evaluation would indicate that the citizen-action programs of NCCD have been influential in bringing about change in the correctional programs of a number of states. In 1957, the work of an NCCD citizen group in Texas was pivotal in the development of a parole system for that state. More recently, a probation-subsidy bill was fostered by a similar group in California. In several other states, broad-scale revisions of entire correctional services were brought about because of citizen-action programs.

These programs primarily draw their strength from an appeal to a select group of persons of power in the community, rather than from a broad base of support. Persons of the desired status for service on state committees do not volunteer extensive amounts of time for direct services with clients. Instead, they prefer to work on problems in the context of their own social contacts. Above all, they require skillful and substantial staff assistance.

The success of these programs lies in their ability to enlist and maintain the interest of persons of influence. An NCCD staff member of considerable experience contends that the key to this depends upon the program being perceived by the citizen as: (1) important, (2) not achievable without his unique contribution, and (3) resulting in a visible payoff. These criteria may comprise a key to effectiveness for all types of citizen-action programs.

THE GATEKEEPERS OF OPPORTUNITY

The third citizen group to be discussed here are the custodians of access to important social institutions—employers, school administrators, and welfare directors. Corrections has sporadically dealt with these gatekeepers of opportunity, but only rarely in their roles as representatives of crucial social systems the modification of which is required for meeting the special needs of the correctional clientele.

The concept is not widely shared in corrections. Even though used too little, the roles of the social persuader or volunteer are at least generally recognized. It is easy to perceive them as necessary for helping to provide the climate and facilities in which the correctional expert can work, or to execute necessary, but nevertheless auxiliary, services for him. Note should be taken that, in either case, the work of the professional is central. The gatekeeper role develops from a different set of beliefs about the nature of the correctional mission and the pathways to its accomplishment.

Clarence Schrag describes three "revolutions" in the history of corrections.[30] The first, the age of reformation, replaced corporal punishment, exile, and physical disfigurement with the penitentiary. The second, the age of rehabilitation, assumed that criminals were handicapped persons suffering from mental or emotional deficiencies. In this era, individual therapy, aimed at healing these personal maladjustments, became the preferred style. In the third revolution—the age of reintegration—society becomes the "patient" as well as the offender. Much more emphasis is placed on the pressures exerted on the offender by the social groups to which he belongs and on the society which regulates his opportunities to achieve his goals.

The central task of corrections is to connect the offender with the opportunity systems of the community and to integrate him with the socializing institutions of society. To accomplish that task, corrections must change those systems and institutions to eliminate their tendency to reject him. No matter how many resources are provided to corrections, it cannot, by itself, solve the problems of reintegration. That requires the participation of the community. The problems of crime primarily arise in the interaction between the individual and his community. The solution to those problems requires a modification of the offenders' adaptive behavior and a substantial contribution by those responsible for the community's opportunity system.

Martin and Shattuck contend that the goal of the correctional agent should not be to arrange for the exemption of offenders from the consequences of belonging to a particular segment of society.[31] They would charge corrections with a responsibility to change the power relationship between society and the offender, so that all persons in the community to which the offender belongs would find similar opportunities. Social reconstruction becomes the other side of the coin of social reintegration.

The difference between a professional and a gatekeeper citizen, from a reintegration frame of reference, might best be described as the difference between an "inside" and "outside" treater who share responsibility in the process of reintegration. Each has a unique and necessary contribution to make.

This represents for virtually all of corrections a vastly different way of conceiving of the community. It requires an ability to identify important social systems and to design sophisticated strategies for changes in each. Needed is a special sensitivity to the forces working toward collaboration, and those resisting it, in each of the target systems. Suitable tactics to enlist the gatekeepers of the systems must be undertaken.

Enlisting them requires, most of all, that they not be seen simply as individual citizens willing to help correctional clients. They are not to be coopted into the correctional milieu, but, rather, to be asked to use the power which adheres to their status toward a correctional end. Unexpected resistance to such requests can be expected, for the citizen is being addressed not as a single individual, but as a member of a social group, with all the referent group forces at play which are implicit in such membership.[32]

The social persuader can be an important ally. For example, the Washington State Citizen Council of NCCD became interested in creating employment opportunity for offenders. Because of their prestige they were able to enlist the active help of the governor and the co-operation of some of the largest employers in the state.

Another technique which could be widely emulated is the assignment of specific personnel to work with specific community groups and institutions. Several correctional agencies have assigned staff to develop apprenticeship and vocational training programs with the help of labor unions, with notable success. Parole agencies have designated staff to work specifically with employer groups. Schools have been similarly assigned to juvenile probation officers who have the task of dealing with the entire social complex they represent. Many more opportunities for this kind of specialization are available.

THE INTIMATES

A final group of citizens for whom corrections must develop more effective programs of engagement are those who are significant in the immediate world of the correctional client.[33] By and large, corrections has done little to engage the peer culture of the offender, and even less to engage his community. They may be the most powerful citizen groups of all.

The correctional theory of rehabilitation placed stress upon the personal characteristics of the offender: they were the primary targets for change. This view has been tempered. The peer group has increasingly become an important target.

> We must be more aware of the group context and social occasions that give rise to delinquency and crime, to the continuing structures of interaction in which they are embedded. The implication is that, instead of trying to tear individuals out of the networks of interaction from which they now gain meaning, these networks themselves must become the targets of change. New rules, new styles of play, new rewards and punishment must be provided.[34]

A dilemma posed for corrections is how to deal with offenders' peer groups when they are not themselves subject to correctional restraint. There has been some experimentation in dealing with these groups within a correctional setting,[35] but few attempts have been made to move beyond *ad hoc* groups created in a correctional setting and to deal with the traditional community peer groups of offenders.

To undertake this task, corrections will probably need to work much more closely with community agencies directly involved with peer groups on a nonofficial basis. The gang-workers projects in New York City constitute one example of such an attempt.[36] The Youth Services Bureau concept advanced by the National Crime Commission may be another useful device. As envisioned, the Bureau would deal with all youths in a given community, whether adjudicated delinquent or not. It would thereby create a vehicle through which correctional authorities could work in dealing with the offenders in their natural context. The Joint Youth Development Committee in Chicago is an outstanding example of correctional agents working very closely with community workers in dealing with traditional peer groups.[37]

Relating to the offenders' broader community presents other problems. They are problems which must be overcome; the offenders' neighborhood and community, in too many cases, act as powerful forces against any program of reform. Gus Tyler describes the community of most offenders:

These are the areas that compose the "other America," standing outside the affluent society and hungrily looking in. Denied the delights of economic and social democracy, this "other" and "under" world breeds its marauders who turn to crime and redistribute the wealth, to voice their frustrations and to express the mores of the disinherited, distressed and disturbed.[38]

Logic demands that the correctional worker be concerned with the well-being of the community of the offender if he is going to be of any realistic help to him. Martin and Shattuck argue that the correctional worker of the future, as well as being a therapist, must act as a community worker concerned and participating with citizens of the community to improve it. Moreover, they contend that the correctional worker should become increasingly an advocate for the community, advancing its general causes.[39]

Already some examples of this kind of citizen involvement are seen in a few correctional programs. The Forsyth County Domestic Relations Court, in North Carolina, has recently undertaken the reorganization of its staff on a test basis. One position being created is that of community-action specialist. Among the requirements for that person are the following:

> To move through areas of high delinquency, interviewing clients and client families before the court to assess the contribution of neighborhood problems to delinquency in general, and specific delinquent acts in particular; to work with others active in community action, such as the police, poverty workers, etc., to develop and carry out planned efforts to change community conditions; to co-ordinate and expand the court's volunteer programs and develop new ways to engage people in the community in the treatment and prevention of delinquency.[40]

This notion of concern with the offender's community as well as with the offender has another important aspect when considering programs in the ghetto areas. Here the correctional agency can easily be perceived simply as the white man's chosen instrument of conformity, an instrument of an essentially racist policy. Agencies offering "help" can have little credibility in clients' eyes within that frame of reference. The problem, indeed, is very much the same as in correctional institutions, where the official structure is seen as antithetical to the inmate culture and is resisted as such. And, as in an institution, part of the solution to the problem must involve the breaking down of those divisions, if there is going to be a legitimization of constructive work with the representation of the dominant community.

Indeed, the notion of decentralizing probation and parole offices and correctional community centers to the ghetto areas, as is now widely recommended, will encounter some very difficult problems unless it comes to grips with the realities of those communities. And the first of these is the necessity to develop some identity of interest with them if community correctional enterprises are to be seen as anything but outposts of an implacable enemy.

Perhaps one of the most effective ways yet undertaken by correctional agencies in meeting these problems is through the use of "new career" personnel in correctional activities.[41] Some correctional departments are making special efforts to enlist citizens from the ghetto community as workers. The city of Seattle, Washington, has such a program; another is being undertaken in Austin, Texas. Such programs create career opportunities in corrections for the citizen of deprived areas and establish bridges between the correctional agency and the community, to permit effective work with the client groups in those areas. They may represent some of the most important citizen programs yet undertaken by corrections.

29 *The Prison of the Future*

DANIEL GLASER*

The prison of the future will differ drastically from today's prison, if it is
rationally designed for goals which already are generally accepted. These
goals are:
  (1) to evoke in offenders an enduring identification of themselves with
       anti-criminal persons;
  (2) to enhance the prospects that released prisoners will achieve
       satisfaction in legitimate post-release activities.
The pursuit of these two goals, in the light of today's common knowledge
about criminals, would lead one far from traditional approaches to prison
design and management. Already, there are signs that such movement
has begun.

One of the most immediately evident differences between tomorrow's
prison and that of today will be in location. The prisons of the future will
be located in the communities from which most of their inmates come.
This means that most prisons will be in metropolitan areas.

A home community location will have many advantages for a prison. It
will simplify the staff's task of knowing both the anti-criminal and the
criminal and disorderly personal influences in the community which
affect their prisoners. It will permit a graduated release of inmates on a
trial basis, for visiting prospective homes and seeking or even filling jobs
in the community, prior to receiving complete freedom. This graduated
release also will protect society, by providing a better test of the risks in

* From *Crime in the City* edited by Daniel Glaser (N.Y.: Harper and Row, Publishers, Inc.,
1970), pp. 261–266. Copyright © 1970 by Daniel Glaser. Reprinted by permission of Harper
and Row, Publishers, Inc.

releasing a man than can be had either by observing him only in a prison, remote and different from his post-release life, or by releasing him to traditional parole supervision, where his contacts with his parole agent are few and brief. Such graduated release also will permit the inmates to solve their social and economic problems piecemeal, reducing their prospect of finding themselves in desperate straits soon after they leave the prison, from having to face all their post-release problems at once. Finally, the predominantly urban location of tomorrow's prison will facilitate recruitment of superior employees, both line staff and part or full-time specialists (e.g., teachers and physicians), for there will be a larger pool of potential employees within commuting distance of the prison.

The short-sightedness of current prison labor legislation will eventually be recognized. Therefore, in addition to their new locations, prisons of the future will have many program features distinguishing them from today's prisons. Prisons will operate industries and services comparable to those in which there is post-release employment opportunity for the prisoners. Also, any inmate who engages in the activities considered optimum for his rehabilitation, including school assignments, will get some financial compensation. This will be at a variable rate, to offer incentives for increased diligence and responsibility, and thus, to provide prior to release that sense of achievement which comes from truly earning rewards. An appreciable portion of these earnings will be deposited in a savings account, for gradual use by the inmate during his parole, based on a budget developed during his confinement, but subject to later revision, with consent of the parole staff.

The prison of the future will have extensive links with community organizations. Churches, social and fraternal organizations, service clubs, hobby groups, professional or trade associations, as well as societies and persons aiding each other in the control of vices (e.g., Alcoholics Anonymous), will participate in the prison more actively than heretofore. This is in addition to the great encouragement of visiting by non-criminal relatives and friends of the inmates. Many of these outsiders will be actively involved in prison treatment programs, and in the institution's social and recreational life.

The staff of the prison of the future will not have many of the sharp distinctions now characterizing prison employees. Whatever their job classification, they all will be treatment personnel, and all will also be concerned with maintaining whatever level of custody proves necessary. The prison staff may even include some ex-prisoners, who have demonstrated clear rehabilitation, and whose crime and reformation experience gives them unusual counseling propensities. Most of the parole supervision staff probably will have offices adjacent to, or in, the scattered urban prisons.

While there may be some formal group counseling programs, most of the treatment impact will arise from the face-to-face relations of line staff with small groups of inmates in the course of routine work, study, and play activities. The line staff will also be intimately involved in the diagnostic decisions of prison management on such matters as the custodial security required for each inmate, the optimum program for his rehabilitation, and his readiness for gradual release; the traditional central classification committee, limited to top institution officials, will be a thing of the past. Most group decisions seriously affecting the place or program of an inmate's imprisonment will be made in groups comprising the staff who know him best.

To facilitate this kind of program, the prison of the future will be small. There will be many institutions, of diverse custodial levels, within any metropolitan area. There will also be a few in rural locations for inmates of that background. Location may not be so critical for prisons to hold offenders considered so highly committed to crime or seriously disturbed as to long be dangerous. However, all inmates will be housed, for an appreciable number of months before their release, in an institution near their release destination, to procure the diagnostic and treatment benefits of community contact and graduated release.

The small institution will reduce the necessity for regimentation, and increase the extent to which most of the staff know most of the inmates on a personal basis, and know each other well. The prisons of the future, because they will be small, can be highly diverse, both in architecture and in program. For example, a graduated release establishment, or other prisons in which custodial security is not a difficult problem, may house as few as fifteen or twenty men, and can be located in large YMCA-type hotels, in sections of a low rental apartment development or in an ordinary family-type house. Where custodial security is needed, for society's protection and to prevent concern with escape from distracting inmates, custody will be achieved by having continuously connected or yard-enclosing buildings, or by having only a single edifice, so that there are few points of possible exit. Custodial emphasis can then be mainly peripheral and invisible; it will impose few restrictions on inside activities. The entire institution generally will house less than one hundred inmates, plus whatever school, work or other facilities are appropriate for the inmates housed there.

There will be less emphasis in the prison of the future on separating inmates by age than now prevails in prisons. The bulk of felony arrestees have long consisted of persons in a period of transition from childhood to adulthood. Their crimes express their prolonged difficulties, as youth, in trying to pursue independent adult roles. It is in this socialization sense, rather than in biological traits, that many offenders can be considered immature. This socialization immaturity is protracted when their social contact is primarily with persons of their own age. Older unadvanced offenders will certainly be better influences on youthful inmates than their delinquent age peers, for the most criminalized of the latter tend to set the standards of accepted behavior when they are in homogeneous age-groups. Tomorrow the most delinquent youthful inmates will be scattered and isolated from each other insofar as possible. Staff will be oriented to maximize the rewarding contact of such prisoners with those inmates least vulnerable to deleterious influence, and most likely to have a long-run anti-criminalizing effect.

In the prison of tomorrow there will be much concern with utilizing the personal relationships between staff and inmates for rehabilitative purposes. This means varying staff modes of interaction with inmates according to the individual inmate orientations towards staff. Thus, the manipulative or aggressive inmate will be met with firm but fair reactions, making violence or fraud unsuccessful, but rewarding legitimate effort. The dependent or neurotic inmate will receive acceptance and ego-support, but with encouragement of self-analysis and self-reliance. Most counseling will not be in formal programs, although these will exist; counseling will occur mainly as it is evoked by problem-revealing events in institutional life, as well as by discussions of the inmates' future plans. This means that both group and individual counseling will involve primarily the line staff, rather than clinical specialists; the latter, neither now, nor in the future, can be sufficiently numerous to be the major source of direct treatment influence on most of the nation's confined criminals.

It should be stressed that most efforts at personality influence of staff on inmates will not be considered as ends in themselves, but as means toward achievement of the two basic purposes cited in opening this paper: evoking identification of offenders with anti-criminal persons—such as staff—and increasing inmate capacity for success in maintaining satisfactory personal relationships with anti-criminal persons, in legitimate employment and other pursuits after release. The major focus in inmate-staff relationships, therefore, will be the staff's contribution to the inmate's development of a conception of himself as opposed to crime, and accepted and successful in a non-criminal life. Many types of personality may make these shifts without profound change in other aspects of their basic modes of psychological reaction.

The prison of the future will only evolve fully in the form described here, as the society of the future changes. This will be reflected in a growing interest of both government, and private groups and persons, in assisting their fellow men, not just with kindness, but with understanding. This means that research will be an integral part of the administration of the prison of the future. The research will include both routine monitoring of the effectiveness of ongoing operations, in terms of their relationship to post-release criminality, and controlled experiments for testing new measures.

If punishment is ever justified in future prison management, it will be only because of objective demonstration that for certain people, and under certain circumstances, it promotes an enduring change of behavior. In this sense, it will be a dispassionate negative reaction to proscribed behavior, administered within legal controls, and in conjunction with positive reactions to favored conduct. Of course, any restriction of freedom for inmates considered dangerous is inherently punitive. However, punishment beyond the minimum restriction essential for custodial purposes will only be imposed deliberately if its merit can be scientifically demonstrated in a given case, and it will then be subject to tight controls.

The prison of the future described here is not really so far away. We already see it foreshadowed in such enterprises as the Federal Pre-Release Guidance Centers, the Work Release programs of the North and South Carolina and Maryland prisons, and the Community Treatment Centers which the California Youth Authority has experimentally substituted for training school commitment from the Sacramento and Stockton areas. We see all of these features even more developed in new types of community institutions for treatment of mental disorders; most features of prisons once characterized mental hospitals, but the latter changed first, in many respects, with prisons following later. This sequence of change is likely to recur in the future, but as it does, the difference between a mental and a criminal commitment will be further reduced: both will be oriented to preparing their subjects for as safe and quick a release to the community as possible, yet both will continue to have custodial concerns.

The prison of the future, clearly, will be part of a society in which rationality is institutionalized, and goodness, truth, and beauty are cardinal goals. Such a society cannot be realized instantaneously. It has been evolving gradually, at least since the Enlightenment, but with many temporary delays and regressions. It will evolve more rapidly and with less interruption, the more clearly we envision it, the more adequately we comprehend the problems confronting its achievement, and the more diligently we work to procure it.

Scientific Guidance
of Institutional Policies

Introduction

What is scientific may be subject to much argument. Philosophers are more certain as to what constitutes the "scientific method" than they are as to what is "science". A possible definition of scientific might include any results which are derived from the use of the "scientific method". However in the consideration of issues surrounding the treatment of offenders, as well as in the determination of the constituents of an offense, the moral becomes mixed with the scientific in an uneasy interaction.

Experimentation, if the term is used in its "scientific methodology" meaning, has several requirements which must be strictly met before valid inference is possible. In the field of criminal justice, as in the area of politics, the term experiment has been used with a quite different meaning—an innovation or the trying out of some hunch. There are certain conditions under which reform may, after the event, be treated as experiments by means of sophisticated statistical analysis: in such cases the quality of the inference may be little impaired by the lack of a prior research design. But the range of the information gained by these methods (although sound within limits) is restricted to little more than global statements about the operation, scheme or phenomenon. To obtain data which have real strength, a formal research design must be part of the experimentation.

Problems of vested interest and frozen imagination impeding innovation in the use of offenders and ex-offenders are discussed by Donald R. Cressey, a leading sociological criminologist who has been in the vanguard of those promoting use of ex-offenders as change agents with

435

offenders. Law professor Norval Morris and sociology professor Gilbert Geis discuss the ethical and legal issues raised by the scientific requirements of experimental procedure in corrections. Some practical strategies for using research to advance correctional administration are proposed by sociologist Daniel Glaser. The book concludes with a comprehensive and systematic survey of the methodological problems involved in evaluating penal measures. It was prepared by Leslie T. Wilkins, a statistician long active in penal research in Britain and America, and in graduate instruction in criminology in the United States.

We have not included in this chapter many studies which might have some indirect reference and value for the guidance of institutional policies. Much fundamental research has been carried out in laboratories with both animal and human subjects. There is, of course, no reason to believe that results obtained under laboratory conditions will apply in an actual institution, and there may be less reason for assuming that there is a close analogue between animal behavior and human behavior. Yet many of the laboratory studies of learning, frustration, limited sensory deprivation and decision-making may have an interest in that they can suggest hypotheses and explanations which might be examined in the prison setting.

It is to be hoped that there will be a time when there will be a continuous and frequent trading between laboratory experimentation and field observation, data collection and analysis. Many problems are too complex to be studied in the field setting, but it is often possible to extract and simplify subproblems which can be researched in the laboratory. When the results of the laboratory experiments are known, the field problem may be reconstituted and further studies made, perhaps again to cycle through the laboratory and back again. Much has been learned in other fields of human behavior and pathology by the use of laboratory methods and of the analogies derived from animal experimentation.

The physical laboratory is not the only currently available form of approach towards the examination of subsets of complex field problems. We have still to explore the utility of computer simulation of organizational structure and process. It is, of course, difficult to find a model which possesses the characteristics of the field situation with a sufficient degree of similarity. It is, indeed, possible to argue the inadequacy of any model which might be used to investigate almost any aspect of the human condition or activity. Our ability to operate with complex concepts, whether in the field or the laboratory, is distinctly limited. Our limitations are similar in either case. Some persons can think better in terms of field data, others may think better about the same kinds of problems in terms of laboratory or simulated data. The question is not whether the field situation is more realistic than that of the laboratory but whether the thinking is more effective in relation to the relevant problem solving; and this is by no means the same thing!

All problems can be reduced to absurdity by over-specification. As one of the editors has noted elsewhere:

> Persons who vary in ways that are in the main unknown (variable X_1), live in situations (X_2), and are exposed to cultural influences that vary in unknown ways (X_3). They sometimes commit deeds (X_4) which vary in many ways, except that they are classified by the laws of society as crimes, and these laws (X_5) also vary both in content and interpretation. Some persons are detected by systems that vary in unspecified ways (X_6); these are dealt with by persons or courts that also vary in their policies (X_7) and are allocated to institutions (X_8) that also differ from each other in many unknown ways. They are committed for varying periods of time (X_9), and their interaction with the treatment (X_{10}) is expected to vary. In most cases they may be expected to interact with other persons (X_{11}) also undergoing treatment. Eventually, they are released to situations that vary both in themselves and in terms of the expected interaction with the personality of the former inmate (X_{12}). In consideration of recidivism, this process may be seen as repeated many times. Frequently in discussion of recidivism the number of times the circuit has been completed remains unspecified.[1]

At the present time there is a conflict of views between those who would claim that we must attempt to think in terms of all the complexity which we can specify, and hence must use subjective or even intuitive approaches to all problems of penal administration, and those who have a lesser regard for their abilities to deal with the complexity and seek to use methodologies appropriate to the specific task. Perhaps the main function of methodology is to uncouple the observer as much as possible from the phenomena observed. It must do this without also uncoupling the data from the problem of concern. In this particular task the scientific imagination is as important as the methodology from which the well-informed scientist must select his tools.

There is a need for the development of more and possibly quite different kinds of tools for the study of criminal justice, but there is also a need for a wider knowledge of the tools which already exist and from which it is now possible to select. Few of the known methods have been applied to issues of scientific guidance of institutional policies. The sample of articles which follows is meant to stimulate thinking in this area.

30 Sources of Resistance to Innovation in·Corrections

DONALD R. CRESSEY*

There are four principal and interrelated sources of resistance to innovations in the field of corrections. These are: conflicting theories regarding efficiency of measures for maximizing the amount of conformity in the society; the social organization necessary to administering correctional programs; the characteristics and ideologies of correctional personnel; and the organization of correctional clients with respect to each other and to correctional personnel. In each case, the basis of the resistance to correctional change in general has special implications for resistance to change which would permit and encourage offenders and ex-offenders to serve as employees of correctional agencies, especially as rehabilitators.[2]

CONFLICTING PENAL THEORIES

The governing of persons who have some degree of freedom is no easy task, even in a small organization such as a family, a business firm, a university, a probation agency, or a prison. In a larger organization such as an army or a nation, it is even more difficult.

Two basic problems confront all persons who would insure that others follow rules. One is the problem of obtaining consent to be governed.

* From *Offenders as a Correctional Manpower Resource* (Washington, D.C.: Joint Commission on Correctional Manpower and Training, June 1968), pp. 31–49. Reprinted by permission of the author and publisher.

Governors must somehow get the governed to agree, usually unwittingly, to the governors' definition of morality, deviance, and deficiency. In this context, at least, it is correct to say that whoever controls the definition of the situation controls the world.

The second problem is one of maintaining the consent of the governed once it has been obtained. Those who are attempting to maximize conformity must be prepared to cope with nonconformity. This means that they must constantly be seeking appropriate measures to control those members whose conduct indicates that they have withdrawn, at least partially or temporarily, their consent to be governed. In utilizing these measures, governors must not inadvertently take actions which significantly diminish the degree of consent that has been given. In child-rearing, to take a simple example, parents must not punish their disobedient children so severely that the children rebel and become even more disobedient. In crime control, governments must not take actions which alienate solid citizens. All correctional devices must be administered in such a manner that the behavior of criminals is changed but the consent of the governed is not lost. Official punishment of criminals, especially, must be exercised with caution. If punishment of criminals is to be accepted by the recipients and by citizens generally, it must be imposed "justly," in measures suitable to correcting deviation without stimulating rebellion.

The rule-making bodies of social groups seldom have a unitary ideology regarding the procedures to be used for inspiring and maintaining conformity. A father, for example, may at one time spank his son for violating family rules and at another time overlook known violations, all the while believing that whatever action he takes is "for the good of the child" or "for the good of the family." In a nation, comparable inconsistencies in implementing a desire for a maximum amount of conformity are found in criminal law and in correctional agencies, owing to contradictions in the penal law theory which lies behind them. Since correctional agencies are, by and large, creatures of legislative processes, one who would understand resistances to correctional innovation must understand the theory on which legislatures operate in criminal matters.

One body of theory maintains that conformity to criminal laws is maximized by swift, certain, and uniform punishment of those who deviate. The "Classical School" of criminology which developed in England during the last half of the eighteenth century and spread to other European countries and to the United States, popularized this notion. The objective of the leaders of this school was to provide advance notice that crime would have punishment as its consequence and to make the imposition of punishments less severe and less capricious than it had been.[3]

According to the ideology popularized by these men, all persons who violate a specific law should receive identical punishments regardless of age, sanity, social position, or other conditions or circumstances. The underlying principle of behavioral and social control developed here is the idea of deterrence. By means of a rational, closely calculated system of justice, including uniform, swift, and certain imposition of the punishments set by legislatures for each offense, the undesirability and impropriety of certain behavior is emphasized to such a degree that it simply does not occur to people to engage in such behavior.

Although this set of theory is not now—and never was—used in its pure form, it is one of the pillars of our contemporary system of corrections. This becomes apparent whenever legislators demand a harsher penalty for some offense, whenever the very existence of probation and parole systems is attacked, and whenever correctional leaders are castigated for trying to introduce changes based on the view that offenders are in need of help. All developed societies maintain a powerful legal organization for corporate imposition of measured amounts of suffering on offenders. By acting collectively to take revenge on criminals, society is said to reinforce its anti-criminal values. In this setting, the notion that criminals themselves should be used as correctional agents is especially vulnerable because it implies that a criminal deserving of punishment will be utilized to mitigate the punishments deserved by other offenders.

A second body of theory is based on the belief that law violations and law violators must be handled individually so far as punishment is concerned. The extreme idea of equality promoted by the Classical School was almost immediately modified at two points. First, children and "lunatics" were exempted from punishment on the ground that they are unable to calculate pleasures and pains intelligently. Second, the penalties were fixed within narrow limits, rather than absolutely, so that a small amount of judicial discretion was possible. These modifications of the classical doctrine were the essence of what came to be called the "Neo-Classical School." The principle behind the modification remains as another of the pillars of our contemporary system for administering criminal justice. The basic idea was, and is, that the entire set of circumstances of the offense and the entire character of the offender are to be taken into account when deciding what the punishment, if any, shall be. "Individualization" of punishment has extended the principle of exemptions to persons other than children and the insane, and this means, of course, that judicial discretion is to be exercised officially.[4]

Our basic conceptions of justice are closely allied with these two contradictory sets of penal theory. These conceptions of justice, intermingled with the two sets of theory, have taken the form of ideologies regarding the "proper" measures to be used for securing and maintaining the consent of the people to be governed by the formulators and administrators of the criminal law. When implemented, the ideologies become directives for action on the part of correctional personnel. But since both the ideologies and the theories behind them are contradictory, we cannot logically expect correctional workers to be consistent in their methods of dealing with lawbreakers and potential lawbreakers. Correctional workers are called upon to play a game they cannot win. They are to ensure that punishments are uniformly imposed on those who violate the law. We are confident that this action will maximize the amount of conformity in the society. But they also are to adjust the punishments to individual cases, thus ensuring that punishments are neither so lenient nor so severe that the degree of conformity will diminish.

The first set of theory implies that, if the price of crime is low, everyone will buy it. Legislatures state, symbolically at least, that crime and criminals must be abhorred or the crime rates will rise. Attempts to handle criminals as if they have basic human rights are therefore resisted. Handling them as if they were capable of serving as correctional workers compounds the resistance. But correctional workers also are to ensure that the price of a crime is not so high that exacting it will result in loss of control of offenders and others. When punishments are too severe or otherwise unjust, citizens may not openly demonstrate their withdrawal of consent. But in a pattern of passive resistance they may well shield criminals from the law enforcement process. Even if they do not commit crimes, they may learn to overlook crimes, with the result that the law's effectiveness in maximizing conformity diminishes.

We assign to each correctional worker the difficult task of striking the delicate balance between leniency and severity of punishments, and between imposing punishments uniformly and imposing them irregularly. This delicate task, it may be argued, cannot be assigned to criminals or ex-criminals because their prior experiences have made them incapable of being disinterested. Traditionally, any grouping of criminals or ex-criminals has been viewed as undesirable, on both custodial and rehabilitative grounds. Association among prisoners meant, and still means, a banding together of dangerous men who could plot for some nefarious purposes. To avoid such association, prison workers have, by and large, substituted psychological solitary confinement for the physical solitary confinement characterizing the early Pennsylvania institutions.[5] In probation and parole, it has from the beginning been against the rules for offenders to associate with each other, partly because it was feared that any association would lead to criminal conspiracies, thereby decreasing the security of the society. It also was assumed that, if offenders were allowed to associate, the more criminalistic of them might contaminate the less criminalistic. The question of why the reverse would not be true has rarely been raised.[6]

In recent times we have, in addition, asked correctional personnel to "treat" criminals. To the degree that treatment is an alternative to punishment, not a supplement to it, its introduction into the correctional process is an attempt to mitigate penalties with a view to maximizing the degree of consent of the governed and thus the amount of conformity. Probation, prison, and parole workers are expected to execute the penalties "prescribed by law" so that offenders and others will learn that they cannot get away with law violation, thus increasing the amount of conformity. But correctional workers also are expected to modify those penalties so that offenders will be "treated" and the amount of conformity thereby increased. Introduction of treatment programs is resisted because they mitigate prescribed penalties. At the same time, correctional workers are accused of inefficiency if criminals are not rehabilitated.

SOCIAL ORGANIZATION OF CORRECTIONAL WORK

Because our society and its penal law theories have been ambivalent about what should be done with, to, and for criminals, it is not surprising to find that correctional work has been, almost from the beginning, characterized by ambivalent values, conflicting goals and norms, and contradictory ideologies. However, such a state of flux is not necessarily an impediment to correctional innovation. Viewed from one perspective, a state of disorganization or unorganization provides unusual opportunities for innovation. For example, an analysis of the Soviet industrial system concluded that conflicting standards and selective enforcement of an organization's rules permits supervisors to transmit changes in their objectives to subordinates without disrupting the operation of the system; permits subordinates to take initiative, be critical, make innovations, and suggest improvements; and permits workers who are closest to the problem field (usually subordinates) to adapt their decisions to the ever-changing details of circumstances. The following comment about the last point is especially relevant to corrections:

The very conflict among standards, which prevents the subordinate from meeting all standards at once, gives him a high degree of discretion in applying received standards to the situation with which he is faced. Maintenance of conflicting standards, in short, is a way of decentralizing decision-making.[7]

As conceptions of "the good society" have changed, conceptions of "good penology" and, more recently, "good corrections" also have changed. This has meant, by and large, that new services have been added to correctional work and new roles have been assigned to both correctional workers and their clients. Moreover, these additions have been made without much regard for the services and roles already existing. The process seems different from that accompanying similar growth of manufacturing and sales corporations, for the new roles have been organized around purposes that are only remotely related to each other. This could mean, as in the case of Soviet industry, that anything goes.

But in correctional work change has been slow and sporadic despite conflicting principles which seem to make anything possible. Ambivalence and conflict in social values and penal theories have produced correctional organizations inadvertently designed to resist change.

In the first place, a shift in correctional objectives now requires changes in the organization, not merely in the attitudes or work habits of employees. In prisons, for example, there is a line organization of custodial ranks, ranging from warden to guard, and salary differentials and descriptive titles (usually of a military nature) indicate that a chain of command exists within this hierarchy. Any prison innovation whose goals cannot be achieved by means of this hierarchy must either modify or somehow evade the organization of custodial ranks.

Positions for prison school teachers, industrial foremen, and treatment personnel are not part of the chain of command. Neither do such sets of positions make up a "staff organization," in the sense that positions for experts and advisors of various kinds make up a staff organization in a factory or political unit. The persons occupying positions outside the hierarchy of ranks in correctional systems do not provide persons in the hierarchy with specialized knowledge which will help them with custodial and management tasks, as staff personnel in factories provide specialized knowledge which assists the line organization with its task of production. In corrections, the "staff organization" actually is a set of separate organizations which competes with the line organization for resources and power. Systems of non-line positions, such as those for treatment, training, and industrial personnel, are essentially separate organizations, each with its own salary differentials and titles.

The total structure of corrections consists of three principal hierarchies—devoted respectively to *keeping, using,* and *serving criminals.* But the total system is not organized for the integration of the divergent purposes of these three separate organizations. In this situation, innovation by members of any one of the three organizations is necessarily a threat to the balance of power between them and the members of the other organizations.

Resistance to using criminals as correctional workers is to be expected because this role, in fact, is part of *none* of the three separate organizations. Further, the role is a threat to the authority structures and the communication and decision-making patterns of all of them.

Secondly, most innovations in correctional work can be introduced and implemented only if the participation, or at least the cooperation, of all employees is secured. In factories, there are separate but integrated hierarchies of management personnel and of workers, and many kinds of orders for innovation can flow freely downward from management offices to factory floors. For example, if the manager of an aircraft factory decides to innovate by manufacturing boats instead of airplanes, a turret-lathe operator can readily accept the order to change the set-up of his machine in such a way that part of a boat is manufactured.

But in correctional work, management is an end, not a means. Accordingly, management hierarchies extend down to the lowest level of employee. The correctional worker, in other words, is both a manager and a worker. He is managed in a system of controls and regulations from above, but he also manages the inmates, probationers, or parolees in his charge. He is a low-status worker in interaction with his warden, chief, or director, but he is a manager in his relationships with inmates or other clients. Because he is a manager, he cannot be ordered to accept a proposed innovation, as a turret-lathe operator can be ordered. He can only be persuaded to do so.

Criminals or ex-criminals serving as correctional workers, even if unpaid, must be given the management responsibilitites assigned to all correctional workers. Addition of this role to a correctional organization is subject to a kind of veto by any of the correctional workers in the organization, for each plays a management role.

But even though all correctional employees are managers as well as workers, the agencies and institutions which they manage are not owned by them. Each correctional agency has a number of absentee owners, and these owners have varying conceptions about policy, program, and management procedures. If they were questioned, it is probable that each would have a distinct opinion about using criminals and ex-criminals in correctional work. Because of differences in theoretical conceptions in the broader society, the contemporary environment of correctional agencies contains overlapping groups with interests in seeing that physical punishments are imposed, groups with interests in reducing physical punishments, and groups with varying ideas for implementing the notion that criminals can be reformed only if they are provided with positive, non-punitive treatment services. The interests of such groups converge on any particular correctional agency, and the means used by correctional administrators for handling their contradictory directives gives correctional agencies their organizational character.[8]

We have seen that, to some degree, resistance to correctional innovation resides in the internal order of the system, especially in the structure requiring that all employees and some clients share policy. But, to an even greater degree, resistance resides in the network of competing or cooperating interest groups, which vary from time to time. Caplow has pointed out that we should expect to find the strictest control of even *non*-occupational behavior attached to those occupations which have important role-setting obligations in the society, are identified with sacred symbols, and have relatively low status.[9] Correctional work qualifies on all three criteria. Factionalism among employees which develops whenever a significant change is made in the work of a correctional agency, is closely linked with changing interests of authorities external to the agency.

Correctional agencies are in a very real sense "owned" not by "the public" at large but by specific outside groups. Punitive, custodial, and surveillance activities are supported and maintained by a different convergence of interests than are production activities, educational activities, religious activities, and counseling and therapeutic activities.

One type of interest group emerges when an existing group sees existing or possible activities of the correctional program as a means for achieving its own objectives.[10] For example, inmate leaders sometimes operate as an interest group and press for control over routine decisions because such control gives them additional power to exact recognition and conformity from other inmates. Political leaders become an interest group when they see a parole agency as a resource for discharging political obligations, and they demand that the agency be so organized that the skills of political appointees, not experts, can be used. Church groups sometimes band together to support or oppose a correctional program on moral grounds. Because there is a strong belief in our society that "doing a good job" is a reward in itself and that laziness and lack of "self-discipline" are sinful, such groups tend to support custody, work programs, and training rather than "treatment." Prison guards become an interest group when they perceive that prison discipline for inmates is becoming so relaxed that the guards might be in danger.

Another type of interest group is directly concerned with preventing innovations which threaten its existing activities or plans. Police often constitute an interest group of this kind. They, even more than correctional workers, are charged with keeping the crime rate low, and they tend to oppose any correctional change which might reduce the degree of custody and surveillance. Similarly, social welfare groups and educational groups oppose any correctional changes which threaten to upset treatment and training routines; industrial groups oppose any organization of employment or employment services which will compete with them; and labor groups oppose any innovation which might reduce the number of jobs for non-criminals.

Other interest groups exist as such because they are obligated to groups directly involved in correctional activities. A group interested in family welfare, for example, may side with prisoners' aid societies and put pressure on correctional administrators by means of speeches, newspaper publicity, and endorsements. In response, still other groups side with correctional interest groups organized around different values. The innovation or lack of innovation which is the issue in conflict may be lost in the political dispute between the various coalitions.

In this situation, effective action on the part of a correctional administrator depends upon realistic assessment of the power possessed by interest groups. When he makes a commitment to any given group or to any coalition of groups, his freedom of action is henceforth limited. If, at the same time, he decides not to commit himself to other groups or coalitions, his freedom to introduce innovations is limited even more. He is able to make some innovative moves because the mandates given by correctional interest groups ordinarily are stated in broad terms and consequently have broad tolerance limits. For example, the directives coming from interest groups usually specify objectives but ordinarily do not spell out in great detail the means to be used for achieving them. Accordingly, the correctional administrator can "compromise" by adjusting in minor ways the networks of interest groups which differ in significant respects from each other.

The conservatism of corrections is in part a reflection of the necessity for caution in making such compromises. As power and influence are redistributed in the network of interest groups, new forms of correctional activities emerge. These become routinized as a new compromise, a new balance of interests. Such routinized activities, then, are at any given moment what Ohlin has called "the crystalized solutions of the problematic or crisis situation from which they emerged."[11] Correctional personnel at all levels participate in routinized activities and in that way are allied with correctional interest groups, whether they know it or not. This is the situation in which all employees share policy-making functions with management, making innovation extremely difficult.

If he is skillful, and if his organization is big enough, the correctional administrator can segregate his audiences by giving one part of his organization to one interest group while giving another part to a group with conflicting interests. For example, an interest group made up of social workers might be maneuvered so that it concentrates its concern on the boys' school or on correctional work with children generally, while an interest group composed of law enforcement personnel might have its interests reflected in one prison. Even one entire unit of a correctional agency, such as a prison or a parole unit, may be given to interests supporting a welfare and treatment policy, while another unit is given to interests supporting a punitive and surveillance policy. But the specialization of correctional units should not be overemphasized. Every unit reflects the interests of many different groups, making change difficult.

It is significant, however, that no important interest group has been pressuring for the use of correctional clients as rehabilitation agents. On the contrary, the moral and almost sacred character of correctional work encourages existing interest groups to oppose such an innovation. Any innovations proposed by correctional workers are subject to veto by some of the influential owners of the agencies employing them.

CONSERVATISM OF CORRECTIONAL PERSONNEL

Perhaps it is ambivalence and conflict in penal theory, together with a complex structure of correctional organizations, that underlies the most striking attitude among correctional workers—an attitude of "standing by." The ambivalence in theory has permitted various interest groups collectively to establish organizational structures which are extraordinarily difficult to change. But interest groups often can be pacified by external appearances and a display of organizational charts, and perhaps it is for this reason that internal pressure for significant innovation rarely occurs.

There certainly is variation from state to state and from agency to agency, but if one looks at correctional workers as a whole he sees among them very little concern for the design of innovations which would put real rehabilitative processes into the "treatment" organizations of prisons and probation-parole agencies. These structures were created some years ago in response to pressures from interest groups. As indicated, however, the mandates given correctional administrators by interest groups tend to be stated in broad terms. Consequently, the mere creation of "treatment" organizations within correctional institutions and agencies pacified some of the groups pushing treatment as a correctional objective. By and large, groups pressuring for "treatment" of criminals have left invention of the processes for administering "treatment" up to the correctional workers themselves, and correctional workers have not been innovative. Rather than experimenting with techniques based on rehabilitation or treatment principles specifically related to corrections, they have used processes vaguely based on general psychiatric theory. The resistance to innovation here has been more in the form of indifference than in the form of planned conservativism. There are two simple kinds of evidence that this kind of resistance is present in corrections.

First, the establishment of "treatment" organizations has permitted workers to engage in "treatment services" without ever defining them. It is extraordinarily difficult to define and identify "rehabilitation techniques" and even more difficult to measure the effectiveness of such techniques.[12] The objective of "treatment" programs in corrections is to change probationers, prisoners, and parolees so that they will no longer be law-breakers. Yet, so far as I know, no correctional worker has ever been fired because so few of his clients have reformed. Perhaps this indifference to employee efficiency arises because a scientific technique for modification of attitudes has yet to be stated and implemented. Instead of precise descriptions of techniques for changing attitudes, the correctional literature contains statements indicating that rehabilitation is to be induced "through friendly admonition and encouragement," "by relieving emotional tension," "by stimulating the probationer's self-respect and ambition," "by establishing a professional relationship with him," "by encouraging him to have insight into the basis of his maladjustment," etc. We need to know—but we do not know—how these things are accomplished and, more significantly, how, or whether, they work to rehabilitate criminals. Two practicing correctional workers who turned textbook writers have commented:

> Stripped to their essentials, these "instructions" boil down to exhortations to treat, to befriend, and to encourage. In effect, our treatment personnel are often told little more than to *go out there and rehabilitate somehow*—precisely how is not indicated. A military commander who confined his strategic orders

to the commands, "Be brave, be careful, and be victorious" would be laughed out of uniform. Often, however, the technical directions given to correctional workers are scarcely more specific.[13]

Because treatment structures have been introduced in defiance of interest groups demanding that corrections be organized for punishment, custody, and surveillance, there has been a tendency on the part of correctional workers to define "treatment" negatively. Rather than identifying what treatment is, they have been content to assert what it is not: Any method of dealing with offenders that involves purposive infliction of pain and suffering, including psychological restrictions, is not treatment. This premise obviously must create strain in a total correctional organization that is expected to be restrictive and punitive. In the processes designed to implement it, there seems to be a mixture of social work and psychiatric theory, humanitarianism, and ethics of the middle class.[14]

Second, because correctional administrators must justify all aspects of their total organization to one interest group or another, the research undertaken by research bureaus located in correctional agencies tends to be somewhat programmatic, rather than the kind that provides the basis for real change in the techniques used to change criminals. For example, research in California indicated that if parole caseloads are reduced to 15 and parolees are accorded "intensive supervision" during the first 90 days after release and then transferred to the normal 90-man caseloads for regular supervision, only slight reductions in parole violation rates occur.[15] But no one knows *why* this experiment, like others, turned out the way it did, principally because no one knows what, specifically, was involved in "intensive supervision" or "intensive treatment" that is not included when the procedure is not "intensive." The experiment seemingly was introduced as much to reduce caseloads as to determine whether a correctional innovation was effective.

Correctional workers should not be blamed or attacked for what appears to be a lack of progress in developing basic principles on which to build sound correctional practice. The condition seems to be rooted in the very nature of the occupation, so that it is not easily changed. At least an attitude of "standing by" seems to be rooted in correctional work in a way that experimental and innovative attitudes are not. Four principal conditions seem to be associated with this conservatism: humanitarianism, poor advertising, bureaucracy, and professionalization.

Humanitarianism as "Treatment"

One of the principal handicaps to developing and utilizing new rehabilitation techniques in modern corrections arises from the fact that we introduced and continued to justify humane handling of criminals on the ground that such humanitarianism is "treatment." One significant consequence is a confusion of humanitarianism and treatment. In speaking of prisons, for example, we now are likely to contrast the "barbaric" conditions of the eighteenth century with the enlightened "treatment methods" of our time, especially in California. Yet we do this knowing that an insignificant proportion of all persons employed in American prisons are directly concerned with administration of treatment or training. We do not know what percentage of probation and parole workers is engaged in treatment and training, and what percentage is engaged in mere surveillance. Neither do we know what percentage of an individual worker's time is devoted to each of these activities. We are inclined to say that *all* probation and parole workers are engaged in treatment and that *all* of a worker's time is devoted to this end.

On what do we base this notion that holds, essentially, that probation and parole are, by themselves, treatment? Perhaps we base it on a logic that goes something like this: Humanitarianism is treatment. Parole is humanitarian. Therefore, parole is treatment. Thus, when we say that criminals are being "treated," we mean something like "They are being treated well," *i.e.*, handled humanely. It has been shown that, in prisons, a pattern of indulgence among employees is itself considered "treatment" by professional personnel serving as administrators.[16]

Correctional workers are increasingly being asked to show the effects of "treatment," but they can produce little evidence of efficiency because much of what has been called "treatment" is merely humanitarianism. Budgets for "treatment" have been doubled in some states, but the recidivism rate has remained constant. Over the years, punitive measures, custodial routines, and surveillance measures were relaxed on the ground that such humanitarian relaxation is treatment. Now it is becoming necessary to try to show why this "treatment" has not been more effective. Occasionally someone argues, usually in connection with a budget request, that no treatment principles have been invented and that, therefore, treatment has never been tried. More often, it is indirectly argued that humanitarianism disguised as treatment has not worked because "inhumane" persons and policies in corrections and in society have opposed it. It would appear that correctional leaders have been so busy defending humanitarianism, on the ground that it is treatment, that they have not had time to develop treatment principles and practices. For that matter, they have little time to study the possibilities of applying principles developed by outside psychologists and sociologists.

Poor Advertising

The second condition associated with conservatism in correctional theory and practice, poor advertising, is closely related to the first. Humanitarians have left to correctional agencies themselves both the problem of justifying humanitarianism on the ground that it is treatment, and the problem of implementing that humanitarianism. But correctional workers are by their very nature poor propagandists for the humanitarian view, even if it is called "treatment." Correctional agencies are political units whose budgets and activities are, in the last analysis, controlled by politicians. And most politicians who want to continue being politicians must be opposed to crime as well as to sin and man-eating sharks. It simply is not expedient for a governmental worker to advocate being "soft" on criminals, even if he thinks he can show that being "soft" is somehow more efficient than not being "soft."[17] Police and prosecuting attorneys are excellently organized for promotion of the view that criminals should be dealt with harshly, but correctional workers are not, and probably cannot be, as efficiently organized for the humanitarian point of view.

Bureaucracy and Housekeeping

The third condition associated with the conservatism about theory and practice in correctional work is the bureaucratic organization necessary to the continuation of correctional agencies themselves. In the "good old days" of corrections, the probation-parole worker, at least, was somewhat of an individualist who played it by ear. Some of these workers got a variety of wild ideas about rehabilitation from a variety of sources and then tried them out on specific probationers and parolees. Most of the ideas did not work, but some of them seemed to be effective, and a few of those that seemed effective changed the course of correctional work.

This style of individualism is rapidly disappearing, especially in large agencies located in urban areas. Instead of rather independent workers who are trying out wild ideas, we have men who are not allowed to go into the field until they have proved to a training officer their ability to recite and adhere to agency policy, who are given "professional supervision" so they will not deviate from that policy, who are the recipients of newsletters that tell them what the "team" is up to, and who are expected to be familiar with the standard operating procedure set forth in manuals written in the home office for the guidance of men in the field. Like prison guards in the olden days, probation-parole workers are becoming strapped down by bureaucracy.

There is no reason to believe that the bureaucratization of correctional work should involve processes different from the processes of bureaucratization elsewhere.[18] One effect of bureaucratization is conservatism and routinization. On a simple level, the work done by employees must be performed within the framework of an 8-hour day and a 40-hour week, and this means that it must, by and large, be performed at a special work station. On a more complex level, it may be observed that in a bureaucracy there are bureaucrats, and a bureaucrat is primarily concerned with housekeeping. It is for this reason that one keen observer of the American scene calls bureaucrats "women in men's clothing." The male principle, he argues, is that of wasteful and reckless experimentation, risk, and creation. The female principle is that of compromise, conservation, monopoloy, complacency, and "results."[19] In correctional work, it appears, we have become housekeepers rather than reckless experimenters. Perhaps this is in part why outsiders are likely to view correctional workers as "weak sisters" and "old women."

Experimentation and innovation have traditionally involved individualistic processes quite different in nature from bureaucratic administrative processes. In fact, some of the most significant inventions made in the last two centuries were made by men who did not have the qualifications for making them. That is, these innovators were individualistic and creative, but not formally trained for or employed in the area of science or technology where their discoveries were made. The inventor of the cotton gin was an unemployed school teacher, the inventor of the steamship was a jeweler, the inventor of probation was a shoemaker, and the inventor of conditional release and parole was a sailor. Innovators and experimenters are not necessarily good "team men." A famous chemist, Cavendish, had an immense dislike of people, and he dismissed any maid working in his house if he so much as laid eyes on her. Darwin, who had no formal scientific training, withdrew to a country house and had very little association with professional colleagues or anyone else.

In correctional agencies that have grown to the point where professionalism and concordant bureaucracy have appeared, individual innovation, experimentation, and attempted implementation of wild ideas must necessarily be controlled. If this is not done, organizational routines might be embarrassingly upset. One control procedure is creation of a "research team," a "research division," or a "planning and development section," which is to contain the experimenters. This custom can block innovation, for the larger the team, the more difficult it is to get concurrence that radically new concepts are worth risking the team's reputation on. After all, if the new plan goes sour, is attacked, ridiculed, and deprecated, the time and energy of all the team members, not just one crackpot, are brought into question. In corrections, a research team is not necessarily conducive to development of radically new procedures, such as using offenders and ex-offenders as correctional workers. Someone has said that sociology has been characterized by a retreat into methodology, meaning that sociologists have refused to take stands on social issues and have instead increasingly been concerned with the methods by which they arrive at conclusions. By the same kind of reasoning, we can observe that correctional innovation might be starting to experience an analogous type of retreat—a retreat into research.

Profession vs. Occupation

The fourth condition associated with conservatism among correctional workers is professionalization. Because professional personnel such as social workers, psychologists, and psychiatrists have constituted an interest group pressuring for "treatment" in corrections, it is somewhat paradoxical to observe that strong resistance to further change is characteristic of this group. There is no doubt that professional personnel have been instrumental in diminishing the punishment-custody-surveillance aspects of corrections, largely in the name of "treatment." However, the same personnel tend to be conservative with reference to changes in professional practices themselves. "Professionalization" implies standardization of practice, with the result that the kind of bureaucratization just discussed is perhaps more characteristic of professional personnel than anyone else in corrections.

Among the characteristics of a profession is monopolization of specialized knowledge, including theory and skills.[20] When an occupation is professionalized, access to its specialized knowledge is restricted, definition of the content of the knowledge is uniform, and determination of whether a specific person possesses the knowledge is determinable by examination. Further, professional personnel ordinarily establish formal associations, with definite membership criteria based on possession of the specialized knowledge and specifically aimed at excluding "technically unqualified" personnel. The name selected by the association generally is unusual enough so that not just anyone can use it, again indicating a monopoly on a piece of theory and a set of skills. If the profession has developed a code of ethics, as professions eventually do, the code consists of a number of interrelated propositions which assert the occupation's devotion to public welfare and, more important to conservatism, stipulate standards of practice and standards for admission. Neither practitioners nor trainees can be allowed to "go it alone" in such a way that new or different standards are developed. They must learn the established code and behave according to the standards it implies. They must, in other words, accept the professional culture. In most instances, professions make their conservatism legal by gaining legislation which limits practice to those who have passed a state-administered examination or who are certified by the state upon completion of a specialized course of study, usually in a university. Often it is a crime for uncertified persons to perform the acts reserved to members of the profession. Concurrently, practices such as the privilege of confidentiality might be reserved for professionals.

In correctional work, these characteristics of professionalization are especially relevant to the proposition that correctional clients themselves should be used as workers and managers of the rehabilitation process. "Professionalization" of correctional work has stressed monopolization of knowledge of "treatment," "rehabilitation" or "reformation" processes, not of knowledge about custody, management, surveillance, and repression. Accordingly, "professionalization" has come to stand for the ideology of "professional personnel" such as psychologists, psychiatrists, and social workers.

The proposal that clients be used as correctional rehabilitators boldly asserts that persons characterized by professional correctional personnel as "laymen" or "subprofessional workers" can achieve what professionals say can be achieved only after years of specialized training. After having participated in a half-dozen or more years of pre-professional and professional training and after having worked his way up in a hierarchy of occupational and professional ranks, the professional in corrections is likely to take a dim view of any suggestion that what he is doing could be done as efficiently (or perhaps more efficiently) by a person without his training and experience.

Moreover, "professionalization" implies that personnel will *not* engage in certain practices, just as it implies that certain practices are reserved to an elite group of personnel. Status as a professional person implies a position of high rank involving little or no dirty work. An admiral does not expect to chip paint, and a doctor does not expect to carry bedpans. As nursing has become professionalized in recent years, nurses do not expect to carry bedpans either. And as social work has become professionalized, social workers do not expect to carry baskets of food to the poor. Such activities are "unprofessional." In correctional work, innovations which would require the professionals to perform the equivalent of chipping paint, carrying bedpans, and carrying baskets of food to the poor are bound to be resisted by the professionals. Yet since World War II almost everyone working in the field of rehabilitation has argued that involvement in this kind of work, especially in "milieu therapy," is essential to rehabilitation.

It also should be noted that correctional administrative positions are increasingly being assigned to professional personnel. When this is the case, an administrator's income and status often depend upon his ability to maintain professional practices which over the years have been defined as "standard" and "good." One who is the director of a correctional rehabilitation program or crime prevention program does more than try to rehabilitate criminals or prevent crime. He administers an organization that provides employment for its members, and he confers status on these members as well as on himself. In other words, personal and organizational needs supplement the societal needs being met by administration and utilization of various correctional techniques. The personal and organizational needs are met by correctional institutions, agencies, and programs. By utilizing or advocating use of "professional methods" in correctional work, a person may secure employment and income, a good professional reputation, scholarly authority, prestige as an intellectual, the power stemming from being the champion of a popular cause, and many other personal rewards. An agency organized around administration of "professional methods" may fill such needs for dozens, even hundreds, of employees.

Because of personal and organizational investments, personnel dedicated to rehabilitating criminals are likely to maintain that criminality is reduced by whatever it is they are doing. Vague statistical measures of efficiency are valuable and useful because they decrease the range of points on which disagreements and direct challenges can occur.[21] Yet any suggestion for radical change is an implicit or explicit criticism, and it therefore is helpful if the efficiency question can be avoided by announcing that the proposed change would introduce procedures that are "substandard" or "unprofessional."

More specifically, acquisition and preservation of the knowledge and ethics of the social work profession is becoming an essential characteristic of what we are beginning to call "the corrections profession" and "the professional correctional worker." Education for the corrections profession has been considered the province of schools of social work. The assumption generally has been that students being educated for participation in the social work profession are, at the same time, being educated for the corrections profession. This means that students of social work cannot be given specialized knowledge and skills which are peculiar to correctional work but which are, at the same time, inconsistent with the ideology, theory, and standards of social work. Further, it is commonly but erroneously assumed that correctional work is so desirable that we can afford to require larger and larger proportions of all correctional personnel to have social work degrees, as we have been doing in recent years.

The individualistic theory of rehabilitation promulgated by social workers and other psychiatrically oriented personnel implies that until one has had at least six years of university training he is not qualified to try to rehabilitate a criminal. Since a highly educated staff has been considered a good staff, more highly educated personnel are sought. But this trend toward professionalization blinds professionals and non-professionals alike to innovations which would involve a lowering of educational standards for correctional workers. Use of offenders as correctional workers is resisted because, considered from the traditional viewpoint, such personnel do not possess indispensable social work skills.

OFFENDERS' RESISTANCE TO INNOVATION

Correctional clients are notoriously resistant to correctional innovations which would change them to significant degrees. In the first place, they usually have good reasons for not trusting the personnel paid to implement any rehabilitation program. It is a fact that some procedures used in the administration of criminal justice are based on the theory that society must be hostile toward criminals in order to emphasize the undesirability of nonconformity. Criminals are committed to the care of correctional agencies against their will, and no amount of sugar-coating hides from them the fact that the first duty of correctional personnel is to protect society from criminals, not to rehabilitate individual criminals. Criminals often find it difficult to distinguish between correctional procedures designed to punish them and correctional procedures designed to help them.

Similarly, they are not at all confident that correctional personnel ostensibly engaged to help them are not actually engaged to assist in punishing them and keeping them under control. They note, for example, that in most prisons the treatment and rehabilitation specialists are subordinate to officials who emphasize the necessity for maintaining order, even if maintaining order interferes with treatment practices. They know that the prison psychiatrist or social worker might have the task of stopping "rumbles" and "cooling out" threatening inmates, rather than rehabilitating criminals. They know that revocation of probation or parole depends as much on the attitudes of the probation-parole officer as on the behavior of the client. Further, they know that the pressures put on them to reform or become rehabilitated have as much to do with the good of "society" or the good of middle-class property-owners as they have to do with the good of the individual criminal himself. Most criminals have very little confidence that the immense amount of data collected on them will be used for their benefit. As a sophisticated ex-convict has written, "The prisoner's need to live and the system's attempt to live for him (and off him) can never be reconciled."[22] In current correctional circumstances, clients have a minimal sense of obligation to the personnel controlling their fate. If, as McCorkle and Korn argued some years ago, criminals are intent on rejecting their rejector,[23] correctional programs will succeed only if the degree of rejection by society is diminished.

Second, neither criminals nor ex-criminals are convinced that they need either existing correctional programs or any program which might be invented in the future. They cooperate with correctional workers, not in order to facilitate their own reformation but in order to secure release from surveillance as quickly as possible and as unscathed as possible. Prisoners, for example, participate in group therapy, group counseling, and individual "intensive treatment" programs as much from a belief that doing so will impress the parole board as from a conviction that they, as individuals, need to change.

Once a criminal has gone through the impersonal procedures necessary to processing him as a law violator, about all he has left in the world is his "self." No matter what that self may be, he takes elaborate steps to protect it, to guard it, to maintain it. If it should be taken away from him, even in the name of rehabilitation or treatment, he will have lost everything. Old-fashioned punishment-custody-surveillance procedures were designed to exterminate each criminal's self. New-fangled correctional programs are designed to do the same thing. Although many criminals, especially inmates, favor "rehabilitation," strong resistance occurs when the rehabilitation technique hints at "brain-washing" or any other procedure which would change the essence of "what I am." A pill or an injection which would change a criminal into a non-criminal without changing the rest of him probably would be accepted with enthusiasm by most criminals. But attempts to change criminals into non-criminals by significantly changing their personalities or life styles threaten to take away all they have left in the world.

Third, probationers, parolees, and even ex-offenders are not likely to become very excited about any program which expects them to look upon the task of rehabilitating themselves as a full-time job. Taking a pill or an injection would be so much easier. Criminals, like others, have been taught that efforts at rehabilitation involve "technical," "professional," or even medical work on the part of a high-status employee, not hard work on the part of the person to be reformed. Moreover, for most criminals crime has been at most a moonlighting occupation or a brief, temporary engagement, and it follows that any personal involvement in their own rehabilitation also should be a part-time affair. Charles Slack demonstrated that it helps if delinquents are paid to perform duties believed by the experimenter to be rehabilitative.[24] But some criminals would resist even if they were offered training for full-time paid employment as people-changers. The market for their skills is vague. Further, delinquents and criminals commonly assume, perhaps correctly, that rehabilitators play a feminine, sissy role. Finally, many criminals and ex-criminals fear that even if they accepted employment as correctional workers they would find the work dull and boring, as some non-offenders do.

Fourth, a special kind of resistance to rehabilitation attempts is encountered in prisons, where inmates are in close interaction and have developed their own norms, rules, and belief systems. Wheeler has shown that inmate attitudes are not as opposed to staff norms as even inmates believe.[25] Nevertheless, for most prisoners, adjustment means attachment to, or at least acceptance by, the inmate group. Moreover, an inmate participating in a rehabilitation program, no matter what its character, is likely to be viewed as a nut, as a traitor, or as both. Strong resistance will be encountered when efforts to change individual criminals would, if successful, have the result of making them deviate from the norms of their membership groups and reference groups.[26] Even among probationers and parolees there is likely to be attachment to the values and beliefs of persons participating in what Irwin and Cressy have described as the "thief subculture," because this subculture stresses norms of "real men" and "right guys."[27]

It should be noted further that even when correctional programs are organized so as to make socially acceptable groups available to offenders, members of socially acceptable groups including some correctional workers are not always ready to accept socially unacceptable offenders. When criminals and ex-criminals do band together to form anti-crime societies such as Synanon, they usually are shocked and then discouraged by finding that few persons, especially professional correctional workers, share their enthusiasm for their "cause."

Fifth, the special handling of some criminals is resisted by other criminals because the special handling is viewed as unfair. Criminals, perhaps more than other citizens, are concerned with justice, and one conception of justice views "special treatment" as unjust "special privilege" or "special favor." In prisons, especially, the punitive-custodial-administrative view is that all prisoners are equal and equally deserving of any "special privileges." They are not, of course. But when treatment criteria cannot be understood, handling inmates as special cases is likely to be interpreted to mean that the inmates in question are being given special privileges with reference to restrictive punishment. A prisoner who is released from prison because he has become "adjusted" or "rehabilitated" is not, from a treatment point of view, being granted a special privilege. But as he is being discharged for treatment reasons, he also is being released from the restrictions deliberately and punitively imposed on him. Accordingly, the discharge is likely to be viewed as a "reward" for good behavior. If, in the eyes of other inmates, the prisoner being discharged is no more deserving of release from punishment than they are, then the discharge is considered unjust special privilege. Similarly, an inmate who is a bad actor in prison might be assigned to what inmates regard as a "good job" as therapy for his misconduct. Because it is often assumed that an inmate will begin to behave responsibly if he is given a position of responsibility, he might even be given a job as a correctional worker. But this therapeutic manipulation of the individual's environment might be viewed by inmates as an unjust reward for misconduct.

If this attitude were held by many inmates it would be a serious threat to institutional security. Inmates might rebel in response to the "injustice" of "special privilege." Or, on the other hand, they might start misbehaving so as to win for themselves a similar "reward." Were "inmate need" the sole criterion used for distributing goods in short supply, then inmate cooperation in meeting institutional needs would be minimal.

Treatment programs which would create such problems, or which threaten to create such problems, are roundly resisted by administrators and inmate leaders alike. The same thing is true in correctional work with probationers and parolees, but perception of special handling as unjust is limited because these clients are not in close association with each other. In prisons, the basic interpersonal relationship among inmates is one of dominance and subordination. This relationship is the foundation on which peace and order are maintained. But, as McCleery has shown, both the relationship of dominance and subordination and the social order supported by it depend upon an official policy of treating all inmates as equals.[28] If the dominant inmates' demands for equality among all inmates were not met, the whole inmate social structure might be upset every time a busload of new inmates arrived.

In other words, peace in prisons depends upon a system in which inmates, not officials, allocate status symbols and special privileges. Any rehabilitation program which would require officials to allocate these symbols and privileges is likely to be viewed as unjust and therefore to be resisted.

31 Impediments to Penal Reform

NORVAL MORRIS[*]

. . . On the theme of penal reform my testament is easy to make and unchallengable: We need more knowledge of the efficacy of our various penal sanctions in their deterrent and educative roles in the community at large and with the individual offender. None will challenge this; but its affirmation does not achieve much. It has truth but lacks momentum. The point has been made with wearisome repetitiveness.[29]

So I would like to pursue a narrower question. Why is it that so little headway is made? What are the impediments to the acquisition of these types of knowledge? It is probable that here, too, progress presupposes some degree of clarity in recognition of the obstacles to progress. I do not mean to dwell on the political and economic obstacles to penal reform. That these may on occasion be massive, no one can doubt. I have in mind rather the impediments of inadequate theory and the gaps in our knowledge that may well in the long run prove more intractable than the political exigencies and the chronic shortage of men, money, and materials with which a selfish community burdens its penal reformers.

It is to be noted that the handicaps of a defective theory and of exiguous information about our penal methods, to which I will point, have not precluded the development of an appreciably powerful and effective penal reform movement; there is no paradox here, since the mainspring of penal reform has been neither empirically validated knowledge nor a developed theory. Decency, empathy, the ability to feel

[*] From *The University of Chicago Law Review*, 33, 4 (Summer 1966): 627–656. Copyright © 1966 by the University of Chicago. Reprinted by permission of the author and publisher.

461

at least to a degree the lash on another's back, the removal occasionally of our customary blinkers to human suffering, a respect for each individual springing from religious or humanitarian beliefs—these have been the motive forces of penal reform and not any validated knowledge concerning the better prevention of crime or recidivism. We have built an intellectual superstructure to our developing sense of identity with all fellow humans, criminals and delinquents not excepted, but it is an edifice of rationalizations. Perhaps this is an overstatement, perhaps a more precise analysis of this relationship between mind and heart in penal reform is that our uniform experience, critically analyzed, seems to be that we can indulge our sense of decency, of the reduction of suffering even by criminals, without any adverse effects on the incidence of criminality. The history of penal reform thus becomes the history of the diminution of gratuitous suffering.

Capital punishment moves from being the basic punishment for all felonies to an exceptionally inflicted indecency in which we place little trust and have little confidence. And the change is not the product of research studies that would satisfy the empiricists of this law school. The same is true of all the ornate and obscene forms of corporal punishment which constituted our heritage of penal sanctions for non-capital offenses. Likewise, that convicts ceased to be transported to the southeastern shores of this continent and to the pleasant sunny climes of Australia had little to do with any assessment of the effectiveness of the sanction of transportation in deterring men from criminal conduct. Yet again, many of the indignities and cruelties of that American invention, the prison, to be found in the original Auburn and Pennsylvania systems, have been eliminated or ameliorated, not because of developing knowledge about the more effective prevention of crime or of recidivism, but because they inflict needless suffering. The crime and recidivist situations at least did not deteriorate upon our casting aside the gallows, the lash, the lock-step, the broad arrow, and the rules of solitude and silence. And much indeed yet remains to be done along these lines. The diminution of gratuitous human suffering, gratuitous in the sense that no social good whatsoever flows from it, that it in no wise diminishes the incidence or seriousness of crime and delinquency, remains an important purpose of penal reform. One does not have to travel far from this place today to find thousands of convicted persons, adult and juvenile, subjected needlessly to such suffering and for grossly protracted periods. Moreover, most such suffering is more than useless; it is harmful to us. It tends to increase the social alienation of those we punish beyond our social needs, and it is highly probable that we pay a penalty in increased recidivism and increased severity of the crimes committed by those who do return from such punishment to crime. Studies of the inmate culture have confirmed the alienating effect of the prison, its creation of a community of the self-identified as aggrieved. The inmate culture has high efficiency in communicating criminal and anti-conventional values in a situation ideal for their transmission and consolidation. The prison engenders more than social alienation; it fosters and confirms maladjustment.

These, then, have been our main guidelines to penal reform: the humanitarian diminution of gratuitous suffering and the self-serving reduction of social alienation. It becomes clear, however, that these guidelines are gradually becoming insufficient. New directions must be charted. The Swedish adult correctional system provides an excellent case study in this impending need. In terms of the amelioration of penal conditions little remains to be done. There obtains in that country as little interference as reasonably possible with the convicted criminal's life, an energetic attempt is made to preserve his social ties by probation systems, and, if it should be necessary to incarcerate him, to do so briefly and in conditions of reasonable comfort with as little disruption of those social ties as possible. No large penal institutions; regular home leave; over a third of prisoners held in open conditions lacking bolts, bars, and walls; adequate work and vocational training; a sense of near equality in the relationships between prisoners and staff; these have become the hall-marks of the Swedish prison system. Along this path, in Sweden, they have gone about as far as they can go. Not quite; there are still a few remaining traditional lock-ups to be eradicated; there still remain a few needless indignities and hardships. Nevertheless, in the broad, the guidelines of empathy and minimizing alienation have served to their limit. Further guidance will not come from the heart; the head must be more directly engaged. And that means a program of research and training which is in Sweden hardly officially envisaged, let alone pursued. The same is true, though at a much earlier stage of development, in this country. Take, for example, the half-way house movement which is spreading so rapidly. It shortens prison sentences, it sometimes serves as an alternative to institutionalization, it provides a bridge between the institution and the community, it supports probation and parole arrangements for some offenders, and there is great enthusiasm for it. Yet, in my view there is no established information showing that it better protects the community or better reforms criminals than the sanctions it is supplanting. We are enthusiastic about it because it assists us to avoid harm; not because we know that it assists us to achieve positive good. It was for this same reason that we eliminated the lash.

What, then, are the limitations on this process of ameliorating the prisoner's lot and of reducing the punishment of the convicted criminal and young offender? Limitations there must be, else no punitive action whatsoever would be appropriate. We must recognize our present penal reform movement as an uneasy series of compromises between punitive aggression and rehabilitative empathy and build towards correctional systems, for adult and young offenders, rationally related to our social purposes. Penal reform must stretch beyond its traditional humanitarian purposes to achieve a larger social protection from crime and recidivism. There are obstacles to this effort; I propose to consider certain of them under the following four headings: deterrence; less eligibility; the limits of the rehabilitative ideal; and the ethics and strategy of research.

I. DETERRENCE

As Sir Arthur Goodhart recently wrote, if punishment "cannot deter, then we might as well scrap the whole of our criminal law."[30] Indeed, to my knowledge, every criminal law system in the world, except one,[31] has deterrence as its primary and essential postulate. It figures most prominently throughout our punishing and sentencing decisions—legislative, judicial, and administrative. We rely most heavily on deterrence; yet we know very little about it.

Ignorance of the consequences of penal sanctions on the community at large is a constant inhibitor of penal reform. Punishment sometimes deters, sometimes educates, sometimes has an habituative effect in conditioning human behavior; but when and how? Our ignorance is a serious obstacle, whatever our regulatory objectives. And of equal importance, we are hesitant to think only in terms of what the individual convicted offender needs to turn him away from crime because we fear that to do so would sacrifice the general deterrent, educative, and habituative effects of our penal sanctions. Thus, if penal reform is to become rational, it is essential that we begin to learn the extent to which our diverse sanctions serve prospective public purposes apart from their effects on the sentenced criminal; absent this knowledge, striking a just balance between social protection and individual reclamation is largely guesswork.

The deterrence argument is more frequently implicit than expressed; the debate more frequently polarized than the subject of a balanced discussion. When I listen to the dialogue between the punishers and the treaters, I hear the punishers making propositions based on the assumption that our penal sanctions deter others who are like-minded from committing crime. And I hear the treaters making propositions concerning the best treatment for a given offender or class of offenders which are based on the assumption that our penal sanctions do not at all deter. There is rarely any meeting of the minds on the issue central to the discourse. And it is not as if such knowledge is unobtainable; it has merely not been sought with anything like the energy and dedication that has been given to the expensively outfitted and numerous safaris that have searched for the source of criminality. The polar argument becomes a bore; a modest beginning on the search for more knowledge becomes a compelling need. We have endured a surfeit of unsubstantiated speculation, continuing quite literally since man first laboriously chipped out his penal codes on tablets of stone or scrawled them on chewed and pounded bark. It is time we did better. To do so it may be wise first to get our terms clear, then to assess what we now know, and then to suggest a strategy for our search.

European criminologists draw a distinction between special and general deterrence which is helpful to our purposes. By special deterrence they refer to the threat of further punishment of one who has already been convicted and punished for crime; it may be the same medicine that is threatened as a method of dissuading him from recidivism or it may be a threat of a larger or different dose. Special deterrence thus considers punishment in the microcosm of the group of convicted criminals. General deterrence looks to the macrocosm of society as a whole (including convicted criminals). It would seem hard to deny that for some types of crime and for some types of people, the individual superego is reinforced and to a certain extent conditioned by the existence of formal punishments imposed by society, and that we are influenced by the educative and stigmatizing functions of the criminal law. Further, it seems reasonable to aver that for some people and for some types of crime the existence of punishment prevents them as potential offenders from becoming actual offenders, by the very fear of the punishment that may be imposed upon them. These two broad effects can be regarded as processes of general deterrence. For purposes of research it may, of course, be necessary to separate these various strands that I have woven together in the concept of general deterrence.

The acquisition of knowledge concerning special deterrence may be achieved by substantially the same methods that will be suggested hereunder as means of dispelling our ignorance of the reformative effects of our treatment methods. In the meantime, this gap in our knowledge is less inhibitory of penal reform than our uncertainty about the general deterrent effects of criminal sanctions and of the possibly adverse consequences of too rapid a shift to predominantly reformative processes.

What, then, do we know of general deterrence? In September, 1965, at the Fifth International Congress of Criminology, held in Montreal, Professor Johannes Andenaes of Oslo University gave a paper, *Punishment and the Problem of General Prevention*[32] which better answers that question than anything else I know in the literature. My comments now are therefore confined to this reference to Professor Andenaes' paper and to an effort to underline its central theme which was that "the problem is not one of determining whether . . . [general deterrent] effects exist; it is one of determining the conditions under which they occur and the degree to which they occur."[33]

Perhaps the capital punishment controversy has produced the most reliable information we have on the general deterrent effects of a criminal sanction. It seems to me well established, as well established as almost any other proposition in the social sciences, that the existence or non-existence of capital punishment as a sanction alternative to protracted imprisonment for convicted murderers, makes no difference to the murder rate or the attempted murder rate. Suppose this is true; there is a temptation to extrapolate such a proposition to other crimes. This temptation should be resisted for it is quite easy to demonstrate contrary situations for other crimes where increased sanctions (maintaining stable reporting, detection, arrest, and conviction rates) lead to reduced incidence of the proscribed behavior. For example, by way of extreme contrast to murder, parking offenses can indeed be reduced by an increased severity of sanctions if one is determined about the matter. And, even with regard to capital punishment for murder, if the secret heart of an abolitionist must be bared, general deterrence still probably functions peripherally.

It seems to me probable that even here general deterrence continues to operate, but in a perhaps unexpected way. It is likely, taking all the available evidence into account and yet using the room for speculation that it allows, that the existence or non-existence of capital punishment for murder is irrelevant to the number murdered or attempted to be murdered but is marginally relevant to who they are. I am suggesting that the difference of sanctions conditions not the rate but in a very few cases who shall be the victims; that the ambit of the circle of victims remains the same but the difference of penalty influences peripherally the victim selection process. In the Report of the Ceylon Commission on Capital Punishment[34] I offered some reasons in support of that conclusion which need not be rehearsed; all that needs to be said for my present theme is that here too a better understanding of the operation of our general deterrent processes could lead to more effective social control.

We need a series of soundings in deterrence, studies aiming at measuring the general deterrent processes of the criminal law in a variety of areas of social control; and we are now beginning such soundings in the Center for Studies in Criminal Justice. The slaughter on the roads might well be reduced were we to have more understanding of the ways in which criminal sanctions might inhibit drunken and dangerous driving—the design of empirical studies to acquire this knowledge lies well within our competence. It is my submission that such soundings could and should be made for all those many efforts we pursue to achieve social control by means of deterrent criminal sanctions. To fail to define our purposes for punishing any human being is to make Pilate's choice; to define our purposes and yet to make no effort to test the capacity of our means to attain them is a similar though a lesser sin against the light. Nor are we as bereft of insights as I may so far have suggested. Professor Andenaes has outlined what knowledge of this type has been gained by the criminologists; but on this topic there are several other disciplines, further advanced than are we, capable of guiding our search. Philosophers have, of course, long speculated about these problems; more recently, other disciplines, particularly psychology and psychiatry, have begun to contribute the chips of knowledge which will make up the mosaic of general deterrence. Kurt Lewin and his followers working on Field Theory; those studying the concept of cognitive dissonance; the educational psychologists and those interested in animal behavior (only somewhat disparate fields) all have contributions to make to our manipulation of criminal sanctions for general deterrent purposes. And the psychiatrists, both those of Freudian orientation and their collectivist colleagues, more interested in conditioned behavior, have knowledge relevant to our task. Indeed, one of the problems in this search for understanding of this basic postulate of the criminal law—that its sanctions deter—is the collation of information from such a disparity of disciplines that the capacity of any one man to draw it together is impossibly strained. Happily there are methods of handling even this difficulty and of achieving interdisciplinary collaboration on the acquisition of the fundamental knowledge of penal sanctions which Hammurabi really needed but did not have before he leapt to that codifying exercise which has sustained his name and inspired his equally unsure successors.

Let me conclude this theme by a possibly too whimsical allegory. Some people tell me that the world is flat; that if you punish one, that will deter the others. And it is plainly clear that for a variety of purposes they are correct, just as for many purposes—tennis, building a house—the world is clearly flat. But there is a certain roundness alleged by some dreamers. They claim that if you sail in one direction you get back to where you started. They suggest it is their long and tragic experience that those who would deter others from acting by threatening or even demonstrating that they will suffer, often experience the very action they seek to deter; that those who would reduce crime by terror often live deeply fearful of violent crime. Let us kill one in ten; that will stop their resistance! Hang the murderers; that will reduce the murder and attempted-murder rates! Bomb their cities; that will bring them to the conference table! And I conclude, on this topic, as I hope you do, that those who would pin their larger faith to deterrence are unwise; and that those who deny its operative relevance in many mundane and smaller areas of behavioral control are likewise unwise. What we need are some soundings in deterrence, some tracings of this shore, so that we shall begin to know where the flatness of the human personality is relevant and where the roundness; for what purpose this particular world is flat and for what purposes round. Given these insights, a massive impediment to penal reform would be cast aside.

II. LESS ELIGIBILITY

The principle of "less eligibility" is the reverse side of the coin of deterrence. Sidney and Beatrice Webb defined this principle, in relation to the 19th century Poor Laws in England, as follows: "The principle of less eligibility demanded that the conditions of existence afforded by the relief [of the pauper] should be less eligible to the applicant than those of the lowest grade of independent labourers."[35] When applied to penal sanctions, and certainly to prisons and reformatory institutions, it means that the conditions of the convicted criminal should be "less eligible" than those of any other section of the community. Jeremy Bentham, in his *Panopticon,* adopted this principle: "[T]he ordinary condition of a convict . . . ought not to be made more eligible than that of the poorest class of subjects in a state of innocence and liberty."[36]

The principle of less eligibility has, as you see, an attractive simplicity. If the conditions of the convicted criminal are to be better than those of any other group in the community, then that group, when they know of this fact, will hurry to join their more fortunate brethren—and the gates lie open via crime. Far from being deterred, they will be attracted. In 1939, Hermann Mannheim regarded this principle of less eligibility as "the most formidable obstacle in the way of penal reform." [37] In the years since Mannheim wrote, the principle seems to have declined in significance, certainly at the administrative level. The Federal Bureau of Prisons has for years in its institutions for younger adults and other youths been providing vocational training programs which are only now gradually being emulated by the Job Corps and which have long been superior to the vocational training opportunities which would have been available to the inmates had they not been convicted of federal offences; and these training opportunities are offered in material and physical conditions manifestly superior to those in which otherwise all but a few would be living. The same is true in many prisons and reformatories,— for example the forestry camps run by the Illinois Youth Commission. The conditions there are certainly not luxurious, but they are better physically than those in which many of the youths live in the depressed neighborhoods from which they come.

And if one goes further afield to test this, say to Polynesia, in the jail at Fiji a bell would ring loudly at five in the afternoon to summon the prisoners working on the docks, it being well understood that those who were not within the walls by five fifteen would have to fend for themselves that night—and would be arrested the next morning. They rushed to jail at the summons of the bell; but few were thereby expressing an affection for jail life. And in the Nukulofa, on Tonga, in the Friendly Isles, the capital of the last kingdom in Oceania, where the unsylphlike Queen Salote has recently been succeeded by her son, King Tupou II, the main prison, an open institution, is known as "Government College."

The truth is that at all levels of cultural development we seem to accept that compulsory treatment, with the stigma of crime, and pursuant to a judicial sentence, is not likely to be positively attractive to other than those who by long institutionalization have been habituated to it.

Thus, though the principle of less eligibility remains a rationalization for the punitive emotions of men, it is not at present a serious bar to penal reform. There is, however, one other aspect of this principle of less eligibility that may merit a passing glance. Assume that to keep a prisoner costs the community about $2,500 a year. It may be cheaper, if our prediction instruments were at all reliable, to leave him at large and by weekly subsidy of $40 to reward his virtuous avoidance of crime; like a reverse income tax, a reverse crime prevention contribution. It may be cheaper, but it won't soon happen. We may doubt the deterrent efficacy of a sanction but we had better, for the time being, not make our punishments positively attractive. Nor do I fear that my successors in this chair will have serious difficulty in avoiding any problems of less eligibility as they discover and define the rules of sound penal practice in relation to our deterrent and reformative purposes.

III. THE LIMITS OF THE REHABILITATIVE IDEAL

A new but nevertheless serious impediment to penal reform is our growing skepticism about the wisdom of indulging in practice our desire better to treat convicted criminals by mobilizing for that purpose the developing skills of the relevant social sciences. We have come to fear that by so doing we will sacrifice many of the traditional and important values of justice under law. The rehabilitative ideal is seen to import unfettered discretion. Whereas the treaters seem convinced of the benevolence of their treatment methods, those being treated take a different view, and we, the observers, share their doubts. The jailer in a white coat and with a doctorate remains a jailer—but with larger powers over his fellows. It is clear that absent definition of the proper limits of the rehabilitative ideal, this lawyer-like skepticism of ours is a serious theoretical and practical impediment to penal reform.

No one has deployed for our consideration better than our colleague, Francis Allen, in *The Borderland of Criminal Justice*,[38] the potentiality for injustice that lies within the rehabilitative ideal. He has demonstrated how the rhetoric of treatment may cloak the realities of persecution and how claims to therapy may conceal mass banishment to institutions devoid of treatment processes and profoundly insensitive to human rights. But we cannot repudiate this whole approach to punishment; we cannot nowadays reject rehabilitative purposes and take refuge in the prayer for judges in the Book of Common Prayer, so close in spirit to that of the developing Common Law, that "they may truly and indifferently minister justice, to the punishment of wickedness and vice, and to the maintenance of . . . true religion and virtue." Inexorably our purposes become forward looking, and inevitably we must incorporate into our sentencing and correctional processes large measures of the rehabilitative ideal.

The dangers of abuse of the rehabilitative ideal are real, but they must not tempt us to inaction; we must not let our skepticism of the reformer's simplistic enthusiasm lead us to a flat and unproductive opposition. We must not be entirely sicklied o'er with the pale cast of thought. Throughout all developed legal systems the rehabilitative ideal sweeps steadily over the jurisprudence of the criminal law and it is regrettable for lawyers to oppose it. We may be skeptical of any rounded Positivist theory, cautious of the School of Social Defence, and even doubt that Marc Ancel's recent graceful study of the penal philosophy of that school accurately phrases correctional realities; but we can hardly oppose their aim or doubt their future significance.[39]

I do not seek to rebut the thesis that the rehabilitative ideal can be abused and has frequently been abused; it seems to me proper to look with suspicion on those who seek power over the lives of others, including the criminal and the juvenile delinquent, on the ground that it will be exercised for their own good and hence for the larger social good. I offer, rather, some suggestions of principle by which we may have our cake and eat it—I hope to suggest principles by which the rehabilitative ideal may be accepted as a guide to social action while at the same time its threats to human rights, its 1984-ish potentialities, can be avoided.

Speaking in 1961 at this law school, on the occasion of the celebration of the enactment of the Illinois Criminal Code, I tried to sketch the dangers of abuse of human rights from assumptions of power for rehabilitative purposes and then offered the following two principles to avoid these dangers:

1. *Power over a criminal's life should not be taken in excess of that which would be taken were his reform not considered as one of our purposes.* The maximum of his punishment should never be greater than that which would be justified by the other aims of our criminal justice. Under the power ceiling of that sentence, we should utilize our reformative skills to assist him towards social readjustment; but we should never seek to justify an extension of power over him on the ground that we may thus more likely effect his reform. This principle should be applied to the exercise of legislative, judicial, and administrative power; it should be applied to substantive law as well as to procedural processes.

2. *Correctional practices must cease to rest on surmise and good intentions; they must be based on facts.* We are under a moral obligation to use our best intelligence to discover whether and to what extent our various penal sanctions do in fact reform.

Few will oppose this second principle or deny the need to establish empirically valid foundations for the methods we use in preventing and treating crime; and no one will doubt that the more secure this foundation the more possible it will be to avoid abuse of human rights from ill-founded claims of rehabilitative capacity. In the next section of this paper I shall deal with some problems of the ethics and strategy of research in this field; let me, however, now offer some comments on the first principle—that rehabilitative purposes cannot justify an extension of power over the individual offender.

In 1964, in *Studies in Criminal Law*,[40] Colin Howard and I again offered this principle of the punitive ceiling for consideration. Two commentators have since criticized this principle—Professor Sanford Kadish and Mr. Richard F. Sparks. Professor Kadish described it as "debatable";[41] Mr. Sparks more curtly categorized it as "mistaken."[42] Professor Kadish pursued his criticisms by means of interrogatories to which I shall now file a reply. He asked, "why should the rehabilitative purpose be subordinated to the deterrent, vindicatory, and incapacitative purposes so that the former may be accomplished only within the limits of confinement appropriate to the latter?"[43] My reply is: whatever their historical roots, these other purposes now function also as a ceiling to punishment, whereas the rehabilitative ideal does not. It is true that the price-list of deterrence and retribution varies greatly from jurisdiction to jurisdiction, and from time to time within any one jurisdiction, but within that price-list, excessively inflated though it may be, we do have a concept of an excessive punishment. That is not true of reform. It is open ended; it cannot be excessive; if we are acting for the good of the subject of the action there need be no limit to our benevolence; it is untrammelled by any sense of injustice.

Professor Kadish rounds out his interrogatories by this comment: "Now if . . .[the] limiting principle [is] to govern only pending the development of proven therapeutic knowledge and techniques, the answer may be a political and practical one: namely, that during this period (which may, of course, not pass for generations, if ever) the historic function of deterrence and incapacitation provide the most likely practical protection against the great potentialities for extended deprivations of freedom in open-ended rehabilitative programs. . . . [But] the ground becomes much shakier if . . . [the] principle [is] to operate even on the assumption of assured rehabilitative success."[44] Mr. Sparks makes the same point,[45] rejecting the offered principle on an assumption that precise reformative and predictive skills will ultimately be available. Their concession is large indeed, and perhaps I should bear their strictures with equanimity, for if the principle I have offered can serve as an insulation from the dangers and excesses of the rehabilitative ideal until our reformative capacities are effective, measurable, and predictable in the individual case, then it is an important principle indeed with a healthy and long life ahead—a principle which demands the allegiance of Professor Kadish and Mr. Sparks and not their distant condescension, for it will see them and me to our graves.

Let me go further, however, and argue for the longer applicability of this principle by testing it beyond that span of years, whatever it be, and by assuming circumstances of certainty of rehabilitative success. Is the ground then really much shakier, as Professor Kadish suggested? I would ask—does the state in which criminology has reached that eminence of knowledge compulsorily apply its certainly reformative processes to people identical with the criminal in all respects, of equal danger, of equal reformative need, differing only in the fact that they have not been convicted of a crime? If yes, then act under whatever such powers, consensual or imposed, you have over the non-criminal and do not needlessly clutter up sentencing and correctional processes in this way. If no, then to exert these larger reformative powers only over the criminal is a gross injustice.

I appreciate that I am advocating a natural law type of limitation to punishment, not easily capable of formulation in terms which exclude an imprecise individual and community sense of injustice; but that does not preclude its being a sound rule for avoiding the potentiality for injustice in the rehabilitative idea. The late C. S. Lewis was, it seems to me, clearly right when he argued:

> [T]he concept of Desert is the only connecting link between punishment and justice. It is only as deserved or undeserved that a sentence can be just or unjust. I do not here contend that the question "Is it deserved?" is the only one we can reasonably ask about a punishment. We may very properly ask whether it is likely to deter others and to reform the criminal. But neither of these last two questions is a question about justice. There is no sense in talking about a "just deterrent" or a "just cure." We demand of a deterrent not whether it is just but whether it will deter. . . . Thus when we cease to consider what the criminal deserves and consider only what will cure him or deter others, we have tacitly removed him from the sphere of justice altogether; instead of a person, a subject of rights, we now have a mere object, a patient, a "case."[46]

The principle I have offered would, I submit, allow ample room for indulgence of our rehabilitative purposes without risking injustice. It may be thought that this suggested principle suffers from too little thrust; that it is almost axiomatic. I would deny this. It is not academic and remote. Had it guided reform, the unjust excesses of insufficient procedural and substantive protections of the purportedly reformative treatment of juvenile offenders and adult sexual criminals, of narcotic addicts and mentally retarded or disturbed offenders, the improper use of the indefinite and indeterminate sentences, and the degeneration of parole systems, all of which have been so widespread, so wicked and so socially harmful, would not have occured. A more cogent criticism of the principle I have offered may be that it is too restrictive; that, if seriously applied, it would preclude reformative and community protective processes which all would regard as desirable. Let us test this.

Could such a rule apply to the gravely psychologically disturbed criminal or to the mentally defective criminal who may have to be detained indefinitely? I think it could and should. I would argue that the gross defects in the sexual psychopath laws of this country were and are exactly of this nature. I would submit that grave injustice flows from combining the two concepts of criminality and mental ill health when one is quantifying the duration of custodial control that the state may properly exercise over people having both deficiencies.

This argument has recently received high judicial support. In *Baxstrom v. Herold*,[47] the Supreme Court held that the petitioner, a convicted criminal who had been civilly committed as his term of imprisonment approached its end, "was denied equal protection of the laws by the statutory procedure under which a person may be civilly committed at the expiration of his penal sentence without the jury review available to all other persons civilly committed in New York."[48] The Court expressly rejected the argument that the state had legislatively created a reasonable and therefore constitutional classification of the "criminally insane" for this purpose, as distinguished from the "civilly insane." "For purposes of granting judicial review before a jury of the question whether a person is mentally ill and in need of institutionalization, there is no conceivable basis for distinguishing the commitment of a person who is nearing the end of a penal term from all other civil commitments."[49]

For the crime he has committed, if that be proved, the offender, sane or insane, should properly be punished or treated (call it what you will) for no longer than would be regarded as a just and deserved punishment were his sanity or psychological balance or social dangerousness not in issue. If he is to be held for any period in excess of that, we should apply to him only the other existing powers that a state takes over all its citizens, criminal and not criminal, on grounds of their mental ill health. If it be argued that this is playing with words, I would suggest that the contrary is true and that the present situation reflects gross abuse flowing from failure to maintain necessary separation between two appropriately distinct processes of state control over the individual. The protections that we have accorded the non-criminal citizen in relation to his commitment to mental institutions, may or may not be adequate; but at least they are likely to be more clearly defined than those available to the convicted criminal, and their application will minimize the double stigmatization which is such a fertile source of injustice.

Could such a principle apply to young offenders who may, it is argued, for relatively minor offences have to be held protractedly under the control and protection of the state? I think it could and should. The late Paul Tappan has compellingly demonstrated the abuses to the rights of the child that have flowed from the unfettered benevolence of the juvenile court movement in this country.[50] There are at present two contrary movements in the common law world with reference to the juvenile court, both of which have tendencies conforming to the principle I have offered, though they are diametrically opposed movements. On the one hand, there is in this country an increasing insistence on due process in the children's and juvenile courts, and a movement towards the provision of counsel for those children and their families.[51] Involved in this movement is a strong suggestion that such great powers over a child's life cannot be justified by the court's benevolent purposes. There is, I would hope, an effort to incorporate a concept of a maximum or a ceiling of a deserved sanction as applicable to the child, in relation to the harm that he has inflicted on society, and an endeavor to move beyond that limited power over him only when either there is agreement by all parties (if possible, including the child) concerning the wisdom of certain retraining processes, or when such processes are justified entirely apart from his criminality and under powers that the state holds over all children, delinquent and non-delinquent alike.

The contrary movement, but also tending to conform to my offered principle, is to be found in a recent White Paper published by the Home Office in the United Kingdom[52] recommending the total abolition of all juvenile courts for children under sixteen in the belief that the problems they present can be best handled on a consensual basis between child, parents, and the welfare authorities of the state; and that the hearing, the day in court, and the sentence are not necessary. Absent a continuing consensus on the best treatment, from time to time, there would be a power of reference to new family courts to be established for the sixteen to twenty-one age group which would also serve several other functions of a family court. Here again, but working from the other end of the spectrum, there is a deliberate effort to divorce deserved punishment from desired treatment, and the effort is much to be welcomed.

In sum, I would suggest that there is a clear difference between the medical, social welfare, psychiatric, and child care functions of the state and its police and correctional functions. There is too much confusion of purposes and too frequently a sacrifice of justice when we combine the several justifications the state may have for taking power over a citizen's life and in so doing expunge or attenuate the existing limitations and controls of power that each has developed. This confusion, productive of injustice, is frequently to be observed. I saw it first ten years ago in a most virulent form in the institution for defective delinquents in Bridgewater, Massachusetts (I hear it has much improved since then), where men were held for a combination of crime and retardation much longer and in grossly less attractive circumstances than they would have been had these labels not been combined. In the sexual psychopath laws of this country the mental health power has infested the judicial power over criminals with like result. The juvenile court suffers a similar and needless confusion of heads of authority. And many plans advanced to meet the problem of narcotic addiction, not the least being recent so-called Civil Commitment Legislation in New York,[53] suffer pathologically from this unjust cumulative mixture of state powers. I am not preaching a sterile separation of powers which would impede penal reform. The rehabilitative ideal has luxuriant opportunity to contribute to human welfare and the diminution of individual suffering without arrogating to itself such extra power. Its leading qualities for decades at least, and probably permanently, should be a modest diligence. But, limited in this way, the rehabilitative ideal demands the lawyer's energetic support, not his distant criticism, for amongst our purposes of punishment it alone offers hope for a more decent, safer, and happier community.

Let me go beyond defense of this principle of punitive ceiling and try to take the matter one step further by offering an outline of another process which seems to me to bear on our agreed aim of rehabilitation without tyranny. Perhaps, as one method of avoiding the injustice of the unfettered benevolence of the rehabilitative ideal, we should make more use of administrative controls of punishing-treating processes rather than to pursue only the separation of powers theme I have advanced. I confess to uncertainty about this, but nevertheless think it proper to offer it for your critical consideration.

Perhaps the Scandinavian Ombudsman[54] is the type of administrative control we should use in our efforts to obtain the advantages of penal sanctions turned towards better reform and more efficient community protection without risking the manifest individual injustices that can ensue. Certainly, the Ombudsman does appear to have this effect in the Scandinavian systems. Complete freedom of access of the prisoner to the Ombudsman and his staff allows one agency of the state, with the high degree of autonomy that the Ombudsman has achieved, effectively to protect the prisoner from any excesses in the rehabilitative purposes which guide another agency of the state, the prison authority. The same is true of the appointment of the "next friend" to all prisoners sentenced in Denmark to indefinite terms; this mechanism allows such a prisoner, through his next friend, easy access to a court to seek his release from custody on the ground that the treatment purposes claimed as justification for the indeterminate custody that is being exercised over him have either been fulfilled or are not being seriously attempted. It may be, therefore, that by administrative processes we could greatly reduce the threat of injustice in the rehabilitative idea; but certainly until such administrative processes were entrenched and efficiently functioning I would reaffirm the principle that power over a criminal's life should not be taken in excess of that which would be taken were his reform not considered as one of our purposes.[55]

IV. ETHICS AND STRATEGY OF RESEARCH

Earlier I noted gaps in our knowledge of deterrence and suggested means for filling them. Knowledge of the deterrent efficacy of various punishments is, however, only half the basic necessary information, for if rational decisions are to be made concerning penal sanctions we need also to know the likely effect of the proposed punishment on the particular person to be punished. This likelihood can be judged at present only as a combined statistical and clinical prediction, and then only in terms of probability. Here too the gaps in our knowledge are chasms and we must consider how they can be filled.[56] It will be found that some serious obstacles of an ethical and strategic nature stand in the way of an easy acquisition of this knowledge.

Before considering them, it should be noted that these two areas of information relevant to any punishing decision (general deterrence and rehabilitative potential) interrelate differently at different stages of the punishing process, and interrelate differently for different types of crimes. Thus, the legislator when addressing himself to the definition of the available sanctions for a given type of criminal behavior will be thinking largely in terms of available knowledge concerning deterrence and to a lesser extent will need to take into account problems of individual treatment and rehabilitation. By contrast, the prison administrator or the probation administrator rarely has to give much consideration to problems of deterrence but stands in larger need of information about the likely therapeutic effects of his decisions on the individual offender. The judge imposing sentence faces a more complex balance between the deterrent and individual treatment processes of the criminal law. And for the judge, the relationship between these two processes, rehabilitative and deterrent, cannot be stated as an equation applicable to all crimes; it varies greatly from one type of crime to another. For example, many murderers could safely be released from the court without further punishment on the day that they are convicted of their murder. Deterrence will, however, be a primary and usually controlling consideration precluding such a decision. By contrast, a criminal frequently previously convicted of a relatively minor offense who has just been convicted for this offense again will raise problems in which his individual needs and the needs of society for protection from him will bulk very much larger than any questions of deterring others from the type of behavior of which he has been last convicted.

Though this interrelationship between the deterrent and treatment purposes of the criminal law is thus dynamic and diverse, in most sentencing situations a rational balancing can be achieved only if some information relevant to both aspects is available.

It has recently become fashionable to stress our lack of knowledge of the relative efficacy of our various treatment methods and I do not wish on this occasion to retrace that melancholy story. The central question eludes us: which treatment methods are effective for which types of offenders and for how long should they be applied for optimum effect? Criminological research has been unwisely concentrated on the search for that will-o'-the-wisp, the causes of crime, glossing over the likelihood that crime is not a unity capable of aetiological study. "What are the causes of disease?" is surely as hopelessly wide and methodologically inappropriate a question as is the question "what are the causes of crime?" At last, however, there is widespread verbal agreement (if not action) that we must critically test our developing armamentarium of prevention and treatment methods, and that to do so requires testing by means of controlled clinical trials. Follow-up studies, association analysis, predictive attributes analysis[57]—no matter how sophisticated other research techniques we apply, we cannot escape the need for direct evaluative research by means of clinical trials. And this leads me to the next impediment to penal reform—clinical trials themselves raise important ethical issues that demand consideration.

In medical and pharmacological research the clinical trial is well established and has proved of great value in the development of therapeutic methods. Where there is genuine doubt as to the choice between two or more treatments for a given condition, efficient experimentation requires that the competing methods be tested on matched groups of patients. Of course, the analogy between the doctor's "treatment" and the court's or penal administrator's "treatment" is imperfect. Both the subject of medical diagnosis and the criteria of successful treatment are better defined, and the patient consents to treatment while the criminal does not. Problems of abuse of human rights thus obtrude when it is sought to apply the clinical trial to correctional practice. Is it justifiable to impose a criminal sanction guided by the necessities of research and not the felt necessities of the case?

The experience of this law school with the Jury Project[58] underlines the need carefully to consider the ethics of social experimentation. Clearly there was no unethical experimentation in that project, but it did reveal the deep emotional and irrational anxieties in the community that empiricism stirs when directed towards social processes which are strongly believed in. One must not, without reckoning the risk, gaze into the face (or even, like my colleagues, an orifice) of the Oracle!

There is, however, a respectable and reasonable ethical argument against clinical trials of correctional treatment methods which must not be burked in our enthusiasm for the acquisition of knowledge. It runs like this: Terrestrially speaking, man is an end in himself; he must never be sacrificed to some self-appointed superman's belief that knowledge about man's behavior is of greater value than respect for his human rights. This is particularly true if the sacrifice is made without his uncoerced and fully informed choice. The explorer may, choosing thus freely, risk his life in the pursuit of knowledge. The citizen may, under certain controlled conditions, risk his life and physical well-being in furtherance of medical experiments. But when hint of coercion, or restraining or unduly influencing pressures appear, it is (choose your epithet) sinful, unethical, socially unwise, to permit such sacrifice of the individual to the supposed collective good.[59] The argument shifts, of course, in wartime; but then the threat to the collectivity is seen as the overwhelming value.

Put in less pretentious terms, the proposition is: given that our knowledge is exiguous, nevertheless, we must at all times act in the way that within that knowledge is thought best for the individual we are treating. When the problem of his treatment raises (as it does generally in relation to criminal sanctions) the issue of the proper balance between the community's need for protection from him and people like him, and his treatment needs if he is to be reestablished as a member of society, conforming sufficiently to avoid criminal conduct, the same principle holds true; we are never justified in applying other than our best judgment concerning that balance for the sake of experimentation aimed at expediting the acquisition of knowledge of how to handle like cases in the future.

It is my view that the ethical argument against clinical trials is not convincing and that, given certain safeguards, it is entirely appropriate, indeed essential, for evaluative research projects of this type to be built into all new correctional developments. The two safeguards that I have in mind may not in perpetuity solve the problem, but they do at least provide sufficient protection of human rights for many decades of correctional research.

First, we do not have to apply such research techniques at the stage of judicial sentencing; they can well operate within the sentence that the judge has determined to be the just and appropriate sentence. Secondly, by applying a principle which might be called the principle of "less severity," abuse of human rights can be minimized.

Experiment at the judicial stage is not necessary since correctional sanctions already include wide diversities of treatment within the judicially imposed sentence. A defined term of imprisonment may in any one state involve a commitment to possibly extremely different types of institutions having substantially different reformative processes and with appreciably different degrees of social isolation. And given the operation of discretionary release procedures, including parole, most prison sentences permit widely differing periods of incarceration. Likewise, a sentence of probation can lead to a close personal supervision or to the most perfunctory experience of occasional reporting. The range of subtreatments within each correctional treatment is thus very wide; so wide that ample room for evaluative clinical research into these subtreatments exists without interference with judicial processes. Of course, as information relevant to sentencing emerges from such administratively created clinical trials, it will be fed back into the judicial process and will then create new opportunities for further evaluative research. And knowledge will grow without experimentation at the judicial level.

"Less severity" is the other safeguard. By this I mean that the new treatment being studied should not be one that is regarded in the mind of the criminal subjected to it, or of the people imposing the new punishment, or of the community at large, as more severe than the traditional treatment against which it is being compared. To take a group of criminals who otherwise would be put on probation and to select some at random for institutional treatment would be unjust; conversely, to select at random a group who would otherwise be incarcerated and to treat them on probation or in a probation hostel would seem to be no abuse of human rights. Applying this principle it is possible to pursue many decades of valuable evaluative research.

There are many methodological problems in evaluative research. I do not wish to deal with them now, but rather to continue to focus on these ethical issues. Have these two principles of administrative rather than judicial experimentation and "less severity" sufficiently disposed of the ethical problems? Let us probe this question by the classroom method of a hypothetical case. Last night this problem was on my mind when I went to sleep and I had a dream which still troubles me. I dreamt that I observed and heard a conversation between a furious burglar sitting in his cell and a garrulous social scientist. Physically, each was a Lombrosian stereotype, and their speech too was a caricature of what one would expect from their widely different backgrounds and experiences. I cannot precisely recall their words, and perhaps it is a mercy that neither the sociologese nor the scatological blasphemy have remained in my mind. I can, however, describe the situation in which they found themselves and, later, in less colorful terms than theirs, tell you the substance of their conversation.

In my dream I saw the furious burglar sitting in his cell. He was part of our control group. The experiment had been impeccably and carefully designed. We desired to test the wisdom of releasing a defined group of offenders some three months earlier than they would otherwise be released by sending them to a recently established halfway house where daily they would go out to work and where their evenings and leisure time would be devoted to guided group interaction, using the most modern techniques, and to other processes designed for their easier and more effective resettlement into the community. This relatively new type of facility had been legislatively and administratively established as an "experiment" which, as you know, is the name of all new penal developments. This experiment differed from the usual experiment in that the social scientists were allowed to make it an experiment.

The group of offenders thought suitable for this new type of treatment had been carefully delineated in terms of their personalities and background. Since the halfway house could accommodate only twenty people it became necessary to discover how many such offenders would be found in the prison system. A careful assessment of the prison population and cautious predictions of its likely future shape led to the view that there were at any one time forty prisoners precisely matching the criteria for selection for this new treatment facility. It was therefore decided that that diagnostic center would be responsible for the selection of the prisoners who fell and might fall within this category; that they would be given a code number; and that chance would be allowed to condition whether a man fell within the T group, and would go to the new halfway house, of the C group, and would be treated just as he would have been had the facility not been built. It was, of course, early and necessarily decided that the C group must never know that this had happened and that the T

group must never know that they were part of a controlled experiment—
though, of course, it would be clear to them that new opportunities were
being given to them. They must believe that they were given these
opportunities because the staff of the diagnostic center had convinced the
parole board of their peculiar suitability for the halfway house. They
might prefer to believe that they had conned the diagnostic center and
the parole board, this being an even better belief, experimentally
speaking. My furious burglar fell within the C group. My social scientists
had been garrulous indeed, and a series of indiscretions had led to him
revealing this fact to the burglar. That is why the burglar was furious.

FB (Furious Burglar); You mean you're holding me here because of
     some . . . experiment?

GSS (Garrulous Social Scientist): Yes.

FB: Why didn't you tell me?

GSS: It would spoil the experiment . . . the Hawthorne effect, you
     know.

FB: Habeas corpus? What chance?

GSS: That is a somewhat difficult question. I am told that it has some
     constitutional aspects to it. To my knowledge the matter has never
     been tested. You should ask our Legal Aid Division.

FB: Wasn't it tested in the Nuremburg Trial?

GSS: Everyone knows that was different.

FB: How different?

GSS: Well, you see, the Nazi experimentation met our criterion that
     the decision must be administrative and not judicial but it did not
     meet the important and to my mind determinative criterion; that
     is, that the new treatment we are testing must be, in our eyes, and
     in your eyes, and in the eyes of all right-minded members of the
     community, a lesser infringement on freedom, a lesser suffering,
     then the traditional punishment against which it is being tested
     and which would otherwise be applied to everyone. You have not
     lost anything; twenty people just like you have gained, but you
     have not lost. And think what good you do for others. We will
     learn how to develop better release procedures; earlier release for
     some is a likely result; crime will be diminished. You should be
     thanking me, not complaining.

FB: I'm complaining. Obfuscate it as you will, because of your . . .
     experiment, I'm here. Have I an action in false imprisonment
     against you, or the warden, or the governor?

GSS: That too is a matter for our Legal Aid Division but I don't think
     you do. We have not increased the maximum of your legally

prescribed punishment in any way. Why are you complaining? You had a fifty per cent chance of getting out three months ago; we were quite fair; without us you would have had no chance.

FB: You lie. The halfway house would have been set up whether you had anything to do with it or not. The prison administrators are not conned by you social scientists; that's just the way they get federal subsidies. I know and you know that I am peculiarly suited to release to a halfway house and that I can talk well to the parole board and that if you had kept your white coat out of it I would have had at least an eighty per cent chance of being sent to that halfway house. By grouping me with those other thirty-nine and tossing coins, you reduced my chances to fifty per cent. Surely it must be clear to you that it is thirty per cent likely that I am here because of your . . . experiment.

GSS: All of us must suffer in the cause of science, you know. Your error lies in failing to appreciate that men must fall into categories for purposes of social research, they cannot be seen entirely as individuals, and we treated you fairly as part of your appropriate category.

And then the garrulous social scientist stalked out of the cell mumbling, "How else will we ever learn?" and slammed the cell door shut behind him, which awakened me. The dream continues to trouble me. I think there were one or two more things that the garrulous social scientist should have said in his own defense, but I am not sure that they are finally convincing. He should have pointed out the randomness of the whole edifice of correctional sanctions. He might well have stressed that repeated studies over the past forty years have beyond a doubt established the gross irrational variations in sentencing practice, even within the same courthouse, and should have tried to persuade the burglar that this type of experimentation was one effective way of acquiring knowledge relevant to the elimination of such unjust disparities. He might have more strenuously argued that the need to devise treatments suitable to categories of individuals sometimes of necessity involves an insufficiently fine balancing of differences between them, and that the burglar's differences from the other thirty-nine in the punishment control group were so slight as to be immeasurable in the macrocosm of the sentencing and punishing jungle. I think he should have tried more diligently to persuade the burglar of the need for such groupings of individuals, if knowledge of rational treatment methods is ever to be acquired. I doubt that he would have succeeded, and I am convinced that it is unwise to employ a garrulous social scientist.

Some have suggested that one way of avoiding this dilemma is, in an experiment of this type, to have arranged that both the treatment and the control groups obtained an advantage over the traditional punishment. That is, that in the previously considered experiment, twenty should be sent to the halfway house three months before their otherwise planned release and twenty should be completely released at the earlier time. Though this minimizes the ethical problem, it does not eliminate it. Now the furious burglar who is complaining is to be found in the halfway house bewailing the fact that he is under the degree of control that he is there. And also, it becomes a different experiment, and it will be necessary if effective knowledge is to be gained from the experiment to compare both our freely released group and our halfway house group with some control group still in the institution if the maximum knowledge is to be gained from the experiment—and they have cause for complaint.

In their *Delay in the Court*, Zeisel, Kalven, and Buchholz devote a chapter to "The Case for the Official Experiment." They consider the possible constitutional limitations on freedom to mount a controlled experiment and point out the tendency of the results of such experimentation to diminish discrimination:

> Paradoxically . . . if the purpose of the experiment is properly pursued, any discrimination that it might have brought about during its operation would be eliminated after the experiment is ended. Whichever treatment emerged from the experiment as superior would become the general rule, thus not only ending discrimination but also improving the law for all. If, on the other hand, the experiment should not reveal any difference in the two treatments, any claim of discrimination is authoritatively disproved.[60]

This may well be true as a matter of constitutional analysis, but not in terms of the possible discriminations of sanctions which chance will allocate between individuals during the experiment. This, the authors of *Delay in the Court* expressly recognize: "In setting the limits within which they may permit legal experimentation, the courts will, as always, weigh the good which it attempts against the evil which, if only temporarily, it may bring about."[61]

In conclusion, let me say that it is my position that the ethical difficulties in empirical evaluation research are so slight as not to constitute a serious impediment to it. I confess that I feel happier when such projects test differences of practice within existing treatments, so that no burglar will bother to be furious, but I know that is no answer. My final reason for not being persuaded by the furious burglar, even in his precise situation, is this: the whole system of sanctions, from suspicion to arrest to trial to sentence, punishment, and release is now so full of irrational and unfair disparities that marginal arguments of the type the furious burglar produces are to me lost in the sea of injustice from which in the long run we can only be saved by these means. Yet I remain on his side to the extent that I abhor experimental design which is not anxiously perceptive of these ethical problems and does not do its utmost to minimize them.

Putting the ethical obstacles aside, I come to one last but serious strategic impediment to the immediate potentiality of empirical evaluative research to lighten our ignorance of treatment methods. It is peculiarly difficult to organize an effective evaluative program from outside the penal system itself. It may be that only from within the administration can effective and continuing research programs be mounted; and it is certain that it cannot be mounted from without unless there is enthusiastic and strong support for it from within. Thus, California is now producing more meaningful evaluative research than any other state or country in the world. One reason is that the Adult and Youth Authorities in that state have built their research programs deeply into their administrative structures. The same thing is in very small part true in the United Kingdom and to some degree in the federal systems and some of the more progressive states; but it is the rare exception and certainly not the rule.

Let me mention some of the difficulties of "outside research"; for example, research mounted by a university department with the permission of the relevant correctional authority. Let it be supposed that the senior administrators of that authority are wholly and fully persuaded of the need for such quality control of their product. Even so, what is in it for the front of the line staff who must be involved in the project? What effect does the project have on, for example, their mileage allowances? What can they gain from it for themselves? How can their quiet insidious lack of enthusiasm be reconciled with the supportive needs of an active research project? Only if research skills and supportive efforts are part of the career line to promotion is it likely that they will be fully supportive. Within the universities, where they are a part of the normal career promotion and status lines, it is well and easy to talk of the high challenge and value of the acquisition of this type of knowledge. It may appear quite otherwise when one is daily engaged in the treatment of criminals, particularly when the knowledge itself which is being sought is likely to be such as to cast a serious doubt on the social value of one's own efforts.

Politically, if the results of research evaluative of an existing practice are adverse to it, one's opponents and critics may use it unfairly to discredit not only those administering the correctional system but also the appointing authority who is politically responsible. Political battles may be fought while mounted on the charger of research. Further, in the usual overcrowded, understaffed, exiguously budgeted correctional agency, the unanticipated extra work that is created by a research project for an already fully occupied staff leads not only to lack of enthusiasm for the research project, but may change the nature, methods, and objectives of the research.

These problems are multiplied when the responsible administrators are not totally persuaded of the value of such research but rather are convinced of the socially useful quality of their product as it stands. They need no quality controls of their product—they daily see that it is good. They have, in short, a vested interest in the preservation of current practices. I do not mean offensively to imply that those in charge of correctional agencies or institutions want, for any financial or personal reasons, to preserve inefficiencies in the system. If it were such a corrupt vested interest it would be a less serious obstacle to penal reform. The point is that their motives are of the best. They have total confidence in the quality of their agency or institution. They are ignorant of developments elsewhere and of existing theoretical speculations and research. They are suspicious of the outsider claiming research skills and critical capacities who yet obviously lacks comprehension of the day-to-day difficulties of correctional work. Many are fine people, devoted to minimizing human suffering, pursuing their work as a humanitarian dedication. Their salaries are not high nor is their status in the eyes of the community. Psychological mechanisms must come to their aid to convince them of the social value of what they are doing. Dr. Schweitzer would not have been easy to persuade that he was doing more harm than good in the Congo; and the analogy is close in the mind of the devoted and ambitious correctional officer and administrator.

Like the other impediments to penal reform to which I have pointed, this one is not an impossible obstacle. There is an increasing movement amongst the leading correctional administrators of the world gradually to incorporate some evaluative research programs into their new developments. The swell is slight, but it is perceptible. There will be setbacks, but the shape of future growth is clear. Likewise, the "outsider" in the university need not at all dispair of gaining collaboration from those daily involved in correctional practice in his research enterprise, provided he realizes that it is necessary when designing his experiment to take into account the material and psychological needs not only of the subjects of his experiment but also of those involved in their treatment. It is no good persuading correctional administrations to allow a research enterprise to be pursued within their organizations unless the collaboration includes the clearest understanding about the roles of those employed in that administration and incorporates advantages to them which will not adversely affect the experiment as an experiment but will provide an incentive for their interested collaboration.

V. CONCLUSIONS

1. To date, our guidelines to penal reform have been humanitarian and aimed at diminishing the prisoner's needless suffering and reducing his social isolation. This sentiment now provides an insufficient frame of reference for penal reform.
2. The fundamental postulate of the criminal law is that punishment deters, yet we have only random insights into the deterrent efficacy, if any, of our diverse sanctions. This knowledge, seriously pursued, would not long elude us.
3. The principle of "less eligibility" is no longer a practical impediment to penal reform.
4. There are no dangers in our espousing the rehabilitative ideal provided
   a) power over a criminal's life is not taken in excess of that which would be taken were his reform not considered as one of our purposes, and
   b) all supposedly reformative processes are subjected to critical evaluation by empirical research methods.
5. Provided experiments are designed with an eye to avoiding abuse of human rights, and for the time being avoid clinical testing at the judicial stage and adhere to the principle of "less severity," the clinical trial is as appropriate to penal reform as it is to medical therapy.
6. Research directed towards penal reform is a responsibility of the penal administrator. The outsider, the scholar in a university, may be a useful collaborator but only if the penal administrator is convinced of the necessity of such research and will organize his staff and their promotion lines to encompass research activities.

32　*Ethical and Legal Issues in Experimentation With Offender Populations*

GILBERT GEIS[*]

The problems involved in research with and upon human beings are ironic, vicious, and often intensely paradoxical. The subject itself is pervaded with a good deal of piety and self-righteousness, and with two sets of antipodal values, neither of them inherently superordinate, which clash fiercely at times. Adherents who press for experimentation in the face of hesitation by others are apt to proclaim proudly that they are "scientists" and that their antagonists are "anti-intellectual" and "fuzzy intuitionists." Their opponents often find the experimenters lacking in compassion and human feeling, without sound comprehension of the legal elements basic to a democratic society. They believe that the experimenters sometimes use the scientific ethos as a camouflage for the infliction of gross indignity and deprivation upon helpless and uninformed people.

The irony lies, of course, in the exigencies of everyday existence, in which all sorts of injustice prevail as the consequence not of scientific experimentation but of happenstance. For most of us, it would be unthinkable that a sample of armed robbers be divided into two groups on the basis of random assignment—one group to spend 10 years in prison, the second to receive a sentence of 2 years on probation. Nonetheless, at a recent federal judicial conference, after examining an elaborate presentence report concerning a bank robber, 17 judges said they would have

From *Research in Correctional Rehabilitation* (Washington, D.C.: Joint Commission on Correctional Manpower and Training, 1967), pp. 34–41. Reprinted by permission of author and publisher.

imprisoned the man, while 10 indicated they favored probation. Those voting for imprisonment set sentences ranging from 6 months to 15 years.[62] From the offender's viewpoint, the vagaries of random assignment for experimental purposes might seem preferable to the lottery of exposure to the considered judgment of a member of the judiciary.

COMPETING VALUES

The difficulty involved in attempts to gain consensus on working principles for correctional experimentation with offender populations stems in part from the fact that both major competing values have almost total support. Few persons are opposed to verified, accurate information; and few persons are opposed to the idea of human decency and justice. The dispute centers about the point at which one value is to be given priority, and it is also involved in judgments regarding the true character of the experimental intervention, the statistical likelihood of different outcomes, and the general importance of the findings, measured in terms of their cost.

The dilemma of correctional research, therefore, arises with great intensity not in the extreme cases but in those where both sides of the value equation are almost equally matched. Few persons, for instance, would be apt to say that the cause of science is sufficient to support an experiment in which, without exception, persons convicted of first-degree murder during a given year are executed in order to determine whether capital punishment does in fact have a deterrent impact when categorically applied. Probably just as few persons would maintain that it is unjust to allow a convicted offender to choose between probation in the jurisdiction where he committed his offense and probation in one a thousand miles away, because an investigator wants to determine whether there is a deterrent factor in voluntary removal from the eliciting scene of criminal circumstances.

A HYPOTHETICAL ILLUSTRATION

But how do we judge a situation in which a foundation grant permits attorneys to be supplied for all cases being heard by a juvenile court where attorneys have previously appeared only in rare instances?[63] A fundamental study hypothesis may be that the presence of an attorney tends to result in a more favorable disposition for the client. This idea may be tested by comparing dispositions prior to the beginning of the experiment with those ensuing subsequently, though it would be more satisfactory to supply attorneys to a sample of the cases and withhold them from the remainder, in order to calculate in a more experimentally uncontaminated manner the differences between the outcomes in the two situations.

The matter takes on additional complexity if the researchers desire to determine what particular attorney role is the most efficacious in the juvenile court. They may suspect that an attorney who acts as a friend of the court, knowingly taking its viewpoint as *parens patriae* and attempting to interpret the court's interests to his client, will produce more desirable results than one who doggedly challenges the courtroom procedure and the judge's interpretation of fact, picks at the probation report, raises constant objections, and fights for his client as he would in a criminal court. But what results are "more desirable"? Perhaps, the argumentative approach will win dispositions more in the client's immediate interest, but the cooperative approach might in the long run better serve society and the client too by decreasing recidivism and by contributing to such measurable items as employment and earnings, marital stability, and general social adjustment.

Persons favoring the experimental use of divergent attorney roles—such roles can readily be inculcated in the attorneys by standard training techniques—might stress that, without the project and its foundation funds, no juvenile would be apt to have an attorney and thus any kind of representation is an improvement over normal conditions. They might also insist that the attorneys' views of their clients' best interest represent little more than a combination of myth and supposition, particularly in so uncharted an area as that of the juvenile court. In the long run, they could argue, all juveniles stand to benefit from this empirical determination of the consequences of diverse attorneys' roles.

Opponents of the experimental program, relying first on what they regard as an immutable professional obligation of the attorney, would be apt to suggest that it is unconscionable to deprive a single person of the effort that an attorney regards as his best in the interest of an experimental design. Failure to appeal a case to a higher court when the attorney suspects that an appeal is in order but the research blueprint does not call for intensive pursuit of technical legal points in stipulated cases, may result in commitment of a juvenile who otherwise would have been set free. That the deprivation of liberty may be in the juvenile's best interests, the opponents of the experiment would probably say, is the kind of pious cant that underlay the Inquisition and that provides paving for that well-traveled historical highway to perdition.

The dialogue could be carried further to convey the subtle nature of the issues involved in the manipulation of a situation suffused with ethical and legal considerations, in order to obtain empirical data. It might be suggested, for instance, that the appeal of a case would result in the freedom of a given juvenile but such a tactic could so antagonize the judge that he would handle all subsequent cases with greater harshness. Perhaps this view could be countered with one suggesting that to soar far beyond the given situation moves the debate into realms so remote that they are beyond speculative redemption. Perhaps it might be said that each juvenile must be allowed to determine for himself his own best interest and that, if attorneys are available, they must be available for all who desire them.

But suppose that there are only enough attorneys to handle half of the cases, the experimenter says. Then why cannot a random assignment schedule be employed to determine which cases they will handle? No, it is countered, a fairer method would be to decide which cases can most benefit from the services of an attorney and to see that these are given representation. Would anyone object, the experimenter counters, if the foundation grant had allowed for the hiring of ten attorneys and all ten were assigned to one court, while in a neighboring jurisdiction no lawyers were assigned, and then comparing the results between the two sites? If this seems reasonable, then certainly it must be reasonable to use other arbitrary techniques of denying representation for the greater good of science and the acquisition of experimental knowledge.

In such matters, the delicate ethical problems of correctional research become evident. Perhaps the only resolution lies in a series of loose dicta. The unjust vagaries of human existence are one thing. The matter at hand is that an experimenter is under the obligation to inflict no further injury or deprivation upon his subjects than necessary, and that the ends of science are irrelevent if they contribute to unreasonable human hurt. Presumably, it must be given to the intelligence and to the conscience of the individual researcher to fill in the teasingly non-specific components of his ethical obligations.

NECESSITY FOR INFORMED CONSENT

Informed consent by an offender who participates in a correctional experiment vitiates to some extent the allegations that his captive condition is being exploited for scientific ends, that he is being manipulated as an object rather than treated as a human being. Informed consent means consent given by a subject who has been provided with adequate information regarding the nature of the experiment, who is fully aware of the possible outcome, and who is free to choose alternative courses without incurring the risk of added disabilities.

There are major difficulties involved in the matter of informed consent in correctional experimentation. For one thing, it often appears self-defeating to convey to the subject the nature of the experimental undertaking, because such information is apt to distort the outcome. As Campbell has indicated:

> In any of the experimental designs, the respondents can become aware that they are participating in an experiment, and this awareness can have an interactive effect, in creating reactions to X which would not occur had X been encountered without this "I'm a guinea pig" attitude. . . . Such effects limit generalization to respondents having this awareness and preclude generalizations to the population encountering X with non-exprimental attitudes. The direction of the effect may be one of negativism, such as an unwillingness to admit to any persuasion or change.[64]

In addition, there are correctional experiments in which the deliberate aim is to hide from the subject what is being done to him in order to arouse anxiety and thus, it is hoped, to impel him toward what is believed to be a more mature and enabling confrontation of the necessity for him to resolve his own difficulties, rather than to depend upon previous self-defeating modes of adaptation.[65] Presumably, under such conditions, informed consent could extend only to acceptance of the rather vague outline of the program, not to its underlying camouflaged elements. Since the outcome is apt to be quite uncharted, little could be told the subject regarding the possible benefit or harm of participation. It is arguable whether such an experiment meets minimum requirements of ethical acceptability, but it seems clear that the subject would have to be accorded the option of leaving the experiment at any time, with no penalty attached to such departure.

In addition, of course, restriction of subjects to volunteers, particularly in correctional research, may undercut the usefulness of the experimental findings. A stricture consistently leveled against Synanon, the facility in California run by former narcotic addicts for addicts, is that its subjects are highly motivated toward success; in fact, the screening process deliberately excludes persons who do not appear to possess adequate desire to remain drug-free. Under such conditions, claims by Synanon that various elements of its program are productive of success and that its program has general utility for the treatment of addiction, are susceptible to the charge that its work has demonstrated only that persons who desire strongly enough to cease use of narcotics are able to do so, to an unknown extent (for Synanon is inordinately vague about its success and failure rate). Corrections is more apt to want to know whether a given arrangement can benefit all of its clientele or stipulated segments of it—not merely whether it is advantageous for volunteers—because corrections is obligated not only to aid the individual but also to protect society from harm and from unnecessary expense.

Informed consent also implies that there be no coercion involved in an experimental subject's participation. Direct coercion is, of course, rather readily recognized, but the particularly vulnerable status of correctional subjects makes them notably susceptible to subtler forms of persuasion. It is clearly established in the law that confessions induced by hints of leniency cannot be regarded as voluntary statements, though the translation of this fundamental principle to correctional research poses difficult issues.

Perhaps the point might be illustrated by the use of prisoners in medical experimentation, for it is in the area of medicine that the subject of ethical behavior has received its most intense scrutiny and soul-searching examination. In the United States, the first use of correctional subjects for medical experiments took place at the Mississippi state prison in 1914, when researchers attempted to discover the relationship between diet and pellagra.[66] The Governor of Mississippi promised pardons to persons volunteering for the experiment. The situation may be contrasted to a more recent experiment in New York in which eight prisoners were inoculated with a venereal infection in order to test possible cures. For their voluntary participation, the subjects in their own words "got syphilis and a carton of cigarettes."[67]

It is difficult to draw a hard line at the point where the hope of reward moves from the realm of the reasonable into that of the unreasonable. All human behavior includes self-serving elements. The suspect who confesses may do so to relieve feelings of guilt, to avoid further questioning, to gain attention or to obtain the quixotic satisfaction involved in pleasing one's accusers. As Justice Holmes suggested: "Nature makes self-love an instrument of altruism and martyrdom, but the self-lover is not required to know it, although he is more intelligent if he does."[68]

The hope of favorable parole action may seem quite acceptable motivation for voluntary participation in an experimental undertaking, both to the prisoner and to the experimenter. Ivy has suggested as a working rule the following proposition:

An excessive reduction which would exercise influence in obtaining the consent of prisoners to serve as subjects would be inconsistent with the principle of voluntary participation.[69]

494   *Scientific Guidance of Institutional Policies*

Presumably such words as "excessive" and "undue" have to undergo meticulous examination in terms of the nature of the experiment and its risks, as well as in terms of the correctional status of the volunteer. It is probably sufficient for the moment to reiterate a principle often over-looked in correctional research that, for a desperate man, hope of reward is apt to undercut his freedom of choice and the requirement of voluntary participation necessary as an ethical stipulation for correctional research.

Lessons from medicine provide corollary guidelines for correctional research. The experiments on human subjects, many of them convicted criminals, which were conducted during the Hitler regime by medical doctors, will always serve as a reminder of the potential abuse inherent in power given to the state over captive groups.[70] Standing beside these gruesome episodes in medical annals are stirring examples of research designed for human betterment that were conducted with rigid ethical etiquette. Suffice it to mention, as a suggestion for correctional research-ers, the example of Walter Reed, who participated as a subject in his own experiments on yellow fever because he could ask no subject to undergo anything that he himself was not willing to suffer.

FOR THE BENEFIT OF THE SUBJECT

In the absence of voluntary consent—either because it is unavailable or because the nature of the experiment precludes its being sought—no correctional subject should be required to participate in an experimental program that does not redound to his advantage, both as he and as impartial persons would be apt to see that advantage. In corrections, this principle demands that no added restraints be placed upon persons for experimental purposes. A new condition of parole, designed to test its efficacy, could not be imposed upon a random sample of parolees, nor could sentences arbitrarily be increased to 15 instead of 9 months in order to measure deterrent impact. The requirement demands that careful attention be paid to the relative advantages of correctional dispositions and particularly to the subjects' convictions concerning these advantages.

There is, of course, something of a dilemma implicit even in so straightforward a principle because it neglects the relative disadvantage falling upon persons unfortunate enough not to fall within the experi-mental group. It is possible to suggest that such persons are suffering no consequences which ordinarily would not have come their way; perhaps, for example, they had been sentenced to a 15-month prison term. If so, they should have anticipated serving the usual amount of time involved in their sentence. That their confreres, drawn by random lot, are being released much earlier is not their ill fortune but rather the others' good fortune. So the matter would appear in logic. To the unchosen inmate, however, it may seem quite different and, interestingly enough, such perception might provide another of those experimental situations where the design itself conditions the results of the experiment. Persons released early may perform in superior fashion only as they perceive such beneficence as a matter of luck; those left behind may do less well only so long as they view their misfortune as a testament of the cold-blooded random-number mentality of the system.

Fewer ethical issues are presented when eased conditions—or even harsher conditions—are imposed upon *all* persons falling into the categories effected. Constitutional requirements of equal protection are usually met when correctional conditions, imposed as part of administrative discretion, bear some reasonable relationship to the end being sought. In practice, most correctional change encompasses all relevant subjects uniformly, with common sense—that is, the view that "it certainly sounds like a good idea"—or work done elsewhere, such as in mental hygiene, providing the impetus for rearrangements. Evaluative work, of necessity, depends upon measurement of subsequent outcomes in comparison to those prevalent prior to the inauguration of the new program. The difficulty, of course, is that extrinsic circumstances rather than program ingredients may have conspired to produce the results.

Such possibilities pressure the researcher into demands for experimental-control research designs, despite anguished cries by service personnel that it is despicable to deprive claimants of services which are obviously—or, at least, almost obviously—of merit. Experimenters may recall the early days of work with the Salk vaccine when only first-graders were inoculated as part of the task of determining the value of the new drug, because only a limited amount of the vaccine was available. Purists in the ranks of science might insist that only a random sample of first-graders should have been included in the experiment. Parents of children below school age and of children in other grades who that year contracted infantile paralysis are not likely to gain solace from lectures regarding the value of pure research or the requirements of controlled experimentation. For correctional researchers, the polio experience may provide grim support for the thesis that verified knowledge is sometimes dependent upon rigid adherence to an adequate research undertaking. But, researchers should also keep in mind, sound ethics requires that experimental-control designs be undertaken only when alternative evaluative methods clearly fall short of requirements. If adequate alternatives are possible, experimental control designs should be used only when limited resources are all that are available.

SUMMARY AND CONCLUSIONS

There are few legal restraints upon experimentation with prisoners, probationers and parolees, and juveniles largely because there exist few sophisticated court considerations of the due process implications of these statutes.[71] Tort law suggests that persons may be treated in diverse ways, within limits, so long as their treatment is related to some reasonable therapeutic theory.[72] Untoward consequences generally will not result in liability if the authorities were acting satisfactorily in terms of their delegated responsibility. Thus, when a prisoner escaped from a minimum security farm and procured a weapon with which he threatened a civilian, who died of a brain hemorrage possibly brought on by fright, the court dismissed the claim for damages from the state for its alleged negligence. It would be against public policy, the judgment states, to "dissuade the wardens and principal keepers of our prison system from continuing experimentation with 'minimum security' work details which provide means for encouraging better-risk prisoners to . . . prepare themselves for their eventual return to society."[73]

Nonetheless, administrative discretion is no excuse for the neglect of ethical considerations in correctional research. For one thing, it is evident that the courts are beginning to look much more intensely at those areas of criminal justice heretofore peripheral to appellate scrutiny, and that due process protections will inevitably be extended into the prisons and parole in the manner that they recently have been catapulted into the juvenile court.[74] Clearly the days are numbered, for instance, for such administrative judgments as that in a recent case in a western state. In this case, which is probably not atypical, a twice-convicted burglar, sentenced for a period of three to fourteen years, was accused by prison authorities of sodomy. He was tried in the county court and acquitted. Though burglars normally are released in three or four years, the prisoner was retained for the maximum period of his sentence, with the justification that it would be a disservice to society to permit a known aggressive homosexual to be set loose.

The ethical difficulties involved in correctional research lie predominantly in the nature of corrections as a social enterprise. Corrections has recourse to diverse forms of suasion, such as reward and argumentation, but, most persuasively, it uses force and deprivation to achieve its aims. Its goal is fairly clear: to protect the society by deterring convicted persons and others from engaging in illegal conduct. Ethical difficulties emerge most pointedly when the aim becomes so insistent that it blurs judgment of the means by which it is being achieved or may acceptably be achieved.

In the United States, the most pressing ethical concern of corrections appears to involve the utilization of programs upon involuntary subjects who do not adequately comprehend them. Presumably no correctional program employing suasion beyond that point at which it can be demonstrated that such suasion produces a desirable result should be allowed to continue. Programs must be examined in terms of whether they achieve things which would not occur were they absent. Unless it is clear that persons choosing to avoid group therapy and educational programs, for instance, represent more serious threats to the society without having such experiences than they do with them, it would appear indefensible to require these activities on an involuntary basis. Obviously there is an amount of coercion necessary for the maintenance of any operation, and it is reasonable to expect that individuals do certain things or do without other things. But this is not the same as deprivation of free choice based on unsubstantiated claims of social advantage.

There are a number of concluding observations which may set the subject into clearer perspective. They insist upon the importance of research, but upon research tied to ethical responsibility. They warn us that well-meaning attempts to aid individuals against their will may be a form of tyranny and, if so, should be zealously resisted. Finally, they suggest that, however vital and important a goal scientific exactitude and experimentation may be, there are dangers inherent in uncritical adherence to its values, as there are in uncritical adherence to any dogma. [75]

Justice Holmes, among many others, has pointed out the pressing need for experimentation in the area of criminal justice: "What have we better than a blind guess to show that the criminal law in its present form does more good than harm?" Holmes asked. "Do we deal with criminals on proper principles? Is it idle to talk of deterring the criminal by the classical method of imprisonment?" [76]

George Santayana, approaching the matter from another side, entered further reservation about programs without specified and monitored purpose. "Fanatics," Santayana said, "are those who redouble their effort when they have forgotten their goal." [77] What can happen under such circumstances was indicated by Holmes' colleague, Louis D. Brandeis.

Experience should teach us to be most on our guard to protect liberty when the Government's purposes are beneficient. Men born to freedom are naturally alert to repel invasion of their liberty by evil-minded rulers. The greatest dangers to liberty lurk in insidious encroachment by men of zeal, well-meaning but without understanding.[78]

33 Five Practical Research Suggestions for Correctional Administrators

DANIEL GLASER*

My chief impression from a quarter-century of moving back and forth between correctional administration and criminological research is that these two worlds are deplorably out of touch with each other and poorly attuned to the general public. This article suggests ways in which the administrator may use research to improve both correctional services and his communication with those segments of the general public and those legislative and executive agencies of government most significant to him. Enumerating five suggestions as the topic of this article is arbitrary; these could have been subdivided and others added.

PROCURING POSTRELEASE INFORMATION

The first suggestion is simply: *Procure the most complete postrelease information obtainable on offenders in your custody or under your supervision, and work to make this information more complete.* When legislators or journalists ask for proof that specific correctional measures prevent crime, the correctional administrator is typically at a loss, having been reluctant to gather postrelease statistics because of the imperfections of any he could get. While bewailing the lack of information on recidivism, he overlooks the potential value of his own agency's records as a minimum data source.

Even a minimal tabulation from these records can begin to show

From *Crime and Delinquency* 17,1 (January 1971): 32–40. Reprinted with the permission of the National Council on Crime and Delinquency.

whether there is a difference in post-release crime rates for prisoners of a given type who are in different programs. Merely as a first step, it can show the number of persons released in past years who were recommitted to his correctional system. While such information certainly does not reveal all recidivism, it imparts far more knowledge than do subjective impressions for estimating trends in recidivism rates or comparing these rates for different types of offenders or for similar offenders subjected to different types of treatment (e.g., work release, intensive vocational training, or programed education). This is useful for any correctional administration—county, state, or national—and records can be designed to simplify such compilation.

That all criminal record information will be incomplete is inevitable, since one can know only about the offenses for which a man is caught. In all statistical comparisons, one assumes that the degree of incompleteness is approximately evenly distributed over all categories of offenders being compared. One can then examine relative postrelease criminality rates to see which categories have high rates and which lower. For example, if one can show that, among offenders of a given type, those granted work release had less criminality recorded locally two years later than those released without it, he will have a strong foothold on evaluative knowledge. Even without absolutely complete postrelease crime figures, such comparisons provide a factual basis for policy guidance. Gradually this knowledge can be improved by information covering longer follow-up periods, larger numbers of cases, more specific categories of offenders or treatments, and, ideally, a larger range of jurisdictions.

FOCUS ON COST-EFFECTIVENESS

This brings us to the second suggestion: *Focus presentation of postrelease data on the responsibilities the correctional agency must meet, especially on cost-effectiveness.* Converting a felon into a saint is a great achievement, but correctional agencies fulfill their primary responsibility if they merely reduce the probability of his committing further felonies. Even a change from felonious behavior to occasional misdemeanors represents partial success. One of the major sources of obfuscation in parole and probation outcome statistics is the counting of all types of postrelease offenses or infractions under a single label, such as parole or probation "violation." Although even nonfelonious violations disappoint those who grant parole or probation to an offender, major felonies are a much more serious disappointment to the general public.

Postrelease statistical differences between groups of offenders given special assistance and comparison groups without such aid are often much greater if expressed in terms of the amount of time which passes before violations are committed or in terms of the seriousness or persistence of violations, instead of in terms of the percentages committing violations of any kind. The variety of possible crimes and rule infractions and the diversity of their consequences for the offender are so great, however, that it is difficult to generalize about the effectiveness of correctional programs by separately enumerating every type of post-treatment maladjustment. Nevertheless, a single index which reflects both time before violation and seriousness is the percentage of time spent reconfined in a given post-release period. Therefore, an administrator may most effectively contrast a special treatment group with a control or comparison group not by their gross violation rates but by their average total months of reconfinement in a given number of years after release.

A major advantage of this index is that it can easily be expressed in terms of *cost* of reconfinement per postrelease year, decade, or other period. This has been shown most effectively by Stuart Adams in his report on the PICO Project, and in his subsequent research.[79] Since prison treatment in most systems costs approximately ten times as much as supervision in the community, an administrator can present strong economic justification for any extra expenditures which reduce the time of reconfinement for a given group of offenders in a postrelease period. If $1,000 of reconfinement costs are saved by $500 for added community services that reduce reincarceration, there is a 100 per cent return on investment. This is not to imply that economy is the major moral argument for a correctional program, but reconfinement time during a postrelease period is about as satisfactory a statistical index as one can obtain to indicate a society's total moral outrage with a group of released offenders. Furthermore, in these days of government financial stress, cutting costs is a crucial and persuasive consideration, particularly in the many states with antiquated and regressive taxation systems.

ECONOMIC PROBLEMS OF RELEASEES

This point is also relevant to my third suggestion: *The economic problems of releasees can be remedied if they are known.* It is relatively meaningless to argue that the economic reasons for recidivism are more important than the psychological or that either are more important than social or cultural reasons. Certainly all are intertwined, and a good criminological theory would generalize on the nature of their interrelationship. Suffice it to note here (1) that we can demonstrate statistically a close relationship between economic hardship and crime in the careers of most felons and (2) that unemployment is closely related to crime, especially among adult offenders.[80] One should also note that over 90 per cent of felonies reported to the police involve the taking of someone's money or property. Furthermore, unlike more abstractly conceived psychological problems, the economic dilemmas of ordinary people can be understood, without special training, by almost everyone.

It is surprising that correctional literature almost completely ignores the economic difficulties of men released from confinement. What evidence we have suggests that this problem limits correctional effectiveness much more than does the size of caseloads or the shortage of psychiatrists. Though acute economic need does not characterize all releasees, the massive statistical dimensions of the economic problem must be a vital consideration in any overall effort to make correctional investments more fruitful.

Studies indicate that about a third of federal parolees and mandatory releasees find no work in their first month out of prison, and a sixth find none for three months after release. Furthermore, since whatever work they may get at first is often temporary and followed by unemployment, a quarter were without jobs when contacted during their third month after release. Almost half the federal releasees earned less than $50 during their first month out of prison.[81] Fortunately, the majority of releasees receive some assistance with room and board from their families, but this is not a satisfactory solution for long. Considering the clothing and other possessions that most newly released prisoners lack, their financial needs in many ways exceed those of men never confined. Considering also the combination of low income, limited resources, accumulated needs, pent-up desires, and prior criminality, it is remarkable that at least nine out of ten adult offenders spend at least their first month out of prison trying to solve their problems by legitimate means; in most jurisdictions for which data are available, a majority seem to persist indefinitely.

Data from research on the postrelease economic problems of federal parole and mandatory release violators have helped promote several post-prison assistance measures, such as increased funds for release gratuities and an added number of employment placement officers, prison employees whose sole function is to seek jobs for releasees. But by far the most significant development for economic and other aid was the creation of the Federal Community Correction Centers in New York, Chicago, Detroit, Los Angeles, and a half-dozen other cities, to which federal offenders are transferred about three months before they start parole.

Prisoners residing in these centers go out to seek jobs, start to work at those they procure, and visit their future homes before moving out to begin parole. A full-time employment counselor aids the twenty to thirty residents of each center. These programs create a dramatic increase in employment rates for youthful recidivist parolees, and the follow-up studies thus far show an especially great drop in this group's postrelease felonies. Counseling a youth about job-getting on the very day he is to seek employment, or on job-holding when he is concerned about this, is much more effective than counseling him about hypothetical postrelease situations while he is still in prison. Gradual departure from prison thus permits prisoners of all ages to organize their postrelease life much more adequately than when they must move abruptly from being completely cared for in a prison to being entirely on their own, with limited resources, in the city.

Perhaps the major contribution of community correction centers, work release, or work furlough is one least often cited—their diagnostic value. Traditionally, the duration of confinement is determined by the judge's interpretation of presentence information and later by the parole board's assessment of this information plus additional reports from prison personnel. Such decisions are tested, however, by the released offender's noncriminality in the community. The economic, personality, and social problems of those endeavoring to support themselves legitimately and the criminal inclinations of others are much more quickly evident to staff in these graduated release programs than in either the artificial environment of the prison or the formal and infrequent contacts of regular probation or parole supervision. Graduated release programs protect the public not just by aiding rehabilitation but also by providing more immediate and relevant surveillance than is possible in other correctional programs. That is why federal judges are relying increasingly on community centers as places for thirty to ninety days of presentence study in cases where they are uncertain whether to impose probation or imprisonment.

ADDRESSING THE OFFENDER'S TOTAL CIRCUMSTANCES AND PERSPECTIVES

Despite the statistically frequent importance of economic conditions, tracing thoroughly the chain of events culminating in any individual's return to crime usually provides support for my fourth suggestion: *Both correctional administration and research should try to comprehend the total circumstances of an offender's current situation and his view of these circumstances.* For example, some releasees are successfully placed in jobs but are too lonely and restless when not at work to resist the ease and welcome they can find in drug use, heavy drinking, or professional criminal social circles. More familiar and accepting companions are especially attractive to them in any period of discomfort, humiliation, conflict, or other stress or when they are required to deal with bureaucratic, more educated, or ethnically different persons at work, in probation or parole offices, and elsewhere. Solutions to economic problems may be necessary for most offenders, but they are not sufficient to prevent recidivism in all.

While research indicates that the majority of ex-prisoners who return to felonies do so only after some effort to "make it on the legit," there is also a significant minority whose perceptions of their competence and prospects in criminal activity are so great that they disdain from the start, or soon thereafter, what they view as their legitimate alternatives to crime. For them a drastic change of experience at legitimate pursuits—in learning and using a skilled trade, for example—may be possible only with long confinement in an optimum program and extensively graduated release. Contrastingly, another noteworthy minority have so predominantly identified themselves with anticriminal persons before their arrest, are so deterred from crime by their arrest and penalty, and have so little prospect of further ties with criminals if released abruptly that most correctional measures—including graduated release—are either irrelevant or somewhat deleterious to their high prospects of nonrecidivism.

What is suggested here is a prescriptive penology which varies both assistance and control with the offender. But this implies learning and taking into account the offender's view of his world at the times that are critical to him. To do so requires changing the qualifications and functions of correctional personnel in both institutions and community-based services. A sound prescription requires that the view of the client be based less exclusively on office interviews or formal test scores and more on familiarity with his daily social circumstances, reactions, and expectations, around the clock, in *his* usual situations.

In federal prison research we asked inmates to think of the prison employee whom they liked best and to bear him in mind while we asked questions about him, but not to reveal his name. We then asked several questions about this person, including the type of position he held. We repeated this inquiry regarding the prison employee the inmate disliked the most. One of our findings was the great predominance of work supervisors among prison employees most liked. Although another finding indicated that prison caseworkers were the most disliked more often than the most liked, they did not compose a high percentage of either designation. The data suggest that work supervisors and line custodial officers have much more impact on inmates than do caseworkers, and I infer that this is because their relationships with inmates are more continuous, cooperative, and personal than those of caseworkers. This was dramatically indicated by studies of successful releasees from prison who were asked to trace their change from criminal to noncriminal concerns. About half said that they changed during imprisonment, about half of these credited a staff member as the most influential person in this change, and in over half of these cases the staff member so credited was a work supervisor.[82]

On the basis of this interpretation it was suggested that caseworkers (1) cease segregating their offices within a single part of the prison and, instead, scatter them, each in a separate work or residence unit of the prison, to make them more accessible to inmates and better located for observation of prison life; (2) cease to have inmates assigned to them randomly from all over the institution and, instead, have caseloads comprised of all inmates assigned to the units where their office is located so that they may more readily know all parties in the social relationships of their clients; (3) each serve as part of a classification team consisting primarily of line officers from these units, but with some representation from prison school, industry, and management, to replace the traditional single institution classification committee of top prison officials, who necessarily must meet hastily and infrequently on most inmates.

The measures described above have now been adopted, with variations, in many federal and state correctional institutions. They bring much more spontaneity, frankness, and even affection to many inmate-caseworker relationships. Classification teams not only meet several times as often on the average inmate as do institution classification committees and operate with more thorough knowledge of the inmates but also greatly enhance communication among the various components of the prison staff.[83] While it would be naive to assume that these measures permit staff to address the *total* prison circumstances of each inmate, they certainly increase the proportion of these circumstances that staff are likely to take into account.

As already indicated, graduated release programs give correctional staff a fuller and more immediate knowledge of the offender's community situation than is usually possible with abrupt release to parole or probation. In the latter, the officer's opportunity to know his caseload more thoroughly might conceivably be enhanced by reduced caseloads, but time studies and controlled experiments suggest that reduced caseloads tend to increase time in paperwork more than in fieldwork, and in presentence more than in postsentence activity.[84] A partial remedy, pioneered in Chicago, is decentralization of parole and probation offices from a single downtown center to scattered neighborhood units, each housing a variety of municipal, county, state, and private correctional, law enforcement, and social service agencies. This facilitates their collaboration, and also permits, through some sharing of staff and files, provision of some personnel for night and weekly duty.

The most adequate solutions to the problem of addressing the total circumstances of offenders stress three specific goals: (1) *supplementing professional casework staff with paraprofessionals of the same sociocultural and neighborhood background as the clients;* (2) *directing assistance at the entire family of the offender;* (3) *being available for crisis alleviation twenty-four hours a day, seven days a week.*

One way of approaching these goals is exemplified by the Probation Officer-Case Aide Project of the U.S. Probation Office in Chicago. The probation officers in this project have part-time aides who are available in the clients' own neighborhoods during evenings and weekends. Frequently ex-offenders themselves, the aides are of the same background as their clients and, in the one to three cases to which they are assigned, can readily become familiar with the clients' total life styles and reputations and offer immediate assistance. In emergencies they can telephone the probation officer at the latter's home, but they routinely make automatically tape-recorded phone calls to the probation office to report their observations and activities on each case.

A more thorough approach to these three goals is represented by the "RODEO" project, an acronym for Reduction of Delinquency through Expansion of Opportunity, of the Los Angeles County Probation Department. Here each probation officer has two full-time paraprofessional aides from the neighborhood. Each three-man team serves no more than thirty juvenile offenders who would traditionally have been institutionalized. Offices for these teams are in the clients' neighborhood and include space for community meetings. The teams treat the entire family of each client. They may help the parents get employment, welfare service, or medical assistance and often also transport them to the offices involved. They may provide emergency baby-sitting or pitch in to help a mother clean up her apartment as a first step in teaching her how to handle her household problems. The emphasis is on helping all family members learn to cope more successfully with a difficult environment, as well as with medical, educational, or other handicaps.

Appropriately titled "Community Workers," the RODEO project's aides to probation officers now have civil service status. They are given considerable responsibility and autonomy as they demonstrate their capacity for it. When the program began, early in 1967, it was centered in a predominantly black area encompassing Watts, but after it demonstrated marked success in reducing confinement costs, it was expanded to include an office in predominantly Mexican-American East Los Angeles and is currently being further augmented by two new offices in integrated areas. Its original supervisor, Mrs. Ruth L. Rushen, is now applying its principles to the still larger area of the Model Neighborhood Program and to probationers of all ages. This new program is called "Harambee," Swahili for "Let us all work together."

PROPOSE CHANGES AS PIECEMEAL EXPERIMENTS

This brings us to my fifth suggestion: *Correctional improvement proposals will be most readily supported if they are introduced piecemeal and include procedures for measuring effectiveness.*

The major source of knowledge in medicine, the most rigorously scientific of treatment sciences, is the controlled experiment. Where randomly selected experimental and control groups with double-blind procedures have not been feasible, medicine has relied on quasi-experimental comparisons of similar people receiving different treatment due to different circumstances in former periods or other areas. Rigorously controlled experiments are possible in correction more often than is usually assumed, but where they are not feasible, the quasi-experimental use of comparison groups can improve knowledge greatly if a minimum of appropriately standardized and concise records is maintained.[85] The records most valuable for evaluating a program can also be the most efficient and useful for correctional operations.[86] Planning and pretesting of standardized, efficient, and relevant records should be part of the first stage in any new correctional program, rather than an afterthought, just as a bookkeeping system should be established when a business begins, rather than later when one wonders where the money went.

Without appropriate records and their analysis by an approximation of the experimental method, any argument on the effectiveness of a correctional program is no more conclusive than a statement of one man's impressions against another's. Legislators and executives in control of government expenditures for coping with crime obviously are not convinced that any group of experts has a guaranteed solution for these problems. In recent years federal and state agencies have granted money for innovations only when the measures were proposed as small-scale experiments with planned evaluation. Research is prominent today in all fields, and legislators can be readily persuaded of the value of correctional research if its prospects for expanding knowledge on crime control are made reasonably clear.

For those correctional administrators who think they know what they need to make their services more effective, a government which vetoes proposals for new programs can be frustrating. But administrators who follow the five suggestions set forth here will, I believe, by justifying their financial requests more adequately, become better able to procure necessary funds.

34 *Evaluation of Penal Treatments*

LESLIE T. WILKINS*

Society pays for its prisons and its penal services through taxation. What do people think they are buying for their money? Should the people who pay have any say in what goes on, or should this be left to the 'experts' or to professional politicians and pressure groups to sort out among themselves?

INFORMATION AND PUNISHMENT

There have never been many people who demonstrated an interest in the penal system, and today there may be fewer than ever. When the ordinary citizen could see the local villain, or nuisance who was personally known to him, placed in the village stocks or other place, some interest in the procedures was evident. Perhaps such interest was of the same order as the interest in cock-fighting in the yard of the adjoining inn. By a primitive 'audience research' the authorities could assess the reaction to the punishment of offenders if only by observing how many deserted one show for the other—like switching television channels! By this means some information about the working of the system was fed back into the system.

Now most people would repudiate the idea that penal sanctions are intended for the satisfaction or amusement of society or of such as may

From *The Sociological Review,* Monograph No. 9, "Sociological Studies in the British Penal Services, edited by Paul Halmos (Keele, Great Britain: University of Keele, January 1965), pp. 237–252. Reprinted by permission of the author and publisher.

attend any public humiliation or obtain satisfactions indirectly through the descriptive techniques of mass media. We have substituted sophisticated methods, but society has lost information in the process.

Although the idea of amusement may be repudiated, people are unaware of their motives, or unwilling to think through the basis of their behaviour. Is it true that all traces of public amusement have been removed from current penal practices?

MASS MEDIA AND CRIME

The press know how to apportion the amount of space they devote to different types of penal subject matter. What determines the size of the headlines? Is there not some component of consumer interest reflected here? Suppose, for example, that all press reporting on criminal matters were to be reduced to matter-of-fact statements of procedures and in terms of legal definitions; what would then be the reaction of the interested parties? Of course, information about the processes of justice is part of the concept of justice, but does this concept explain everything that is done in the name of free press reporting?

Some may claim that at the present time the majority of the entertainment value of crime in the Western world is derived from fictitious crimes. And a very large amount of the material of the entertainment industry is obtained from this area. But the entertainment value covers only a part of the whole story. There can be few plays, films, television shows or books which follow the story from the criminal act to the finding of guilt, through the court procedures, sentence, penal establishment and release and rehabilitation of the offender. Nor are these different aspects of the process given proportional representation. There seems to be little entertainment value in the problems of resettlement and after-care of prisoners, nor in the impact of the penal processes on those closely concerned with the offender.

In the majority of stories it is not possible so much as to ascertain whether the guilty person was married or single, nor are the facts about his background frequently illustrated. Moreover, little prominence is given to the victim, usually it is sufficient that he is properly dead! Murder stories can conclude after the sentence has been pronounced. Readers, viewers and listeners can then feel that the story is ended—particularly while we have the death penalty. It is all most simple and pleasant. The determination of 'guilty' or 'not guilty' 'saint' or 'sinner' results in the simple consignment for eternity to either heaven or hell.

THE PROBLEM OF OBJECTIVES

The simple black-white, true-false, right-wrong type of universe is only slightly complicated by the fact of social class. We are, of course, all against sin, and particularly against working-class sin. This seems to be the very basis of our social control system. It will stay that way until there is sufficient stimulus for rethinking. Such rethinking must consider the whole process from the commission of the act, including the role of the victim, through to the rehabilitation of the offender in society. This is a long and complex process-continuum. From the point of commission of the act of which society disapproves onwards, a large number of decisions are made by persons having different roles. Each of these decisions could be subjected to investigation by known rigorous research methods. There are not sufficient funds (perhaps because there is not sufficient public concern) to investigate all of these processes, indeed, there are other inhibiting factors to the carrying out of any such study. The objectives which are sought in the different decisions are not by any means all sufficiently explicitly stated, nor is there consensus regarding the aims of the sub-sections of the total system. There are vast problems of communication and criteria. The total system has been divided up into different professional interests. This cannot be deplored; it must be accepted as an inevitable consequence of other social factors.

If change comes, it must come through some sector of the professional interests. Any one professional sector will be influenced by other sectors, and influence other sectors. Perhaps changes in respect of the system in regard to the victim may be expected mainly to arise from those who have direct personal contact with victims, and changes in respect of the treatment of offenders from those who have direct contact with offenders. It is through personal contact that information may be obtained; and rational change must be based on information. If that information can be systematised by research techniques, then it can be the more powerful as a valid basis for change.

OPERATIONAL OBJECTIVES

In this paper we shall discuss only the problems of the treatment of offenders; a field of professional endeavour where there is a pressing claim for investigation of existing procedures. This does not mean that other sectors are not equally important if the problem of crime and its control is to be faced. After the finding of guilt, society can hide its deviants in penal institutions—at least those perceived to be the worse cases. Hiding problems does not solve them, and not all people can consign their responsibility to others.

The treatment of offenders is a specific role of the penal system. It is those professionally concerned who are charged by society with responsibility for the rehabilitation of the offender. Although the function of punishment and treatment are not well differentiated, at least a large measure of agreement can be reached regarding objectives, namely, that one of the main aims of treatment must be to minimise the probability that the offender will again commit crimes. In a word, the reduction of recidivism is the major objective of the penal system.

TREATMENT V. JUSTICE

It is well known that there are considerable variations in the sentencing policies of courts, and that differences in the nature of the disposals of offenders cannot be completely explained in terms of the differences between offences or offenders. Some critics have seen in this variation a conflict with their views of justice. There is an assumption that the same type of offence, committed by the same type of offender against the same type of victim should receive the same type of sentence. This is not a question which the research worker concerned with the evaluation of the penal system finds to be within his terms of reference. The differences between courts can be used to provide evidence as to the different values of different treatments or treatment policies. It is sufficient for research workers to accept the variance within the system. If the people who are generating the variation are doing so in good faith and in terms of their concept of justice, punishment, treatment or other, this is not the research worker's concern as a research worker; as a citizen he may take a different view. If there is any question of ethics here, it seems to be in that it is unethical to fail to do research to try to find out the nature of errors and to seek remedies. Ethical decisions like rational decisions can be assessed only in terms of information. As research advances, the variations which provide the data necessary for the utilisation of the scientific method may, perhaps, tend to be reduced and research may become more difficult. At present this presents no scientific problems in the field of evaluation, since evaluation means the measurement of the degree to which what is attempted is in fact achieved.

EXPERIMENT AND EVALUATION

Unless and until it comes to be regarded as ethical to carry out controlled experimental variations in the penal system, the existing system must be explored by means of operational research methods. Operational research methods of course, will always be attended by some measure of doubt regarding the validity of the inferences from the existing (as against the controlled) variations. But newly developed techniques can reduce this margin of uncertainty. And uncertainty itself can be dealt with scientifically, that is to say, it can be measured. We need not deceive ourselves by false assumptions about degrees of certainty, they can, and indeed should, be assessed. Such assessment involves the use of statistical techniques of estimation and confidence intervals which, unfortunately are rather less generally known than tests of significance. It is necessary to go beyond the concept of significance and to say something about the meaning of significance—the significance of what, and even the 'so what'!

It is impossible to see how efficiency in any treatment system can be improved, or how evaluation may begin, without some basis derived from a clear statement of the goals of the system, and the reduction of this statement to some measurable or orderable set. Perhaps the reason why so little work of evaluation has been done is the implicit necessity to state exactly what good it is one is seeking. Good doing is much more pleasant if it can remain vague.

Whether this is also the reason why some respected authorities in the criminological field reject the concept of evaluation is irrelevant. Generally the rejection of the claims of the scientific method to investigate penal processes is based on the superiority of 'personal experience'. It is claimed that the human intelligence alone (and presumably unaided!) can correctly assess situations involving human emotions. 'No one can test my methods unless he has himself been trained in them' is a frequent claim. Fink protests that there was no substitute for 'human judgement'.[87] 'I am', he says, 'inclined much more to the judgement of a judge who is wise, human and just, than to the efficiency of prediction tables'. Similarly, Teeters discussing the prediction method writes, 'the parole petitioner is a person, not merely a digit, and this presents a hazard of losing sight of him as a living personality'.[88] But what is meant by 'wise', 'just', 'human'? What is the objective of the wisdom, humanity, and justice? These and all similar arguments against the application of rigorous techniques of evaluation seem to miss the basic issue. The issue is, not *how* the task is done, but *how well* it is done, and, of course, what the task is. Most critics seem to be saying that because they have a distaste for the means, the ends must also be wrong (i.e. inefficiently attained). But if the end is known, this is a matter for assessment. Exactly similar arguments have been used for a century or more to support the claim for reforms—it is right (ethical), therefore it must be true (effective). If measurement systems do not enable the objective to be achieved, and achieved more efficiently than other systems, they should be rejected. But these methods cannot be rejected *as such,* that is to say without reference to the objectives.

Perhaps Popper (1945)[89] made the best rejoinder to those who make such claims when he asked, 'Who . . . shows the greatest concern for the sanctity of human life—the scientist who devotes himself to discovering step by step, always ready to submit to facts, always aware that even his boldest achievements are never more than a stepping stone for those who come after him, or the mystic elite who reject measurement and are thus free to maintain anything because they need not fear any rigorous testing of their beliefs?'

It must be recognised that those of us who wish to evaluate social action, to test the effectiveness of penal treatments or other forms of social work, want to do this for the very same reasons as those who administer or carry out the field work of the social services. Research is no substitute for action, and action no substitute for research.

THE PREREQUISITES OF EVALUATION OF PENAL TREATMENTS

Evaluation cannot begin until a number of conditions are satisfied. It may be desirable to note these points briefly before further developing the discussion of the methods of evaluation itself. The conditions are:

1. The objectives of the treatment (or other event) have been worked out within the framework of the general social ethic. A statement of a general ethic will not suffice. A large measure of consensus regarding the objectives must be obtained, and the language of description of the aims must be precise.
2. The sub-problems have been identified and related to the specific activity which it is expected will modify the particular behavior or remedy the specific situation.
3. The ways in which the sub-objectives relate to the general objective have been thought through and a rational strategy, including provisional priorities has been decided upon. Sub-objectives may be

means towards the main objective, or they may not. Such differences should be distinguished.

4. The proposed activities (penal treatments, etc.) have been devised, described, and standardised. Alternatively, variations in the activities have been carefully noted and the expected nature of the differences in the outcomes associated with the variations in the activities indicated.

5. The nature of the expected change, both positive and negative and short and long term has been described in some detail.

6. Tests have been made, where necessary, to ensure that the statements made in regard to 1—5 above are satisfactory as a basis for further development and are not merely assumptions. For example, it may be necessary *to test* the assumption of degree of concordance in the main objectives; *to test* whether the concepts used are communicable; and so on.

When these conditions are satisfied, it is possible to consider moving on to the final two stages of evaluation, namely, to

7. develop means for measuring the degree of change in the direction specified in 5 above.

8. develop systems whereby identified changes can be related to the particular activity and separated from the effects of other origin, or random variation.

If the above conditions are really necessary, it may be questioned whether it is yet possible to get started with evaluation of any forms of social action. Can the objectives of penal treatments be stated with sufficient confidence and concordance? If not, who has the right or duty to state what the objectives should be? It may be necessary to avoid some of these questions and to start with operational definitions and even operational criteria because more satisfactory definitions are not forthcoming. Once the process of evaluation is started, it can continue to be improved and made more powerful. The information derived from evaluative studies provides the information which can be the mechanism facilitating the evolution of the system. Unless information about the working of a system is fed back into the system, the system lacks the means for its self-development.

THE INPUT-OUTPUT PROBLEM

The nature of the raw material conditions the product of any system or organisation. The input to the different treatment facilities within the penal system varies in quality—that is to say in the prior probabilities of further conviction after treatment. The so called 'prediction methods' (a form of multi-variate analysis) enable the prior probabilities of recidivism to be estimated. (See, for example, Mannheim 1955).[90]

Until recently the majority of studies which had examined the nature of the output of a penal treatment in terms of the input (and there were very few), failed to reveal any differences in outcome. That is to say, the recidivism rate for probation was greater than that for cases fined, and cases put into prison had a higher rate than that for probation, but the difference was only that to be expected from the type of offender given the different type of treatment (Wilkins 1960).[91] It came to appear that it did not matter what was done, offenders recidivated or not quite independently of the type of treatment. Or to be more precise, when the expected recidivism rate for a given 'input' was related to the recidivism of the 'output' of two different types of treatment, the variation in the output between the treatments could be explained in terms of the variation in the input. This sort of finding, of course, falls far short of proving that 'treatment makes no difference'. There are four quite straightforward hypotheses which could underlie these findings, namely,

H1. There is no difference between treatments.

H2. The difference between treatments is of a higher order. For example, it might be that when taken into consideration with ·types of offenders, treatments show different interaction effects.

H3. The differences in treatments are offset by similarities in the 'culture of the prison', or other sub-cultural influences. It may be that the social consequences of crime are more important than the official consequences.

H4. The basic components of all treatments are the same, hence, no differences in treatments are expected (e.g. if it is argued that only personal contact can influence change in offenders and that system or organisational differences are of no consequence, and that all forms of penal treatment attract the same qualities of staff.)

There are three types of problem involved at a very simple level—whether the main effects are postulated to be

(a) offender on offender,

(b) system on offender, or personality of treatment staff on offenders,

(c) an interaction between types of offenders and types of treatment.

It follows that, if there is an interaction between types of treatments and types of offenders and no overall treatment effect can be isolated, some offenders are being 'made worse' and others 'improved' by the treatment currently being given to them, even though the treatment is regarded as being the same for both types of offenders. Variations within a 'treatment' system may account for differences in outcome, but if this is postulated, then there are two or more 'treatments' and not one. One treatment, plus an interaction, must mean that there are compensating factors present if the general outcome is not differentiated. An example of an interaction of this kind is given later (see Table 1). Since there is some evidence for interaction effects, and since if some persons are being made worse it should be possible to stop doing whatever it is and get an immediate pay-off (!), hypotheses regarding types of interaction (types of treatment x types of persons) appear worth investigation. If other types of hypotheses are sustained, the pay-off decision does not seem to be so simple or so immediate. But there is the important question to be explored of what is meant by 'types of offenders'.

THE PROBLEM OF TYPOLOGY

It has, of course, to be noted that offenders subjected to different treatments which are to be compared in terms of recidivism, are compared in terms of their 'prior probabilities of recidivism'. Information has also to be obtained from similar sources to determine typologies. Clearly, if all risk groups performed better after treatment A than treatment B, the hypothesis of an interaction would not be required. A would be a superior treatment. But if, say, both high and low risks did better under treatment A, and medium risk categories under treatment B, the case for an interaction would be supported. If only two categories, high and low risk, were differentiated, it would be difficult to demonstrate an interaction. Suppose that the better risk class were less often recidivists after treatment A than after treatment B, and the worse risk categories were less often recidivists after treatment B, but the differentiation between persons after treatment B were greater than for treatment A, it might be suspected that some factor in relation to the *information* regarding persons subjected to treatment A had tended to reduce the efficiency of the estimation within that treatment group. It is possible that bad recording of information might show a treatment to be inferior in respect of the bad risks and superior in respect of the good risks, merely because information regarding *all risks* classes in that treatment was not so well recorded! That is to say, the regression line for one treatment may differ from that for another because of random errors in the recording of *information*.

In general, however, it may be assumed that the *nature* of the information used for purposes of differentiation between persons with respect to estimates of prior probabilities of recidivism is not influenced by the nature of the treatment process. This assumption may not be justified where two or more treatments are compared but the persons involved in carrying out the treatment were not subjected to the same discipline of record keeping.

The use of information for the purpose of placing subjects in risk categories and for typologies of other kinds at one and the same time, raises many problems of the nature of inference which cannot now be discussed. If the same information is used twice for two different purposes, its power for these purposes cannot be assumed to be the same as if the items of information were independent.

AN EXAMPLE OF AN INTERACTION SITUATION

Perhaps the first to demonstrate the relationship between treatment outcomes and types of treatments was Grant (1960).[92] Grant *et al.* were able to randomise treatments for United States Navy delinquents from a pool of available personnel. The research design was a factorial model, but the basic input 'material' was randomised—as indeed it had to be. Before allocation to the different treatments, numerous measurements of personality, by interviews and sundry other procedures were carried out. There was thus no question of assessing the differences in the input to the different treatments, except for the purpose of investigating the possibility of interaction, since randomisation ensured that the expected recidivism rate was approximately equal for all treatments. Grant was able to use a very satisfactory criterion of the outcome of treatment—the successful return to Navy duties and satisfactory performance therein for a period after release from the correctional institution.

The initial results of this research looked much the same as others. There could be no question that the treatments were very different treatments in terms of the percentage success. One treatment (T1) was a most intensive 'living group therapy unit' and another (T3) was much the same as the normal retraining routines of a Navy correctional establishment. Certainly the cost of the different treatments was very significantly different, and the personnel employed in the treatments were differently trained and differently orientated.

The majority of the personality tests, which had been applied to the cases before allocation, revealed no significant relationship with the outcome, nor was there any demonstrated interaction—except for one measure. This was a 'social maturity scale' based on perceptual process theory, with particular regard to social perception. Classifying offenders according to whether they were of high or low social maturity, the results shown in Table 1 below were obtained.

TABLE 1
Showing the Results of Different Types of Treatment of U.S. Navy Delinquents, by Different Types of Personality Assessment

Offender's Personality Type	Treatment Type % success		
	T1	T2	T3
Socially mature	70	72	61
Socially immature	41	55	60
All	59	65	61

It is obvious that the high social maturity cases were able to benefit from the intensive therapy routine, or, to use a term now current in case work, they were 'therapy ready'. But those who were classified as of low social maturity were more likely to become successes if they were not given the 'living group therapy', but the more conventional, and doubtless more authoritarian treatment (T3). Whether the particular ingredient of the treatment which gave rise to the difference was related to the factor of authoritarian or non-authoritarian structure or to some other factor is not yet determined. Certainly the conventional treatment was less complex in terms of the interpersonal relationships and the degree of linguistic sophistication demanded.

It is reasonably clear, however, that the underlying factor has something to do with perceptual processes—the ways in which different people try to make sense of the world, particularly the world of other people. It may lie in the connection between language and perception. (Bernstein 1961).[93]

Whatever the reason for the difference, it seems that questions which merely ask whether a particular form of treatment 'is good' are meaningless questions. It is even doubtful whether questions which relate to the punitive element of different types of punishment for different types of persons can be meaningful without reference to the different types of persons subject to the punishment. The typology of offenders is an area of study which must now be developed if further progress is to be made in the treatment of offenders with a view to reduction of recidivism.

TREATMENT INTERACTIONS

In the Grant studies it may be assumed that each treatment type was sufficiently specific to be described as a 'treatment', and not two or more interwoven types in one. At least the 'living group therapy' routines were based on a detailed statement of personality theory. In other cases it may not be true to assume that a treatment, although known by one name, is sufficiently unitary to withstand research analysis in the manner of the United States Navy study. Probation may mean different things to different probation officers, and different offenders placed on probation may experience different routines, but if the offender stays with one officer during his period of supervision, he will obtain a consistent image of probation treatment. But in certain cases, treatments are intentionally mixed by the court's decision. In the United States, for example, it is often a requirement of 'probation' that the offender first spends some time in prison. In this country, the Attendance Centre disposal is frequently combined with probation.

It seems generally to be assumed that if (x) is a good treatment and (y) is also good, then treatment (x + y) must be better, or at least as good. This does not follow. Indeed it seems that different treatment types may interact, with the result that the outcome is less desirable than where one treatment alone is given. Some indication of this is to be found in the Cambridge Institute of Criminology's study of Attendance Centres (McClintock 1961).[94] Where probation was given with Attendance Centre requirements, the outcome was always worse than expected—after, that is, making allowance for differences in the input by means of pre-sentence probability estimates.

Perhaps these results can be related to those of a number of research investigations into the 'cause of delinquency'. In general it is assumed that parental discipline is a factor in predisposition to delinquent acts. The beliefs that it is 'good' to have a strict or lax discipline, however, have not been supported, rather it has emerged from several studies that inconsistency of disciplinary action is a factor predisposing towards delinquency. The term 'inconsistency' has evaluative overtones and this may be unfortunate. It is possible to consider 'inconsistency' as representing a *more complex* system of control, and this may involve the individuals subjected to these systems with sophisticated role-playing if they are to cope. A similar explanation might underly the findings of the U.S. Navy Non-conformists study. The more complex the system, the more complex the information which individuals subjected to it have to be able to handle.

It so happens that social case work methods and in general, the 'more progressive' treatments are the *more complex*. More information has to flow in 'progressive treatment' systems than in authoritarian systems. The socially immature may not be able to cope with the amount of information in the 'living group therapy' treatment, and the 'authoritarian' system may show better results with these persons, *not because it is authoritarian, but because the information is less complex.*

The combination of two treatments into one sentence presents a more complex information set to the offender than one treatment. It may be that this accounts for the less satisfactory results.

RESEARCH DESIGNS AND DECISION MODELS

It seems to be fairly safe to conclude that interaction between types of offenders and types of treatment, and interactions between types of treatments cannot be ignored in research designs in penology. It does not follow that other hypotheses will not withstand testing. There may still be an 'offender on offender' effect as well as a 'system on offender' effect. It is also possible that the time of exposure to different systems will have some contribution to the variance of the outcomes, although in most studies, time has failed to show any significant pattern.

The nature of the hypotheses which now seems most tenable must influence the nature of the research designs which should now be considered. The simple randomisation of input, although a powerful research design, answers some types of questions inefficiently or not at all. Factorial designs, which still require basic randomisation are more powerful, but what levels of what measurements to treat as factors is not yet clear. It is obvious that if input is randomised to each form of treatment, the sub-cultural hypotheses cannot be tested, since by design, the 'mixture' within each treatment is controlled *to be* equal. Merely measuring it and finding it so at the conclusion demonstrates only that the randomisation was done properly in the first place ! Similarly, control and experimental designs may 'design out' certain factors which are correlates of the factors used as control information. The 'control' of certain sociological factors designs out certain psychological factors. Similarly, the control of certain psychological factors designs out certain sociological factors. If all offenders of any one type are placed together in one treatment, even if there is provision for a cross-over in the design, the hypothesis that the 'like with like' may produce different results from the 'like with unlike' cannot be tested.

Many hypotheses may be put forward as to what factors it would be worth while to attempt to control or to insert in factorial designs. Even the concept of 'likeness' without reference to the dimensions of 'likeness' is not a simple matter. Even quite complex designs can take into account only two or three levels on any factor, and assumptions of linearity are too easy to make and difficult to prove.

This may seem to be leading to a counsel of despair—there is nothing that research can do if it is to be valid; the situation is too complex. If this is the inference, then the matter is being approached with an incorrect (dysfunctional) philosophy of science. It is necessary to question the philosophy of research itself.

Perhaps we should now ask why we want to do research into penology. If we reply that we want to understand the process of social change which may take place in offenders, or to find out how to generate desirable social change we will be formulating questions which, to say the least, are going to be extremely difficult and costly to attempt to answer, even if answers can be expected to such questions. What, it may be asked, characterises successful research? Is there any satisfactory way for measuring degrees of 'scientific understanding'? If not, what can be adopted as a criterion for the effectiveness of research? It cannot be claimed that the subjective satisfaction of the 'scientist' is an adequate criterion of the value of his work.

If, on the other hand, we are prepared to change the research philosophy to a decision model, the problems are very much simplified and a strategy for research emerges. The decision model proposes questions for research which are linked with the strategy of social action. In the former case there are no boundaries to the possible action which might be proposed, and there are no boundaries to the information which can be considered to be likely to be of interest. In the decision case the criterion is one of prediction and of pay-off in terms of the 'action' variables rather than the 'scientific' variables. It is true that these 'action' variables are related to or derived from the present value structure of society, but is this important?

The 'decision' model allows of the use of operational definitions and of 'as if' statements which avoid otherwise intractable concepts. Items of data, initially believed to be 'information' can be demonstrated to be no more than 'noise'. By this method an evolutionary process can be developed—more information leading to more control, and more control leading to more information. Of course, it means that the concept of pay-off to be sought by the social scientist is some one else's concept of pay-off—the concept of the social administrator or social workers. But the division between action and research is a recent invention. Whether we like it or not, social scientist, administrator and social worker are all members of the same society. If we had been subjected to different social forces, would our science have been the same, would there not have been different concepts of 'truth'? The pursuit of independence is not realistic, the pursuit of superiority for one group over another is not functional. We shall get further with social science, social administration and social work when we find ways to work together towards a common goal, with the determination of which, all interests have been concerned together as equals. This means, that evaluation of the present systems of social action has claims to be the main focus for research effort in the immediate future, and perhaps for longer than that.

None the less, social research is itself, in this light, a social activity. Hence, by this argument, social research should itself be subjected to evaluation. Research into research may seem like the beginning of an infinite regress, but most things we value could be analysed in the same way.

THE PROGRESSIVE LOOP

This system of 'decision' research models in relation to social action is a dynamic model. It makes no claim to be ideal, indeed the concept of an ideal is not accepted. The penal system needs no ideal but a mechanism which will enable it to pursue continuously and effectively the changing ideas of ideals. An organisation which has a built-in pursuit mechanism should be able to keep 'in advance' (whatever is meant by that!) of systems which lack any such mechanism.

The infinite regress or circle looked at in terms of three dimensions, may be seen as a spiral. A step-by-step strategy should facilitate the statement of goals and give some indication of the sign-posts that will help us to place our position, so that we can check where we are moving and say whether we perceive this as desirable in terms of the current social ethic. If it is demonstrated that the information needed to arrive at rational decisions is too complex for the existing systems for information handling, new systems can be devised. The same argument applies to the methods of science itself as to the social action or social administration component. Neither science, action nor administration can claim a superior status or greater independence of role than the other. The decision model is a learning model, it is collaborative not competitive. It is, as Lord Hailsham (1962) said, necessary that society should 'bear within itself the means of constant change, endlessly adjusting itself to the alterations of technology and education and other social changes as they endlessly occur, automatically providing the basis for new advance.'

NOTES

Section I: History and Current Status

1. Cesare Bonesana, Marchese di Becarria, Italian jurist and reformer, 1738-1794.
2. John Conrad, *Crime and Its Correction: An International Survey of Attitudes and Practices* (Berkeley & Los Angeles: University of California Press, 1965).
3. The Joint Commission on Correctional Manpower and Training, which completed its studies under this grant in the Spring of 1969.
4. U.S. President's Commission on Law Enforcement and Administration of Justice, National Crime Commission, *The Challenge of Crime in a Free Society* (the General Report) (Washington, D.C.: U.S. Government Printing Office, 1967), Chap. VI.
5. "Declaration of Principles of 1870," as Revised and Reaffirmed at the Sixtieth Annual Congress of the American Prison Association, held at Louisville, Kentucky, October 10-16, 1930.
6. Maes, "La peine de mort dans le droit criminel de Malines," *Revue Historique de Droit Francais et Étranger* 28 (4th ser., 1950): 372, 383.
7. I. Leon Radinowicz, *A History of English Criminal Law* (1948), pp. 142, 147.
8. Francois Marie Arouet de Voltaire, *Idée Républicaines* (1762), p. xi.
9. Cesare Bonesana Becarria, *Dei Delitti e Delle Pene* (1764), par. 2.
10. Arthur Koestler, *Reflections on Hanging* (New York: Macmillan Company, 1957).
11. Edwin Powers, "Massachusetts Department of Correction," *American Journal of Correction* 27, 4 (July-August 1965): 16-25.
12. Austin H. MacCormick, "The Prison's Role in Crime Prevention," *Journal of Criminal Law and Criminology* 41, 1 (May-June 1950): 36-48.
13. William Paley, "The Principles of Moral and Political Philosophy," in *Eighteenth Century Penal Theory,* James Heath, ed. (New York: Oxford University Press, 1963), p. 258.
14. Negley K. Teeters, *They Were in Prison* (Philadelphia: John C. Winston, 1937), p. 30.
15. Gustave de Beaumont and Alexis de Tocqueville, *On the Penitentiary System in the United States and Its Application in France* (Carbondale: Southern Illinois University Press, 1964), p. 48.
16. Federal Bureau of Prisons, "Prisoners in State and Federal Institutions for Adult Felons," *National Prisoner Statistics* (November 1964): table 2, p. 13.
17. American Correctional Association, *Manual of Correctional Standards* (New York: American Correctional Association, 1966), p. 366.
18. Gresham M. Sykes, *The Society of Captives* (Princeton, N.J.: Princeton University Press, 1958), p. 36.
19. Paley, *op cit.*
20. Daniel Glaser, *The Effectiveness of a Prison and Parole System* (New York: Bobbs-Merrill, 1964), p. 113.
21. *Ibid.*, p. 235.
22. *Ibid.*, p. 113.
23. For a description of this program, see Columbus B. Hopper, "The Conjugal Visit at Mississippi State Penitentiary," in *Readings in Criminology and Penology,* David Dressler, ed. (New York: Columbia University Press, 1964), p. 556.
24. Glaser, *op. cit.,* pp. 490-503.
25. This generic term, used throughout, includes camps and other training facilities.

26. Osborne Foundation and National Council on Crime and Delinquency, *A Report of the Juvenile Institutions Project* (preliminary draft) 1966.

27. For the sake of convenience, the total will be designated as "52 jurisdictions."

28. "Statistics on Public Institutions for Children: 1964," *Children's Bureau Statistical Series 81* (Washington, D.C.: U.S. Department of Health, Education and Welfare, 1965). The remaining 14 percent not included in the present survey consists of 83 locally operated programs located in 16 States. In 1965 these had a projected capacity of 6,634 and an average daily population of 6,024. Approximately half of these programs are in California, where they are partially State subsidized.

29. Two State systems have no treatment staff at all.

30. "Institutions Serving Delinquent Children: Guides and Goals," *Children's Bureau Publication No. 360* (Washington, D.C.: U.S. Department of Health, Education, and Welfare, revised 1962), p. 52.

31. American Psychiatric Association, "Training Schools for Delinquent Children," p. 19.

32. *Ibid.*

33. Louis N. Robinson, *Penology in the United States* (Philadelphia: John C. Winston, 1921), p. 32.

34. Sol Rubin, *The Law of Criminal Correction* (St. Paul, Minn.: West Publishing Company, 1963), p. 170.

35. Myrl E. Alexander, *Jail Administration* (Springfield, Ill.: Charles C. Thomas, 1957), p. 311.

36. Paula K. Drucker, "Short-Term Education in a Short-Term Penal Institution," *Crime and Delinquency* (January 1966): 58-69.

37. See "Report on the Pilot Project for Women, Westchester County Jail," Westchester Citizens Committee of the National Council on Crime and Delinquency, Valhalla, New York, January 1965.

38. Mark S. Richmond, "The Jail Blight," *Crime and Delinquency* (April 1965): 134.

39. C. E. Ares, *et. al.*, "The Manhattan Bail Project: An Interim Report," *New York University Law Review* (January 1963): 67-95.

40. Richmond, *op. cit.*, p. 139.

41. "The Criminal Offender—What Should be Done?" Report of the President's Task Force on Prisoner Rehabilitation, April 1970.

42. Joseph F. Fishman, "Crucibles of Crime, a Shocking Story of American Jails," in *Series on Criminology, Law Enforcement and Social Problems* No. 35 (Patterson-Smith Publishers, 1969).

43. *Task Force Report: Corrections,* President's Commission on Law Enforcement and Administration of Justice (Washington, D.C.: U.S. Government Printing Office, 1967), p. 53.

44. *The Correctional Trainer,* Newsletter for Illinois Correctional Staff Training, (Fall 1970): 109.

45. "The National Sheriff," Publication of the National Sheriffs' Association, October-November, 1970.

46. *Task Force Report: Corrections,* pp. 77-81.

47. Hans W. Mattick and Ronald P. Sweet, *Illinois Jails, Challenge and Opportunity for the 1970s,* summary report based on *The Illinois Jails Survey of 1967-68,* conducted by the Center for Studies in Criminal Justice, The Law School, University of Chicago.

48. *Task Force Report: Corrections,* p. 79.

49. *Handbook of Correctional Design and Construction* (Washington, D.C.: U.S. Bureau of Prisons, 1949), p. 2.

50. Personal comment to author.
51. Howard B. Gill, *Prisons,* U.S. Attorney General's Survey, Vol. 5, 1940, p. 1.
52. Harry E. Barnes and Negley K. Teeters, *New Horizons in Criminology,* rev. ed. (New York: Prentice Hall, 1945), p. 532.
53. *Ibid,* Chapter 26, "The Cruelty and Futility of the Modern Prison."
54. *Contemporary Correction* (Tappan, ed. 1951), pp. 277-296.
55. *Ibid,* p. 193.
56. Harry E. Barnes and Negley K. Teeters, *New Horizons in Criminology,* 2nd ed. (New York: Prentice Hall, 1952), p. 498.
57. *Handbook of Correctional Design and Construction,* pp. 44-59.
58. *Ibid,* pp. 32, 64-65, 67, 69.
59. *Recent Prison Construction 1950-1960* (Washington, D.C.: U.S. Bureau of Prisons, 1961).
60. *Handbook of Correctional Design and Construction,* p. 14.
61. *Ibid,* p. 48.
62. *Ibid,* pp. 97, 99, 103, 118, 119, 130, 133.
63. *Ibid,* pp. 18, 21-22, 35, 38, 53.
64. "Prisoners in German Institution Employed by Private Employers," *Federal Probation* 24 (December 1960): 80. See also *Prison Labor* (New York: U.N. Department of Economic and Social Affairs, 1955).
65. Terrence Morris, "Worldwide Concern With Crime," *Federal Probation* 24 (December 1960): 21, 27.
66. Some data may have become obsolete through the actions of state legislatures in session in the spring of 1967.
67. The department supervises *all* state institutions.

Section II: The Correctional Institution as a Community

1. Piri Thomas, *Down These Mean Streets* (New York: Alfred A. Knopf, Inc., 1967), p. 281.
2. "Gleaning" is one term which is not natural to the prison social world, and the category itself is not explicitly defined. Convicts have recognized and labeled subparts of it, such as "intellectuals," "programmers," and "dudes on a self-improvement kick," but not the broader category which I have labeled gleaners. However, whenever I have described this category to convicts, they immediately recognized it and the term becomes meaningful to them. I chose the term gleaning because it emphasizes one very important dimension of this style of adaptation, the tendency to pick through the prison world (which is mostly chaff) in search of the means of self-improvement.
3. David W. Maurer, *Whiz Mob* (Princeton, N.J.: Princeton University Press, 1964), p. 196.
4. Erving Goffman has described this mode of adaptation, which he calls "playing it cool" in *Asylums* (Garden City, N.Y.: Doubleday Anchor Books, 1961), pp. 64-65.
5. Thomas, *op. cit.,* p. 280.
6. John Irwin and Donald Cressey, "Thieves, Convicts, and the Inmate Culture," *Social Problems* (Fall 1962): 150.
7. Black, *You Can't Win,* pp. 104-105.
8. Donald Clemmer, *The Prison Community* (New York: Holt, Rinehart & Winston, 1966), pp. 123, 127.
9. Malcolm Braly, *On the Yard* (Boston: Little, Brown and Co., 1967), pp. 106-107.

10. Fifteen percent of the 116 ex-prisoners were classified as "jailers."
11. Irwin and Cressey, *op. cit.*, p. 149.
12. Claude Brown, *Manchild in the Promised Land* (New York: Macmillan Company, 1965), p. 412.
13. In the sample of 116 ex-prisoners, the records indicated that 19 percent had followed a gleaning course in prison.
14. Malcolm X and Alex Haley, *The Autobiography of Malcolm X* (New York: Grove Press, 1966), p. 171.
15. *Ibid.*, p. 173.
16. *Ibid.*, pp. 173–174.
17. This movement was foretold by Malcolm X (see *The Autobiography of Malcolm X*, p. 183).
18. See Walter Reckless, *The Crime Problem* (New York: Appleton-Century-Crofts, 1955), pp. 24-25.
19. Gordon Allport, *The Nature of Prejudice* (Garden City, N.Y.: Doubleday Anchor, 1958), pp. 337-338.
20. Clemmer, *The Prison Community*, pp. 87, 299-301.
21. For fuller evaluation see Gresham M. Sykes, *The Society of Captives* (Princeton, N. J.: Princeton University Press, 1958), Chapter 4.
22. Clarence Schrag, "Leadership Among Prison Inmates," *Sociological Review* 19 (1954): 40.
23. Clemmer, *The Prison Community*, pp. 136-143.
24. Elmer H. Johnson, "Bureaucracy in the Rehabilitation Institution: Lower Level Staff as a Treatment Resource," *Social Forces* 38 (1960): 355-359.
25. Sykes, *Society of Captives*, Chapter 3.
26. Harper, "The Role of the 'Fringer' in a State Prison for Women," *Social Forces* 31 (1932): 53-60.
27. Otto Von Mering and Stanley H. King, *Remotivating the Mental Patient* (New York: Russell Sage Foundation, 1957).
28. Clemmer, *The Prison Community*, pp. 117-133.
29. Sykes, *Society of Captives*, pp. 5, 89–90.
30. For material concerning the social relations of persistent offenders see D. J. West, *The Habitual Prisoner* (New York: Macmillan, 1963); W. H. Hammond and E. Chayen, *Persistent Criminals* (H. M. S. O., 1963); D. H. Stott, "Delinquency, Maladjustment and Unfavorable Ecology," *British Journal of Psychology* 51, 2 (1960): 157-170. Representative theoretical discussions will be found in D. H. Stott, *Delinquency and Human Nature* (Carnegie, 1950); J. Bowlby, *Forty-four Juvenile Thieves* (Bailliere: Tindall and Cox, 1946); L. E. Hewitt and R. L. Jenkins, *Fundamental Patterns of Maladjustment* (State of Illinois, 1946).
31. See W. Goldfarb, "Psychological Privation in Infancy and Subsequent Adjustment," *American Journal of Orthopsychiatry* 15 (1945): 247 et. seq.; M. D. Ainsworth, *et. al.*, *Deprivation of Maternal Care* (W.H.O., 1963).
32. Gordon B. Trasler, "Criminality and the Socialization Process," *Advancement of Science* 21 (1965): 94.
33. Gordon B. Trasler, *The Explanation of Criminality* (London: Routeledge and Kegan Paul, 1962).
34. Some indirect evidence of this is to be found in K. Friedländer, *The Psycho-analytical Approach to Juvenile Delinquency* (London: Routeledge and Kegan Paul, 1947); W. Aichorn, *Wayward Youth* (New York: G. P. Putnam, 1936); and J. D. Grant, "A Group Dynamics Approach to the Treatment of Nonconformists in the Navy," *Annals of the American Academy of Political and Social Science* (1959).

35. See references to relevant sources in *The Explanation of Criminality*, Chapter 4.
36. R. A. Cloward, *et. al.*, *Theoretical Studies in Social Organization of the Prison* (New York: Social Science Resources Council, 1960); Terrence and Pauline Morris, *Pentonville* (London: Routeledge and Kegan Paul, 1963).
37. A. K. Cohen, *Delinquent Boys* (London: Routeledge and Kegan Paul, 1956).
38. The qualification is important; certain recognized patterns of interaction between inmates and staff tend to emerge in which there is tacit, *ad hoc* collaboration to defeat some official rule which is mutually inconvenient. Cf. Terrence and Pauline Morris, *Pentonville*.
39. See Gordon B. Trasler, "Re-socialization in Penal Institutions," *Cambridge Opinion* 38 (1964): 20-21.
40. For example see Gresham M. Sykes, *Society of Captives*, pp. 68-83, and Erving Goffman, *Asylums*.
41. See Gresham M. Sykes and Sheldon L. Messinger, "The Inmate Social System," in *Theoretical Studies in Social Organization of the Prison*, pp. 5-19; Howard W. Polsky, *Cottage Six* (New York: Russell Sage Foundation, 1962); and George H. Grosser, "The Role of Informal Inmate Groups in Change of Values," *Children* 5 (January-February 1958): 25-29.
42. For extended discussion and description of these treatment concepts and problems primarily directed to mental hospital patients, see Maxwell Jones, *The Therapeutic Community* (New York: Basic Books, Inc., 1953); Harry A. Wilmer, *Social Psychiatry in Action* (Springfield, Illinois: Charles C. Thomas, 1958); John Cumming and Elaine Cumming, *Ego and Milieu* (New York: Atherton Press, 1962); and among prison inmates see Joseph W. Eaton, *Stone Walls Not a Prison Make* (Springfield, Illinois: Charles C. Thomas, 1962); Robert H. Scott, "The Therapeutic Community in Prison," *Journal of Social Therapy* 7 (1961): 197-203; and Gene G. Kassebaum, David A. Ward, and Daniel M. Wilner, *Group Treatment by Correctional Personnel*, Monograph No. 3 (Sacramento: California Department of Corrections, 1963).
43. Harold Garfinkel, "Conditions of Successful Degradation Ceremonies," *American Journal of Sociology* 61 (March 1956): 421-422.
44. A former inmate of a prison for women in England described her experience: "Reception! A word that can conjure up a variety of functions. The wedding celebration; the formal party; the ovation that may greet the appearance of any public figure. The average person would never connect it with prison. To me, now, it can never mean anything else. Even to those who have been 'inside' ten years or more the first few hours of imprisonment are as indelibly printed on their minds as though they had happened only the day before." Joan Henry, *Who Lie in Gaol* (London: Victor Gollancz, 1952), p. 17.
45. There is an exception when the ring has no stones.
46. The quoted remarks are taken from a private conversation with a staff member.
47. The patient arriving in another total institution, the hospital, undergoes a similar experience: "Not knowing what to expect, the patient fears the worst, and the process of hospitalization during the first hours after his arrival lends to such fears the support of reality. The series of procedures that follow immediately after admission are perceived by the patient as an attack on his body. As a first step he is deprived of body symbols . . . he now has to surrender his clothes and his jewelry, and he may be given a hospital gown. Depriving the patient of all his body symbols is a way of stripping status and self-assurance from him." Rose L. Coser, *Life in the Ward* (East Lansing: Michigan State University Press, 1962), pp. 42-43.

48. Serapio R. Zalba, *Women Prisoners and Their Families,* Departments of Welfare and of Corrections, State of California (June 1964), pp. 35-36.
49. For an extended discussion of this particular point based on experiences of Korean prisoners of war see Albert D. Biderman's "Social-Psychological Needs and 'Involuntary' Behavior as Illustrated by Compliance in Interrogation," *Sociometry* 23 (June 1960): 120-147, especially pp. 135-138.
50. These roles among male prisoners are described by Sykes, *op. cit.,* pp. 91-93, 102-105.
51. In a similar vein Ward has criticized studies of homosexuality in prisons for males on the grounds that they, "ignore the important part that homosexual behavior plays in defining the social role of a boy in a training school society which is organized along a continuum from strength to weakness." Jack L. Ward, "Homosexual Behavior of the Institutionalized Delinquent," *The Psychiatric Quarterly Supplement* 32 (1958): 303-304.
52. Sykes, *Society of Captives,* p. 80. See also Terrence and Pauline Morris, "The Experience of Imprisonment," *The British Journal of Criminology* 2 (April 1962): 351-352.
53. Another adaptation which is akin to rebellion is "manipulation." "The manipulator is more rational than the rebel, not only seeking his own ends without coming into conflict with authority, but in contriving to outwit it. He recognizes the virtual impossibility of ameliorating the system by appeals to authority, so he acts on his own initiative." Terrence and Pauline Morris, *Ibid.,* p. 353.
54. Terrence and Pauline Morris, "Experience of Imprisonment," p. 350-351. Some of the consequences of becoming so adjusted to institutional life have been described by Robert Sommer and Humphry Osmond, "Symptoms of Institutional Care," *Social Problems* 8 (Winter 1960-61): 254-263.
55. The varied reactions to confinement of patients in a mental hospital have been described by Dembo and Hanfmann as a primitive drive to get out of the hospital by blind attack, insight into the basic factor of hospitalization, refusal to accept the reality of the hospital situation, preoccupation with psychosis, finding the hospital to be a place of refuge, and focusing on concrete aspects of confinement but not hospitalization as such. Tamara Dembo and Eugenia Hanfmann, "The Patient's Psychological Situation Upon Admission to a Mental Hospital," *The American Journal of Psychology* 47 (July 1935): 381-408.
56. For a discussion of the threat to collective solidarity posed by narcissistic, dyadic and familial withdrawal, see Philip E. Slater, "On Social Regression," *American Sociological Review* 28 (June 1963): 339-364.
57. Alfred C. Kinsey, *et al., Sexual Behavior in the Human Female* (Philadelphia: W. B. Saunders Company, 1953), pp. 642-689.
58. Alfred C. Kinsey, *et al., Sexual Behavior in the Human Male* (Philadelphia: W. B. Saunders Company, 1948), pp. 327-393.
59. Paul H. Gebbard, *et al., Sex Offenders* (New York: Harper & Row, 1965).
60. From a preliminary analysis of the differences between the pre-institutional and the institutional sexual outlet of adult male prisoners interviewed by the Institute for Sex Research, the institutional rates are only one-tenth of one-fifth of noninstitutional rates. For some males, the institutional rates are nearly zero.
61. For a discussion of the necessity of socially facilitating cues for sexual arousal and performance, see John H. Gagnon and William Simon, "Pornography: Raging Menace or Paper Tiger," *Trans-Action* 4, 8 (July-August 1967): 41-48; and William Simon and John H. Gagnon, "Pornography: The Social Sources of Sexual Scripts," a

paper presented at the 17th Annual Meeting of the Society for the Study of Social Problems, San Francisco, August 1967.

62. Alfred C. Kinsey, *et al., Sexual Behavior in the Human Male,* pp. 497-509.

63. Estimates may be found in the following sources: Joseph Fishman, *Sex in Prison* (New York: National Library Press, 1934), pp. 30, 40 percent; Gresham Sykes, *Society of Captives,* 35 percent; Donald Clemmer, "Some Aspects of Sexual Behavior in the Prison Community," *Proceedings of the American Correctional Association* (1958), 40 percent. Preliminary estimates from the Institute for Sex Research data are 35-45 percent.

64. The notions of "active" and "passive" in homosexual relationships are more obscuring of the actual conditions of the behavior than they are enlightening. The psychiatrist Irving Bieber has suggested the words "insertor" and "insertee" be substituted for active and passive, since these latter words assume that role behavior in sexual act has major meaning in psychological personality terms. *(Homosexuality* New York: Basic Books, 1962, pp. 238-254.) For an attempt at clarification of this confusion see William Simon and John H. Gagnon, "Homosexuality: The Formulation of a Sociological Perspective," *The Journal of Health and Social Behavior* 8, 3 (September 1967): 177-185.

65. Robert Lindner, "Sexual Behavior in Penal Institutions," in *Sex Habits of American Men,* Albert Deutsch, ed. (New York: Prentice Hall, 1948), pp. 201-215; Arthur Hoffman, "Sex Deviation in a Prison Community," *Journal of Social Therapy* 6, 3 (1955): 170-181; George Devereaux and M. C. Moss, "The Social Structure of Prisons and the Organic Tensions, *Journal of Criminal Psychopathology* 4, 2 (October 1942): 306-324.

66. See Seymour L. Halleck and Marvin Hersko, "Homosexual Behavior in a Correctional School for Adolescent Girls," *American Journal of Orthopsychiatry* 32, 5 (1962): 911-917; Rose Giallombardo, *Society of Women: A Study of a Women's Prison* (New York: John Wiley & Sons, 1966); David Ward and Gene Kassebaum, *Women's Prison: Sex and Social Structure* (Chicago: Aldine, 1965); Sidney Kosofsky and Albert Ellis, "Illegal Communications Among Institutionalized Female Delinquents," *The Journal of Social Psychology* 48 (August 1958): 155-160.

67. The two volumes are Ward and Kassebaum, *Women's Prison,* and Giallombardo, *Society of Women.* For an excellent comparative discussion, see the joint review of these volumes by Sheldon Messinger, *The American Sociological Review* 32, 1 (February 1967): 143-146.

68. F. J. Roethlisberger and W. J. Dickson, *Management and the Worker* (Cambridge, Mass.: Harvard University Press, 1939); Edward A. Shils and Morris Janowitz, "Cohesion and Disintegration of the Wehrmacht in World War II," *Public Opinion Quarterly,* 12 (1948): 280-315. Informal organization has also been found to contribute positively to economic organizations by reducing absenteeism, and negatively to military ones by generating norms which foster "goldbricking." Lewin's study contrasting the consequences of different patterns of control upon informal relations specifies in more detail relationships between organizational parameters and informal relations (K. Lewin, R. Lippitt, and R. K. White, "An Experimental Study of Leadership and Group Life," in *Readings in Social Psychology,* rev. ed., G. E. Swanson, T. M. Newcomb, and E. L. Hartley, eds. (New York: Holt, Rinehart & Winston, 1952). For an excellent study dealing with similar concerns in juvenile institutions which was published too late for comment in this paper, see David Street, "Inmates in Custodial and Treatment Settings," *American Sociological Review* 30 (February 1965): 40-56.

69. The replicated study was: Oscar Grusky, "Organizational Goals and the Behavior of Informal Leaders," *American Journal of Sociology* 65, 1 (July 1959): 59-67. Sociology is characterized by a lack of replication studies, particularly in the area of social organization. In his analysis of replication studies, Hanson noted fewer than twenty-five such studies in the field of sociology, with fully one-third of these refuting the original hypothesis. This would appear to leave sociology in the position of having relatively few sets of propositions which have been independently tested in different research sites. This condition neither contributes to the development of a cumulative fund of reliable knowledge, nor does it permit of the development of a set of standardized instruments which can be used to compare different types of organizations. See Robert Hanson, "Evidence and Procedure Characteristics of 'Reliable' Propositions in Social Science," *American Journal of Sociology* 63 (January 1958): 357-71. This replication was enhanced by the use of the same instruments in two new prison camps in addition to a repeat investigation of the prison originally studied by Grusky. Moreover, we utilized Grusky's questionnaire items and Guttman scales.
70. It is important to keep in mind that all three prison camps would be located on the treatment end of the continuum if compared with maximum-security institutions.
71. One cannot overlook the possible importance of the size of the prisons, which could provide an additional explanation to the one offered in this paper. However, the fact that Benign almost doubled in size between the original study and the replication, while inmate attitudes remained relatively unchanged, casts some doubt on its usefulness in accounting for our findings. Also, similar data collected on three other juvenile institutions did not show attitudes to be related to size as such; rather, it confirmed the importance of organizational goals. This is not to discard the importance of size, since it may have important ramifications for organizational structure which, in turn, influences informal organization. There was also a selectivity in the inmates sent to Benign, which will be dealt with in this paper.
72. Donald Clemmer, *The Prison Community,* Chapter 2; Donald Clemmer, "Observations on Imprisonment as a Source of Criminality," *Journal of Criminal Law and Criminology* 46 (September-October 1950): 311-19; R. J. Corsini, "A Study of Certain Attitudes of Prison Inmates," *Journal of Criminal Law and Criminology* 37 (July-August 1946): 132-42; Donald Cressey, ed., *The Prison: Studies in Institutional Organization and Change* (New York: Holt, Rinehart & Winston, 1961); Lloyd W. McCorkle and Richard Korn, "Resocialization Within the Walls," *Annals* 293 (May 1954): 88-98; Hans Reimer, "Socialization Within the Prison Community," *Proceedings of the American Prison Association* (1937), pp. 151-55; Sykes, *The Society of Captives,* Sykes and Messinger, "The Inmate Social System," pp. 5-19; Robert Vinter and Morris Janowitz, *op. cit.*
73. In comparing Grusky's results with our own, there was remarkable agreement in the percentages of positive responses.
74. In an excellent study of socialization within the prison, Wheeler demonstrates similar findings in regard to "prisonization," a phenomenon related to both attitudes toward society and the prison. His findings show that the longer the time the inmate spent in the prison, the less conforming his attitudes were with those of the staff, reflecting his internalization of the prison culture. See Stanton Wheeler, "Socialization in Correctional Communities," *American Sociological Review* 26 (October 1961): 697-712.
75. It should be pointed out that a smaller proportion of fairly recent (0-3 months) inmates of Partial than those from the more custodial Lock demonstrated favorable attitudes toward the staff. However, the percentage of favorable responses increased steadily with experience in the former institution, and decreased steadily in the latter. A

greater proportion of favorable responses was evidenced at all time periods among inmates of the highly treatment-oriented Benign than among those of both the other prisons. We inferred that inmates of Benign were apparently more receptive to the staff initially, their receptivity then declined, but ultimately were most favorable among those inmates with eight or more months of experience. Of course, the sample survey design which we used has the weakness of providing data only for a particular slice of time. Resurveys or panel studies are required to assess clearly the effect of prison experience on attitudes.

76. Wheeler, "Socialization in Correctional Communities," found a similar U-shaped pattern in regard to conforming attitudes held by inmates and attributed this to the stage of the inmate's institutional career. Inmates in the last phase of their institutionalization were believed to shed prison culture as they anticipate leaving the prison and returning to society.

77. The total time spent by the inmate in confinement in any institution was also found to be related to negative attitudes; the longer the time spent in custodial institutions, the more negative the attitude. This, of course, supports the argument that it is the prison experience as such which is largely responsible for the development of negative attitudes. Selectivity did exist, however, in that all inmates sent to prison camps to begin with were not believed to be security risks by the prison officials. It should be pointed out in this connection that inmates in all camps were, as a whole, positively oriented toward their institutions, staff, and programs. Whether this finding can be attributed to an initial selectivity in inmates sent to camps, or whether this is a reflection of the differences between maximum- and minimum-security prisons, generally, cannot be settled by this research design. The amount of variance accounted for by characteristics of members in an organization has not been clearly established by research findings.

78. Wheeler's study also demonstrated a relationship between the speed and degree of "prisonization" and involvement in formal inmate organization.

79. Clarence Schrag, "Leadership among Prison Inmates," *American Sociological Review* 19 (February 1954): 37-42.

80. Leaders were designated in accordance with Grusky's and Schrag's studies, *op. cit.*

81. In the typical custodial prison, social rejection; pervasive and rigid social control; and loss of liberty, autonomy, respect, affection, heterosexual relationships, security, and self-esteem have been identified as problems which inmates experience. Because these problems often require the cooperation of others for their solution, strong pressures for a collective response are built up. As cohesion develops among the inmates, a reduction of deprivations is experienced and, conversely, as it decreases, an increase in the irritants of prison life is experienced. In this manner systematic pressures for a collective solution are created (cf. Sykes and Messinger, "The Inmate Social System").

82. Cf. Albert K. Cohen, *Delinquent Boys* (Glencoe, Ill.: Free Press, 1956), Chapter 3 for a penetrating analysis of the formation of subcultures.

83. McCorkle, for example, has argued that the major problem the inmate social system attempts to cope with is social rejection and that inmates defend threats to their self-esteem by "rejecting the rejectors," a process which allows inmates to maintain favorable self-images in a situation where the formal organization imposes self-definitions which are unacceptable or threatening. This is accomplished by devaluing either the importance or legitimacy of persons imposing such definitions. L. S. McCorkle and R. Korn, *op. cit.*, pp. 86-95.

84. Gresham Sykes, *Society of Captives;* Richard Cloward, "Social Control in the Prison,"

in *Theoretical Studies in Social Organization of the Prison* and others have pointed out problems endemic to the custodial institution in maintaining social control, the most important of these being the lack of an internalized sense of duty on the part of inmates, the limitations upon the use of force, the difficulties involved in segregating rule violators, the lack of effective inducements, and the strains inherent in the role of the guard.

85. See Richard McCleery, "Communication Patterns As Bases of Systems of Authority and Power," in *Theoretical Studies in Social Organization of the Prison,* for a discussion of relations between formal and informal power structures.

86. In part, some of the differences between camps in the proportions of top leaders was a function of the numbers of nominations made by respondents in the different camps. Whether the number of nominations reflects the number of actual leaders is directly linked to the difficult problem of validity in the use of sociometric techniques which cannot be dealt with here.

87. Leaders were more authoritarian than nonleaders at Lock and less authoritarian than nonleaders at Benign. At Lock, 48.3 percent of the leaders as compared with 39 percent of the nonleaders gave authoritarian responses to a question asking if they would harshly discipline an angry employee while, at Benign, only 33.3 percent of the leaders as compared with 47.6 percent of the nonleaders responded in such an authoritarian fashion. At Partial, 40.5 percent of the leaders and 52.0 percent of the nonleaders responded in an authoritarian fashion.

88. Leaders were also less well liked and more socially distant from nonleaders in the custodial institution. At Benign, 77.4 percent of the leaders were also chosen as a "best buddy" by other inmates as compared with 66 percent of the leaders at Partial and 40.6 percent of those at Lock. The same pattern was found in regard to being chosen as "best liked" by other inmates, where 77.8 percent of the leaders at Benign, 52 percent of the leaders at Partial, and only 48 percent of the leaders at Lock were so chosen. These relationships were also found to hold in regard to a question asking who they would discuss personal problems with in the prison, where inmates at Lock were much less likely to discuss personal problems with their leaders than were inmates at Benign.

89. For example, Elliott Jaques, *The Changing Culture of a Factory* (New York: Dryden Press, 1952); Ronald Lippitt, "An Experimental Study of the Effect of Democratic and Authoritarian Group Atmosphere," *University of Iowa Studies in Child Welfare* 16 (1940): 43-195; Ralph White and Ronald Lippitt, "Leader Behavior and Member Reaction in Three 'Social Climates,'" in *Group Dynamics,* Dorwin Cartwright and Alvin Zander, ed. (Evanston, Ill.: Row, Peterson & Co., 1953), pp. 583-611; Rensis Likert, *New Patterns of Management* (New York: McGraw-Hill Book Co., 1961); and Norman R. F. Maier and John J. Hayes, *Creative Management* (New York: John Wiley & Sons, 1962). Much of the work in this area is summarized in the books by Likert.

90. See Peter M. Blau and Richard W. Scott, *Formal Organizations* (San Francisco: Chandler Publishing Co., 1962), pp. 186-92; Theodore Caplow, *Principles of Organization* (New York: Harcourt, Brace & World, 1964), pp. 156-58; Robert Dubin, George C. Homans, Floyd C. Mann, and Delbert C. Miller, *Leadership and Productivity* (San Francisco: Chandler Publishing Co., 1965), pp. 1-50; Robert L. Hamblin, "Punitive and Non-Punitive Supervision," *Social Problems* 11 (Spring 1964): 345-59; and the suggestive findings and comments in Joan Woodward, *Industrial Organization* (London: Oxford University Press, 1965).

91. The research on prisons is summarized in Cloward *et al., Theoretical Studies in Social Organization of the Prison*. References to the original research reports are given in

Sykes and Messinger, "The Inmate Social System," footnote on pp. 5-7. For mental hospitals, see Ivan Belknap, *Human Problems in a Mental Hospital* (New York: McGraw-Hill Book Co., 1956); William R. Morrow, "A Persisting Clique of Chronic Mental Patients," *Human Organization* 20 (Spring 1961): 32-35; and Richard F. Salisbury, *Structures of Custodial Care* (Berkeley: University of California Press, 1962).

92. See especially Richard A. Cloward, "Social Control in the Prison," and Richard McCleery, "Communication Patterns as Bases of Systems of Authority and Power," in Cloward *et al., op. cit.,* pp. 20-48, 49-77. For additional findings, see Richard McCleery, "Authoritarianism and the Belief System of Incorrigibles," in *The Prison: Studies in Institutional Organization and Change,* Donald R. Cressey, ed. (New York: Holt, Rinehart & Winston, 1961), pp. 260-306; Terrence Morris, Pauline Morris, and Barbara Biely, "It's the Prisoners Who Run This Prison," *Prison Service Journal 3* (January 1961): 3-11; Joseph C. Mouledous, "Organizational Goals and Structure Change: A Study of the Organization of a Prison Social System," *Social Forces* 41 (March 1963): 283-90; Sykes, *Society of Captives;* and Stanton Wheeler, "Socialization in a Prison Community," *American Sociological Review* 26 (October 1961): 697-712.

93. Bernard B. Berk, "Organizational Goals and Inmate Organization," (in this volume see pp. 233-247); Oscar Grusky, "Treatment Goals and the Behavior of Organizational Leaders," *American Journal of Sociology* 65 (July 1959): 59-67; Daniel Glaser, *The Effectiveness of a Prison and Parole System,* (Indianapolis: Bobbs-Merrill Co., 1964); McCleery, "Communication Patterns." David Street, Robert D. Vinter, and Charles Perrow, *Organization for Treatment* (New York: Free Press, 1966); and Mayer N. Zald, "Organizational Structures in Five Correctional Institutions," *American Journal of Sociology* 68 (November 1962): 335-45.

94. William Caudill, Frederick C. Redlich, H. R. Gilmore, and E. G. Brody, "Social Structure and Interaction Process on a Psychiatric Ward," *American Journal of Orthopsychiatry* 22 (April 1952): 314-34; William Caudill, *The Psychiatric Hospital as a Small Society* (Cambridge, Mass.: Harvard University Press, 1958); Milton Greenblatt, Daniel J. Levinson, and Richard H. Williams eds., *The Patient and the Mental Hospital* (New York: Free Press, 1957); Milton Greenblatt, Richard M. York, and Esther L. Brown, with Robert W. Hyde, *From Custodial to Therapeutic Care in Mental Hospitals* (New York: Russell Sage Foundation, 1955); H. Rowland, "Interaction Processes in a State Mental Hospital," *Psychiatry* 3 (April 1938): 323-37; and A. H. Stanton and M. S. Schwartz, *The Mental Hospital* (New York: Basic Books, 1954).

95. Street, Vinter, and Perrow, *Organization for Treatment,* pp. 225-27.

96. Erving Goffman, *Asylums.*

97. For the general social-psychological model used here, see Daniel J. Levinson, "Role, Personality and Social Structure in the Organizational Setting," *Journal of Abnormal and Social Psychology* 58 (March 1959), 170-80, and Theodore R. Sarbin, "Role Theory," in *Handbook of Social Psychology,* Gardner Lindzey, ed. (Cambridge, Mass.: Addison-Wesley Publishing Co., 1954), pp. 223-58.

98. It should be noted that a sharp distinction is being made here between role expectations institutionalized and supported by sanctions in the organization, on the one hand, and the attitudes evoked in the individual by these expectations, on the other.

99. See, for example, Goffman, *Asylums* and Sykes and Messinger, "The Inmate Social Systems."

100. The fourth logical type, congruence of goals without reliance on organizational activities, should be unstable and hence empirically rare.

101. See James G. March and Herbert L. Simon, *Organizations* (New York: John Wiley & Sons, 1958), Chapter 6. "Decisions" are construed here as involving "search" activities or "absorption of uncertainty."
102. In addition, a third type of management, autocratic, can be identified that seems to be common in custodial institutions. Autocratic management is characterized by relatively little emphasis on rational administration of rules and heavy emphasis on what Weber has called "Kadi" justice, in which the superior makes decisions on the basis of *ad hoc* judgments suited to the particular persons involved and the practical ends the superior seeks to attain. In such a case, a subordinate influences decisions primarily through his particular relation with the superior, since there is no rational system of rules on which the subordinate can depend irrespective of the personal views of the superior.
103. The institution and demonstration project are described in detail in Elliot Studt, Sheldon L. Messinger, and Thomas P. Wilson, *C Unit: Search for Community in Prison* (New York: Russell Sage Foundation, 1968). In that report, cooperative and opportunistic adaptations are referred to as "problem solving" and "wise," respectively.
104. Details of the selection procedure are given in Studt, *et al., C Unit.* The chief possible source of bias is that certain inmates with extremely bad behavior records acquired either in the reception center or in other institutions before arriving at the institution under study were excluded from the eligible pool. These inmates usually were segregated from the general population on their arrival and often spent much of their stay in segregated housing. Thus, they tended to be somewhat underrepresented in the nonhonor units and seldom gained honor status. At worst, this bias might affect comparisons between the participative and nonhonor units, and there is some reason to believe that this effect is negligible. See Studt, *et al.,* Appendices A and D.
105. The survey samples in the two bureaucratic units were drawn randomly with a sampling ratio of one in three, yielding fifty-seven and sixty inmates in the nonhonor and honor units, respectively. The C Unit sample of 120 inmates consisted of all inmates who had been in C Unit for at least two weeks at the time of the survey. See Studt, *et al.,* for further details.
106. Complete details are given in Studt, *et al.* Each inmate was asked two sets of questions about each role relationship he was involved in with staff; counselor, day and evening housing-unit officers, morning and afternoon work supervisors, any one "other" named by the inmate, and participation in supervised groups.
    As an example, for the counselor, the first set contained two items. "When you see your counselor, there are a number of things you could talk about. One kind of thing is about procedures, requests, classification, assignments, board reports, and so on. How much of your contact with him is about things like this—would you say over half or less than half? (Probe: Almost all? Over half? About half? Less than half? Very little?)," and, "Do you ever 'talk serious' with your counselor? (Probe: How much do you talk serious with him? A lot? Some? Or not very much?." If an inmate indicated that not all of his contact with his counselor was about procedural matters and that he "talked serious" a lot or some of the time (i.e., discussed matters the inmate felt to be important in a relatively open and frank way, as opposed to "shucking" the counselor), his attitude toward the counselor was scored as positive on a "shared goals" index. In a similar way, indexes of shared goals were constructed for the attitudes of an inmate toward each of the staff members to whom he was related.
    A second set of questions was used to develop a "working relationship" index for the counselor "How well do you think he understands you and your problems?" "When you really need something done, can you count on him to help you out?" And, "On

the whole, how do you get along with him?" If an inmate responded positively to all three questions, his attitude toward the counselor was scored as positive on the working relationship index. Again, parallel questions were asked concerning the inmate's attitudes toward other staff members.

Inmates' attitudes toward a given staff member were then classified as "cooperative" (working relationship and shared goals), "opportunistic" (working relationship but not shared goals), "nonscale" (shared goals but not working relationship), or "alienated" (neither working relationship nor shared goals). Since shared goals should be unlikely to persist in the absence of a working relationship, it was anticipated that the nonscale category would be rare. This proved to be the case, since less than 9 percent of the respondents gave nonscale responses toward any given staff member. Consequently, these were combined with the opportunistic responses.

Finally, to obtain the over-all index of type of adaptation, the indexes describing attitudes toward the several staff members were combined: "cooperative" *adaptation* (cooperative attitudes toward two or more staff members), "opportunistic" *adaptation* (opportunistic attitudes toward two or more staff members, or opportunistic attitudes toward one and cooperative attitudes toward one staff member), and "alienated" *adaptation* (neither a cooperative nor an opportunistic adaptation).

107. The following questions were used: Have you talked with any staff in the past several weeks about something that was really on your mind?" "In an institution there are bound to be procedures a man won't like—for instance, unlock procedures that make men wait too long, petty rules, too many shakedowns, TV rules that make for a lot of hassle. When something like this gets really bad in the unit, do you talk with other inmates about it? Do you talk about it with any staff?" And, "There'll be some inmates who do things that bother the other men in the unit—like too much noise, fires, maybe some racial tension. When things of this sort get really bad, do you talk with other inmates about it? How about with staff?"

108. Inmates were asked to think about the other inmates they associated with most often and to assign them fictitious names. The following question was asked about each such associate. "On the streets would you want him as a close friend, a friend but not really close, just an associate, or wouldn't you want to associate with him?" Positive responses were "close friend" or "friend but not really close."

109. "Thinking over the past several weeks, have you talked with inmates about something that was really on your mind?"

110. The factors controlled were legal status, race, father's occupation, age, intelligence, psychiatric diagnosis, alcoholic history, opiate use, nonopiate drug use, homosexual experience, family-arrest history, prior prison terms, prior jail terms, present offense, having a fixed parole date, time in institution, and time in housing unit. See Studt *et al.,* for details.

111. It may be noted that this pattern of findings also argues against the possibility that the findings are the result merely of contamination between the indicators of type of adaptation and communication with staff.

112. Findings suggestive of this same idea are reported by Arthur Kornhauser, *Mental Health of the Industrial Worker* (New York: John Wiley & Sons, 1965).

113. As an example, see Melville Dalton, "The Industrial Rate-Buster: A Characterization," *Applied Anthropology* 6 (1948): 5-18.

114. Charles Perrow "A Framework for the Comparative Analysis of Organizations," *American Sociological Review* 32 (April 1967): 194-208. See also Woodward, *op cit.,* for an extremely important study of the effects of technology.

115. Clemmer, *The Prison Community,* pp. 298 ff.
116. *Ibid.,* pp. 107, 123 ff.
117. Clarence Schrag, "Social Types in a Prison Community" (Unpublished M.S. thesis, University of Washington, 1944).
118. Morris G. Caldwell, "Group Dynamics in the Prison Community," *Journal of Criminal Law and Criminology* 46 (January-February 1956): 648-657.
119. Gresham M. Sykes, *Society of Captives,* Chapter 5; Gresham M. Sykes, "Men, Merchants and Toughs: A Study of Reactions to Imprisonment," *Social Problems* 4 (October 1956): 130-138.
120. Samuel M. Strong, "Social Types in a Minority Group," *American Journal of Sociology* 48 (March 1943): 564.
121. *Ibid.,* p. 563.
122. Richard A. Cloward, "Social Control in the Prison," Chapter 2 in *Theoretical Studies in Social Organization of the Prison;* Schrag, "Social Types in a Prison Community;" Sykes, *Society of Captives.*
123. Fred E. Fiedler and Alan R. Bass, "Delinquency, Confinement and Interpersonal Perception," *Technical Report No. 6,* Group Effectiveness Research Laboratory (Urbana: University of Illinois, 1959).
124. Stanton Wheeler, "Social Organization in a Correctional Community" (Unpublished Ph.D. Dissertation, University of Washington, 1958).
125. Richard A. Cloward, "Social Control and Anomie: A Study of a Prison Community" (Unpublished Ph.D. Dissertation, Columbia University, 1959).
126. Donald L. Garrity, "The Effects of Length of Incarceration Upon Parole Adjustment and Estimate of Optimum Sentence: Washington Correctional Institutions" (Unpublished Ph.D. Dissertation, University of Washington, 1956); and Donald L. Garrity, "Statistics for Administrative and Policy Decisions, I," *California Youth Authority Quarterly* 10 (Fall 1957), 40-47; and Chapter 9, above.

Section III Specific Programs in Correctional Institutions

1. *Handbook on Classification in Correctional Institutions* (New York: American Correctional Association, 1947), p. 10.
2. Some parole officials believe that *parole classification procedures* should be developed utilizing institution classification information as basic source material and integrating it systematically with treatment and training needs and facilities which are based in the community. Adequate "continuity of care" would seem to require such a development.
3. Several of these studies are summarized in my book, *The Effectiveness of a Prison and Parole System* (Indianapolis: Bobbs-Merrill, 1964), Chapter 12.
4. See John Clark and Eugene Wenninger, "Social Class, Area, Sex and Age as Correlates of Illegal Behavior Among Juveniles," *American Sociological Review* 27 (December 1962): 826-834; Albert J. Reiss, Jr., and Albert L. Rhodes, "The Distribution of Juvenile Delinquency in the Class Structure;" *ibid.,* 26 (October 1961): 720-32.
5. Published in 1961 by the Viking Press, and republished by them in 1964 in paperback as Compass Books No. C 168.
6. *Ibid.,* pp. 34-45.
7. *Ibid.,* pp. 89-95.
8. John M. McKee, "Reinforcement Theory and the 'Convict Culture,'" Proceedings, American Correctional Association, 1964, pp. 171-178.

9. *Manual of Correctional Standards,* (New York: The American Correctional Association, 1959), p. 232.
10. Daniel Glaser, "How Institution Discipline Can Best Serve Correctional Purposes," *American Journal of Correction* 27, 2 (March-April 1955): 3-6, 22.
11. American Correctional Association, *op. cit.,* pp. 298, 303.
12. Stuart Adams, "Interaction Between Individual Interview Therapy and Treatment Amenability in Older Youth Authority Wards," in California Board of Corrections Monograph No. 2, *Inquiries Concerning Kinds of Treatment for Kinds of Delinquents* (Sacramento, 1961), pp. 27-44. Republished in Norman Johnston *et al., The Sociology of Punishment and Correction* (New York: John Wiley & Sons, 1962), pp. 213-224.
13. See Norman Fenton, *An Introduction to Group Counseling in State Correctional Service* (New York: American Correctional Association, 1958).
14. Robert M. Harrison and Paul F. C. Mueller, "Clue Hunting About Group Counseling and Parole Outcome," *California Department of Corrections Research Report No. 11,* (Sacramento, 1964).
15. O. F. Lewis, *The Development of American Prisons and Prison Customs, 1776-1845* (Albany: Prison Association of New York, 1922), pp. 169-170.
16. *Ibid.*
17. O. F. Lewis, "Inmate Self-Government a Century Ago," *The Delinquent* 8 (1918): 9.
18. Zebulon R. Brockway, *Brockway, Fifty Years of Prison Service: An Autobiography* (1912), p. 96.
19. Helfman, "Antecedents of Thomas Mott Osborne's 'Mutual Welfare League in Michigan," *Journal of Criminal Law and Criminology* 40 (1950): 597.
20. *Ibid.*
21. Calvin Derick, "Self-Government," *Survey* (September 1, 1917): 473.
22. Reported in Enoch C. Wines, *Punishment and Reformation: A Study of the Penitentiary System* (Lane rev'n, 1923), p. 408.
23. Thomas Mott Osborne, *Society and Prisons* (1916), p. 164.
24. Frank Tannenbaum, *Crime and the Community* (1938), p. 416.
25. Wines, *op. cit.,* pp. 397-398.
26. *Ibid.,* pp. 407-408.
27. Howard B. Gill, "The Norfolk State Prison Colony at Massachusetts," *Journal of Criminal Law and Criminology* 22 (1931): 107.
28. *Ibid.*
29. Lewis, *Development of American Prisons and Prison Customs,* p. 36.
30. "The Inmate Advisory Council," 1955 Proceedings, American Correctional Association, p. 142.
31. Hermann Mannheim, *The Dilemma of Penal Reform* (London: George Allen & Unwin, Ltd., 1939), p. 56.
32. Max Grunhut, *Penal Reform* (Oxford: Clarendon Press, 1948), p. 209.
33. Frank T. Flynn, "The Federal Government and the Prison-Labor in the States, I: The Aftermath of Federal Restrictions," *Social Service Review* 24 (March 1950): 20-21.
34. Selig Perlman, *A Theory of the Labor Movement* (New York: Augustus M. Kelley, 1949), pp. 182-200.
35. O. F. Lewis, *The Development of American Prisons and Prison Customs,* p. 48.
36. Howard B. Gill, "The Prison Labor Problem," *Annals of the American Academy of Political and Social Science* 157 (September 1931): 84.
37. Attorney General's Survey of Release Procedures, Vol. 5, *Prisons* (Leavenworth, Kansas: Federal Prison Industries Press, 1940), pp. 29-30.

38. Blake McKelvey, *American Prisons* (Chicago: University of Chicago Press, 1936), pp. 103-104.
39. *Ibid*, pp. 98, 105.
40. Flynn, *op. cit.*, pp. 20-21.
41. Manuel Lopez-Rey, "Some Considerations of the Character and Organization of Prison Labor," *Journal of Criminal Law, Criminology, and Police Science* 49 (May-June 1958): 10-28.
42. John C. Burke, "A Warden's View on Vocational Education in Correctional Treatment," *Proceedings of American Prison Association, 1946*, p. 137.
43. Wade K. Springsted, "Industries on the Treatment Team," *Progress Report* 10 (April-June 1962): 11.
44. "Policies Relating to Inmate Industrial Assignments," *Progress Report* 8 (April-June 1960): p. 10.
45. Wesley O. Ash and Walter L. Barkdull, "California's Trade and Advisory Councils," *American Journal of Correction* 23 (May-June 1961): 10.
46. F. Emory Lyon, "Prison Labor and Social Justice," *Annals of the American Academy of Political and Social Science* 46 (March 1913): 149-50.
47. Springsted, *op. cit.*, p. 12.
48. Lyon, *op. cit.*, p. 149.
49. Louis N. Robinson, *Penology in the United States* (Philadelphia: John C. Winston Co., 1923), p. 181.
50. Daniel Glaser, *The Effectiveness of a Prison and Parole System* (Indianapolis: Bobbs-Merrill Co., 1964), pp. 234-35.

Section IV: Fusion of Institutional and Community Programs

1. *Task Force Report: Corrections,* The President's Commission on Law Enforcement and Administration of Justice (Washington, D.C.: U.S. Government Printing Office, 1967), pp. 6-7.
2. "Correction in the U.S.," A Survey for the President's Crime Commission by the National Council on Crime and Delinquency, pp. 247-252.
3. *Task Force Report: Corrections,* p. 154.
4. See Lloyd W. McCorkle, Albert Elias, and F. Lovell Bixby, *The Highfields Story: An Experimental Treatment Project for Youthful Offenders* (New York: Henry Holt & Co., 1958). See also Paul Keve, "Imaginative Programming in Probation and Parole" (Minneapolis: University of Minnesota Press, 1967), pp. 137-173, and J. Robert Weber, "A Report of the Juvenile Institutions Project" (unpublished report to the Osborne Association and the National Council on Crime and Delinquency, September 1966), pp. 123-126, 223-230.
5. For further discussion of Pinehills and Essexfields, see LaMar T. Empey, *Alternatives to Incarceration,* Office of Juvenile Delinquency and Youth Development Studies in Delinquency (Washington: U.S. Government Printing Office, 1967), pp. 37-40.
6. Weber, *op. cit.*, pp. 225-226.
7. *Ibid.*, 173.
8. *Ibid.*, p. 176.
9. *Ibid.*
10. *Ibid.*, p. 179. Cf. Keve, *op. cit.*, pp. 250-251.
11. Communication from Keith Griffiths, chief, Division of Research, California Youth Authority, December 1966.

12. The development of the Community Treatment Project is reported in "Community Treatment Reports" issued by the Division of Research, California Youth Authority, Sacramento, Nos. 1-7, 1962-66.
13. Data provided by the California Youth Authority.
14. *Ibid.*
15. Data in this section communicated to the Commission by Milton Luger, director, New York State Division for Youth, December 1966.
16. *Citizen* is defined here to mean, generally, persons other than correctional clients or those hired primarily to give a service in relation to them.
17. See, for example, International Prisoners' Aid Association, *International Directory of Prisoners' Aid Agencies,* 1968 (Milwaukee, Wisconsin: International Prisoners' Aid Association, 1968).
18. U.S., President's Commission on Law Enforcement and Administration of Justice (National Crime Commission), *The Challenge of Crime in a Free Society* (the General Report) (Washington, D.C.: U.S. Government Printing Office, 1967), p. 159.
19. Benedict S. Alper, *Community Residential Treatment Centers* (New York: National Council on Crime and Delinquency, 1966), pp. 6-10.
20. Gordon H. Barker, "Volunteers in Corrections," consultant paper prepared for the U.S. President's Commission on Law Enforcement and Administration of Justice (National Crime Commission) (Washington, D.C.: U.S. Government Printing Office, 1967), pp. 16-19.
21. Joe Alex Morris, "Royal Oak Aids Its Problem Youth," *Reader's Digest* 87 (October 1965): 163-167.
22. See Jack Otis, "Correctional Manpower Utilization," *Crime and Delinquency* 12 (July 1966): 261-271.
23. *Task Force Report: Corrections,* p. 104.
24. *Ibid.,* p. 103.
25. See Robert K. Merton, *Social Theory and Social Structure* (Glencoe, Ill.: Free Press, 1957), p. 199; and W. Richard Scott, "Theory of Organizations," in *Handbook of Modern Sociology,* Robert L. Faris, ed. (Chicago: Rand, McNally, 1964), p. 510.
26. *Task Force Report: Corrections,* p. 109.
27. U.S., Joint Commission on Correctional Manpower and Training, *The Public Looks at Crime and Correction,* Washington, D.C., February 1968.
28. Frank Remington, "The Jurist Frame of Reference in Parole" (New York: National Parole Institutes, 1963). (Mimeographed.)
29. George B. Leonard, "A New Liberal Manifesto," *Look* 32 (May 28, 1968): 29.
30. Clarence Schrag, "Towards a Correctional Model," an unpublished paper submitted to the National Crime Commission.
31. John M. Martin and Gerald M. Shattuck, "Community Interventions and the Correctional Mandate," consultant paper prepared for the U.S. President's Commission on Law Enforcement and Administration of Justice (National Crime Commission) (Washington, D.C.: U.S. Government Printing Office, 1967).
32. See Howard Becker and Blanche Geer, "Latent Culture: A Note on the Theory of Latent Social Roles," *Administrative Science Quarterly* 5 (September 1960): 304-313.
33. The family, although an obvious focus of important interventions, is excluded from this discussion.
34. Lamar Empey, "Peer Group Influences in Correctional Programs," consultant paper prepared for the U.S. President's Commission on Law Enforcement and Administra-

tion of Justice, (National Crime Commission) (Washington, D.C.: U.S. Government Printing Office, 1967), p. 22.

35. McCorkle, *et. al., The Highfields Story;* Lamar T. Empey and Jerome Rabow, "The Provo Experiment in Delinquency Rehabilitation," *American Sociological Review,* 26 (October 1961): 679-696.

36. See *Reaching the Fighting Gang* (New York: New York City Youth Board, 1960).

37. See "Proposal Submitted to Office of Economic Opportunity, 1968—Corrections," Joint Youth Development Committee, Chicago, 1968. (Mimeographed.)

38. Gus Tyler, "The Criminal and the Community, *Current History* 53 (August 1967): 104.

39. Martin and Shattuck, *op. cit.,* pp. 34-36.

40. "Case Management Project: A New Approach to the Management and Delivery of Court Services" (Winston-Salem, North Carolina: Forsyth County Domestic Relations Court, 1968), p. 8. (Mimeographed.)

41. See Judith G. Benjamin, Marcia K. Freedman, and Edith F. Lynton, *Pros and Cons: New Roles for Nonprofessionals in Corrections* (New York: National Committee on Employment of Youth, 1965).

Section V: Scientific Guidance of Institutional Policies

1. Leslie T. Wilkins, *Evaluation of Penal Treatments* (New York: Random House, 1969). (In this volume see pp. 509-523.)

2. The theory regarding the efficacy of using criminal groups as media of change and targets of change has been spelled out in a series of articles over a period of almost 15 years, and this theoretical discussion will not be repeated here. See the following articles by Donald R. Cressey: "Contradictory Theories in Correctional Group Therapy Programs," *Federal Probation* 18 (1954): 20-26; "Changing Criminals: The Application of the Theory of Differential Association," *American Journal of Sociology* 61 (1955): 116-120; "Social Psychological Theory for Using Deviants to Control Deviation" in *Experiment in Cultural Expansion: Proceedings of a Conference on the Use of Products of a Social Problem in Coping with the Problem* (Sacramento: California Department of Corrections, 1964), pp. 139-152; "Social Psychological Foundations for Using Criminals in the Rehabilitation of Criminals," *Journal of Research in Crime and Delinquency* 2 (1965): 49-59. See also Rita Volkman and Donald R. Cressey, "Differential Association and the Rehabilitation of Drug Addicts," *American Journal of Sociology* 69 (1963): 129-142; and Donald R. Cressey and Edwin H. Sutherland, *Principles of Criminology,* 7th ed. (Philadelphia: J. B. Lippincott Company, 1966), pp. 378-380, 548-557, 675-680.

3. See Leon Radzinowicz, *A History of the English Criminal Law and Its Administration from 1750,* I (New York: Macmillan, 1948), pp. 268-449.

4. We cannot here discuss the arguments of the "Positive School" of criminology whose leaders in the nineteenth century popularized individualization by denying individual responsibility and advocating an essentially nonpunitive reaction to crime and criminality. See George B. Volk, *Theoretical Criminology* (New York: Oxford University Press, 1958), pp. 27-40; and Cressey and Sutherland, *Criminology,* pp. 56-58, 313, 354-355, 683-684. The idea of individualization had elements of novelty in its formulation, but Cohen has pointed out that to a considerable degree "it was but a reassertion of the old idea of equity *(epieikia)* as the correction of the undue rigor of the law, a

542   *Notes*

corrective to the injustice which results from the fact that the abstract rule cannot take into account all the specific circumstances that are relevant to the case. It assumes its simplest and oldest form in the pardoning power. . . . Some religions, indeed, make God's forgiveness His most glorious attribute." Morris R. Cohen, *Reason and Law* (Glencoe, Ill.: Free Press, 1950), p. 53.

5. See Donald R. Cressey, "Prison Organization" in *Handbook of Organizations,* James G. March, ed. (New York: Rand-McNally, 1965), pp. 1023-1070.
6. See George H. Grosser, "External Setting and Internal Relations of the Prison," in Richard A. Cloward *et al., Theoretical Studies in Social Organization of the Prison* (New York: Social Science Resources Council, 1960), pp. 130-144.
7. Andrew Gundar Frank, "Goal Ambiguity and Conflicting Standards: An Approach to the Study of Organizations," *Human Organization* 27 (1958): 8-13.
8. See Philip Selznick, *Leadership and Administration* (Evanston, Ill.: Row Peterson, 1957); and Mayer N. Zald, "The Correctional Institution for Juvenile Offenders: An Analysis of Organizational 'Character,'" *Social Problems* 8 (1960): 57-67.
9. Theodore Caplow, *The Sociology of Work* (Minneapolis: University of Minnesota Press, 1954), p. 129.
10. See Lloyd E. Ohlin, "Conflicting Interests in Correctional Objectives," in Cloward *et al, op. cit.,* pp. 111-129.
11. *Ibid.,* p. 126.
12. See Donald R. Cressey, "The Nature and Effectiveness of Correctional Techniques," *Law and Contemporary Problems* 23 (1958): 754-771.
13. Richard R. Korn and Lloyd W. McCorkle, *Criminology and Penology* (New York: Henry Holt, 1959), p. 593.
14. See Donald R. Cressey, "Limitations on Organization of Treatment in the Modern Prison," in Cloward *et. al., op. cit.,* pp. 78-110.
15. Ernest Reimer and Martin Warren, "Special Intensive Parole Unit: Relationship between Violation Rate and Initially Small Caseload," *National Probation and Parole Association Journal* 3 (1957): 1-8.
16. See Cressey, "Prison Organization," p. 1059.
17. See Donald R. Cressey, "Professional Correctional Work and Professional Work in Correction," *National Probation and Parole Association Journal* 5 (1959): 1-15.
18. See Robert K. Merton, *Social Theory and Social Structure,* 2d ed. (Glencoe, Ill.: Free Press, 1957), pp. 198-199.
19. David Cort, *Is There an American in the House?* (New York: Macmillan, 1960), pp. 175-176.
20. See Caplow, *Sociology of Work,* pp. 139-140; and Cressey, "Professional Correctional Work and Professional Work in Correction," pp. 2-3.
21. See Donald R. Cressey, "The State of Criminal Statistics," *National Probation and Parole Association Journal* 3 (1957): 230-241.
22. W. H. Kuenning, "Letter to a Penologist" in *Prison Etiquette,* Holley Cantine and Dachine Rainer, eds. (Bearsville, N.Y.: Retort Press, 1959), p. 132.
23. Lloyd W. McCorkle and Richard Korn, "Resocialization within Walls," *Annals of the American Academy of Political and Social Science* 293 (1954): 88-98.
24. For a summary statement regarding this experiment, see Ralph Schwitzgebel, "A New Approach to Understanding Delinquency," *Federal Probation* 24 (1960), 31-35.
25. Stanton H. Wheeler, "Role Conflicts in Correctional Communities" in *The Prison: Studies in Institutional Organization and Change,* Donald R. Cressey, ed. (New York: Holt, Rinehart and Winston, 1961), pp. 229-259.

26. See Harold H. Kelley and Edmund H. Volkhart, "The Resistance to Change of Group-Anchored Attitudes," *American Sociological Review* 27 (1952): 453-465.
27. John Irwin and Donald R. Cressey, "Thieves, Convicts and the Inmate Culture," *Social Problems* 10 (1962): 142-155.
28. Richard McCleery, "Communication Patterns as Bases of Systems of Authority and Power" in Cloward *et. al., op. cit.,* pp. 49-77.
29. Most emphatically I do not wish to be misunderstood as suggesting that we do not now have knowledge that could be applied to the better prevention and treatment of crime. There is a culture lag here too. The knowledge of the criminologist may be exiguous, but it is ample indeed compared with that of those who are responsible for our legislation and practice in this field.
30. Arthur Goodhart, book review, *The Listener* 74 (1965): 1006.
31. *Kriminalloven Og de Vestgrønlandske Samfund* (Greenland Criminal Code, 1962).
32. This paper is reprinted in Andenaes, "The General Preventive Effects of Punishment," *University of Pennsylvania Law Review* 14, 114 (1966): 949.
33. Johannes Andenaes, "Punishment and the Problem of General Prevention" (September 1965), p. 60. The quotation is from a summary by Professor Andenaes which was not reprinted in Andenaes, *supra* note 32.
34. *Report of the Commission of Inquiry on Capital Punishment,* Sessional Paper 14 (Ceylon, 1959), pp. 42-52.
35. Sidney and Beatrice Webb, *English Poor Law Policy* (London: Kelley, 1963), p. 11.
36. Jeremy Bentham, *Works,* John Bowring, ed. (London: Russell, 1893), pp. 122-123.
37. Hermann Mannheim, *Dilemma of Penal Reform* (Patterson-Smith, 1939), p. 59.
38. Francis A. Allen, *The Borderland of Criminal Justice* (Chicago: University of Chicago Press, 1964).
39. Marc Ancel, *Social Defence—A Modern Approach to Criminal Problems* (1965).
40. Norval Morris and Colin Howard, *Studies in Criminal Law* (New York: Oxford University Press, 1964).
41. Sanford Kadish, book review, *Harvard Law Review* 78 (1965): 908.
42. Richard F. Sparks, "Custodial Training Sentences," *Criminal Law Review* 44 (1966): 96.
43. Kadish, *op. cit.,* p. 908.
44. *Ibid.,* pp. 908-909.
45. Sparks, *op. cit.*
46. C. S. Lewis, "The Humanitarian Theory of Punishment," 6 *Res Judicatae* 225 (1953).
47. *Baxterom v. Herold,* 382 U.S. 107 (1966).
48. *Ibid.,* p. 110.
49. *Ibid.,* p. 110-111.
50. U.N. Department of Public Information, *Survey of Juvenile Delinquency, Part I: North America,* rev. (1958).
51. *Kent v. United States,* 383 U.S. 541 (1966).
52. *The Child, the Family and the Young Offender,* Great Britain Home Office (1965), Cmnd. 2742.
53. New York Session Laws (1966), Chapter 192, pp. 200-213.
54. See Walter Gelhorn, "The Swedish Justice Ombudsman," *Yale Law Journal* 75 (1965): 1.
55. Every legal system provides for extending the periods of imprisonment for recidivists and habitual criminals. Such an increase of punishment is justified by the purpose of "warehousing." Our aim here is not reformative, though we preserve the hope that the deterrent effect of the more protracted imprisonment and the reformative efforts that may be made during it will in some cases have the effect of leading the persistent

offender to a law-abiding life. In fact, of course, the processes of growing older, of maturing, eventually lead virtually all such hardened, repeated offenders to a marginally conforming noncriminal life. Our "warehousing" does give opportunity for this reform to take effect by effluxion of time. See Terrence Morris, *The Habitual Criminal* (1951).

56. It would be a disservice to exaggerate our lack of knowledge of the efficacy of certain penal sanctions. Cynicism is a cheap commodity and gives a spurious air of wisdom. We have, for example, reasonably securely established that there are large categories of criminal offenders, adult and juvenile, who can be treated better on probation than in institutions. By "better" here I mean that they have no higher recidivist rate (though their closer supervision would make it likely that a larger proportion of their offenses would be detected—that their "dark figure" of crime would be less than that of those sent to prison and observed after release), that it is cheaper to treat them on probation than in prison (quite apart from other welfare costs that are also minimized), and that when probation is given to this category of offenders there appears to be no consequential increase in the rate of crime for which the criminal sanctions alternatively used might be thought to have a deterrent effect. This type of knowledge is important, and has emerged from a multitude and variety of studies. It guides social planning to a degree, and there remains much to be done on the basis of the already acquired knowledge of this type and range. Yet it is not cynicism to mention its defects. It suffers from too gross a grouping of personality types and persons subject to social pressures, and omits any analysis of the dynamic relationships between personality and community processes relevant to human behavior. It is highly probable that within the gross groups so tested there are some who need prison and not probation. And further, probation and prison are not unities, in themselves, but are rather diverse bundles of treatment and custody methods. The step from our present too broad analysis of competing treatment methods toward the gradual development of a treatment nosology demands much more refined and narrow controlled experimentation, and is an inevitable precursor of rational penal reform.

57. See Leslie T. Wilkins, *Social Deviance* (New York: Prentice Hall, 1965), Chapter 9.

58. Harvey Kalven and Hans Zeisel, "The American Jury and the Death Penalty," *University of Chicago Law Review* 33 (1966): 627; Friendly, book review, *University of Chicago Law Review* 33 (1966): 844.

59. See "Do We Need New Rules For Experiments on People," *Saturday Review,* February 5, 1966, pp. 64-70.

60. Hans Zeisel and Harvey Kalven, Jr., *Delay in the Courts* (Boston: Little, Brown and Company, 1959), p. 246.

61. *Ibid.,* p. 247.

62. "Test Presentence and Summary of Ballot," 27 *Federal Rules Decisions* 383 (1961).

63. This hypothetical situation owes its genesis to discussions of the advisory committee for a study conducted by the National Council of Juvenile Court Judges, when that committee met in Washington, D.C. in 1966.

64. Donald T. Campbell, "Factors Related to the Validity of Experiments in Social Settings," *Psychological Bulletin* 54 (1967): 304.

65. See Lamar Empey and Jerome Rabow, "The Provo Experiment in Delinquency Rehabilitation," *American Sociological Review* 26 (1961): 679, and the subsequent exchange of letters in 27 (1962): 256.

66. Joseph Goldberger, "Pellagra: Causation and a Method of Prevention," *Journal of the American Medical Association* 66 (1916): 471; Goldberger and G. A. Wheeler, "Experi-

mental Pellagra in White Male Convicts," *Archives of Internal Medicine* 25 (1920): 451. Cf. the account by Ralph L. Smith, "Research behind Bars," *New York Times Magazine,* December 4, 1960.

67. Quoted by Howard A. Rusk in "Medical Research and Prisoners," *New York Times,* November 15, 1962.

68. Quoted by Mark DeWolfe Howe in *Justice Oliver Wendell Holmes* (Cambridge, Mass.: Harvard University Press, 1963) II, p. 49.

69. A. C. Ivy, "History and Ethics of the Use of Human Subjects in Medical Research," *Science* 108 (July 2, 1948): 5. Dr. Ivy was responsible for drawing up the provisions of the Nuremberg Code on this subject, which were based on his experiences at the Nuremberg war crimes trials. See also Irving Ladimer and Roger W. Newman, eds., *Clinical Investigation in Medicine: Legal, Ethical, and Moral Aspects* (Boston: Law-Medicine Institute, Boston University, 1963); Henry K. Beecher, "Ethics and Clinical Research," *New England Journal of Medicine* 274 (1966): 1354; and Note, "Legal Implications of Psychological Research with Human Subjects," *Duke Law Journal* (1960), 265.

70. See Fredric Wertham, "The Geranium in the Window" in *A Sign for Cain* (New York: Macmillan, 1966).

71. Cf. Sanford F. Kadish, "The Advocate and the Expert Counsel in the Correctional Process," *Minnesota Law Review* 45 (1961): 803. See generally Norval Morris and Colin Howard, "Penal Sanctions and Human Rights" in *Studies in Criminal Law;* Paul A. Freund, "Is the Law Ready for Human Experimentation?" *Annals of Psychology* 21 (1967): 394; Oscar M. Ruebhausen and Orville G. Brim, "Privacy and Behavioral Research," *Columbia Law Review* 65 (1965): 1184.

72. See *Jackson v. Burnham,* 20 Colo. 532, 39 Pac. 557 (1895), and Note, "Legal Implications of Psychological Research with Human Subjects."

73. *Williams v. State,* 308 N.Y. 548, 127 N.E., 2d 545 (1955).

74. *In re Gault,* 387 U.S. 1 (1966), See also Comment, "Rights of Prisoners While Incarcerated," *Buffalo Law Review* 25 (1965): 397.

75. See further Richard A. Brymer and Buford Farris, "Ethical and Political Dilemmas in the Investigation of Deviance: A Study of Juvenile Delinquency," in *Ethics, Politics, and Social Research,* Gideon Sjoberg, ed. (Boston: Schenkman, 1967), 297-318; and Solomon Kobrin, "Legal and Ethical Problems of Street Gang Work," *Crime and Delinquency* 10 (1964): 152.

76. Oliver Wendell Holmes, Jr., *Collected Legal Papers* (New York: Harcourt Brace, 1921), pp. 188-189.

77. Quoted in Walter Gelhorn, *American Rights* (New York: Macmillan, 1960), p. 94.

78. *Olmstead vs. U.S.,* 277 U.S. 479 (1927).

79. Stuart Adams, "The PICO Project," *The Sociology of Punishment and Correction,* 2nd éd., Norman Johnston, Leonard Savitz, and Marvin E. Wolfgang, eds. (New York: John Wiley & Sons, 1970), pp. 548-61; "A Cost Approach to the Assessment of Gang Rehabilitation Techniques," *Journal of Research in Crime and Delinquency* (January 1967): 166-82 (with Barbara Cantor); *The Cost of Correcting Youthful Offenders,* Research Report No. 6, District of Columbia Department of Corrections, September 1968. For other outstanding cost-effectiveness studies, see *The Saginaw Probation Demonstration Project,* Michigan Crime and Delinquency Council, 1963, and Virginia McArthur, Barbara Cantor, and Sara Glendenning, *A Cost Analysis of the Work Release Program,* Research Report No. 24, District of Columbia Department of Corrections, May 1970.

80. Daniel Glaser and Kent Rice, "Crime, Age and Employment," *American Sociological Review* (October 1959): 679-86; Belton M. Fleisher, *The Economics of Delinquency* (Chicago : Quadrangle Books, 1966); Daniel Glaser, review of Belton M. Fleisher, *The Economics of Delinquency* in *Journal of Research in Crime and Delinquency* (January 1968): 89-90.
81. For more detailed data, see Daniel Glaser, *The Effectiveness of a Prison and Parole System*, abridged ed. (Indianapolis: Bobbs-Merrill, 1969), Chapter 13; George A. Pownall, *Employment Problems of Released Prisoners* (Washington: Manpower Administration, U.S. Department of Labor, 1969), Chapters 6 and 7.
82. Glaser, *op. cit.*, Chapter 5.
83. *Ibid.*, Chapter 8. See also Charles R. Hagan and Charles F. Campbell, "Team Classification in Federal Institutions," *Federal Probation* (March 1968): 30-35, and Lloyd E. Ohlin, "The Reduction of Role Conflict in Institutional Staff," *Children* (March-April 1958): 65-69.
84. Glaser, *op. cit.*, pp. 299-303, 310-315. See also Joseph D. Lohman, Albert Wahl, and Robert M. Carter, *The San Francisco Project, Final Report* (Berkeley: University of California School of Criminology, 1969), Chapters 8 and 9, and Stuart Adams, "Some Findings from Correctional Caseload Research," *Federal Probation* (December 1967): 48-57.
85. See Donald T. Campbell and Julian C. Stanley, *Experimental and Quasi-Experimental Designs for Research* (Chicago: Rand McNally, 1963).
86. This point is elaborated in Daniel Glaser, "Automated Research and Correctional Practice," *California Youth Authority Quarterly* (Winter 1965): 24-31.
87. A. E. Fink, 'Current Thinking on Parole Prediction Tables,' *Crime and Delinquency* 8, 3 (1962): 227.
88. Negley K. Teeters, "Current Thinking on Parole Prediction Tables," *Crime and Delinquency* 8, 3 (1962): 237.
89. Karl R. Popper, *The Open Society* (London: Routledge and Kegan Paul, 1945), p. 231.
90. Hermann Mannheim and Leslie T. Wilkins, *Prediction Methods in Relation to Borstal Training* (London: H.M.S.O., 1955, includes bibliography).
91. Leslie T. Wilkins, "A Small Comparative Study of the Results of Probation," *British Journal of Criminology* 8, 3 (1960): 201.
92. J. D. Grant, "The Treatment of Nonconformists in the Navy" *Annals of the American Academy of Political Science* (March, 1960).
93. B. Bernstein, "Aspects of Language and Learning in the Genesis of the Social Process," *Journal of Child Psychology and Psychiatry* 1 (1961): 313.
94. F. H. McClintock *et al, Attendance Centres* (London: Macmillan, 1961).

INDEX OF NAMES, ORGANIZATIONS AND PROGRAMS

Adams, S., 501
Aderhold, G. W., 383, 385–400
Alcatraz, 331
Alcoholics Anonymous, 50, 83, 177, 186, 234, 307, 366, 429
Allen, F., 470
American Bar Association, 95
American Correctional Association, 6, 279, 329, 335
American Prison Association's Committee on Riots, 30
Ancel, M., 471
Andeaes, J., 467
Ashurst-Sumner Act, 47, 360
Auburn System, 111–13, 344, 462

Bad Check Association, 50
Baker, J. E., 280, 340–55, 365–71
Barnes, H. E., 112
Becarria, C. B. di, 11, 15, 36
Beck, B., 147, 233–47
Bentham, J., 15, 468
Bernstein, B., 519
Black, J., 177
Boston Common Council, 342
Braly, M., 179
Brancale, R., 120
Brockway, Z. R., 48, 342, 359
Brown, C., 181
Bureau of Prisons Community Treatment Center, 104
Bureau of Prisons Employment Placement Service, 379
Burger, W., 95

Caldwell, M., 265–66
California Prisons, 31, 90, 146, 178, 188, 363, 449–50
    California Department of Corrections, 336–38
    California Study of Correctional Effectiveness, 336–37
    Pilot Intensive Couseling, 336
    Synanon, 50, 492–93
California Youth Authority, 411–13, 432, 485
Campbell, D. T., 492

Canlis, M. H., 89
Caplow, T., 445
Center for Studies in Criminal Justice, 93
Central Classification Committee, 193
Clemmer, D., 178, 196–97, 200, 265–66
Cloward, R. A., 266, 269
Cohen, A. K., 208
Commission on Correctional Facilities and Services, 95
Commission on Law Enforcement and Criminal Justice, 88
Community Correctional Center, 399
Community Representatives Staff, 105–6
Congressional Committee (1929), 99
Cooley, C. H., 233
Corrections Task Force of the President's Crime Commission, 389, 392
Cressey, D. R., 149, 435, 438–60
Curtis, J., 342

Department of Corrections, 31
Department of Institutions, 133–34
Department of Justice, 105, 326
Department of Mental Health and Corrections, 135, 391
Department of Public Safety, 134–35
Department of Welfare, 132–33, 139
Derick, C., 343
Division of Health Services, 103
Division for Youth, 414
Dixon, J. D., 233
Draper Prison, 323

Economic Opportunity Act, 49, 83
Elmira Reformatory, 26–27, 29
Ellis, W. J., 113
England
    The Classical School, 439
    in the 1800s, 18
    Poor Laws, 468
    prisons in, 146, 485
Essexfields Project, 403

Federal Bureau of Prisons, 40, 48, 51, 99–100, 105–6, 110, 124–25, 364, 407, 409, 469

547

Federal Community Correction Centers, 502

Federal Correctional Institutions, 102–3

Federal Elementary and Secondary Education Act, 49

Federal Institute for Women, 126

Federal Pre-Release Guidance Centers, 432

Federal Prison Industries, Inc., 48, 101–2

Federal Prisoners Rehabilitation Act, 104

Federal Reformatory for Women, 102–3

Fifth International Congress of Criminology, 466

Fink, A. E., 513

Fishman, J. F., 88

Franklin, B., 20, 36, 110

Frontera Prison, 214–20

Gagnon, J. H., 147, 221–32

Garfinkel, H., 214

Garrity, D. L., 263, 272

Geis, B., 436, 488–98

George, W. R., 343

Gill, H. B., 345–46

Glaser, D., 147, 263–73, 279–80, 318–28, 329–39, 384, 428–432, 499–508

Glueck, B., 113

Goffman, E., 214, 219, 249

Goodhart, A., 464

Grant, J. D., 518, 520

Grunhut, M., 357

Grusky, O., 234–35, 241–42, 247

Halmos, P., 203

Harper, R. A., 197

Harris Poll, 421

Hatch, H. F., 342–43

Haviland, J., 111

Hawes-Cooper Act, 27, 47

Heyns, G., 128–41

Highlands Project, 403–4, 414

Hlanas, P., 509n

Holmes, O., 493, 497

Howard, C., 472

Howard, J., 111

Illinois Criminal Code, 471

Independent Departments, 135–38

Information Center of the National Council on Crime and Delinquency, 51

Institute for Defective Delinquents, 126

Institute for the Study of Crime and Delinquency, 51

International Prison Congress, 26

Irwin, J., 145, 173–91, 458

Janowitz, M., 233, 235

John Howard Association, 126, 417

Johnson, C. H., 345

Johnson, E. H., 146, 193–202, 279, 280, 356–64

Johnson, H., 343

Johnson, L. B., 88

Joint Commission on Correctional Manpower and Training, 419

Kadish, S., 472–73

Kalven, H., 484

Kassebaum, G., 146, 213–20

Kelley, T., 127

Kindall, A. F., 256

King, S. H., 197

Kinsey, A. C., 147, 222–24

Korn, R., 457

Law Enforcement Assistance Administration, 88, 105

Leavenworth Prison, 101, 363

Lewin, K., 467

Lewis, C. S., 473

Lewis, O. F., 352

Lopez-Rey, M., 361

Lynds, E., 111–14, 118

MacCormick, C. H., 6, 110

Malcolm X, 184, 189

Mannheim, H., 356, 468–69, 516

Manpower Development and Training Act, 48

Martin, J. M., 423, 426

Massachusetts, 19–20

McCleery, R., 459

McClintock, F. H., 520

McCorkle, L. W., 457

McGee, R. A., 6, 88

McKeon, O., 180

Medical Center for Federal Prisoners, 103, 126

Mexicans (Chicanos), 187–89

Moore, F., 343
Morris, N., 436, 461–81
Multnomah County, Oregon-Correctional
   Institution, 84

Narcotics Anonymous, 50
National Anti-Contract Association, 359
National Association of Junior Republics,
   343
National Council on Crime and Delin-
   quency, 418, 422, 424
National Crime Commission, 417, 419, 421,
   425
National Institute for Mental Health, 51,
   85, 337
National Prison Association, 6, 26
National Sheriffs' Association, 89
National Survey of Corrections, 405
Negroes (Blacks), 187–89
New Jersey Penitentiary, 26
New York House of Refuge, 342
New York State Prisons, 25, 474

Ohlin, L. E., 447
O'Leary, Vincent, 384, 417–27
Omnibus Crime Control and Safe Streets
   Act, 105
Opportunities, Inc., 50
Osborne Association, 417
Osborne, T. M., 28, 113, 343–45

Parkland Project, 404–5
Pennsylvania Prisons, 19–20, 26, 36, 441,
   462
Pennsylvania System at Eastern Penitentia-
   ry, 111–12
Perlman, S., 358
Perrow, C., 249, 262
Philadelphia Society for Alleviating the Mis-
   ery of Public Offenders, 36
Pilgrims, 19
Pinehills Project, 403–4, 416
Pinel, P., 14
Popper, K. R., 514
President's Commission on Law Enforce-
   ment and Administration of Justice,
   92, 383
President's Committee on Juvenile Delin-
   quency and Youth Crime, 417

Psychiatric Institute, 248–49, 298
Public Health Service, 103

Quakers, 19–20, 40, 110

Rattigan, W., 344
Reed, W., 494
Report of the Ceylon Commission on Capi-
   tal Punishment, 466
Richmond, M. S., 383, 385–400
Robinson, L., 71–2
Romilly, S., 18
Root, W. T., 113
Rush, B., 13, 36, 111
Rushen, R. L., 507

Safe Streets and Omnibus Crime Control
   Act, 399
St. Paul, Minnesota,
   work-school programs, 82 –83
San Diego County, California,
   honor camps in, 84–85
Schrag, C., 145, 149–72, 182, 195, 241,
   265–66, 272, 423
Sellin, T., 3
Sexton, P. C., 319–20
Shattuck, G. M., 423, 426
Shils, E. A., 233
Simon, W., 147, 221–32
Sing Sing, 113, 344
Slack, C., 458
Sparks, R. F., 472
State Division of Correction, 94
State Divisions of Institutions, 94
State Department of Correction, 94
State Industrial for Women, 126
Stratton, J. R., 147, 263
Street, D., 249
Strong, S. M., 266
Sykes, G. M., 182, 196, 213, 243, 266

Tannenbaum, F., 344
Tappan, P., 475
Teeters, N. K., 112, 513
Texas
   prisons in, 30, 384
   Seagoville Prison, 325
Thomas, P., 174

Trasler, G., 146, 203–11

U. S. Bureau of Prisons, 100–6
U.S. Courts, 100, 105
U.S. Industrial Commission, 360
U.S. Penitentiary
  Georgia, 106
  Pennsylvania, 366
  Washington, 102
U.S. Probation Service, 100
U.S. Public Health Service, 100

Velde, R., 88
VERA Institute, 386, 388
Vinter, R., 249
Von Mering, O., 197

Walnut Street Jail, 111, 341, 353
Ward, D. A., 146, 213–20

Warden's Association of America,
  353
Webb, B., 468
Webb, S., 468
Weber, R., 266, 405–6
Westchester County, New York
  prison education in, 83–84
Wheeler, S., 268–70
Whites, 187–89
White House Task Force on Prisoner Reha-
  bilitation, 95
Wilkins, L. T., 436, 509–23
Wilson, T. P., 147, 248–62
Wirth, L., 266
Women's Division of the Federal Correc-
  tional Institute, 103
Work Furlough Plan, 32

Zeisel, H., 484

INDEX OF SUBJECTS

attorney, 451, 490–91

bail system, 86

citizen, 479
  corrections and, 417–19
  types of
    opportunity, 422–24
    social persuader, 420–22
    volunteer, 412–20
classification, 113, 301–3, 316–17, 345, 505
  diagnostic, 306
  objective of, 304–5
  procedures, 307–17
colonial prisons, 25
community (society)
  correctional services, 383, 388–89,
      401–2, 429
    foster home, 402–7, 412, 416
    group interaction, 402–4, 457, 497, 521
    intensive treatment, 402, 410, 412–13,
      457
    prerelease guidance, 402, 407–9,
      414–15,
    reception center parole, 402
  mental health services, 389
  prisons and, 365
  protection of, 3, 21
  work release, 503
community workers, 507
correctional education
  academic, 49, 100–1
  corruption in, 324–25
  effectiveness of, 318–22, 328, 497
  research, 325–28
  student and, 322–23
  vocational training, 48–49, 100–01,
      357–58, 360–62, 383, 424
correctional institutions (adult)
  categories
    board, 130–31, 138, 140
    ex-officio boards, 131–32, 138
  counseling, 49–50
  discipline, 46, 329–33, 415
  diversification, 32–33
  families, 50, 263–64
  goals, 3, 150, 249

latent functions, 3–4
local, 6
manifest functions, 3
organization, 39–40, 444
personnel, 41–46, 150–57, 291
physical plant, 40–41, 395–97
postrelease programs, 366–79, 384,
    407
prerelease programs, 372–79, 499–500
security, 398–99, 430
variations of, 145–46
See also jails, prisons
correctional services, 95
courts, 15, 23, 512
crime
  capital offenses, 18
  cause of, 14
  general deterence, 4, 23, 462, 464–66,
      472–73, 477–78, 497
  individual deterence, 4
  special deterence, 465
  victims, 510–11
criminals, 149
  behavior of, 150, 439
  as correctional workers, 444–45, 453
  habitual, 203–4, 272

death penalty, see punishment (capital)

Federal prisons systems, 29, 31, 90–101
  architecture of, 110, 112, 120, 123, 394
  counseling, 335
  discipline, 330–33, 346
  health services, 102–3
  inmate employment, 102
  management of, 101
  personnel, 99, 104, 106, 505
  religion and, 103–4, 270, 289
  training in, 296
  work-release, 104–5, 388
  See also correctional education, manage-
    ment
felony, 35, 37–38, 90, 190, 389, 500
freedom, 15, 244

Golden Age of Penology, 6, 26
The Great Law, 19

halfway houses, 38, 388, 401, 407, 412, 416, 416, 463, 481, 484

inmates
    antisocial role, 151, 157, 194
    attitudes of, 234–38, 242
    rats, 146, 194–95, 197, 202
    self-government, 340, 342–47
        negative, 341
        positive, 341
    socialization, 236, 241
    special privilege, 459–60
    subcultures, 243, 245, 463
    unassimilated, 196, 201
        flaccid, 199
        mentally maladjusted, 199
        unsocialized, 199–200
interest groups, 446–49
    church groups, 445
    inmate leaders, 445
    political leaders, 445, 451, 461, 485

jails (local), 36, 71–72
    age of, 75, 80
    cost of, 75–76, 389, 394, 407, 415
    county, 32, 94
    management of, 392–93
    number of, 73–74, 92
    offenders, 72, 90
    personnel, 76–80, 88
    physical plant of, 79–80, 89
    pretrial releases, 86–87
    programs, 87–90
    punishments, 72
    purpose of, 72–73
        future, 385–89
    remedies for, 91
    scandals and, 89, 98
    state, 81–82, 393–94
    See also, correctional institutions
justice system, 16, 95, 277
    correctional agencies, 97
    courts, 97
    criminal, 89, 278, 387, 399–400, 436–37, 456
    police, 97
    See also law enforcement
juvenile delinquent, 35, 301
    antisocial, 171

prosocial, 171.
    See also community (correctional services)
juvenile institutions
    administrative resources, 68–69
    average stay, 59
    corporal punishments, 55
    cost of, 60–61
    housing and, 65–68
    overcrowding in, 57
    programs in, 58–59, 70
    pseudofamilies, 230
    purpose of, 55–56
    security in, 55
    staff in, 61–65
    training schools and, 52–54
juveniles, 53
    correctional institutions and, 140, 229, 475
    See also juvenile institutions

law, (criminal), 15, 20–21, 467, 478, 497
law enforcement, 23, 506
    municipal, 93–94
    police and, 451
    See also justice

management
    of law offenders, 89–90, 97
    patterns of, 248, 250, 252, 256, 260–62, 329
    prison rules of, 282–300, 444
    problems in, 92–94
maximum security, 117, 119, 333, 336
medium security, 33, 85, 116, 119
mentally insane
    crime and, 24, 38, 474
minimum security, 33, 84–85, 116, 119, 234
    experimentation, 496

offender, 5, 9
    adult 25, 94, 97, 336
    conformity of, 269
    dealing with, 8, 21–22
    postrelease of, 336
    rehabilitation of, 3–6, 21, 24–25, 29, 32–34, 48, 99, 106, 223, 264, 356, 361–64, 385, 503
    release of, 503–4

offender (*cont.*)
   types of, 24–25, 236, 268
   See also prisoners, programs, punishment
organization, 443
   formal, 233–34, 244
   informal, 233–34, 240–47

parole, 21, 27, 38, 91, 94, 139–40, 171, 263, 271, 302, 315–17, 326, 330 338, 384, 389, 408, 411–13, 418, 429, 442, 448, 450, 458, 494, 500
penal legislation, 16
   See also interests groups
penal philosophy, 111–15, 120–23, 126
penal progress, 26
   See also prisons (future)
Penal reform
   guidelines, 463–65
   obstacles, 461–62, 468, 470
penal system, 16, 280
penitentiary, 37
   See also correctional institutions, jails, prisons
penology, 15, 27, 48, 115, 340, 443, 522
   modern, 110, 330
   penologists, 24
   progressive, 116
phenomenon, 10, 14, 189, 225, 435
prison society
   asocial inmates, 165–67, 170.
   codes in, 159, 161–62, 177, 190–91
   peer groups, 209, 212, 248, 256, 261, 423
   prosocial prisoners, 164, 166–170
   pseudosocial inmates, 165–71
   roles of prisoners, 160–63, 182, 265–66
   social contacts, 208, 265, 504
   social system, 159, 207–8
   See also inmates, prisoners
prisoners, 24, 29, 33, 118
   adaption of
      alienated, 250, 252–52, 255
      co-operative, 249–50, 252, 254–56, 258
      disordered criminal, 187
      doing time, 174–77
      dope fiend, 178–79, 183, 185–86
      gleaning, 174–75, 183–86
      heads, 183, 186
      hustler, 179, 182–83, 185–86

      jailing, 174, 180–81
      lower class, 180, 183, 186
      lowriders, 182, 185
      old con, 191–92
      opportunistic, 249, 252–55, 258, 260–61
      post release, 270–73
      regular, 191
   behavior of, 151, 153, 162, 173, 251, 271
   sexual adjustment of, 222–23, 229
      heterosexual, 224–26, 228
      homosexual, 225–26, 231–32
      passive, 227–28
      masturbation, 224
   treatment of, 117–19, 266, 281, 294, 301
   unconvicted, 298–99
   See also, inmates, offenders, puinshment
prisonization, 195, 263
prisons
   types
      classification, 199–200
      custodial, 114, 119, 147, 170, 196, 234–49, 353
      professional, 115–16, 119–20
      progressive, 114–15, 119
   bureaucracy, 452
   changes in, 5, 29–31, 113
   communications, 154, 157, 170, 252, 255–56
   as a community, 121, 147, 155, 172, 193, 210, 365
   costs of, 11, 501, 509
   crime reduction, 22
   force in, 155–58
   future, 428–31
   industry and, 356–57, 362–64
   labor in, 32, 112, 356–61, 363, 429
   new prison, 126–27, 178, 429–30
   penalties and, 157, 423
   role of, 278
   rule enforcement, 158, 260
   staff personnel,
      administrative, 121–22, 125, 137, 154–55, 192, 449, 455, 486
      executive, 121
      professional, 122–23
   treatment in, 123, 147, 234–35, 241–42, 247, 249, 251, 442–45, 448–50, 454

probation, 21, 94, 96, 140–41, 330, 371, 373–74, 388–89, 404, 413, 415, 418, 442, 448, 450, 458, 480, 489, 500, 520
programs
  conservatism in, 446–47, 451–54
  rehabilitation, 277, 449, 451, 456, 470–73, 476–77
  See also offenders
psychoneurotic, 195
psychopathic, 195
punishment, 14, 342
  and the accused, 85–86
  capital, 10, 12–15, 18–19, 25, 111, 213, 278–79, 462, 466
  corporal, 10–11, 13, 15, 19, 25, 46, 111, 289, 342, 423
  individual treatment and, 14–15, 32–33, 113, 294–95, 348, 440–41
  laws and, 15
  purpose of, 8–9, 22, 287, 439, 473
  sentiment against, 12, 509

reformatory, 53
  See also juvenile institutions
riots, 30, 174, 337, 350

scientific method, 437

experimentation, 435–36, 478–80, 482, 484, 487–88, 490, 495–96,
  informed consent, 491–94
  medical, 493–94, 507
research, 436, 484–86, 488, 490, 508, 513–14, 518, 523
security
  types of 116–17
  See also, correctional and juvenile institutions
solitary confinement, 36–37
state government, 95, 98, 105
state prisons, 31, 128–29
  See also correctional institutions

woman's prisons
  bisexual, 218
  colonization, 219–20
  emotionally disturbed, 219–20
  family separation, 215
  heterosexual, 218
  homosexual relationships, 146–47, 217–20, 230–31
  inmate codes, 216–17
  man role type, 217
  penal confinement, 214, 216
  pseudofamilies, 230